Praise for *Entwined Lives*

"Dr. Segal knows more about the literature of twin research and more remarkable twin pairs than anyone of my acquaintance, and she reveals what she knows with clarity, accuracy, and humor. I have been studying twins for nearly thirty years and yet I learned something new and intriguing from every chapter of *Entwined Lives*."
—David Lykken, Ph.D., professor emeritus,
Department of Psychology, University of Minnesota

"What E. O. Wilson did for ants, Nancy Segal has now accomplished for twins. Our fascination with twins and their power for understanding the human condition are wonderfully documented in this unique compendium . . . Researchers, clinicians, parents, students, and anyone interested in what twins tell us about human behavior will devour this book."
—Irving I. Gottesman, Ph.D., Sherrel J. Aston Professor,
Department of Psychology, University of Virginia

"A definitive book on a fascinating subject. A delight to read."
—Frank J. Sulloway, author of *Born to Rebel*

"Highly readable . . . The wealth of research findings and human stories illuminate every chapter."
—Elizabeth M. Bryan, M.D., author of *Twins, Triplets, and More*

"An exhaustive analysis . . . powerful."
—*The Orange County Register*

NANCY L. SEGAL is professor of developmental psychology and director of the Twin Studies Center at California State University, Fullerton. She is a fellow of the American Psychological Association, a contributing editor and member of the editorial board for the journal *Twin Research,* and a member of the advisory board for the Twins Foundation. Dr. Segal served as assistant director of the Minnesota Center for Twin and Adoption Research from 1985 to 1991.

ALSO BY NANCY L. SEGAL

Uniting Psychology and Biology
(edited with Glenn E. Weisfeld and Carol C. Weisfeld)

Nancy L. Segal, Ph.D.

Entwined Lives

TWINS

AND

WHAT THEY

TELL US

ABOUT

HUMAN

BEHAVIOR

A PLUME BOOK

For my family—

and for twins who have contributed so much
to what we know and can know just by being themselves

PLUME
Published by the Penguin Group
Penguin Putnam Inc., 375 Hudson Street, New York, New York 10014, U.S.A.
Penguin Books Ltd, 27 Wrights Lane, London W8 5TZ, England
Penguin Books Australia Ltd, Ringwood, Victoria, Australia
Penguin Books Canada Ltd, 10 Alcorn Avenue, Toronto, Ontario, Canada M4V 3B2
Penguin Books (N.Z.) Ltd, 182–190 Wairau Road, Auckland 10, New Zealand

Penguin Books Ltd, Registered Offices: Harmondsworth, Middlesex, England

Published by Plume, a member of Penguin Putnam Inc. Previously published in a Dutton edition.

First Plume Printing, April, 2000
10 9 8 7 6 5 4 3 2 1

 REGISTERED TRADEMARK—MARCA REGISTRADA

The Library of Congress has catalogued the Dutton edition as follows:
Segal, Nancy L.
    Entwined lives : twins and what they tell us about human behavior
/ Nancy L. Segal.
        p.   cm.
    Includes bibliographical references and index.
    ISBN 0-525-94465-6
        0-452-28057-5 (pbk.)
    1. Twins—Psychology.   2. Nature and nurture.   I. Title.
BF723.T9S44   1999
155.44'4—dc21   98-51460
                                                      CIP

Printed in the United States of America

Contents

Acknowledgments

Entwined Lives was a book waiting to be written. I could not have imagined a more perfect project, nor a more perfect time in which to write it. Twin studies are moving in exciting directions, and it is important to convey these events to the people whose lives they most affect.

My agent Angela Rinaldi and my editor Deb Brody have offered me that chance. I am grateful to them both and to everyone at Dutton for a remarkable writing experience. Catherine Johnson added style and polish to my early drafts, setting a fine example.

I am indebted to colleagues who generously reviewed sections and chapters in their areas of expertise. Thank you, David Allison, William Bauman, Thomas J. Bouchard, Jr., E. Steven Dummitt III, Bryan Hecht, Owen Jones, Barbara Luke, David Lykken, Kevin MacDonald, Colleen McCann, Matt McGue, Linda Mealey, Walter Nance, James O'Neill, Jr., Laura Roberts, Kimberly Saudino, Ann Spungen, Frank Sulloway, P. Tony Vernon and Kimerly Wilcox. Thomas J. Bouchard, Jr., David Rowe and Michael McGuire read the manuscript in full.

Other colleagues and friends performed a host of invaluable services. Mike Miller kept me informed of relevant media reports posted on the Internet. Stanley Kohn shared insights on Einstein's famous "twins paradox." Meg Keyes provided up-to-date publications on twins reared apart. Bonnie Birnbaum commented extensively on the penultimate version of the book.

My family was always there for me in countless vital ways. My father Al Segal was my best research assistant, sending me virtually every twin-related article from the *New York Times, Wall Street Journal, New Yorker,* and other publications. My mother Esther Segal was my steady source of encouragement, listening patiently and with good humor to regular progress reports. My twin sister Anne was with me from the start (pun intended!), an amazing supporter, a great critic, a trusted ally. Together we savored the sweetness of some of our old twin jokes which writing this book inevitably revived.

The Psychology Department at New York University offered an ideal environment for the partial completion of this project during the fall of 1997. The remainder of the book was written at California State University, Fullerton, where I have been a faculty member since 1991. I am grateful for the one-year sabbatical leave allowing me the time and freedom to write.

The success of *Entwined Lives* relied on the thoughtfulness of people too numerous to name. Their acts of kindness included sending a clever news clipping, locating an obscure study, sharing unpublished research results, loaning a cherished photograph, and finding a difficult to find book. I have yet to meet some of these people to thank them properly for all they have done. Like my twinship, their deeds fashioned a forceful, ever-present background that impressed me at every step along the way.

Foreword

Book extraordinaire! As the subtitle, "Twins and What They Tell Us About Human Behavior" indicates, this book is about much more than twins. It is a book about *us* and what makes *us* who we are. It is a scientific book in the best sense of the term, drawing on a large verified body of knowledge, integrating that knowledge with the best available theories, and proposing thoughtful testable hypotheses relevant to issues we wish to understand. Unlike much writing in the behavioral sciences, it is intelligible, informative, and fun to read.

Why study twins to understand human behavior? A standard procedure in many scientific disciplines is to find a model system that can be systematically manipulated (experimented with) and studied in detail. Such studies reveal underlying regularities and lead to the discovery of causal mechanisms. Chemists create pure samples before conducting their analyses under varied physical conditions. Nonhuman animal geneticists work with inbred strains of organisms that have been specially developed to disclose nature's many mysteries. Such systems are unavailable to students of humanity for obvious reasons. As Sir Francis Galton pointed out long ago, however, nature has provided us with an approximation to such a model system: identical and fraternal twins. Twins are a great experiment of nature, allowing insights into the genetic and environmental influences underlying behavioral development.

Because of their utility as a tool or method, twins are often referred to informally as the "Rosetta Stone" of behavior genetics. Indeed, I keep a reproduction of the Rosetta Stone mounted on the wall of my home office as just such a metaphor. Nancy Segal knows that, like any metaphor, this one can be misleading. The twin method, especially when combined with the adoption study (an experiment of society), can help bridge the gap between the language of the genes and the influence of the environment on mind and behavior. Twin methods cannot, however, tell us the whole story. Nancy Segal has learned how to interpret this Rosetta Stone in ways of which no one else has dreamed. In addition to thoughtful interpretations of the standard use of twin designs, she has implemented novel variations of these designs which she discusses in this book. She has also suggested many innovative research strategies that, while not yet implemented, serve as thought experiments to help us comprehend the complexities and intricacies of behavioral science research more thoroughly. For example, she extends the logic of twin methodology to the pseudo-twin design (same-age unrelated individuals reared together), correctly pointing out that we understand something even better when we understand its complement—another fundamental tool of the scientific process. She goes well beyond Galton, however, to show how twins can address fundamental issues in the new discipline of evolutionary psychology. She uses the tools of evolutionary analysis with verve and imagination, bringing the nonspecialist reader right along brilliantly, and explicating why the answers to seemingly academic questions asked by evolutionary psychologists are so fundamental to understanding the everyday behaviors and feelings of human beings.

Both the specialist and the lay reader will quickly understand why the simple learning theories and socialization theories of the recent past have, when used in isolation from genetic, evolutionary and biological considerations, completely failed to explicate why we are the way that we are. They fail to take into account how we came to be! Nancy Segal explains to us how twins' spurts and lags in behavioral development are influenced by genes "turning on and off" (developmental synchronies), phenomena that only twins can elucidate. Data on the friendship patterns of twins and the loss of a twin, drawn from the discipline of *social genetics* (study of genetic influences on social behavior and social relationships) are interpreted in the context of evolutionary theory. This effort throws entirely new light on the universal phenomena of friendship and bereavement. The social and ethical consequences of creating multiples via the new fertility treatments are discussed with sensitivity and professional acumen. The insightful analysis of other fascinating topics (e.g., twin-based insights on athletic skills; relevance of twin research for legal decision making), highly relevant to our everyday life, goes on and on.

All of this is accomplished in a natural and nondogmatic style that fully recognizes our lack of knowledge about many topics and the complexities of the task ahead. At the same time, we are provided with an enormous amount of knowledge that will be valuable to specialists and nonspecialists alike. This is a useful book, an enjoyable book, a book full of golden nuggets. No thoughtful reader will go away unfulfilled. It would have been impossible to find anyone more qualified to write this book, and what a book it is. It is a gem. Nancy Segal takes us on a journey through the realm of twin research that leaves all other recent treatments of the topic in the dust. This is not a surprise to anyone who knows her. This book establishes Nancy Segal as one of the world's most knowledgeable authorities on twin studies. Indeed, she is the source to whom I turn when faced with difficult "twin questions." This book reflects her encyclopedic store of biological knowledge, her fundamental grounding in the social sciences, her unique clinical skills, and her elegant writing style. It is a stunning achievement.

Thomas J. Bouchard, Jr., Ph.D.
Professor of Psychology, University of Minnesota
Director, Minnesota Center for Twin and Adoption Research

Preface: Not Like Me

Twins and twin research have been my natural passions. After twenty years the multiple thrills—designing studies, evaluating data, meeting twins, talking to parents—have only grown stronger. Perhaps we love most what we come to know best. . . .

I cannot recall my first conscious awareness of being a twin. I only know that this knowledge was always present and somehow set my sister Anne and me apart from the much larger population of nontwins, or what psychologists call *singletons*. In our case, the distinctive features of twinship, such as matching faces and forms, were never obvious that is, no one would ever have guessed we were twins, given our striking physical and behavioral differences. In fact, the residents of our New York City apartment building assumed that the twins on the seventh floor were Safi and Michelle Newman, the sisters who lived next door to us! Safi and Michelle differed in age by twenty-two months, but were near equals in height and build and had the same hair color and texture. In contrast, since childhood Anne and I have stood four inches apart in height and have always had very different builds. Her hair is medium brown and curly, while mine is dark brown and straight. Because our twinship was virtually hidden from view, the feeling of being "different" from my friends was mostly a personal perception, rather than a consequence of special treatment by others. Maybe it was the stunned surprise on the faces of those who learned of our twinship that pleased me most and gave rise to feelings of being special. "I have something you don't have!" was a sure way to capture the respect of childhood peers.

Anne and I are fraternal, or nonidentical, twins. Like ordinary siblings, we share approximately half our genes by descent. Given our natural differences in appearance and behavior, twinship was downplayed in our family, even overlooked, and the two of us lived separate lives. We did homework in the same room, took part in family excursions to museums and plays, and spent several summers as cabinmates at overnight camp. But beyond this our paths rarely crisscrossed intentionally and our shared experiences were due more to circumstance than to choice. Our parents did not deliberately "decide" that this was the best way to raise twins; instead they responded to our natural differences in personality and temperament that emerged over the years.

Young children sometimes grasp concepts they lack the words to articulate, and so it was with my understanding of nature and nurture. How is it possible, I wondered, for two children to be born on the same day, to share the same family, to inhabit the same educational and cultural environments,

My fraternal twin sister, Anne, (left) and I at age four, during a family vacation to Beach Haven, New Jersey. Our height difference was evident at an early age. PHOTO CREDIT: OUR DAD.

and then to diverge so dramatically in abilities, temperamental traits, interests, and friendships? Our parents were the fanatics of fairness—we were their only children and opportunities offered to one of us were always offered to the other. However, it was clear early on that objectively similar opportunities held different meanings for us: I delighted in ballet classes, Anne read books with lightning speed. Mathematics was a struggle for me, but it came naturally to Anne. I loved to dive; Anne feared diving, but was a stronger swimmer. I was outgoing; Anne was reserved.

As a child I decided we had different "stuff"—that each of us had come into the world with "something different." My child's mind had discovered genes, those pieces of DNA that are the building blocks of life. Nevertheless, it would be some time before I translated these thoughts into the formal scientific concepts that describe these complex processes.

We know genes interact with environments to produce the behaviors that uniquely define each individual: Our genetic makeup may selectively steer us toward environments and events that we find most compatible. Free spirits may seek exotic voyages to faraway lands, while careful planners may prefer itineraries with a predictable course. Variation is the hallmark of human behavior and we need look no further than outside our front door to find the liveliest mixture of personalities, talents and temperaments. Paradoxically, the same family environment may be quite different for each child in a fam-

Our childhood friends and neighbors, Safi (left), age four, and Michelle, age two, the "twins" on the seventh floor. PHOTO COURTESY OF FRITZI AND DAVE NEWMAN.

ily. Despite parents' claims that "each child receives equal treatment," equal does not necessarily mean the same. Equal means that parents respond effectively to the natural inclinations of each child. Anne and I were different and our parents treated us differently. What twins teach us about these processes is an exciting story—twin research is not solely about twins, it is a model that helps all of us find answers to questions of who we are and how we got there.

Twins would seem to be natural allies since, in addition to shared heredity and environment, they share birthdays. I remember the birthday parties. The small tables that sat four were arranged in a spiral with the head table (Anne and I, each with a best friend) in the center. There were my friends and her friends, with few in common. This was surely a partial function of attending different classes at school, yet these friends rarely became mutual comrades despite weekend visits to our home. Why? Our choice of different friends apparently reflected our genetically based individual tastes and preferences in people. In fact, during our childhood years, my friends were typically my playmates of choice over my twin sister. Unlike most identical twins, we were not natural allies; "ships passing in the night" comes closer to the mark. Appreciation of the critical biological and psychological distinctions among the different types of twins is so crucial for rearing twins successfully. Professional and personal experience has now taught that parents should seek scientific confirmation of twin type—an issue I will examine in some detail.

Whenever I am asked how and why I began to study twins, I return to my senior year at Boston University. A term paper on personal adjustment was a required assignment for a class I was taking in abnormal psychology. In casting about for a topic, I recalled family decisions surrounding the placement of Anne and me in separate classes (an event that occurred in the second grade) and, ultimately, in different schools when we reached junior high. At that time in New York City, classes within each grade were ordered according to student ability. For example, the second grade consisted of classes 2-1 (brightest), 2-2 (next brightest), and so on. Anne and I both qualified for the "1" class, but her higher test scores dropped me into second place. As a child I accepted this decision amicably, but later it filled me with anger and resentment. This experience did, however, furnish the needed paper topic: "Twin Relationships and Their Implications for School Placement." Reviewing the literature on twin development was a completely engaging and insightful academic task. There was no question that human development from a twin research perspective would be my area for graduate study in psychology at the University of Chicago.

The use of twins in research is an ever-expanding enterprise. Twin studies are assisting discoveries into the bases of human intelligence and personality, and the genetic components of complex diseases, such as multiple sclerosis and schizophrenia. Economists use twins to uncover ability and educational factors affecting annual income, and psychologists are now recruiting multiples to explore the foundations of human happiness, marital satisfaction, and love styles. In my own work I have been fascinated to find new areas of interest continually emerging, often in surprising ways:

- Application of twin research findings to assist legal decision making in wrongful death, injury and custody cases involving twins.
- Comparing responses of identical and fraternal twins to the loss of their twin sibling.
- Assessing behavioral similarity in "pseudo-twin" pairs (unrelated children of the same age who are reared together from infancy).

Current advances in molecular genetics promise a new series of tantalizing questions about human development that twin studies can help to address, and researchers eagerly anticipate them. New methods for conceiving twins, in addition to a host of unusual "twinlike" sibships, are available and are raising countless thought-provoking, often difficult, ethical and medical questions for families and physicians.

On the personal side, the fact of twinship is still ever-present in the corners of my mind, still setting me/us apart. Anne and I are now close sisters, a circumstance that we view with some surprise and amusement in light of the past. She is a corporate attorney, living in New York City, and while we rarely find ourselves in the same area, we keep in touch at least once a week by telephone and, most recently, by e-mail. This new friendship is not a "twin thing"—many nontwin siblings grow closer over the years as the importance of family ties acquires new value. But perhaps this process is easier when you share your birthday (March 2, 1951: Nancy, 7:29 P.M., Anne, 7:36 P.M.; Boston, MA).

Introduction

Why are we the way that we are? Why are we tolerant or temperamental, happy or sad? Why do we love the way that we do?

Most people would simply say that we are a product of our environment, with our behaviors, attitudes and beliefs fashioned by parents, friends, the neighborhoods we lived in and the schools we attended. This is an understandable notion. Yet insights gleaned from the study of twins show that it is incorrect. Aiming the research spotlight on the lives of identical and fraternal twins captures vital clues to solving the behavioral riddles that each of us pose.

Twin studies are simple and elegant. The significantly greater similarities between *identical twins* (twins formed from the splitting of a single fertilized egg, who share all their genes) than between *fraternal twins* (twins born from two separate eggs and two separate sperm, who share half their genes, on average) demonstrate that we are not just a product of nurture, but also of nature—our unique genetic makeup. This blend of nature and nurture raises provocative questions that speak to the core of what it is to be human: To what degree are we the authors of our own actions? Does genetic inheritance limit our free will or our range of possible behaviors?

As participants in scientific investigations, twins touch us all. Few singletons are unaffected by the many recent developments in our understanding of human behavior that derive from twin studies. The extraordinary similarity and intimacy of identical twins, and the relative dissimilarity of fraternal twins, hold answers to the knotty ambiguities found within the nature-nurture debate. Some psychologists and psychiatrists reject nature versus nurture arguments, claiming that they portray a false dichotomy. Their position is that human behaviors result from the inseparable influences of genes and environments, a view called *interactionism*. This perspective confuses individuals and populations because, while genetic and environmental effects cannot be disentangled for single people, they can be separately estimated for groups. According to evolutionary psychologists Martin Daly and Margo Wilson, "The nature-nurture debate has been pronounced dead many times, but it won't stay buried."[1] A new preferred formulation of nature versus nurture is nature via nurture, the concept that genes predispose individuals to seek certain environments and experiences during development.[2] Books on shelves and pictures on walls, previously considered strictly environmental, reemerge as genetically influenced pieces of the environment because they reflect the interests and personality of whoever put them there. At the same time, nurture via nature captures another side of this debate, the idea that parenting is largely guided by children's genetically influenced temperaments and talents. In other words, parents' disciplinary practices appear to be driven partly by their children's individual behaviors, as well as by parents' own behaviors and beliefs.[3]

Twins offer a natural experiment that allows exploration of genetic and environmental influences upon human development. From twin studies we learn that athletic prowess attributed to emulating one's father may be partly explained by also acknowledging inherited factors associated with speed and strength. Mathematical wizardry in a young child may reflect unique gene combinations, assisted by the efforts of dutiful tutors.[4] Twin studies are not limited to physical or mental abilities, but address the origins of personality traits, social attitudes, medical conditions and religious interests. This information is profoundly affecting our views of ourselves, our relationships with family members, our methods for raising children and our outlook on human potentials and possibilities.

In recent years, psychologists have begun to see behavior through fresh lenses. Two new behavioral science fields, *behavior genetics* and *evolutionary psychology,* have yielded new findings that challenge traditional theories of human behavior. *Behavior genetics* lies at the intersection of genetics and psychology.[5] It is concerned with the extent to which genes and environments explain individual differences in various traits. We all differ from one another in intelligence, in sociability and in athletic skill because we differ in our genetic makeup and in our environments. Genes and environments are inextricably intertwined within individuals, but the twin design is a cornerstone of behavioral-genetic methodology that can estimate relative genetic *(heritability)* and environmental influence to explain why people differ from one another in particular traits. Twin studies show that genetic influence affects virtually every human characteristic and that the gene-environment balance differs across behaviors. We know, for example, that genes explain a greater proportion of individual differences in intellectual abilities than in personality traits. This means that personality traits are more susceptible to environmental influence than intellectual abilities.

Charles Darwin's 1859 theory of evolution transformed scientists' views of the nature and origin of human and nonhuman physical and behavioral variation.[6] In recent years the relevance of Darwin's theory for investigating human psychological issues has been increasingly recognized. *Evolutionary psychology* is concerned with the origins and functions of human behavior. Evolutionary psychologists peer into our evolutionary past to try to determine which behavioral strategies best served humans by improving chances for survival. Survival, in evolutionary currency, means genetic survival—living into adulthood and passing on genes to children who will, in turn, pass on those same genes to their own children. At first glance this view suggests that people should be concerned primarily with their own welfare and less

sensitive to the needs of others. However, there are many examples of cooperation, even sacrifice, on the part of relatives for one another. In 1964,
British evolutionary biologist William Hamilton reasoned that helping close
relatives with whom genes were shared was equivalent to "helping" one's
own genes to survive.[7] Close relatives do not perform genetic calculations in
their head before acting cooperatively or lending assistance. Instead, evolutionary psychologists assert, people come equipped with genetic predispositions to behave as if they perform these calculations, because caring for kin
has increased chances for survival in the past.

Evolutionary theory offers a new and exciting framework that enables us
to attach function and meaning to human behavior. Combining twin studies
with evolutionary psychology may help to explain why we get along well
with one sibling and not another, why we grieve more for a sister than for a
distant cousin, and why we tend to maintain loyalties to family members, especially in times of danger or need. This is because twin research methods,
based on the difference in genetic relatedness between identical (100%) and
fraternal twins (50%, on average), offer powerful tools for testing evolutionary hypotheses concerned with social relatedness. This work might also explain why many identical twins and some fraternal twins who were separated
at birth and reunited as adults feel closer and more familiar to each other than
to the adoptive siblings with whom they were raised. Evolutionary accounts
do not diminish social-psychological explanations, but offer an additional,
more complete way of thinking about the "why" of behavior because they
take human history into consideration. For example, children may acquire aggressive tendencies through learning, but evolution may have predisposed
males to be more susceptible than females to aggression learned through observation.[8]

Less universal, but still striking, is an exploration into the curious world of
twins themselves. The remarkable behavioral and physical similarities of
identical twins hold a special fascination for us all. This fact alone speaks to
some aspects of our human nature. There is persuasive evidence that friendships and marriages derive from, rather than result in, certain similarities of
the partners, a process called *assortment*.[9] Our tendencies to seek out others
who resemble us in some way may explain the enormous interest in what
makes twins tick. It may also explain why twins are often used to develop
themes of interdependence and individuation in classical literature, science
fiction, film and the visual arts. Shakespeare's *Comedy of Errors* and *Twelfth
Night* were humorous, yet revealing, tales of mistaken identity involving
pairs of identical and opposite-sex twins (Shakespeare was the father of
opposite-sex twins, Judith and Hamnet). Thornton Wilder, himself a twin, au-
thored *The Bridge of San Luis Rey,* in which identical twins, Manuel and Esteban, struggled with their twinship until the death of Manuel caused Esteban
to experience true loneliness. Readers were riveted by Ira Levin's *The Boys
from Brazil,* in which ninety-four genetic replicas of Adolf Hitler were placed

in families similar to that of the infamous führer in an evil attempt at recreating his despicable self. They were also captivated by Ken Follett's *The Third Twin,* which stretches the possibilities of genetic manipulation to new limits by involving eight genetically identical males, born on the same date to different mothers, in an intriguing story of experimentation and conspiracy. Visitors to the Capitoline Museum in Rome are captivated by the statue of mythological twins, Romulus and Remus, being suckled by a she-wolf, while students of West African art are enticed by figurines depicting twin-specific themes of loss and fertility.[10] Most everyone is drawn like a magnet to a stroller, a park bench or a photograph bearing a matched pair. Perhaps this is because near-duplication of body and mind challenges a cherished belief in the individuality of all people, posing a fascinating exception to the general rule. However, some people may feel disturbed or even threatened by identical appearances, possibly rooted in survival needs to distinguish kin from nonkin and friend from foe.

Still, despite their genetic identity, identical twins are surprisingly much less alike than most people believe. Consider the following conundrum drawn from a number of identical twin studies: Some identical twins who were not separated at birth turn out to differ dramatically in certain traits. How can this be? Researchers do not know the entire answer as to why this happens, but they do know that explanations must reside in the environment. Twin studies of homosexuality, for example, indicate that only about one-fourth to one-half of homosexual identical twins have homosexual cotwins. Similar identical cotwin differences are true of many genetically influenced medical disorders, such as multiple sclerosis (MS), schizophrenia, Crohn's disease and type two (adult onset, non-insulin-dependent) diabetes.[11] Identical twins who differ in important ways have helped to identify the critical environmental keys that can unlock certain behaviors in one twin, but keep them "closed" in the twin brother or sister.

Heated controversies and great debates have periodically swirled around twin research. Evidence of genetic influences upon antisocial behavior has provoked emotionally charged exchanges, especially among people concerned with social policy issues.[12] If it could be shown that a predilection for criminality is genetic in some people, does this mean that the individual committing the crime is not at fault? Are genetic engineering methods a likely or promising solution? Furthermore, it was not so long ago that the theory and methods behind twin research were seriously abused and misconceived. Such was the case in the Auschwitz concentration camp in the 1940s, when the infamous physician Josef Mengele conducted his brutal and dehumanizing twin experiments.[13] Hundreds of helpless twins and disabled individuals from across Europe were subjected to painful injections, X rays, blood transfusions and other horrendous procedures masquerading as science. These experiments, ostensibly aimed to support the Aryan view of a master race, set twin research back for many years. The field's reputation has since been restored, but concerns associated with Mengele's activities, such as whether twin research findings could be used to support the biological superiority or inferiority of some groups of people, occasionally resurface even now. Today there are new ethical dilemmas raised by ongoing twin studies, many linked to evidence of a genetic basis to alcoholism and schizophrenia, and to the new reproductive technologies that can result in unusual "twinlike" sibling relations.

I would argue that research that informs us about human behavioral development, even if controversial, is important and worth pursuing. Now is the time to place twin-based genetic research into its proper perspective. Twin methods and findings have clearly withstood the test of time, due to their power to lay bare the basis of human behavior. More than ever before, the greatest care and circumspection must be brought to studies concerned with how genes and environments mesh, and with the methods that create twins artificially. A hard look at some of the misuses and misconceptions of twin research, as well as its benefits and promises, deserves the utmost public and professional attention.

Entwined Lives brings together an array of topics on twin research and twin development that has never before been included in a single volume. Some of the topics are so unique and timely—legal issues (e.g., death of a twin and custody of twin children) and "pseudo-twins" (e.g., unrelated children of the same age reared together, who share a special twinlike relationship)—that they have received coverage only in specialized journals. My goal is to bring twins and twin studies to life for the millions of people who will be more enriched, informed and enlightened by the messages they hold. This book is not just for twins or for parents of twins, it is for everyone who is curious about the events that shape us from conception and throughout our lives.

Entwined Lives concludes with a hard look at the current role of twin research in psychology. There is no question that twin research can reveal much more about human behavioral development than is available from other sources. Although some of the findings are controversial and politically unpopular, the most valuable information we can ever hope to gather are the facts that explain why we are the way that we are. Identical and fraternal twins will continue to serve as critical guideposts in this most important quest.

1

Identical and Fraternal Twins: Living Laboratories

I feel a rush of excitement waiting in my laboratory for nine-year-old twins, Rocky and Tony Novak, and their mother, Linda, to arrive for their research visit. For the next two hours the four of us will be players in a great discovery game, a search for how and why people grow and develop as they do. I wonder how alike Rocky and Tony will look to one another, how similarly they will respond to problems and questions, and how much they enjoy being twins. It will be fascinating to learn how their answers and test scores, and those of other twins, illuminate areas of human development that remain in the dark.

Occasionally, I am asked to recall a "favorite" pair, or a pair that was especially memorable in some way. I always answer that it is the pair I last studied in my laboratory whose particular personalities and preferences still linger in my mind. Each individual twin pair is a fresh and fascinating take on what it means to be human. It is, however, the collective story, repeated countless times and in different ways by each set, that tells us who we are and how we got there. It was extraordinary to discover that the "Jim twins," the first pair of reunited identical twins studied at the University of Minnesota, had sons with the same name, enjoyed woodworking and bit their fingernails to the nub. It was also striking to find other examples of highly matched idiosyncratic behaviors in many other reared apart identical pairs, and to find them so infrequently in reared apart fraternal pairs. The parallel paths of identical twins, and the diverging paths of fraternal twins, strongly suggest that human development proceeds according to a plan that is largely guided by our genes. Twins are truly living laboratories.

Twins offer a natural experiment for studying how behavioral and physical traits are shaped by nature and by nurture. In fact, when twins are not included in human developmental research, the findings may actually be sus-

Identical twins, Tony (left) and Rocky Novak, age eighteen, with identical twin partners, Brooke (left) and Tiffany Engen, age seventeen. Dancing as "Two Twins" they captured third place in the 1997 Show Biz National Talent final in St. Paul, MN. PHOTO COURTESY OF LINDA NOVAK.

pect. The classic twin method was first described in 1875 by Sir Francis Galton, a gentleman-scholar from London. According to Galton, "It is, that their history affords means of distinguishing between the effects of tendencies received at birth, and of those that were imposed by the circumstances of their after lives; in other words, between the effects of nature and nurture."[1] Greater resemblance between identical than fraternal twins, in height or IQ, shows that genetic factors affect the development of that trait. This conclusion is reasonable because the members of identical and fraternal twin pairs are the same age and were raised together in the same home, so the only critical difference is their biological relatedness. Nature has provided science with a convenient assembly of human subjects that allows control over factors that may affect the way we mature and develop.

If the entire twin chronicle were so tidy we could stop here, but twin research has endured a mixed reception in behavioral science research. Throughout history, the twin method has been treated as both honored guest and social outcast. Supporters have reveled in the rich body of knowledge that only twin studies provide concerning the development of intelligence, special abilities, personality, psychopathology, diseases and virtually any human trait that can be measured and studied. However, detractors have pointed to "flaws" in the research design, and misuse of findings. For example, some people have argued that identical twins are so alike because they are treated more alike than fraternal twins, violating the *equal environments assumption* of the twin design, and that their more similar genetic makeup has little to do with it. Other people have worried that gene-behavior relationships will be used to discriminate between different groups of people or to deny the usefulness of programs designed to improve child care or educational opportunities. I will return to these important issues in the last chapter. Actually, it is only in the last two decades that the twin method has achieved its stunning comeback. This is partly due to greater appreciation for what twin studies can accomplish and to improved methods for interpreting results.[2]

What produces twins, who has twins and how twins differ from singletons, or nontwins, are among the vital questions that have fueled debates over the role of twins in scientific investigation. The biological events responsible for twinning are a good place to begin to sort through these issues. Identical (*monozygotic* or one-egg) twins result when a single fertilized egg, or *zygote,* divides between the first and fourteenth day after conception.[3] Further splitting can lead to identical triplets, quadruplets, quintuplets or sometimes more. The identical Dionne quintuplets, born in Canada in 1934, resulted from a single fertilized egg that split four times.[4] Based on the quints' relative likenesses in palm prints, hair whorl, handedness, facial form and ear shape, the University of Toronto research team constructed a "continuous chain of similarities," suggesting the position of each sister in the succession of divisions: Annette, Yvonne, Cécile, Marie and Emily.

What causes the fertilized egg to divide remains a mystery. One early theory linked identical twinning to delayed implantation of the fertilized egg in the uterus.[5] More recently, Dr. Judith G. Hall from the University of British Columbia, Canada, suggested that the early developing mass "senses" an error, attempts to "rid itself of" the abnormality, and may produce identical twins in a minority of cases.[6] Other possible explanations include time of fertilization and different inactivation patterns in female twins' X chromosomes. Some of these theories continue to be explored.

There is little evidence that the tendency to produce identical twins is tied to the genes.[7] Identical twinning seems to occur randomly so such twins might show up in virtually any family at any time. The fairly constant rate at which identical twins occur worldwide (approximately 1/250 births) is also evidence against a genetic influence on this type of twinning.[8] Nevertheless, the birth of more than one identical pair in some families has not gone unnoticed, and a closer look at the distinguishing features of these unusual families is worth doing. Identical twinning and left-handedness appear to occur together among the relatives of some identical twins,[9] although increases in birth abnormalities have not been observed in twins from such families.[10] A few investigators have proposed that a single gene whose expression varies may be responsible for identical twinning in some families.[11] These observations, while intriguing, are tentative at best.

Fraternal (*dizygotic* or two-egg) twins result when two different eggs are fertilized by two different sperm cells so that, genetically speaking, their relationship is the same as ordinary brothers and sisters. These twins come in two varieties: same-sex and opposite-sex. Fertilization of three, four or even five eggs at the same time is possible, although these "higher order multiples" occur less frequently than twins. Many combinations of identical and fraternal "supertwin" partners are possible.

A great deal more is understood about what causes fraternal than identical twinning, and some of the more surprising factors might well affect family planning decisions once they are more widely known. Fraternal twinning happens most often to women who bear children between the ages of 35 to 39 years.[12] The catalogue of other characteristics linked to fraternal twinning includes:

- *Maternal height and weight.*[13] Mothers of fraternal twins are taller and heavier, on average, than mothers of identical twins and mothers of singletons. Height and weight, per se, may not influence fraternal twinning, but may reflect hormonal or other factors.
- *Oral contraceptives.*[14] Evidence of links between oral contraceptive use and fraternal twinning is mixed. One study found that the chance of having fraternal twins increased if conception occurred within two months after contraceptive medication was withdrawn. Other studies showed that oral contraceptives decreased fraternal twinning or had no effect.
- *Social class membership.*[15] There is some evidence that fraternal twins occur more often in lower social classes, partly because family sizes are larger. Mothers with many children may be likely to express twinning tendencies because repeated pregnancies may accentuate these tendencies. This trend is not constant across studies, partly due to variable classification of families and exclusion of illegitimate births.
- *Birth order.*[16] Fraternal twins are likely to be among the last-born children in the family. This is because the chance of fraternal twinning increases with parity (number of previous children). One study found that because older mothers tend to have more children than younger mothers, the parity effects vanished when age was controlled.
- *Genetic transmission.*[17] A genetic predisposition for fraternal twinning occurs in families, but it is difficult to precisely predict who will bear twins. It is also unclear if the tendency to produce twins is passed only through the mother's family, or if the father's family may be involved. The genetic factor may involve hyperstimulation by follicle-stimulating hormone (FSH), suggested by elevated FSH levels in premenopausal mothers of fraternal twins.
- *Nutritional and food supply.*[18] The dietary habits of mothers of fraternal

twins do not differ from those of other mothers. There is, however, speculation and suggestive evidence that the Nigerian Yoruba tribe's high frequency of fraternal twinning (about 1/22 births) is explained by yams, a
food with estrogenlike substances. (Some studies have challenged this
particular theory.) Higher and more constant food sources may explain
the increased fraternal twinning rate in southwest Finland's archipelago
of Åland and Åboland, relative to the mainland.

• *Intercourse following periods of sexual abstinence.* [19] There is some evidence that fraternal twins are likely to be conceived following periods of
sexual abstinence. This effect has been observed when soldiers return
home to their wives following wartime service. It has also been observed
in orthodox Jewish families whose religious practices prescribe intercourse after two weeks' abstinence during menses and the next seven days.

• *Frequency of sexual intercourse.* [20] A link between more frequent sexual
intercourse and fraternal twins has been observed, based partly on a high
incidence of fraternal twins conceived illegitimately and before marriage. It is possible that, in some women, intercourse stimulates ovulation, and that frequent ovulation leads to the release of more than one
egg. Increased fraternal twinning has also been associated with an increased number of marriages which may offer more opportunities for intercourse and ovulation.

• *Seasonality.* [21] A British study reported a higher number of fraternal twins
and triplets born in December than in June. However, evidence of seasonal effects on twinning is inconclusive at best.

• *Emotional stress.* [22] Stressful events may lower sperm count and sperm
motility in males, cause menstruation to stop in females, and curb sexual desire in both sexes. These factors may have reduced fraternal twinning between the 1930s and 1970s in Western nations.

• *Environmental pesticides.* [23] There is speculation that fraternal twinning
rates are partly linked to the presence of chemical agents in the environment. They would have the effect of reducing sperm count, thus de-
creasing the frequency of fraternal twinning.

Whenever I review these points with parents of twins the response is a
blend of recognition, amusement and bewilderment. It is the bewildered parents, those whose family characteristics do not match those listed above, who
need explanation. The key concept here is that, while certain background factors may be important, fraternal twinning is influenced by a complex mix of
events. Therefore, it is hardly expected that all parents of twins will conform
to a certain type. An especially interesting question was raised by one mother
who puzzled over how her triplets could include an identical female pair and
a fraternal male cotriplet, since these two events are apparently unrelated.
One answer is that because identical twinning occurs randomly, it may be
simply a matter of chance when it occurs together with fraternal twinning.

However, Charles Boklage, a biologist at the University of East Carolina and the father of twin girls, believes that the biological origins of the two types of twins may have a lot in common, a finding that twin researchers view with interest.[24] This view, while not proven, is partly based on the high rates of left-handedness among parents of both identical and fraternal twins.

Misconceptions concerning the causes of fraternal twinning abound. Fraternal twinning does not "skip" generations, although this might occur in some families. Unfortunately, this area of research is plagued with difficulties because of questionable reports concerning twin births and twin types. Many couples I know pay attention to twins in their family trees only after the birth of their own twins, and twin type in these cases is often just a guess. Furthermore, family-planning decisions, such as restricting the number of children to two, or postponing the child-bearing years, may conceal natural reproductive patterns. A practice worth examining is how often people limit their families after delivering twins, especially if the twins' birth rank exceeds three or four. Some mothers whose first pregnancy produced twins yearn for a singleton child, believing they missed the intimacy that evolves from caring for a single infant. Several years ago, I received a surprised and somewhat distressed telephone call from a mother of fraternal twins who, on the advice of her physician, became pregnant in hope of having a nontwin child—but age, parity and genetics combined to produce her second twin pair.

Twins occur in only one out of eighty births in Western nations, yet the recent frenzy of scientific and media attention has persuaded us that they are everywhere. Among Caucasians, identical twins represent only about one-third of all twins, or 1/250 births. Fraternal twins represent the other two-thirds of the twin population, or 1/125 births. (These conventional estimates are being revised due to the new reproductive technologies, as I discuss in Chapter 10.) The identical twinning rate is fairly constant across populations and ethnic groups, while the fraternal twinning rate is as low as 1/330 among Asian populations, and as high as 1/63 among African populations. Twins are celebrated among Western Nigeria's Yoruba tribe, in which one in eleven people are part of a pair. One study found that fraternal twins comprised over 95% of Yoruban twins.[25] Among interracial couples, the chances of fraternal twinning are usually decided by the woman's background so that a black mother and a white father would be more like to produce fraternal twins than a white mother and a black father.

In 1996, the number of live births in the United States was 3,914,953; the number of infants born as twins was 100,750; the number of infants born as triplets was 5,298; the number of infants born as quadruplets was 560; and the number of infants born as quintuplets or more was 81.[26] I have estimated that there are 73 million twin pairs, or 146 million individual twins in the world.[27]

Why aren't twins more frequent than they are? An evolutionary perspective

suggests that the birth of same-age infants unduly burdens fa
of parental care, especially when there are other children in th
over, because twins are often born prematurely and show e
lems, they may press parents' emotional and financial res
limits. Multiple pregnancies may also pose serious health hazard
Nature sometimes offers "solutions" to such problems, for example, the spo
taneous abortion of one twin, although researchers disagree over whether
twins are eliminated more often than nontwins. The "Vanishing Twin Syndrome" occurs when one twin fetus is reabsorbed by the mother during the
first trimester, resulting in a singleton pregnancy. This event may be another
natural remedy when a multiple pregnancy becomes life-threatening.[29] The
rate of twin "disappearance" ranged from zero to 78% at medical centers in
which women pregnant with twins received a series of ultrasounds. This finding suggests that the human twinning rate is actually much higher than one
in eighty births. Many more of us start out as twins and parents of twins than
we know.

Dramatic cases involving infanticide of twins, usually the weaker twin or
the female in opposite-sex pairs, have occurred in some societies when removal of the child improves chances for the survival of parents or other siblings. In these societies twins are not at greater risk of infanticide than
singletons because the motivations are the same in both cases. The disturbing
findings that child abuse is elevated in families with twins urges serious re-
thinking of support services available to new parents.[30] A conversation with a
mother of several young children and infant twins is burned indelibly into my
brain. One of the twins was handicapped, and given the tensions of child care,
she admitted to being "this close" to becoming abusive. We will return to this
topic in the final chapter.

Most people assume that identical twins occur more frequently than fraternal twins, but this is true only in Asian populations where the fraternal
twinning rate is low. If identical twins appear to be more plentiful than fraternal twins, it is because their physical likeness makes them easy to spot. In
contrast, many fraternal twins blend into the background with their twinship
virtually hidden from view. I was amused to learn that when seven-year-old
fraternal female twins, Abigail and Rebecca Moore, attended a Girl Scouts
meeting they were "introduced" to one another by a member who assumed
they were unrelated. Their difference in appearance is one of the most dramatic I have ever seen because Abigail was a tall, sturdy blonde and Rebecca
was a petite, "pixie" redhead. Seeing them together with their older brother,
Adam, who resembled Rebecca, gave me the impression that the "wrong"
people had been born together. In contrast, some fraternal twins look very
much alike. I recall the intensity with which I stared at one young pair, Katie
and Becky Mitzuk, searching for a distinguishing feature, since I knew that a
blood test confirmed their fraternal twinship.

Very different looking fraternal twins, Abigail (left) and Rebecca Moore, with their older brother, Adam. Rebecca looks more like her older brother than her twin sister. PHOTO COURTESY OF KATHRYN MOORE.

The fact that some fraternal twin pairs look quite different, while others look quite similar, highlights a very interesting, often overlooked, feature of fraternal twins, namely that they vary on a "spectrum" of genetic relatedness. Fraternal twins share half their genes on average, but members of some pairs share genes for a greater number of traits than others. It is simply a matter of chance if fraternal twins inherit the same genes from each parent: Each person carries two forms of each gene and passes one of them to each child with a ½ probability. Fraternal twins, therefore, have a 50% chance of resembling or not resembling one another. This same process affects every one of our genes, and also explains why some siblings resemble one another in many traits or in only a few.

Assortative mating, the tendency for "like to marry like" in traits such as height, intelligence and personality, can affect fraternal twin similarity. If traits are influenced by genetic factors, then fraternal twin similarity in those traits may increase beyond the expected 50%. This is because when parents have the same genes for certain traits, they pass on the same genes to each child. Assortative mating would not affect identical twin resemblance, because identical twins share 100% of their genes, a situation unaffected by their parents' mating patterns.

Behavioral geneticists distinguish between *discrete* and *continuous* traits.[31] Discrete traits such as Huntington's chorea (progressive brain disease beginning in middle age) and Tay-Sach's disease (metabolic disorder causing blindness, mental retardation and death in infancy) are associated with single genes. They are considered to be "either-or" traits because peo-

Unusually similar looking fraternal twins Becky (left) and Katie Mitzuk. Based on their appearance, I was certain that these twins were identical. When their blood tests indicated fraternal twinning, I had them repeated to be sure. PHOTO CREDIT: DIANE MITZUK.

ple have them or they do not have them. The transmission of these traits in families follows the laws worked out by a Moravian monk, Gregor Mendel, in 1866. Huntington's chorea is a *dominant* trait, so only one copy of the gene (either from the mother *or* from the father) appears in affected individuals. Tay-Sach's disease is a *recessive* trait, so two copies of the gene (one from the mother *and* one from the father) are required for its expression. Continuous traits such as verbal skill, extraversion and depression are associated with many genes whose combined effects affect the appearance of the trait. The separate genes are, however, inherited, according to Mendel's laws.

Identical twins are not identical in every way and, in fact, show differences in virtually every trait that has ever been studied. The myriad of differences between identical twins is explained only by differences in their environments or by unusual events occurring soon after fertilization, a topic explored more closely in Chapter 2. The variations among both types of twins sometimes challenge the ability of scientists, family members and even twins themselves to know for sure if they are identical or fraternal.

One of my favorite cartoons shows a couple preparing to go out for the evening to visit friends who are parents to a pair of twins. "Don't ask them what kind of twins they have," the woman warns her partner, "or we will be debating that all night!" It is a great surprise to many people to encounter ambivalence among some parents and twins, even physicians, in response to queries about twin type. It is unfortunate that scientific procedures for twin-typing are not routinely applied following twin deliveries because mistakes lead to inaccurate accounts of how the gene-environment balance influences behavior. It is also disturbing that descriptions of methods for determining twin type are occasionally missing from scientific reports.

Knowledge of twin type is vital for individuals dedicated to the care of twins. Developmental discrepancies between twins might warrant different interpretations and treatments depending on twin type. If the musical talents of one fraternal twin foreshadowed a Beethoven or a Bach, while the twin brother or sister turned in a less polished performance, there may be small cause for alarm. This difference, while dramatic, might reflect a difference in genetically influenced ability which, in turn, may affect the amount of effort invested in musical activity. Most fraternal twin differences are natural and expected, and do not reflect "unfair" parenting. In contrast, marked differences in appearance or ability between identical twins might be the residue of a prenatal nutritional deficit, or a childhood illness, and would warrant serious attention. Knowledge of twin type can also inform emergency medical decisions involving blood transfusion or organ transplantation. It can additionally guide, but not dictate, decisions concerning classroom placement, recreational pursuits and other activities because the nature and extent of social closeness varies with twin type. Medical insurance does not cover the costs of blood-typing or DNA analysis for classifying twins, but Patricia Malmstrom, Director of Twin Services, in Berkeley, California, is attempting to reverse this policy.

It is curious that some parents prefer to remain in the dark over their children's twin type. This reluctance may come from worry that such information may affect how they treat their children. The stunned reaction of Rachalle Spears to learning that her twin daughters, Natalie and Noel, were really identical and not fraternal underlines this concern. She lamented that everyone, from teachers to camp counselors, had been told that the twins were fraternal, so she feared adjustment of their attitudes and practices toward her children. This concern is understandable, but is probably not justifiable. There is considerable research evidence that behavior toward twins is largely influenced by the twins themselves, and is generally unrelated to opinions of twin type. Even when parents of identical twins believe that their twins are fraternal, their personality ratings, warmth and criticism of their twins do not differ from those of parents who have correctly identified their children's twin types.[32]

Apologies to parents of twins, but mothers and fathers are among the least accurate judges of twin type. Members of one of the first participating pairs in my doctoral research were, according to their mother, very different in appearance and clearly fraternal. I was to study seven-year-old Jodie and Katie on consecutive days. On the second appointed day I waited with anticipation for the arrival of twin number two, wondering how she might differ from her obedient and somewhat shy sister. Anticipation turned to bewilderment when I caught sight of the child—why was the mother bringing the first twin back? It turned out that this second twin was identical to the first, but not in her mother's mind.

That parents are often incorrect in this important part of their twins' development flies in the face of common sense since they had the children, raised them from birth, and wrestled with so many decisions affecting their health and well-being. I suspect that parental misperceptions reflect acute sensitivity to subtle behavioral and physical differences between identical twins, perhaps a slightly broader smile or more animated facial expression, which escape the initial notice of an investigator or stranger. I have also learned that older siblings of identical twins possess an uncanny ability to tell them apart.

I confirmed this lesson in a 1984 study, using forty-seven identical and six fraternal twin pairs whose twin type had already been scientifically established (see below).[33] Based upon my first impression of physical resemblance, I correctly classified 94% of the twins, in contrast to parents who were accurate only 74% of the time. Even more striking, forty-two physicians (whose judgments were provided by mothers) ended up trailing the field with a shocking 67% accuracy. The observations of two blood-typing experts, Ronald Race and Ruth Sanger, anticipated my own experience: "For many years, Mr. James Shields of the Genetics Unit at the Maudsley Hospital [in England] has been sending us samples of blood from the twins. We find that the blood groups practically never contradict the opinion of such a skilled observer of twins."[34]

The most common error made by parents in this study was the misclassification of identical twins as fraternal, rather than the other way around. Given the probable sensitivity of parents to small differences between twins, look-alike fraternal twins are unlikely to be confused at home, although they might be confused by teachers, friends and especially distant relatives. Some look-alike fraternal cotwins may have difficulties fulfilling the similar expectations held by others, because there is no necessary connection between physical and behavioral resemblance.

Whenever I address gatherings of mothers of twins, I am besieged with requests to examine photographs of children and to render an opinion: identical or fraternal. I am still astonished, but no longer surprised, by the general lack of agreement between the mothers and me. Fortunately, a number of very reliable procedures are available for classifying same-sex twins as identical or fraternal. Opposite-sex twins are, of course, diagnosed as fraternal due to the sex difference.

• *Examination of blood group systems.* One of the most accurate methods for determining twin type is comparing cotwins' similarity in red blood cell factors. In addition to the familiar A, B, O and RH positive or negative (Rhesus) blood groups, twins may be tested for factors such as Kell, Duffy and Kidd. Cotwin comparison of eight blood group systems discriminates identical and fraternal twins with less than 2% error. Fraternal twins might match on a single blood group, so multiple comparisons are necessary to avoid their misclassification as identical.

When differences in any of the blood groups are detected the twins are diagnosed as fraternal with complete confidence. Fraternal cotwins do not have the same genetic makeup, so blood group differences always indicate nonidentical twinning. In contrast, identical cotwins have the same genes, so identical twinning is virtually certain if all their blood groups match. Identical twinning is *not* completely certain because, on rare occasions, fraternal twins can inherit exactly the same blood groups from their parents. Fortunately, I had seen such a pair during the course of my studies and, based upon their differences in eye color and height, which are strongly influenced by genetic factors, I reassigned them as fraternal twins. Many studies do not enable close contact between researchers and twins, but using large numbers of twins probably dilutes the effects of misclassifying a few pairs.

How accurate are the results from blood-typing? David T. Lykken, a twin researcher at the University of Minnesota, showed that when twins are compared across eighteen blood group factors, in addition to various physical measures, such as similarity in the ponderal index (height/cube root of body weight) and fingerprint ridge count, the probability of misdiagnosis is less than .001.[35]

• *Physical resemblance questionnaires.* Physical resemblance questionnaires can be used for twin classification if blood-typing is not possible.[36] These forms request information about twins' similarity in genetically influenced characteristics, such as hair color, eye color, height and weight. Other items may concern how often twins are confused by parents, teachers and friends. This method shows approximately 95% agreement with results from blood-typing analyses.

• *Fingerprint analysis.* Fingerprint analysis refers to the number of lines, or ridges, that are formed on the tips of the fingers during the second trimester of pregnancy. The total number of ridges across all ten fingers is genetically influenced, as revealed by the much greater resemblance between identical than fraternal twins. Identical twin resemblance is rarely perfect because intrauterine disturbances, such as viruses, may affect the formation and similarity of the ridges.

The palm and fingerprint characteristics of identical twins who differ in mental disorder are especially interesting because they may flag the effects of prenatal disturbances. Dr. H. Stefan Bracha reasoned that since fingerprint patterns and some phases of brain development occur during the same prenatal periods, identical twin differences in prenatal insult (e.g., infections or unequal blood supply, shown by cotwin differences in health or body size) may lead to differences in schizophrenia (mental disorder characterized by disordered thinking and disordered emotion) and in fingerprint characteristics in predisposed pairs, a relationship he was able to demonstrate.[37]

Some identical twins are partners in crime, but an innocent cotwin need not fear punishment for his sibling's misdeed. He or she can count on his fingerprints.

• *Molecular genetic techniques.* Techniques that can reveal the identity of individuals based upon unique characteristics in genetic material are extremely accurate. A procedure called DNA Fingerprinting, developed in the early 1980s by Dr. Alec Jeffreys at the University of Leicester in Great Britain, has been used to establish twin type, as well as paternity and identity.[38] DNA, or deoxyribonucleic acid, is present in all cells of the human body. Genes, the hereditary units that are transmitted from parents to children, are actually segments of DNA. Scientists can obtain DNA from blood samples and examine the segments to determine unique patterns for each individual.

Examining DNA profiles is ideally suited to classifying twins as identical or fraternal because it would be extremely rare for two people to show exactly the same patterns. Identical patterns indicate identical twins with near certainty, but it is theoretically possible for a fraternal pair to also show identical patterns.

Buccal cells, obtained by scraping the inner cheek with special brushes and swabs, can also be used for DNA testing.[39] It is a much less expensive procedure than analysis of blood-derived DNA. Cell samples can be obtained at home and mailed to laboratories for examination in specially prepared kits.

• *Examination of the placenta and fetal membranes.* The *placenta* and fetal membranes provide less information on twin type than many people realize. Once the sperm has penetrated the egg, the new cell develops very rapidly. This is followed by implantation in the uterus between days six and eight, the formation of two protective fetal membranes called the *amnion* and *chorion,* and the development of the placenta. The placenta connects the mother and fetus via the umbilical cord, enabling exchange of nutrients and waste products between them. The placenta is also one of the most misunderstood structures from the point of view of classifying twins as identical or fraternal.

All fraternal twin pairs have two placentae, two amnions and two chorions, but so do one-third of identical twins. Consequently, knowing that twins have "two of everything" is not informative with respect to twin type. Approximately two-thirds of identical twins share a placenta and chorion, but have separate amnions. Some identical twins share an amnion, chorion and placenta, but this is found in only .1–4% of the pairs. When division of the fertilized egg is incomplete, the result is the rare occurrence of *conjoined twins* (identical twins who are connected physically), most of whom are female.

Additional complications are posed by the chance that two placentae may fuse, opening a window for misdiagnosing fraternal twins as identical. Martin G. Bulmer, author of *The Biology of Twinning in Man* (1970), found

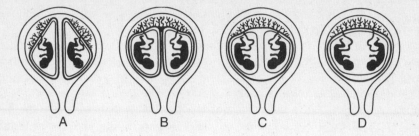

(A) Identical or fraternal twins with separate amnions, chorions and placentae. (B) Identical or fraternal twins with separate amnions and chorions, and fused placentae. (C) Identical twins with separate amnions, and a shared chorion and placenta. (D) Identical twins with a shared amnion, chorion and placenta. Source: (A–C) from Fundamentals of human reproduction *by E. L. Potter (1948). McGraw-Hill; (D) from* Principles of human genetics *by C. Stern (1960). 2nd ed. W. H. Freeman and Company.*

that 42% of fraternal twin pairs have fused placentae, hardly a trivial number. Fused placentae have also been observed among approximately 43% of two-chorion identical twins, but this situation would not lead to misdiagnosis.

I love talking to gatherings of parents of twins. These mothers and fathers have rare access to those living laboratories that are so precious to psychological and medical science. Parents know well what many professionals fail to see, namely that raising twins differs from raising singletons, and that genes explain a great deal about how people develop and why they differ. My visits to twins clubs are, by now, very predictable events: Following a thirty-minute lecture on some aspect of twinning, I field questions and comments for close to twice that time. It is at forums like these that I am privy to new bits of information and new threads of thought that sharpen my thinking about where research should be headed. One member casually noted that her identical twin daughters delighted in using their own private words and gestures to communicate, behavior sometimes called "twin language." Her inability to understand her twins was easily solved when an older child in the family proved an able interpreter. This was exciting news because a clever investigator could include older siblings in research programs to advance understanding of the nature of twins' private speech. This is an important problem to resolve, because twins, on average, perform below nontwins in general intelligence tests, especially in verbal abilities.[40]

Fortunately for twin researchers, there is an extensive network of local, state, national and international organizations for families with multiples. The members are highly dedicated to promoting work that will advance knowledge about human behavior and parenting. There are many informative ways to use twins in research. If some of the methods sound familiar, it is probably because informal versions of them are applied in homes, schools and workplaces everywhere.

• *Cotwin control studies.* Scientists may be interested in the power of a drug to prevent disease, or the effects of a new teaching style on achievement. The effects of drugs or teaching would be revealed most clearly if the comparison simultaneously included the same person both treated and untreated, but this is obviously impossible—or is it? It is possible only if identical twins are included in the research design. In the method of cotwin control, training or treatment is given to one identical twin and not to the other, or different treatments are provided to each pair member.[41] This procedure offers a new look at the relative contributions of maturation and experience to behavioral development. If twins show similar behavioral change or no change after training, this suggests that the treatment or intervention did not make a difference, and that biological maturation was the most important factor. If differences are observed, this suggests that training had an effect. Cotwin control studies have shown that maturation is the most important influence on stair-climbing and block manipulation at forty-two weeks of age,[42] and that Vitamin C has little effect on preventing the common cold.[43]

Sometimes unexpected events happen, producing cotwin control studies au naturel. A dramatic case involved ten-year-old identical twin boys, one of whom suffered from a near drowning accident.[44] Testing revealed a near absence of neuropsychological deficits in the affected twin, as compared with his brother, indicating excellent recovery, information that only an identical twin could provide.

• *Fraternal twin designs.* Genes explain both similarities and differences between family members. Several researchers have used fraternal twins to see if partners sharing higher proportions of genes also show increased behavioral or physical resemblance.

One of the more interesting studies of this kind found that fraternal twins who were uncertain or mistaken about their true twin type had a higher proportion of shared blood groups than pairs who classified their twin type correctly.[45] This index of biological similarity is very approximate because blood groups represent a small fraction of the many thousands of human genes. Some researchers feel that such efforts are unproductive because it is hard to find associations between complex behavior and a small amount of genetic variation. Remember that behavioral differences between fraternal twins are explained by both genetic and environmental factors, while identical twin differences are explained only by environmental factors. Recent breakthroughs in the *Human Genome Project,*[46] whose purpose is to determine the role and function of every human gene, may heighten the value of fraternal twin designs because of the greater precision that can be achieved in studying specific gene-behavior relationships.

• *Longitudinal twin studies.* Imagine a row of snapshots of the same person, one taken on each day of life, lined up one by one. As a child, I imagined that such a procedure would disclose the moment at which an infant grew into a toddler, or a teenager matured into an adult. Developmental changes are, however, too gradual and complex to be captured in this way so, instead, psychologists follow the same group of individuals over time to record changes in behavioral and physical traits. Unusual patterns of development have often been explained by environmental events, such as an illness or a move to a new neighborhood. Adding twins to longitudinal designs has shown that genetic factors affect the nature and timing of developmental ups and downs.[47]

A longitudinal twin study is launched the minute twins are born. Parents, teachers and friends are witnesses to the unfolding of development according to a finely calibrated, genetically influenced clock. Not all genes are active all the time, but instead exert their effects at certain times, such as at adolescence, causing male voices to deepen and hormones to surge. How certain genes get "turned on and off," and how these biological events translate into everyday behaviors, such as the infant's first word or the adolescent's final growth spurt, are among the exciting issues challenging scientists today.

• *The twin-family design.* Families with identical twins are like transformers, the popular children's toy of the 1980s that assumes new identities when its parts are rotated into new positions. These families add new layers to old relationships: When identical twins marry and raise families, each twin becomes a "genetic parent" to their nephews and nieces (their twin's children). These nieces and nephews become their aunts and uncles' "genetic" sons and daughters. This happens because identical twins are *clones,* making them biologically "interchangeable." (Clones derive from a single organism through asexual reproduction, making them genetically identical to that organism. Human identical twins arise from a sexually produced zygote which then divides or clones itself. I will expand on clone/twin issues in Chapter 10.) In other words, each twin carries the same genes involved in the production of his or her twin brother's or twin sister's children. Now consider that ordinary half-siblings result when a man or woman marries twice and bears children with each spouse. Next consider that in ordinary families, siblings' children are first cousins, but that in identical twin families cousins become "genetic half-siblings." The extraordinary parallel in these twin families comes from the fact that the two sets of children have the "same" mother or "same" father.

The plethora of unusual relationships generated by these families is captured by thirty-five-year-old identical twins Debbie Apodaca and Terri Bugbee, their husbands Mark and Dean, and their children, Kari, Katie and Steven. Debbie is Kari and Katie's biological mother, as well as Steven's aunt and "genetic mother;" Terri is Steven's biological mother, as well as Kari and Katie's aunt and "genetic mother." Kari and Katie Apodaca are Steven Bugbee's cousins, as well as his "genetic half-siblings."

The twin-family design disentangles heredity and environment in several ways. One way is to compare behavioral similarity between identical twin

Identical twin full sibling family. Pictured (left to right) are identical twin couples Pauline and Peter Collister, and John and Pat Collister. Pauline and Peter's children and Pat and John's children are "genetic full siblings." Pauline and Peter's daughter, Jennie, and John and Pat's son Tom were born on the same day (less than one hour apart!), making them "genetic fraternal twins." Their infant sons Joe (left) and Jack were born six weeks apart. PHOTO CREDIT: NANCY L. SEGAL.

mothers (or fathers) and (1) their own children and (2) their nieces and nephews. Identical twin parents are equally related to their own children and to their twin's children, but only share home environments with their own children. It is also possible to compare similarity among full-siblings who live together and between "half-siblings" who live apart. Most identical twin families live in separate homes, but the Apodacas and Bugbees share a five-bedroom house. They would *not* be ideal candidates for separating genetic and environmental influences on development because their children live with their aunts *and* their mothers.

Identical twin parents have commented on the confusion displayed by young children when confronting their aunt/mother or uncle/father. "Unky-daddy!" proved a clever compromise from one small family member. The power to identify actual parents is, however, truly tested when identical twins marry identical twins. Children resulting from these rare couplings are "genetic" full siblings, as well as double first cousins. In fact, opposite-sex "fraternal twins" were born in Great Britain to identical twin sisters who married identical twin brothers and delivered their son and daughter on the same day. The male infant "siblings" were born six weeks apart.

• *Twins as couples*. Couple effects, the subtle and intricate ways in which twins influence and react to one another, are well-known to twins and their families because they are expressed daily and in so many ways. Identical twin students, Tammie and Tapatha, students in one of my larger lecture classes in developmental psychology, arrived each week in tandem, selected adjacent seats, and scribbled notes in each other's notebooks. They seemed held together by an invisible glue that enabled effortless communication and understanding. Identical twins may be prototypes of cooperation at its finest, and we can hope to learn from them.

The "twins as couples" design can help us decide why some relationships work effortlessly, while others impose strain at every juncture. In this approach, researchers compare the social-interactional events and outcomes of identical and fraternal twin pairs as they engage in joint activities. The object of interest is the behavior of the pair—e.g., their level of cooperation or competition—rather than the separate behaviors of the individual twins, as in traditional twin studies. Differences in social relations between identical and fraternal twin pairs alert us to the possibility that genetic relatedness, perhaps in the form of similarities or differences in information processing strategies or temperamental styles, may affect twins' joint behaviors. How and why this may happen continues to challenge evolutionary psychologists, and twins are among the newest recruits to this research enterprise.

• *Partially reared apart twins*. Understanding how twins' psychological effects on one another may influence their behavioral similarity involves comparing twins living apart and living together.[48] Living together might make identical twins more alike in some behaviors, given opportunities for interaction and imitation. Alternatively, living together might whittle away at similarity as twins strive to achieve separate identities, especially during adolescence. It would also be important to know how living together or apart affects fraternal twin similarity.

Educational opportunities and career choices separate many twins, often for the first time. Partially reared apart twins are, therefore, liberally scattered throughout universities, workplaces and countries around the world. Many people are daily witnesses to the significance of separation in twins' lives and, over the years, I have encountered many identical and fraternal twins who have embraced, rejected or shown ambivalence toward the freedoms and responsibilities that separation brings. These themes are conveyed in Diane LeTourneau's 1990 film, *Like Two Peas in a Pod,* which follows the lives of three identical twin pairs: the charming Jean and Luc, who live and work in different cities; the endearing Alphonse and Louis, who live together in the same home; and the engaging Christiane and Christine, who react quite differently to their self-imposed separation. I recall that my twin and I viewed our choice of different colleges as a natural bend in our diverging pathways, but, fortunately for purposes of comparative study, some fraternal twins remain together. The partially reared apart twin design, which is highly under-used, has the potential to gather a great deal of the information we need to know about how environments and behavior work together.

• *Twins reared apart.* Scenes of identical and fraternal twins convey the inescapable impression that they belong together. Perhaps this is why the stories of reunions between separated twins move us to happy tears. Lucky Collins and Diane Clark, identical redheaded twins, were videotaped at their first reunion when they were thirty-four years old. They have the same marvelous laugh and a shared affection for horses and dogs. I cannot watch their first moment together without feeling a lump in my throat, and I have watched that tape many times. Scientists who study reared apart identical twins agree that they constitute the most potent, naturally occurring research design for disentangling genetic and environmental influences on behavior. If identical twins are separated early in infancy, and raised in contrasting environments, they provide a direct estimate of genetic influence on behavior. This is because the only factor they share is their genes. Studying fraternal twins reared apart tells us if similar rearing environments lead to behavioral resemblance. If, for example, fraternal twins are raised in similar environments, but still show differences in measured traits, this diminishes the estimated contribution of environmental factors to the development of those traits.

Identical twins reared apart are a favorite among journalists and talk show hosts. The idea that two people can be so similar after having been separately reared all their lives strikes many people as absolutely incredible, with some individuals turning to mental telepathy as the only likely explanation. However, twin researchers explain the many fascinating phenomena with reference to genetic relatedness and the tendency for people with similar genes to seek similar environments. All of us have chosen places to live, work and play, and these choices are partly fashioned by our genetically based interests and preferences. There are probably many other places and activities that would please us, but some that we could never imagine choosing. This concept can help us to understand why most reared apart identical twins end up being so similar, and why most reared apart fraternal twins do not. Unfortunately, fraternal twins are not a favorite on talk shows or in the printed media because they lack the visual interest of identical twins. Investigators see them as a vital comparison group—without them twin research would not be the same.

"Which one of you is older?" is a dreaded question of secondborn twins. Every minute becomes precious as the "older" twin lauds seniority over the "younger" sibling. It is right at delivery that birth order may assert its effects on twins, although whether its early imprint differs for identicals and fraternals is unknown. There is substantial evidence that firstborn twins are biologically advantaged, relative to secondborn twins, who are more susceptible to oxygen deficiency and other traumas.[49] Reduced respiratory exchange between the second fetus and placenta, due to reduced uterine size following the first twin's birth, or reduced placental function or blood volume following clamping of the first twin's umbilical cord are possible explanations. First-born and secondborn twins do not, however, differ in the frequency of new-born death.

In contrast, with secondborn twins' generally less favorable birth circum-stances, firstborn twins tend to contract HIV infection from affected mothers more often than secondborn twins. The twin closer to the uterine opening may experience greater exposure to infected blood than twins located higher in the womb, regardless of delivery route.[50] Some studies have also reported higher rates of HIV infection among twin infants, relative to nontwin infants,[51] and higher rates of infection among fraternal than identical twin infants.[52] Greater frequency of HIV infection among fraternals could be explained by the link between fraternal twinning and increased sexual activity.[53] Mothers of HIV-infected fraternal twins may engage in frequent sexual activity with multiple partners, increasing their risk for contracting the infection.[54] There is, of course, a difference between frequent sexual activity with one partner versus several partners. Individuals engaging in frequent sexual activity with one partner may be more likely to conceive fraternal twins, but not to contract HIV. It is also possible that because twin pregnancies require more care than non-twin pregnancies, AIDS cases among twins are identified more often.[55]

Consistent associations between twins' birth order and behavioral differ-ences have not been found. It is possible that lingering birth order effects from delivery are slight among the surviving twin pairs who comprise most research samples. I will return to this topic in later chapters.

Reverberating loudly between the lines of the scientific writings of most researchers, myself included, is reverence for and wonderment at the out-comes from the natural experiments in which twins take center stage. Rocky and Tony, the nine-year-old twins who visited my laboratory, turned out to be identical with perfectly matched freckled faces and punk-style haircuts. They have passions for jazz dancing and for each other. They showed a one-and-one-half-inch height difference, a half-pound weight difference, and a two-point IQ difference, all characteristic of identical twins. These similarities in identical twins, contrasted with the relative dissimilarities in fraternal twins, provide an elegant demonstration of genetic influences on these traits and on many others. However, Rocky was left-handed while Tony was right-handed, a nongenetic difference that affects approximately 25% of identical twins.[56]

The basic biology of twinning and twin research designs provide the im-portant backdrop for appreciating the wonderful ways that twins teach us about human development. There are many fascinating and informative vari-ations on the twin theme, and making sense of them is a giant step toward making sense of ourselves.

Identical, but Not the Same: Differences Between Identical Twins

Identical twins Mohammad and Ali Hidari came to the United States from Iran in 1984 with their parents, Daryoush and Azar. They are hardworking young men with close ties to family and friends. These brothers have remained faithful friends throughout their twenty-six years, and the joy they derive from their relationship always makes me smile.

Their mother, unaware she would be delivering twins, had selected a double name, Mohammad Ali, in the event of a son. This proved to be a lucky choice, because when two names were needed she had one that was easy to divide.

My association with Mohammad and Ali began in 1991 when Ali enrolled in a developmental psychology course that I would be teaching. This particular section was filled to capacity several days before classes started. There was a knock on the door and there stood Ali with a question for me: Would I admit his identical twin brother into the class? Even as I explained that this required me to waive the rules, I knew I would let Mohammad in! How could I resist the opportunity to observe the social exchanges, mannerisms and body postures of these identical individuals for three hours each week?

The physical resemblance of these twins overwhelms me, as it does most onlookers, and it is only with some effort that I can distinguish between them. However, despite their genetic identity, they are not perfect copies. They are like the same scene cast in different lights, the same tune played in different keys. Identical twins share their fundamental building blocks, but environmental influences operating soon after conception sometimes continue throughout early development. They may leave a legacy of behavioral and physical differences, some slight, others more apparent. Mohammed and Ali are virtually identical in height, but Mohammad is left-handed, while Ali is right-handed. Mohammad weighs 155 pounds, while Ali weighs 145 pounds, and they point out that Mohammad, who weighed six and one-half pounds at birth (one-half pound more than Ali), has been the heavier twin since infancy. Most recently, Mohammad had his appendix removed, but Ali did not, and the twin's initially identical eyesight is starting to differ. However, this pair displays only a few of the remarkable behavioral and physical differences that may be displayed by identical twins.[1] Some twins (identical and fraternal) even celebrate birthdays in different months or years because the second twin arrived on the other side of midnight.

Mothers of twins try desperately to be fair, but their control over many intrauterine events before birth is limited. An expectant mother of twins may follow a healthy dietary plan, but cannot insure that each developing fetus receives an equal share. Differences in the quantity of nutrition reaching each twin might produce size differences that could persist or affect other developmental features. How and why the genetic plan sometimes nods to the will of the early prenatal environment cannot always be known. Some significant experiences in our lives may well occur long before our parents greet us at birth.

Knowing that identical twins are not truly identical sends the important message that early life events influence the unfolding of genetically based developmental plans. These difference-producing events may occur before birth, at birth, after birth or involve all three. Some investigators favor replacing the terms *identical* and *fraternal twins* with *monozygotic (MZ or one-egg)* and *dizygotic (DZ or two-egg) twins,* as in the professional literature.[2] There is support for their reasoning, as I will show. In the interest of familiarity and convenience, I have retained the terms *identical* and *fraternal,* with the understanding that differences between *both* types of twins are varied and complex.

Some identical pairs share distinguishing features with certain other pairs, but not with all, prompting hard thinking over whether identical twins should be "lumped" together and studied as a single group. The more that is discovered about identical twinning, the more the answer is *no*. There are many very interesting variations of identical twinning which favor grouping of these pairs according to a number of informative schemes. Refinement of twin groups according to chorion type or sex is ultimately a great idea because it paints a clearer picture of how some traits are affected by specific birth and life history events.

Researchers recognize four varieties of identical twins:

- identical twins with two placentae, two chorions and two amnions
- identical twins with fused placentae, two chorions and two amnions

$\frac{1}{3}$ of identical twins "early-splitters"

- identical twins with one placenta, one chorion and two amnions
- identical twins with one placenta, one chorion and one amnion

$\frac{2}{3}$ of identical twins "late-splitters"

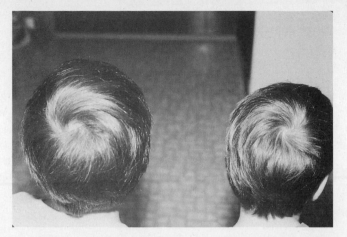

Eight-year-old identical twins, Tony (left) and Nick Notto, display their reversed hair whorls—Tony's is clockwise, Nick's is counterclockwise. Both twins are right-handed. PHOTO CREDIT: NANCY L. SEGAL.

These four identical twin types have been organized according to when the fertilized egg divides. Chorions develop by day four or five after conception, and amnions develop by day seven.[3] It is, therefore, reasoned that twins with two sets of membranes and placentae are "early-splitters" and twins with shared membranes and placentae are "late-splitters." (Early-splitters are thought to result from division at the two-celled stage, while late-splitters are thought to result from duplication of the inner cell mass.) Presumed relationships between twinning and placentation may, however, be less straightforward than has been believed and therefore require confirmation.[4] Research by Belgian investigators, discussed below, has brought new insight to when identical twinning events occur.

According to Dr. Walter E. Nance of the Medical College of Virginia, families with two or more identical twin pairs may also hold keys to enigmas surrounding the varieties of identical twinning. Only a few of these rare families have been investigated, but placental type (one or two placentae) has varied. This view of identical twinning would see these different identical twinning events as part of a common process.

Late-splitting (splitting after day seven) has been a common explanation of twin partner reversals in some physical traits.[5] Again, embryological complexities prevent firm conclusions regarding events causing "mirror-imaging" effects in identical twins. Time and location of the split may well be involved. It is also possible that splitting causes, or is caused by, developmental instability of the embryo. This could lead to abnormal or random reestablishment of left-sidedness and right-sidedness in some identical cotwins.[6]

The most obvious reversed effects in some identical twins are direction of

Eight-year-old identical twin sisters with cleft lip and palate on opposite sides of their faces. The girls show no other signs of physical reversal. PHOTO CREDIT: NANCY L. SEGAL.

the hair whorl (clockwise in one twin, counterclockwise in the other twin), location of physical marks (opposite birthmarks and moles) and preferred writing hand (twin "A" is left-handed, twin "B" is right-handed). Approximately 25% of identical twins show some form of mirror-image reversal. Eight-year-old identical twins Nick and Tony Notto display the most perfect example of opposite hair whorls I have ever seen (see photo page 23).

Identical twins may also show reversals in dental features (opposite cross-bites), fingerprints (patterns on twin "A's" left hand mirror patterns on twin "B's" right hand), facial features (twins show cleft lip and palate, i.e., fissure in the upper lip or palate, on opposite sides), visual characteristics (reversed abnormal optic nerve development) and disease symptoms (cancerous cells on opposite lungs).[7] In rare circumstances, identical twins may show reversals in internal organs or *situs inversus* (e.g., hearts on opposite sides of the body). Specific links between twinning and situs inversus have not, however, been found. One of the most unusual clusters of reversed features I have observed was presented by eight-year-old Peter and Brian Smith, the "Buddy Holly" twins, whose shaggy hair, horn-rimmed glasses and guitars recall the legendary rock star. Their mother, Nancy, noted that her boys favored different hands, were diagnosed with amblyopia (dimness of sight) in opposite eyes, and showed reversed congenital inguinal hernias (rupture of the lower abdomen at birth). Mrs. Smith delivered redheaded identical twins, Kevin and Robert, two years after her first set.

Splitting of the fertilized egg has also been associated with more extreme twin differences in physical features. In some cases, only one identical twin displays a cleft lip or palate, spina bifida (exposure of the spinal cord through the backbone), symmelia (severe limb malformation) or heart defects, while the twin partner remains unaffected. Maria and Kelli Ann Ellis, eight-year-old identical twins, looked dramatically different when I first met them because Kelli Ann's cleft palate and subsequent surgeries had substantially altered her facial contours. (Sadly, Kelli Ann, the secondborn twin, passed away at the age of fifteen years from bone cancer.) Interestingly, identical twins show an increase in early major structural malformations, over and beyond fraternal twins and singletons. When a major defect occurs in identical twins, it is estimated that in 80% of the cases only one twin is affected.[8] The frequency of symmelia (developmental anomaly in which the legs appear to be fused) is 100 times higher among identical twins than among singletons.[9] Why should identical twins be especially prone to these difficulties? It has been suggested that the middle area of the fertilized egg, where splitting occurs, has a tendency to be weak. In fact, when identical twinning was artificially "induced" in mice and in fish, it created midline abnormalities in the resulting organisms.

No one can boast that the left and right sides of his or her face, body and limbs are identical mirror images of one another. This departure from perfect body consistency, or *fluctuating asymmetry* (FA), is a new research interest of evolutionary psychologists.[10] Greater FA, as measured by greater right-left differences in facial width, ear length or wrist circumference, is thought to reflect greater developmental instability caused by stressful biological and environmental events. People with greater FA are judged to be less attractive and tend to have fewer sexual partners than people with lower FA, characteristics associated with reproductive success.

A recent controversy revolves around the extent to which genetic fitness (the ability to produce viable children) may be genetically influenced and the extent to which FA may be one indicator of fitness. A solution to this debate might be found if identical twin differences in FA were linked to differences in fitness because the twins' genes associated with fitness are the same. A study by Linda Mealey, on leave at the University of Queensland in Brisbane, Australia, showed that lower FA identical twins were judged more attractive than their higher FA cotwins.[11] Identical twins also offer a superb test of controversial evidence that left-handers die sooner than right-handers because of more frequent birth-related deficits, immune deficiencies and accidents.[12] Identical twins share genes associated with disease susceptibility and other health characteristics, so the earlier death of left-handed cotwins or higher FA cotwins could offer insight on factors affecting longevity.

It is amusing that body asymmetries should now emerge as a serious topic for human behavioral investigation. Twins and families have long known that some twins find it difficult to identify themselves in snapshots, even if they have not known why. Perhaps some twins' faces in mirrors match cotwins' faces in photographs. Another facial difference between identical twins, the system of blood vessels laid out in uniquely branching patterns, is even more challenging to the naked eye. A new scanning technique reaches beyond identical foreheads, cheeks and chins to produce a *thermogram,* an imprint of individual differences in temperature caused by individual variability in blood vessel patterns.[13] Three-dimensional modeling of identical twins' facial features can also reveal the effects of disease differences. A female teenage twin who had infant cardiac illness showed smaller facial height than her sister, as well as a reversal in the normal larger facial height to facial width ratio.[14]

Faces, bodies and even the brains of identical twins are subject to the secrets and uncertainties of development occurring as early as the two-celled stage. New technology has revealed that *convolutions,* the folds and spirals decorating the surface of the human brain, show contrasting patterns in normal identical twin pairs. Recent studies found that identical twins show little resemblance in the shape of the *planum temporale,* a brain structure possibly associated with language.[15] Colleagues and I observed that opposite-handed identical cotwins showed similar patterns of brain involvement on most verbal and nonverbal tasks, except for finger-tapping combined with verbal problem-solving.[16] Why some differences in brain-behavior relationships were observed remains a mystery. Nobel laureate Gerald Edelman believes that the dynamic nature of nervous system development guarantees individuality in neural connections, so that even identical twins would show significant differences.[17] A true challenge for the future will be to determine if, and how, these brain differences predict dissimilarities in identical twins' behaviors.

The presence of separate or shared chorions surrounding twins opens windows into their early developmental world. Indiana University researchers found that four- to six-year-old identical twins who shared a single chorion (the "late-splitters") were more alike in personality measures, such as self-control and social competence, than identical twins with separate chorions. These findings match personality data collected on adult twins.[18] Differences in six types of mental abilities were, however, not detected between the two identical twin groups. Other studies comparing intellectual resemblance between one-chorion and two-chorion identical twin pairs have either found greater similarity in the one-chorion group, or no differences at all. The findings are somewhat surprising because one-chorion twins sometimes end up with size and health differences due to shared fetal circulation, yet their mental skills and personality traits are more alike than those of two-chorion twins. Perhaps one-chorion twins who make their way into psychological studies are those who have successfully weathered the prenatal storms.

According to conventional wisdom, identical twins differing in handedness should be the late-splitting variety, that is they should share a chorion. Two recent studies failed to confirm this relationship.[19] I wonder if the explanation is that researchers did not separate the twins according to their

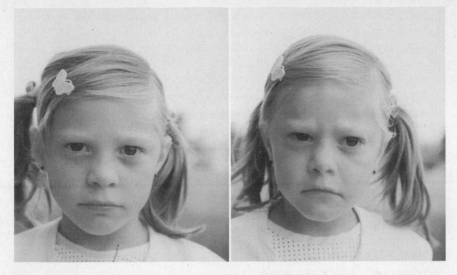

Prenatal trauma and delivery difficulties explain the striking physical con-trasts between eight-year-old identical twins, Missi (left) and Kelley Seemuth. Now, at age twenty-seven, Missi is seven inches taller and thirty-seven pounds heavier than her sister. PHOTO CREDIT: NANCY L. SEGAL.

source of left-handedness. Some types of left-handedness may be explained by birth trauma,[20] a finding with implications for identical twins, who face more birth problems than nontwins. This means that some two-chorion iden-tical cotwins may show reversed hand preference because of "pathological left-handedness" in a twin initially destined to be right-handed. Secondborn twins would be expected to show increased pathological left-handedness,[21] al-though increased left-handedness among firstborn twins has also been re-ported.[22]

I compared the IQ scores of opposite-handed identical twins, assigning them to groups according to whether left-handed twins weighed more or less at birth than their right-handed cotwins.[23] It turned out that the lighter left-handers scored lower than all the other twins, suggesting prenatal difficulties. It is also possible that these twins resulted from unequal splitting of the fer-tilized egg, such that one twin developed from fewer cells than the other. In contrast, heavier left-handers were the highest-scoring group, suggesting that their left-handedness reflected the time and/or location of zygotic splitting. Organizing identical twin pairs according to handedness *and* possible source of opposite-handedness may disclose previously hidden information.

Some early studies (1920–1976) found that about 20% of twin individuals are left-handed, as compared with 10–12% of singletons.[24] More recent in-vestigations have both upheld and refuted this finding.[25] One early investigator, Charles Lauterbach, proposed that all left-handed people were originally part of a twin pair, but there is little factual basis to this claim.[26]

Extreme situations, such as those involving prolonged oxygen deprivation or a detached placenta, may produce more obvious developmental differences between identical twins, especially the secondborns. As a graduate student, I studied blond identical twins, Missi and Kelley Seemuth. Their mother, Barbara, had experienced premature labor several times in her pregnancy, but when delivery contractions ceased during the birth of Kelley, the second twin, they caused Kelley to stop breathing. Furthermore, Kelley's placenta was marginally attached so prenatal nutrition was probably inadequate. Both handedness and birth weight showed mirror-image reversal— Kelley was right-handed and four pounds six ounces, Missi was left-handed and six pounds four ounces. At age eight, these sisters showed a height difference of five inches and a weight difference of nine pounds, yet their facial features and body form were completely identical. Kelley scored eleven IQ points below her sister, a difference typical of fraternal rather than identical twins. She showed borderline seizure disorder at age seven and possible heart problems at age eight, likely consequences of dire events before and during birth.

The fetal transfusion syndrome, or shared blood circulation between identical twin fetuses, can also lead to differences in health characteristics. The chronic, or long-term, form of this condition involves blood imbalance due to transfusion between identical twins who share a chorion. Single chorions have connecting blood vessels, so blood sometimes passes from one twin to the other, but not back again. Some pairs may be more severely affected than others. Elizabeth Bryan, pediatrician and medical director of the Multiple Births Foundation in London, explains that the donor twin is typically the smaller one, whose development is then affected by loss of nutrition.[27] Large discrepancies in size, or even death to one or both fetuses, may result. The acute form of this condition, which occurs during labor, also affects identical twins with a single chorion. Twins in this case may, or may not, be similar in birth weight, but immediate treatment of both twins is usually required to avoid cardiac failure. Most studies find that identical twins with one chorion are more likely to be born early, differ in birth weight, and suffer early death compared to identical twins with two chorions.[28] A substantial difference in the number of fingerprint ridges may reflect physical size differences midway through the pregnancy.[29] Some very rare cases of identical twin transfusion have resulted from fusion of separate placentae.[30]

It may seem surprising that identical twins may show greater birth weight differences than fraternal twins because their genetic commonality suggests otherwise.[31] This finding is undoubtedly tied to unusual intrauterine conditions, especially fetal transfusion syndrome, that affect some identical twins. However, identical twins gradually become more and more similar in size, largely offsetting some of these early effects, while fraternal twins show the opposite pattern. If identical twins differ in birth weight by less than 25%, it is unlikely that the difference will persist later in development.[32]

Whenever I lecture to students in behavioral genetics and evolutionary psychology courses, I explain that identical twins are genetically identical because they split from a single fertilized egg—but are they genetically identical all the time? Unknown to few outside the medical community, some extremely rare cases of identical twins with different genetic conditions, even sexes, have been reported. Chromosomes, the threadlike structures in the center of our cells which contain our genetic information, sometimes fail to separate properly during cell division. Every primary sperm and egg cell includes that person's 46 chromosomes, organized into pairs, but these cells divide before fertilization. The two products, therefore, contain just one chromosome from each pair, or 23. The later joining of sperm and egg restores the normal human chromosome number to 46. Sometimes two chromosomes from the same pair end up in a mature sperm or egg, or an X chromosome never enters the sperm or egg. If a mature egg (or sperm) lacking an X chromosome is joined with a normal sperm (or egg), the result is a Turner Syndrome female (45, XO). This condition is characterized by short stature, webbed neck, low-set ears, underdeveloped sexual organs and poor directional sense. Turner Syndrome occurs in about 1/2,500 live female births, but 99% of the fetuses are miscarried.[33]

There have been identical female pairs in which only one sister was affected with Turner Syndrome. An especially interesting case included twins who were *mosaics*.[34] Mosaics are individuals with two or more distinct cell populations arising from a change (mutation) or chromosomal error in genetic material soon after conception. This is followed by replication of both altered and original cells. In this case, both twins' blood revealed a patchwork of cell types, mostly normal, but some with a missing X chromosome. Only one twin displayed Turner Syndrome, making it likely that splitting of the inner cell mass (cells that become the embryo) and loss of the X chromosome in only one twin occurred almost simultaneously. Shared blood circulation during fetal development may have caused cell exchange between the twins. The unaffected twin did not display the condition because abnormal cells transfused from her sister were foreign to her, and because in mosaics abnormal cells often grow more slowly than normal cells.

Some researchers believe that Turner Syndrome and identical twinning are linked in some families, but this has not been fully confirmed.[35] There have also been reports of normal identical twins whose partners suffer from Down Syndrome or trisomy 21 (inheritance of an extra twenty-first chromosome marked by mental retardation, protruding tongue, short stature and other physical features) caused by cell error or gene mutation soon after splitting, or who show various multiple malformations.[36] Down Syndrome occurs less often in identical twins than in singletons, possibly because stress from a chromosomal disorder plus zygotic splitting leads to loss of these conceptions.

Surely the most dramatic dissimilarities between identical twins involve differences in sex. How is this possible if identical twins share all their genetic material, including the two sex-determining chromosomes, XX for females and XY for males? If one of two inner cell masses, initially destined to become male, loses a Y chromosome, this can result in a Turner Syndrome female and a normal identical male twin. A number of such cases have been described in the medical literature. Even more compelling is a set of identical Italian triplets composed of two normal males and a female with Turner Syndrome.[37] It is believed they are the first and only identical triplets to show a sex difference.

The rarity of these unusual twins and triplets prevents a systematic survey of how their sex differences affect development. These multiples do, however, offer an informative look into what can happen when atypical events tamper with nature's plan. This is because these naturally occurring studies come equipped with perfect genetic controls. The little girl from the Italian triplet set retained a Y chromosome in some of her cells, so she was expected to grow taller than other children with her condition, but not as tall as her brothers. Another rare but possible occurrence is identical twins with different mitochondrial DNA. Children's mitochondria, which are inherited through their mother, are tiny cell structures that convert food to energy. Mitochondrial DNA is the same for identical and fraternal twins, so cotwin differences would be due to rare mutations (gene changes). If mutations occurred in a few mitochondrial cells and they were differently distributed between identical twins, they could produce differences. Mitochondrial mutations have been found in the cells of some patients with Alzheimer's disease,[38] a condition in which twins show a 67–78% similarity.[39] Identical cotwin differences in behavioral or medical traits have not been conclusively linked to mitochondrial differences. This possibility was not, however, ruled out in a case of identical male twins discordant for adrenoleukodystrophy (paralysis and sensory loss).[40]

In the midst of the research interest that sex-discordant and disease-discordant identical multiples inevitably attract, we should never forget that these tragic cases ensnare families in escalating emotional and financial struggles. Dilemmas faced by families with affected members undergo significant revision when identical twins are involved because the normal "version" of the affected partner is always present. Along with questions such as, What could have been? What should have been? Why us? Why him? Why her? are the questions, Why not me? Are we still twins? that are uniquely replayed throughout the life history of the family. Nowhere are these themes conveyed more forcefully than in the story that follows.

First some background. While preparing this chapter I made a note to myself to mention a most remarkable case of male-female identical twins whose sex difference was caused not by the occasional whims of human biology but by an extraordinary medical mishap. The *next day* a comprehensive followup report to that case, first published nearly thirty years ago, appeared in newspapers across the country.[41] An attempt to correct a problem with the foreskin of an identical infant male twin led to accidental removal of the child's penis, and the decision to rear him as a girl. Years of surgical reconstruction, hormone therapy and parental "push" toward femininity by way of dolls and dresses followed.

The case was initially viewed as a noteworthy scientific achievement, proof that gender identity was a product of learning and adolescent hormones. However, Joan (now John) ripped dresses, rejected feminine toys, and even attempted to stand while urinating. Ceaseless ridicule from classmates culminated in suicidal feelings until the truth was finally revealed when he was sixteen years old. "All of a sudden everything clicked."

Surgery and hormone treatments have now restored John's male identity, as well as his ability to have intercourse and achieve orgasm, and he has married and adopted his wife's children. The important lesson is that his brain had been masculinized by the time of his birth, a process that was not to be undone by experience. It did not take a twin to show this, but his untreated identical twin brother provides an important gauge against which to judge the impact of the surgery, hormones and rearing practices. Little has been revealed about the social relations between the brothers, probably out of respect for their privacy.

The random fancies of biology have left other fascinating identical twin differences in their wake, some of which affect female twins only. About six to eight days after conception (at the time of implantation) one of the two X chromosomes in each cell "shuts down." Which one does so is determined by chance.[42] This process, called *lyonization,* does not affect males who have one X chromosome and one Y chromosome. The sole "switch" that causes the shutdown is the *Xist gene,* discovered in March 1997 by Laura Herzing and colleagues at the Institute for Cancer Research in London.[43] There is no guarantee that the same X chromosomes shut down in both twins, opening up the possibility for differences in traits found on the X chromosome.

Elizabeth Tuckerman at the Queen Elizabeth Medical Centre in Birmingham, England, described identical twin sisters, one of whom showed above average intelligence, while her twin was diagnosed with Fragile X Syndrome. This condition is marked by mental retardation and revealed by breaks and tears in the X chromosome.[44] Both twins had inherited one normal X chromosome and one abnormal X chromosome, but the shutting down process kept the abnormal X active in only one twin. It is hardly surprising that their parents believed they were fraternal twins because, while they were indistinguishable at one year of age, they showed dramatic differences in facial features by age ten.

The strange ways of the X chromosome can also explain reports of identical female twin differences in Duchenne muscular dystrophy, a weakening and wasting of the muscles; gonadal dysgenesis, the abnormal development of the ovaries; and color-blindness, the inability to discriminate between certain hues.[45] Only two of the identical Dionne quintuplets of Canada were color-blind even though all five carried the gene.[46] These rare cases may help to explain some oddities in the inheritance patterns of our own families. Marked differences between sisters, or the sudden appearance of a previously silent characteristic or condition, may make sense if we discover which X chromosomes are fortuitously turned on or turned off. Pairs showing marked differences in X-linked traits will attract medical attention, but disease similarity in identical female twins carrying the genes for X-linked disorders has *never* been observed.[47]

A "timely" issue in twin research is: Does identical twinning occur *before* or *after* X-inactivation? Researchers have shown that the blood cells of one-chorion (presumably late-splitting) twins show more similar X-inactivation patterns than those of two-chorion (presumably early-splitting) twins.[48] This suggests that twinning may proceed *or* follow inactivation of X chromosomes. Alternatively, late-splitting twins' cell patterns could be more similar because of their shared prenatal blood supply. Belgian researchers found, however, that X-inactivation patterns in identical female cotwins' buccal mucosa cells (cells from the inner cheek which do not circulate) matched those from blood analyses.[49] Hypothesized relationships between twinning events and chorion type are thus supported by this finding.

Dr. Nance proposed that even if twinning occurs after X inactivation it could magnify any differences in twins' X chromosomes. Because the fertilized egg splits, identical twins originate from a smaller number of cells than nontwins so they must "catch up" in growth. Greater catch-up should produce larger cell patches in affected female cotwins who may have been smaller from the start. Citing a supportive case study, Nance concluded that "twin lyons have larger spots!"[50] How often unequal splitting may explain MZ cotwins' X-inactivation differences is, however, unknown.[51]

An intriguing new discovery is that genes on the X chromosome may be implicated in sensitivity to social cues.[52] British researchers observed that Turner Syndrome girls had more friends, were more aware of others' feelings, and were happier if their single X chromosome came from their father rather than from their mother. This phenomenon, called *genomic imprinting,* occurs when the same stretch of genetic material is expressed differently in a child, depending upon which parent it came from. (Imprinting activates a gene on one chromosome, but silences the same gene on the corresponding chromosome.) The X-inactivation process in females means that twin researchers will need to take a second look at the social similarities of female identical twins.

*   *   *

What if it were possible to peer into the hidden world of the womb to take an inventory of the future baby's behavior? Alessandra Piontelli has provided twin researchers with a ringside view of twin-to-twin behavior and interaction before birth.[53] Beginning at the eighteenth week of pregnancy, she used ultrasonic procedures to periodically visualize and record the head and small body parts of each twin. Most remarkable were the stable individual and twin pair behavioral patterns that emerged over time, which included kicking, punching and gentle stroking. Observations of twins after birth demonstrated that behaviors displayed in prenatal life continued. In the womb, identical twins, Giorgio and Fabrizio, had "lived in a 'tangle' from the start" and their general lack of activity suggested a "parasitic life." However, Fabrizio, the smaller twin, occasionally initiated some movement that would be repeated by Giorgio, his larger twin brother. As young children they displayed an intense interdependence, with Fabrizio continuing to assume the leadership role. Alessandra Piontelli's "double features" are a joy to behold, but caution urges additional work to firmly establish these reported relationships.

I was treated to another series of intrauterine twin films at the 1998 International Twin Congress in Helsinki. Professor Birgit Arabin of the Sophia Ziekenhuis, the Netherlands, presented scenes of fetal twins engaged in slow body contacts (88th gestational day), complex contacts or "embrace" (99th gestational day) and mouth contacts "kiss" (110th gestational day).[54] How prenatal interactions may affect twins' postnatal behaviors might be learned through this medium.

Scattered reports of congenital syphilis and congenital rubella syndrome in one identical twin, leading to developmental abnormalities, also show prenatal differences in twins' susceptibility to infections. Reasons for such differences are unclear, but unequal intrauterine blood supply may explain twins' differential disease resistance both before and after birth. These findings are interesting to researchers concerned with viral explanations of schizophrenia, and with why less than 50% of affected identical twins have affected twin siblings. A link between birth order and schizophrenia in differing twins has not been supported, but some birth factors have been implicated as I discuss in Chapter 5.

In December 1997 an intriguing "medical mystery" was posted on the Internet.[55] The mystery featured a photograph of forty-three-year-old identical female twins with distinct facial differences. The twin on the left appeared normal in contrast with her sister who looked dark, gaunt and aged. One month later over 800 readers had suggested (1) Addison's disease (a hormonal condition causing weakness, low blood pressure and darkened skin pigmentation) in the woman on the right, (2) right facial weakness in the woman on the left, (3) both of these and (4) autoimmune disorder. Dr. Jerome P. Kassirer, one of the physicians who posed the riddle, believed the combined diagnosis (choice 3) was best, but left us guessing: "Only further followup can determine whether this diagnosis is correct."

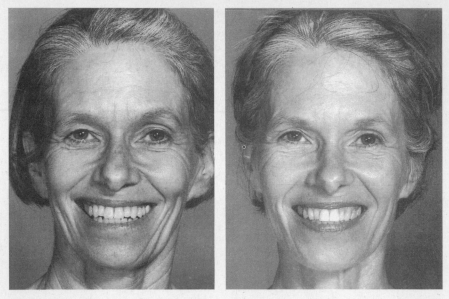

Years of smoking and sun exposure accelerated aging processes in identical twin Gay Block (left). They caused Gay to appear older than her sister, Gwyn Sirota, although the twins themselves did not see this. PHOTO CREDIT: DARRICK E. ANTELL.

Equally dramatic identical twin differences can occur when one twin lies in the sun and the other twin sits in the shade. Sixty-year-old identical twins, Gay Block and Gwyn Sirota, lived outside Baltimore, Maryland, until age twenty-one, when Gay moved to California. Years of intense sun exposure and smoking caused Gay's skin to wrinkle more noticeably than Gwyn's—although the left side of each twin's face showed greater signs of aging than the right side. Both twins told me they were unaware of their different appearance, but New York plastic surgeon Dr. Darrick E. Antell saw it immediately. He chose them from among other twins to take part in his research on what causes skin to age. The twins underwent cosmetic surgery in April 1998 for "the adventure, the contribution to science, and the opportunity to share with one another." Now they look younger and more alike.

The vast majority of identical twins end up being very much alike in be-havior and physique, despite nature's tendency to create contrasts. Over the years, some initially disadvantaged twins have "caught up" to their more ad-vantaged partners.[56] This speaks to the resiliency of human beings, especially their ability to tolerate stresses and strains within certain limits.

The environment is so much more than our schools, workplaces and com-munities. It is also the small universe we inhabit during the nine months from conception to birth, which may include any number of unexpected, incidental and idiosyncratic events. Sometimes we carry indelible marks from these experiences, while in some cases the effects are fleeting. Identical twins are the reflecting pools whose altered images teach us how the range of environmental influences shape developmental outcomes.

Natural Experiments: Unusual Twin Types

In March 1997 Craig Fujii, a photographer from the *Los Angeles Times,* took snapshots in my laboratory of two identical twin sets to accompany an article detailing research activities at California State University's Twin Studies Center. He is also a twin, a member of a male-female pair, and this circumstance of birth made the assignment especially attractive for him. It was remarkable that the six of us were all twins, and Craig and I joked that our being fraternal made us "second-class twins," minor league players, in contrast with the elite identicals who always captivate crowds.

To many people fraternal twins are less alluring than identical twins because they lack the behavioral and physical likeness that is so powerful and seductive. Over the years I have always encouraged members of the media to include fraternal twins in talk shows and in newspaper articles, yet identical twins remain the multiples of choice. Unbeknownst to many, however, scientists have been accumulating extraordinary observations about fraternal twins that promise to capture the public's fascination and direct attention to these neglected pairs. Some of the findings increase our understanding of unusual birth histories, parental favoritism and gender nonconformity among both twins and nontwins, while others explain why some twins and siblings can be so very different from one another.

The more widely I have studied the phenomena of twins and twinning, the more often I have encountered compelling observations and reports:

- In 1810, a report in the medical literature announced the birth of a pair of twins with different fathers. Not only that, the twins differed in ethnicity: one was white, the other mulatto.[1]

- Some fraternal twins may be more closely related on their mother's side than on their father's side.[2] Some of these twins may fall "in between" ordinary identical and fraternal twins in genetic relatedness.
- Mandy Charnock is black and her husband, Tom, is white. In 1982, Mandy delivered fraternal twins: Wesley, who looks white, and Thomas, who looks black.[3]
- Fraternal twins can be conceived at the same time, but their birthdays can be days, weeks or even months apart. In 1996, Peggy Lynn from Danville, Pennsylvania, delivered fraternal opposite-sex twins Eric and Hanna eighty-four days apart.[4] Fraternal twins can also be conceived at different times, but born in unison.[5]

These tidbits show that fraternal twinning is far from simple. In addition to the usual processes of double ovulation and fertilization that produce fraternal twins are some extraordinary variations and perturbations. The examples provided above are just some of the naturally occurring consequences of fraternal twinning in humans. These events seem to be rare, but in truth little is known about how frequently they occur. Scientists, eager to explore the research potential of these "natural experiments," may be uncertain of how to insert these pairs into ongoing studies. In fact, some pairs place considerable strain on the definition of what it means to be a twin.

Little is known about the frequency of unusual fraternal twins because they are often born "without fanfare," making their atypical features easy to miss. For example, a woman may release two eggs simultaneously, but only one might be fertilized at a particular time. It may require another coital act, taking place within three or four days after the first, for fertilization of the second egg to occur. A woman might also release eggs at different times within the same menstrual cycle, again opening up the possibility for fertilization during separate coital acts. Such twins are called *superfecundated twins*.[6] If the same male fathers both children, it is extremely unlikely that the twins' origin would be known, and that is why superfecundation may occur more often than most people believe. Japanese researchers may be especially attuned to this issue because, even if separate fathers are involved, the limited differences in skin color and other physical characteristics of most residents in that country make superfecundation virtually impossible to detect. It is, therefore, all the more remarkable that a likely case of superfecundated twins was discovered in Japan. The twins' difference in crown-to-rump length detected at ten weeks into the pregnancy, rather than questionable paternity, brought it to light.[7]

Superfecundated twins may well be noticed when different males have fathered each child, especially if their ethnicities differ as occurred in the famous case in 1810. In this instance, one twin was white and the other twin was mulatto. There has even been reference to triplets representing three different races. If parents from the same ethnic background have twins whose ethnicities differ from them, and from each other, it is virtually certain that they are unrelated on their father's side, making them genetically equivalent to half-siblings. This situation repeated in 1982 when a Caucasian mother sought medical attention for her four-year-old fraternal twin girls who differed greatly in complexion, appearance, and features of fetal hydantoin syndrome.[8] Fetal hydantoin syndrome, characterized by craniofacial and skeletal abnormalities, has been linked with prenatal exposure to phenytoin, a substance the twins' mother received for epilepsy treatment at thirteen. The less severely affected twin had black hair, dark skin and Negroid features, while her more severely affected cotwin had brown hair, fair skin and Caucasoid features. The mother admitted that the twins may have been fathered by men of different racial origin. The putative fathers' unavailability precluded confirmatory blood group analysis, but the twins' bloods showed race-specific factors consistent with their having different fathers.

Fathers need not differ in ethnicity in order for superfecundation to be revealed. If infant twins look "different enough," and mothers keep track of sexual partners, the possibility of two fathers may be raised. This happened to an Arizona family in a case that led to a bitter custody dispute. Upon learning that she was pregnant, Brenda Taylor did not know if the true father of her children was Dean, her current husband, or Peter Tonnessen, her former husband.[9] Upon delivering twins, Megan and Lauren, on September 2, 1994, she was relieved to see that firstborn Megan resembled Dean. Pleasure turned to pain when she recognized the resemblance between Lauren and Peter. Peter tried to obtain custody of Lauren, while Dean was willing to be father to both girls. Peter was eventually granted limited visitation rights and the twins stayed together.

The phrase "Mommy's babies, daddy's maybes" captures an essential feature of this case, namely that women can be certain of who their children are, while for fathers it may be a guessing game. Evolutionary researchers have been interested in this concept of *paternity uncertainty* and how it affects a father's devotion to his child.[10] One suggestion is that fathers unconsciously gauge the degree of physical resemblance between themselves and their children, and use it as a kind of "proof" of relatedness, especially during the first year of life. The greater the resemblance, the greater the investment because it only makes sense to "invest" in one's own genes and not in someone else's. Of course, such parental favoritism would not operate at a conscious level since, as evolutionary psychologists assert, people may possess genetic predispositions to be sensitive to who their kin are since caring for kin improved survival in the distant past. Interestingly, Nicholas Christenfeld found greater resemblance between children and fathers than between children and mothers during the child's first year of life, but not beyond, a possible natural insurance plan to promote child care by fathers.[11] Paternity uncertainty is not specific to twin births, but the presence of twins, especially fraternal, enables good tests of relationships between perceived father-child resemblance and fathers' behavior toward children because twins are the same age. It is time for someone to take on this research task in a formal way.

Nonpaternity rates are estimated to be between 5 and 30%,[12] so a substantial minority of children are not related to presumed fathers. Reasoning from group statistics to individual cases may raise unwarranted paternity doubts among some fathers, especially if they perceive differences between themselves and their children. A close look at interracial and interethnic couples with twins and singletons is an excellent way to show that physical discrepancies are not always grounds for questionable paternity.

Mixed couples no longer turn heads, but apparent racial or ethnic differences between parents and children, or between siblings, often attract our attention. The whims of genetic transmission sometimes dictate that children from interracial or interethnic couples closely resemble one parent or the other, rather than appear as a fair compromise of the two. Mixed couples with one child may know this well. A blond, fair-skinned friend of mine, formerly married to a dark-skinned Latino, has a twelve-year-old daughter who resembles her so closely that seeing them together is to witness live, time-lapse photography. Other mixed couples with fraternal twins, such as Mandy and Tom, whose seemingly "black" and "white" fraternal twin boys made news around the world, experience this situation more profoundly. Over the years I have learned that these "interracial" twins are not so exceptional after all. One of my students showed me a photograph of his fraternal twin nieces, Jamisha and Lacresha, who are stand-ins for their black mother and white-Filipino father, respectively. These examples remind us that genetics accounts for both similarities and differences among family members.

Fraternal twinning may also "straddle" lengthy time intervals. Some pregnant women undergo the release and fertilization of a second egg several weeks following the first conception, leading to a twin pregnancy. This process, known as *superfetation,* occurs in both human and nonhuman mammals. Unlike their superfecundated counterparts, *superfetated twins* are easier to spot, even when the same male is responsible for both infants, because deliveries may include full-term infants separated by weeks or months, or the birth or abortion of twin infants who differ in developmental maturity. In 1974, Sam Rhine and Walter Nance (formerly of the Indiana University Medical School in Indianapolis) described a family with six twin pairs, born over four consecutive generations, all of which included one normal twin and either one malformed fetus, one stillborn twin or one premature infant twin.[13] In order to explain the repeated occurrence of this event, they suggested a gene for superfetation, passed down through either the maternal or paternal branches of the family. The gene would work to reverse the usual ovulation inhibition that commences after conception. It is also possible that delayed implantation of one embryo in the uterus, rather than superfetation, could

Seven-year-old Lacresha (left) resembles the twins' white-Filipino father, while her sister Jamisha resembles the twins' black mother. Family members call them the "salt and pepper twins." PHOTO COURTESY OF ANGELA WILLIAMS.

produce marked developmental differences between fraternal twins, but the Rhine-Nance theory accounts for superfetated twins and twinning on mothers' or fathers' side of a family.

Surprisingly, superfetation can even occur following conceptions brought about by the new reproductive technologies. In an unusual case, transfer of three eggs and thirty thousand sperm into the Fallopian tube of a thirty-three-year-old woman culminated in a twin pregnancy, later diagnosed as a triplet pregnancy. Unfortunately, none of the conceptions survived due to a partial spontaneous abortion during the fifteenth week of pregnancy. An autopsy report confirmed the presence of two embryos, two fetuses and a fetal remnant. The enormous differences in the developmental stages of the embryos and fetuses suggested that the embryos resulted from a later ovulation.[14] Debbie Gilbert of England, believed to be the sixth person in the world to conceive twins (naturally) a month apart, was expected to deliver a healthy boy and girl.[15] A second ultrasound identified a second fetus four weeks younger than the first. Seven pound, four ounce Lucy and five pound, four ounce Timothy arrived on November 25, 1997. Their growth patterns, followed from early in the pregnancy, were normal but one month apart.

More people than we realize probably started out as part of a twin pair, yet were destined to live lives as singletons. It is difficult to know the proportion of "silent" twins among us, although improved medical technology and more frequent prenatal examinations may provide answers. It is now estimated that over one in eight natural pregnancies begin as twins and that there are six singleton twins for every liveborn pair.[16] I have listened to many lone twins whose twin siblings did not survive the birth process, and while most do not dwell on past events, they express an unmistakable sadness when the topic arises. I have sometimes wondered if the participation of surviving twins in singleton studies of cleft palate or family relations has affected the findings in unknown ways. Medical and psychological researchers might screen singleton samples for surviving twins whose biological beginnings render them questionable candidates for certain investigations.

The "third twin type" is, by now, a buzzword that has made the rounds of twin clubs and computer chat rooms to describe twins who appear less alike than ordinary identical twins, but more alike than ordinary fraternal twins. Some parents in a quandary over whether their twins are identical or fraternal have embraced this convenient solution, but do we really need another twin type? The answer is *yes,* because there is convincing evidence of a special class of biological events that give rise to a unique "third" type of twin. Interestingly, in 1919, as modern twin research was getting under way, a prominent statistician, Ronald A. Fisher, claimed that twin data sorted more naturally into three groups, rather than into two groups;[17] however, he rejected this claim in 1925 when his theory failed to fit some twin data. Since then, some intriguing case reports have added substance to his initial observation, although some researchers are still skeptical.[18]

The concept of the third twin type is fraught with misunderstandings, even among twin researchers. The third twin type is an umbrella for three types of twins, not all of which fall "in between identicals and fraternals."[19] What happens is that the oocyte (primary egg cell) divides twice on its path to maturity, yielding egg cells and polar bodies at different stages along the way. Three polar bodies (which result when the primary egg divides on its way to maturity) are usually smaller than egg cells and do not play a meaningful role in reproduction. Occasionally, polar bodies are large enough to be fertilized. Depending on the interplay of chromosomes, fertilization of both the mature egg and a polar body may result in fraternal twins who span the range from unusual genetic similarity to unusual genetic dissimilarity. This third type of twinning is also called *polar body twinning.* According to Martin Bulmer, the most similar polar body twins would share all their mother's genes, but only about half their father's genes—making them a rare breed of "three-quarter siblings"—more alike than most fraternal twins, but less alike than most identical twins. These twins would involve division of the ovum, followed by fertilization. Dr. Walter Nance has, however, suggested that deficient cytoplasm (material surrounding the cell nucleus and associated with maternal inheritance) in the polar body twin might mask any increased similarity from shared genes. At the other end of the spectrum are twins resulting from fertilization of primary and secondary oocytes and polar bodies. These twins would be unlikely to share all their maternal genes because of chromosomal exchanges between the egg cell and polar body. They would, therefore, be less alike genetically than the "three-quarter siblings," and some pairs might be among the least similar fraternal twins.

The only way to tell for sure if twins belong to this exotic class of twinning is to perform genetic analyses of twins and their parents to see which parent contributed which genes to which twin. Evidence of polar body twinning comes from a 1981 case that included a normal male twin and a grossly malformed female fetus.[20] Most remarkable was the presence of only one chorion, a feature thought to be unique to identical twins. Extensive testing suggested that the mature egg and an early polar body had been fertilized by different sperm. It was not revealed if the mother had conceived naturally or had taken fertility drugs. I wondered if Clomid, a drug that stimulates ovulation and boosts the chances of a multiple pregnancy, might have been involved.

In the late 1970s and early 1980s, it seemed that every mother of twins whom I interviewed had taken Clomid. Terri Godlewski, mother of eight-month-old twins, Michael and Matthew, presented conflicting information about her sons' twin type. Shared blood groups, a single chorion, fetal transfusion syndrome and matching birthmarks favored Michael and Matthew as identical twins. Contradictory evidence in the form of small differences in hair and eye color and slight variations in ear shape was puzzling. The twins are now eleven, and while tests on additional blood groups have yielded identical results and their eye color difference has lessened, their twin type remains a riddle. Tests of the twins' DNA could provide an answer.

It was with great interest that I listened to a 1979 presentation by Karen Fisher and Herbert Polesky linking Clomid to polar body twinning.[21] Sixteen twin pairs whose mothers had taken this drug showed remarkably high similarity in blood groups (three pairs completely matched across a series of red cell antigens), although comparing heritable features, such as eye color and earlobe shape, indicated nonidentical twinning in all cases but one. I remember the lovely pictures of the different pairs flashing across the screen, and being so impressed by the facial resemblance of some of the partners, even as I was aware of their physical differences. The relationship between fertility drugs and twins is complex, and new research suggests that Clomid and other ovulatory-inducing substances may trigger both identical and fraternal twinning.

I urge parents not to assume the third kind of twin when twin type seems uncertain or at odds with what physicians or child care manuals report. Twins may have inherited many of the same genes for a number of traits, which also explains why some biological siblings, who are genetically equivalent to ordinary fraternal twins, can look or behave very much alike. It is also possible that prenatal factors caused developmental differences in ordinary identical twins, causing them to look different. No one knows the number of "walking third twins," nor do we know whether all theoretically possible third twin types are viable, because only medically significant cases attract attention.

The third twin type may not always be the easy label for hard-to-type twins, but it might solve a different vexing question, namely why as many as 25% of fraternal twins are opposite-handed. Logic tells us that fraternal twins may differ in handedness either because of inherited differences, or because one twin experienced birth trauma. However, these two explanations cannot explain why so many fraternal pairs include a right-handed twin and a left-handed twin. It took the keen eye of Charles Boklage to suggest an association between polar body twinning and reversed handedness in fraternal twins.[22] Specifically, a division leading to near equality of an egg cell and polar body might well provide the missing piece to this story. His theory is not yet confirmed, but opens up new ways of thinking about what may be happening in the wombs of some women.

A *chimera* may be an imaginary being composed of incongruous parts or a fabrication of the mind. A chimera is also an individual whose different cell types come from different people. What does this have to do with twins? In cattle, prenatal blood exchange between fraternal twins occurs often, causing sterility in 90–95% of the females from opposite-sex pairs.[23] This circumstance is called the *freemartin effect* and the sterile females *freemartins*. Such *partial chimerism* occurs when the blood vessels of a fused placenta become interconnected. Cattle twins (but not human twins) can have single chorions despite being fraternal because the dividing chorial membranes fuse and disappear.

In 1975 evidence of more than one blood type was found in the members of twenty-five fraternal twin pairs.[24] By 1995 only about forty cases had been described, leading researchers to assume that human chimerism was rare. The following year, however, Dutch researchers reported blood group chimerism in 8% (32/415) of fraternal twin pairs and 21% (12/57) of fraternal triplet sets, showing that it occurs more commonly than was realized.[25] Using a sensitive fluorescence technique, they detected very low proportions of foreign cells in twins' blood.

In humans, the "foreign fetal blood" received by one or both twins is not rejected, but is tolerated throughout their lifetime.[26] Some male twins from opposite-sex pairs have even shown white blood cell characteristics typical of females, and some females have shown the male chromosomal constitution, or XY, in their white blood cells.[27] Chimeric twins can accept skin grafts from one another. There is, however, no evidence of infertility in female twins from opposite-sex chimeric pairs.

Chimerism is easy to confirm when both twins are alive and available for testing, but it could understandably raise eyebrows when detected in a single individual. (Chimerism in twins was first reported in 1953, twenty-five years after a male cotwin died in infancy, leaving his blood cells to survive in his twin sister![28]) The possibility of an early history as a twin cannot be ruled out when chimerism is detected. Its presence can also complicate decisions surrounding twin type, as in a case involving a normal male whose twin sister had Down Syndrome.[29] The twins' blood groups were the same, consistent with identical twinning, so the Down Syndrome could have been caused by a biological error after splitting. However, the twins differed in sex so their similar blood groups were probably caused by exchanges before birth. Note that these twins are not more alike genetically than ordinary fraternal twins. Most importantly, the sex difference identified the twins as fraternal—had they been same-sex, they would have been classified as identical, which probably would have been wrong.

John Barth, the author of *The Sot-Weed Factor, Lost in the Funhouse* and, ironically, *Chimera,* is also the "Jack" in a "Jack and Jill" twin pair. Either as a twin, or as an observer of human nature, or both, he has astutely noted that less is known about what he calls "opposite-sexers" than about other types of twins.[30] Researchers have preferred to contrast the similarity of identical twins with that of same-sex fraternal twins to avoid the bothersome "sex difference." Speaking with parents, I frequently find myself caught between defense of, and apology for, this omission. Recent statistical methods can, however, disclose sex differences in gene expression in studies using same-sex and opposite-sex twin pairs.

I call them the "unseen twins" because their lives as twins are camouflaged. Like other multiples, opposite-sex twins share the womb, their date of birth, their first day of school and all their graduation days. Their sex difference, however, runs contrary to fundamental themes of twinness, namely similarity and synchrony. In truth, the mental, social and physical development of males and females differs in many important ways. However, information from new sources is stirring up excitement among twin researchers who are using opposite-sex twins in creative ways to learn how males and females function.

The newfound popularity of opposite-sex twins comes from surprising places. There has been a rediscovery of the freemartin effect and similar observations in other species.[31] Female mice positioned between males in the uterus are heavier and more aggressive than females positioned between females.[32] Gerbils also add to this story because males positioned between two females sire smaller litters, are less likely to impregnate females, and are less likely to elicit scent-marking by females.[33] Hormonal transfer occurring in the womb seems responsible.

These findings are not new, yet word of them has spread rather recently among researchers dedicated to deciphering relationships between hormones and behavior in humans. Until recently, the power and potential of twin designs were probably underappreciated by many investigators outside behavioral genetics. Behavioral geneticists, recalling the sting of early criticisms of their theories, focused on restoring the reputation of the field by examining genetic influence on behavior through carefully constructed twin and adoption designs. This situation may have temporarily halted opposite-sex twin research because genetic effects were most clearly revealed by studies comparing identical and same-sex fraternal twins. Now, in addition to applying new analytical methods to study sex- and gender-related behavioral differences, researchers have taken a fresh look at opposite-sex twins as a unique natural experiment—a possible human analogue to situations posed by some nonhumans.

Females from human opposite-sex twin pairs do not differ in obvious ways from other females. There are only a few hints of behavioral and reproductive effects possibly tied to prenatal coexistence with an opposite-sex twin. An Australian study showed that average age at first menstruation and first pregnancy, length of menstrual cycle, and body height were slightly higher for opposite-sex female twins than same-sex female twins.[34] These measures are most comparable to those suggesting hormonal masculinization in female rats and mice. Questions concerning birth were answered only by twins who had children, so the possibility that opposite-sex nonrespondents experienced greater reproductive difficulty than same-sex nonrespondents remains. Another twin study found no difference in fertility, age at first birth, or feminine interests between Finnish female twins from opposite-sex and same-sex pairs.[35]

The new research opportunities offered by opposite-sex twins have proven intoxicating to some investigators who have produced a potpourri of curious and compelling findings and ideas. Sensation-seeking, the desire for thrill and adventure, is behavior in which males usually outscore females, but Susan Resnick showed that females from opposite-sex pairs score higher than females from same-sex pairs.[36] Dennis McFadden found that females with twin brothers produce far fewer of the continuous tones, or "hums," emitted by the human ear, compared with other female twins and nontwins, and do not differ from their brothers. These hums, or *spontaneous otoacoustic emissions (SOAE),* are discharged by hair cells in the inner ear intended to raise the volume of weak sounds to make them audible.[37] Shirley Cole-Harding found that while males typically outperform females on some spatial ability tasks, female twins are on a par with their twin brothers, and obtain higher initial scores than same-sex female twins.[38] Ed Miller noted that elevated rates of myopia (nearsightedness) in opposite-sex twins were reported in early studies.[39] Charles Boklage claimed that a co-ed fetal environment offers special protection against fetal and newborn death, and brain damage due to oxygen deficiency at birth, especially for male twins.[40] Even more intriguing, Boklage has developed a set of adult facial measurements that can tell if someone is male or female, but these measures do not work for opposite-sex

twins. In other words, a rule based on typical male-female differences in left-
and right-side dental measures misclassified 70% of males and 90% of females from opposite-sex pairs. His novel findings encourage greater attention to the origins, development and classification of twins from fraternal
pairs.

A comprehensive theory uniting handedness and hormones, put forth by
Norman Geschwind and Paul Behan in 1982, proposed that left-handedness
and immune disorders are associated with fetal exposure to elevated testosterone levels.[41] Testosterone was thought to affect the brain by delaying left
hemisphere development, and enhancing right hemisphere development and
immunity via the thymus gland. This complex model has been both positively
and negatively received. Norman Geschwind passed away suddenly in 1984,
but his creative insights, some tentative but well-reasoned, are preserved in a
special 1985 issue of the *Archives of Neurology*. I was particularly drawn to
speculations that male twins from same-sex pairs and female twins from opposite-sex pairs should show increased left-handedness, due to increased levels
of fetal testosterone. He suggested that this effect may begin with their mothers, who are more often left-handed than mothers of singletons, possibly due to
high testosterone-producing tendencies in their families. A recent British study
of 33,000 twins and singletons found the highest frequency of left-handedness
among male twins, followed by female twins, male singletons and female singletons,[42] somewhat consistent with testosterone "overdosing" in same-sex
male and female opposite-sex twins. Few studies have examined handedness
within opposite-sex pairs, although Dutch researchers reported more left-
handedness among opposite-sex than same-sex fraternal twins.[43] Understanding of prenatal biological influences on hand preference and other behaviors
should benefit from fresh attention to opposite-sex twin pairs.

In a 1966 study of five- and six-year-old twins, Helen Koch found that
girls from opposite-sex pairs did not appear to be "masculinized" by their
brothers' influence so much as boys seemed to be "feminized" by their sisters' influence.[44] Male twins from opposite-sex pairs were more responsible,
more obedient and less active than nontwin boys, although these differences
were less pronounced relative to same-sex fraternal boys. Female twins
showed only a "very slight hint" of greater masculinity than same-sex fraternal twins when judged by teachers, but they were socially dominant over their
brothers and tended to boss them. These results seem contradictory to findings of greater risk-taking tendencies in females from opposite-sex pairs, but
the younger age of twins in this study may explain the difference.

Maybe twin researchers are now onto something exciting that will ultimately explain unforeseen behavioral and developmental detours among
nontwins. Perhaps slight hormonal excesses or deficiencies present before
birth, coupled with certain environmental events, may heighten spatial visu-

alization or risk-taking tendencies in females. However, is this new opposite-sex twin perspective the best approach to understanding sex- and gender-related behavioral differences?

Not all research bears out the predictions generated by the redesigned opposite-sex twin model. In a study of childhood sex-role behaviors, males with twin sisters scored slightly lower than males with twin brothers, but no differences were observed among females.[45] In a more recent study, Brenda Henderson and Sheri Berenbaum showed that young females with twin brothers did not spend more time playing with boys' toys than did females with twin sisters or females with older brothers.[46]

A different explanation for many of the male-female twin findings may be just as compelling, namely that daily social interactions between opposite-sex twins blur behavioral differences between them. For example, female twins might partake in the thrill-seeking activities of their brothers. Reviews of this field by Marcia Collaer and Melissa Hines, and by Michael Bryden and colleagues,[47] remind us that not all human behaviors are equally affected by prenatal hormones, and that the lengthy gap between hormonal exposure in utero and behavioral measurement in childhood, renders this research enterprise somewhat tenuous. However, the reduced number of "hums" from female ears seems to require input from hormonal theories.

An appropriate and challenging goal is zeroing in on research designs that separate early hormonal influences from child-rearing experiences. A little hard thinking, plus an inventory of the vast array of available twin and twin-like partnerships, may identify the necessary tools. I suggest recruiting two unique kinships whose biological and environmental situations are complete opposites:

- *Male-female twins raised apart.* Opposite-sex twins separated in infancy and raised in separate environments can demonstrate the effects of early exposure to cross-sex hormones in the absence of a shared rearing environment. It is assumed that the twins' new adoptive homes would not include a near-in-age opposite-sex sibling.
- *Male-female unrelated siblings of the same age raised together.* Opposite-sex unrelated siblings of the same age raised together from infancy, which include two adoptees or one adoptee and one birth child, can reveal the effects of growing up with a different sex partner in the absence of early exposure to cross-sex hormones.

The availability of these two kinships, in addition to ordinary fraternal twin pairs, could ignite a series of exciting comparisons, each of which would allow for the important separation of biology and experience. If, for example, female twins reared apart from their brothers are more active or more skillful at spatial visualization tasks than females raised with an adoptive brother of the same age, this would tell us that early hormonal influences, rather than common rearing with a male, affect the development of those behaviors. Such evidence would not conclusively settle the question of whether fetal hormones shape behavior, but would sharply define targets for future investigation, such as when and for how long hormones must take effect. Brain imaging studies comparing male and female twins and nontwins might shed insight on these issues.

Twins reared apart are rare, but ongoing studies in Minnesota and in Scandinavia promise that a sufficiently large sample of opposite-sex twins can be found to allow informative comparisons. At first glance, unrelated siblings of the same age also seem scarce, but since finding my first pair in 1989 I have located over 100 such pairs. (Much more will be said in Chapter 8 about the valuable contributions to human developmental research offered by these sibships.) Some people might wonder why some researchers studying behavioral sex differences would take the trouble to track down these unusual cases. The answer is that twins, especially if combined with same-age adoptees, offer the best control over the effects of genetics and rearing.

There is so much more to twin types than just the identical-fraternal distinction, and there is greater complexity to the definition of a twin than most people realize. The various pairs, ranging from superfecundated to polar body to chimeric, offer so many new, intriguing angles for studying how genetic relatedness may affect behavioral similarity and social relations. How similar are twins with different fathers, relative to full siblings who differ in age but who share a father? Do twins with different fathers squabble more than ordinary fraternal twins or siblings? The varied hues and textures of twinship make us better positioned to understand who relatives resemble and with whom they get along.

A downside to twins' failure to sort neatly into two exclusive groupings concerns attempts to estimate genetic influence on behavior. If, for example, a twin study of running speed compared an identical twin group to a fraternal twin group which included a large proportion of superfecundated twins with different fathers, the "fraternal twins" would be less alike than expected, overestimating genetic influence. Researchers are generally unconcerned with this potential wrinkle, and find safety in large numbers of twins. It may be time to take a fresh look at studies whose findings conflict, or which report larger than expected identical twin–fraternal twin differences. Twins may not always be what they seem to be, and depending on one's definition, twins with different conception dates or different birthdays may not be twins at all.

4

Developing in Tandem: Intelligence and Special Mental Skills

T he person on the other end of the receiver was clearly agitated. The father of identical twin college seniors explained that his sons had been wrongly accused of cheating on a class assignment and risked failing grades and expulsion from their university. A professor had detected an identical error in their work and, believing these mistakes were too unusual to have been produced without collaboration, referred the matter to a university committee. The twins' father had hired an attorney to argue on behalf of his boys who, to his knowledge, had always been honest and dedicated students. He wondered if similar findings and observations, so vital to his sons' predicament, were contained in the psychological twin literature.

The events of this case are not surprising. A vast number of studies reveal striking similarities between identical twins in general intelligence and special mental skills. Most importantly—and this point is often missed—the degree of intellectual resemblance between identical twins, while remarkable, is less impressive than their consistently greater resemblance relative to fraternal twins. Longitudinal studies show that during the first six months of life, identical and fraternal twins are equally similar on mental development measures.[1] After that, identical twins become more alike until two years of age, when their degree of similarity becomes very high and remains high throughout childhood and adolescence, even increasing somewhat in adulthood. IQ *heritability* (the extent to which genetic differences among people explain their IQ differences) is estimated to be 20% in infancy, 40% in childhood, 50% in adolescence and 60% in adulthood.[2]

Heritability increase with age means that individual differences in intelligence become more closely tied to genetic factors. It also means that the amount of variation due to environmental factors is changing. *Shared environments* have less of an impact on IQ over time, while *nonshared environments* continue to be important, explaining about 30% of IQ differences among adults. *Shared environments* include events common to family members which make them alike (such as eating a vegetarian diet or vacationing in Europe). *Nonshared environments* include events uniquely experienced by individual family members which make them different (such as winning a race or contracting an illness). In addition to showing increase in IQ heritability, research also shows that genetic influence on IQ is stable from age to age. This seems contradictory—how can genetic influence increase *and* remain stable over time? The answer is that (1) waning of shared environmental influence causes genetic influence to increase over time, *and* (2) genetic effects on intelligence at one age affect intelligence at another age. For example, genes underlying verbal ability at age three also underlie verbal ability at age four. There is evidence that new sources of genetic influence are also expressed during development, notably at ages one, two, three and seven.[3] Dutch researchers found genetic influence on intelligence at age seven, but questioned whether new genetic effects arise at that age.[4]

Heritability estimates are not magical, nor are they unchanging. They are based on correlations (measures of relationship) between the test scores of pairs of twins, siblings, and parents and children. A *correlation* expresses the extent to which two or more things may be related. Correlations range from −1.0 to +1.0. A positive correlation for height and weight would mean that as height increases (or decreases) weight also increases (or decreases). A negative correlation for marital age and family size would mean that older parents have fewer children. A zero correlation (0.0) between two things means that they are unrelated. Correlations *do not* tell us why two things are related or unrelated, only that they might be.[5]

IQ correlations equal to 1.0 would mean that cotwins' test scores correspond precisely. If one twin had a high IQ the other twin would also have a high IQ. IQ correlations between twins or between other relatives are never 1.0, but they are generally higher when people share a higher proportion of genes. Typical IQ correlations are .86 for identical twins reared together, .75 for identical twins reared apart, .60 for fraternal twins, .42 for parents and children and .15 for cousins.[6] IQ correlations for adoptive relatives are generally lower then those for biological relatives. They reflect the effects of shared environmental influences on intellectual development. Psychologists usually specify a range of IQ heritability values (.30–.70) rather than a single estimate.

Heritability has nothing to do with how high or how low people score on a test. It concerns the *differences* among people's scores, namely the extent to which genetic and environmental influence explain these differences. Heritability estimates can be high or low regardless of the population's average—improved training can raise the population average, but does not eliminate individual differences in skill. Heritability estimates refer only to how much genes and environments affect the behavioral variation of *populations,* not the behavior of *individuals*.

Genes explain intellectual change as well as intellectual stability. The late Ronald Wilson added insight and dimension to the Louisville Twin Studies with a longitudinal twin design.[7] Repeated testing of twins between three months and fifteen years of age revealed greater coordination of developmental "ups" and "downs," or age-to-age changes, among identical twins than fraternal twins. The more recent Colorado Adoption Project has revealed major "transition points" in intellectual growth at about ages two, three and seven (when new genetic effects appear; genetic effects stabilize by age four).[8] Researchers also showed increasing genetic influence and stability in high-scoring twins at ages fourteen, twenty, twenty-four and thirty-six months.[9] These findings show that in addition to level of intelligence, the timing and sequencing of intellectual growth and development are genetically influenced. This approach to intelligence is part of a new research area, *developmental behavior genetics,* which aims to understand the unfolding of behavior over time, and the processes leading there.

A clever twist to the Louisville study was the introduction of near-in-age singleton siblings of the twins. These siblings showed different developmental contours than the twins, despite being raised together. The rare triplet sets composed of one identical pair and one fraternal cotriplet capture this effect even more dramatically because age differences do not intrude and, in fact, the predicted patterns have been shown for height.[10]

All the while that identical twins are becoming more alike and staying alike, fraternal twins are becoming less alike—a discovery which tells us that genetic influence upon intelligence *increases* as we age. Recent longitudinal twin studies suggest that events uniquely experienced by each twin, such as school absence or world travel, may substantially affect IQ, but briefly, and that genes play a more substantial role across the life span.[11] A monumental study using Swedish twins over eighty years old shows that genetic influence on intelligence is high even in later adulthood, yielding a heritability estimate of .62, similar to that for younger adults.[12] Intuitively, it seems that environmental influences should count for more, not less, as people broaden their intellectual experiences and opportunities. It appears, instead, that with age we acquire greater freedom to fashion our environments in ways that are compatible with who we are, and in doing so we become "more like ourselves" every day.

No single study delivers the last word on the controversial issue of how genes and environments influence mental development. Ultimately, this story is told most faithfully by the hundreds of carefully executed twin studies that find greater identical than fraternal twin similarity across many types of mental ability measures. At the same time, corroborating anecdotal evidence breathes life into the "hard data." The college twins pose one revealing situation in that their identical errors may reflect similar genetically based patterns of thought, rather than cheating or chance. Identical twins Mark and Scott Kelly offer another insight by having withstood a grueling competition against 2,400 candidates for two of thirty-five places in NASA's 1996 astronaut class.[13] This, and the fact that both were among ten individuals chosen for the shuttle pilot program suggest that genes bear some responsibility for the blend of intellect, stamina and perseverance that was "right" for NASA. These stories are fascinating and informative, but because they might miss what is taking place among the thousands of twins in the population, evidence concerning intellectual development must come from the full set of psychological investigations.

There are probably more twin studies of IQ, the intelligence quotient representing general mental ability, than any other behavioral measure. This is partly due to the tremendous value placed upon intellectual performance in modern society. Amid the great debate over how much genes and environments explain individual differences in mental ability is the often neglected point that IQ tests were developed without any notion that genetic influence might affect test scores. The first modern intelligence test was devised in 1905 by French psychologists Alfred Binet and Theodore Simon, to identify children unlikely to succeed in the general school system.[14]

As a young investigator in 1982, I compared the IQ similarity of sixty-nine identical and thirty-five fraternal same-sex twin pairs. When IQ correlations of .85 for identical twins and .46 for fraternal twins flashed across the computer screen, my own data reaffirmed that genetic factors substantially contribute to individual differences in general intelligence—these values are consistent with correlations of .86 and .60 reported in other twin studies.[15] Twins in this study were between five and twelve years of age and, as they put forth their best effort to answer the problems presented to them, I smiled to think that they were really on a more important mission, telling us about the nature of the human mind.

Studies of identical twins reared apart provide the most stunning evidence that genes influence intelligence. My affiliation with the Minnesota Study of Twins Reared Apart, at the University of Minnesota, offered a ringside view of identical genes guiding developmental processes even if twins are oceans apart. When results were available for forty-eight pairs they confirmed what studies of ordinary twins were already telling us:[16] Separated early in life and reunited as adults, these identical twins are just slightly less alike in IQ than identical twins reared together, and considerably more alike than pairs of fraternal twins, brothers and sisters, parents and children, half-siblings and cousins—demonstrating genetic influence on intelligence. Reared apart volunteer fireman twins, Jerry Levey and Mark Newman, scored only two IQ points apart, despite meeting for the first time at age thirty-one. Remarkably, both twins pursued interests in firefighting and in forestry years before they met, and both advanced to high ranking positions within their fire stations. Their special brand of intellect and drive is reflected in these choices and achievements. This is true for most individuals, but the parallel paths traced by identical twins reared apart makes a more convincing case for the role of genetic factors.

One of the most compelling contributions from twin studies has been the knowledge that living together does not make people alike in intelligence. Such a discovery deepens our appreciation for the nature and origin of individual differences within families. Moreover, Thomas J. Bouchard, Jr., director of the Minnesota study, believes that the slightly greater IQ similarity in identical twins reared together rather than apart is explained by their being tested as children living in the same home, while twins reared apart were tested as adults. In other words, families may affect how children learn while they are at home, but their influence wanes once the children leave. The trick is to compare adult twins who have been reared together with adult twins who have been reared apart; some recent work shows comparable similarity in these two twin groups.

Fraternal same-sex and opposite-sex twins show the same degree of IQ similarity. Fraternal twins also tend to be more similar in IQ than nontwin siblings, possibly due to their more similar rearing circumstances. Adoptive siblings show some IQ resemblance in childhood (.29–.34 correlation), suggesting a modest but real contribution from the shared environment.[17] When adoptive siblings are studied in adolescence and adulthood, however, their IQ correlation reduces to zero (below the .15 cousin correlation), showing that shared environmental effects on intelligence diminish as they age.[18] I have been gathering IQ scores on rare pairs of adoptive siblings *of the same age* who are essentially raised as twins, and their modest resemblance confirms findings from other adoption studies.[19] Studies of twins and same-age adoptive siblings may actually inflate the importance of common rearing for intellectual development because they share experiences not shared by siblings of different ages.

The same degree of IQ resemblance between identical twins reared apart has now been shown across five different studies, conducted between 1937 and 1992 by investigators in the United States, Great Britain, Denmark and Sweden.[20] This level of consistency is rare in human developmental research, matched only by the finding that identical twins are nearly as alike in IQ as the same person tested twice.[21] Twins' life histories and human interest stories are appended to the American, British and Danish studies, illustrating how similar abilities often blossom despite differing life circumstances. My favorite is the tale of Ed and Fred who were adopted by different families, but who attended the same school until age eight when the families separated.[22]

While in school together they noted physical similarities between them, but were not close friends. They did not meet again until age twenty-five when Ed was mistaken for Fred and their twinship revealed. Invited to the University of Chicago for study, they met reared apart twins, Esther and Ethel, and the identical couples aroused great interest from onlookers. Twins in both pairs performed similarly on ability tests, although different educational experiences might have explained Esther's superior performance in some areas. Confidentiality requirements make it unlikely that future reared apart twin studies will include details of the twins' lives.

The other meaningful message from twin studies is that genes do not act alone, but work in concert with the environment, and environmental influences upon intelligence are pervasive. We know this because IQ resemblance between identical twins if never perfect, even if they are reared together. The same accelerated math course, inspiring teacher or vacation abroad might leave variable impressions on identical twins' developing minds, but how these objectively similar opportunities translate into different experiences and different IQ scores, and for how long, is unknown. It is easier to understand that fraternal twins and siblings react differently to classes, teachers and excursions because genetic differences partly fashion the talents, attitudes and beliefs they bring to their experiences. Sometimes family dynamics propel identical twins to separate along academic lines, especially during adolescence when questions of identity and individuation become paramount. Terms like *difference* and *separation* acquire new meaning with reference to identical twins, however, because their "different" interests or occupations may simply be variations on a theme.

Differentiation for identical twins Jill Sigel-Greer and Judy Sigel-Freeman meant that one became a commercial artist and the other a visual artist. College-bound seniors Julie and Lisa Grinfeld named different high schools and universities as evidence of significant differences between them, but close consideration suggests otherwise. Both twins are talented in performing arts, but Julie specialized in dance and Lisa specialized in drama, capitalizing on the strengths of their respective high schools. Identical male graduate students Bill and Bob Green are pursuing careers in film and in law, areas that appear quite diverse, except that Bill is specializing in entertainment law. An identical quartet, Alison, Brooke, Claire and Darcy Hansen, recent graduates of Baylor University in Waco, Texas, claim two Fulbright scholarships and two internships for study in Spain, Austria, the Netherlands and England.[23] The twins and quads have followed alternate routes to comparable destinations.

Environments also include a catalogue of events in the womb, such as nutritional supply, viruses, fetal crowding and other factors that may affect brain development. Increased attention to prenatal influences on intelligence is important, but similar conceptualization of identical and fraternal twins' intrauterine environments is misleading. A recent review of 212 twin, sibling and family IQ studies concluded that there was a greater prenatal effect on IQ than was previously thought, reducing estimates of genetic influence to 48%.[24] It also claimed that fraternal twins' shared intrauterine conditions may be the key to their intellectual similarity, suggesting two maternal womb environments, one for twins and one for siblings. However, identical twins, but not fraternal twins, may experience shared placentae, fetal transfusion syndrome or adverse consequences of delayed splitting, factors that may be implicated in behavioral and physical *differences* between them. This information is not always clearly or accurately presented.[25] I have always been impressed by the consistently greater IQ similarity of identical twins than fraternal twins *despite* their exposure to more trying prenatal circumstances.

The search for factors that create distance between identical twins' IQ scores has been a kind of scavenger hunt because the list of candidates has yielded interesting and sometimes surprising findings. Birth weight has been a popular choice in this search because twins are more often born prematurely (before thirty-seven weeks gestation) than singletons (44.5% twins vs. 9.4% singletons), twins have lower birth weights (less than 2,500g or 5.5 pounds) than singletons (50% twins vs. 6% singletons), and twins may show substantial birth weight differences.[26]

Twins' birth weight–IQ relationships are not simple. Some work suggests that birth weight differences between identical twins may be important for IQ differences only when one twin is above five pounds and the other is below five pounds.[27] A study by Ronald Wilson showed that identical twins differing in birth weight by over one and three-quarter pounds maintained their size difference at age six years, but did *not* show marked IQ differences as might be expected.[28] Of course, subtle mental processing dysfunction not apparent in overall IQ scores may have affected some lighter twins. Wilson suggested that developing organisms come equipped with "buffering mechanisms" that shield them from early insults and that some organisms resist insults better than others.

Buffering mechanisms have long been mysterious, but new research suggests that fetuses experiencing moderate nutritional deficits undergo adaptational changes, namely accelerated maturation of the brain and lung that ready them for premature birth and life outside the womb.[29] Infants with accelerated lung function may show advanced development in other organs and functions—as much as a ten-week advantage—with the brain usually showing the greatest degree of growth. Surprisingly, the smaller of two identical twins shows more accelerated development, especially when fetal transfusion has taken a toll, since larger twins experience delayed lung development. Like so many other behaviors, fetal and newborn response to modest stress is best gauged by studying identical twins in which only one twin is affected, a natural cotwin control design. A mother of identical left-handed female twins described the difficult moments when her secondborn twin was ensnared by her sister's umbilical cord. This caused the infant's heart rate to plummet, but the twins' nine-year IQ scores were only two points apart and well above average. Of course, very stressful environments may overwhelm the positive outcomes of adaptational change.

Answers to the puzzle of IQ differences between identical twins may also reside in their brains, particularly the variable patterns of neural connection and structures established before birth and throughout infancy. Identical twins show greater similarity in brain volume than fraternal twins, but they do not show greater similarity in their patterning of convolutions (folds) on the brain's surface.[30] Prenatal events affecting twins' brain structures are unknown, but both human and nonhuman researchers have shown that infants' levels of environmental stimulation affect brain development. Some experts have concluded that the more time parents spend talking and singing to infants the more complex the circuitry of the developing brain.[31]

This argument, if substantiated, has important implications for families raising twins. Perhaps one infant twin demands greater attention than the other, emerging as the primary player in parental social exchange, eventually edging ahead of the other twin in mental functioning. Janet Mann found that mothers' attention and vocalization were directed more frequently toward healthier twins than toward less healthy twin partners by eight months of age.[32] If these "healthier" twins ultimately outperformed their twin brothers and sisters on mental tasks it would be difficult to know if differences in maternal vocalization or differences in health histories played a bigger role.

Several caveats are in order. First, the connection between environmental stimulation and brain circuitry is known from 1960s animal research, so despite the extraordinary 1990s preoccupation with this finding it is not a new discovery. Second, evidence that increased stimulation yields better brain functioning than adequate stimulation is uncertain. Much of the research on brain circuitry has been on animals, not on humans, so there is a danger of overinterpreting the findings.[33] It may be that we know more about environments necessary for normal brain development, rather than enhanced brain development. Third, while increased parent vocalization may be linked to improved child learning, expectations of equal intellectual gains across different children are groundless. If parents with richer vocabularies produce children with richer vocabularies it is largely because they transmit both the genetic factors and environmental opportunities associated with superior skill.[34]

Another potentially informative finding, not yet applied to twin studies, is the association between fluctuating asymmetry (FA) and IQ, namely that individuals with lower IQ tend to have higher FA.[35] As indicated in Chapter 2, increased FA, measured by greater right-left physical differences, may reflect greater developmental instability. It is possible that identical twins showing a greater than average IQ difference (more than six points) might differ partly because of differences in FA.

*   *   *

A classic study of 850 adolescent twin sets includes some of the best data for looking at how differences in identical twins' lives may explain differences in their test scores.[36] Differences in subtests from the National Merit Scholarship Qualifying Test showed little relation to differences in illnesses, parental attention, birth order and birth weight, and only a small relationship to differences in school grades. Identical twins raised apart bring sharper focus to this issue because of their nonoverlapping environments. Educationally and socially advantaged reared apart twins in an early study had an intellectual edge over their twin siblings, but this finding has been wrongly used to dampen genetic explanations of mental development.[37] Despite their differences, these twins were still remarkably similar to one another *and* different from twins in other pairs. In other words, IQ difference *within* pairs is compatible with genetic difference *among* pairs. The Minnesota study could not find connections between twins' IQ similarity and the similarity of cultural and intellectual resources in the rearing home, parental education, father's socioeconomic status, twins' impressions of parental treatment, or time living part before reunion. In both studies, however, some reared apart identical twin pairs showed larger IQ differences than others, even as large as twenty-nine points, so different environments may have major effects on intelligence in individual cases.

Twin research does not diminish the importance of how environments influence intelligence. Instead, it challenges beliefs about what people usually think is important for intellectual advancement. Children's achievements might still be the same even if they were raised by different parents in different settings as long as their best abilities were encouraged and their emotional development supported. This assertion by Dr. Sandra Scarr has met with controversy for seeming to diminish parental responsibilities, but I believe it underlines the significance of caretaking roles. This information has been reassuring to parents concerned with "doing the right thing." Scarr makes the crucial point that we know more about restoring deprived conditions to the normal range, but far less about altering supportive environments when development goes awry.

Twin research teaches us that the home environment differs for every child, and that, with appropriate guidance and encouragement, children seek experiences and opportunities that best serve their talents and interests. Many psychologists now believe that this process explains the extraordinary IQ similarity seen in identical twins raised by different families, such as Jerry and Mark. In my view, the most remarkable outcome of all is that, despite the many factors creating intellectual differences between twins, the intelligence test scores of identical twins still turn out to be so alike.

*   *   *

There are gifted identical and fraternal twins in every area of human
achievement, such as Donna Shalala (United States Secretary of Health and
Human Services), the late Paul Tsongas (former Democratic senator from
Massachusetts), Elvis Presley (legendary rock and roll star) and Iva and
Malvin Albright (twentieth-century American painters). Also notable are
thirteen-year-old identical twins Anastasia and Alba Somoza of New York
City who, despite confinement to wheelchairs due to cerebral palsy, boast IQ
scores in the top 2% of their age group.[38] It is also true that twins' average IQ
score dips below the average IQ score of the population of nontwins. The
twin-singleton IQ difference of 5 to 10 points is consistent across studies
with twins scoring about 90–95 and singletons scoring 100.[39] This information is often misrepresented and misinterpreted, and I groan inwardly to think
of the concern experienced by new mothers and fathers.

The truth is that when the IQ scores of many twin pairs are averaged and
compared with the singleton average, the twins' score is lower. There is still
considerable variability within both groups, meaning that some twins obtain
higher scores than some singletons, and vice versa.[40] It does not mean that all
twins score below all singletons, or that it is possible to predict someone's IQ
score by knowing that he or she is a twin or a nontwin.

How much do twins' and siblings' IQ scores differ? The average IQ difference is six points for identical twins, ten points for fraternal twins, fourteen
points for full siblings and seventeen points for unrelated individuals picked
at random.[41] Approximately 80% of identical twins differ in IQ by less than
ten points, probably due to minor environmental effects, while 20% differ by
more than ten points, probably due to more severe traumas.[42] Some identical
twins differ by as much as full siblings, and some fraternal twins differ by
only a point or two. These rare cases disguise the bigger picture, namely that
genetic influences do affect measured intelligence. Whatever is responsible
for identical twin IQ differences seems to push one twin down more than it
raises the other twin up. Whether or not comparable environmental factors
mostly lower singletons' IQ scores is uncertain.

The 5–10-point reduction in twins' IQ scores, relative to nontwins' IQ
scores, is probably *not* due to the minority of severely retarded twins unlikely
to be included in psychological studies, but to biological and rearing influences unique to multiples. Many psychologists and educators have devoted
their careers to figuring out why some twins obtain lower than average IQ
scores, and what this may mean for intellectual achievement among nontwins. This inquiry has targeted two possible explanations, twins' more difficult birth situations and twins' experiences with the twin relationship and
with parental "time-sharing."

Extreme conditions before or after birth can reduce twins' IQ scores, but
when birth stress is more modest, it may not significantly affect later intelligence. Some researchers have failed to find important links between birth

events and intelligence in twins. Consequently, attention has turned to the distinguishing features of growing up as an identical or a fraternal twin, particularly the social relationships uniquely shared with twin partners and parents, and how they affect learning and performance.

A natural experiment resulting from a sad event, the loss of a twin at birth, was used by British investigators to see if eleven-year-old twins growing up as "singletons" showed better verbal reasoning ability than twins growing up together.[43] Singleton twins performed slightly better than ordinary twins, suggesting that twins' social closeness might restrict their development of verbal skills. However, this finding was not confirmed in a similar study of general intelligence conducted in the United States with four- and seven-year-olds.[44] These 1970s studies have not been repeated, but I would expect higher singleton-twin than intact-twin scores, especially in verbal skills which suffer most from reduced language opportunities. It would also be important to determine the twin type of surviving twins because singleton fraternals may outscore singleton identicals due to generally lower birth stress.

Other natural twin experiments may help decide how much birth events, rearing as a twin, or both may affect intelligence. No one has recognized that reared apart identical twins are really singletons whose birth histories remain those of twins. This special class of multiples may be a better IQ comparison group than the surviving British twins because their twin type is known, and because their prenatal environments are more like those of ordinary twins since both survived. The Minnesota study reported an above average IQ score of 108,[45] suggesting that rearing as a singleton improves test performance. In contrast, some earlier reared apart twin studies found the opposite result. The Minnesota data may not, however, offer the best test of twin vs. singleton status on IQ. It is likely that the twins' average IQ is somewhat inflated because of the continued widespread rise in scores since 1930. This trend, called the "Flynn Effect" after its founder, James R. Flynn of the University of Otago in New Zealand, refers to the 1.8–12.5-point increase in scores when the same test is taken by people in later decades.[46] Reared apart twins in Minnesota completed the original 1955 Wechsler Intelligence Scale for Adults (WAIS), not the updated 1985 Wechsler Intelligence Scale for Adults-Revised (WAIS-R), a factor which may partly explain their superior performance.

Another attack on this problem involves inspecting the IQ scores of unrelated siblings of the same age raised together since infancy. These rare sibships can uniquely reveal the IQ consequences of rearing as a "twin," but without the complicating prenatal factors of multiple birth. If a twinlike rearing situation produces IQ deficits then unrelated same-age siblings should score below 100, but these sibs obtained an above average IQ score of 106.[47] A caveat is that participants in this study and in the Minnesota study do not include the less advantaged twins and adoptees in the general population, possibly inflating the scores of available samples.

Language deficits are primarily responsible for the average lowering of

twins' IQ scores, although the proportion of affected twins is hard to estimate. Unfortunately, definitive answers to the birth event–twin rearing IQ debate elude us. It is probably closest to the truth that both factors affect the IQ
scores of twins with varying contributions across pairs. At the same time, the
hurtful effects of twinship on the language skills of some young twins continue to be documented by many investigators, especially when they look at
how twins talk to each other and how parents talk to twins.

"Who wants to go first?" I asked when I arrived at the Askeland home to
test Stephani and Brenna. The identical little girls stared hard at each other
for several moments without speaking a word until Stephani came to my side
and Brenna turned to leave, all in beautifully coordinated fashion. This is a
marvelous example of "twin speech," the private gestures, words and phrases
that about 40% of twins, most likely identical, develop on their own for communicating with each other.[48] Variously called *autonomous language, cryp-
tophasia* and *idioglossia,* twins' speech may be slightly distorted or even
unintelligible to anyone outside the twinship. Some parents find that older
siblings are able translators, even though they do not participate in these extraordinary exchanges. Most investigators have focused on twins' verbal utterances and structures, but the nonverbal pieces are often key to the decision
or joke that is passing between them. Near-in-age siblings may also develop
idiosyncratic speech patterns due to a "twin effect." Lois Bush, mother of
four-year-old unrelated siblings, Samantha and Jaclyn, wrote that, "We have
always believed that they communicated in their own way, but it wasn't until
this summer that we actually caught them in a conversation to confirm it."

Some people refer to twins' unusual speech as *twin language.*[49] This is a
poor term because it misleads parents, teachers and everyone else about the
nature and significance of twins' verbal behaviors. There is nothing unique
about the grammar or sentence composition that sets twins' speech apart
from the language of their culture, so we are not witnessing a new language
in the making. This point was highlighted in a case involving six-year-old
identical twins, Ginny and Gracie, whose unusual speech was likened to a
tape recorder played on fast forward.[50] San Diego's Children's Hospital investigators initially suspected the birth of a new language, but closer analysis revealed a complex blend of English and German constructions, partly
owing to the twins' rearing by their German-speaking grandmother. The
twins had a vocabulary of "hundreds of exotic words" and were too intelligent for the schooling they were initially provided. Another striking case of
twins' unusual speech was reported in 1903, in the *Fremont Journal.*[51] A list-
ing of unusual words employed by prominent identical twins, Mrs. Nellie
Bell and Mrs. Lillie Wright, was provided, for example skebble = able and
kriskird = easy. The sisters seemed able to converse easily with individuals
outside their twinship, but often responded in unison.

I believe we are seeing the products of twins' spontaneous verbal responses to new objects and events, their pleasure in speech sounds, their delight in shared social experience, and their tacit agreement to use their new "words" in the future. Young twins can be wonderful companions for one another, surrogate sitters who free parents while they happily engage in joint activity. The stage is, thus, set for creating new sound combinations which, according to one mother, involved each twin's holding up an object, making a sound, exploding with laughter and repeating this routine. Many nontwin couples, such as spouses, business partners and friends also enjoy words or expressions that trigger memories or understandings derived from shared experiences. Nontwins' special phrases may not differ that much from what occurs between twins, except that many twins discover such communication early, and it comes easily and frequently.

Some features of twins' speech directly reflect their status as twins. Pat Malmstrom, mother of identical twins, Krista and Kelda, described their early use of double names in reference to themselves (Krista-Kelda) and others (Mommy-Daddy), and preferences for team pronouns ("Mommy, if you sit between *me,* then you can reach *me* better" and "Which one of *me* is this [in the picture]?").[52] These unusual speech qualities do *not* suggest retarded intellectual development, but rather a normal variant of mental functioning.

Bringing mothers and fathers into the language arena underscores the unique features of parent-twin triads.[53] Twins as young as one to two years of age use fewer words and fewer types of words than singletons, show less turn-taking behaviors while conversing, and engage in more "short" conversations and fewer "long conversations." Less talking by mothers and less encouragement of twins' attention to the environment, as well as less attention by twins to mothers, may explain this difference because at four months of age twins and singletons do not differ in active looking and in positive vocalization. Paradoxically, mothers of twins speak and interact with their children as much as, or more than, mothers of singletons. Because of parental "time-sharing," however, individual twins receive less speech and shorter utterances, participate in fewer joint attention episodes, have fewer and shorter conversations, and receive more nonverbal (gestural) messages than nontwins. Mothers of twins also tend to be more controlling and less affectionate than mothers of singletons, and supply less encouragement to continue a new topic.

A new "maternal economics" may be at hand.[54] If mothers of twins are more controlling than mothers of singletons it is probably because two children are harder to manage than one. If mothers do not always continue a conversation with one twin it is probably because dividing attention fairly is uppermost in mind. Some mothers confess that their involuntary, but necessary responses to "butting in" by one twin can dispel attempts at fairness. Siblings in general, and twins in particular, are exquisitely sensitive to who receives the "bigger half" of the cookie or the ten extra seconds of parental time. As noted in the introduction, caring for two same-age children strains the parenting process, engaging twins and parents in two-way and three-way contests over available resources. In a small way, the language laboratory shows us evolution at work in the form of sibling-sibling and parent-child conflict. Each child tries to secure the lion's share of family goods, but parents also wish to attend to other children who will ultimately reproduce and pass on the parents' genes. It is usually beneficial for parents to invest more in older children who have weathered the uncertainties of infancy and toddlerhood, and are more likely than younger children to thrive and to reproduce. (As older children mature parental attention is redirected to developing younger children.) Twins add a wrinkle to this process because they are the same age, causing parents to divide attention between them, sometimes with a verbal price to pay.

Esoteric speech also has unique benefits. There is power in numbers and even more so when twins' communications successfully control the behaviors of others. Twins' pleasure at manipulating parents and friends may encourage them to resist relinquishing their verbal armor. Several case studies of language-delayed identical twins show that placement in different school classes, coupled with speech therapy, is an effective route to improved verbal behavior. Other studies show a lessening of twin-singleton differences in language skills once past early childhood.[55] A recent study found that when twins are two, mother-twin triads increase children's opportunities for conversational turn-taking, although only four twin pairs were observed.[56]

It is essential to note that *not* all twins display language difficulties, nor are the different types of twins equally susceptible. Identical twins appear to be at higher risk than fraternal twins for problems in vocabulary and rate of speech, probably reflecting their closer social relationship. Even though identical twins' birth situations are more hazardous than those of fraternal twins, recent studies implicate the twin situation (identical twins' relationship to one another and to their parents) to a greater degree in their speech difficulties.[57] In contrast, fraternal female twins and twins from opposite-sex pairs generally perform on a par with singletons, possibly due to more varied social experiences with parents and with individuals outside their twinship. Fraternal male twins seem to fall in between, a finding variously explained by lower social class, mild mental impairment, and competition for parental attention.

Some rare cases of unusual language behaviors in twins elude easy solutions. The weight of the unspoken word was powerfully captured in Marjorie Wallace's 1986 book, *The Silent Twins,*[58] which detailed the unhappy story of Jennifer and June Gibbons. These twins' withdrawal and failure to communicate was matched by their growing dependence on each other, reinforced by words and phrases intelligible to them alone. They eventually turned to a life of crime, culminating in sentencing to the Broadmoor prison in England and the later death of one twin.

Over the years, I have heard from parents whose identical twins display *selective mutism,*[59] the failure to speak in some situations despite adequate speech abilities in other situations. I was curious about this condition in view of twins' increased language difficulties. In September 1997, I met with Dr. E. Steven Dummit, psychiatrist at St. Luke's–Roosevelt Hospital Center in New York, who has investigated this rare condition. Selective mutism is *not* considered a language disorder, but a social anxiety disorder, specifically an exquisite sensitivity to interactions with individuals outside the family. It is usually evident by about age three when children are in new verbally inter-active settings, such as preschool. Girls are affected twice as often as boys. Most of the fifty children evaluated in Dr. Dummit's study came from middle-class families.

Sue Newman and Carol Miller, both mothers of affected identical twin daughters, cofounded and codirect the Selective Mutism Foundation, Inc. in Sunrise, Florida.[60] Sue told me that approximately twenty families with affected twins have joined the organization—350 people subscribe to the newsletter, but the organization has been contacted by hundreds more. Systematic twin research on selective mutism has not been undertaken, probably because the number of affected twins is small. Only about one in a thousand school children are affected so the chance that an affected child is also a twin is about one in forty thousand (1 person in forty is a twin). Sue also told me that both cotwins in all the identical pairs are affected, whereas in many instances only one twin in the fraternal pairs is affected. This observation, and the presence of selective mutism, anxiety disturbances, social phobias and shyness in the relatives of affected children suggest genetic influence on this disorder.

The possibility that twins suffer more frequently from selective mutism than nontwins is uncertain. Dr. Dummit and his colleagues identified three affected identical twin pairs who comprised 12% of the individuals (or 6% of the families) in his study, exceeding the 2.5% of twin individuals and .8% of identical twin individuals in the population. Families with twins (5.7%) are also overrepresented among subscribers to the Selective Mutism Foundation's newsletter. Most behavioral disorders do *not* occur more often in twins than in singletons, as I discuss in Chapter 5. Twins affected with selective mutism may be more likely to attract professional attention than nontwins, elevating the numbers that get reported. Information on the twin-nontwin balance among families not receiving the newsletter would be helpful, as would population-based surveys of affected individuals.

Treating identical twins with selective mutism may be more difficult than treating fraternals or nontwins, due to their close social relations. A mother of affected fourteen-year-old identical girls, Kay Klatt, who contacted me in 1988, believed her daughter's mutual reinforcement of their language behaviors explained their persistence. Dr. Dummit agreed that this could happen, indicating that once the behavior begins "it takes on a life of its own."

Dr. Dummit has reported encouraging results from treating affected children with the drug fluoxetine for a nine-week period.[61] In his group of twenty-one five- to fourteen-year-old children, 76% showed improvement, namely reduced anxiety and increased speech in public places. Younger children did better than older children. He has also treated several twin pairs, and finds that observing them when they are unaware reveals the flavor of what is going on between them. Some twins show "secret signs," suggesting that each is closely attuned to what the other is thinking. Selective mutism is a rare disorder and should not be confused with the private words and gestures displayed by many young twin pairs.

Some people are "good" in arithmetical reasoning and "poor" in vocabulary while others show a reversed pattern. Twin researchers have compared the profile or patterning of identical and fraternal twins' performance across the various verbal and nonverbal subtests that make up IQ. Verbal abilities include general information, concept formation, vocabulary, social comprehension and arithmetical reasoning. Nonverbal skills include visual reasoning, visual organization, visual-motor coordination, perceptual organization and short-term memory. Several studies, including one of my own, found that identical twins show greater similarity in their scattering of verbal and nonverbal scores than fraternal twins.[62] This suggests genetic influence on the patterning of special mental abilities, but less than on overall intelligence. We can also appreciate why some fraternal twins, nontwin siblings or unrelated people may obtain similar IQ scores, but show different aptitudes and talents.

I was impressed when nine-year-old Dean described a complex design as a "bottle with an apron," a concept his identical twin brother David grasped immediately. Researchers have also administered special mental ability tests to reared apart and reared together twins to assess genetic and environmental influences on verbal, spatial, perceptual and memory abilities. Reared apart twins studies demonstrate that about 50–55% of individual differences in these skills is explained by genetic factors, with the remainder explained by environmental factors. Studies on twins reared together show lower genetic influence on memory, so additional analysis will be needed to resolve this difference.[63] Genetic influence on special abilities makes it understandable that, in the Minnesota study, identical reared apart twin sisters were among the highest scorers on a difficult spatial task, and that the identical twin college students independently produced the same flawed solution to a problem. Knowing that intelligence is partly configured by genetic factors helps explain the origin of "natural" abilities and our attraction to activities requiring them.

Twin studies of creativity have shown little genetic influence. It is suspected that any resemblance for creativity is really due to resemblance in special mental skills.[64]

*   *   *

Some studies have moved beyond IQ testing in search of how people process the information around them. Everyone differs in the amount of time taken to respond to a problem or to find a solution, and this may be one approximate measure of how differently people's brains function.[65] Researchers have recorded the speeds with which identical and fraternal twins name objects, colors and numbers, and the speed with which they detect similarities and differences among letter combinations.[66] Genes appear to influence speed of processing, and people who process information faster have higher IQs. An intriguing observation is that the time taken to decide if two letters are the same or different is a good predictor of verbal skill. Another component of information processing is memory capacity, the "working space" available for handling different bits and pieces of material.[67] Greater memory capacity is also associated with higher IQ scores, but because it enables consideration of alternative answers to problems it sometimes reduces processing speed. Twin studies have shown that the genes affecting information processing abilities and general intelligence may be the same.

Identical twins' similarity in IQ and information processing skills may be tied to common genes, but differences may reside in the anatomical details of their brains. This view makes it possible to understand why identical twins often, but not always, encounter similar learning difficulties.

Learning disabilities are language disorders resulting in listening, thinking, spelling, mathematical or other problems that are not caused by physical handicaps or environmental disadvantages.[68] Everyone knows that these problems run in families, but twin studies show that many people know this for the wrong reasons. Twin research shows that the roots of learning disorders are partly genetic, not just experiential.[69] Identical twins reared apart further illustrate these findings: Earl and Frank spelled poorly and transposed letters, while Clara and Doris experienced difficulties in school.[70] I recall being puzzled when reared apart identical twin sisters in the Minnesota study failed to return letters while we were arranging their visit, but it turned out that both had similar reading and spelling problems.

Some very intriguing findings have come to light.[71] Dorothy Bishop's British twin studies revealed a possible connection between speech impairment and maternal toxemia (blood poisoning) during pregnancy. This study also found that twins with language problems came from larger families, tended to be later-born, and had mothers with less education than twins without language problems, but the separate contributions of these different factors are hard to disentangle. Philip S. Dale's twin research showed substantial genetic influence on language delay in children scoring in the lowest 5%, relative to the full sample. Twin studies have suggested new reasons for learning disabilities, thereby lightening guilt and self-blame among parents and alleviating frustration among sufferers. Having a learning disabled parent, sibling or even an identical twin is not a sure sign that someone will develop similar symptoms, but may heighten awareness of telltale signs. Nontwin siblings of both identical and fraternal twins are more likely to show language difficulties when both twins are affected, rather than just one. Slight memory problems or reading difficulties may assume different significance depending on the behaviors of those around us.

Sometimes very low levels of general mental functioning come packaged together with extraordinary skill in a few specific areas. This rare group of *autistic savants* combines mental subnormality with near superhuman talents in music, mathematics or memory. (The name *autistic savants* is preferred to *idiot savants* because most affected individuals are autistic. *Autism* is a severe childhood disorder marked by failure to communicate and to develop social relationships.[72]) Autistic savants who are identical twins are so rare that only one case study, from 1965, is available.[73] Identical twins, Charles and George, the "calendar calculators," could identify the years in which April 21 fell on a Sunday or the date of the fourth Monday in February in a given year, abilities in which George held a slight lead, but neither twin was able to add up to thirty or multiply three by six. Neither Charles nor George was aware of how their calculations were executed, simply explaining that "[it's] in my head." Visual components are probably involved as evidenced by a young savant who "sees the pages" as he performs calendar calculations. The information processing skills of such individuals have been described as "computerlike mechanisms" that appear at about age six years, mostly in males. Close study of the twins by neurologist Oliver Sacks led him to conclude that they relied on a "prodigious panorama," enabling them to retrieve and to visualize all they had witnessed and experienced.[74] His sympathetic remarks on the mutual elation the twins felt when engaging in "number play" acknowledge a humanity that was often neglected by those around them, and we regretfully learn that their enforced separation (to foster more socially acceptable behavior) diminished their remarkable skills and the pleasure it provided.

David Lykken has suggested that complex gene combinations, or *emergenesis,* might explain the one-time appearance of an unusual mental skill, personality trait or physical characteristic of a family member.[75] Emergenic traits are a special class of *polygenic traits,* affected by many genes. In some polygenic traits such as IQ, genes work *additively,* meaning that they sum to produce their effect. In emergenic traits, such as leadership ability, genes work *nonadditively,* meaning that interactions occur among the unique configurations affecting the trait. Emergenic traits are unlikely to reappear in later generations because the required gene combination dissolves when a parent transmits only half his or her genes to children; the children of conductor Arturo Toscanini did not display the same musical talent as their famous father. Parent-child resemblance is due to additive genes, not to nonadditive genes, because children do not inherit rare gene combinations from their parents.

It is tempting to attribute the rare talents of Charles and George to emergenesis. However, the development of such skills in people following brain trauma at birth or later has been observed and these twins did show convulsions in early infancy. It will be many years until the birth of another pair of autistic savant identical twins, but the presence of even one pair raises the possibility that genetic factors may contribute to this rare behavior.

George and Charles's research team wisely noted that motivation may extend unique ability, but cannot explain its basic structure, a concept that also applies to school achievement. Final exam scores, report card grades and academic test rankings improve with effort, but the greater similarity of identical than fraternal twins shows that school achievement test scores and grades are also affected by genetic factors.[76] It is, therefore, not surprising that people show varying results following completion of the same required classes or "crash" courses.

Many people wonder what it means to say that intelligence and special skills are influenced by genetic factors. It means that while we are all born with potentials for learning and achievement that require nurturant, supportive environments to fully develop, we differ in the ease with which these traits express themselves. This is why classmates rarely receive identical grades and why each school produces only one valedictorian. Everyone has enormous room for refining different skills, but improvement proceeds at different rates and in different ways. I often remind people that they may have great untapped potentials, such as abilities in math or mechanics or language, that they know nothing about simply because they missed the class or teacher or trip that would have made the difference. The gifted mathematician Ramanujan had little formal education, but access to several math primers apparently fueled his incredible talents and drive. Dominique Dawes, the renown United States gymnast, undertook gymnastics because enrollment in a preferred sports class was complete.

Most twin studies of intelligence have used IQ tests and special ability tests, but there are other diagnostic tools and a growing number of new and provocative theories of what it means to be intelligent.[77] Unlike IQ testing, newer views such as Daniel Goleman's emotional intelligence theory (which considers intelligent behavior as the ability to get along and to make appropriate personal decisions) have not endured decades of scientific scrutiny. A twin perspective might add an informative twist to views that emphasize emotional intelligence, planning ability and other nontraditional measures. Exciting work is also taking place in molecular genetics laboratories in which researchers have found a link between reading disability and genes on chromosome six[78] and are continuing to scan chromosomes for genes associated with low, intermediate and high IQs and other intellectual traits.[79] Once these genes are identified the intellectual similarities and differences between fraternal twins, nontwin siblings, and parents and children will be better understood.

Evolutionary psychologists are refining our understanding of human intelligence by conceptualizing people as possessing specialized problem-solving strategies that reflect the types of problems faced in early human history. Successful problem-solvers were more likely to survive and to have children than unsuccessful ones.[80] Twin studies can enrich this enterprise by identifying the most genetically influenced abilities and those most susceptible to change. Twin studies of birth order and mental ability have yielded a mixed picture,[81] but cleverly designed twin studies might enhance understanding of the roots of achievement and creativity. Achievement and creativity have recently been linked to being a laterborn in *Born to Rebel* by Dr. Frank Sulloway, formerly of the Massachusetts Institute of Technology. Laterborn children, in the evolutionary race to reap the parental resources extended to firstborn children, may distinguish themselves by carving out new areas of interest. Studying identical twins reared apart who fall into similar and different birth order positions in their adoptive families might reveal the blend of genetic and environmental factors that propels one twin and not the other toward immortality.[82]

What are the practical sides to twins' intelligence issues? The advisability of same or different classrooms for twins' educational and social advancement is one of the most commonly raised questions by concerned parents. About twenty-five years ago psychologists and educators emphasized separation of twins at school to foster development of their "separate identities." Unfortunately, this policy was not research-based, nor was the concept of "separate identity" clearly defined, but the practice lingers. I was distressed reading a 1991 newspaper article in which a school principal cited research showing that twins do better when separated.[83] I contacted the principal only to learn that his views did *not* reflect research findings, but were based on events at his own school. In 1992 I completed a small study showing that more mothers of identical twins than fraternal twins favor common classrooms during the early years, although most agreed that decisions should be made on a case-by-case basis.[84]

It is curious that many school administrators believe twins (identical and fraternal) will fail to develop "individuality" if assigned to the same classroom, even though research shows that nontwin children attending school with friends adjust earlier than children coming alone.[85] Twins are given the more difficult task of separating from their parents, as well as from their familiar and comfortable twin relationship, and this can prove devastating. A concerned mother told me that one of her identical twin boys, Tim, adjusted well to kindergarten on his own, but that his brother Sean literally "shut down." I have always believed that same classrooms, but different play groups, might be an answer to early school placement dilemmas. I was delighted when the Oklahoma state legislature considered a resolution in 1993 asking school districts to set separation policies allowing for individual review of each twin pair's situation. According to Dr. Ramona Paul, Oklahoma

State Assistant Superintendent, "It's tradition that we do [separate twins], but no one has ever studied it and asked, 'Why?' "[86]

Placing twins in different grades is sometimes proposed by educators if one twin lags behind. This situation has been mentioned to me most often by parents of school-age male-female twins who are concerned about their sons. Males tend to mature less quickly than females, so these male twins may suffer from early comparisons with their socially, physically and intellectually precocious sisters. Instead of separate grades, I suggest tutoring and other assistance to avoid damage to male twins' self-esteem and to buffer insensitive comments from others. We have traveled full circle in our thinking about keeping twins together or apart, first leaning toward inseparability, then pushing toward individuality, and now easing toward a happy balance in which two people enjoy themselves and each other.

Why intellectual differences among people persist is an unresolved question.[87] If the survival of human populations depends on the varied talents of their members then perhaps our genetically based differences serve a vital role. We know that the wealth of abilities we see every day is a partial reflection of our genetic diversity, and that without genetic differences the world would probably be a less vital place in which to live.

Unfolding Lives: Personality Traits, Mental Disorders and Atypical Behaviors

A marvelous painting of identical female twins, *Léa e Maura,* hangs in the Museu Nacional De Belas Artes in Rio de Janeiro.[1] We find a vision of perfectly matched twin sisters with perfectly matched printed dresses and wavy hairstyles. Penetrating stares, taut lips and semirigid bodies are mirrored in duplicated faces, bodies and hands, suggesting personalities that combine attentiveness with timidity, and intensity with reserve. A discerning observer would, however, note slight differences in the strength of the stare, the positioning of the mouth and the stiffness of the shoulders and hands, suggesting less than perfect similarity in the twins' personalities and temperaments. No doubt Brazilian artist Alberto da Veiga Guignard knew these twins well.

Twin studies of personality are not new. Some of the most instructive observations are found in 1870s letters gathered by Sir Francis Galton, who viewed identical twins' corresponding emotions and habits, and occasional "interchangeable likeness" as reflecting an inherited plan, variously modified by environmental circumstances.[2] These letters anticipated a story that has been repeated more scientifically and persuasively over the years due to advances in psychological and biological methods and theories. Countless twin pairs have now completed personality questionnaires and inventories, and participated in videotaped experiments and interviews designed to reveal if—and the extent to which—happiness, aggression, empathy, extraversion, neuroticism, sensation-seeking and other traits are shaped by genetic and environmental factors. The answer is that identical twins are not exactly alike, but they are much more alike than fraternal twins or any other pair of relatives, demonstrating genetic influence upon personality development. Approximately 20–50% of individual differences in personality are genetically based,[3] so genes have a somewhat

Alberto da Veiga Guignard Brasil, 1896–1962. Léa e Maura. *Oil on canvas.*
Museu Nacional de Belas Artes, Rio de Janeiro, Brazil. REPRODUCED BY PER-
MISSION OF PEDRO M. C. XEXÉO, TECHNICAL COORDINATOR.

lesser impact upon personality traits than they do upon intellectual skills.
Parents, close friends and twins themselves tune into the differences, but
anyone meeting identical twins for the first time cannot deny that their
personalities often blend.

The personality story is still unfolding, leaving new insights and challenges along the way. A turning point in behavioral genetic research occurred
in 1987 when Robert Plomin and Denise Daniels summarized research showing that twin resemblance in personality was mostly due to shared genes, not
to shared environments.[4] This news prompted a steady stream of studies combining more and different types of kinships, such as identical twins reared together and apart, fraternal twins reared together and apart, biological
siblings, half-siblings, adoptive siblings and step-siblings, to tease apart the
network of biological and rearing factors. Fascinating spin-offs from this
work have included twin- and sibling-based forays into the origins of divorce,[5] altruism,[6] shyness,[7] social attitudes,[8] religiosity,[9] love styles,[10] parenting,[11] television watching,[12] response to stress,[13] accident proneness[14] and age
at first intercourse,[15] all of which may reflect personality traits at some level.
Evolutionary psychologists have begun to use psychological twin findings to
explore new ideas about the structure of human personality, the adaptive significance of species-specific behaviors, and how and why people differ.[16]

Molecular geneticists are linking personality traits, such as novelty-seeking,[17] to specific genes on specific chromosomes.

My own reverence for the role of twins in modern personality research dates back to a slim volume by Peter Mittler, *The Study of Twins* (1971).[18] This collection gave scientific meaning to many unusual and compelling observations of twins' personality traits that were familiar, but misunderstood by many. If identical twins are more alike than fraternal twins in imaginativeness and anxiety, as well as in habits and gestures, even when raised apart, this suggests that genes play an important role. Subsequent research has refined this first wave of findings to provide a better understanding of how genes and environments work together, and to dispel notions that physical resemblance, parental expectations or coincidence explain personality similarity in identical twins and relative personality dissimilarity in fraternal twins.

Behavioral geneticists think about personality as a set of traits or dimensions along which people vary. Trait theorists show that personality may be carved up among the "Big Five" personality traits of Extraversion, Agreeableness, Conscientiousness, Emotional Stability (Neuroticism) and Openness to Experience. All Big Five traits measured on adult twins show genetic influence, but Extraversion (Dominance—Submissiveness) edges slightly ahead at 49% and Agreeableness falls slightly behind at 39%.[19] The table below lists specific characteristics associated with each of these dimensions.

Big Five Personality Traits*

TRAIT	DESCRIPTION
Extraversion— Introversion	Sociable, dominant— Retiring, withdrawn
Agreeableness— Lack of Agreeableness	Cooperative, sympathetic— Quarrelsome, cold
Conscientiousness— Lack of Conscientiousness	Organized, efficient— Disorderly, careless
Emotional Stability— Emotional Instability	Calm, stable— Distraught, unstable
Openness to Experience— Resistance to Experience	Imaginative, inventive— Narrow, simple

*Adapted from Rowe (1994).[20]

Individual differences in personality influence how people think about each other, and judgments differ depending on the roles people play in our lives. Dominance may be appreciated in a supervisor, but not in a coworker.

Differences in people's personality traits can be considered a resource environment because they provide the social cues we rely on when making crucial decisions about how to lead our lives. Evolutionary psychologist David Buss has suggested that the Big Five personality traits form the dimensions of this "adaptive landscape" because they help us decide what we need to know in order to prosper.[21] Extraversion—Introversion and Agreeableness—Lack of Agreeableness underlie social bonding that is crucial for survival.

Everyone differs in personality and in how accurately they evaluate personality traits in other people. Individuals sensitive to the stature or trustworthiness of others are probably more destined for success than those who are less discerning. Personality variation is welcome because it allows different people to occupy a range of niches, safeguarding the population in the face of changing environmental conditions. People at the positive and negative extremes of personality dimensions are rare and may represent maladaptive versions of the different traits. Dr. Jerome Barkow notes that excessive pride or anger would be maladaptive because of disrupted social relations and inapproriate goals.[22] The "negative" side of personality dimensions is clearly useful in some circumstances which may explain why "negative" genes remain in the population. Extraversion benefits social bonding, but some reserve is probably prudent in novel situations. Intriguing parallels have been drawn in the world of medicine—fever is unpleasant but fights infection, and morning sickness is distressing but may protect fetuses from harmful substances.[23]

Classic twin studies show that a substantial portion of individual differences in personality is explained by genetic differences. Studies of identical twins living or reared apart can show whether and how different environments affect personality. A number of researchers who once focused on the genetic side of the personality equation are relying on twin studies for insights on the environmental side. Several concepts are of interest:

- *Active gene-environment correlation.* Do people with certain genetic backgrounds choose certain professions or recreations? Identical twins reared in separate households both became firemen and both love to party. In contrast, fraternal twins reared in the same household individually favored psychology versus law, and movies versus plays. Individuals apparently seek experiences congruent with their genetically influenced personality traits, offering insight into why family members differ.
- *Reactive gene-environment correlation.* Why do people react to or respond to us as they do? Identical twins' matched personality traits elicit similar reactions in others, but this similar treatment does *not* appear to cause their similarity. The message is that childrens' genetically influenced personalities shape parental treatment, and that tailoring treatment to different children may sometimes be appropriate.
- *Gene-environment interaction.* Does the same environment differently af-

fect people with different personality traits? Some reared apart identical Swedish twins showed high extraversion despite rearing in different low-controlling and high-controlling families.[24] However, some low-extraversion identical twins came from high-controlling families, while their more ex-traverted twin siblings came from low-controlling families. These findings suggest that rearing styles (the environment in this case) affect some indi-viduals differently (extraversion level in this case) depending on the type of parental control.

- *Special identical twin environments.* Is personality similarity affected by the unique identical twin relationship? Identical twins show much higher simi-larity than fraternal twins in some Big Five traits, such as Conscientious-ness and Agreeableness. Controversy concerns whether this is due to their special rearing situation or to emergenesis, the unique combinations of genes shared by identical twins but not by fraternal twins. Evidence favors emergenesis, explaining why siblings (who are gentically equivalent to fra-ternal twins) can differ so greatly from one another.

- *Twins' perceived differences in experience.* Are identical twins' perceived differences in parental treatment and experience linked to behavioral dif-ferences between them? Adolescent twins perceiving higher parental nega-tivity were higher in depression and higher in antisocial behavior than their twin siblings.[25] Studying identical twins in this way shows how environ-mental events impact behavior because they are perfect genetic controls.

Researchers organize personality investigations around naturally occurring variations in twins' lives to include twins living together and apart, twins raised together and apart, or identical twin half-sibling families (families cre-ated when identical twins marry and have children). Twins are also used to study the origins of temperament, a part of personality concerned with be-havioral style and expressivity.

Big Five twin studies and twin studies of other personality and tempera-ment traits have produced a remarkable assembly of results:

Identical twins generally show greater similarity than fraternal twins, begin-ning in infancy and continuing throughout the life span, informing us that genes influence our varied preferences and responses to people, activities and events.

The Louisville Twin Study, which originally revealed so much about twin similarity in IQ in the 1970s and 1980s, did the same for personality in the 1980s and 1990s. At three days of age identical and fraternal twins (both same-sex and opposite-sex) show similar levels of resemblance in irritability, soothability and activity. This suggests that environments before and during birth overshadow some genetically based effects on infant termperament.[26] Then, slowly but surely genetic effects become evident, starting out modestly over the first year, but increasing during the second year and during early childhood.[27] Personality studies concentrating on adolescence and adulthood

report escalating genetic influence which eventually stablizes until late adulthood before diminishing somewhat, probably due to accumulated individual experiences. In fact, most personality change has been linked to environmental factors, while personality stablility has been linked to genes.

Happiness and shyness exemplify personality stability and change. Happiness measures are more alike for identical twins than for fraternal twins, showing that we have genetically influenced happiness levels or characteristic "set points."[28] Most striking is that identical twin A's happiness was more closely associated with twin B's later happiness than with A's marital status, educational attainment or income—this means that happiness stability is also genetically influenced. Fortune and disaster can cause happiness levels to fluctuate, but their effects are not lasting, partly explaining why psychotherapy or changes in scenery may not lift unhappy moods.

Even infants only a few days old show individual differences in arousal level when a blanket is placed over their face, and when their heel is pricked to obtain blood.[29] Infants also vary when they are shown novel stimuli at four months,[30] and when they receive inoculations during the first six months.[31] Early arousal differences following stimulation suggest that children's underlying physiological factors differ. These differences may predispose some children to be wary of novelty (shy or inhibited) and others to embrace it (outgoing or uninhibited). Genetic influence on shyness (inhibition) is indicated by greater similarity of identical than fraternal twin infants and children.[32]

Environmental events, both in the womb and beyond, can cause behavior to deviate from the genetically influenced plan. Adjusting daily environments can help unhappy and shy people overcome day-to-day difficulties, but transforming them into exuberant or outgoing individuals is unlikely.

Twin studies would border on boring if all they did was extend the list of genetically influenced traits. However, a marvel of twin research is its ability to show us what environments mean and do not mean for personality development. Like twins, environments come in two varieties, *shared* and *non-shared,* a distinction very important to recognize. This new take on the environment has produced thought-provoking results:

Shared environments make a small contribution to personality similarity among relatives. It seems hard to imagine that growing up together does not make people alike, and that personality traits shared by siblings are explained by common genes and not by common environments. Actually, the finding that shared environments do not significantly affect personality development emerged over twenty years ago when researchers showed that identical twins who dressed alike or played together were no more alike in personality than identical twins who did not.[33] Twin studies also show that identical twins tend to enjoy similar friends and activities, as well as each other, even when their parental treatment differs. A genetic view of human behavior is still absent from many university psychology departments, but some students and faculty are heeding the lessons taught by the growing number of twin-based studies of personality.

*   *   *

As a research associate at the University of Minnesota I participated in a study comparing personality similarity in identical and fraternal twins raised apart and raised together.[34] This simple, but sensitive design was poised to reveal if personality development was significantly altered by life histories that were separate or shared. About fifty reunited pairs of twins passed through the psychology department during my tenure in Minnesota. Diane and Lucky were outgoing and vivacious, especially when discussing their favorite subjects, namely raising dogs and raising horses. One twin exhibits purebred dogs and rode horses as a child while the other twin exhibits show horses and owns dogs, suggesting that how interests are specifically expressed may be linked to nonshared (individual) experiences.[35]

Mark and Jerry were playful but serious-minded, traits they respectively reserved for their free time with friends and their volunteer firefighting responsiblities. Their impatience with poor chefs was their trademark, Jerry's more so than Mark's, as I recall from two dining experiences with them in New York. Roger and Tony were energetic and full of fun. They showed unlimited enthusiasm for the people they liked, the activities they enjoyed and the company of each other.

Daily interactions with the twins over each week-long investigation gave the impression that separated twins' personality similarities were greater than expected. In fact, some colleagues were unprepared for what the questionnaire data were to reveal: Identical twins reared apart and together are about as similar as identical twins reared together in personality traits such as Well-Being, Stress Reaction and Aggression. In contrast, Social Closeness (affiliation) was more susceptible to the shared environment than the other traits. A surprise was that Traditionalism, the endorsement of traditional family and moral values, did not show common family effects. In other words, living with someone does not lead to agreement on standards of conduct or parenting practices. The last decade has witnessed a run of twin studies that have generally confirmed these findings.[36]

The bottom line is that living together does not make people in a family alike and that similarities are explained primarily by shared genes. Fraternal twins, even if raised together, are much *less alike* than identical twins reared apart. Of course, extremely potent environments such as those found in families of high position and power, or families facing unusual stress or trauma, might transcend the genetically based individual differences found in typical families.[37] Children of politicians may gain confidence from participation in public events, while children of abusers may be extra fearful and suspicious.

Personality traits of children born to prominent parents have not been systematically studied, making it easy to draw false conclusions from the children who have achieved prominence themselves. Children whose interests

match those of their remarkable parents often believe opportunities were offered to them, but were not forced upon them, thus holding environments responsible for their accomplishments. However, I challenge these children to
decide where their interests came from, and why their interests may not be
shared by all of their brothers and sisters. Psychological data are available for
some abused children and do reveal shame, hostility and aggressivity.[38] Nevertheless, separating genetic and environmental effects in these families is
difficult because parents provide the genes *and* the environments underlying
behavior, a concept called *passive gene-environment correlation*.

Not all studies agree that shared environments play minor roles in personality development. One study found greater similarity in Extraversion and
Neuroticism among identical twins reared apart than identical twins reared
together.[39] This result was supported by some, but not all, early twin studies
comparing personality similarity in twins living together and twins living
apart for five years.[40] This finding is highly counterintuitive because it makes
sense that people living together should be more alike than people living
apart. Some researchers have proposed that twins living apart express themselves more freely because they are not influenced by their twin, while twins
living together "create" differences in the interest of individuation. A more
recent Finnish study reported greater similarity in Extraversion, Neuroticism
and alcohol consumption among both identical and fraternal twins who were
living together or spending more time together, compared with twins living
apart or spending more time apart.[41] The present weight of evidence supports
the view that personality similarity *leads* to spending time together, rather
than the other way around.

The finding that shared environments contribute little to personality development has never surprised me. This is because it captured a view of personality development that I had sensed all along. I know that my sister shares
this view because when a friend introduced her fraternal twin toddlers, little
boys who differed in size and in social demeanor, she observed, "They are
just like us."

The shared environment has a flip side, and that is the nonshared environment, the accumulated experiences and events that uniquely affect individuals in families and make them different from everyone else. If genes explain
20–50% of the variation in personality and shared environments have a modest impact, then nonshared environments must account for the rest.

Environmental experiences unique to individuals in families (events that
happen to only one member) explain the greatest amount of their personality
differences, but just slightly more than what is explained by genetic factors.
Children growing up together rarely follow parallel paths, as suggested by the
title of a recent book, *The Separate Social Worlds of Siblings*.[42] It is becoming increasingly clear that family homes are replete with behavioral nooks

Nine-month-old firstborn identical twin Thomas Bryant (right) appears to prevail over his secondborn twin brother, Lucius. PHOTO COURTESY OF MRS. EVELYN BRYANT (LUCIUS'S WIFE).

and crannies with space for just one, so that within the same four walls siblings migrate to different locations that reflect their unique personalities and tastes. Even identical twins may differentiate somewhat by displaying different levels of a trait, a concept called *polarity*. Some twins may be slightly more assertive or more decisive than their cotwins, possibly exchanging roles in different situations. Identical twins have been referred to as "doer" and "watcher," and "aggressor" and "clinging vine," quantitatively different characters acquired in relation to one another.[43] In contrast, fraternal twins have been described as "terror" and "professor," indicating qualitatively contrasting identities expressed apart from, and in relation to, their cotwin. Differentiating identical twins along behavioral continuums is a convenient way for parents and others to distinguish them, but this can exaggerate twins' slight discrepancies. A judicious scheme might include terms such as "frequent doer" and "less frequent doer" to preserve twins' basic personality plan.

Research on systematic nonshared environmental influences on personality is progressing. Recall that more depressed adolescent identical twins judged their parents to be more negative than did their twin siblings. Another study found that adult identical twins with higher hostility scores described their parents as exerting greater hostile control than did their lower-scoring cotwins.[44] Whether or not parents really treat twins differently may be less important for their behaviors than *twins' judgment of that treatment*.

Birth order is another family feature that is not shared by siblings, or even by twins, but is of great interest to everyone because everyone has one. Birth order has been resurrected as a shaper of the personalities and achievements of children within families. In *Born to Rebel,* Frank Sulloway[45] argues that firstborn children should identify with parental authority and values, maintaining favored status in the family. In contrast, laterborns should be less traditional, engaging in risk and rebellion to fashion a unique family niche in order to deflect resources from the elder sibling. He reasons that because firstborns often act as surrogate parents they score higher than laterborns on the Big Five factor of Conscientiousness. Sibling personality differences are consistent with the evolutionary view that they would reduce competition for family resources, possibly leading to greater reproductive success in families.[46] This compelling theory has stirred lively debate among colleagues.

Some people might object that twins' birth order is meaningless for personality development because they are the same age. *Born to Rebel* urges a fresh look at old findings, as do the stirring words of seventy-six-year-old secondborn identical twin Lucius Bryant, following the death of his identical twin brother, Thomas. Gazing at a childhood photograph, shown on page 78, he commented:

> The picture shows a pair of shining-smile, happy, supremely innocent, supremely confident little fellows, looking the camera in the eye with a directness which is disarming. That is the way it was generally seen by the older and wiser. Just see the little hand resting upon brother's shoulder, in love, affection and a gesture of protection. . . . But I, having experienced that gesture, saw it differently. . . . A restraining gesture, almost a shove, that said, "Get back there where you belong, Buster! And stay there. There's no room for both of us up front here, and it's my place! So you stay back there for now. . . ." (Note that firstborn Thomas is also holding the larger toy. . . .)

A 1969 birth order study of young twins with singleton siblings, some older, some younger, is worth another look.[47] Firstborns in these threesomes were described as adult-oriented and mature, secondborns were described as easygoing and lighthearted, while thirdborns were described as emotional and distrustful, supporting some of Sulloway's evolutionary predictions. A summary of a 1971 Japanese study showed that firstborn and secondborn identical male twins display the "typical cultural and educational differences" of older and younger siblings in Confucian families.[48] Other twin studies present a mixed picture of birth order–personality relations. Similar to a suggestion in Chapter 4, a creative approach would compare scores on Openness to Experience and on the other Big Five personality dimensions in two types of reared apart identical twins: one group in which twins' birth order positions were the same in their respective adoptive families, and a second group in which twins' birth order positions differed.[49] Predicted personality differences between twins in the second group would be an exciting demonstration of how birth order effects may be modified in genetically identical people. A closer look at specific parenting practices might also reveal if small treatment differences have big personality consequences later in life. I wondered how young Charlie, a firstborn identical twin and keeper of the key to the twins' home, might differ from his brother due to his enviable status.

The real significance of birth position for behavioral development is far more complex than order of arrival, as demonstrated by fraternal twins. Anne and I were nearly seven years old before my mother disclosed that I was the firstborn twin, a subject she avoided by insisting we were "born at the same time." A neighborhood friend, also a twin, convinced us that twins could not be born simultaneously so we pressed hard for the truth. Learning that I was the firstborn twin was a short-lived triumph, more of a surprise, because being smaller and the last to come home I had always "felt" like a secondborn. One of the most fascinating new findings is that size or health may override actual birth order, thereby "reversing" position and personality to yield "functional" firstborns or laterborns. Functional birth order is the position one occupies because of circumstance, rather than actual birth order. I believe I am a functional secondborn because of being smaller than my twin. Personality studies of identical and fraternal twins who differ in size or other characteristics associated with birth position in nontwins would be welcome.

Personality studies discussed so far have relied mainly on twins' self-reports. However, ratings of twins by parents, friends, teachers, laboratory observers and each other round out the picture. Parental ratings of child temperament generally show genetic effects because identical twins are usually rated more alike than fraternal twins. However, parental ratings of behavior also illuminate the ways parents *think* about how similar or different their identical and fraternal twin children may be. Interestingly, physical similarity is *unrelated* to personality similarity in identical twins; one study found that the most frequently confused identical twins were rated *least* similar in behavior, suggesting that parents accent minor differences.[50] Peers' perceptions of adult twins' personality generally agree with twins' own ratings, and twins themselves are qualified judges of their partners' behaviors, with identical twins showing greater agreement with what their siblings reported than fraternal twins or nontwin siblings.[51]

I was imprinted on an observational study of infant twins conducted by my graduate student advisor, Daniel G. Freedman,[52] and have since taken a shine to watching what twins do naturally. His landmark study found greater identical than fraternal twin similarity in social orientation and fearfulness during the first year of life, demonstrating that some of the earliest personality traits have a genetic basis. Some of the most interesting findings concerned identical twin differences, such as the contrasting social sensitivities of more out-going Lori and more reserved Lisa. Reasons for these contrasts may reside in prenatal factors, birth history events and/or unknown sources.

Other observational studies have captured twins' reactions to people, objects or events in laboratories and playground situations. A drawback is that occasional glimpses of behavior on a certain day may be misleading or un-representative, in contrast with questionnaires and inventories that focus on "typical" or "average" tendencies. However, observational methods alone can capture the arresting subtleties and complexities that arise outside standard research settings.

Twin research over the last several years has found that happiness has a genetic basis, but there are no single genes for happiness. It has also shown that divorce has a genetic basis, but there are no genes for divorce. These complex human behaviors are *polygenic* which means they are shaped by many genes, each of which contributes a small effect, in combination with particular social and cultural experiences. (In contrast, single gene traits such as color vision are influenced by only one pair of genes.) People fall naturally along a trait continuum so, for example, there may be "high" risk-takers, "intermediate" risk-takers and "low" risk-takers. Divorce would seem to be an "either-or" trait (either you are divorced or you are not divorced), but the predisposition to divorce may be continuous, with some people more likely to separate from their spouse than others.

Chance of divorce is affected by many factors, but is greater among people low in traditionalism (following rules and authority), high in alienation (feeling mistreated and used) or high in dominance (being masterful and forceful). Genetic factors shared by divorce risk and personality structure may affect marital relationships in ways leading to divorce in some cases and to marital stability in others, although the social processes linking personality traits and divorce risk are unknown.[53] A significant byproduct from this work is appreciation for children's variable responses surrounding family breakup, namely that children reacting negatively may do so partly because of the very same inherited personality traits that proved problematic for their parents—not solely because of disturbed family dynamics. Such children may experience similar marital difficulties later in life, so the observation that divorce "runs" in families acquires new meaning.

A clever twin study by Drs. Susan L. Trumbetta and Irving I. Gottesman took a new look at marital status by asking the question: Why are some people single?[54] Rephrasing the issue in this way addresses behavior departing from the usual pair-bonding patterns found in many species. Pair-bonding facilitates the evolutionarily adaptive processes of reproduction and child care, so factors underlying single status are of interest. Genetic influence was highest for ever marrying versus never marrying (45%); genetic influence was least for ever divorcing versus staying married (21%). The nature of the genetic influence affecting marital status is uncertain, but may include personality factors such as introversion and alienation.

When it was first reported that religiosity and social attitudes were genetically influenced, many psychologists were incredulous, arguing that individuals simply assume the religious identity and values of the families in which they find themselves. This may be true for a person's religious affiliation, such as Judaism or Catholicism, but religious interest and commitment to certain practices, such as regular service attendance or singing in a choir, partly reflect genetically based personality traits such as traditionalism and conformance to authority. This knowledge was revealed, in part, by my colleagues at the University of Minnesota who showed that identical twins reared together and apart showed greater similarity in religious interests and occupations than fraternal twins reared together and apart.[55] Knowing this suggests that when religious parents produce religious children, it is partly because they share personality traits relevant to religious interest and responsibility. At the same time, having religious parents does not guarantee religious children because some children do not inherit the blend of traits that make religious activities interesting or pleasurable.

Having a television in the home does not necessarily turn people into couch potatoes, while its absence may not discourage faithful viewers from following their bliss elsewhere. A future challenge will be to determine how genes, which explained 45% of the variation in television watching, affect behaviors leading some children to favor TV over tennis. It is not surprising that shared environments increased young siblings' similarity in television hours, but it is remarkable that shared experiences explained just 20% of the variation.

Some people's lives are a monotony of misfortunes, while other people's lives are relatively tragedy-free. Twin studies are showing us that things do not just happen, but that personality traits may affect the sequence of life events. Swedish twin researchers found that genetically influenced personality traits of Neuroticism, Extraversion and Openness to Experience were the genetic underpinnings of controllable life events, such as marriage and divorce, for older females, but not for older males.[56] This gender difference in personality–life event links may be due to gender differences in perceiving and interpreting experiences. In this study, uncontrollable life events, such as accidents or illnesses, were primarily due to environmental factors, but different results might emerge using younger age groups. Twin studies of accident proneness in children[57] and sensation-seeking in adults[58] show that both are genetically influenced, and that personality traits such as activity and impulsivity, and extraversion and conscientiousness, may partly provide the genetic basis. Therefore, it may not be total chance if individuals high on these behaviors find themselves in dangerous or stimulating situations, due to poor judgment, physical ineptitude or thrill-seeking tendencies. Seemingly "uncontrollable" events, such as getting lost, falling off a cliff or bucking a thunderstorm while parachuting from a plane, may be fundamental to the life course of some people.

A provocative new study found greater similarity between identical than fraternal twins for age at first intercourse, with stronger genetic effects among twins under forty years of age.[59] Younger twins, having grown up in less sexually restrained climates than older twins, probably had greater freedom to act as they wish, thereby expressing genetically based tendencies more fully. Sexual behavior is most likely affected by a blend of physical characteristics, social customs, cultural values and personality traits. Sociability and impulsivity are natural personality candidates for explaining genetic influences on sexual behaviors and, in fact, early sexual activity has been linked to these traits. Twin studies have also opened our eyes to the possibility that genes affect sexual orientation.

The view that probability lies between genes and behavior seems challenged by an early report finding 100% resemblance for homosexuality in identical twins,[60] but a closer look suggests otherwise. The data themselves are not debatable, but the methods for identifying participants have been suspect. Many members of the thirty-seven male twin pairs were found in correctional facilities, psychiatric institutions and bars attracting gay individuals so the twin sample is probably unrepresentative of the larger homosexual twin population. In other words, it is likely that when both cotwins are homosexual one or both would be found in these settings more frequently than twins who differ in sexual orientation.

Reports on a small number of twins reared apart have produced uncertain conclusions regarding sexual orientation. Early studies described a pair of identical female twins with possible differences in sexual preference (Marjorie and Norah),[61] a pair of identical male twins with attachments to older men during adolescence (Peter and Palle), and a pair of identical male twins in which one cotwin tried to caress and kiss his cotwin (Kaj and Robert).[62] A recent pool of ninety-five reared apart twin pairs, *not identified for sexual preference,* yielded a pair of identical male twins similar for homosexual orientation, a dissimilar pair and a pair with mixed sexual histories. In contrast, five identical female pairs, one fraternal male pair and one fraternal female pair were dissimilar for homosexuality.[63] Findings from this study raised the possibility of genetic influence on male homosexuality and social acquisition of female homosexuality. However, more comprehensive 1990's twin studies have suggested genetic influence for both males and females.[64]

Recent studies conducted by Dr. J. Michael Bailey at Northwestern University in Chicago found a similarity rate of about 50% for identical male and female twins, in contrast with 22% for male fraternal twins, 16% for female fraternal twins, 9% for nontwin brothers of male twins, 14% for nontwin sisters of female twins, 11% for adoptive male siblings and 6% for adoptive female siblings. (The 9% similarity of nontwin brothers of male homosexual twins is lower than the 22% rate reported in another study so it may be an anomalous finding.)[65] When these findings were first announced, an uneasy parent asked me: Are half of all twins really homosexual? The studies actually showed that homosexuality occurs in about 4–10% of males and 2–3% of females, with a 52% chance *if* one's identical male twin is homosexual and 48% *if* one's identical female twin is homosexual.[66]

Estimates of genetic influence on homosexuality, based largely on twins recruited through homosexual groups, may now require downward revision. Using an anonymous survey, an Australian national twin study found modest genetic influence on male sexual orientation and no genetic influence on female sexual orientation.[67] It seems we have traveled full circle in our study of female sexual preference.

In 1991, I visited the University of New Mexico as lecturer in a psychiatry seminar series at the invitation of psychiatrist Jay Feierman. Feierman argued that identical twins probably do not differ in sexual orientation to the degree that twin studies were revealing. He suggested that physiological responses to sexually explicit material (such as nude photographs of same-sex individuals) would be better measures of sexual preference than questionnaires, and would probably show more similar results in identical twins with apparently different orientations. His comments raise the question of atypical sexual behaviors in heterosexual identical twins with homosexual twin siblings. Dr. Scott Hershberger identified a fascinating case study of identical male triplets, one of whom was homosexual.[68] The homosexual triplet displayed slight gender noncomformity as a child (e.g., reduced interest in sex-typical activities), but his heterosexual brothers did not. Twin research has found gender noncomformity in both members of male and female identical pairs concordant for homosexuality, but only in homosexual members of pairs discordant for homosexuality.[69]

One of the most intriguing findings to sweep through academic corridors in 1991 was that anatomical differences in the brain distinguished male homosexuals from male heterosexuals, but it was unclear whether differences in brain structures were the cause or consequence of homosexual practices.[70] This news was succeeded in 1993 by another remarkable study in which thirty-three out of forty homosexual nontwin brother pairs shared genes on the X chromosome which they inherited from their mothers.[71] This intriguing finding is under further study in some laboratories.

There are other plausible explanations of homosexuality in which twins and siblings can, and have, played featured roles. Hormonal theories suggest that prenatal exposure to cross-sex hormones might affect sexual preferences by "masculinizing" or feminizing" developing fetal brains.[72] Beth Zemsky joined my twin loss study after losing her twin brother Bob to AIDS, and I was fascinated to learn that both twins were homosexual. I wondered if prenatal hormonal exposure may have simultaneously masculinized the male's brain and feminized the female's brain, causing sexual attraction to same-sex individuals. However, opposite-sex twins are not the optimal choice for studying hormonal influences on sexuality because of confounds with twins' shared social experiences. Reared apart opposite-sex twins would avoid this problem, but few pairs have been identified. None of the reared apart opposite-sex pairs studied so far have been concordant for homosexual orientation.

Meaningful twin research on sexual orientation requires attention to the level and timing of hormonal exposures soon after conception, in conjunction with childhood and adolescent social experiences, as noted in Chapter 3. Homosexuality does not occur more often among male-female twins relative to other twins and singletons, and for those male-female pairs including one or two homosexual members there are no simple answers.

Psychodynamic views of homosexuality implicate distant parent-child relations as a causal influence. A recent developmental theory suggests that children's perceived differences from same-sex peers cause feelings of attraction, i.e., "exotic become erotic."[73] These theories may be ultimately tied to genetic and other biological factors that influence childhood personality and social relationships. Interestingly, laterborn males with a high proportion of brothers are overrepresented among homosexual samples, possibly reflecting hormonal insufficiencies linked to maternal stress during pregnancy.[74] These theories are useful, yet inconclusive, and if substantiated would most likely represent alternative routes to behavior as complex as homosexuality.

I recall a mother's bewilderment when describing one young identical twin daughter's fondness for feminine clothing and accessories, in contrast with her sister's liking for masculine attire and her discomfort when seen wearing a dress. Isolated signs are not sure signals of sexual preference, but twin research has found links between homosexuality in adulthood and sex-atypical behaviors in childhood. We should never forget that adult sexual orientation is affected by both genetic and environmental factors, even while understanding of how these factors mesh is incomplete.

Behavioral geneticists are delighted to discover behaviors that lack genetic influence or show shared environmental influence, possibly because it strengthens their belief that twin studies teach us as much about the workings of the environment as they do about heredity. This may explain the enormous attention focused on a twin study of love styles which failed to find genetic influence on being swept off one's feet, or falling in love more slowly and steadily.[75] This was a surprising finding because it is easy to suppose that imaginativeness or impulsivity or extraversion might fashion the course of love relationships. Love relations take two and perhaps in this one special area we become exquisitely attuned to the needs and desires of our present love objects, so the particular nature of these needs and desires dictates how intimacy evolves. The novel findings on love styles should stimulate additional research. I wonder if genetic influence may affect more specific features of loving, such as frequency of gift giving and time spent together.

The finding that personalities are genetically influenced has been resisted by some people whose alternative views have not withstood scientific scrutiny. One of the more memorable of ABC's *Nightline* programs of 1989 included interviews with identical reared apart triplets Bobby Shafran, David Kellman and Eddy Galland, Minnesota twin study staff and other guests.[76] Just by being themselves the triplets embodied the critical message from personality research, namely that growing up together does not forecast personality similarity between family members. They came to this belief because they differed from their adoptive parents and siblings, but were like each other in ways unrelated to their rearing. A critical guest geneticist objected that physical appearance and the response it elicits from others must surely explain similiarities between identical twins, as well as individual differences among singletons. Physical features, while similar in identical twins, are *not* linked to personality traits so even if similar responses are triggered by corresponding faces and figures they will have little effect on the developing personality.[77] In other words, unless similar treatment affects biological functions underlying personality it will not affect similarity of measured traits. Identical twins show resemblance in personality, despite occasional differences in appearance, misclassification by parents, or insistence by twins themselves that they are different. This is more telling and more consistent with the growing pool of findings which support genetic effects.

Alberto da Veiga Guignard's painting *Léa e Maura,* and many other portraits and photographs of identical twins, are fine expressions of the striking personality similarities and differences that researchers study and write about. There are also stories of twin resemblance in behaviors beyond the range of what is considered usual, but which cast a strong light on the origins of these pathologies and atypical tendencies in nontwins.

The Genain Quadruplets taught an unforgettable lesson about the interplay of genes and experience underlying schizophrenia and other psychotic disorders.[78] I was privileged to spend the summer of 1974 under the tutelage of the late Dr. David Rosenthal of the National Institute for Mental Health (NIMH), in Bethesda, Maryland.[79] Ten years earlier he had completed a monumental case study of genetically identical quadruplet sisters, all of whom were diagnosed with schizophrenia. Genain is not the actual family name, which was disguised for confidentiality, nor were the sisters' real names Nora, Iris, Myra and Hester. Names were assigned according to birth order and the first four letters of the institute (NIMH) where they lived for three and a half years while participating in a comprehensive study of their illness. *Genain* has a Greek derivation, meaning "dreadful birth" or "dire gene." The pressing search for the sources of influence that unleash the auditory hallucinations, disordered thought processes and distorted sense of self that define the schizophrenic syndrome was what motivated researchers conducting this unique investigation. The Genain quadruplets were a genetic revelation when they were studied in the 1960s because they challenged more popular environmental theories of schizophrenia. They remain a dramatic illustration of genetic influence on psychopathological predisposition and environmental influence on symptomatology which foreshadowed information from current twin and adoption studies.

My role in the follow-up study of the Genain Quadruplets was to review a decade's worth of their letters to Dr. Rosenthal and to organize them according to subject categories. There were clear differences among the four sets of correspondence with respect to frequency and types of symptoms. This was not surprising because, despite their common diagnosis of schizophrenia, Nora, Iris, Myra and Hester varied in the timing, symptoms, progress and outcome of their illness. Psychiatric researchers explain the imperfect match between genes and psychopathology by a diathesis-stress model, the idea that individuals inherit a predisposition (diathesis) for disease which may be triggered when environments turn stressful, or which may remain subdued so long as environments stay stress-free. Environments include the sum total of events affecting us before, during and after birth. Similarly, candidates for coronary conditions are susceptible to attacks when physical and emotional health are neglected, but they may forestall life-threatening episodes through exercise, diet and psychological well-being.

Predisposition for schizophrenia and for other major psychiatric conditions most likely involves many different genes. Therefore, the chance of becoming affected varies as the number of telltale genes varies. Approximately 1% of the population is at lifetime risk for schizophrenia, but if a person is affected, the risk rises to about 6% for his or her parents, 9% for his or her siblings, 13% for his or her children, 17% for his or her fraternal twin and 48% for his or her identical twin.[80] These figures show that developing schizophrenia is more likely with increasing genetic relatedness to the affected individual. The less than perfect resemblance between identical twins tell us that environments also mediate the life course of individuals at risk for this condition.

Bipolar disorder, marked by bouts of mania and depression, also affects approximately 1% of the general population. This condition shows a family risk pattern similar to that of schizophrenia, although lifetime risks are higher—individuals with affected identical twins have a 50–79% risk, while individuals with affected fraternal twins have a 5–19% risk.[81] Family risks for unipolar depression, episodes of depression without mania, are lower than family risks for bipolar depression,[82] and higher for females than males, but the trend toward increased susceptibility with increased genetic relatedness to a depressed individual holds true.

Escalating disease risk among close family members is consistent with both genetic and environmental explanations of abnormal behavior because families share genes as well as social and learning environments. In fact, the prevailing wisdom of the 1960s was that schizophrenia was transmitted by impaired family dynamics, especially conflicting messages communicated from "schizophrenogenic mothers" to children.[83] However, when features of these interaction patterns were also observed in some families without schizophrenia, disengaging genes and environments in the onset of major mental disorders became paramount. A very clever use of the twin-family design (married twins with children), conducted by Drs. Irving I. Gottesman and Axel Bertelsen, tracked schizophrenia in children born to normal identical and fraternal twins and their schizophrenic twin siblings ("discordant" pairs).[84] Remarkably, children of both well and ill identical twins showed the disorder with near equal frequency (17.4% and 16.8%), while children of well and ill fraternal twins differed greatly (2.1% and 17.4%). These findings confirm that identical twins inherit the same genetically influenced disease predisposition that can be passed to children even by a twin who does *not* express the disease, and that living with a schizophrenic parent is not necessary for a disorder to appear in a child. The lesson for nontwin families is that parent-to-child transmission of abnormal behavior may occur as a quiet tendency in the parent that is expressed in the child.

Discordant identical twin pairs are a valued population for teasing out specific birth factors and life events that may activate illness in one twin and silence it in the other. Contrasting the backgrounds and behaviors of discordant identical twins with twins who are both normal or both schizophrenic ("concordant" pairs), or twins who have other psychiatric conditions such as bipolar disorder, can identify unique features of the schizophrenic syndrome. The quest for the keys to the origins of this disorder have led researchers to examine twin differences in prenatal complications, delivery events, handedness, fingerprint and handprint characteristics, brain function, brain insult and viral infections. A monumental 1994 study by Dr. E. Fuller Torrey and colleagues found that affected identical twins from discordant pairs generally showed more frequent birth delivery problems, smaller left and right brain structures associated with mood and memory, reduced blood flow to the brain's frontal lobes, and some degree of intellectual and neurological impairment, but basic personality features were the same.[85]

The 1994 study and others also showed that discordant identical pairs had a larger fingerprint ridge count difference (difference in total number of ridges across all ten fingers) relative to normal identical twins, and that nine pairs with the greatest differences had lower birth weights and more haz-

ardous deliveries. Fingerprint and handprint differences in discordant identical pairs may reflect prenatal trauma which triggered the disease in only one twin even though both inherited the predisposition. For example, even though identical twins share identical genes, a detached placenta or infection in one twin might activate an inherited tendency in that twin only.

The 1994 study also found that twins in identical pairs, both discordant and concordant for schizophrenia, showed greater neurological difficulties than normal twins. Interestingly, well twins in discordant pairs displayed more neurological impairment than normal twins, suggesting common genes for schizophrenia or common early insult. This might explain the increased "personality quirks and idiosyncrasies" found among these well twins compared with normal controls or "supernormals." Affected twins in pairs discordant for bipolar disorder also showed greater birth complications than their well twin siblings, and showed brain changes similar to those shown by schizophrenic twins, but to a lesser degree. Previous reports of links between schizophrenia and left-handedness were not confirmed, and associations between viral infections and schizophrenia appeared possible, but preliminary.

Affected twins and well twins in discordant pairs showed few differences in childhood predictors of schizophrenia when compared as groups. Reading skills, school grades and peer relationships in primary and in junior high school were similar in discordant pairs. However, affected twins were somewhat more disruptive and somewhat less motivated in school than unaffected twins. Neurological dificulties, such as developmental delays, were the clearest warning signs of psychopathology among affected twins in eight discordant pairs. In four of these sets affected twins were shy and socially withdrawn, and in the other four sets affected twins showed learning and language problems. There was some suggestion that well twins assumed childhood leadership roles, but the trend was slight.

The organization of the Genain Quadruplets into favored and disfavored pairs by their parents provides unique insight into how inter-quad relations may have affected symptom severity. Heading the hierarchy was Nora, the firstborn and tallest, whose leadership role may have severely stressed a fragile personality structure. Paired with Nora was Myra, the thirdborn and healthiest sister, whose position conferred favorable status without responsibility. Lower in the pecking order was Iris, the secondborn, whose rightful rank alongside Nora was preempted by larger, livelier Myra. Paired with Iris was Hester, the lastborn and most severely debilitated of the four.[86] These divisions, generated by differences in birth size and development, fashioned roles as leader (Nora), mother (Myra), clown (Iris) and baby (Hester). The varying clinical pictures painted by the Genain Quadruplets cannot be reduced to a simple formula, but suggest a delicate interplay among genetic liⁿbility, prenatal events and early health, all of which may have contributed to ⁿling status. The birth order–personality scenarios discussed earlier may

also play out among twins and siblings with psychiatric predispositions, a point that further research may clarify.

Future twin studies of schizophrenia and depressive disorders will no doubt focus on specific prenatal and birth events, brain structures, viruses, genes and genetic markers associated with these illnesses. Genetic markers are inherited traits that tell us about the inheritance of particular behaviors or traits in families. A genetic marker for schizophrenia should appear in affected and unaffected relatives of schizophrenic patients. It should appear in an unaffected twin from a discordant pair because this twin would carry the genes that might express the disease. Some twin and family studies have identified impaired eye tracking,[87] the inability to maintain visual focus on a moving target, as a marker (or "genetic flag") for schizophrenia, but other studies disagree.[88] Dr. Torrey and his colleagues found eye tracking differences between well identical twins and their ill cotwins, but found an *absence* of differences between these well identical twins and normal identical control twins.

Twin studies have generously contributed to knowledge of psychopathology and atypical behaviors, leading some people to wrongly assume that abnormality is more frequent among twins than nontwins.[89] This falsehood partly arises from the extraordinary professional and public attention similar twin pairs inevitably attract, a sentiment fueled by more dramatic examples of concordant triplets and quadruplets. Double suicides in twins are noticed, but Dr. Niels Holm, Scientific Codirector of the Danish Twin Registry, found a 28% reduction in suicide among twins, relative to nontwins. He speculated that the social support twins may offer one another may offset suicidal tendencies if they are at risk.[90] Some popular reports of atypical behaviors and major mental illnesses slight the environmental side of the equation (prenatal traumas, infections, social experience) which may affect the behavior as much as, or more than, the genetic side. This imbalance in presentation might reflect devotion to new findings, but may ultimately entertain or disturb readers rather than inform them.

It is possible that psychiatric disorder is elevated in twins whose cotwins died, compared with twins who are both living. A 1981 British study by Dr. Adrienne Reveley found mental disturbance among 24% of twins with deceased cotwins (most of whom died before age two), compared with 11% of twins with surviving cotwins.[91] She suggested that birth factors causing the death of one twin may have triggered psychosis in his or her cotwin.

A rare triplet set came to my attention in 1985 while I w...
sity of Minnesota. The set consisted of fifty-seven-ye...
twins with a fraternal triplet brother, all three of who...
from two months of age without contact for forty-sev...
turn visit by one of the sisters there was mention of a cu...

toms common to all triplets. These symptoms included motor tics (eye blinks and facial twitches), phonic tics (grunts and coughs) and repetitive motions (arm and finger movements). For example, in childhood one triplet twirled continuously to the right while descending a spiral staircase, while another engaged in right leg kicking at 5–15 minute intervals. These behaviors are symptoms of *Gilles de la Tourette disorder,* a neuropsychiatric syndrome first described in 1825, which occurs before eighteen years of age, and 1.5–3 times as often among males as females. It affects about .04–.05% of the population.[93]

The presence of Tourette disorder in reared apart triplets is compelling evidence of genetic influence, a view upheld by its appearance in one sister's two children, and in the triplets' biological father and uncle. Twin studies of Tourette's are few in number and modest in size, but they also support a genetic contribution. Using strict diagnostic criteria, 53% of identical twins and 8% of fraternal twins are concordant, figures that climb to 77% for identical twins and 23% for fraternal twins when criteria include "any tics," not necessarily vocal ones.[94] (Transient tics unrelated to Tourette disorder occur in about 6–12% of children.) Identical twin similarity in autism also climbs when criteria change from strict to broad.[95] Little is known about nongenetic factors causing identical twins to differ in the expression or severity of these disorders, but environmental agents or developmental periods of increased vulnerability presumably play a role. Environmental agents might include prenatal toxins or bacterial infections,[96] while increased vulnerability in one twin may be associated with fetal positioning or oxygen supply.

A 1986 letter in the *American Journal of Psychiatry* from Dr. Alec Roy caught my attention: "There has been a good deal of interest recently in the genetic factors of suicide. . . . I would be most grateful to hear from colleagues who know of a twin who committed suicide."[97] I was aware of such twins, having launched the Minnesota Twin Loss Study in 1983 with Prof. Thomas J. Bouchard, Jr. Some participating twins had lost their twin siblings through suicide, a disturbing familial and societal problem occurring in about 11.4/100,000 people, more often in males than in females.[98] Twins' potential contribution to understanding the causes of suicidal behaviors was clearly articulated in Alec Roy's request, and we have been research partners ever since.

Our first study, published in 1991, included sixty-two identical twin pairs and 114 fraternal twin pairs.[99] The proportion of cases in which both twins had committed suicide was 11.3% for identical pairs and 1.8% for fraternal pairs, and combining our study with three previous studies produced similar results (13.2% vs. 0.7%). Suicide occurs among about 1% of males and .5% of females, so a 13.2% similarity rate in identical twins is high in a relative sense. Detailed life history information from eleven pairs showed that most twin suicide victims had been treated for a psychiatric disorder and had a close relative who had also received psychiatric care. Our second study found suicide attempts among ten of twenty-six identical twins, but among none of nine fraternal twins, whose brothers and sisters had committed suicide. These findings show that identical twins are more likely than fraternal twins to share a genetic predisposition for suicide.[100] A recent Australian survey of intact twin pairs found that identicals showed greater similarity in suicidal attempts and thoughts than fraternals, consistent with our results.[101]

A genetic interpretation of suicide has been dismissed by some investigators who favor environmental transmission of suicidal tendencies within families. In fact, several colleagues suspected that more frequent suicides or attempts by surviving identical than fraternal twins reflect a deeper sense of loss, rather than a shared genetic predisposition. This view was perfectly compatible with our findings. I wondered if an answer lay hidden in our sea of data when the elusive research strategy became clear: It was important to compare suicidal attempts between identical twins and fraternal twins whose partners' deaths were *not* due to suicide. An equal and low frequency of suicidal attempts among these particular identical and fraternal twins would show that, despite their grief, they lacked a predisposition for suicide. Only three out of one hundred and sixty-six identical twins and three out of seventy-nine fraternal twins had attempted suicide soon after their twin's death, providing support for our initial conclusions.[102]

Many unanswered questions revolve around suicide, especially the behavioral mechanisms underlying suicidal behavior—in other words, what exactly is transmitted within families leading someone to take his or her own life? Psychiatric disorder or low stress tolerance, joined to poor impulse control, may be one route to suicidal behavior.[103] Recent evidence suggests that reduced levels of the neurochemical serotonin may be implicated in suicide, and Dr. Roy has launched an investigation of this substance in identical twins at risk. Preliminary data from seventeen surviving Swedish twins suggest modest support for a link between serotonin level and suicidal predisposition.[104]

My files include a striking photograph of extremely handsome identical twin brothers whose suicides were separated by a thirty-year gap. Early academic disappointment triggered suicide in one twin, while intolerable stress decades later triggered suicide in his cotwin. This case shows that the same inherited tendency may be activated at different times and in different ways, and that gene-behavior relationships are probabilistic, not deterministic.

Parental treatment, social experience and genetic probability are well-debated themes in the origins of criminal and antisocial behaviors. Attention has been lavished on identical partners in crime, probably because the idea of two people performing the same unconscionable acts in unison is so fantastic. Professional football players twenty-eight-year-old Mike and Mark Bell, served 1986 federal prison sentences in Duluth, Minnesota, on cocaine charges.[105] Mike was convicted of two felony counts of using a telephone to try to purchase cocaine and one misdemeanor count of trying to obtain cocaine. His twin brother Mark was convicted on the same day of one felony count and one misdemeanor count. Mike was a Kansas City Chiefs defensive end and Mark had played six seasons, also as a defensive end, for the Indianapolis Colts and Seattle Seahawks before leaving the sport. Death-row inmate Carey Moore and theft convict David Moore switched places at the Nebraska Penitentiary until their ten-pound weight difference gave them away.[106] The twenty-seven-year-old twins had requested a meeting to discuss family matters, and had used this opportunity to switch clothes and places. Authorities were uncertain if the change was a prank or an escape attempt. Luis Pedro Ajete-Terra of Minnesota committed a traffic violation while his twin brother, Pedro Luis, was charged with cocaine possession, but both claimed identities as Luis Pedro who was linked to the lesser offense.[107] The twins, who were twenty-four, claimed that their identities were confused during the booking, which happened at the same time and place.

Shocking role reversals between guilty and innocent twins have also occurred as shown by Donald Anderson, who served three jail sentences for his identical brother, Ronald, and even substituted for him in the military.[108] "The judge asked me why I did this, and I said my twin needed help." Even more incredible, Southern California witnessed the attempted murder of twenty-two-year-old identical twin Sunny Han by her sister, Jeen.[109] Jeen apparently hoped to assume her sister's good name to erase an infamous past featuring stolen credit cards. This was not a case of "good twin" and "bad twin," a romantic notion without scientific support, especially since credit card fraud and a brief jail stint by the "good" twin was revealed.

Over the years, twin studies of criminality in the United States, Europe and Japan have been unanimous in finding greater similarity among identical than fraternal twins. A 1997 summary of seven twin studies of adult criminality found concordance rates of 52% for identical twins and 23% for fraternal twins, evidence of genetic influence.[110] However, type of crime makes a difference as shown by a Danish twin study indicating genetic effects on serious crimes punishable by loss of liberty after age fifteen years, but not on misdemeanors.[111] Twin studies have generally failed to find genetic influence on juvenile delinquency, although a recent study found genetic effects on self-reported delinquent behaviors.[112]

Identical twin similarities in criminal acts are impressive, but differences are also instructive. Dramatic case reports of criminality in identical twins reared apart show that antisocial tendencies may vary across environments.[113] A pair of identical male twins, separated at age eight, were placed into unfavorable foster homes. Both pursued criminal activities until the military enlistment of one twin and the marriage of the other twin to an "energetic and strong-minded woman" ended these exploits. A second case concerned twins who stole, but whose variable involvements in criminal life were linked to differences in the favorableness of their childhood homes. Still another case involved identical twins separately reared by religious natural parents and by alcoholic foster parents in a nearby slum district. Both twins were "gentle, intelligent and gifted," but the slum-raised twin engaged in repeated theft and embezzlement. These examples show that antisocial tendencies may sometime be channeled into socially acceptable behaviors through appropriate parenting, career options and emotional support.

Environments of twins raised together are surely more alike than those of twins raised apart, but subtle differences in the rearing home or beyond may spell huge differences on the street. A telling example came in the form of a phone call from an identical twin housewife and mother, Debra Mapes, whose twin sister, Diane Bowerman, was jailed for first-degree aggravated murder.[114] Their childhood home included physical and sexual abuse by a stepfather, but the twins remained close until Debra married Chuck Mapes, after which Diane withdrew and hooked up with undisciplined, abusive crowds. Similar features of home environments are not always the same for cohabitants, not even identical twins, and may trigger different responses. I wonder if Debra's marriage left Diane grieving for her absent twin, providing the trauma that activated her diathesis (predisposition) for criminal behavior. Some identical twins experience a form of mourning when their twin marries, but this experience may conceivably be extremely stressful if combined with a pathological predisposition.

What is the nature of genetic predispositions to antisocial behavior? Candidates include brain abnormalities, altered enzyme levels and birth complications. Dutch investigators attracted worldwide attention when they found reduced levels of the enzyme monoamine oxidase (MAO) in five male relatives showing impulsive aggression, arson, attempted rape and exhibitionism.[115] The genetic mutation was located on a precise portion of the X chromosomes of the men in question. No subsequent study has identified this MAO mutation in other families, so it must be quite rare. Nevertheless, this study, which unites behavioral and molecular genetics, exemplifies the future course of twin and family studies of antisocial disorders.[116]

Years ago I supervised a puzzle completion session in which one identical twin boy spoke out of turn, worked in short spurts, and continually "horsed around," while his cotwin worked willingly and cooperatively, admitting embarrassment at his brother's antics. The pair recalled Simon and Garfunkel's "voices out of rhythm, couplets out of rhyme," from the song "The Dangling Conversation," about two lovers who had lost their early intimacy and rapport. These boys were evidence that identical twin children can differ in problem behaviors, such as social difficulties and aggression, making differences in some pairs as engrossing as the similarities because of potential insights into environmental effects. Problem behaviors reflect a mix of genetic influence, shared environmental events and individual experience, but this three-part division is not constant at all ages or for all behaviors or for all studies. For example, twins and siblings' shared experiences appear to have greater effects on anxiety during childhood and adolescence than at age three.[117]

Twin studies have illuminated factors affecting Conduct Disorder, characterized by repetitive and persistent behaviors violating age-appropriate social rules such as harming people or property.[118] A recent study of adult identical and fraternal twins' reports of such behavior in childhood found substantial genetic influence and modest shared environmental effects,[119] while another study found the opposite, possibly due to differences in samples and procedures.[120] Most studies agree that genetic influence does affect risk for Conduct Disorder, and that externalizing problems are more common in males than in females.

Interest in childhood predictors of adult antisocial behaviors has been overwhelming in recent years, one reason why relevant twin research has proliferated. Not all delinquent adolescents were delinquent children, but children displaying severe and frequent problem behaviors are at risk for delinquent tendencies at older ages. Identical twins, Ali and Alquan S. from New Jersey, who became famous at only seven years of age for fires, thefts and property damage, have already revealed one factor contributing to their shared misadventures: Ali blamed Alquan for being the "leader" and for constructing maps of their untoward plans.[121] An interesting sidelight from adolescent twin research is that both identical and fraternal twins may coax their twin siblings into joining delinquent acts,[122] a theme well illustrated by the seven-year-olds. Of course, social pressures toward criminality or other antisocial behaviors, pathologies and atypical tendencies may only work in predisposed individuals. Attempts to discourage instigators might be the way to discourage followers.

A final link in the chain uniting twin research on psychopathology and atypical behaviors is the question *why*. Why do so many debilitating behaviors remain in the human population when they bring apparent pain? In the past some researchers speculated that individuals with low doses of genes underlying psychopathology, such as relatives of schizophrenic patients, enjoy enhanced creativity, fertility or longevity which ultimately benefits individuals, families and populations.[123] A similar explanation was proposed for autism, a heartbreaking condition affecting 5–10 out of 10,000 children[124] that involves rare use of language, inappropriate eye contact and inappropriate response to others. This rare disorder was diagnosed in the children of five theoretical physicists in California, suggesting a "price" was paid for their parent's exceptional mind.[125] More recently, fathers and grandfathers of autistic children were found to be overrepresented in the field of engineering. Such explanations are intriguing, but have found little empirical support when applied to other disorders, and therefore warrant further study.[126]

Evolutionary psychologists have recently argued that features of anxiety, fear, obsessive-compulsive behaviors, anger, grief and other seemingly mal-adaptive behaviors may have benefited humans during the course of evolution. Fear of heights protects people from injury, emerging shortly before crawling begins, while obsessive or compulsive tendencies may represent extreme motivations to prioritize behaviors.[127] Antisocial personalities and personality disorders have been conceptualized as alternative strategies or life-styles which, depending upon circumstances, may allow "cheaters" to achieve desired goals at reduced personal cost.[128] These individual benefits may explain the low but continued presence of antisocial behaviors in the population. These explanations are novel ways of thinking about human behavior that are slowly gaining attention even as they are raising challenging questions. Twin studies can help by showing which disorders are genetically influenced, whether genetic effects are similar in males and females, and how environments modify behavioral expression.

Twin studies have now been conducted on a wide range of mental disorders and atypical behaviors. They include hyperactivity,[129] anorexia nervosa (self-imposed starvation),[130] bulimia (extreme overeating combined with purging),[131] febrile and afebrile seizures (seizures with and without fever),[132] alcoholism,[133] cigarette smoking,[134] panic attacks[135] and Alzheimer's disease,[136] all of which reveal contributions from genetic and environmental sources. Premenstrual Syndrome (PMS) is also attracting attention from twin researchers. An eight-year longitudinal twin study found varying degrees of genetic influence on the persistence of perceived difficulties during menstruation (77%), pain (55%) and menstrual flow (39%).[137] There is evidence of genetic influence on autism, not just from twin studies,[138] but from case reports of identical triplets concordant for infantile autism and for a related disorder called Asperger's Syndrome.[139] Family studies linking autism to a specific gene controlling a particular brain chemical are especially important for identifying individuals at risk.[140]

Knowledge that genes contribute to autism and other childhood behavioral disorders has reassured many parents who believed they were somehow responsible for their children's behaviors. It is now known that parents may treat autistic children differently from their unaffected siblings, but this treatment is largely a response to, not a cause of, their behaviors. Twin studies have helped guide us toward this crucial understanding, and to much of what we know about the genetic jurisdiction of atypical human traits. Families have also gained hope as genetic researchers now search for the causes and treatments of behavioral difficulties.

Friendship Extraordinaire: Twins' Special Relationship

My boys were thrilled to learn that they are definitely identical twins. Why, I don't really know, but it is a big deal to them.—A mother of twins

They [identical twin brothers] are more important to each other than I am to either of them.—A nonidentical male triplet with identical twin brothers

The boys who were "thrilled" when test results confirmed that they were identical twins were probably unable to articulate why they had these feelings. Similarly, words could not express why the fraternal triplet who, feeling different from his brothers, sensed that three can be a crowd.

These observations are not surprising, they are consistent with how identical and fraternal twins act toward each other. Explaining why the bond between identical twins—a *friendship extraordinaire*—is stronger than the bonds between other siblings, even to the extent of making a fraternal triplet feel excluded, is not so simple. Studying twins can also provide insights into what it takes to get along with others. A new way to accomplish this task is by uniting twin research with evolutionary psychology to show how the social relationships of identical and fraternal twins inform us about our own family attachments.

Some researchers have capitalized on the difference in biological relatedness between identicals and fraternals to probe the genetic and environmental foundations of human social behavior. Many different theories and methods have been applied in this area, but the results are nearly always the same: Identical twins share closer social bonds than fraternal twins. This simple finding carries the broader message that biology affects how we behave toward one another. Understanding why and how this happens is a fascinating story.

We begin with Charles Darwin's theory of evolution, first proposed in 1859.[1] In its classic form, Darwin's theory emphasized the differential survival and reproduction of individuals. This process, known as *natural selection,* is regarded as basic to the evolution of all living things. Evolutionary biologist Robert Trivers reminds us that in Darwinian theory, reproduction means giving birth to surviving offspring; activities, such as sexual behavior, friendship and leisure time, are organized around fulfilling this aim.[2]

Yet an enigma that was not to be resolved for another hundred years was the occurrence of countless displays of altruism or selfless behavior within species. If evolutionary theory emphasized the welfare of the individual, then acts benefiting other individuals would seem contradictory. Then, in 1964, William D. Hamilton, a graduate student at the University of London, published a series of papers that were destined to change forever the way that many psychologists and anthropologists view human social behavior.[3] Hamilton reasoned that helping biological relatives who share your genes "helps" your own genes to survive. His vital insight was that natural selection is not just about the reproductive success of the individual, but the replication of an individual's genes, whether or not those genes reside in the individual or in a relative. This concept is called *inclusive fitness.* Consider that mothers directly transmit 50% of their genes to each of their children. It makes "evolutionary sense" for them to act altruistically toward their own children, as compared to unrelated children, as a way of preserving copies of their genes in future generations. Another, indirect way for individuals to transmit their genes is through collateral relatives, such as cousins, who descend from the same family, but in a different line—recognizing that genes could be preserved in this way was Hamilton's unique contribution. This new view of behavior, which focused on the gene rather than the individual carrying it, launched the new science of evolutionary psychology and a new series of predictions about human behavior, especially altruism.

Altruism is commonly defined as unselfish behavior or devotion to the welfare of others and, indeed, this is how most people understand it. To evolutionary psychologists altruism means behavior that results in assistance to someone *at the actor's expense.* Child care is an example of altruistic behavior because it is costly to parents, but benefits their children. Altruism can wear many faces. Richard Dawkins, author of *The Selfish Gene,* cautions that how we construe the "credits" and "debits" of helping behavior matters.[4] Some behaviors which appear to benefit the recipient actually benefit the donor. In this sense, parental care may acquire a "selfish" cast since caring for a child is, in fact, a means of passing on one's own genes. "Selfishness" does not reside in parents whose genes predispose them to love their children, not does it reside in genes themselves. "Selfishness" is the effect of genes promoting behaviors leading to the genes' replication.

Some evolutionary psychologists speak about "genes for altruism," but this is misleading. Anthropologist Jerome Barkow explains that the phrase "genes for altruism" really refers to inherited factors, possibly combinations of certain genes, responsible for psychological processes that increase a person's chances for being altruistic.[5] Close genetic relatives, such as siblings, are more likely to share genetic factors related to altruism than individuals who are more distantly related, such as cousins. Twin studies have found genetic influence on altruism, as well as on empathy and nurturance.[6]

Evolutionary theory predicts that identical twins, who share 100% of their genes, should be more mutually helpful than fraternal twins who share about 50% of their genes,[7] half-siblings who share about 25% of their genes, and cousins who share about 12.5% of their genes. In other words, genes influencing individuals to favor others likely to carry these same genes would be a way to transmit the genes into future generations. Parents, twins and other close relatives do not consciously think about genetic relationships before lending assistance or performing a favor. Psychologist Steven Pinker said this well by distinguishing individuals' "real motives" and genes' "metaphorical motives."[8] Remember, genes replicate because they foster behaviors favorable to their preservation, not because individuals carrying the genes make replication decisions. Evolutionary psychologists assert that people come equipped with genetic predispositions to behave as if they perform these calculations.[9] Why is this so?

In the course of evolutionary history, those who helped and received help from their biological relatives were likely to survive and to have children, while those who did not were less likely to survive or to reproduce. In this sense, parents act like a "selfish" lot since caring for a child is a way of preserving one's own genes, through children and through children's children. At the same time many adoptive, foster and surrogate mothers and fathers love their children as much as natural parents love their children, and work hard on their behalf, behavior possibly attesting to the strong human need to assume parenting roles. David Barash suggests that such "internal whisperings" explain why adoption is a natural and desirable alternative to many childless couples.[10] Some fertile parents choose adoption over reproduction to provide needy infants with loving family environments,[11] although raising biological children remains the preferred arrangement.

Altruism is also influenced by immediate circumstances, such as having the skills or resources required by the person you wish to help. Altruism is further affected by cultural norms and ethical principles, such as guidelines restricting the use of medical data collected on Holocaust victims even if it might save a life. Such social factors explain exceptions to the evolutionary predictions described above. Unfortunately, there are also a minority of biological parents who neglect children's needs, a heartbreaking situation which may variously reflect psychological and biological disturbances in these families.

*   *   *

Interpretations of behavior by evolutionary psychologists are novel and captivating. They do not replace explanations based on socialization theories, but they may breathe new life into social explanations as we know them.[12] Why do parents all over the world endure, even welcome, the difficult challenges of raising children? Why do many infertile couples invest thousands of dollars in the hopes of conception? Most likely it is because caring for children is exquisitely and uniquely pleasurable to most parents, and the pleasant emotions that parents feel as a result of taking care of children guarantee that caretaking occurs. Even in trying moments, most couples agree that having children is "well worth it." These sentiments may be the critical driving force that keeps the human race going, and twin studies can tell us more about this process. Evolutionary views of behavior are also contentious and controversial, raising worries that researchers have slighted environmental effects. I will return to this theme in the final chapter.

Twin studies, coupled with evolutionary psychology, extend the range of new and surprising answers about who spends time with whom, who avoids whom, who misses whom and why. The special intimacy shared by many identical twins has been convincingly demonstrated by many different studies. An early investigator, Dorothy Burlingham, described the identical twin bond as the "closest tie between two individuals," a theme repeated in recent analyses.[13] The view that one is and should be closer to the twin than to other siblings has been expressed more often by identical than by fraternal twins.[14] A study of high school–age twins found that identicals and fraternals, as groups, did not differ in their feelings about being a twin, as measured by satisfaction with the twinship and frequency of fighting.[15] Within pairs, however, identicals were more likely to *agree* with each other about their experience of twinship. In other words, the fraternal twin group included more pairs in which one twin was contented with the twinship while the other was not. As one colleague put it, these striking differences in satisfaction may speak to the more similar "powers of perception" and finely tuned system of communication that appear to characterize partners who share all of their heredity, as compared with those who do not.[16] Identical twins often agree even when they argue, as revealed by an identical triplet who anticipated his brothers' retorts.

A landmark study published in 1971 by Martha McClintock showed that women living together in college dormitories synchronized their menstrual cycles, and that this tendency was stronger for friends than for acquaintances.[17] No one has undertaken a twin study with this in mind, but I expect that identical female twins would show greater menstrual synchrony than fraternal female twins, reflective of their greater emotional investment in one another, as well as time spent together. Identical twins show greater similarity in age of menarche (onset of menstruation) and cycle regularity, suggesting genetic effects,[18] but possible social-interactional influences have not been considered.

Why are identical twins closer than fraternal twins? There is evidence that parents and caretakers do not bear the primary responsibility for twins' similarities or how they relate to one another. Instead, many studies demonstrate that parents respond to, rather than create, behaviors expressed by identical twins. In my cooperation and competition study discussed below, identical and fraternal twins' behaviors were unrelated to parents' judgment of twin type, membership in a twins club and encouragement toward behavioral similarity or dissimilarity.[19] It is counterintuitive, but true, that identical twins who are treated alike *do not* show greater behavioral resemblance than identical twins who are treated less alike.[20] Parents and others may magnify or downplay traits and tendencies, but the twins are the movers and shakers.

Identical twinship is not perfect harmony since identical twins, like everyone else, have clashes. One study found that, on average, identical and fraternal male and female twins fight "sometimes" as revealed by a three-point scale ranging from "usually" to "sometimes" to "rarely or never."[21] I believe we should look at the nature and severity of twins' arguments, and the possible differential significance of arguments for identical and fraternal twins' feelings about one another. Mothers of some identical twins tell me that their twins constantly bicker, yet are quick to defend each other against "outside attack." I have known twins who seem to enjoy being each other's exclusive combatants, but who are in frequent contact. Dr. Daniel G. Freedman of the University of Chicago has wisely noted that aggression and altruism are not mutually exclusive, and then even "warring" twins may be inseparable due to mutual understandings.[22] Identical twins may, thus, come closer than anyone else to achieving the coordinated, harmonious relations for which we all strive. An identical twin may not have all the answers to his or her cotwin's questions. On balance, however, an identical twin may be the best source for most types of assistance for which we would normally rely on other people, such as emotional sustenance or investment decisions. This is because, genetically speaking, helping an identical twin is like helping oneself, i.e., helping one's own genes to survive. This may sound selfish, but remember that evolutionary psychologists do not accuse caregivers of having motives, selfish or otherwise. Behavior is labeled "selfish" only to the extent that it results in the passing on of genetic material.

In contrast with identical twins, fraternal twins are not as close, nor are their lives as intimately entwined. Just as parents do not create identical twin similarities, parents play a modest role in the development of fraternal twin differences. If fraternal twins receive differential treatment from parents, this is because they are genetically different and, therefore, behaviorally different and their parents respond to their uniqueness. Some fraternal twins, even siblings, are quite close, however. According to Donatella Versace, sister of the late fashion designer Gianni Versace, when they were together there was a "spooky electricity that flowed between them—the kind that links twins."[23] Studying these exceptional pairs may identify unique factors affecting social relations, such as unusual behavioral or physical resemblance or early loss of a parent.

Some people might wonder how identical twins who "hate each other" fit into the picture. Some television talk shows have featured identical twins who professed to loathe their twin sibling. As mentioned in Chapter 5, a recent case in California involved Asian identical twin sisters, one of whom was clearly troubled and had been arrested for credit card fraud. As the details unfolded, it turned out that this sister had tried to murder her twin in order to assume her identity and start a new life. In a *Los Angeles Times* interview, I commented that the twin bond is generally quite strong and that this case was a clear exception to the rule.[24] The fact that such events make it to the airwaves underlines their novelty. Not all twins conform to type in terms of their social relations, but it is the difference between groups of identical and fraternal twins, rather than the exceptional pairs, that most informs our understanding of broad patterns of human social relationships. The exceptional pairs remind us that human behavior is flexible and not necessarily predictable from genetic background or genetic relatedness.

Studies that use twins as couples can be very revealing about what goes into making a relationship happy or discontented. Observing twins as couples while they are conversing with one another, playing a game or confronting the decision to donate an organ to their twin tests whether social relations differ if partners share all their genes or half their genes. Researchers are interested in knowing if cooperation, mutual enjoyment and degree of participation differ between identical and fraternal twins in these situations. This approach to studying twins (as couples) differs from the classic approach I described before in which the degree of behavioral similarity of identical and fraternal twins in IQ, personality or job satisfaction is compared. According to evolutionary psychology, greater cooperation is expected between identical than fraternal twins. Such findings can be used to try to understand why some siblings get along better than others, why some parents and children agree more than others, and even why some business associates are more congenial than others.

A 1934 twin study conducted by the German investigator Helmut von Bracken showed in great detail how identical twins cooperate more than fraternal twins when they work together.[25] Young identical and fraternal twins were asked to independently complete arithmetic problems and coding tasks (matching numbers and symbols according to a given scheme) under two conditions: in the same room and in different rooms. Identical twins performed more alike when they were together than when they were apart. In identical pairs showing the greatest differences when working apart, the more skilled identical cotwin allow the less skilled cotwin to catch up when working together. In contrast, those fraternal twins who perceived ability differences between them were unmotivated to try very hard when working in each other's company—they seemed to lack the cutting edge. Fraternal partners who perceived that they were matched in skill became rivals. In fact, when the difference between two fraternal twin boys was artificially equalized, the more skillful twin tried desperately to outscore his brother, even inventing answers to increase his speed and work output. Professor von Bracken suggested that ". . . the understanding between the two members of an identical pair is much greater than that between either member and other persons. With fraternals . . . the intimate understanding due to similar hereditary disposition is not present to the same degree."

I was inspired by this study, and by J. Paul Scott's animal research showing greater cooperation between dogs from genetically similar vs. genetically dissimilar breeds.[26] Based on the theories and methods of this work, I observed young identical and fraternal twins as they completed a puzzle together.[27] The identical twins demonstrated greater cooperation during this activity than the fraternal twins, as expected. In particular, identical twins were more likely to complete the puzzle successfully than fraternal twins, and to position the puzzle more equally between themselves. Most compelling were the very gentle physical restraints, such as those shown by nine-year-old identical twins Dean and David. Dean placed his hand lightly on his brother's arm before quietly removing a puzzle piece from his hand and placing it himself. In contrast, pushing and shoving were more typical of fraternal twins. Seven-year-olds Gina and Tammy seemed to inhabit separate worlds, as when Gina moved the puzzle pieces to her side of the table and placed her arms around them to deny her sister access.

Like other children, twins can be self-centered, but identicals seem to keep these tendencies under wraps to a greater degree than fraternals. This finding was apparent in a second study I conducted in which young twins earned points for themselves by tracing a series of shapes as fast as they could.[28] The situation was then changed by instructing children to earn points for their twin, i.e., they had to hand over their earnings to their twin siblings. Both identical and fraternal twins worked harder for themselves than for their twin siblings, but the difference between work done for the self and for the twin was much smaller for identical twins. More recently, Dr. Scott Hershberger of California State University, Long Beach, and I observed the same pattern of behaviors by teenage and adult twins in a comparable game situation.[29] Cooperation and competition are quite closely intertwined features of behavior when we realize that identical twins may cooperate more than fraternal twins by competing less. Identical twins' responses toward one another may include a "greater restraint of selfishness" than fraternal twins' strategies.[30]

What lies behind the cooperation and generosity that identical twins show toward one another? It is not enough to know that genetic relatedness may matter—the real question is: How does genetic relatedness translate into psychological processes underlying social behavior? Psychologists have not yet pinned this down, but there are some clues. We know that identical twins are more similar than fraternal twins in general intelligence, personality and physical appearance. It is conceivable that twins who are matched in intelligence and in personality are more likely to work together productively than those who are not. In the puzzle study, identical and fraternal twins in each pair were matched in general intelligence. Remember, two people can have the same intelligence level, while differing in their patterning of abilities. Identicals show more similar ability patterns than fraternal twins, so their approach to puzzle-solving may have been more alike. Perhaps they both began by sorting the pieces according to size, or by painting a "mental picture" of the finished product. In contrast, many fraternal twins show contrasting ability profiles, and so may have brought different skills to the task. Complementary abilities may have enabled some fraternal pairs to cooperate, but a "sorter" and a "mental artist" might have easily clashed with one another.

Cooperation and productivity can result from complementary behavioral styles. In other words, it would be incorrect to suppose that all identical twin pairs cooperated by working in exactly the same way. In some cases twins "took turns" at placing the puzzle pieces, while in others each twin "assumed responsibility" for different parts of the task. These kinds of differences between identical twins are most likely quantitative, e.g., one is more assertive and the other is less assertive, while these kinds of differences between most fraternal twins and nontwins may be qualitative, e.g., one is assertive and the other is submissive. It is likely that identical twins can cooperate despite these differences because of similarities in other behaviors, such as how they process information and how much they enjoy an activity. Not all fraternal twins, such as those in von Bracken's experiments, or nontwins may be similar enough to cooperate across situations.

The important point is that behavioral differences in identical twins are often "variations on the same theme"[31] so, for example, a slightly more assertive twin might "direct" puzzle activity, while a less assertive twin might "carry out commands." It is easy for identical twins to organize themselves in this way because they are so similar to begin with. Fraternal twins are generally less alike and may encounter difficulty when trying to mesh their contrasting styles. Some evolutionarily minded researchers have suggested that because identicals "intuit" the actions or intentions of their cotwins better than fraternals they should show greater cooperation regardless of how much they value their partners. I would argue that twins' sensitivity to their cotwin's behaviors lays the basis for a harmonious relationship, joining understanding and cooperation closely together.

What do these findings tell us about joint activities between nontwin partners? Think about your business associates—surely there are some with whom you enjoy positive, productive relations, while there are others with whom life is a constant struggle. What qualities about each of you underlie these relations? Research on cooperation in the workplace shows that coworkers who are also friends collaborate more often than those who are

just colleagues. Coworker skills also include the ability to draw on each partner's special skills, and a feeling of commitment to the group's goals.[32]

Watching and listening to twin pairs has revealed a great deal about cooperation in joint endeavors. Feeling the same way, thinking the same way, "knowing that the other person can take care of you if you don't want to do something" is how many identical twins describe their shared professional and personal relationships.[33] Some fortunate nontwins have discovered similar qualities in their own working lives. Movie director Mike Nichols and screenwriter Elaine May have been called "inner twins." According to Nichols, "She's [May] the person to whom I have to explain nothing."[34] Within most families, certain parent-child and sibling pairs also stand out as more cooperative than others. I would expect that nontwin partners' cooperation is limited to situations they both enjoy, while identical twins' cooperation is more pervasive.

The von Bracken study and the puzzle task were "semi-naturalistic" studies, situations made to feel like real life. What if twins were observed in unstructured settings to see whom they chose to be with, and what they chose to do and for how long? In 1984, I observed the behaviors of eight young identical twin pairs and four young fraternal twin pairs during recess periods at school.[35] The physical closeness and social exchanges of the twins were recorded at ten-second intervals. As expected, identical twins showed greater physical and social closeness than did fraternal twins. Several fraternal twin pairs were never once spotted together during the entire observation period, which is not surprising given the more formal twin studies reviewed above.

Some events observed during this "twins in the wild" study lend richness and texture to twin relationship data obtained from questionnaires and interview studies. Seven-year-old identical twin boys Matthew and Michael entered the play area at different times. Michael, who appeared first, looked about anxiously until his brother emerged. Once he spotted him, he broke into a marvelous grin, ran eagerly toward his brother, and the two boys began to swing around a pole in perfect synchrony. Other identical twin boys, Dean and David mentioned above, were involved in a ball game. When they were separated they could be seen looking around for one another every once in a while. The slight tension in their faces when they searched disappeared once they caught sight of their brother. This type of behavior is like the interactional melodies, the finely tuned relationship patterns, observed between parents and children in parks and playgrounds around the world, in which separations are followed by searches and, eventually, joyful reunions.

These observations have implications for relationships between classmates and friends. Child development researchers are aware that friends display similarities and, more importantly, that these similar behaviors are usually present prior to the establishment of the relationship.[36] In other words, close associations do not make friends alike, they are alike before meeting and are

perhaps drawn together because of their similarities. Identical and fraternal twin comparisons illustrate this point quite nicely. Think about who your best friends are and what brought you together. It might be because you have "a lot in common." There are probably certain activities, traditions, habits, even jokes, that you mutually enjoy, but which others might find silly or pointless. Family members also have their own "cultures," consisting of certain practices or rituals that reflect shared interests and experience, such as favorite songs or yearly outings to obscure historical landmarks.

A colleague has suggested that identical twin pairs can be viewed as "cultures," namely miniature inbred populations with their own special understandings and ways of doing things: "Perhaps to the extent that the fine tuning is alike in sender and receiver, two may feel as one, and the two can consequently sacrifice for one another."[37] The relationships between reared apart identical and fraternal twins after reunion offer striking examples of identical "twins as cultures." Investigators affectionately referred to the "Giggle Twins," sisters who laughed incessantly only when they were together; the "Jim Twins," brothers named Jim who shared interests in carpentry and police work; the "Fireman Twins," brothers who independently chose to become volunteer firemen; and the "Twins with the Seven Rings," sisters who both arrived at the study wearing seven rings, three bracelets and a watch. Similar labels were distributed far less frequently among reunited fraternal twins.

There are no single genes for laughing or for wearing rings. There are genetic factors affecting personality traits, intellectual abilities, physical features and vocational interests. As discussed in Chapter 4, distinctive behavioral patterns may reflect unusual combinations of many genes or *emergenic traits*.[38] If identical twins show a high degree of similarity for a particular behavior and fraternal twins show a very low degree of similarity, this suggests that the behavior is emergenic.[39] Such behaviors surely fashion each identical pair's special brand of behavior or "culture," contributing to the intimacy and rapport that most identical pairs share. Fraternal twins remind us not so much of cultures as of "mixed populations," given their more distinctive tastes and talents. A marvelous example of the mixed population motif comes from the fraternal triplet who felt at odds with his identical brothers. He described his two brothers' unusual habit of "packing," in which they would intentionally consume huge quantities of food, a practice that he did not endorse.

The family arrangement consisting of married identical twins, their spouses and children can test the idea that genes may affect similarity, affiliation and conflict within families.[40] Recall that children born to identical twins add intriguing twists to family trees: Full siblings from the two families, shown in the diagram, are "genetic half-siblings" because their mothers are identical twins. Genealogists could spend lifetimes trying to unravel the unique relationships generated by families resulting from the marriages of

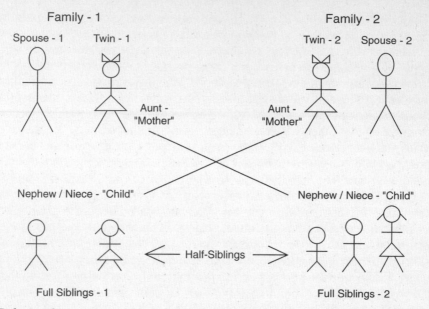

Relationships generated by identical twin "half-sibling" families. This natural "experiment" begins when identical twins marry, allowing researchers to track similarities between couples and spouses. The birth of children makes the research design complete. FIGURE DESIGN BY KELLY DONOVAN.

identical triplets or quadruplets, especially in the event of divorce and remarriage.

The twin-family constellation begs for analysis of social relationships.[41] For example: *Greater altruism should be shown to nieces and nephews by twin aunts and uncles in identical half-sibling families than in fraternal twin families.* Tests of such predictions can reveal whether individuals respond to the genetic relationship or to the cultural relationship. Perhaps both identical and fraternal twin aunts occasionally provide child care for their nieces, with identical twin aunts doing so more often. It is possible that the higher proportion of genes shared between identical twin aunts and their nieces, as compared with fraternal twin aunts and their nieces, might "drive" the relationship, resulting in more contact. Here we have perfect parallels with the parenting role discussed earlier, namely that twin aunts would not consciously consider the genetic relatedness of nieces before acting altruistically and that the pleasurable feelings resulting from providing care would maintain the relationship. It was already shown that close relations may not necessarily result from increased contact, but that similarities already present between relatives may lead to more constant companionship, as is true for friends. In the case of identical twins, it is now believed that more similar twins choose to spend more time together, rather than the other way around.

These findings may explain why biological relatives, such as dad's brother, may be a more frequent and helpful guest than his wife, an aunt by marriage.

Identical twin "half-sibling" families also include a potential for conflict. Disapproval by the nontwin parents over favors provided to their children by identical twin aunts or uncles may cause bickering within couples. In one such family, an identical female twin wished to assume responsibility for her nephew, or "son," following the death of her sister. This decision met with strong objection from the child's father, who was understandably committed to raising his own child, and a schedule of visits was eventually agreed upon. The woman's plan to raise the child was not based on genetic calculations, but on her feelings that the child was somehow "hers." The physical resemblance of the "half-siblings" is striking. This case was resolved outside court and is an example of the unusual legal snarls that can happen in families with twins which I discuss in Chapter 14.

What do cases like this say about what goes on behind the scenes in our own families? Maybe we feel greater interest in the children of a biological sister than those of an adopted sister. Or as stepparents we may take slight interest in stepchildren from a spouse's previous marriage, despite feeling that we should regard these children as our own. Or perhaps it seems more meaningful to spend the holidays with parents than with in-laws. The same exercise can be applied to individuals who inhabit our "extended households," such as grandparents, aunts and uncles, nieces and nephews, cousins and in-laws. Look around the table at a family wedding or graduation party to see who is seated next to whom and why this arrangement was important. Close relatives are probably clustered together and seated closest to the head of the table. Examine the holiday gifts you have purchased for your relatives and think about the effort and expense that went into each one. It is likely that you thought more and spent more for relatives who are closest to you. Would you react differently to news of serious injury to different family members? The answer to this question is probably also yes. Studies of identical and fraternal twin families conducted with these issues in mind can bring varying family loyalties and coalitions into sharper focus. Listening to twins whose cotwins were severely injured made me think seriously about such questions.

Identical twin Kari Krumweide was paralyzed when she was hit by a falling tree at the age of thirty-one. She and her sister, Kathi Nordgaard, talked to me by telephone on November 25, 1997. Always the best of friends, they became part of a special twin group holding clues to spinal cord injuries' effects and treatments. The accident's aftermath did not separate them, but bound them more closely together. Kathi began practicing wheelchair maneuvers with Kari so as to stay part of her world. She also accompanied her sister to the August 1997 Ms. Wheelchair America Pageant where Kari placed in the top ten and captured the Ms. Congeniality title.

The December 1, 1997, high school shooting by student Michael Carneal in Paducah, Kentucky, killed some students and injured others. It touched the

lives of fifteen-year-old identical twins Mandy and Missy Jenkins, revealing special twinship qualities that laboratory studies only approximate. I spoke with them by telephone on April 16, 1998.

"I'm glad the damage happened to me, not to her. I can handle it better if it's me—if something happened to her I don't know what I'd do." Carneal's bullet hit Missy Jenkins at the end of a prayer meeting as students prepared to pick up their backpacks before leaving. The injury left Missy paralyzed, but her relationship with her twin sister Mandy stayed strong. The sisters were never separated for a single day until the accident, sharing their thoughts with one another in ways that set them apart from their brother and three sisters. Since December, Mandy has spent much of her time at the Lexington, Kentucky, hospital with her sister until she returned to Paducah in mid-April. According to Mandy, "I love her with all my heart. . . . She [Missy] is still my sister and I take her everywhere I go." The only effect of the accident was that Mandy now helps Missy with things she cannot do for herself. The twins' selflessness is really an extension of the relationship they always enjoyed. Missy admitted that when Mandy developed a crush on someone and the feeling was mutual, she [Missy] was more excited than her sister. This theme may seem foreign to some nontwins, but is familiar in many identical twins' lives.

Mandy's devotion to her sister's comfort, and Missy's pleasure in her twin's social successes rests on recognizing that they are close relatives. This is an important concept in evolutionary psychology. How people know who their relatives are, and whom to help, is partly a function of whom you grow up with. Evolutionary psychologists have also proposed a matching process in which people gauge the similarity between their own features and those of others, using it as an approximate guide to their degree of genetic relatedness. A series of studies found that perceived altruism was associated with perceived similarity in personality, but not appearance, in parent-child and grandparent-grandchild pairs.[42] Extending these analyses to twin and sibling relationships would be informative. Missy and Mandy looked very much alike, did most things together and shared many interests. Their perceptions of similarity may have affected the strong ties they felt for one another. Identical twins looking or acting less alike, or having less sensitivity to their similarities, may be less close.

I believe that Missy and Mandy's bond is a major factor in Missy's positive outlook and adjustment. These twins (and Kari and Kathi) show us so much about caring. I wonder how the twins' other siblings were affected by the injury, and how Missy and Kari might have fared had they not had a twin sister. I am also interested in knowing if and how Missy and Mandy's relationship may change as they approach young adulthood. Perhaps Missy will nurture Mandy in ways allowing her twin to raise additional children, behavior biologically benefiting Missy because these children would be genetically hers as well. Kari had four children at the time of the accident and Kathi had two children, but this issue may still apply in their case because they are within their reproductive years.

Understanding that our concern or our willingness to help may vary with genetic relatedness does not justify neutral feelings toward distant relatives or nonbiological relatives in need. It also does not imply that nothing can be done to improve social relations.

It is instructive to pay attention to exceptional cases, such as adoptive parents and parents whose children were conceived through assisted reproductive techniques (ART). Studies conducted in several European countries have variously reported that adoptive and ART parents show a superior quality of parenting and higher emotional involvement with their children than fertile couples. Therefore, they concluded that genetic ties are less important for family functioning than the desire to become a parent. How can we reconcile these results with the increased child abuse observed in nonbiological families? It is wise to separate adoptive parenting in which couples choose to raise children, and stepparenting in which one parent did not choose to raise children. People are predisposed to care for their own children, so that forced rearing of an unrelated child may pose unwelcome obligations. Stepparenting is a potential risk factor in abusive parent-child relationships,[43] but there are many happy outcomes, testimony to the range and flexibility of human behavior. Comments from some adoptees suggest that physical similarities between adoptive parents and children contribute to successful relationships and this might be true in stepfamilies as well.[44] Research along these lines would be welcome.

Despite the knowledge that similarities may foster attraction between people, that friends are similar before they become friends, and that months and years of shared companionship at school, at the workplace or at home do not make people alike, it is likely that some people will question these findings. As counter evidence, skeptics may point out that their closest associations are those that have lasted the longest. It is for this reason that we turn to one of the most powerful and provocative experiments of nature: identical and fraternal twins reared apart from birth. A hard look at the feelings of familiarity and friendship among these reunited couples will bring clearer vision into who enters our private social world and why they stay.

> The brothers shook hands stiffly, when they saw each other for the first time. Then they hugged and burst into laughter. 'I looked into his eyes and saw a reflection of myself. . . . I wanted to scream or cry, but all I could do was laugh.' (Jim Springer, one of the "Jim twins.")[45]

Reunions of reared apart twins reveal that intimacy need not depend on shared experience. Most reunited identical twins, and some reunited fraternal twins, establish close lasting bonds despite an absence of previous familiarity. This is a powerful and provocative observation. Although time spent to-gether is needed for filling in life events, the basis for a close relationship is often present at the moment of meeting. It is as if the twins "knew each other all along," without having to be introduced. This process may be akin to re-lationships with friends we see infrequently, but with whom we share great rapport.

"I am him and he is me," remarked identical twin Mark Newman, who had been reared apart from his brother, Jerry Levey. Jerry elaborated this senti-ment by noting that his brother seemed only to have "been on a trip" for thirty-one years, and now that he had "returned" they were able to "pick up where they had left off." These twins participated in the Minnesota Study of Twins Reared Apart at age thirty-two, several months after their chance re-union in September 1985. Jerry, who installed burglar alarm systems and vol-unteered for the Tinton Falls, New Jersey, fire department, stopped for lunch while attending a volunteer firemans' convention. He noticed someone star-ing at him. It was firefighter Jimmy Tedesco, who finally approached him to ask: did he have a brother? what was his birthday? Jerry replied that he did-n't have a brother and that he was adopted. He also answered that he was born on "tax day" (April 15), although he did not reveal the year (1954). Several days later Tedesco called Jerry to ask if April 15, 1954, was special, causing Jerry to drop the telephone because that date was his birthday. Tedesco worked at the Paramus fire station with Mark Newman, Jerry's identical twin, and his keen eye and detective work were about to bring the twins together. In addition to being a volunteer fireman, Mark installed chemical fire sup-pression systems, a job similar to Jerry's.

Tedesco arranged for the brothers to meet at Jerry's firehouse sixty-five miles away. In order to heighten the suspense, he told Mark that they were making the trip to inspect new firefighting equipment. Mark shook Jerry's hand, but walked past him to find the new machinery. When Tedesco brought him back, Jerry removed his hat, revealing the same bald head as Mark's perched on a similar six-foot four-inch frame. This time Mark noticed the re-semblance and expressed total surprise and shock. The brothers stood before a mirror to compare their sideburns, mustache and other features which, de-spite their eighty-pound weight difference, were perfectly matched.

I remember when Mark and Jerry first met. Elena Serock from *Firehouse Magazine* called Professor Bouchard for information on reared apart twins.[46] She was writing an article about identical volunteer fireman twins who just met one another after a thirty-one-year separation. We were eager to invite them to Minnesota, promising to wait for her article to be published so she would be credited with revealing their reunion. We learned more about these twins over the next several weeks, such as their love of Budweiser beer and joy in pulling pranks—they appeared on the *David Letterman Show,* causing a stir when they downed Budweisers on live television. I also remember meeting Mark and Jerry at the Minneapolis airport. By this time the twins had received considerable media exposure so their arrival brought excited commotion to the terminal. Several years later I met Jimmy Tedesco and heard him retell his story of the twins' reunion as tears welled up in his eyes.

At the time of their assessment, approximately ten months after meeting, both Mark and Jerry felt "as close as best friends" and perceived their twin to be "more similar than a best friend." Each had adoptive siblings in their families. Despite their common rearing, one adoptive sibling was rated "as close as someone I meet for the first time" and "as familiar as a casual friend," while the other adoptive sibling was rated "as close as a casual friend" and "more familiar than a best friend." These questions have been completed by other reunited twins and, while my analysis is still ongoing, the results suggest greater expectations of social closeness and perceptions of greater immediate familiarity among reunited identical than fraternal twins.

These findings, which I return to in the next chapter, are especially compelling because they come from twins reared apart, many of whom did not know they were a twin until contacted by the other. Most who were aware of their twinship did not know if they were identical or fraternal. Some twins who initiated a search for biological relatives did so with the intention of locating mothers and fathers, but after learning of their twinship, refocused their energies on finding the twin. Why should a twin, a parent or a sibling be so important to locate? Why might a search for a reared apart twin take precedence over a search for a parent or nontwin sibling? Cultural and societal norms which lead us to value such relationships play a role, but where did these principles come from in the first place? What fuels the search for close relatives while lowering enthusiasm for distant uncles and cousins? Perhaps relationships vary in importance due to biological, as well as social and cultural factors, although these sources of influence are not truly separable. Just as genetic relatedness may differentially drive social relations with relatives we know, it may differentially prompt searches for those who are missing. Underlying it all may be the imperative to pass on our genes even while we do not think about it.

I sometimes ask people if they would search for a cousin or distant uncle they have never met. The response is usually an uncertain grin. In contrast, the idea of searching for a parent or sibling evokes a great deal of enthusiasm. A reared apart identical twin is met with an unmistakable gleam in the eye, a smile and an excited "yes!" The idea of meeting and having a genetically identical twin, someone just like "me," seems impossible for most people to resist, and why this is true is a tricky matter. When we realize that the children and grandchildren and great-grandchildren of an identical twin are "ours," too, then our rush of emotions makes sense. In other words, although you do not really think about it, this relationship has important long-term results, i.e., getting your genes into future generations. I do not believe there is a special process for responding to one's identical twin. Instead, increased closeness between twins may be an extension of the general principle of directing increased altruism toward close relatives.

Many adoptees show interest in searching for biological relatives, despite having loving adoptive families. This interest, which ranges from simple curiosity to all-consuming desire, becomes more comprehensible because of what twin studies reveal: Biological links can be powerful. Many wonderful reunion experiences between separated relatives have been reported, but not all stories have happy conclusions. Rewards and disappointments might be better understood by looking at the degree of similarity between the two parties. We are still in the process of defining the factors that may explain the positive and negative outcomes of twins' reunions. Along these lines, a most intriguing phenomenon has recently been described, namely genetic sexual attraction (GSA). GSA refers to the strong sexual connection experienced by some separated biological mothers and sons, fathers and daughters, and brothers and sisters, following reunion. In the words of one such mother, "Our knowledge about this brought us to the conclusion that the attraction happens between the two who are the most alike. They seem to have the most common gene pool." It is "as though you have met a part of yourself." Others have commented that it "seems to be a type of self-love. One you never knew about or could understand before."[47] Studies of GSA would be of interest.

Feelings of similarity could end up as sexual attraction between opposite-sex relatives who grow up apart and meet as adults. In contrast, researchers find that when brothers and sisters are raised together, this generally prevents feelings of attraction from developing between them. Evolutionary researchers explain this "incest taboo" by noting that some degree of "out-breeding," or mating with someone genetically different from ourselves, is necessary to achieve genetic variability in the population so that enough individuals have different skills to meet environmental challenges. Furthermore, all of us carry some single genes for unfavorable traits, such as phenylketonuria (a metabolic disorder that could lead to mental retardation) and Tay-Sachs disease (a disorder causing blindness, mental retardation and death in infants), but these conditions are not expressed unless two copies of the gene end up in the same individual.[48] Close relatives are likely to have single genes for the same unfavorable traits, so children they might have are at an increased risk for inheriting these conditions. Interestingly, unrelated boys and girls raised together on the Israeli kibbutz (cooperative community) never marry as adults. The decision to marry someone outside the kibbutz is not a conscious one, but the individuals have described a "vague discomfort" with the idea of marrying a childhood friend.[49] A study of Taiwanese "minor marriages" (marriages between biological sons and near-in-age adoptive daughters) showed that the least successful unions occurred when girls were adopted before thirty months of age.[50]

Evolutionary psychologists Nancy and Randy Thornhill have suggested that when children or adults are socialized with a young child who is in the sensitive stage (between two and six years), this should lead to sexual aversion between them.[51] This phenomenon has been termed the Westermarck Effect after Edward A. Westermarck, who proposed it in the late 1800s. Evolutionary biologist Edward O. Wilson suggests that the Westermarck Effect may be due to genetic evolution by natural selection because it reduces inbreeding and occurs in other primates. However, further study of this issue is needed. The psychological processes promoting incest avoidance, such as particular childhood experiences or events, are also unknown.[52]

Newspaper accounts of datings and matings between biological relatives who were unaware of their true relationship are available. In 1985, after twenty years of marriage, Frederick and Susan Machell from Australia were astonished to learn they were twins separated at birth.[53] Both knew they had been adopted, and were amused to discover that they were born on the same day at the same hospital. When one of their children was diagnosed with a hereditary birth defect, they launched an investigation to learn more about the medical histories of their biological families. One day letters arrived informing them of their true relationship but, despite the incredible shock, they remained together. In 1986, Swiss newlyweds, identified only as Marguerite and Hans, learned that they, too, were twins separated at birth.[54] Both knew that they were twins and had planned to search for their missing siblings, but the search ended sadly when Marguerite showed Hans's aunt a baby photo that was identical to one in the aunt's own home. The couple separated despite being deeply in love. In 1990, Gertrude Hardy set out to search for the boy and girl twins she had given away at birth.[55] Little did she know that, following a college romance, the twins had married and raised several children. News of their true relationship was traumatic but, despite investigation by authorities for incest, they stayed together.

We may feel distress, even revulsion, at the idea of sexual attraction between reunited family members, regardless of whether the genetic relationship was known or unknown. These behaviors run counter to the practices and norms of virtually all societies. Understanding the origins of such attraction may help individuals come to terms with their feelings, and enable therapists to provide more informed psychological support.

The possibility that some separated relatives could be attracted to one another and eventually marry urges serious thinking about possible consequences from the new medical techniques that help some infertile couples have children. Suppose that sperm donated from the same man were used to father children in a small town—boys and girls resulting from this procedure would be genetic half-siblings. Should such individuals meet and become romantically involved with one another, we might witness a reenactment of the scenarios described above. The films *Fool for Love* (1985) and *Lone Star* (1996), while fictional, dramatically depict the intense attraction that is possible between separated half brothers and half sisters who are unaware of their true relationship and fall in love. These films have been successful be-

Twist of Fate:
Twins Reared Apart[1]

It usually starts with a telephone call, a newspaper article or a radio interview, but the first time it happened it was on the front pages. In February 1979 newspapers around the world announced the incredible reunion of identical twins, Jim Lewis and Jim Springer, after a thirty-nine-year separation.[2] Reared apart since infancy by different adoptive families in Ohio, they met shortly after Jim Lewis contacted Lima County court officials who located his twin through officials in Dayton. Jim Lewis's adoptive mother told him he was a twin at age five, but "it never soaked in" until he received adoption papers just before his thirty-ninth birthday. Jim Springer's mother told him he was a twin at age eight when he overheard her conversation about his adoption, and he asked her to explain what it meant. However, his parents were told his twin had died so there was no reason to search. Ultimately, it was Jim Springer who made the first telephone call to his brother on February 9, 1979, after learning his twin was alive. It was a great day. Three weeks later Jim Springer served as best man at his identical twin brother's wedding.

The circumstances of Jim Lewis and Jim Springer afforded an ideal opportunity to directly disentangle genetic and environmental influences on behavioral and physical development. The twins' reunion stunned Margaret Keyes, a graduate student at the University of Minnesota, who had been studying the nature and origin of human individual differences with Professor Thomas J. Bouchard, Jr., in the Department of Psychology. She shared the news with Bouchard, who lost no time mobilizing the university's resources and a research team that would bring the "Jim twins" to Minneapolis for a week of psychological and medical study. No one could have predicted that the joining of Jim and Jim would so profoundly affect our thoughts about intelligence, personality and physical health, as well as what we could learn cause they capture a realistic, if little discussed, aspect of human relations. The potential for uncomfortable outcomes from fertility treatments should *not* discourage their further use because these procedures have brought indescribable joy to many infertile couples. Recognizing the potential misuses of these procedures is key to their proper administration.

Meetings between relatives who grew up apart possess a special poignancy that deeply affects us all. These responses enlighten us about the significance of current connections with family members, and evolutionary theory suggests new reasons for why this is so. Psychological processes set in motion by perceived similarities (e.g., social attraction) may have long-term consequences (i.e., assuring a place for one's genes in future generations). The pathway from genes to behavior remains a complex puzzle. We have some distance to travel before grasping how genetic factors may actually shape the infrastructure of our social relations.

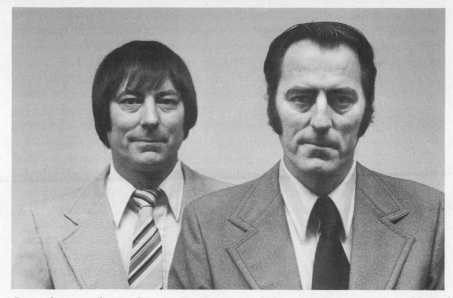

Reared apart identical twins Jim Springer (left) and Jim Lewis launched the Minnesota Study of Twins Reared Apart in March 1979. PHOTO CREDIT: THOMAS S. ENGLAND.

about the bacteria on our gums, the structures on our retinas and the positioning of our hands while drinking a beer.

There was much excitement surrounding the Jims' reunion, but they were not the first identical reared apart twins to capture the interest of psychological investigators. Nineteen sets were studied at the University of Chicago in 1937, forty-four sets were studied at the Maudsley Hospital in England in 1962, and twelve sets were studied at the University of Odense in Denmark in 1966.[3] The Jim twins were special because they arrived amidst impassioned controversy over how and how much nature and nurture contributed to behavioral development, providing a stringent test of popular environmental suppositions. For example, in 1981, Walter Mischel, an eminent personality theorist, concluded that, "Genes and glands are obviously important, but social learning also has a dramatic role. Imagine the enormous differences that would be found in the personalities of twins with identical genetic endowments if they were raised apart in two different families—or, even more striking, in two totally different cultures. . . ."[4] Earlier studies of twins reared apart and together showed that genetic influences on personality were important, but Walter Mischel's opinion reflected the prevailing environmental view of behavior at that time.

The Jim twins were also special because almost no one believed that twins were still being separated. This was not the only surprise awaiting investigators. The Jim twins produced a list of psychological and medical similarities, impressive even to the Minnesota researchers who were well-versed in twin and adoption studies, having worked in these areas since the 1960s and early 1970s. When the twins first met, both were 6 feet tall and weighed 180 pounds, but closer inspection provided these compelling details:

- Jim and Jim had each been married twice. Their first wives were named Linda; their second, Betty.
- Each twin had a son with the same name, but spelled differently: James Alan and James Allan.
- As children, each twin had a dog named Toy.
- Both had taken family vacations independently to the same three-block strip of Florida beach, called *Pas-Grille,* without ever meeting. They both arrived in light blue Chevrolets.
- Each had worked part-time in law enforcement as sheriffs.
- Both smoked Salems, and both savored an occasional Miller Lite beer.
- Both bit their fingernails, and since age eighteen both suffered from mixed headache syndrome, a combined tension and migraine headache.
- Both scattered love notes to their wives around the house.

Identical twins are not exactly alike, and the Jim twins were no exception:

- One twin expressed his thoughts better in speaking, the other expressed his thoughts better in writing.
- One twin wore his hair straight down over his forehead, the other twin wore his hair back with sideburns.
- One Jim remarried for a third time, to a woman named Sandy (which may, understandably, cause concern for the other couple!).

Television talk shows and magazine coverage fascinated the public with the twins' similarities before these findings found their way to scientific journals. This turn of events yielded unexpected benefits and unfair criticisms. The most important long-term benefit was the identification of new reared apart twin pairs, both identical and fraternal, enabling systematic examination and confirmation of what the Jim twins suggested, namely that genetic influence lies behind virtually all behavioral and physical traits. The three earlier reared apart twin studies purposefully did not include fraternal twins, a decision that risked excluding dissimilar identical twins and computing inflated estimates of genetic influence, so attracting both types of twins was crucial. In other words, if during recruitment identical twins differing in appearance were excluded because investigators suspected they were fraternal, the sample would include too many extremely similar identical twins, leading to very high genetic estimates. Interestingly, the Minnesota researchers had no intention of launching an ongoing study of twins reared apart, hoping instead to identify a few pairs besides the Jim twins for a short series of case studies. Bouchard admits that once fifteen twin pairs had been found the mix of compelling findings and the promise of fresh interesting cases made further investigation irresistible. Fraternal twins, both same-sex and opposite-sex, would be an important addition to the new Minnesota Study of Twins Reared Apart.

An unfortunate short-term consequence of so much public attention to early reports was misinterpretation of goals and findings. Specifically, there were some claims that the project focused on twins' similarities and genetic explanations for them, neglecting twins' differences and the environmental side of development.[5] One critic suggested that the findings were "romantic stories" that people find hard to believe.[6] These misconceptions were resolved in scientific papers which the investigators wisely delayed publishing until testing a sufficient number of reared apart pairs. Vital themes running through these papers are that genetic influence affects a greater variety of behaviors than was previously believed, but that environmental factors, especially idiosyncratic or serendipitous events unique to individuals, also shape every measured human trait. Winning a lottery may be largely luck, but some people have the hope and tenacity to enter often, raising their prospects even if slightly. In some situations, but not all, we may be partly responsible for whatever chance events affect us. In contrast, separate rearing from a twin seems a clear twist of fate and reunion for many is just as unplanned.

Distinctive twin pair similarities did appear, such as both twins using the same rare Swedish toothpaste, *Vademecum,* wrapping rubber bands around their wrists and dangling key rings from their belts. The noteworthy part is that these similarities occurred far more often among separated identical twins than fraternal twins. This is vital information because, while specific genes do not affect preferences for toothpaste, rubber bands and key rings, the greater frequency of unusual similarities among identical than fraternal twins suggests that the same complex gene combinations may end up as extraordinary traits repeated in identical people. As a nine-year member of the research team, I learned that such rare behaviors cannot be studied across twin sets because lack of variation would render the study pointless. If I conducted a toothpaste study, I would probably (hopefully!) find that both identical and fraternal twins use toothpaste, and I might find that more identical than fraternal pair members both prefer Colgate or both prefer Crest. Greater identical twin preference for a common product is mildly interesting—reared apart identical twins Tony Milasi and Roger Brooks both used Vitalis hair tonic when reunited at age twenty-five—but because there is a limited selection from which to choose, and because many people use the product, little can be said about genetic influence. The matched presence of highly unusual or exceptional traits in identical twins, such as Roger and Tony's choice of *Vademecum,* however, suggests that characteristic quirks and signature behaviors may partly reflect each person's unique genetic mix.

Unusual similarities were also observed in reared apart identical twins

Oskar Stohr and Jack Yufe, a pair whose rearing differences were staggering. Their parents' divorce divided them across continents when they were infants.[7] Oskar was raised by his Catholic mother and grandmother in Czechoslovakia's Sudetenland and had planned to enter the Hitler Youth before World War II ended; Jack was raised by his Jewish father in Trinidad and had joined a synagogue and spent time on an Israeli kibbutz. Their initial reunion at seventeen was unsuccessful, but they visited Minnesota in 1979 at age forty-six. We learned that they both read books from back to front, flushed the toilet before and after using it, and enjoyed sneezing loudly in crowded elevators. Perhaps these behaviors reflected the twins' shared personality tendencies such as impatience (eagerness to know the story's outcome), squeamishness (sensitivity to germs), and gregariousness (fondness for attention). Their similarities did not extend to their political or social outlooks—Oskar's traditionalism and Jack's liberalism were largely fashioned by their different backgrounds. They came to terms with their pasts, and Oskar's passing away in 1997 was traumatic for his twin. An insightful and moving 1995 film, *Oskar and Jack,* chronicles their separation, their reunion, and their remarkable similarities and differences.[8]

The Minnesota Study of Twins Reared Apart now includes about 135 pairs (triplets are counted as three pairs each), but they do not comprise a sample in the strict sense. Samples result from systematic selection of cases from an available pool, perhaps by surveying birth records, to assure that the final group represents the larger population. Participants in the Minnesota study are identified in many different ways, including the media, adoption registries, social services, professional colleagues and the twins themselves, so it has been important to show they are not unusual in any way. Our research team compared reared apart twins to reared together twins in height, weight, IQ and other traits, showing that they do not differ significantly, and that findings can be viewed confidently.[9]

Scandinavian nations are better equipped than the United States to assemble true samples because each individual is linked to public registers concerned with twinship, adoption, psychiatric disorder and other characteristics. The twelve pairs included in Niels Juel-Nielsen's 1966 study comprised the entire population of living identical reared apart twins born in Denmark between 1870 and 1910. Ongoing Finnish and Swedish studies of reared apart twins also enjoy this advantage. Researchers in these countries have gathered many more hundreds of separated twin pairs than our Minnesota staff, but only a small proportion were separated as early as 5–6 months like most twins studied in Minnesota.[10] The Kinki Adult Twin Registry in Osaka, Japan, has also yielded reared apart twin pairs, but few who were separated before age five.

For me, working on the Minnesota Study of Twins Reared Apart was a dream job that was a natural extension of my doctoral research on twins' co-

Reared apart fraternal twins Dewayne Gramley (left) and Paul Forbes display gifts at their first birthday party together—their seventieth. PHOTO CREDIT: NANCY L. SEGAL.

operation and competition at the University of Chicago. The Minnesota study had been in progress for three years when I joined in 1982. During that time I watched the progression of participants, procedures and findings, and sampled two delicious tastes of what reared apart twins and reunions were all about. In November 1979 Bouchard and the Jim twins appeared on *Friday Night,* a WLS-TV program originating in Chicago. Sitting in the audience, I was captivated by their similar voices, hand gestures and mannerisms that printed pages cannot capture. That same year I delivered a twin research seminar at an adoption agency where I learned that twin girls had been separated at birth. I notified Bouchard, and with the cooperation of the agency the identical twin women, Gina and Ellen, were reunited for the first time in September 1980 at the Minneapolis airport. Driving them to their hotel, Bouchard recalls, he noticed their excitement at discovering their physical similarities and parallel life events, although their hairstyles, dress and marital status differed. Gina, who then lived in a tropical setting, wore her hair long and loose, walked barefoot, and chose light floral patterns. Ellen, who then lived in a rural environment, wore her hair short, preferred shoes, and picked plain practical outfits. Bouchard noted the remarkable ease of their interactions soon after meeting and wrote that, "They were very lovely ladies, and we had a beautiful week."

Gina and Ellen ranked "highest quality" among the separated sets for quite a while. They had had no contact until arrival in Minnesota at age thirty-two and had grown up unaware of being a twin, providing the "purest" possible estimate of genetic handiwork. This status eventually shifted to other twins whose separations exceeded fifty, sixty and even seventy years. Contrary to what logic suggests, we learned that similarity in intelligence was unrelated to years of separation, contact time and age at reunion.[11] In other words, twins who were apart for twenty years, spent vacations together, or were reunited at a young age were no more alike than twins who had been apart for fifty years, had little contact with one another, or were reunited late in life. We also learned that identical twins reared apart were as similar in personality traits as identical twins reared together, demonstrating that shared genes, not shared environments, primarily underlie family members' personality similarity.[12] These findings are important because they uniquely demonstrate genetic influence on identical twins' coordinated development. They also explain why children sometimes resemble parents and siblings even when living apart for many years.[13]

Jim and Jim, and Gina and Ellen set an exciting stage for the many reunions and assessments in which I was to take part from September 1982 to August 1991. Learning about newly reunited twins, tracking them down, making the first phone call and setting the date for their arrival required a great deal of work, but it came with an undeniable thrill that went beyond just getting the job done. It had to do with the opportunity to follow the incredible events leading to their reunion, and to vicariously experience the overwhelming joy, excitement and uncertainty of their first meeting.

One of my favorite parties was one we held for fraternal twins Dewayne Gramley and Paul Forbes. They celebrated their seventieth birthday, *their first one together,* at the University of Minnesota in February 1987. Dewayne had been adopted from the Nebraska Children's Home Society in Omaha by the Reverend and Mrs. Luther Gramley when he was five months old.[14] At first the couple did not feel they could afford to raise two children, but they changed their minds later, only to discover that Dewayne's twin brother, Paul Forbes, had been adopted by another family. In 1956, Dewayne tried finding his brother through the adoption agency, but the staff was not helpful. He tried again in 1986, and this time he was successful. The twins had an exciting, but "not too emotional reunion." These fraternal twins differ in their builds (Dewayne is slim and Paul is stocky) and in their outlooks (Dewayne is a liberal and Paul is a fundamentalist). Nevertheless, meeting their twin was a significant life event for which both brothers are grateful.

Both Dewayne and Paul came to Minnesota with their adopted sisters who took part in some of the testing. Reared apart twins' adoptive siblings are a valuable group to study because they reveal how much shared environments affect unrelated siblings' resemblance. If Dewayne and his sister showed less similarity in spatial skill or in extraversion than Dewayne and Paul, this would demonstrate genetic influence on those traits. Siblings' results are not yet available because too few have participated, possibly because siblings feel less personal investment in the project than the twins.

Dewayne and Paul were responsible for the most memorable reared apart recruitment I undertook. It began with a glance at the 1990 *Guinness Book of World Records,* where I expected to see reference to Dewayne and Paul as the world's longest separated twins. They were surpassed by seventy-seven-year old twins, Iris Johns and Aro Campbell, from New Zealand, who had been reunited at age seventy-five. This was the first time I had heard of this pair, and while Bouchard thought the chance of finding them was slim, I located them two telephone calls and five minutes later. Iris and Aro arrived for testing soon after I left Minneapolis for Fullerton, but I arranged to meet them at the Los Angeles Airport on their return trip to New Zealand. They had not known each other long, but they interacted with such ease I remember thinking that they belonged together.

Separating twins and siblings strikes most people as unkind, unfair and unnatural. Most twins in the Minnesota study were separated due to illegitimacy, but some were separated due to the death of a parent, divorce, poverty, wartime crisis and even "switching" at birth.[15] A dramatic example concerns identical male twin infants, George Holmes and Brent Trembley, placed in a temporary foster home for several months.[16] No one knows how this happened, but when their birth parents came to claim them they received George and an unrelated little boy, Marcus, whom they raised as fraternal twins, fully believing both were their sons. Meanwhile, Brent was adopted by a family living only seven miles away. The true relationship between George and Brent and George and Marcus was revealed when Brent was mistaken for George while attending Carlton University in Ottawa. The reunion was happy for George, but not for Marcus who felt bereft of a family history. His adopted parents, Randy and Laura, assured Marcus that "he is their son."

The "slings and arrows of outrageous fortune" also separated some pairs. A Chinese twin's separate rearing by her grandmother (with yearly visits to her twin) was advised due to the twins' early health differences. This arrangement proved the start of a thirty-nine-year separation when political circumstances in the 1940s forced her family to leave the mainland without her when the twins were five. Sometimes adoption agencies could not find families financially suited to raising two children. Twinship was, however, often unappreciated so best efforts were not always made. With one exception described in a later chapter, I have strongly supported common placement of twins in custody cases. Twins and other multiples are still being separated today, probably less often because of extramarital delivery, which is now less socially stigmatized, but because of new reproductive technologies that introduce twins, triplets, quadruplets and more into families unable or unwilling to care for them. In 1988, an infertile woman sought the assistance of a surrogate mother for bearing children, but when opposite-sex twins were born she accepted only the girl.[17] She relinquished the male twin to the surrogate parent when her doctor advised her against the stress of raising too many children—but she said that she would have raised the second twin if it had been female. The attorney in this case believed that this was the first instance of surrogate-born infant rejection due to the child's gender. I also learned of an alleged baby-selling scheme in Greece involving hundreds of adopted children and their families, including twins.[18] According to Christo Pantelidis who was reunited with his nontwin brother at forty-six, "It was often the case . . . that a twin was taken so that the mother would be left with a child."

There are also fascinating cross-cultural examples of twins reared apart, reflecting differences in national attitudes and customs. Distaste for twins among Japanese nobility once meant that multiple births were kept secret and the second twin given away.[19] Lyle Steadman, Professor of Anthropology at Arizona State University, who lived among the Hewa of New Guinea in the mid-1960s, learned of an infant male twin given away because of milk intolerance.[20] The affected infant was named *Mompama* which means "doesn't drink milk." Poor living conditions in some cultures have resulted in cross-cultural adoption and separation of some twins. Some of these cases have come to my attention through my study on same-age unrelated siblings, discussed in Chapter 8.

Everyone is fascinated by twins' reunions and this widespread interest suggests a simple but profound truth about human nature, namely that family matters. Efforts expended on finding parents, children and siblings exceed efforts expended on finding uncles, nieces and cousins. Parent-child reunions affect us deeply, while cousin reunions may go relatively unnoticed. Some sibling and half-sibling reunions are nearly as dramatic as those involving twins. Steven Jobs, adoptee and famous founder of *Apple Computers,* was first reunited with his biological parents and sister at forty-one years of age.[21] His sister, Mona Simpson, is an acclaimed fiction writer, and despite accomplishments in different fields, this brother and sister may have inherited similar intellectual and motivational blueprints for achievement. According to Jobs, "She's one of my best friends in the world." This theme is repeated by half sisters Darlene Meadows and Jeanette Pyden, who worked side by side in the food department of a Kmart store in Marysville, Michigan, unaware of their true relationship.[22] Darlene toyed with the possibility that Jeanette might be her sibling because of Jeanette's similarities to an aunt. A search by Jeanette's daughter revealed the truth to the pair whose friendship had already blossomed.

Many separated twins who were unaware of their twinship began a search for mothers and fathers, but redirected efforts toward finding the twin once this news was disclosed. According to evolutionary psychologists, small social groups based on kinship are common living arrangements since they probably offered the best access to physical and emotional resources needed for survival throughout history.[23] The nature and impact of twins' reunions

Reared apart triplets (left to right), Eddy Galland, David Kellman and Bobby Shafran were the first identical threesome to visit the University of Minnesota. PHOTO CREDIT: THOMAS J. BOUCHARD, JR.

may well reflect this basic human theme. Reunions between friends, colleagues and war buddies are also irresistibly sweet, perhaps because they replay elements of companionship, support and familiarity characteristic of close relatives.

Twins have found one another in many surprising ways. Identical twins Caroline and Margaret Shand lived only twenty-one miles apart in Scotland, but their paths did not cross for sixty-four years.[24] One day Margaret and her friend visited a church and, finding it locked, Margaret's friend rattled the door. Next, they walked around the building to a gravesite. Hearing the sound, Caroline, who worked at the church, came to the door and finding nobody outside searched the premises until she spotted Margaret. Realizing their resemblance she asked, "Is your name Shand? Are you my sister?" at which point they hugged and cried. Neither twin had married and after meeting they were thrilled to live together.

Mistaken identity and chance reunited nineteen-year-old identical triplets, Bobby Shafran, Eddy Galland and David Kellman.[25] Eddy had enrolled for a brief time in Sullivan County Community College in New York, but after leaving the campus his brother, Bobby, arrived the next semester. Friends were curious as to why "Eddy" had returned, and when Bobby insisted he was not Eddy one of Eddy's friends, Michael Dominitz, reunited them that night. They enjoyed being twins for about one week until David was shown a newspaper photograph of his brothers and made it a threesome. Bouchard described them as "three versions of the same song." Intelligent, extraverted and slightly rambunctious, the triplets worked part-time at Sammy's restaurant on Manhattan's Lower East Side before opening Triplets Roumanian Steak House a few blocks away. The three partners were perfectly suited to a business requiring outgoing personalities, trustworthy partners and clout. I visited the restaurant and was impressed with the brothers' ease in drawing diners into songs and entertainment.

There are dark sides to the triplets' story. They may have been part of a child development experiment in which identical twins and triplets were placed in separate homes from birth allowing their behaviors to be followed. I met with Stephanie Saul, a staff writer for *Newsday,* who investigated this possibility. She learned that Mrs. Kellman, David's mother, contacted the Louise Wise Adoption Agency in New York when she wanted to adopt a little boy; she had adopted her daughter from the agency two years earlier.[26] She was told there would be a wait, so she was surprised when a baby boy was available six weeks later. She was also told that he was part of a study and would be periodically observed at home by research staff. The other triplets' families had similar experiences and none were told of their sons' multiple birth status. Interestingly, all three families had an adopted daughter two years older than the triplets, suggesting that the researchers tried to keep the family structures constant. Saul located some other pairs separated by the agency and spoke to one of the investigators, Dr. Peter Neubauer. Neubauer claimed that the adoption agency believed in the benefits of separating twins and had advised him of the extraordinary research opportunity to track the twins' development from birth. Details about the study are murky, although some findings appear in a single case report and book.[27]

The triplets and their parents were understandably distraught that their true backgrounds were concealed. Bobby, Eddy and David were lucky to have found one another, especially at a relatively young age. The search process for some other twins is a series of stumbling blocks and blind alleys. Jean Perkin, a fraternal twin, set out to find her sister, Yvonne, but Yvonne's adoptive family had changed her first name (to Jean!), a decision that set the process back for years. The twins eventually found each other in their early fifties. Another female fraternal twin experienced similar frustration because, while she and her sister were born minutes apart they were also born in different months. Other twins never find each other, their thin portfolios never leaving Bouchard's lower file drawer.

Twins who find each other are the lucky ones because, despite regret or anger at the loss of shared childhood, they have opportunities to build relationships, compare medical histories and extend families. Some twins recreate the stolen years by dressing alike or by enjoying childlike pranks and

Reared apart identical "giggle twins" Barbara Herbert (left) and Daphne Goodship from England. Each twin inspires continuous laughter in the other, but what sets them off is a mystery to everyone else. PHOTO COURTESY OF THE TWINS.

schemes, exemplified by Dewayne and Paul's "first" birthday party hosted by the investigators, complete with party hats and favors. Certainly the magic of twins' reunions inspired British social service official John Stroud to develop a unique specialty in this area, having reunited the famous "Giggle Twins," Barbara Herbert and Daphne Goodship. Stroud was a brilliant and gentle man with a true gift for bringing people together, providing Bouchard with many twins. Over the years he hosted several gatherings of British reared apart twins at the Briggens House Hotel, an idyllic setting in Hertfordshire, north of London. I attended two of these unique events, one in 1983 and one in 1996, and was overwhelmed by the connectedness and understanding among the many pairs whose different pasts were linked by early separation from a twin sibling. John Stroud passed away in 1989 and is sorely missed by the investigators, the reunited twins and maybe most of all by twins in search.

No one knows how many separated twins there are, but reunited identical twins in the Minnesota Study outnumber reunited fraternal twins at a steady rate of two to one, consistent with Lykken's *Rule of Two-Thirds*.[38] Greater media attention to reunited identical than fraternal twins may have also quickened discovery of these cases, but I also suspect that reunited identical pairs are more common because identicals have an easier time finding one another than fraternals. Many identical twins were reunited because of mistaken identity, while fraternal twins were at the mercy of adoption agencies, attorneys, reunion registries and chance. There were several remarkable exceptions among both twin groups. Reared apart fraternal females Kerry Keyser and Amy Jackson looked so much alike that when Kerry moved to Burlington, Vermont, at the age of twenty-five, she was often called Amy.[29] Frustrated, but curious, she tracked Amy down and after visiting the adoption service, they learned they were twins for the first time. Their twin type posed a fascinating riddle and while they were initially judged as "unalike" identicals, by the week's end they seemed to be "look-alike" fraternals, and blood tests confirmed this. Both displayed a rare genetic condition in which hair turns brittle and breaks off before reaching an inch in length, a characteristic that contributed to their remarkable physical resemblance. They are a wonderful example of how similar some fraternal twins can be.

I also recall two identical pairs who differed greatly in size and form, due to documented birth trauma in one case and probably birth trauma in the other case. Mistaken identity could not have reunited twins in these pairs and, in fact, their meetings resulted from search procedures typical of fraternal twins. Profound physical differences between identical twins are rare, but even while most identical twins look very much alike, a range of physical variation is found across pairs. Identical twin disparities are probably accentuated by the frequency and intensity of prebirth and postbirth differences.

Amy and Kerry's greater than average fraternal twin resemblance warns that genetic and environmental contributions to behavioral traits cannot be properly judged by extraordinary similarities or dissimilarities in individual twin pairs. Two years after the Minnesota study began, a Charles Addams cartoon appeared in the *New Yorker* magazine, depicting a pair of male identical twins seated outside a patent attorney's office, their eyes intensely fixated on one another.[30] Both sport eyeglasses around their necks, scissors in their breast pockets and moles on their left cheeks, and juggle the same curious invention on their laps. The legend reads, "Separated at birth, the Mallifert twins meet accidentally." This composite pair contains some elements of fact, as demonstrated by reared apart identical twin firemen who favored huge belt buckles, heavy key rings and work boots, but the final product does not ring true. Identical twins reared apart are very similar, but it is not perfect similarity and some behaviors show greater resemblance than others. Five full days and two half-days of rigorous psychological and medical testing revealed these important outcomes and a great deal more.

We called them "Twin Weeks." They began on Saturday when twins and significant others arrived in the "Twin Cities" from their homes across the country, but they could start on Friday if twins lived outside the United States and needed recovery time from jet lag. Dr. Bouchard or other staff members were at the airport in St. Paul to greet twins and to escort them to their hotel. This was an exciting time because after weeks of correspondence, the twins were so familiar to us that meeting them was like catching up with an old friend. I did not pick up Caroline and Margaret Shand who flew in on a Friday from Scotland, but I identified them from their newspaper photograph as they wandered through Minneapolis on their free Saturday. I approached them enthusiastically, but they did not know me and were shocked to be recognized so far from home.

I also found the start of "Twin Weeks" exciting because every pair came differently packaged, promising new insights, fresh leads or affirmation of emerging trends. A pair of identical female twins preferred drinking "hot" drinks warm, suggesting genetic influence on temperature sensitivity. Simultaneous unexplained weight gain by identical male twins raised the possibility of underlying genetic mechanisms that switch on at certain times in the life span—a finding that may justify frustration when faithful dieters are disappointed. A two-point IQ difference between identical male twins added to data supporting genetic influence on general intelligence. The endings of "Twin Weeks" were exhausting, but exhilarating, because so much had been learned from such extraordinary people. Wonderful science was taking place because answers to inventories and tracings from treadmills, never before completed by reared apart twins, would be added to responses from other pairs for statistical analysis, a primary activity during "nontwin" weeks. The research team examined the data for differences in resemblance between identical and fraternal twins, and between male and female identicals and fraternals. Identical and same-sex fraternal twins share age and gender, a situation that boosts similarity even among unrelated people, so special analytical procedures removed this effect from the data, allowing a clearer picture of genetic influence.

There was also a human side to the study and that was the twins' satisfaction at advancing scientific knowledge, learning why they were nearsighted or short-tempered, and connecting with their twin after so many years. Most twins got along well, some famously, but even those who did not were grateful to have gained vital personal insights by visiting a past they never knew. Varied circumstances explain why some twins did not become close, such as contrasting life styles and differences in sexual orientation, but some pairs with differing life styles or differing sexual preferences got along well. Human social relationships are complex, diverse and often unpredictable, especially when twinship and separation are added to the mix. I believe the larger twin group best communicates the important message that close relatives have the capacity and the potential to form close social ties despite nonshared life histories. My review of sixteen of nineteen early case studies of reared apart identical twins revealed that twins in six pairs chose to live together and/or to embark upon shared careers and that twins in nine pairs stayed in touch after meeting. Twins in only one pair, the "two Paul Harolds," did not pursue a close relationship. Their separate rearings in urban and rural environments apparently placed a social rift between them, explaining why they acted like "mere acquaintances." The fact that they shared first and second names may reflect a clerical error by the foster agency when their new parents came to claim them, but this is speculative. The investigators commented on how strange it was to hear both twins refer to each other as Paul.

The majority of reared apart twins were adoptees and, while many enjoyed warm, loving relationships with adoptive parents and siblings, they lacked the luxury of learning the source of their interests and talents. Life events may kindle curiosity about family in some people, or dampen it in others, but tracking biological relatives may reflect the importance of kin and kin relations in the human behavioral repertoire. Searching for biological relatives per se is not an evolved behavior—in early human history families usually stayed together so such efforts were unnecessary—but current family separations and rearing arrangements may trigger this behavior in relatives living apart. I was captivated by this feature of reared apart twinship and will say more about it later.

The twins' assessment schedule was comprehensive and demanding, having expanded greatly over the years to accommodate new tests and interviews. I believe the success of the program was due to a superb team of highly skilled and committed investigators and assistants, and of course to Bouchard, whose special brand of intellect, motivation and charm was the essential driving force. People following the study in the popular press or in professional journals may be surprised to learn just how many psychological and medical tests are completed by twins. Some intellectual and personality traits were measured in more than one way to be certain that findings were not specific to a particular procedure. Occasionally, we were surprised to discover something missing from the schedule, such as a skin exam or a question about shoe size, but these reared apart twins were studied more extensively than reared apart twins in the past. "Twin Weeks" put a lock on our lives because there was little time for anything else, but the experience was well worth it. I took part in over seventy assessments which began on a Sunday afternoon. . . .

• *Day 1: Sunday.* Sundays were half-days, beginning in the early afternoon and lasting until six o'clock in the evening. We began in the Psychology Department, in particular the "Twin Room," a large area with a big table holding freshly sharpened pencils, a plate of cookies, consent forms, and folders bearing the personality questionnaires and interest inventories participants would complete throughout the week. A separate folder was prepared for each twin and companion, usually a spouse, and while periods were set aside for working on these materials, the packet was always available to fill time while waiting for medical appointments or interviews. It is estimated that each twin answered over 10,000 questions over the course of fifty hours before going home.

Inviting spouses or significant others to Minneapolis was not just an incentive to encourage twins to participate in the project, but served several useful functions. First, it was a way to obtain average or typical responses from nontwins on tests that had not been widely administered. Some forms, such as recreational and religious interest inventories, were specially constructed for the study so it was important to know if the reared apart twins might differ in any way from the general population. Second, similarities and differences between twins and spouses were examined for evidence of *assortative mating*. Similarity across couples suggests that a particular behavior may affect choice of spouse in a nonrandom or purposeful way, while dissimilarity indicates that a particular behavior may be less important in mate selection. For example, spouses show greater resemblance in intelligence and in years of education than they do in height and personality.[31] Third, scores of twins' spouses were compared to see if husbands and wives of identical twins are more alike than husbands and wives of fraternal twins. This would suggest that identical twins are more highly attracted to similar people than fraternal twins, illustrative of *active gene-environment correlation,* the process by which people purposefully seek or construct environments compatible with genetically influenced tendencies.

The jury is still out on the reared apart twin data, but both identical and fraternal reared together twins are *less* like their spouses than might be expected.[32] Partners showed only slight similarity across seventy-eight personality, educational, occupational, attitudinal and recreational measures, and modest similarity across ten. Most interesting was that wives of identical twins were not especially attracted to their brothers-in-law, and both husbands and wives of fraternal twins were more negatively than positively disposed toward their spouses' twins. In contrast, husbands of identical twins felt some attraction to their sisters-in-law, although only 13% said "[I] might have fallen for her myself." The surprising message from this study is that mate selection seems largely governed by romantic infatuation, distinguishing it from other choices which reveal our behaviors and interests more fully. Of course, partners generally match in age, social class and years of education, but there may be many satisfying prospects within the "eligible pool." Anyone who has been in multiple relationships may better understand why they feel attracted to people with little in common, or why their two best friends never hit it off.

An informed consent procedure offered an overview of the weeks' activities and opportunities for participants to ask questions about the different procedures. Twins were then escorted to an adjacent room where an assistant administered the first series of special mental ability tests, including vocabulary, visual memory, subtraction and multiplication, spatial rotation and other skills.[33] Intelligence tests were purposefully scheduled early in the morning or afternoon when twins were alert and well rested. They were seated back-to-back on opposite sides of the room to prevent awareness of how quickly or slowly their twin was progressing. Still, the watchful eyes of the examiner (often mine) could detect if portions of the test seemed equally challenging to twins, and identicals usually responded with more comparable enthusiasm or frustration than fraternals.

Life history interviews were individually administered following the mental ability tests. Sections of the booklet covered birth and separation from the twin, rearing family background, places of residence, educational attainments, marriages and relationships, occupational history, current family background and religious activities.[34] Specific information gathered in these sessions was eventually used to explore a broad array of hypotheses and questions concerning genetic and environmental influences on behavioral and physical traits. These meetings were also opportunities to savor the incredible details surrounding childhood, searches and reunions overlooked by the media. One male twin did not learn he was adopted until entering the military at eighteen years of age, but was sensitive to temperamental differences between himself and his parents. He wondered if he truly belonged to them. Carole and Sylvia grew up continents apart, but Sylvia's Australian friend recognized Carole as Sylvia's twin when visiting Carole's small town in England. Both twins had brown hair, but Carole's natural blond streaks were a puzzle, especially because she came from less sunny surroundings. I believe these tidbits of perception and chance will trigger new thoughts in everyone's mind about life events and developmental outcomes had he or she been raised in different circumstances.

Life history interviews were followed by the first wave of scheduled inventories, with each form reviewed by an assistant to catch missing items. Final events on Sunday consisted of height and weight measurements and photographs, wise choices because these activities were not mentally demanding to twins who were starting to tire. The photograph series, which included unposed individual and pair snapshots of front views, left and right profiles, hands, eyes and ears, yielded some of the most fascinating findings. Glancing across the pairs it was clear that identical twins naturally assumed more similar body postures than fraternal twins, such as arm-folding or hand-crossing. It is often assumed that we model the physical movements of those around us, but reared apart twins suggest that genetic factors underlie the shape and form of torsos and limbs, explaining why we like to cross our arms or lean to the left.

Dr. Bouchard usually drove twins back to their hotel at the end of the first day, often joining them for dinner. It was important and pleasurable for twins to spend free time together, especially those who had recently met, but critics suspected that twins might discuss tests or compare answers. All participants were advised to avoid discussing any part of the study until both had

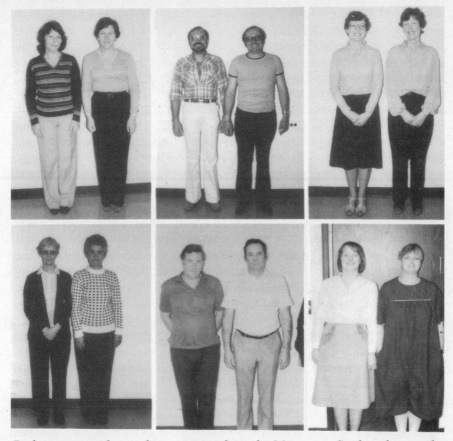

Body postures of reared apart twins from the Minnesota Study, taken on the first assessment day. Without instruction from researchers, the three identical twin pairs (top row) naturally assumed similar standing positions, in contrast with the three fraternal twin pairs (bottom row) who posed differently. PHOTO COURTESY OF THOMAS J. BOUCHARD, JR.

completed it; in fact, the schedule was designed so that twins generally finished the same tests on the same day. They clearly comprehended their critical role in insuring the scientific integrity of the data.

• *Day 2: Monday.* Monday marked the first of three days at the University of Minnesota Hospitals where twins completed an extensive battery of medical and psychophysiological tests.[35] They received a general physical exam, chest X ray and lung function test before proceeding to the heart hospital for vectorcardiograms (recordings of changes in the heart's electrical activity) and echocardiograms (ultrasonic displays of the heart's activity while beating).[36] Naip Tuna conducted the physical exams and is memorable for his warmth, intelligence and slight tardiness. Lunch was followed by a visit to David Lykken's psychophysiology laboratory where twins were again photographed and fingerprinted. One twin remained there for computerized testing of word knowledge and problem-solving ability, brain wave measurement, and electrodermal response (skin conductance) testing.[37] Brain wave patterns and skin conductance tests revealed psychophysiological reactions to music, voices, sudden noises and other stimulation. The resting brain waves of identical twins reared apart and reared together are only slightly less alike than those of the same person tested twice, while those of fraternal twins show less average resemblance.

Meanwhile, the other twin completed extensive medical life history and psychiatric interviews in a different laboratory. Medical life history interviews included a review of symptoms, illnesses, injuries and surgeries. The psychiatric interview consisted of the *Diagnostic Interview Schedule* (DIS) which covers major diagnoses recognized by the *American Psychiatric Association,* such as schizophrenia, substance abuse, compulsive gambling and sexual dysfunction. In most cases the DIS was administered to twins by different examiners to avoid bias from knowing the other twin's history. The generally good mental health of the reared apart twins meant that few psychiatric disorders would be detected, so we used individual symptoms rather than formal diagnoses in analyzing data. Information on thirty-two identical reared apart twins revealed genetic influence on substance abuse, childhood antisocial behavior and adult antisocial behavior, but not on alcohol use.[38] Larger studies of male and female twins reared together have shown genetic influence on alcohol use, so the absence of genetic effects in the reared apart twins may reflect the small number of pairs.[39]

By Monday afternoon most twins had completed the Minnesota Multiphasic Personality Inventory, or MMPI, a lengthy form that includes personality measures related to expressions of psychopathology, such as depression and paranoia.[40] Twins reared apart generally showed the same degree of genetic influence across the different scales as twins reared together. A particularly fascinating finding concerns members of two identical twin pairs reared on different continents, in countries with different political systems and different languages: Each pair's average cotwin difference across thirteen scales was *less than* the average cotwin difference based on all reared apart identical twins in the study. This result, while provided by only two pairs, is striking given the twins' different backgrounds, and supports evidence showing that shared genes rather than shared environments explain personality similarity between relatives. Nevertheless, some identical pairs drew attention to events causing divergence between twins. Two exceptional identical pairs showed marked differences on the MMPI, traceable to the development of psychiatric disorder in one case, and probable brain damage due to head injury in the other case.

• *Day 3: Tuesday.* Tuesday morning brought the most controversial aspect of the study, the assessment of each twin's IQ.[41] In order to avoid examiner bias or between-twin discussion, two professional psychometrists in the Neuropsychology Department of the University of Minnesota Hospital (who were not part of the research team) administered the Wechsler Adult Intelligence Scale (WAIS) to twins at exactly the same time. (Spouses or significant others completed the WAIS immediately after twins, with each examiner testing the husband, wife or partner of the other twin—that is, each examiner tested one twin and the other twin's spouse to avoid bias from testing both twins, both spouses or both members of a couple.) This was an important procedural decision, one that was not followed by previous reared apart twin investigators, causing considerable criticism over the years.

I once conducted a mini-investigation of the same tester–different tester issue by comparing the IQ similarity of reared together pairs in which both twins were tested by me, and pairs in which one twin was tested by me and the other by my assistant.[42] Identical twins showed greater similarity than fraternal twins as expected, but the numbers hardly changed across conditions, showing that standard tests with well established administration and scoring rules yield stable group differences in similarity regardless of the tester. Of course, examiner characteristics such as personality (warm or distant) may occasionally affect the performance of individuals, a point to consider in assessing learning disabilities or other problems. I advocate separate examiners for twin and sibling studies, given the bitter debates that genetic views of intelligence can provoke.

The reared apart twin studies report nearly identical correlations for IQ similarity. They range between .64 and .78 across the five studies, averaging .75.[43] This means that intellectual differences in a population are, to a considerable degree, due to genetic differences among the members. It also means that there is room for improving intellectual abilities, although it is unlikely that everyone will advance at the same pace or end up at the same level. Close to one-third of the differences are explained by environmental effects, for example quality of education or encouragement. Of course, these findings only apply to people in the normal range of rearing environments represented by the twins, not to people from deprived or impoverished situations.

The 75% estimate of genetic influence based on adult twins reared apart is higher than the 50% estimate based on young sibling and parent-child pairs. This effect is probably explained by findings that genetic influence on intelligence increases with age, as well as the observation that different ways of calculating genetic influence yield a range of values, usually 30–70%.[44] The 75% estimate of genetic influence on general intelligence is also higher than the 50–55% estimate of genetic influence on special mental skills, such as vocabulary and spatial visualization, because IQ tests are more reliable (or less subject to measurement error) than tests of separate abilities.

IQ correlations for fraternal reared apart twins have been reported by only two recent investigators. They are lower than those reported for identical reared apart twins, as expected. The Swedish study found a value of .32 for forty-five pairs and the Minnesota study found a value of .47 for twenty-eight pairs, averaging .38.[45] This value is slightly below the .47–.50 values typical of first-degree relatives, such as parent-child and sib-sib pairs. Bouchard cautioned that the Minnesota data are preliminary and require further analysis.

The consistency of the IQ findings from the different identical reared apart twin studies is compelling because the information was gathered by different investigators, using different tests, in different countries, at different times, and from different twins. Some people are unaware of the early studies, but are familiar with a highly publicized case of alleged scientific fraud involving reared apart twin IQ data which has, unfortunately, biased some interpretations of recent findings.[46] Sir Cyril Burt, a British psychologist, published five papers between 1943 and 1966 on identical twins reared apart. Even though the number of pairs increased in each report, his .771 correlation remained constant. Adding more pairs to each analysis should have changed the correlation somewhat, but the fact that it stayed the same does not establish professional dishonesty. This unusual observation, nevertheless, unleashed accusations of deception from colleagues who did not support genetic views of intellectual development, as well as from the media, so Burt's case was effectively tried in the public press. He was accused of fabricating twin pairs, fabricating research assistants and fabricating data. More judicious attempts to investigate this matter have since taken place, and while some questions remain, two investigations published in 1989 and 1991 cast doubt on Burt's supposed scientific transgression.[47] Arthur R. Jensen of the University of California, Berkeley, who has defended Burt, showed how rounding the numbers may have led to the repeated .771. The battle over Burt, nevertheless, continues.[48]

Burt's work is no longer cited in the psychological literature, but that hardly discredits IQ findings from past or current reared apart twin studies. I believe excluding Burt's studies has no effect on our understanding of the genetic basis of intellectual development because his findings were completely consistent with other reared apart twin studies, including ours, and receive continued support from the wealth of reared together twin and adoption data.

IQ findings from the Minnesota Study of Twins Reared Apart were published in a 1990 paper in the journal *Science,* the first major report on intellectual similarity in identical reared apart twins since 1966.[49] The theoretical significance and educational implications of the work guaranteed intense interest and scientific scrutiny from supporters and critics. The findings also generated hard questions from the media, and from parents facing the challenging task of raising young children. The whole world seemed to be watch-

ing. The study actually went far beyond producing estimates of genetic influence to test alternative explanations for the twins' resemblance. Some remarkable findings emerged:

- Similarity of identical twins' rearing environments was unable to explain similarity in IQ scores. Some critics of reared apart twin studies have argued that common features of twins' prenatal and rearing environments, rather than their shared genes, are primarily responsible for their intellectual resemblance.[50] The Minnesota study found that similarity in childhood physical facilities (e.g., dictionaries, telescopes and original artwork), social status indicators (e.g., father's education, mother's education and father's socio-economic level) and parenting practices (e.g., twins' impressions of parental treatment) was unrelated to IQ similarity. In other words, twins who were matched on some or all of these measures were as similar in IQ as twins who differed. Furthermore, IQ scores showed little relationship to the environmental indices—that is, access to power tools or membership in a high status family did not distinguish between high- and low-scoring cotwins.
- Amount of contact between identical reared apart twins before or after reunion did not affect IQ similarity. Another frequent criticism of reared apart twin studies is that twins who are separated later, reunited earlier, and in greater contact are more alike in IQ.[51] Participants in the Minnesota study showed considerable variability in these measures. For example, twins on average were separated by five months of age, but some were reared apart right from birth and others stayed together until age four. Some twins met for the first time in Minneapolis or en route to the Twin Cities, but most met before participating in the study, some as much as twenty years earlier. Variability in these measures was an important advantage because it was possible to test whether twins' degree of social contact explained IQ similarity, and the answer was that it did not.

Similar challenges were launched against the three early reared apart twin studies. One critic attempted to show that later age at separation, reunion in childhood, rearing by relatives and environmental similarity lead to similar IQ scores.[52] His criteria for grouping twins according to these measures were largely arbitrary; in other words, they did not have a firm rationale so any other scheme might have been substituted. Bouchard reanalyzed the same data according to the same criteria, using a different IQ measure available in each study, but the results did not hold up.[53] Therefore, Bouchard's analysis revealed the inappropriateness of the original grouping plan, and the misperception that environmental similarity leads to IQ similarity. Actually, some of the objections and concerns that have been raised over the years are not farfetched—for example, it seems sensible that greater social contact might lead to greater IQ similarity—but resolution of criticisms is only possible by repeated testing of multiple data sets, and

there is no convincing evidence that social contact or other environmental factors explain IQ similarity in identical twins reared apart. The path from genes to behavior is unclear, but it may be that shared genetic factors steer reared apart twins toward comparable environments and experiences that underlie the psychological similarities we observe and measure—in other words, "nature via nurture." This may be the route we all travel throughout our lives.

IQ testing was followed by stress EKGs (electrocardiograms) for one twin and inventories for the other, after which they rotated positions. Technicians and physicians monitored the progress of each twin as they walked or jogged on treadmills, paying careful attention to symptoms or other concerns detected during medical examinations the previous day. Twins learned a great deal about their physical fitness during these visits. I recall occasional discovery of heart murmurs or other conditions of which twins were unaware, but which could be followed up with personal physicians when they returned home. There were surprisingly impressive treadmill performances by some twins, such as sixty-six-year-old Caroline Shand who explained that, "If you walk slower you can go further." Caroline had walked two miles to and from school each day in her native Scotland.

Tuesday afternoon was identical to Monday afternoon, including completion of psychophysiological tests and medical and psychiatric interviews, except that the twins changed places. I escorted twins to dinner at a restaurant close to campus because they returned an hour later for separate completion of Sexual Life History questionnaires and interviews. Joseph Bohlen and his staff devised and initially administered this part of the study to twins, but research assistants and I assumed responsibility for this in the mid-1980s. A Sexual Meaning Survey examined the personal sexual significance of concepts such as *weak-strong* and *happy-sad*. A Sexual Life History Timeline obtained information about the occurrence and timing of sexual events, such as age at first intercourse and first attraction to a member of the opposite sex. A Sexual Events Questionnaire gathered data on past and current sexual attitudes and practices, such as use of contraception and frequency of sexual relations. Questionnaires were followed by a structured interview enabling twins to elaborate on their developmental, premarital and marital histories. Only a small sample of twins have completed this assessment, and spouses were never included in this part of the study.

The Minnesota study was the first to systematically examine sexual histories in twins reared apart. Genetic influence on male, but not on female, sexual orientation was found, suggested by similarity between reared apart identical male twins and dissimilarity between separated identical female twins, as discussed in Chapter 5.[54]

Twins returned to their hotels that evening with reminders to avoid eating and drinking because fasting blood samples would be taken early the next

morning. They were also given training in how to operate a device that would monitor their blood pressure while asleep.

• *Day 4: Wednesday.* We arranged for twins' blood samples to be drawn upon arrival Wednesday morning for analysis of blood chemistry, fasting sugar levels and twin type, after which they were treated to breakfast. I then escorted them to the heart hospital where a twenty-four-hour Holter monitor was attached, enabling continuous recording of heart activity over the next day and night.[55] Whenever a significant change in activity occurred, such as eating or climbing stairs, they punched a button on the side of the monitor and recorded the time, event and their physical state in a small notebook. Showering was strictly forbidden during this period, a request most twins tolerated with good humor. Our immunological team next examined frequency and severity of allergic reactions by an allergy interview and by skin testing, although skin testing was later dropped from the schedule due to time and other constraints. Skin testing involved inserting common allergens, such as house dust and Timothy grass, under the skin with needles and monitoring response over time.

Resemblance in selected allergic reactions and characteristics was compared between reared apart and reared together twins. Identical twins showed more similar histories of asthma and bronchitis than fraternal twins, regardless of whether they were reared together or reared apart, indicating genetic influence.[56] Even more impressive, identical twins reared apart were as similar in susceptibility as identical twins reared together, suggesting that shared environments are not required for similarity in some allergic responses among relatives. Blood level of total IgE, a protein that fights infection from foreign substances, showed a strong genetic effect; however, levels of specific antibodies (infection fighters) showed a stronger environmental effect. These findings arc somewhat tentative because the number of pairs studied was small, but they may ease bewilderment over variable reactions to chocolate, pollen and house dust among family members. Knowing that identical twins vary in some allergic reactions suggests that differing levels of exposure to environmental substances, possibly combined with general health at the time of exposure, may trigger effects in one twin but not the other.

Scientific study of allergies and other medical conditions dramatically highlights the delicate interplay between genetically based sensitivities and physical response.[57] A 1987 television documentary, *Body Watch,* produced by WGBH in Boston, included a compelling piece on adult-onset diabetes, a genetically influenced condition in which only 50% of identical twins are both affected. In the program, Dr. J. Stuart Soeldner explained that an infection, a dietary factor or other event might activate diabetes in one identical twin, but not the other. This observation was well illustrated by identical twins, Joan and Jane, one of whom developed the disease following an infection, while her sister remained symptom-free, trying to stay as healthy as possible. Identical twins differing in medical traits remind us that environmental triggers are required to activate inherited predispositions. Many people with family histories of heart disease or weight gain use diets or exercise to control potential difficulties, although triggers such as infection in the case of diabetes may be harder to offset than others.

Twins' reactions to the skin testing procedure itself sometimes provided the most interesting findings when, for example, three identical male triplets declined the test due to fear of needles. Genes predisposing people to fear of needles are nonexistent, but there were other striking examples of common fears and solutions in identical twins reared apart. Identical twin sisters were both terrified of fast driving (a fear that was understandably aroused when driving with Bouchard!). Fear of fast driving may not be all that uncommon, so this similarity was less impressive to me than their shared motivation to tell him. These same twins also feared entering the ocean, and before meeting both discovered that backing in slowly before turning around was a successful strategy.[58]

I first thought seriously about genetic influence on dental traits in 1979 when Paula Tachau, mother of opposite-handed identical twins, Joel and Jeremy, noted that her boys had opposite nondescended incisors and each boy had five teeth removed to make room for braces. It is now well known that faithful brushing and good diet improve dental health, but there are individual differences in frequency of cavities, bone loss and other oral problems. Some lucky people are filling free, while others require constant care despite preventative efforts. Standard dental and periodontal exams occurred late Wednesday morning and were unique additions to reared apart twin research, although earlier reared apart twin studies did include dental information on thirty-six sets.[59] Early reports of similar dental structures, location of cavities and history of dental problems anticipated findings from the more systematic assessments conducted in Minnesota.

Dental exams included a clinical examination, X rays, dental models and dental history questionnaire. The principal dental investigator, Michael Till, examined records and tests for all twins. He maintained objectivity by staying "blind" to twin type and to which twins were in which pairs. Studies of twins reared together have produced impressive evidence of genetic influence on frequency of decay, number of teeth, tooth size and other traits, but similar findings in twins reared apart are more compelling evidence that genes affect dental health. Reared apart twins revealed that genetic influence explains 45–67% of variation in number of teeth present, number of teeth and surfaces restored, and caries (cavities) present.[60] These findings encourage a new look at the way diet, oral hygiene and dentists' philosophies interact with genetic predispositions. Dental history questionnaires completed by reared apart twins are under review for clues as to how treatment may modify dental health. I suspect genetic factors directly related to dental status and structure will continue to be important, while treatment may prove less important in explaining individual differences. This does not imply that dental treatment is not important for achieving or maintaining dental health—it implies that dental treatment differences may explain dental health differences less effectively than genetic factors. I also believe genetically influenced psychological traits like conscientiousness (for scheduling regular dental visits) and apprehension (of dental procedures) will play key roles in determining dental health.

What began as an ordinary appointment with periodontologist Marc Herzberg triggered a fruitful ongoing collaboration between the Periodontology Department and the Minnesota Study of Twins Reared Apart. I am one of the unlucky who battle periodontitis, a silent condition of the gums involving buildup of plaque and possible loss of teeth if left untreated. I suspected genetic factors underlie periodontal problems because my fraternal twin sister is relatively free of them even though she is less vigilant about her dental care than I am. During my visit Dr. Herzberg asked what I did, and when I discussed twins reared apart we both realized the valuable role they could play in elucidating the genetic and environmental basis of periodontal diseases, especially gingivitis (inflammation of gums) and periodontitis (loosening and loss of teeth). Bouchard was also enthusiastic, and meetings with Bryan Michalowicz, Bruce Pihlstom and other members of the Periodontology Department incorporated the first peridontological checkup into reared apart twin research. It also launched an important comparison study of twins reared together. Combined analysis of twins reared apart and together revealed genetic influence on probing depth (space between gums and tooth surface), attachment loss and plaque buildup.[61] Estimates are that 38–82% of individual differences in periodontal disease measures may be associated with genetic factors. Periodontists generally agree that bacteria in plaque are the instigators of periodontal difficulties, but they also recognize individual differences in response to these bacteria. Twin studies, by identifying genetic effects on periodontal traits, can explain why some family members may be more susceptible than others.

It is often said that the "eye is the window into the soul." Medical research is not quite as sensational, but reared apart twins may well be windows into the origins of visual structures and disorders. Information on vision available for thirty-five reared apart identical pairs from the early studies included remarkable similarities for wearing eyeglasses or for experiencing nearsightedness, farsightedness and strabismus (eye muscle imbalance preventing the production of a focused image by both eyes at the same time), strongly suggesting genetic influence.[62] The Minnesota study was the first to administer standard, comprehensive eye examinations, under the direction of William Knobloch. Twins were tested for visual acuity, refraction, pressure and muscle balance, after which the eyes were dilated to study the anterior segment (front of the eye) and fundus (interior of the eye opposite the pupil). The final phase included detailed photographs of the optic nerve, macula (oval area in the retina where visual acuity is greatest) and standard fields. Data have been analyzed for only twenty-six identical pairs and eight fraternal pairs, but expected identical twin similarities in refraction (focusing of light rays on the retina) and esotropia (a type of strabismus) were found.[63] Most interesting was a "demonstration of the biological clock," the coordinated timing of visual changes and symptoms in reared apart identicals. Twins in one pair showed early development of estropia and use of eyeglasses before school age, and twins in another pair had strabismus surgery scheduled just one year apart. More provocative, only one member of an identical male triplet set showed macular degeneration, but his two brothers showed early warning signs. Macular degeneration (breakdown of the visual structure surrounding light-sensitive cells) is the major cause of severe vision loss in Caucasian individuals over sixty-five years of age, especially those with blue eyes. Previewing a likely change in medical futures is a benefit specially reserved for identical cotwins and triplets. Genetic effects on macular degeneration are further demonstrated by a 1988 study of a concordant reared together identical twin pair,[64] and a 1998 report of a gene increasing the risks of heart disease, Alzheimer's disease (progressive mental and behavioral deterioration beginning in middle age) and this eye condition. I also recall Dr. Knobloch's impressive observation that twin type could be reliably diagnosed by the similarity of the fine structures of the retina. These features differ widely from person to person, but show remarkable similarity in identical twins.

Birth weight and knowledge of oxygen use were unavailable for reared apart twins so their relationship to visual health could not be determined. Oxygen was once given more freely to premature infants in incubators to assist breathing, but was later limited because of damaging effects on eyesight. I wondered if this procedure might mask genetic effects on vision by "making" fraternal twins alike. In a 1966 study of twins' psychological and physical development, Helen Koch found that five-year-old and six-year-old twin children were more likely to wear glasses than nontwin children, (identical, 13%; same-sex fraternal, 7%; opposite-sex fraternal, 13% vs. nontwins, 4.39%).[65] She also noted that the twin similarity rates for wearing glasses (about 44%) were similar across twin type, and that eye deficiencies paralleled prematurity. Unfortunately, only a few studies have discussed relations between twins' vision and birth events.[66] About ten years ago, Professor Jaakko Teikari from the University of Helsinki told me there was little evidence that twins' early oxygen exposure had contaminated vision research. Recent studies have found greater identical than fraternal twin similarity for most ocular traits, even studies using adult twins whose birth occurred when oxygen was given more routinely to infants in incubators.[67] It is possible that twins experiencing birth traumas that could have affected their vision were excluded from research on normal visual traits.

Twins were dismissed early Wednesday afternoon because their dilated eyes prevented them from reading the inventory questions. Bouchard sometimes used this opportunity to escort twins on a tour of Minneapolis's lovely lakes. Twins were outfitted with special glasses for protection from the sun, but I always wondered if they fully appreciated the beautiful scenery.

• *Day 5: Thursday.* The next two and one-half days brought twins and staff back to the "Twin Room" and to other laboratories in the Psychology Department. The morning included mental abilities and inventories, as well as a new activity, psychomotor testing.[68] Psychomotor tests examine involuntary hand movements and other motor traits while passing a rod through a small space and fitting pegs into holes. Genetic influence on initial ability, and on the extent to which practice improves performance, was measured by our experimental psychology team, headed by Bill Fox. We compared identical and fraternal reared apart twins' scores across three consecutive days. Findings from a rotary pursuit task, in which people learn to track a moving target with a long rod for as long as possible, were remarkable. On day one, identical twins showed greater similarity in "time on target" than fraternal twins, evidence of genetic influence on this psychomotor skill. More compelling was the fact that identical twins improved at more similar rates than fraternal twins, revealing that genetic effects also underlie performance changes associated with practice. Some critics have objected that such findings may discourage efforts to improve ability in difficult tasks, but even twins showing minimal beginning skill were doing better by Saturday. Such findings may actually curb frustration by encouraging people to resist self-blame, avoid blaming others, set realistic goals, and develop alternative practice routines. This information promises new insights for budding athletes, dancers, artists and surgeons, and for their trainers, although it is likely that many have sensed it all along.

Why we move and gesture as we do is a fascinating, but neglected aspect of human behavior. Psychomotor tests and unposed photographs say a thousand words about fine motor skills and still body posture, but videotaped interviews of twins recounting childhood histories, social attitudes and current interests speak volumes about people in motion. One of my favorite tasks was faithfully capturing hand gestures, head positions, foot tapping and energy level in one-hour videotaped sessions of each twin alone, followed by half-hour videotaped sessions of twins together. Twins were also requested to walk across a room, throw a ring of keys and draw a series of pictures. This part of the study was intriguing because twins stepped outside confined laboratory settings to move and gesture naturally. Families are often captivated by physical quirks repeated in different members, such as positioning of hands or raising of eyebrows, but genetic and environmental influences are hopelessly intertwined, hiding the true source of these behaviors.

Reared apart identical twins, Jerry Levey (left) and Mark Newman. The twins are reliving one of their first marvelous moments: comparison of physical characteristics soon after meeting. Note that the twins' little fingers support their cans of beer. Budweiser has always been their favorite brand. PHOTO CREDIT: NANCY L. SEGAL.

Distinctive physical expressions co-occurring in identical twins reared apart suggest that genetic factors are involved. Jerry Levey and Mark Newman, identical volunteer firemen, held pinky fingers under cans of Budweiser beer long before they met. Other pairs were notorious for swaying side-to-side while walking, accenting long slender fingers with abundant jewelry, and belting out warm rich laughter. Like complex psychological traits, finger holding, ring wearing and laughing do not originate from single genes, nor solely from genetic factors, but rather from multiple genes linked to physical and personality traits, interacting with features of the environment. Videotapes were a great way to preserve these behaviors. This valuable archive has yet to be viewed with a scientific eye, but continues to flourish with each new pair.

The interviews ended with a request for twins to tell us something about themselves that perhaps we had forgotten to ask, although after nearly a week of examinations and inventories they could rarely think of a thing. Closing comments were usually words of thanks for the opportunity to gain personal knowledge and to further scientific discovery. Their remarks were sincere and it was a wonderful way for us to end the day.

• *Day 6: Friday.* The twins were very familiar to us all by Friday and I remember feeling a touch of sadness that these people who had shared so much of their incredible lives would soon be gone.

Psychomotor tests resumed on Friday morning, followed by life stress interviews and information processing tests. Life stress interviews asked twins to list and to rate the significance of life changes and stressful events in their lives, such as marriages, separations, births, deaths, occupations, crimes and naturally occurring disasters such as fires or floods. Chapter 5 reviewed twin research revealing genetic influence on stressful life events, as well as links between personality traits and tendencies to experience these events. Studies of reared apart twins extend this work because greater identical than fraternal twin similarity in stressful life events, especially those likely to have been initiated by the individual, suggest mechanisms by which such parallels occur.[69] The similar personalities and physical makeup of identical twins may propel them toward certain experiences over others, despite differences in parental teachings, social pressures and environmental hazards. Like previous twin studies, higher genetic influence was found for controllable life events than uncontrollable life events, a finding well illustrated by several of the pairs. Mark and Jerry, volunteer firemen, admitted to close calls in the line of duty, but could accept these events as part of their job and move on. Identical female twins were honored as valedictorians at age twelve in their separate schools in separate countries, but invitations for public speaking elevated stress even miles apart. Both twins forced themselves to fulfill their obligations, before retreating to more comfortable, private settings.

Information processing included three timed tasks to see if genetic factors influenced speed and accuracy of problem-solving.[70] For example, pairs of figures were presented on a screen and twins decided if they were the same or different, indicating their choice by lifting a finger from the "home button" and pressing a response key. Genetic influence on information processing speed and on spatial speed was slightly over 50%, while genetic influence on acquisition speed was 27%. Studying the basic components of mental functioning is an exciting area because some information processing measures appear related to general intelligence, although the nature of the relationships is not well understood.

Lunch was a welcome break from the morning's activities, after which we administered additional mental ability and information processing tests to twins. Friday afternoon provided excellent opportunities for additional inventories, one of which was the Twin Relationship Survey designed to explore some commonly seen, but profound features of human affiliation.

Every twin reunion was a celebration, but some proceeded more quietly and more privately than others, and it was intriguing to understand the differences. Did reunited identical twins develop closer social relations than reunited fraternal twins, mirroring the *friendship extraordinaire* exemplified by identical twins raised together? How did this new relationship fare when measured against relationships with adoptive siblings who were familiar since childhood? These were just some of the questions that arose as I watched the Minnesota study from the sidelines in the late 1970s and early 1980s.

When the Minnesota study began in 1979, evolutionary perspectives on human behavior were arousing interest, as well as controversy, in psychology departments everywhere. New thoughts on genetic contributions to social behavior, made famous in Edward O. Wilson's monumental 1975 book, *Sociobiology: The New Synthesis,* encouraged reappraisal of the nature and origin of human social relationships.[71] The basis for this approach came from William Hamilton's theory of inclusive fitness, discussed in Chapter 6. At that time, I was participating in a sociobiology study group at the University of Chicago, and while the theory required testing and evaluation, it offered compelling new views of social relationships in general, and twin relationships in particular. In other words, genetically speaking, helping an identical twin is the equivalent of helping oneself. The greater social closeness of identical than fraternal twins might be construed as reflecting increased altruism between close genetic relatives, associated with transmission of shared genes.

How do we know who our relatives are? How do shared genes affect our feelings toward them? As I discussed in Chapter 6, indicators of genetic relatedness might be accomplished (albeit approximately) via *recognition mechanisms,* such as perceptions of behavioral or physical resemblance which would be greater in identical twins.[72] Daniel G. Freedman, director of the study group, suggested that recognizing similar features may foster a "sense of 'we' between ourselves and our fellow tribesmen. Recognition of this sense may trigger a series of emotions whose net effect is tribal unity and the increased chance for altruism."[73] This perspective squared with more common psychodynamic views of social behavior which also acknowledge that similarities attract, but the evolutionary slant promised a richer, more comprehensive picture of why this happens.

Twins reared apart were an experiment out of the ordinary for disclosing how genetic relatedness might affect social interactions in the absence of a shared childhood. Soon after I arrived in Minnesota, Bouchard and I composed the Twin Relationship Survey, a comprehensive form for capturing the twins' adoption experience, search for their cotwin, first moment of meeting, and developing relationship.[74] Administering this survey was one of my favorite activities during the week and the sixty-five identical and fifty-seven fraternal twins and triplets thoroughly enjoyed it. Bouchard occasionally grumbled about the space these surveys occupied in the file drawers, but I knew he was pleased.

Twins responded to four questions concerning initial and current feelings of closeness and familiarity by selecting one choice on a six-point scale, ranging from feeling "closer than best friends" to "less close than most people I meet for the first time," and from feeling "more familiar than best friends" to "less familiar than most people I meet for the first time." The pro-

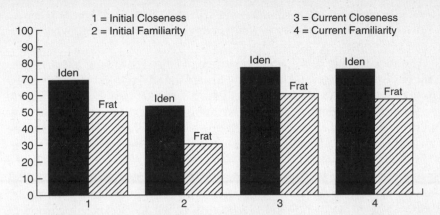

Proportions of reared apart identical and fraternal twins indicating they were "closer than best friends" and "as familiar as best friends." FIGURE DE-SIGN BY KELLY DONOVAN.

portions of identical and fraternal twins indicating they were "closer than best friends" and "more familiar than best friends" were compared because these extremes would probably distinguish most clearly between the two groups.

A first look at twins' responses is dazzling. When meeting for the first time, identical twins were more likely than fraternal twins to: (1) anticipate becoming closer than best friends, and (2) find the twin more familiar than a best friend. Currently (at the time of the study), identical twins were more likely than fraternal twins to: (3) feel closer than best friends, and (4) find the twin more familiar than a best friend.

It is also provocative that even after fraternal twins got to know one another, a slightly smaller proportion felt "closer than best friends" (61%), compared to the proportion of identical twins who felt "closer than best friends" when meeting for the first time (69%). Over one-half of fraternal twins endorsed the highest levels of initial closeness, current closeness and current familiarity, and one-third endorsed the highest level of initial familiarity so these are not trivial numbers. The 50% average genetic relatedness of fraternal twins makes it reasonable for them to feel familiar and close to their twins, although the frequency of highest ratings should be less than for identical twins. Fraternal twins who look and behave alike may develop closer social relations than fraternal twins who look and behave differently, although this has not been tested. A letter sent to me from a separated fraternal twin, Jean Perkin, following the death of her twin sister captures the intense emotional connectedness that can evolve between relatives meeting in adulthood:

I really cannot say exactly how I feel, mostly just 'very sad' is the best way I can describe my feelings. . . . My sister Jean had been ill for so long and suffered so much that I feel poor dear must be at rest now. My only consolation is that I did know her for 12 years and we brought each other much happiness."

The social relatedness findings are more riveting if we look at twins' current sense of closeness and familiarity toward the adoptive siblings they knew all their lives: Only 27% of all twins felt "closer than best friends" and only 36% found their adoptive siblings as "familiar as best friends." (These figures rise slightly when only same-sex pairs are considered.) These results are not immediately predictable because many twins were unaware of their twinship until adulthood, twin type was questionable in some cases,[75] and time spent with adoptive siblings far exceeded time spent with twins. These findings make sense, however, if twins' genetic similarities did, in fact, "trigger" the feelings of familiarity and closeness between them. The proportion of identical and fraternal twins rating adoptive siblings "closer than best friends" or as "familiar as best friends" did not differ, but this is not surprising—both types of twins were reared as nontwin adoptees in their respective homes and being identical or fraternal should not have affected this measure. Clearly, the most revealing finding remains identical and fraternal twins' differing perceptions of their new twinship. Further analyses and additional data are needed, especially ratings from unrelated siblings and from identical and fraternal twins reared together which I have been gathering. This information will be critical for illuminating the relative importance of shared experience and shared genes in shaping social relations. Similar ratings between identical twins raised apart and identical twins raised together, or higher ratings between fraternal twins than between adoptive siblings would downplay shared environments and underline genetic relatedness as factors affecting closeness and familiarity.

Earlier I made the point that identical twin resemblance is less interesting or meaningful than identical twin resemblance compared to resemblance between other relatives. The same principle extends to social relationships—the greater average social closeness between identical twins tell us less than its magnitude relative to fraternal twins, full siblings, adoptive siblings and cousins.

Evolutionary theory adds layers to our understanding of why reunited twins feel closer and more familiar with one another than with adoptive siblings and, more importantly, why identical twins feel closer and more familiar with one another than fraternal twins. More detailed study of factors such as twins' perceived physical resemblance and quality of adoptive home life will sharpen the picture of identical and fraternal twins' relationships at reunion and beyond. Anecdotal evidence suggests that physical resemblance between parents and children contributes to favorable relations between them. Scenes from these dramas are staged in homes everywhere, but reared apart twins play their parts to perfection, making variable attachments to family members more comprehensible.

One night in 1984, I outlined a novel way to assess recognition of relatives whom one had never met and whose relatedness was unknown. This design involves children of identical twins who are genetic "half-siblings" as well as cousins. Photographs of these individuals and unrelated children could be shown to children of each identical reared apart twin who would judge them for physical similarity, feelings of friendship and feelings of familiarity. Higher ratings for "half-siblings" or cousins than for unrelated individuals would suggest links between genetic relatedness and social attraction. Children of fraternal twins should also rate cousins higher than unrelateds, but the difference should be smaller than for children of identical twins because children of fraternal twins are not "half-siblings." This proposed study would be difficult to conduct because the children of reunited twins often meet following their twin parents' reunion.

Friday afternoon closed with a few more inventories, one of which examined morningness-eveningness.[76] "Morning people" rise easily and are alert early in the day, while "evening people" sleep in and are alert later in the day. These behaviors are familiar to most people, but their origin is less certain. Reared apart identical and fraternal twins, combined with reared together identical twins and spouses, participated in the first behavior-genetic study of this tendency. Genetic influence explained slightly over 50% of the variation in morningness-eveningness. Reared apart fraternal twins were unusually similar in this trait, a finding that will be followed as new data are gathered.

The twins were driven back to their hotel, leaving one-half day to go.

• *Day 7: Saturday.* Saturdays have a relaxed feeling even when one is working. The Minnesota study was an exception because many twins would soon be leaving the country, making it difficult to contact them if unanswered questions remained. We redoubled our efforts to be certain that all inventories were completed before lunch. A task left to assistants was copying age-matched pictures of twins taken in infancy, childhood, adolescence and adulthood. This exercise in time-lapse photography revealed better than any other that genes guide gradual changes in physical appearance and form, explaining why most identical twins remain so similar, even into old age, barring accidents or injuries.

Bouchard usually took twins to lunch, accompanied by assistants who later returned to the lab to process remaining material or to prepare for a new pair coming the next day. The "Twin Room" always had an empty quality to it at this time, like the close of a great party whose end is not welcome. It was still satisfying to know that both twins and investigators had come a great distance toward solving their particular medley of behavioral puzzles.

Seven years have passed since my direct association with the Minnesota Study of Twins Reared Apart. I am gratified that twins are still being reunited and studied because this design is surely the most insightful way to probe genetic and environmental influences on development. I have described findings from this study many times in my courses and seminars, and my students have delighted in the theoretical dialogues and personal knowledge this research presents. Commonly encountered questions concern the most amazing or surprising result, and the most memorable or remarkable pair. I have thought long and hard about correct responses to these questions. The answer is that no single finding or particular pair competes with the power and presence of the accumulated findings. If pressed to produce a bottom line, it must be that reared apart twins show that genetic influence is pervasive, affecting virtually every measured behavioral trait, many previously assumed to be environmental in origin, such as religious interests, social attitudes, vocational interests, job satisfaction and work values.[77] This research has truly affected the way we think about our own abilities, shortcomings and potentialities and those of the people we know. Understanding that mathematical skill, social nonconformity and weight gain may be partly genetically influenced is the key to informed appreciation of individual diversity in response to teaching methods, political events and dietary practices.

Identical twins reared apart are a great twist of fate. They were first used by the Roman comic dramatist Plautus (254–184 B.C.), as a literary device in his play *Menaechmi (The Two Menaechmuses)*.[78] Bouchard and I once surveyed psychological journals to find the first reference to separated twins and, contrary to common belief, this idea did *not* begin with Sir Francis Galton.[79] Reared apart twins were first recognized as a window into behavioral development by Paul Popenoe in 1922, in his case report of reared-apart twins, Bessie and Jessie.[80] The twins were separated at eight months (after their mother's death) and did not meet again until they were eighteen. Their matched physical and behavioral traits, including their bouts with tuberculosis, voices, energy levels, administrative talents and decision making impressed Popenoe. Bessie wrote that she and her sister had their hair cut at the same time unbeknownst to each other and this "really took courage, because the majority of our friends do not approve." They were also very attached to one another. ("We have never had a disagreement between ourselves, and while I am fond of my older sister and two brothers, yet they have never seemed as close to me as Bess.")

Bessie and Jessie were studied more thoroughly by geneticist Hermann J. Muller in 1925.[81] He found only a three-point difference in their intelligence test scores (153 and 156) despite the fact that Jessie completed college courses and Bessie had only four years of formal schooling—in fact, Bessie obtained the higher score. Both twins were avid readers, probably compensating for Bessie's sparse education—current researchers would say that she created an environment compatible with her inherited potentials. The twins did not perform similarly on all test items; for example, Bessie did better in arithmetic and Jessie did better in analogies. A more puzzling finding was the twins' limited resemblance on personality tests despite their own and others' perceptions of their traits as similar. Muller suggested that better means might be found for identifying genetically mediated features of personality.

Bouchard once commented that Plautus's play was a striking example of art anticipating science. Another great twist of fate—same-age unrelated siblings—also eluded behavioral geneticists until I learned about them from a mother of an unusual "twinlike" pair.

Another Twist of Fate: Children Adopted Together

Y ou should study my children." It was winter 1989 when Judy Punčochàř (pronounced punch-a-car), a psychology graduate student, insisted that while her boys were not twins I would surely find them fascinating. I was hardly prepared for the story that was to add such depth and dimension to my ongoing twin studies and will, I believe, significantly refine emerging pictures of human development painted by behavioral geneticists and evolutionary psychologists. I can only wonder why this magnificent natural experiment had never been recognized by behavioral-genetic investigators until now.

In 1978 Judy lost her four-day-old infant son who was born prematurely and with complications. She desperately wanted another child, but experienced difficulty conceiving and decided to adopt. With the adoption process in motion she became pregnant and just four days before delivering her son, Jonathan, newborn Carlton became available and she was happy to take him. Carlton was just five days older than Jonathan, and while the two boys were not genetically related their close age and rearing situation transformed them into an unusual "twinlike" pair. At age twelve years Jonathan stood four feet, eight inches tall, and was slight with blond hair and gray eyes, while Carlton towered over his brother at five feet, four inches, and was heavyset with brown hair and brown eyes. During participation in the study, Carlton weighed over twice as much as Jonathan, a difference apparent in photographs taken over the years. Like twins, Jonathan and Carlton joined their family at nearly the same age and time, and have shared many important life events, such as school attendance and first visit to a museum. Their developmental timelines are in greater harmony than those of ordinary full siblings, even those born just one year apart, making them valuable participants in developmental research. Of course, these "pseudo-twins" are more like fraternals than identicals because pseudo-twins and fraternal twins do not look physically alike.

I was stunned as the logic and power of this research design dawned on me. Unrelated siblings of the same age, reared together from early infancy, offer a wonderful way to learn how much shared environments might be associated with behavioral similarity. Individuals who do not share genes may resemble each other only because of shared experiences, providing "pure" estimates of environmental influence. In fact, pseudo-twins are an exact mirror image of identical twins reared apart because pseudo-twins share environments but not genes, while identical twins reared apart share genes but not environments. Pseudo-twins and identical twins reared apart are actually complementary approaches to the same class of questions, namely the extent to which genetic and environmental factors explain individual differences in behavior.

Adoption research is not new as evidenced by countless studies of intelligence, personality and psychopathology that have generally revealed negligible shared environmental influence on siblings' behavioral similarity past childhood. Pseudo-twins offer a new twist to this familiar design because they are the same age, thus smoothing over some bumps and blemishes of ordinary adoption designs. In some studies large age differences between adoptive siblings raise concern that environments may not be truly shared, making it hard to know the extent to which genetic differences or individual experiences explain behavioral differences between them. Siblings born years apart may actually live in two different families because sudden fortune, untimely deaths or other events may alter material resources or emotional support available to each child.

Pseudo-twins also offer a stringent test of a nagging criticism, the view that identical twins are alike because of common treatment, rather than common genes. If similar treatment were the whole story, pseudo-twins should be at least as alike as fraternal twins and full siblings, but if genetic factors affect behavior pseudo-twins should be quite different despite their twinlike existence. Pseudo-twins also have great potential for sorting out evolutionarily based issues regarding genetic and environmental contributions to social relationships. Their unique rearing situation makes it fascinating to learn how their feelings of friendship compare with those of identical and fraternal twins, and how this information squares with new theories of affiliation and loyalty.

These ideas multiplied as I chatted with Judy. I was amazed that experienced colleagues who were so quick to recognize new, informative kinships had not picked up on this one. I was actually close to discovering this new sibship ten years ago when a professional acquaintance, Bill Robiner, mentioned acquisition of an unrelated brother, "a step-twin," just two months younger than himself following his mother's second marriage when he was six years old. I have often reread his moving essay on growing up together:

As far as I know, I was not looking for twinship but essentially became immersed in one anyway. Our relationship was different from most step-family relationships because we were so close in age. As a result I started to feel a special closeness to him. . . . Our uniformity taught me democratic values, a sense of fairness, and gave me realistic self-perceptions. At another level, it felt oppressive when my own individuality was seemingly not prized by others. The twinship created conflict within me between the dual wishes to be alike and to be different. . . . We had identical quilts and bedspreads for our bunk bed, the same furniture and bicycles, and on and on. From elementary school through high school, we were often classmates and got similar grades. Although our parents never encouraged us to dress alike, we developed a similar wardrobe anyway. Some common traits and a growing history of shared experiences were merging us together. . . . We both hold doctorates and work in medical schools. We work too hard and are sometimes too serious. We got married within four months of each other. In many ways we have approached life's milestones in synchrony. . . . A bond of love allows my brother to understand and influence me more than anybody else. Perhaps the love has been the key to our psychological twinship, even though for some cosmic reasons we slipped into different pairs of genes.

Bill's sibship was forged in childhood, so it did not replay the essential twinning theme of mutual arrival in infancy. This notable "imperfection" may explain why the human interest side of his story took over, blinding me to the great research potential here if only the siblings had come together earlier. What I failed to recognize then became crystal clear only minutes after talking with Judy.

I invited Judy to bring her sons to my laboratory where I regularly ran identical and fraternal twin children through mental ability tests and cooperation-competition experiments. I was not sure how I would use information from a single case study, but I was certain that whatever findings emerged would intrigue behavioral-geneticists interested in child development. The boys' intelligence test scores were about as alike as fraternal twins', and their patterning of verbal and nonverbal subtests revealed both differences and similarities. Judy indicated that her boys got along "better than best friends," were very sharing, and preferred to play with each other more than with other friends, although they disagreed somewhat with her and with each other on these issues. One boy preferred the company of his mother to his brother, and both boys preferred playing with and sharing secrets with different friends than with each other. They seemed uninvolved with one another as they worked together on puzzles and story tasks, in contrast with the interconnectedness more typical of identical twins. Despite Judy's perception of her boys' relationship with one another, she emphasized their personality differences, not similarities, which was striking given a rearing situation that was much closer than that of biological siblings. Available twin and adoption studies prepared me well for these observations, but I still wondered if the behaviors of other pseudo-twins would replicate the modest impact of shared experience that Jonathan and Carlton were hinting at, or would reveal more potent effects of common rearing as suggested in Bill Robiner's piece. However, I never imagined that the meeting with Judy Punčochàř was the start of a comprehensive research program on shared environments and behavioral resemblance.

In his essay, Bill Robiner asked, "Who knows how close in age two people have to be to be treated like twins or to fancy themselves bound together in a profoundly close tie?" No one knows the answer to that question. I decided that for research purposes an age difference of nine months was an appropriate upper limit because classmates born in September and June differ by that much, but still fulfill the twinlike criteria of matching academic and social calendars. Despite the "allowable" nine-month age difference it was still a safe assumption that pseudo-twins would be rare because so many families struggle to adopt even one baby. I was, therefore, delighted when Judy referred me to a family with same-age pseudo-triplet sisters consisting of one natural child and two adoptees, the largest age difference between any pair being six and one-half months. This was an exciting find because pairing "A" with "B," "B" with "C," and "A" with "C" yielded three new pairs, quadrupling my sample of one.[1]

Several more encounters with unrelated pairs convinced me that a large scale study of same-age unrelated siblings was feasible. In 1991 I received a call from Megan Doyle a mother with questions about the behavioral development of adopted children. When she casually mentioned that her two sons, Devin and Nathan, whom she had raised as infants, were only three months apart I knew that another great case would be added to the list. Devin and Nathan, studied at age six, were both adorable, but very different in appearance. Devin was tall and slim with fair hair that fell straight into his eyes, while Nathan was smaller and more compact with a smile that made you melt. The next two cases, identified one year later, were packaged as a tripletlike assortment of teenage male fraternal twins and an adopted brother. I was pleased by the prospect of unrelated pairs who were past childhood. This was because studies of adopted children were producing increasing evidence that shared environmental influences associated with modest IQ similarity in childhood essentially evaporated by adolescence, at which time adoptive siblings were no more alike than children raised in different families. This does not mean that smart children grow smarter, or that less intelligent children grow less intelligent—it means that children thrive differently or to different degrees in their environments partly due to genetic differences between them. This effect might be even more dramatically demonstrated if enough teenage and adult pseudo-twins were assembled because of their same age.

Launching a formal study of pseudo-twins was invigorating because it was a novel, and I believed better, approach to questions concerning intellectual and social development whose answers have crucial consequences for parenting and educating children. It was also satisfying to bring these hidden sibships into the investigatory limelight, confirming the value of their research status which had been suspected by many parents all along. In the midst of these events, I was struck by the headline of a December 1991 *New York Times* article: " 'Are the Babies Twins?' 'Well, No. Not Really,' " which debated promises and pitfalls of adopting near-in-age children, but overlooked the research significance of these special couples.[2] Still, the article offered assurance that a reasonable number of pseudo-twins could be identified for scientific study.

Twin researchers know that an effective way to find new twin pairs is to seek referrals from twins and parents of twins who have already participated in research. It seemed reasonable that parents of twins would know parents with pseudo-twins because both families face the special task of raising two same-age children, a situation marked by unique pleasures and pains compared with raising nontwin siblings. Notices about the study appeared in *Twins* magazine and in adoption society publications, such as *People to People* and *Adoptalk*—while most pseudo-twin mothers did not subscribe to *Twins* they learned of the study through mothers who did. Lecturing at mothers of twins clubs also identified pairs known to the membership and, not surprisingly, several parents with same-age unrelated children belong to such associations. I have identified over one hundred pairs from across the United States and around the world, ranging in age from four to fifty. Correspondence from parents has sharpened my thinking about shared environmental influence on behavioral development:

> A mother raising an adopted son and a birth son, born four months apart, delighted in their similarities and differences. Her boys thought they were twin brothers because everyone treated them as twins and strangers mistook them for twins.

> A parent raising one birth daughter and one adopted daughter was fascinated watching their personalities unfold. She often caught herself wondering how different her adopted child would have been if she had lived with her birth family.

> A family with two adopted boys, aged thirteen and sixteen months, was astonished at how different the children were and from what an early age they became complete personalities. The mother suggested that something inherent in the boys' relationship forced them to forge unique behavioral styles, ensuring each one a special place in the family.

It was important that a study of unrelated same-age children examine siblings' similarity in intelligence, personality, interests and problem behaviors.

Karen and Bryan Hochhalter provided me with three same-age unrelated sibling pairs. After arranging to adopt Anna (second from left), Karen learned she was carrying fraternal triplets Andrew (far left), Benjamin and Alyssa. She delivered them just five and a half months after Anna came home. PHOTO COURTESY OF KAREN HOCHHALTER.

All of these behaviors have been studied in the twin and adoption literature, thus providing valuable groups for comparing similarity among different kinship pairs. In other words, I could test the hypothesis that behavioral similarity would be lower between pseudo-twins than between twins and siblings who share genes. I could also determine if unrelated children of similar age were more alike than unrelated children of different age, something that would tell a great deal about how shared environments work. It was also necessary to obtain family background measures, such as age at adoption, number of previous living situations, and parenting practices to see if they were associated with siblings' similarities and differences.

Reading through parents' letters, I was struck by the comment: "We have two 12-year-old sons, both adopted at birth, who are nine weeks apart in age. . . . We sometimes refer to them as 'judicial twins.' " I believe that "judicial twins" captures the idea of twinship generated by legal procedure associated with adopting children. This phrase also embodies the broader concept that the "twinship" emerged fortuitously as a by-product of practices used to identify children and bring them home. Rearing unrelated same-age children is *usually,* but not always, unintentional as I will explain, but it generates unusual twinlike relationships that are valuable in psychological investigation.

The next task was to choose a scientific label for these sets, one that would mesh well with the labels of other informative kinships discussed in the literature. Parents had a colorful collection of titles for their children including "environmental twins," "developmental twins," "synthetic twins," "almost twins," "artificial twins" and "virtual twins," in addition to "judicial twins" and "step-twins." I originally chose SURP, which stands for Same-Age Unrelated Partners; but colleagues persuaded me that UST-SA (Unrelated Siblings Reared Together of the Same Age) was more compatible with acronyms used in twin and adoption studies, for example MZA (monozygotic, or identical twins reared apart), DZT (dizygotic, or fraternal twins reared together), UST (unrelated siblings reared together) and so forth. I decided that UST-SA was a refined version of the more common UST, and have since used it in published papers and conference presentations.

The key goal of the study is to provide another estimate of shared environmental influence on behavioral similarity that is not available in the behavioral genetic literature. A second aim is to compare resemblance among UST-SAs, identical twins, fraternal twins and full siblings. If UST-SAs are much less alike than identical and fraternal twins and siblings this would disconfirm a "purely environmental" explanation of individual differences, but would confirm explanations that refer to genetic factors.

• *Participants*. UST-SAs are created by two adoptive children, or one birth child and one adoptive child. Nobody would discount the rewards of being a parent, but many people are absolutely amazed that some couples adopt two children simultaneously, or adopt a child shortly before or after delivering a child of their own. The emotional and financial difficulties of rearing twins are well known. There are, however, a surprising number of reasons why some families end up with UST-SAs. Infertile couples, weary of the troublesome adoption process, may adopt two children to avoid further aggravation and expense. Older mothers with single children, knowing the uncertain chances for another pregnancy, may favor adopting a second child. I also heard from a mother of three who adopted a child soon after the birth of her youngest son just because she always wanted twins. Couples experiencing difficulties conceiving, or who have children already, may adopt a child only to discover a surprise pregnancy shortly thereafter. Actress Kate Capshaw and her celebrity filmmaker husband, Steven Spielberg, adopted a baby girl, Mikaela, shortly before learning that another little girl, Destry, was on the way, to be born just eight months later.

I spoke with Kate Capshaw by telephone in October 1997 when Mikaela was one and one-half and Destry was ten months old. I was enchanted with her characterization of the little girls and impressed with her appraisal of what raising near-in-age siblings means. "Double delicious, a double ball of ice cream, an absolute delight" is how she described watching her two children grow up together. "They coexist so sweetly," she told me, recalling that one night Mikaela approached her sister, patted her on the shoulder and said,

" 'No, Des, pees' " ['No, Destry, please'], telling her that 'I want Mommy's attention now.' " Kate is awed by their politeness and generosity toward one another, remembering that her five older children who range in age from five to twenty-one were more likely to push and shove their siblings when they wanted attention.

Mikaela was only eight weeks old when Kate learned she was pregnant with Destry. Her first reaction was shock—Kate and Steven silently acknowledged this surprising event, fearing that if they talked they might choose the wrong words. But then they celebrated and laughed because they appreciated that despite being successful adults with control over their lives, things that you simply cannot control happen unexpectedly. Their situation was not unique among families in my study, and when Kate's doctor said "join the club" he disclosed that adoption and conception co-occur more often than we know. Everyone knows infertile couples who "magically" conceive soon after adopting, but there is no causal link between these events. Dr. Bryan R. Hecht, Director of the Division of Reproductive Endocrinology at Canton Ohio's Aultman Hospital, explains that most couples with conception difficulties are not infertile but *subfertile,* so they have a low but definite probability of treatment-independent pregnancy.

Kate elaborated on three thoughts that followed news of her unplanned pregnancy. Her primary reaction was guilty concern for her newly adopted daughter Mikaela, who would miss her full share of individual parental attention. Her second worry was over how she would nurse, diaper and console two babies at the same time. She realized, however, that mothers of twins do this, and that she and her daughters would replay these essential twinship features. This insight led her to her final thought, namely that if she had ever conceived twins she would *not* have felt guilty—so she rejoiced instead. The distinction she hinted at is that guilt does not come from *having* twins or near-in-age siblings; guilt comes from concern over dividing attention fairly between two children.

Does she think of her girls as twins? Kate told me that Mikaela and Destry's appearances and personalities are so different that they rarely remind her of twins. Mikaela is "cappuccino" and Destry is "powdered sugar," is how she conveyed the dramatic contrasts in their coloring. Mikaela is an observer, while Destry is a doer, evidence of their separately emerging dispositions despite their common rearing. However, she agreed that the practical aspects of her children's care are probably similar to those of twins. She likened her kitchen/changing table to an airport launching pad because while she attends to one child the other "circles over" in a characteristic "holding pattern." These amusing episodes also highlight a potentially problematic twinship feature posed by the extra energies involved in caring for two, namely not calling each child by name. Kate admitted that Mikaela and Destry become "this one" and "that one" when things get frenzied, but they both know who they are. Her advice to parents raising or thinking about raising two near-in-age children: Keep a sense of humor, and when they are both crying remember there are times when they are both giggling too.

It was vital to the goals of the study to follow carefully developed rules that would honor the essential ingredients of the twin situation and provide the best quality information possible:

- Both unrelated siblings must have been reared together before one year of age. Mutual entry into the family in infancy is a hallmark of twinship so it was necessary for unrelated siblings to be adopted close in time and early in life. Most twins are brought home by one week of age, although it is not uncommon for some twins to remain in the hospital for several weeks due to birth complications. Arrival in the family by age one was a reasonable compromise, enabling recruitment of a large sample by the first half of infancy.
- The minimum acceptable age at testing was four years. Most four-year-old children attend a preschool or other day care program and would be comfortable in an unfamiliar test situation. Standard tests of general intelligence are available for children of this age, and early testing would allow opportunities to track sibling similarity during development.
- The maximum acceptable age difference was nine months. Nine months is the maximum age difference between classmates who experience educational and social experiences in the same coordinated manner as twins. This situation influenced my decision to include pairs differing in age by nine months or less.
- School-age siblings must have been enrolled in the same grade at the time of testing, but may have attended separate classrooms or separate schools. Twins usually attend the same school grade so it was important that UST-SAs did so, especially because years of schooling may affect IQ scores of near-in-age children.[3] I did accept siblings attending separate classes and schools, given trends toward different classrooms for twins, especially after second grade, and because a minority of twins attend different schools. Same-grade pairs were required to obtain a sample replicating the typical twin situation.
- Pairs in which one or both partners experienced birth difficulties that may have affected intellectual development were excluded. Birth and health histories were reviewed with parents to rule out behavioral differences due to early trauma or neurological deficits. Information on pregnancies and early life events was occasionally missing for adoptees, so decisions were based on current health and functioning. My decision to eliminate pairs with remarkable birth histories was explained by the goals of the study. I wanted to understand if, and how, shared environments are associated with behavioral resemblance, and birth trauma can

introduce important differences between children over and beyond their genetic differences.

- Opposite-sex siblings have been accepted. Approximately one-third of Caucasian twins are opposite-sex so there is reason to include unrelated males and females linked by common age and adoption. Studies of sex-related behavioral differences that might use such pairs are described in Chapter 3.
- Siblings who differ in ethnic background have been included. I recruit UST-SAs differing in ethnicity because some ordinary fraternal twins display striking differences in physical appearance associated with parental differences in ethnic or racial background. Further discussion of these remarkable pairs appears in Chapter 3.

Not all families with near-in-age unrelated children fit the study criteria, and writing "letters of rejection" to enthusiastic parents is always difficult. I have received many communications from parents who are delighted to share observations and insights on their twinlike "experiments." I have also been privy to some incredible new sibships likely to launch future research projects on parenting, sibling relations, self-concept and behavioral growth. An intriguing UST-SA pair was created by a couple whose adopted son was joined by a brother conceived eleven weeks later from a donor's egg and father's sperm. A second family was raising a natural child and his first cousin born only three weeks apart, and a third family was raising two first cousins born three months apart, creating what one child called "almost-twins" who share 12% of their genes on average. A novel twinlike half-sibship was also invented by adoptive parents raising children born nine days apart who shared their fathers, but not their mothers. With the exception of the adoptee/donor egg-father's sperm siblings, these pairs did *not* qualify for the study because the children shared varying proportions of genes.

These situations seem rare, but like UST-SAs other pairs may be awaiting discovery and unforeseen sibships may be forming as family relationships and reproductive technologies continue to change. In fact, premade embryos are now available to infertile couples so multiple pregnancies created by embryos from different families would yield still another novel UST-SA pair, one that shared their intrauterine environment.[4] Soon after I thought about this possibility I learned that it *had* happened. In 1997, a thirty-seven-year-old Italian mother delivered a healthy boy and girl created from the eggs and sperm of two unrelated couples.[5] The children have been called "non-sibling twins,"[6] but I prefer "same-age unrelated co-siblings" to avoid similarity expectations that the term *twins* conveys. Adding the prefix *co* recognizes the children's shared prenatal environment.

*   *   *

Once families are identified, I send parents of young children and adult siblings a packet of questionnaires to complete. They include a:

- Family Background Form, completed by parents or adult siblings, that requests information on adoption, parents' education and occupation, children's educational histories and other background data.
- Child Behavior Checklist, completed by parents of children 4–16 years of age, that reviews interests, abilities and behavioral problems.[7]
- Adjective Checklist, completed by parents, requesting identification of personality traits descriptive of sons and daughters, or completed by adult siblings who describe themselves.[8]
- Sibling Inventory of Differential Experience (SIDE), completed by children age 12–16 years to identify perceived differences in parental treatment, experiences with siblings, experiences with peers and other features of their social worlds during the last twelve months.[9] It is also completed by adult siblings living apart who answer questions with reference to years growing up together in the same home. A brief modified version of the SIDE is available to parents with young children.[10] This information allows exploration of relationships between siblings' different experiences and behavioral outcomes.
- Sibling Relationship Survey (SRS), completed by adolescent and adult siblings who provide past and present feelings of closeness and familiarity toward one another.

Unrelated siblings complete a standard test of general intelligence administered by separate examiners at the same time. Families are scattered throughout the United States and elsewhere, so it has been a formidable task to find local examiners, and I am grateful to colleagues who have provided assistance in this regard. In a few cases the same individual tested both children, but he or she did so in rapid succession to avoid discussion of test items between siblings. Separate testers are easy to arrange for adult siblings living apart and while choosing a common time is tricky, tests are given as closely together as possible. There have been valuable opportunities to visit some nearby families on several occasions to determine if sibling differences at one age remain stable over time, although limited funding has prevented travel to distant locations.

I have studied over fifty pairs and have scheduled new pairs for testing. The average age difference between pairs is three months, but the closeness in age of some UST-SAs is striking. Members of three pairs were born on the same day, even in the same hospital in one case, and members of four other pairs were born just two or three days apart. Birthdays are joint celebrations for these pairs, while some families plan individual festivities, shared festivities, or both. The average age at entering the family is slightly over one month, but just over half the adoptees arrived by two weeks of age or less. Variability in these characteristics and in others, such as pair type (adopted-adopted or adopted-biological), gender (same-sex or opposite-sex), ethnicity (same or different) and classroom placement (same or different), is welcome because it is possible to see if pairs similar in IQ or personality are more similar in these other ways.

I recently published detailed analyses of IQ scores for the first twenty-one UST-SAs, although a peek at the full sample of over fifty has been irresistible.[11] The findings show fairly close agreement between the smaller and larger groups, but I will note some interesting differences and what I think they might mean.

• The most striking result for this study is that IQ scores of same-age unrelated siblings are much less similar than scores of identical twins, fraternal twins and full siblings. The UST-SA IQ correlation (measure of association between siblings in each pair) was .17, in contrast with correlations of .86 for identical twins, .60 for fraternal twins and .50 for full siblings. Remember that shared environment accounts for all the similarity in UST-SA pairs and in this study it explained only 17% of the individual differences. This tells us that shared environment makes a small contribution to the resemblance of people living together, and that genetic factors and nonshared environmental influences account for the remaining 83% of differences among people. The average IQ difference between UST-SAs was fifteen points, a clear contrast to the six-point difference between identical twins and ten-point difference between fraternal twins. It was slightly higher than the fourteen-point difference between full siblings, and slightly lower than the seventeen-point difference obtained by randomly chosen unrelated individuals.[12]

The correlation between UST-SAs jumped to .29 with the larger sample, suggesting that shared environments explain 29% of individual differences in general intelligence. The increase may be partly due to the fact that 67% of the sibling pairs were under age seven, the time when family environments exert potent effects on children's intellectual development.[13] (Young children comprised 58.5% of the smaller sample of twenty-one pairs.) The 29% value is closer to the 25% reported for different-age adoptees, and is a better estimate than 17% because it is based on many more pairs.[14] The more closely matched age and rearing circumstances of UST-SAs might make them slightly more similar in IQ than ordinary adopted siblings, although new cases will help settle this question.

• Adopted-biological pairs are more alike in IQ than adopted-adopted pairs. The IQ correlation for adopted-biological pairs was .36 and the IQ correlation for adopted-adopted pairs was .03. This is an intriguing finding, supported by some but not all ordinary adoption studies.[15] This result was based on six adopted-biological pairs and fifteen adopted-adopted pairs, but I replicated this difference using the sample of sixteen adopted-biological pairs and forty adopted-adopted pairs. There may be reasons why this pattern emerged.

Couples with biological children sometimes adopt children who resemble them, a process called *selective placement*. This can cause unrelated adoptive and biological siblings in a family to be similar. If high IQ couples adopt children born to high IQ biological parents, this will increase IQ similarity between these adoptive children and any biological children in the family because biological children inherit genetic factors from their parents. Unfortunately, detailed information on the biological families of the adoptive children is missing, so this explanation could not be tested. It is also true that biological parents transmit both genes and environments to children and that the two are closely related. High IQ parents transmit "high IQ" genes to children, as well as provide books and other stimulating resources—but they only provide environments to adoptive children. As such, the environments of adoptive children in the home are correlated with the genetic backgrounds of biological children, possibly making them more alike than adopted-adopted sibling pairs for whom this relationship does not occur.

• IQ score differences between UST-SAs are unrelated to most background measures. IQ score differences between UST-SAs are unrelated to sibling differences in age, gender, ethnicity and classroom placement. In other words, siblings more similar in age are not more alike in IQ than siblings who are less similar. IQ differences are also unaffected by number of years siblings attended the same class at school. An exception is that siblings in different classrooms are less alike in verbal skills than siblings in same classrooms, but it is important to determine to what extent verbal resemblance is a cause or consequence of classroom placement. Siblings showing early differences in language ability may be placed in separate classrooms *because* of this difference, rather than the other way around.

The difference in IQ points was the same between adopted-biological siblings and adopted-adopted siblings, a finding that seems contradictory to the greater similarity (correlation) found for adopted-biological pairs. The answer is that the scores of adopted-biological siblings were more closely matched than those of adopted-adopted siblings. In other words, siblings in each adopted-biological pair scored closer to one another than they did to members of other pairs, while siblings in adopted-adopted pairs scored somewhat less like each other and somewhat more like members of other pairs. Members of adopted-biological pairs might score 100, 105 and 120, 125, while members of adopted-adopted pairs might score 105, 100 and 107, 112—in both cases the average pair difference is five points, but adopted-biological siblings' scores are more closely matched than adopted-adopted siblings' scores. Note that the sibling from the adopted-biological pair scoring 100 scores closer to his or her sibling than to members of the other pair; however, the sibling from the adopted-adopted pair scoring 105 scores closer to a member of another pair (107) than to his or her own sibling. Sibling pairs can show fifty-point IQ differences and still yield higher group correlations if they maintain the same rank-ordering relative to one another.

• A surprising finding from the first twenty-one pairs is that siblings' scores on the nonverbal portion of the IQ test were more similar for older pairs. This trend was unexpected because most studies show that siblings become less alike in intelligence as they grow older. In other words, as children age they begin to follow their own genetic blueprints more closely, and encounter more diverse experiences outside their home. Consequently, shared home environments which may have enhanced early sibling similarity may diminish in effect over time. This process may, however, work differently for some special abilities. Perhaps as children's competencies broaden, families acquire new and interesting objects and facilities (e.g., computers and sports equipment) so that home environments offer increased opportunities for shared practice and imitation of nonverbal skills. Further study of this finding is of interest.

Findings from the Child Behavior Checklist (CBCL) are available for forty pairs.[16] This form obtained parents' reports of a wide range of children's interests and activities, as well as social and emotional competencies and difficulties. Questions concern the nature of hobbies, chores and school subjects, and abilities in these areas, as well as frequency of restlessness, anxiety and fatigue. UST-SAs were much less alike than identical twins on all major scales, but they were only slightly less alike than fraternal twins on all but the Social Problems Scale in which they were more similar. (Correlations of the Social Problems Scale were .64 for identical twins, .24 for fraternal twins and .42 for UST-SAs.[17]) The generally small difference in similarity between unrelated siblings and fraternal twins (who were older) may reflect the greater importance of shared environments in younger children.

Problem behaviors in some adoptees have been associated with features of their biological families, birth circumstances or adoption processes, acting alone or in combination. Dr. P. F. Sullivan found that individuals adopted before age one and studied as adults showed increased frequencies of conduct disorder, antisocial personality, and drug abuse or dependence, relative to individuals raised by both biological parents.[18] Teenage mothers relinquishing children for adoption may lack the impulse control to avoid early sexual activity, transmitting these tendencies to their children. Children's feelings of rejection by their biological families may also contribute to adjustment difficulties. Young adoptees and their families also utilize psychiatric services to a greater degree than nonadoptees and their families, but this may reflect parental overprotectiveness or the greater availability of assistance to financially secure couples who are overrepresented among adoptive parents.[19] In contrast, recent analysis of a national sample showed slightly lower *and* higher levels of emotional and behavioral functioning among adoptees, relative to nonadoptees.[20]

Some problem behaviors, such as attentional difficulties, were more frequent among UST-SAs than among some ordinary twins. The comparison twins were drawn from a Norwegian registry, and while the validity of the CBCL has been demonstrated for that population, unknown sample or rater characteristics might explain the findings. It is worth noting that the frequency of UST-SAs' behavioral problems was below that of other children from both clinical and nonclinical populations. This is primarily because I eliminated pairs in which siblings experienced birth difficulties likely to interfere with intellectual performance or who had diagnosed learning disabilities. Furthermore, most families volunteering for the study had children functioning within the normal range of behavior.

On balance, it seems that Jonathan and Carlton, rather than Bill and his brother Mike, are the winners in the shared environment–shared behavior contest, setting the pattern for what UST-SAs reveal as a group. Findings generally suggest that genetic factors and nonshared environments substantially affect intellectual development, consistent with what twin and other adoption studies have shown. Living with someone does not make you resemble them. Bill and Mike were, however, very much alike, at least according to Bill's self-reflections, so how can his situation be reconciled with the more frequent dissimilarities observed between unrelated same-age sibs?

Bill and Mike were brought together by remarriage, not by adoption, so Bill's mother and Mike's father may have mated assortatively, or nonrandomly, for intelligence, educational background and other traits. They may have transmitted these genetically based traits to their respective sons who, in turn, ended up being similar in school performance, work habits and career paths. This family is unusual because none of the UST-SAs in the study were products of "blended" families, famous for exotic combinations of "yours, mine and ours." Bill and Mike also warn against generalizing single case findings to larger groups.

The charge that identical twins are similar in behavior because they are treated alike is weakened by the findings. UST-SAs are raised in the same close quarters as identical and fraternal twins, much more so than full siblings, yet their IQ similarity is far less. Shared environments may play a larger role in some problem behaviors than in intelligence, especially in younger children, but genes have an effect. However, we should never forget that home environments and the parents who maintain them matter a great deal, because all children require warm, supportive families in order to nurture their interests and talents. A common thread running through mothers' and fathers' letters and telephone calls was deep interest in the progress of their children, fascination for what the pair might reveal about human developmental processes, and great enthusiasm for being a parent.

Many parents in this study were in their mid-forties, somewhat older than most parents of young children, and the majority were well-educated. Furthermore, as was true for findings from the Minnesota Study, results from this project apply only to the middle-class families represented, not to families whose children are deprived or impoverished.

I have not yet examined the psychological and emotional benefits and liabilities of membership in a same-age unrelated sibship from the siblings' points of view, but I expect to have some answers once the majority are old enough to speak for themselves. This information can address evolutionarily based predictions that cooperation should be greater between close genetic relatives than between more distant genetic relatives or unrelated individuals. Identical and fraternal twins reared apart dramatically demonstrate that feelings of closeness and familiarity may be linked to genetic relatedness, even in the absence of a shared social history. UST-SAs offer an alternative take on the same question, namely the extent to which common rearing leads to attraction and affiliation. Findings from the Minnesota study suggest that adolescent and adult UST-SAs will experience lower social closeness and familiarity than identical and fraternal twins, on average, but I expect variability. Glancing quickly at the few completed social relationship surveys revealed social closeness and social distance. A woman delighting in her sibship happily repeated both names several times in reverse order: Patsy and Faye, Faye and Patsy, Patsy and Faye, while two brothers agreed that they were generally uninvolved. These individual cases are fascinating, but more are needed to develop the bigger picture.

Parents of young children seem presently focused on the upside of things, especially the care and concern siblings show for one another, despite their differing personalities and temperaments. Not all parents report harmonious relations, but the battles and storms seem typical of those waged by any pair of twins and siblings from time to time. Parents' most trying ordeal really involves explaining their children's relationship to others, especially maintaining composure at the classic shopping mall query: "Are they twins?"

I was disappointed by the dim view of simultaneous same-age adoptions expressed by some counselors in the *New York Times* article and in a 1997 article, "Artificial Twinning," published in *Adoptive Families*.[21] One individual suggested that "artificial twinning" deprives a child of a special place in the family, and another worried that accommodating the different needs of same-age unrelated children may be problematic. Adoptive parents were accused of seeking same-age children to serve their own needs, such as avoiding adoption process grievances or hoping for an instant family, while neglecting the best interests of children. I appreciate the concerns, but disagree that twinning, whether genuine or situational, denies a child a special place in the family. Even identical twins, who generally look and behave very much the same, are individuals in their own right and are appreciated as such by family members. Many families with twins find that pair members assume contrasting roles, so twins are distinguishable both within their relationship and within the family structure. I also take exception to the idea that parents cannot respond effectively to the individual needs of each child. Parents with awareness and respect for individual differences are well poised to offer each child the right amounts of encouragement and assistance. Finally, I do not see a necessary connection between parental attempts to ease strains of adoption and neglect of children's needs.

Reasoning from unsystematic observations may alarm families raising same-age unrelated children and mislead families anticipating raising such children. Data from my study, although based on a small sample, does not support concerns voiced thus far. UST-SAs' IQ scores were above average and behavior problem scores were below those of children in clinical and nonclinical samples. I suggest that judgments concerning advisability of rearing same-age unrelated siblings be delayed until children's intellectual, social and emotional functioning are carefully examined.

Parents' references to their same-age unrelated children as "pseudo-twins" or as "almost twins" was done with good humor and a grin. They did not entertain expectations of similarity or demands for compatibility, which would have been inappropriate and even unfair. Instead, they seemed charmed by the delightful little laboratory in the next bedroom, and by what their children could teach them about each other and about themselves. However, like parents of twins, these parents were also pleased that their children were rarely lonely, growing up side by side with a constant close companion. Twin and twinlike relationships are valued and admired by nearly everyone, most of all by those lucky enough to have them. The flip side is that a great price is paid when the relationship is lost, a difficult topic to which we now turn.

Lonesome Crowd:
Loss of a Twin

In 1985, I lost then and forever my idea of my own immortality. There was this form that looked so much like me, that moved like me, had mannerisms like me. It was a tremendous impression that burned into my brain forever, I'll never forget it.—Jim Wilson, six years after the death of his identical twin brother, Bill (*A Closer Look,* NBC, March 21, 1991)

I first met Jim on Labor Day, 1987, at the annual International Twins Association Convention in Oklahoma City, but I already knew him well. In the weeks preceding this meeting of multiples we had spoken many times by telephone about the death of his twin. Jim learned that I would be addressing a special session at the convention, a gathering of "twinless twins" whose individual tragedies brought them a depth of grief that only other twins could comprehend. We agreed to continue exploring the shock, the isolation, the nightmares and the memories that are the legacy of surviving twins. Jim turned emotions into revelations, conveying profound loss for a much beloved brother ("Bill and I had a closeness like no other I will ever experience again"), but also celebrated years of shared pleasure and fun. I was one of very few people who knew that his exquisite pain was heightened by self-imposed silence about the true circumstances behind his brother's death.

Jim's twin brother Bill had died of AIDS, but to the world outside Cabrini Hospital in New York City his death was caused by hepatitis. In 1985 deaths due to AIDS were discussed reluctantly, so Jim had kept the truth hidden—public knowledge of this fact might have struck an unsympathetic chord. However, social stigmas surrounding AIDS deaths had relaxed over the years, allowing Jim to express himself honestly, knowing his loss would be treated with the dignity it deserved.

The exceptional interest in twins' lives is matched by a remarkable silence

Identical twins Bill (left) and Jim Wilson at age three and a half. PHOTO COUR-
TESY OF JIM WILSON.

surrounding their deaths. I suspect that the loss of a twin arouses the dread and
disbelief that it does because twins enter the world in tandem, and we believe
that somehow they should exit in the same way. Grief counselors and clinical
psychologists have also been curiously quiet concerning twin loss, focusing
upon the more common losses of parents, children, spouses and friends. Consequently, bereaved twins have sought each other out, establishing support groups
such as Twinless Twins International in the United States, Lonesome Dove in
Australia and Lone Twin Network in Great Britain. Many bereaved twins remain
a lonesome crowd, requiring professional attention and information.

My interest in twin loss grew naturally out of research on twin relations,
sparked by psychiatrist George Engel's 1974 Helen Ross Lecture, *Mourning
and Anniversary Reactions to the Death of a Twin,* presented to the Institute
for Psychoanalysis in Chicago.[1] Engel's presentation was a moving interpretation of his blissful years spent with his identical twin brother Frank, his
struggle to balance unification and individuation, his anguish at Frank's untimely death at age fifty-eight from a heart attack, and his resulting preoccupation with birth and death anniversaries.

George and Frank were constant childhood companions, and in Engel's
words "went to extraordinary lengths to regulate and control expression of
physical aggression toward each other." They attended the same college,
medical school and internship, first separating at age twenty-seven to pursue
different specialties. They stayed in touch despite raising families in separate

cities, and when meeting they relished the confused stares from onlookers that only identical twinship can bring. Engel admitted that his lecture was a symbolic attempt to recreate his missing twin relationship. The best speeches are rarely read because speakers envelop them in a love and intimacy that comes from the heart. Engel's performance was exceptional because his audience sat hushed and captivated as he recited his twenty-seven-page text. I wrote to tell him how much I appreciated his presentation, and he replied, "You know why it is meaningful to me to have responses. . . ."

I thought a great deal about Engel's talk, but found little scientific literature on loss of a twin. I discovered a 1954 study asking high school twins to name family members who would be missed most in the event of death.[2] Mothers were selected most often, with twins a close second, and fathers third. Twin siblings were named by 49% of identical twins, by 25% of same-sex fraternal twins and by 13% of opposite-sex fraternal twins. This pattern mirrored the psychological literature on twin relationships showing greater social closeness between identical twins than between fraternal twins. However, this study was not satisfying because the twins' responses were to *hypothetical,* not *actual,* loss and because the procedures used to classify twins as identical or fraternal were not described.

The Minnesota Center for Twin and Adoption Research gave me my first encounters with twinless twins. In 1983, I recalled Engel's moving speech while reading twins' lonely letters and answering their sad telephone calls. I spent time with a bereaved identical twin whose sister had died in a train-car collision. That session painted a picture of unusual events following loss of a twin: becoming a living reminder of the deceased, experiencing the confusion of others, dreading the approach of solitary birthdays, facing decisions alone, and questioning one's status as a twin. I was again convinced that little was known about the nature and management of twin bereavement, and felt ready to launch a study that would provide some answers.

A study of twin loss promised a rich yield of scientific insight, not just for helping bereaved twins and their families, but for understanding whom we mourn and why. Knowing that identical twins generally share closer social bonds than fraternal twins, I suspected this pattern would be reflected in their greater average grief following *real loss,* not just *hypothetical loss* as in the 1954 study—after all, love and sorrow are close cousins. I also wondered how losing a twin compared emotionally with losing parents, grandparents, nontwin siblings, children and spouses. Most bereavement studies recognized death of a spouse or child as the most devastating loss, but twin loss might reorder this ranking. Research also showed that death of a parent (in adulthood) was less traumatic than death of a spouse or child, but identical twins' close bond might lessen the significance of these other losses. I never anticipated that the project would attract over 500 participants, or that the findings would be used in legal battles over twins' wrongful deaths.

A Twin Loss Survey composed with Dr. Bouchard, includes questions on the twin relationship, time shared with the twin, age at loss, circumstances surrounding the twin's death, responses to the loss of the twin and responses to the loss of other relatives and acquaintances. Three forms embedded within the survey include the Grief Intensity Scale (GIS),[3] the Grief Experience Inventory (GEI)[4] and the Coping Scale (CS).[5] Items from a standard physical resemblance questionnaire assign twins as identical or fraternal, sometimes with help from photographs.

Why we grieve is a simple, but profound puzzle concerning the origins of human emotions. Grief brings physical and emotional stress, causing some researchers to question its benefits for human survival. Some believe grief does *not* have adaptive consequences, and is a "by-product" of investing in close relationships that enhance evolutionary fitness.[6] That is to say, the misery of grief may be simply the "price paid" for the advantages of warm, soothing relationships. Similarly, male jealousy following partner infidelity brings anger and humiliation, which are clearly debilitating.[7] It could conceivably be argued that these emotions also serve no positive functions. In contrast, researchers such as Randy Nesse have brought new meaning to emotions by suggesting they serve many purposes.[8] He proposes that grief may "induce low mood, which communicates the need for aid and submissive social withdrawal, and motivates conserving resources and considering other possible strategies or goals." Therefore, there may be future beneficial features to "negative" emotions such as sadness and woe. For example, some bereaved individuals use traumatic experiences to raise awareness of events causing loss of loved ones, such as drunk driving or casual sex. These efforts may transform maladaptive tendencies (such as depression) into positive behaviors which preserve memory of the deceased. In fact, some bereaved twins report that their emptiness and pain have prompted personal growth and development when facing new situations alone. In the case of jealous males, sexual jealousy may motivate steps to eliminate rivals or to keep partners close by.

Evolutionary perspectives have recast the role of emotions in human behavior by suggesting meaningful ends to our stressful states. At the same time, evolutionary perspectives help us realize why eternal bliss is neither possible nor desirable. Jerome Barkow, Professor of Social Anthropology at Dalhousie University in Halifax, Canada, has argued that constant happiness would produce maladaptive and inappropriate behaviors by interfering with our assessment of situations.[9] He suggests that perpetually happy people might not distinguish between friends and acquaintances, or between safe and hazardous situations. Evolutionary psychology has also encouraged us to rethink why we love someone more than someone else, and why we uniquely mourn that person's loss.

I often refer to David Barash's words that in parental bereavement we hear "the wail of frustrated genes."[10] In an evolutionary sense Barash meant that death of a child blocks transmission of one's genes into future generations. However, loss of reproductive potential is *not* what makes parents sad; it is loss of a beloved child that makes parents sad. Uniting evolutionary processes (loss of fitness via survival and reproduction by children) and immediate events (death of a son or daughter) for understanding bereavement is speculative. However, Barash suggests that parental love insures parental care, allowing children to reach sexual maturity and transmit genes. In other words, loving and caring for close relatives feels good, and may be an immediate psychological reason why close relationships are maintained and missed. We do not think about why certain relationships feel good, but perhaps they provide emotional and material benefits, furthering the ultimate function of replicating one's genes.

As I explained in Chapter 6, children of one identical twin are the "genetic" children of the other identical twin. Therefore, caring for identical twins and for their children is a good genetic investment because it is a means for preserving one's own genes in the future. This relationship does not equally apply to fraternal twins who are more closely related to their own children than to their twin's children. (Fraternal twins share exactly half their genes with children, and share one-fourth of their genes, on average, with their twin's children who are their nieces and nephews.) Again, the fact of shared genes is less significant or interesting than the way in which shared genes affect the perceptions and emotions underlying our behaviors. Perhaps studies showing increased closeness between identical twins as opposed to fraternal twins tell us that identical twinship "feels better" than fraternal twinship. Conversely, do these studies imply that loss of an identical twin "feels worse" than loss of a fraternal twin? If love and sorrow are close cousins, then bereaved identical twins should generally grieve more intensely than bereaved fraternal twins, and bereaved fraternal twins should generally grieve more intensely than bereaved half-siblings and cousins. Bereaved fraternal twins might grieve more than bereaved siblings because their age similarity makes sharing experiences more likely; however, their genetic relatedness is the same. The first task was to identify enough bereaved twins to find out.

Bereaved twins have surfaced among my students, colleagues and acquaintances. Sometimes I have known these people a while before discovering they are twinless twins, news that forever changes the way I think about them and their lives. Just as seeing identical twins challenges our beliefs about the uniqueness of behavior and physique, news of lost twinship makes us wonder how there could have been two, and what catastrophic event could possibly have severed the tie. Perhaps death of a twin stirs emotions similar to those following death of someone we consider part of a perfect couple.

Once accustomed to a person as a singleton, knowledge of their twinship unleashes a flood of "what if" questions. Ed Stearns, my former colleague in the Psychology Department at California State University, is a skilled statistician and runner. When I learned that his twin was miscarried in the first trimester, I wondered if they would have been friends or shared talents had the twin survived. I also wondered if Stearns regretted not knowing. He told me he thinks about his twin from time to time, sad that he never knew this "someone" he was meant to know. Stearns, now sixty-six, is a husband, father, grandfather, scholar and athlete, yet twinship remains "part of my background, part of my world—if asked to list important things about my life I'd bring this [being a twin] up." At the same time he is perplexed by these feelings because his lost twin was not part of his conscious experience. It was a revelation to me that early twin loss can be a potent shaper of thoughts and preoccupations.

No one has systematically studied the psychological effects on children of losing a twin before birth or in infancy, but some older twinless twins express sadness or anger over this event, and some introduce themselves as twins. However, links between early twin loss and psychological disturbances, while conceivable in some cases, have *not* been established. A recent biography claims that Elvis Presley's early loss of his twin brother Jesse explains his survivor guilt and drive toward individuality.[11] This is a tantalizing take on Presley's life, but separating truths from guesses is impossible until researchers track emotional adjustment of singleton twins from infancy onward.

Some reared apart twins in the Minnesota study were told that their twins had died at birth. Some adoptive parents of reared apart twins were falsely informed of cotwins' deaths; other adoptive parents fabricated this explanation, perhaps to prevent twins from searching for their twin siblings. It seems, however, that none of these twins showed unusual or abnormal adult behaviors associated with this loss. It is virtually certain that, unlike biological parents, adoptive parents of reared apart twins did not grieve for their children's deceased twins—after all, adoptive parents lacked biological and psychological connectedness to these children. Therefore, it is conceivable that adoptive parents' lack of mourning reduced sadness in their adopted twin children. Conversely, more severe response to twin loss is possible among nonadopted twinless twins whose mothers and fathers' grieving may reinforce their sense of loss.

Some separated twins did *not* believe their cotwins had died. Despite what she had been told, Iris Johns was sufficiently optimistic to believe that her twin brother, Aro Campbell, was alive, finally finding him through a missing persons television broadcast at age seventy-seven. Tony Milasi had also been told his twin had died, but he still asked and dreamed about him.[12] He never tried finding his brother, Roger Brooks, but their incredible reunion at age twenty-four occurred after Roger was mistaken for Tony at a Coral Gables, Florida, Pancake House. Factors motivating some separated twins to ignore news of their cotwins' deaths are unknown, but they may be tied to these twins' hopeful outlooks or to uncertainties surrounding their births.

Some twins lost their cotwin after both participated in my studies so their stories are deeply personal to me. April 1991 brought a letter from Mary Ellis of Chicago, lamenting the loss of her fifteen-year-old identical twin daughter, Kelli Ann, from bone cancer. I remembered her twins well—Kelli Ann and Maria were the only pair for whom my twin type judgment (fraternal), based on their appearance, did not match their blood typing results (identical). Mrs. Ellis wrote that, "it was and still is very hard for Maria to accept what happened to Kelli Ann . . . they were *oh* so close."

After a brief reunion, several reared apart twins also experienced the loss of their cotwins. Their moving comments hinted at interesting associations between relatedness and grief because they knew each other so briefly. Identical twins Margaret Plucknett and Lily Pitwon were separated at six weeks of age, meeting for the first time at age sixty-five. When Lily died suddenly from pulmonary failure, Margaret felt deeply saddened. During our conversation one month after the death she recalled their "four lovely years together," and her happy memories of visiting Minnesota. Interestingly, she had worried that attending her sister's funeral would be awkward because they looked and behaved so similarly.

Fraternal twin Debbie S. lost her twin brother, Charlie W., at age fifty-nine after meeting him for the first time at age fifty-four. Charlie had been hospitalized, but despite signs of recovery he died suddenly. Debbie wrote to say, "I miss him and his phone calls. Life seems so unfair at times—to find him after 54 years . . ." Identical twin Ethel Gaherty was separated from her twin at a young age, after which the twins met only briefly as children and adolescents. Her twin sister, Helen, died when they were sixty-six. "I still go to call her about anything new, exciting, or funny and then remember she is dead and I feel unfulfilled."

One reared apart twin was not deeply affected by losing his twin sister, even though they got along well. "It would take time to develop a close feeling and we did not have that time." This exceptional case underlines bereavement experiences' complexity, but I believe that the real story is told by the majority of grieving pairs. The warm feelings shared by most reunited identical and fraternal twins were matched by extreme anguish among most survivors. These observations are compelling because the twins grew up apart, suggesting that biological connectedness matters.

I also heard from reared together twins who were less affected than others when their cotwin died. One identical twin was relieved when his brother was out of pain, although he had grieved during his twin's illness. Some twins discordant for major physical conditions since birth do not (or cannot) form close relationships, due to communicative or other difficulties, so they are less affected (or are uniquely affected) by loss. A young fraternal female twin lacked opportunities to bond with her mentally impaired sister, so she accepted her twin's death with minimal difficulty. An identical twin whose sister showed Turner Syndrome (diagnosed by a missing X chromosome), grieved for her deceased twin, but felt more like her twin's mother or older sister. At the same time, some twins with handicapped cotwins enjoy close, protective relationships. I recall a letter from an identical twin describing her wonderful relationship with her sister, who was blind. Studying twins discordant for various handicaps would identify behavioral and physical differences disrupting close relations between some identical pairs.[13]

Bereaved twins are a hidden crowd because they no longer come packaged as pairs. However, many twins belong to twin loss support groups which provided half my participants. I located the other half through personal referrals, colleagues, attorneys, members of the media, and other bereaved twins. My results are based upon individuals who lost twins at age fifteen years or later, because they shared childhood years and could recall the loss experience. Even as the sample increased over the years findings remained the same: Identical twins had higher initial grief intensity ratings than fraternal twins. Identical twins also had significantly higher scores on four of eight GEI bereavement scales (Despair, Guilt, Rumination, and Depersonalization) and slightly higher scores on most remaining scales.[14]

In short, identical-fraternal twin differences in bereavement captured the spirit of what we know about twin relationships. Finding consistent results from the different forms included in the larger survey was essential for making sense of twin loss. Interestingly, though identical-fraternal twin differences were statistically meaningful, they were smaller than I had expected. I believe this is so because bereaved twin volunteers do not faithfully represent the full population of bereaved twins. Fraternal twins are born twice as frequently as identical twins, but provided only 35% of the sample. Therefore, those fraternal twins who did participate were probably an especially saddened group of bereaved fraternals. Had I been able to cast my research net more widely, I may have identified fraternal twins who were coping more effectively with their loss, widening the statistical gap.

In evolutionary terms, the interesting twist to twin loss is that identical twins are more closely related to each other than to their own children—so while child loss is devastating, twin loss might be more traumatic for them. In contrast, fraternal twins are about equally related to their children and to their twin, so child loss and twin loss might be similarly devastating.[15] I am not suggesting that fraternal twins grieve more for their deceased children than identical twins grieve for their deceased children, but that *grief following loss of an identical twin might exceed grief for most, or all, other losses*.

It was not surprising, but still compelling, to find higher initial grief intensity ratings for deceased twins (identical and fraternal combined) than for deceased mothers, fathers, nontwin sisters, nontwin brothers, grandmothers, grandfathers, aunts, uncles and cousins. It is striking how quickly grief intensity diminishes as we move from first-degree relatives (parents and siblings) to second-degree relatives (aunts, uncles, nieces and nephews) and third-degree relatives (cousins). Even more provocative, when only identical twins' ratings were used, the difference between grief for deceased twins and other deceased relatives was somewhat greater. Another exceptional finding was that initial grief intensity ratings for deceased twins *equaled* ratings for deceased spouses, a point I return to later.

I also found that GEI scale scores of recently bereaved twins (identical and fraternal combined) were *higher* than those of recently bereaved children and spouses, and *slightly higher* than those of bereaved parents. These findings underline the magnitude of bereaved twins' grief—even though twins' responses were retrospective (their loss occurred one year, or less, before participating), twins had *higher* GEI scores than comparison group members (their loss occurred three months, or less, before participating). Just as identical twin similarity is not meaningful without reference to fraternal twin similarity, I believe ratings of loss alone are less significant than their ordering across different relationships.

Spouse loss is extremely devastating so lack of difference between grief intensity ratings for deceased spouses and deceased twins flags twinship as an extraordinary relationship. Spouses (except in inbred populations) do not share genes by descent, so how can evolutionary psychology explain widows' and widowers' grief and mourning? Perhaps losing a spouse, especially during child-bearing years, represents loss of an investment in reproductive fitness. Spouse loss may, therefore, be more devastating than parental loss because aging parents no longer augment their children's reproductive fitness.

I could not resist looking at identical-fraternal twin differences in spouse ratings, despite the small sample. The average spouse loss rating by seventeen identical twins was slightly *lower* than the average twin loss rating, while the average spouse loss rating by thirteen fraternal twins was slightly *higher* than the average twin loss rating. Why this may be is enormously interesting to researchers and to families, so I was captivated by thoughts from Judy L., an identical twin. Judy L. did not lose her husband, she lost her identical twin sister, Betty S. at age twenty-two in a car accident. Judy L. was also injured and emerged from six unconscious days to find her twin gone. ("All of a sudden I had to survive alone—there was no more Betty!") In strictest confidence she revealed that love for her twin sister exceeded love for her husband, a sentiment she once communicated to Betty by letter. ("This was a *twin thing* and he did not need to know.") Perhaps having an identical twin revises relationships with family and friends in unique ways. Identical twins may invest emotions more exclusively in their cotwins than in their spouses, compared with fraternal twins whose individual tastes and temperaments may facilitate alliances beyond immediate family. This possibility was tentatively raised by this analysis, but it received support when I looked at how grief changes over time.

The thought that "time heals all wounds" comforts some bereaved individuals, but people cope differently with loss. Teasing out the nature and origin of these differences helps us understand who crosses the rockiest paths and why. Some twins dwelled unhappily on the loss of their cotwins, and I wondered if individual differences might be tied to twin type. After all, if identical twins showed higher initial grief than fraternal twins, they might also show less grief reduction over time.

In collaboration with graduate student Sarah Ream I examined lessening of grief among 173 bereaved twins after controlling age at loss.[16] We found less grief reduction for loss of identical twins than for loss of fraternal twins, and less grief reduction for loss of twins than for loss of mothers, fathers, nontwin brothers, grandmothers, grandfathers, aunts, cousins and friends.[17] (Too few bereaved twins in my sample had lost children, sisters or spouses, or had completed past and current GISs, so these comparisons could not be made. Comparing grief of twins who lost a cotwin with grief of twins who lost a child would tell us about the relative magnitude of these losses. However, I believe twins experiencing loss of their twin *and* loss of their child offer more sensitive measures of differences in the nature and level of grief.) These patterns help us appreciate that we may recover more successfully from some tragedies than others, and why. Parents losing teenage children usually experience profound and persistent grief, while teenage children losing great-uncles may feel more modest and transient sadness. These differences would not be directly tied to genetic relatedness, but more likely to degree of physical and behavioral resemblance, perceptions of resemblance, and social attraction that vary approximately with genetic overlap. The differences may also be explained by the greater sharing of experiences between parents and children than by nieces or nephews and uncles, although genetic relatedness may affect frequency of social contact.

Sarah and I also found that identical twins showed less decrease in grief for cotwins than for mothers and aunts, while fraternal twins showed no differences. Just as identical twins may relate differently to spouses than do fraternal twins, analysis suggested that identical twins relate differently to mothers and aunts than do fraternal twins. It is probably not unusual for most people to feel affinity with relatives both inside and outside their immediate families, as fraternal twins do. Of course, identical twins may also feel close to other friends and relatives, while reserving their strongest ties for one another.

Findings from the twin loss study generally supported more severe bereavement response among identical twins than fraternal twins. Since my study began, work in England by Joan Woodward, founder of Lone Twin Network, has produced similar results.[18] Imbalance in identical twin–fraternal twin research participation has been a concern, but I believe the imbalance itself is a crucial finding. That is to say, greater participation by identical twins may reflect their greater stake in twin relations, relative to fraternal twins. In fact, most twins' memoirs have been written by identical twins, not by fraternal twins—*Two or the Book of Twins and Doubles* by Penny Farmer[19] was inspired by loss of her sister, Judith, and *My Twin and I* by Ethel Jones,[20] was a moving remembrance of her sister, Elsie. At the same time, many fraternals miss their deceased twins very much, so despite theoretically interesting twin group differences in grief, care and treatment of bereaved twins should proceed on a case-by-case basis.

Study participants were mostly identical and female, typical of the excesses of identical twins and female twins in volunteer samples. Nearly *three-fourths* of bereaved twins in the study were female, a striking contrast to the real male-female twin ratio of 1,013 liveborn male twins to 1,000 liveborn female twins.[21] I also noted the scarcity of bereaved males from male-female pairs, who represented only 2% of the bereaved twins.[22] This uneven gender distribution is common in nontwin bereavement research, possibly reflecting females' increased expressivity, emotionality and willingness to seek help. Cultural expectations require males to show strength, not stress, so gender differences in grief expression may partly mask male suffering.

An evolutionary view of sex differences also predicts greater female than male participation in bereavement studies. Throughout human history females have been highly involved with child care, situations engaging them in close interpersonal exchanges with relatives and neighbors.[23] Females are expected to invest more effort in child care than males since they are much more limited in the number of children they can bear, and because they can be certain of who their children are. Recent research has, in fact, uncovered sex differences in behavioral traits that could explain why females would be more attracted to bereavement studies than males. Dr. Kevin MacDonald and his colleagues at California State University, Long Beach, found that females' self-ratings of intimacy and warmth items were higher than males', and that females' ratings of the importance of these traits in friends and in leaders were higher than males'.[24] Females are also better at naming relatives, and are more likely to mention family roles (e.g., daughter or sister) than family names when questioned about their close relationships.[25] If grief following the loss of a twin mirrors twins' affection for one another, then feelings of grief may be more frequent and intense for females than males, propelling females toward research opportunities. Gender differences in cultural expectations surrounding grief may *mirror,* as well as *reinforce,* gender differences in bereavement experiences.

Twin loss research may attract only highly bereaved or highly expressive males, but there may be other answers to the puzzle of missing male twins. In particular, I wondered if skewed male-female participation might also reflect earlier male than female mortality (age at death). I was unable to test this hypothesis because my sample was not drawn from the general population. A population-based Danish study did find fewer male twins (46%) than female twins (54%) among pairs in which both twins survived until age fifteen. Males' greater biological vulnerability lasts from conception to death, a finding explained by increased risk for infection and disease, as well as more strenuous and dangerous life styles. In my study, age at death was somewhat younger for male twins (37.4 years) than for female twins (40.6 years), consistent with this view. However, male twins' earlier deaths may have been less responsible for males' reduced research participation than male survivors' tendencies to withdraw socially following loss.[27]

Adding to what we know about bereavement in opposite-sex twins from grief surveys are extraordinary personal accounts of the depth and continuity of grief. Claudette Lantz lost her twin brother, Claude, in the Oklahoma City bombing of the Alfred P. Murrah federal building on April 19, 1995, at age forty-one years, and Beth Zemsky lost her twin brother, Bob, to AIDS in September 1990 at age thirty-one years.

Claude and Claudette were a close pair, staying in touch even after Claude entered military service 800 miles away. Their early connection was evident when their individual difficulties in separate first grade classes reunited them later in the school term. They were grateful that a sympathetic teacher allowed them to sit together. Over the years they led separate lives—Claude was a senior special agent for United States Customs, and Claudette was a social worker—but they spoke often.

Claudette never considered what twinship meant to her—she only knew she could confide in Claude without fearing rejection or ridicule. When Claude entered the Alfred P. Murrah federal building in Oklahoma City on April 19, 1995, shortly before the 9:03 A.M. bombing, Claudette's life changed forever. She spent the day in denial until federal agents located Claude's car in the underground garage, and questioned his secretary who had seen him in the building. His desk faced a window.

Like many twins, Claudette never imagined that she and Claude would be apart, but she has learned to cope with feeling "totally alone." Hers is a special case because she is immersed in reminders of her lost twin. Aside from birthdays, events responsible for the Oklahoma City bombing and its aftermath remain headline news. In addition, Claude was young and healthy, and died suddenly, factors compounding survivors' grief.

The untimely loss of another male twin, Bob Zemsky, from AIDS also revealed unique psychological consequences for his twin sister, Beth. I met Beth in Richfield, Minnesota, in 1991 when she joined a twin loss support group I was advising. Beth was an attractive, intelligent woman who had thought a great deal about the meaning of twinship and the significance of its loss. Her story was memorable because both she and her twin brother were gay, the only case of similar homosexual opposite-sex twins I encountered personally. I met Beth again in 1997 when she visited me in my office at New York University while I was on sabbatical.

They were "Bobby and Beth," dressed in matching outfits as children to emphasize their twinness. Their last name began with "Z," making them the last two students to receive diplomas at their high school graduation. They at-

Fraternal twins Bob and Beth Zemsky at age seven. Being twins made them feel special from an early age. PHOTO COURTESY OF BETH ZEMSKY.

tended the same college where they shared cars and confidences—each was the first person the other told of his/her sexual preference.

　　Bob contracted the AIDS virus at age twenty-nine, surviving for twenty months until his death at thirty-one. Quality of life was important to him, and decisions surrounding life support were made together with Beth, not with other family members. They were always honest with each other during his illness, acknowledging the quality of life Bob wanted. Very quickly he had to decide about resuscitation—so the twins asked everyone to leave the room and they decided together. After Bob's death, Beth felt dramatically alone for the first time in her life. Even though she and Bob had lived apart for many years, she felt part of a unique relationship ("I was [his] special somebody."). Bob's death ended that special relationship, and it was a while until Beth realized she would never experience the same connection with other partners.

　　For Beth, the anniversary of their birth is a cruel day, harder than the anniversary of her twin's death. Friends have encouraged her to celebrate, and she has agreed so long as they choose a different day ("Otherwise it feels too much like *us*."). Still, she prefers to be alone each June 23. In 1996, Beth joined a Chicago AIDS bike trip scheduled on her birthday. She cried for the first one hundred miles—the ride for AIDS gave her a way to grieve, and a way to celebrate life as Bob would have wanted.

My own research focus has been on how and why genetic relatedness may affect bereavement experiences of twins. Little work has been done on their nontwin siblings' response, but I am collecting this information in a childhood and adolescent twin loss study. Parental response to losing a twin is also poorly understood, but some attention has been paid to this misfortune.

I will never forget a conversation with Wendy L., Judy L.'s mother, several years after losing identical twin daughter Betty in the car accident. She gloried in her girls' twinship, feeling continually awed by their dual presence, so it was shocking to learn how people responded to her loss. Some felt she was "fortunate" that Judy L. was also injured because this would "take her mind off [the loss of] Betty." This was not the first time I heard about callous comments because mothers losing infant twins also recounted insensitive remarks from family, friends and hospital staff. The source of these comments is unknown, but some people may reason that the loss is not total when one twin survives. Unfortunately, parental grief has been overlooked due to misperceptions that surviving twins compensate for loss of their cotwins. Wendy L.'s husband, Allen L., was stunned to hear this thought from a parent whose son had died. However, this conviction crumbles at findings of similar depressive reactions in parents losing a twin infant and parents losing a singleton infant, even though twin parents still had a child.[28] In my experience, most parents anticipate multiple birth with enthusiasm and thrill, once the initial shock subsides. Therefore, it would be surprising if pain and sorrow were relieved by the presence of a surviving twin. I believe Wendy L. had it right when she observed that people are ill equipped to respond appropriately when the deceased is a child *and* part of a pair.

Parental loss of a twin child at any age evokes disappointment and desolation that accompanies loss of a singleton child. However, twin loss brings unique features to the family's bereavement experiences. For example, twinless twin children can be bitter reminders to parents of what could have been, and what will never be. Therefore, I was disturbed to read 1986 newspaper headlines announcing, "Hope After Death: Family Finds Solace Awaiting Twin's Birth."[29] Pat Moller of Los Angeles, California, lost twin son Daniel Allen after his removal from the womb due to bleeding in the twins' shared placenta. The focus of considerable media attention, Pat was hospitalized for the birth of Daniel's twin brother, David, due ten days later. "I break down every ten minutes about my son passing away . . . but I feel extremely blessed and optimistic." Unfortunately, there has been less professional attention to the first part of her statement than to the second part, causing parents to mourn silently and alone.

They are the unseen parents of twins, the mothers and fathers whose multiples were lost during pregnancy or soon after birth. However, they are no longer hidden thanks to Jean Kollantai, founder of the Center for Loss in Multiple Birth (CLIMB), in Anchorage, Alaska. Her publication, *Our Newsletter,* is a poignant compendium of letters, poems and memorials to the twin children that were somehow not meant to be, but who linger in the minds and hearts of their families. A "Bulletin Board" keeps members informed of research and resources prepared by staff, but there is a need for greater attention from twin and infancy researchers. My sense is that to the outside world these special parents are not parents of twins because their twins died so soon. However, *Our Newsletter* is larger than ever, a curious trend given improved management of multiple birth pregnancies. Its growth may reflect new sources of twin loss, such as the Vanishing Twin Syndrome (resorption of a twin fetus by the mother during the first trimester), and the gambles of reproductive technologies (methods for helping childless couples conceive, sometimes requiring elimination of one or more multiple fetuses). Another support group for parents of multiples, Twin Hope, counsels families who lost one or both twins to fetal transfusion syndrome (shared blood circulation between identical twin fetuses). The Multiple Births Foundation in London also runs a bereavement clinic for parents.

Little is known about parents' responses to loss in these varied circumstances, nor about twinless twins' reactions to survival. We do know that parents losing an infant twin experience similar levels of depression as parents losing a nontwin infant. Jill MacNiven, President and Founder of Twin Hope in Cleveland, Ohio, lost her twin sons to fetal transfusion soon after their birth. She has observed that families losing one newborn twin may be affected differently than parents losing both twins. Parents raising single twins are often reminded of the infant they lost, an experience reinforced by the admiring remarks of onlookers concerning the *child,* not the *children.* Parents losing both twins (or all multiple birth babies) struggle with the grief of repeated loss and disappointment.

Some twins surviving the prenatal loss of their cotwins may experience guilt, anger, frustration or sadness later in life. The same is possible for twins losing cotwins in infancy due to illnesses or accidents. Both groups of surviving twins are largely unstudied populations. I worked with one family who lost an eighteen-month-old identical male twin in a household accident that occurred while his twin was present. The surviving twin experienced episodes of crying, screaming and sleeplessness, and his two-and-a-half-year-old brother showed increased irritability, helplessness and nightmares. Until we understand young twins' (and siblings') responses to the early loss of a twin, appropriate interventions will be unavailable.

The significance of early twin loss has been underlined in unexpected ways. A children's puppet show, *Nicky, Somewhere Else,* tells the story of Nicky, who learns of his lost twin Noël from a photograph.[30] The reviewer notes that this profound loss is approached with "humor, creativity, immense charm and touching sensitivity."

Occasionally, I hear from people who believe they were born twins, but who lack medical proof of twinship. Common threads to their stories have been lifelong feelings of depression and emptiness, and a sense that "someone else is out there." I wonder if the incredible joy conveyed by reunited twins who appeared in news articles and on television programs accentuated their cravings for warmth and intimacy. Alessandra Piontelli's and Birgit Arabin's films (discussed in Chapter 2) show that twin fetuses experience physical contact, but there is no evidence that this translates into conscious awareness of twinship after birth. Many reunited twins were unaware of being twins until contacted as adults by their cotwins, and they do not show elevated depression. Some parents of infant twinless twins have wondered whether certain behavioral responses shown by their children, such as excessive need for physical comfort, signal searching for the missing other. I sympathize with their concerns, but advise them that proof of fetal twin awareness is unavailable, and overinterpreting infant behaviors may go against the best interests of the child.

Uniting the stories of bereaved twins is the belief that in death, as in life, they would "go together." No one knows if this assumption is more common among identical or fraternal twins, but research has shown that age at death is more similar for identicals than for fraternals. The headline "Twins Die Together While Dining" drew instant attention because time of death is never certain, even among the seriously ill.[31] Therefore, the world mourned in disbelief when identical Australian twins, William and John Bloomfield, suffered fatal cardiac arrest within moments of each other while dining at a casino restaurant. An ambulance spokesman observed that "they came into the world together and died together," but was this due to anything other than coincidence? At the other end of the life span are startling cases of identical twins' simultaneous deaths from SIDS (Sudden Infant Death Syndrome).[32] Perhaps the more closely matching births and deaths of identical than fraternal twins hold a deeper message, namely that our life spans are partly influenced by genetic factors. Consider this amazing birthday celebration described in the *Albany Times Union,* 1989:

> Clayton and Clarence Loucks stopped dressing alike decades ago, and haven't even lived near each other for half a century. But when the twins got together this week to observe their 93rd birthday and to reminisce, it was hard to believe they have lived 3,000 miles apart. . . . "A twin is someone who has the same memories."

Twin and adoption studies find both genetic and environmental effects on longevity with greater influence from environmental factors. The Danish twin researchers found that age at death differed by 14.7 years for identical twins and 18.5 years for fraternal twins. They estimated that 33% of life span differences were associated with genetic factors, while the other 67% were mostly associated with nonshared environmental influences (events separately experienced by family members) such as accidents or adult nutrition.

Twins' frequency and resemblance for accidents and illnesses were not provided in the Danish study. However, information from the Vietnam Era Twin Registry pairs shows environmental effects on injuries and poisonings.[33] Discharge diagnoses indicated that twins in only ninety-three sets (1.2% of 7,276 pairs) were affected, and that concordance was modest for both identical (33%) and fraternal twins (27%). Breast cancer is a good example of an illness showing environmental influence. Twin studies have shown low rates of concordance for both identical (8–15%) and fraternal twins (6–10%), even though genetic factors are involved.[34] These figures could rise if unaffected cotwins show disease symptoms at later dates. Comparing family histories and lifestyles of concordant and discordant identical pairs would help clarify the causes of this condition. Identical twins living in different climates might also illuminate genetic and environmental factors affecting skin cancer. Dr. Caleb E. Finch of the University of Southern California suggests that lifestyle factors have considerable impact on aging and disease, especially at advanced ages.[35]

Few people reach the age of 100, so we marvel when identical twins harmoniously weather the uncertainties and setbacks of aging. Some investigators have wondered whether twins die sooner than nontwins, and whether identical twins die sooner than fraternal twins, both reasonable thoughts in light of twins' (especially identical twins') precarious beginnings. Mormon genealogical records revealed that male twins from same-sex and opposite-sex pairs died one to two years earlier than the group of nontwin male siblings, although differences were not found for females.[36] However, population-based figures from Denmark showed that after age six, disease and death rates were similar in twins and singletons, and similar in identicals and fraternals, posing no threat to the power of twin designs.[37] The representativeness of older twins was also confirmed by the OCTO-Twin Study of Sweden which found that octogenarian twins and nontwins (individuals eighty and older) did not differ across most behavioral and health-related measures.[38]

We can look within our own families for hypotheses, but not conclusions, concerning our life spans. If biological parents die before age fifty from infections or cardiovascular causes, death rates for their adopted away biological children are five times higher than if the children's adoptive parents died from these conditions.[39] If our nontwin siblings reach 100 years of age then we have a four times greater chance of reaching ninety than if our siblings died in their seventies.[40] However, only twin and adoption studies allow separation of genetic and environmental influences on longevity.

Loss of identical twins understandably brings fear of impending death to their cotwins, especially if causes were genetically influenced (e.g., diseases or other physical conditions). This dread formed the basis of Dr. George

Engel's concern with anniversary dates of his brother's (and father's) heart attacks and deaths. Reared apart identical twin Margaret Plucknett also worried after her sister died suddenly: "It does alter your way of living—[before] it did not seem to worry me." However, both twins and nontwins do not necessarily die soon after their cotwins and other relatives, nor do they necessarily die from similar causes. This is because genetic predispositions to disease require environmental factors to become expressed—Engel apparently avoided events that triggered fatal heart disease in his twin brother, Frank. Nevertheless, bereaved identical twins' worries over their own mortality could compound the tragedy of losing their twins.

I once "created" a partnership between two young women who had lost identical twin sisters from sudden illnesses. Both were stunned to find other twins who felt as strongly as they did about twinship and its loss. I often call upon Jim Wilson to contact newly bereaved twins because he eases them through difficult moments better than anyone.

I talked with Jim Wilson again in December 1997, twelve years after he lost his twin. Time dulled his initial shock and grief, but it sharpened his awareness of what he missed most. For Jim, the immediate mental and emotional connection he shared with his twin brother Bill is irreplaceable. ("They know your elation and they know your sadness, and they know if you are rationalizing a decision. . . . When you no longer have this you miss it terribly.") Even now "when something neat happens" he instinctively reaches for the telephone to call his twin—just like reared apart twin Ethel Gaherty. Jim still regrets the lost opportunity for a joint petroleum business venture the twins had planned just days before Bill's death. "We would have made a dynamite duo—he would have handled finances and I would have handled operations." He also misses their fun.

Jim sometimes questions his own status as a twin, acknowledging that these thoughts change with the context. For example, he might feel out of place in New York City's Twins Restaurant, an eating establishment owned and staffed by identical twins. At the same time, approaching twins is irresistible because of the "instant connection" he believes twins feel for one another. He finds talking to twins demands greater effort now than in the past, but it is his way of regaining familiar feelings.

The lonesome crowd can be especially lonely because most twins have never felt alone. Perhaps it is this unique feature of twinship that distinguishes its loss so dramatically from other losses.

Making Multiples:
New Fertility Treatments
and Beyond

It was February 1996. What began as an ordinary evening with mothers of multiples ended with elaborate dramas and surprise scenes. Several members told fascinating stories about new ways of making multiples that brought them twins and more when all hope failed. A woman unable to maintain pregnancy created embryos from her own eggs and her husband's sperm, using a surrogate mother to bring the babies to term. Another woman carried one embryo, giving the second embryo to a surrogate mother while coordinating joint deliveries. In fact, the first American woman to serve as a surrogate for her daughter (who was born without a uterus) delivered opposite-sex twins (her own grandchildren) in 1991. The embryos were created from her daughter's eggs and her son-in-law's sperm.[1]

I was fascinated by these unusual multiples, but wondered how their atypical origins might alter twin research as we know it. Mothers' different hormonal characteristics might affect children's development in the second family, making them less alike than ordinary twins. Future investigators might need to pay closer attention to twins' conception and gestation, studying artificially conceived pairs apart from naturally conceived pairs.

Spectacular finales to infertility treatment feature healthy babies, but infertile couples' paths to parenthood are uncertain, with only 24% of attempts resulting in pregnancy.[2] Of these pregnancies, 78% resulted in live births, while the remaining 22% resulted in unfavorable outcomes, e.g., stillbirths and spontaneous abortions. However, success rates nearly double when older mothers use eggs donated by younger women. Modern medical techniques are estimated to be as high as $10,000 for each treatment cycle.[3] Conception to delivery can be suspenseful and heart-wrenching, but burdens are tolerated because the human desire to have and raise children is overwhelming. This yearning propels the phenomenal medical advances providing children to families all over the world.

The first successful live birth from in vitro fertilization occurred in England, in 1978. It attracted enormous medical attention, leading to a similar birth in the United States in 1981. Assisted/Advanced Reproductive Technology (ART)[4] now offers a remarkable array of procedures allowing infertile couples to have children. In mammals the Fallopian tube (oviduct) carries egg cells from the ovary (female reproductive organ producing eggs) to the uterus (womb) where embryos develop. ART begins with administering fertility drugs to stimulate superovulation in ovulating women:

- Follicle stimulating hormone (commonly called Metrodin, Fertinex, Follistin, and Gonal-F) or human menopausal gonadotropin (commonly called Humagon or Pergonal) is given to ripen/stimulate multiple follicles for ovulation.
- Clomiphene citrate (commonly called Serophene or Clomid) is given to induce ovulation in women who do not ovulate or who show ovulatory dysfunction.

Ovulatory stimulation may be followed by retrieval of mature eggs from follicles (ovarian sacs) by transvaginal ultrasound-directed oocyte (primary egg cell) recovery. Depending on couples' health and reproductive histories, sex cells are donated by both parents, by one parent or by neither parent.

In vitro fertilization went from controversial in 1978 to conventional in 1998. This pattern is being repeated with more exotic assisted reproductive methods developed over the last five to ten years, namely egg donation, cryopreservation (freezing of embryos), and embryo procurement. Despite its increased use, ART is responsible for a very small proportion of births—less than 1%—but an exact figure is hard to determine because not all relevant data are reported.[5]

Assisted Reproductive Techniques

In Vitro Fertilization and Embryo Transfer (IVF-ET) involve laboratory fertilization of eggs by sperm in a petri dish—*in vitro* means "in glass." Forty-eight- to seventy-two-hour-old preembryos are implanted in the uterus.[6] In 1995, IVF accounted for 78% of ART treatments producing live births.[7]

Variations of IVF-ET, based on location and timing of transfer, are also available:[8]

- Gamete Intrafallopian Transfer (GIFT) combines eggs (usually four) and sperm in a petri dish and injects them into the Fallopian tube (oviduct) where fertilization occurs. This procedure is reserved for women with healthy

Fallopian tubes and for men with healthy sperm. Fallopian tubes provide a more supportive environment for developing embryos than the uterus.

- Zygote Intrafallopian Transfer (ZIFT), first used in 1986, transfers fertilized eggs to the oviduct at an early stage (before cell division). ZIFT may be more successful than GIFT because zygotes are helped by an extended stay in the oviduct.
- Pronuclear Stage Transfer (PROST) is similar to ZIFT except fertilized eggs are transferred at the earlier *pronuclear stage*. (In the pronuclear stage the egg and sperm unite, but the egg's nucleus has not fused with the sperm's nucleus.)
- Superovulation, Uterine Replacement, Capacitation, Enhancement (SOURCE) uses ovarian stimulants (such as Clomid) to obtain multiple eggs within a menstrual cycle. SOURCE is recommended for ovulating women unable to conceive, and for women failing to conceive by ordinary ovulation induction. This method may be combined with intrauterine insemination by sperm separated from seminal fluid, making sperm highly fertile.[9]

Knowing reproductive techniques' effects on multiple birth rates is crucial to family planning decisions, but reliable figures are hard to compile.[10] Underreporting of twin births, variable calculation of pregnancy rates, unavailability of fertility treatment outcomes, and varying fertility treatment practices across clinics compromise accuracy of these estimates. Furthermore, some evidence suggests fertility procedures vary in their promise of multiple yields. GIFT may slightly increase multiple birth rates because natural ovulation and fertilization could occur at the same time as oocyte transfer. For example, birth of sextuplets (six children) to a woman following transfer of only four egg cells suggested collaboration between natural processes and medical intervention. However, the *major* cause of multiple pregnancies following GIFT arises from multiple egg transfer.

Newest Assisted Reproductive Techniques

The newest assisted reproductive techniques overpower eggs' inevitable aging which can prevent conception in women past forty. Women's own or others' frozen eggs, younger women's eggs, couples' frozen embryos or other couples' premade embryos now offer amazing pregnancy possibilities. Sperm donors receive approximately $50, while some egg donors receive $5,000 or even more[11]. Egg donors typically receive $2,000–$2,500, but total medical costs can reach $16,000.[12] Success rates are not perfect, partly due to uncertainties of freezing and thawing procedures.

- Frozen eggs, combined with sperm, first resulted in a successful pregnancy in the United States in October 1997.[13] A thirty-nine-year-old woman became pregnant using a twenty-nine-year-old woman's eggs that had been frozen for twenty-five months. (The first birth from a frozen egg occurred earlier in 1997, in Bologna, Italy.) Four of eleven embryos created by mixing the eggs with her husband's sperm were implanted, resulting in healthy twin boys. Of course, women in their twenties and thirties may freeze their own eggs for pregnancies in their forties and beyond. Only a few successful pregnancies have resulted from using frozen eggs so this remains a technique for the future.

- Egg donation, first performed in 1984, allows creating embryos by combining other women's eggs with spouse's or other male's sperm. Two or three embryos are implanted in each attempt to improve pregnancy chances, although occasionally as many as four or five have been used. Success rates are 50% for forty-four-year-old women using donated eggs, compared with success rates of 3.5% for women using their own eggs.[14] Egg and sperm donor information is available in fertility clinics and on web sites, allowing couples to "choose" characteristics they want for their child, possibly matching them to their own traits. Of course, gene-outcome relationships are complex, so results are uncertain.[15] In 1995, egg donation accounted for 8% of ART treatments (attempts per monthly cycle) producing live births.[16]

- Couples' frozen embryos can be used for future pregnancies. These embryos are usually created at the same time as embryos that are implanted immediately, a process producing unusual sibships and high-profile legal proceedings.[17] In 1995, frozen embryos accounted for 14% of ART treatments producing live births in the United States.[18]

- Other couples' premade embryos are being made available to infertile couples who cannot afford the costs of choosing donors.[19] Cost is approximately $2,750 per embryo. Some embryos are unused by couples who created them, while others are made by physicians. Premade embryos are rare and are distributed quietly.

Most ART programs now report data, a new requirement for membership in the Society for Assisted Reproductive Technology (SART).[20] The 1998 Registry Report revealed 2,906 multiple births (from IVF), which accounted for 36.6% of the deliveries in 1995. They included 2,350 twin, 508 triplet and 48 higher multiple birth sets. Similar multiple birth rates have been reported in Australia and in England.

A surprising discovery in the early 1980s was pregnancy in some women from fertility drug treatment alone while preparing for IVF.[21] These women received extra high doses of ovulatory drugs to determine IVF's eventual success rates. Of course, increasing drug doses increased the number of eggs released. Stimulating multiple follicles at one time offered a new fertility route, but the procedure (SOURCE) is controversial because the risk of twins and supertwins (triplets and more) rises. The higher frequency of multiple births with increased numbers of transferred embryos (and oocytes) has also been dramatic. Transfer of eleven eggs to women over age forty caused their pregnancy and multiple-birth rates to equal those of younger women receiving fewer eggs.

Fascination with ART for permitting pregnancy and multiple pregnancy against all odds has been fueled by notable cases. In 1994, in Canino, Italy, Rosanna Della Corte delivered little Riccardo ("Riccardo piccolo") at age sixty-two, becoming the oldest woman in history to bear a child.[22] However, Della Corte was "dethroned" by sixty-three-year-old Arceli Keh from California (originally the Philippines) who delivered six-pound, four-ounce Cynthia on November 9, 1996.[23] Each woman used donated eggs mixed with her husband's sperm. Another notable case is Sue Green from Cambridgeshire, Great Britain, who delivered triplet boys at age fifty following IVF;[24] however, the oldest mother of triplets delivered her children at age fifty-seven, in Italy. In winter 1996, Pnina and Shmuel Klaver of Brooklyn, New York, welcomed quintuplets Bruchy, Saralah, Chayala, Moishy and Chaim into their home, following Pnina's Perganol treatment in her late thirties.[25] We marvel at these rare success stories, forgetting that most assisted attempts fail because natural and assisted pregnancy rates decline with advancing maternal age. Of course, this may not apply to conceptions assisted by egg donation, which enjoy a 50% delivery rate. Egg donation is, however, too recent to judge effects of maternal age on its success.

Rose Della Corte's case sparked both public sympathy and outrage. If biology permits men to become fathers at any age why couldn't women become mothers at any age?[26] Proponents cited research showing mothering skills and maternal satisfaction do not diminish with age, while antagonists worried that children born to older couples would be prematurely orphaned. Della Corte's story also pressed medical advances and concerns to new limits. She raised fresh hopes for other childless couples, but alarmed physicians unfamiliar with assisted conception so late in life. Scientific progress continually moves forward, so I expect Rosa Della Corte's experience will repeat, but very occasionally. Despite her success and contrary to doctors' fears, multitudes of women past age sixty have *not* sought fertility treatment. Similarly, some people worried that embryo preservation would spur couples to store vast assortments of potential progeny, but this has not happened.[27] Technology bypassing some infertile couples' biological constraints does *not* mean that it will be used excessively, or that all eligible couples will choose it. Failure of these concerns to materialize may speak to human tendencies underlying most people's reproductive choices. Potential costs incurred when children go from none to more than one can also affect family planning decisions.

The Klavers faced eviction from their apartment because their building was scheduled for sale. They also faced termination of welfare benefits because Shmuel Klaver's poor health prevented him from looking for work. The family was forced to seek charitable donations. Their situation was more extreme than most, but astronomical expenses are required to raise multiple birth children. The estimated first year cost of quintuplets including fertility treatments, hospital care, feeding, equipment and assistance is $447,680.[28]

Medical expenses can be never-ending when treatment is required for multiples with low birth weights and other delivery complications. Tina and Jerome Hamer had female quadruplets in June 1997, but the babies suffer from blindness, breathing problems and lung infections.[29] Adding to their heartache was the death of one of their newborn daughters, Aubrey Marie, at only five days of age. Potential financial and emotional burdens for prospective couples call for realistic assessment of ART's higher order multiple birth risks. Hospital staff are also concerned that multiple birth infants from assisted conceptions are burdening newborn care services. In 1990 a British neonatal unit admitted ten multiple birth babies, four from two twin pairs and six from two triplet sets; two of the births had resulted from ART.[30] These premature infants represented 23% of infants born before twenty-eight weeks, and all required ventilation. Seven of the babies died, representing 35% of deaths among these premature infants. Twins are also at twice the risk of nontwins for Sudden Infant Death Syndrome (SIDS), the leading cause of infant death in the United States among children between one month and one year of age. These apparently healthy infants stop breathing in the absence of a clear cause.[31] Simultaneous SIDS (both cotwins dying on the same day) has been reported more often than delayed SIDS in surviving cotwins of SIDS victims.[32] We should, however, cautiously examine twins' SIDS cases because some singletons' SIDS cases are now known to be misdiagnosed abuse,[33] behavior that is unfortunately elevated in families with twins.

Twins' medical expenses do not stop when higher order multiples come home. The estimated amount for raising the McCaughey (pronounced McCoy) septuplets over the next eighteen years is $1,000,000, excluding obstetrical expenses.[34] Adding a first year total of $700,000, based on newborn quintuplet costs of approximately $100,000 per child, yields nearly $2,000,000. Fortunately, the McCaugheys can count on help from friends in their small midwestern town, where living costs are somewhat reduced.

The McCaugheys were born on November 19, 1997, the first such set in the United States. Their parents, Bobbi and Kenny, had a two-year-old daughter, Mikayla, when Bobbi delivered Kenneth, Alexis, Natalie, Kelsey, Brandon, Nathan and Joel.[35] Bobbi had taken Metrodin for infertility, the same drug she had used to conceive Mikayla. All seven children survived, weighing two pounds, five ounces to three pounds, four ounces.

Expenses will also be exorbitant for another septuplet set, conceived by Hasna Mohammed Humair, a Saudi Arabian woman taking the fertility drug Clomid.[36] This septuplet set, born in January 1998, was momentarily upstaged by the possible birth of eight or nine babies to Cristina Nunez in Chihuahua, Mexico, also conceived by a fertility drug.[37] Ultrasound and X rays later suggested that Nunez was carrying seven fetuses, but instead she was carrying six and delivered the sextuplets, three boys and three girls, on February 28, 1998. The success of some higher order multiple births is astounding. However, infants' developmental dangers, mothers' physical risks, parents' emotional perils and families' financial concerns, at birth and beyond, cannot be ignored.

Reporting difficulties may have also concealed a recent surprise association between identical twinning and ART. Rachalle Spears's shock at discovering her twin daughters were identical, not fraternal, was noted in Chapter 1, but an important detail was missing: Rachalle's pregnancy was induced by Clomid (clomiphene). As ART's popularity grew, people naturally assumed fraternal twins explained multiple birth increases because ovulatory stimulants increased the number of eggs released, and IVF transfers involved separate embryos and oocytes. However, preliminary data from Belgian and British clinics uncovered significant *increases* in identical twinning with IVF-ET (1%) and with ovulation induction alone (1.2%), relative to the population rate (.4%).[38] Even more dramatic, a University of Iowa ART study reported an eight-fold increase in identical twinning, accounting for 10% of 218 pregnancies.[39] Identical triplets have also resulted from IVF procedures.[40]

Increased identical twinning from ART also explains parental bewilderment when some artificially conceived twins look and act alike. The possibility of identical twinning following ART may not always be raised when counseling infertile couples, but families need this vital information to imagine all possible outcomes. This is especially true now that identical triplets and conjoined twins and triplets have resulted from ART. A chimera (individual whose different cell types originated from separate sources) born to an infertile couple suggests another unexpected risk from IVF.[41] Two of the three transferred embryos (one male, one female) fused, forming a single child. The healthy boy was being treated for a nondescended testicle when an ovary and fallopian tube were discovered—had the fused embryos been same-sex the condition may have gone undetected.

The unexpected occurrence of identical twinning among assisted conceptions has challenged physicians, epidemiologists and twin researchers fixated on ebbs and flows of identical and fraternal twinning rates. How much twinning has increased, and why, lead the list of inquiries, reflecting the public's perceived explosion in twinning rates. Almost everyone knows a school or neighborhood famous for an unusually high number of sets, such as the West Patent Elementary School in Bedford, New York, whose 1995 kindergarten class boasted seven pairs. However, has twinning truly accelerated, and have identical and fraternal twinning rates similarly changed? Has ART masked natural twinning tendencies?

Twinning declined between the 1930s and 1970s in many western nations, showing an upswing in the 1980s. Curiously, fraternal twinning dropped through the 1970s, whereas identical twinning rose slightly, arousing considerable speculation. Reduced fraternal twinning could reflect increased reproductive difficulties in the population, possibly due to climbing rates of testicular cancer and reduced sperm count, or environmental pesticides may have elevated levels of some symptoms.[42] Scottish researchers reported the curious finding of *increased* twinning both in humans and in cattle, associated with air pollution from incinerators.[43] The investigators viewed this finding cautiously.

Maternal stress, reduced body fat from exercise and diet, and delayed childbearing may have also lowered fraternal twinning rates. (Fraternal twinning is more likely to occur with increased parity, i.e., when women have borne previous children. Studies are, however, divided on whether parity is an advanced age effect in disguise.[44]) On the positive side, identical twinning increases were explained by better detection and management of multiple birth pregnancies. Twinning patterns through the 1970s led to several conclusions:

- Fraternal twinning declines were genuine because they occurred despite improved medical practice. In contrast, slight identical twinning *increases* were observed as would be expected given better health care.
- Fraternal twinning declines raised some public health concerns because fraternal twining decreased to a greater degree than identical twinning increased. This is because disease or lifestyle changes that modified twinning rates were negatively affecting fraternal twins only.
- Fraternal twinning is a better barometer of shifting health and environmental conditions than identical twinning. Factors associated with fraternal twinning, such as maternal weight and possibly paternal sperm count, may be affected by environmental events. In contrast, little is known about the causes of identical twinning.
- Overflows of identical pairs among research volunteers may accurately reflect twin type distributions in populations, rather than skewed sampling, thereby raising confidence in findings. In other words, the excess proportion of identical twins in many studies, relative to same-sex fraternal twins, may approach their true proportion.

Twinning decreases in the 1960s and early 1970s were counterbalanced by twinning increases in the late 1970s and beyond.[45] More striking jumps in births of higher order multiples (triplets, quadruplets and quintuplets) were reported in newspapers and magazine everywhere. Holly Taylor's statistical summary showed marked increases in the frequency of multiple births between 1973 and 1994.[46] Twins went from one in eighty-four to one in seventy-eight deliveries; triplets went from one in 6,889 to one in 2,393 deliveries, but the increases were probably not due to ART alone. Twin frequencies and conceptions (both natural and assisted) were monitored between 1976 and 1992 by researchers associated with the East Flanders Prospective Twin Survey, in Belgium. They concluded that natural twinning rates *rose* even as ART also added to the upsurge.[47]

Rising twin rates are electrifying, reflecting the thrill that twins and twins' special qualities bring to so many people. Still, new reproductive techniques cast occasional shadows upon multiple parenting pleasures. Consider that unfavorable outcomes in multiple pregnancies are proportional to the number of fetuses in the uterus.

Multiple embryos improve pregnancy rates, but escalating birth complications are sorrowful side effects. Hazards include premature birth, predisposing infants to low birth weight, respiratory difficulties, and learning disabilities. Cerebral palsy (a developmental brain disorder caused by lack of oxygen or other prenatal injury, and resulting in weak, uncoordinated movements of limbs) affects early-borns (babies born before thirty-two weeks) twenty times as often as later-borns. The biological reality is that women are best equipped to carry single fetuses so two, three, four or more strain mothers' child-bearing resources. Higher multiple birth risks are well illustrated by a British woman who spontaneously aborted eight fetuses—she had been paid by a tabloid press for the rights to her story. Evolutionary researchers speculate that physical and practical difficulties explain why multiple births are relatively rare among humans.

Multiple birth problems have been partly resolved by *multifetal pregnancy reduction (MPR),* termination of some fetuses allowing survival of two or three. In 1985, Dr. Mark Evans was the first American physician to practice this procedure, reducing quadruplets to twins. This maneuver involves injecting potassium chloride into an embryo's chest cavity at 9–11 weeks' gestation, disrupting cardiac function.[48] This procedure also eliminates abnormal embryos threatening the progress of normal embryos. Selective reduction saves mothers' and babies' lives, but it is rife with physical hazards and emotional heartbreak. Surrounding fetuses are at unknown risk for premature delivery, damage or miscarriage. Evans showed that frequency of miscarriage climbs with larger pregnancies even after reduction, rising to 22% for sextuplets. Most favorable outcomes followed reducing triplets to twins, with the inexplicable result that reduction to two was better than reduction to one. I am unaware of research exploring links between fetal reduction and behavioral problems in surviving children. Prematurity of remaining fetuses is likely when the procedure is delayed or not undertaken, possibly leading to learning disabilities or other difficulties.

It is unimaginable for many couples to consider eliminating even one embryo to ease the way for others. Undoing conceptions that have been months and years in the making is troubling, but often inescapable for some families hoping to beat the odds. Location and access (ease of removal) of embryos usually dictate which ones to eliminate, but promise unfulfilled may reside forever in parents' minds. Furthermore, no one has considered selective reduction's later psychological effects on surviving children who may wonder about brothers and sisters they might have had.

The American Society for Reproductive Medicine suggests transferring a maximum of four embryos in women under age thirty-eight years. Physicians favor guidelines over laws because they afford flexibility in meeting needs of clins and patients, but this matter continues to be debated.[49] Ideally, a single embryo with high survival potential would circumvent difficulties posed by multiple implantations. The trick is to extend embryonic development outside the womb because 100-celled blastocysts probably have higher survival rates than 6–10-celled embryos. Researchers are attempting to create the elusive growth medium enabling this to happen.

ART has created extraordinary kin relations whose nature and quality are unknown. Helping people achieve the families they longed for has been gratifying, yet controversial. Redefining roles and relationships between siblings, and between parents and children, has been a legacy of upheavals in creating and bearing babies. Intriguing sibling and parenting relationships have emerged, transforming traditional family structures beyond recognition.

My first introduction to the new world of kinship occurred following a 1990 lecture to Twin Services, in Berkeley, California. A blond woman approached me, not to ask a "twin question," but to ask the name of my fifth-grade teacher. I soon recognized Betty Lou Moglen, an elementary school classmate from New York. Betty and her partner, Barbara, shared parenting responsibilities for four children, two of whom were fraternal twin sisters. Barbara had conceived all four children through artificial insemination using the same sperm donor. Here was an unusual case of twins raised by both biological and nonbiological mothers in the same home! This family offers rare opportunities for comparing similarity between children (the twins) and their biologically related and unrelated parents, *both of whom had been with them since birth and shared their rearing.*

Details of Betty and Barbara's family configuration may not repeat in other households, but some couples may perceive similar features in their own homes. For example, divorce and remarriage means rearing of some children by one biological parent and by one nonbiological parent. Children conceived by ART may be products of one biological parent and one donor parent, or two donor parents. Members of these families are players in a great nature-nurture game whose outcomes partly depend on the age of the child and the particular behavior. Young children may be more intellectually similar to unrelated siblings and to unrelated parents than are adolescents because shared family environments have greater impact on intelligence at young ages.

Resemblance between parents and artificially conceived children is also affected by behavioral matches between rearing and donor parents. A 1997 Discovery program, *Making Babies,* shows that infertile couples can review habits, tastes and talents of potential sperm or egg donors before selection. Judy and Richard Walters were eager to raise a family, but Richard's infertility prevented parenthood so they chose IVF with sperm donation. A donor was partly decided by his joy in "fixing things," a quality suggesting, but not guaranteeing, a good match between child and father, who also liked to tinker. Young Rebecca eventually displayed this behavior, although the extent to which it was inherited from her donor or acquired from her father will never be known because of confounded genes and environments.

Matching egg donors and recipients sometimes misfires. An acquaintance from the midwest, JK, who conceived twin boys through egg donation, sought a donor, D, who was "like her." The match proved too good to be true when autistic tendencies were detected in one twin. It turned out that D carried a gene for autism *and* that autism runs in one branch of JK's family—in fact, JK had an older autistic son.

We are learning that older women can bear children, but poor egg cell quality may be the stumbling block. Seeking eggs from younger donors has been a solution, but I was unprepared for the mixing and matching of relationships generated by one family, revealed in a 1997 talk show segment. An older mother desiring another pregnancy looked no further than her own married daughter for egg donation. Healthy twins were born, but they were not ordinary children because their birth mother was their grandmother, their biological mother was their sister, their stepfather was their brother-in-law and their cousins were their half-siblings. The biological mother-sister denied feelings of motherly love toward her "children," possibly due to lack of hormonal priming crucial to mother-infant bonding. The range of incredible relationships generated by ART families complicates evaluating child outcomes because large numbers of specific pairings probably cannot be found. However, loving parents are the likely key to any child's well-being. Of course, conventional issues of parent-child resemblance in appearance and in genetic predisposition to disease must be resolved in unconventional ways, by looking to sisters, brothers or others for information. Inheritance decisions could assume a life of their own as family members grapple with who is related to whom.

Concepts of twins and twinship invite revision in light of new reproductive technologies. In 1988, Barbara Unell, former editor of *Twins* magazine, sought my view on the multiple birth status of some remarkable children. The world had just witnessed the first successful birth of three infants born twenty-one months apart at the AMI South Bay Hospital in Redondo Beach, California. A couple underwent retrieval and fertilization of ten eggs, four of which were implanted in the mother's uterus, yielding a healthy baby girl. Remaining embryos were frozen for later implantation, resulting in twin daughters. The three infants were termed *triplets* because they were conceived together, prompting Barbara's crucial question: Are the children *truly* triplets? I knew this provocative case anticipated dramatic transformation in research and thinking about twins and twin research findings. However, I never envisioned the fantastic assortment of twin and twinlike pairs I would encounter over the years.

A 1995 letter from Joanne Dennis confirmed that reproductive technologies after the late 1970s changed twinning forever: "My two children,

Stephanie and Becky, are not twins but they are only twenty-two hours apart in age and have lived with us since the beginning. . . . After seven years of infertility and with the biological clock ticking, my husband, Bill, and I found a surrogate [mother] to have our child for us; unexpectedly, I became pregnant at the same time as our surrogate. Bill is the biological father of both our daughters and they have different biological birth mothers. All six years of their lives have been a joy. . . ."

Sharing a father made the girls "genetic half-siblings," but perhaps a twenty-two-hour birth interval qualified them as an unusual type of twins. After all, naturally conceived twins have been born days apart, sometimes with different fathers, so maybe twins could be born with different mothers. This complex question requires identifying unique psychological and biological features of twinship.

I believe defining twinship can help parents struggling with rearing practices and with behavioral expectations for artificially conceived multiples. For example, shared birthday parties are appropriate for twins, but may neglect the individuality of some artificially conceived siblings such as Joanne's. I also believe this knowledge will help investigators puzzling over questions of research design and analysis. Of course, general guidelines on defining twinship could be challenged by unforeseen cases, but I believe attention to exceptional pairs sharpens thinking about the problem. However, no one foresaw that a laboratory error in a village near Arnhem, the Netherlands, would create a pair of little boys that would truly test conceptions of twinning.[50]

They call their twins *duo Penotti,* after the Dutch topping of twisted vanilla and chocolate strands spread on bread. Sitting together in their small bathtub with arms and legs intertwined, the twins were a living image of that popular treat (duo Penotti in een potti—duo Penotti in one little pot).[51] By 1993, in vitro fertilization and embryo transfer were widely practiced so the December birth of twin boys, Teun and Koen, to Wilma and Willem Stuart should have gone unnoticed. However, details of the boys' incredible beginnings became famous through newspapers, magazines and a compelling November 19, 1996, *Dateline NBC* special. The pregnancy Wilma described as "delicious" ended on an uncertain note: cradling her two healthy boys, Wilma noticed that Koen "appeared very brown." Hospital staff dismissed these concerns, and while Wilma's worries quieted they were never resolved.

Genetic testing in November 1994 revealed that Teun was Wilma and Willem's child, but that Koen was Wilma's child only—failure to clean a pipette used to unite sperm and egg of a black couple probably led to fertilization of Wilma's egg by this second father. The black father was originally from Aruba, an island in the Caribbean Sea. Incredibly, Wilma recalled sitting near that family in the waiting room, contemplating the possibility of mismatches.

I have shown *Dateline*'s segment to my psychology classes many times because it is informative and moving. Especially memorable were Willem's avowal that Koen was *his* son, even if not his biological son, and Wilma's devotion to Koen, believing he was somehow meant to be. Wilma is eager for Koen's biological father to teach him about living as a minority member of a predominantly Caucasian nation. She suspects difficult times ahead as Teun and Koen become occasional targets of thoughtless words and unmerciful stares. She was also amused by attention from New Yorkers during taping of *Dateline*'s special, undermining her belief that big cities offer protective anonymity.

Wilma and Willem's story was revealed because of the biological father's differing ethnicity. Had the mistake involved a Caucasian father the error may have remained silent forever.[52] This incredible possibility became obvious to me when I learned of a second twin set whose Caucasian mother and black father underwent medical testing for suspected genetic disease in one twin. The surprising outcome was that sperm had been donated by different fathers, but this time the "foreign" sperm came from a man of the same race as the father. Had genetic testing not occurred this error, too, may have gone undetected. Such mistakes appear rare, but because they may go unnoticed their true frequency is unknown.

ART's occasional whims and fancies can manufacture novel twinlike relationships that challenge our views of what twinship is and means. I believe three defining features distinguish twins from twinlike pairings:

- Twins are conceived at the same time, sharing both parents. Identical twins form simultaneously from division of a fertilized egg or zygote. However, members of higher order identicals, such as triplets and quadruplets, may result from zygotic splitting separated by hours, days or even close to two weeks. For example, identical triplets result when a fertilized egg divides twice in succcssion, and identical quadruplets result when a fertilized egg divides three times in succession (or when both zygotes created by the first division each divide again, or when one zygote created from the first division divides twice). It is also assumed that most fraternal twins result from simultaneous fertilization of two eggs from the same mother by two sperm from the same father, but fertilization intervals are unknown. Furthermore, superfecundation (fertilization of eggs at different times, sometimes by different fathers) and superfetation (fertilization of eggs at different times, due to their separate release in different weeks) mean some fraternal twins are conceived at different times—these pairs are recognized as "superfecundated twins" or as "superfetated twins." Members of exotic identical-fraternal supertwin combinations also appear in sequence as egg releases, fertilizations and zygotic divisions occur.
- Twins share intrauterine environments. Identical and fraternal twins share the womb from conception to delivery so broad effects of maternal diet, health and prenatal care are matched. However, natural details of intrauterine life can dif-

fer dramatically between identical and fraternal pairs, among identical pairs, and between pair members. For example, some identical twins share their outer fetal membrane (chorion), a situation that may adversely affect development from shared circulation. In contrast, all fraternals and some identicals have separate fetal membranes so they experience less hazardous prenatal circumstances. In addition, both identical and fraternal cotwins may vary in access to prenatal nutrition and exposure to some maternal infections, discussed in Chapter 2. Fraternal twins may also be differentially sensitive to prenatal events, due to their differing genetic backgrounds.

- Twins are born at the same time. Multiple births come from single deliveries, leading to joint birthday celebrations, shared family events and common cultural experiences. However, twists of fate in the form of the premature birth of one twin, or rearing of twins by different adoptive families can alter, but not deny, the basic twinning plan. Natural events disrupting common delivery, such as early rupture of one twin's sac, reveal the breadth and scope of twins' unpredictable births. Rearing twins apart is not the norm, but biological twinning processes have run their course when this unhappy decision is made. Even when twins are reared apart their matched age means they experience many life events at the same time, such as entering kindergarten, graduating from high school and earning a driver's license. I also believe that losing a twin at birth or later in life is a variation of natural twinning processes that do not deny these individuals' multiple birth status.[53]

Who among ART sibling pairs qualifies as twins or other multiples? My response to Barbara Unell's question concerning the triplet status of the three children born in Redondo Beach, California, was negative. Despite their simultaneous conception by in vitro fertilization the older child and younger twins were *not* triplets. Born nearly two years apart, the babies did not share birthdays, setting the stage for differing developmental and cultural experiences. Even while they were carried by the same woman, their intrauterine environments may have differed due to changes in their mother's emotional or physical health, or in preferred medical practices of the day. Older and younger newborn siblings vary in their fetal hormone levels, so the twins born twenty-one months after their older sibling probably encountered differing fetal environments.[54]

Concepts of twinship were challenged again by a baby whose February 1998 birth in Tarzana, California, was unusual for two reasons.[55] The infant, Billy, was born from an embryo frozen for seven and one-half years—furthermore, the embryo was created at the *same time* as the embryo producing his older brother. Their parents had forgotten about their unused embryo until they were contacted by the clinic, thus explaining their sons' seven-year age gap. The brothers were described as "technically twins" and "fraternal twins" by reporters and physicians appearing on television news programs. I disagreed with their calling the boys "twins" for the same reasons I disagreed with calling the Redondo Beach twins and singleton "triplets."

Note that siblings born several years apart could theoretically share nearly all their genes in common, depending upon which genes were transmitted from each parent. Most everyone knows siblings showing striking physical and behavioral resemblance, but no one would call them twins. I believe that our lack of names for unusual ART sibships has led us to use existing names inappropriately. The term *fraternal siblings* might describe the relationships between the singleton and twins, and between the two singletons. This label distinguishes them from fraternal twins (Redondo Beach births) and ordinary siblings (Billy and his brother) while conveying their genetic relatedness. Fraternal siblings could also describe infants born together, but from embryos their parents created at different times.

The extraordinary "duo Penotti" pair replays defining features of superfecundated twins and can be considered as such. (Superfecundated twins are conceived near in time by different fathers.) However, a more difficult riddle was raised earlier in this chapter—children born from embryos created at the same time, but carried by different women and delivered apart (on the same day). Are these children twins? Reviewing the three twinship criteria suggests they are *not* strictly twins because they did not share intrauterine environments. I believe they are more accurately considered fraternal siblings. Of course, the best test of prenatal influences on development would involve identical twins carried by different women. This event was considered unlikely until a surprise 1993 report by George Washington University researchers appeared.

What began as an effort to help childless couples conceive became headline news around the world. Moments before revealing their human cloning technology breakthrough to the 1993 American Fertility Society meeting in Montreal, Canada, Drs. Jerry Hall and Robert Stillman vacillated over disclosure of this controversy. Clones are exact duplicates of molecules, cells, plants or animals,[56] although errors in cell replication are possible and mitochondria (cellular structures providing energy to cells) are not reproduced. However, mitochondrial DNA is only one part in 200,000 relative to nuclear DNA, and if women cloned themselves using their own eggs, their children's mitochondria *would* be identical.[57] (Mutations in mitochondrial DNA could occur and have been associated with Alzheimer's disease, Parkinson's disease—a degenerative disorder associated with aging—and some forms of epilepsy.[58]) At that time, nonhuman animal cloning, such as duplicating cattle to boost milk and food production, was routine, but human cloning was controversial due to feared misuses—for example, would families freeze one twin embryo for future organ donation or child replacement? Would identicals born in different years forge close bonds or bitter rivalries? Could identical children born by different mothers meet in the future? Federal funding for human cloning was (and is) banned, but researchers were tinkering with existing methodologies in quiet corners of clinics and laboratories. Opting for scientific discussion, Hall presented his cloning technique ("embryo-splitting") to colleagues, a decision that thrust his work into an unexpected limelight. Actually, he and Stillman demonstrated the *possibility* of creating identical twins, not the reality of creating identical twins, because they chose flawed embryos unable to survive. Overzealous journalistic accounts led to misunderstandings of how far human cloning technology had actually progressed. However, a more extraordinary achievement was only three years away.

The 1996 cloning of an adult sheep, reported in February 1997 by Ian Wilmut and his colleagues at the Roslin Institute in Edinburgh, Scotland, transformed adult nonhuman and human cloning from uncertainty to possibility.[59] Dolly, lamb number 6LL3, produced from a single cell of a Scottish Blackface ewe's udder (mammary gland) and weighing 14.5 pounds, signaled a new era of reproductive advances and challenges. Wilmut named the lamb for Dolly Parton who he joked was known for her mammaries.[60]

Old issues resurfaced and new questions emerged once the potential for cloning existing human beings was revealed. Amidst the turmoil it was often forgotten that the techniques involved in creating Dolly were hardly perfect since Dolly was the only successful outcome among 277 attempts.[61] Dolly's fertility and longevity also remained uncertain because the cell creating her was donated by an older organism. Furthermore, *actual* adult human cloning was *not* demonstrated—rather, *potential* adult human cloning was suggested.

New insight into the "minds" of cells allowed the Scottish team to accomplish their stunning feat. In a process called *somatic cell nuclear transfer,* DNA division and adult donor cell division were arrested, followed by insertion of the adult cell nucleus into an egg whose nucleus had been removed. Cell division was restarted, producing an embryo that was implanted into an unrelated surrogate mother who carried it to term. This embryo produced Dolly, a clone of her original adult donor. The basis for these methods was actually established in 1994 at the University of Wisconsin, when Dr. Neal first produced four identical calves from an early embryo.[62] The technique was then repeated in 1996 by Wilmut's team, creating twins Megan and Morag from embryo cells, the first cloned sheep.

Wilmut and his research team never intended to apply their methods to humans; their plan was to use it to produce "super-cattle" (cattle rich in milk and beef)[63] and new drug sources. In fact, Polly and Molly, sheep later cloned by Wilmut's group, were genetically manipulated to produce milk with a protein helpful to people with hemophilia.[64] (Hemophilia is a hereditary disorder in which blood does not clot properly.) Another stunning cloning achievement since Dolly's birth includes cow triplets Charlie, George, and an unnamed partner, created from fetal cells by University of Massachusetts scientists

James Robl and Steven Stice.[65] A more recently cloned pair are Holly and Belle, identical female calves born in the Netherlands by a new method that froze the embryos before and after cloning, allowing additional study. The Dutch government is banning the technique that created these animals.[66]

How close are we to human cloning? In October 1997 I spoke by telephone with Dr. Steen Willadsen, scientist at St. Barnabas Hospital in East Orange, New Jersey. (Willadsen's methods were also used in Dolly's cloning.) He told me that human cloning is possible now, using embryos to create identical individuals. He also believes that cloning from mature human cells is possible, is vastly the same for any mammal, and may be easier for humans than for other animals. This knowledge may lie behind government efforts to restrict human cloning experimentation until we know more about its social implications and its physical safety. Legislation banning human cloning is workable in theory, but hard to enforce because international restrictions differ, allowing experimentation abroad. It has also been suggested that separate policies for cloning activities serving legitimate goals (treating infertility) versus cloning activities likely to cause harm (narcissistic self-replication) may be preferable to global guidelines.[67]

In February 1997 President Bill Clinton requested Dr. Harold T. Shapiro, Chair of the National Bioethics Advisory Commission and President of Princeton University (also an identical twin[68]), to consider scientific, religious, ethical and legal questions surrounding human cloning techniques, and to prepare recommendations for preventing abuse of this technology. A report, "Cloning Human Beings," resulted from ninety days of analysis and discussion by commission members and testimony from medical, legal and religious authorities. President Clinton imposed a moratorium on federal funding during preparation of the report and requested private researchers to halt human cloning experimentation.

On September 24, 1997, I spoke with Dr. Shapiro in his office at Princeton University. I originally contacted Dr. Shapiro to learn more about how he and his twin brother, Bernard, both became presidents of major universities. (Dr. Bernard Shapiro is president of McGill University in Montreal, Canada; see Chapter 13.) Upon learning of Shapiro's role in federal cloning policies, I was eager to hear his thoughts. Cloning and twinning are related, but not identical concepts, so the debate was meaningful to me and to the families with whom I have worked.

Dr. Shapiro viewed the cloning controversy as a remarkable moment in science history. He was surprised by the astonishment of many scientists following Dolly's birth. Experimentation in the last three decades had strongly hinted that mammalian cloning was coming, with only technical difficulties blocking the way. He was also unprepared for the range of fears and misconceptions expressed in the media, some by prominent scientists. I agreed, recalling the following example: "Might it be possible to clone the dead?"

Dr. Shapiro sees public understanding of cloning's possibilities and limitations as a monumental goal. He explained that fears of Hitler reproductions, largely fed by 1970s fiction and film (e.g., Ira Levin's *The Boys from Brazil*) are scientifically unfounded because they ignore important effects of experience on human development. Drawing upon his athletic zeal, Shapiro suggested that a Michael Jordan clone would be simply a hoop dream. Causal differences between outstanding sports performance and good sports performance may be small—for example, slightly greater height, better lung functioning or more developed muscle mass might ultimately discriminate stars from stand-ins. However, these crucial differences may depend upon significant developmental events (in the womb and beyond) whose identities are unknown and whose replication is impossible. A Michael Jordan clone might be athletically talented, but *not* athletically distinguished. Shapiro believes more and better sports programs (and physics laboratories) chart more efficient routes to increasing the population's Jordans (and Einsteins) than cloning possibly could.

In January 1998 unforeseen events rejuvenated efforts to legally ban human cloning research.[69] A sixty-nine-year-old Chicago physicist announced his intention to establish a clinic that would develop human cloning techniques for conquering infertility. Administration response to his overture was swift. A federal bill to ban cloning was reintroduced to Congress in February 1998, bypassing usual committee hearings.[70] However, its passage has stalled because key issues have left government leaders divided. The bill's supporters fear destruction of human embryos, while its opponents fear restriction of medical research. The psychological consequences of cloning for children and other family members have been controversial.

I believe that there are insights from twin research that are relevant to the psychological situations that would be faced by cloned individuals. This information could influence decisions concerning the use and abuse of the procedure. Therefore, I was pleased when Professor Owen Jones of Arizona State University's Law School invited me to comment on the Bioethics Commission's report for a special issue of the journal *Jurimetrics*.

In my article, "Behavioral Aspects of Intergenerational Human Cloning: What Twins Tell Us," I argued that discussion of psychological issues would benefit from reviewing twin, family and adoption studies of human behavior. Consider a striking statement from a male identical twin, interviewed for Turner Broadcasting's 1997 documentary *Twin Stories*: "We were doing cloning before it became in vogue."

This remark suggests that the concepts *clones* and *twins* are interchangeable, a theme that has, unfortunately, been repeated elsewhere. In her essay on losing a twin, D. S. Barron asserts, "However ordinary someone may be, give him his clone and he instantly becomes engaging [to those around him]." In his provocative column on identical cross-country runners Roger and

Frank Bjorkli, P. A. Linde asks, "Wait a second, who are those clones leading the way? Who are those two lanky guys . . . ?" Understanding clone-twin associations is central to issues raised by the Commission, such as how we might view relations between adults and cloned children.

I believe that *identical twins are clones, but clones are not identical twins*. I take exception to the commission's use of *"delayed genetic twin"* for individuals resulting from cloning techniques, offering *intergenerational clone* (IGC) as a more accurate label for these individuals. Clones are not identical twins because they fail to fulfill the three twinship criteria: simultaneous conception, shared prenatal environments and common birth. Clones generate novel "twinlike" relationships, so the commission's hypothetical situation of cloning a child to serve as bone marrow donor for a terminally ill child would *not* create "identical twins of different ages," but would create individuals who are genetically the same (IGCs). Furthermore, substituting human clones for human twins in psychological research would not yield unlimited informative twin samples, but an unlimited approximation of the real thing. Twins can also clarify other concerns raised by Commission members:

- Would individuality and uniqueness of cloned persons be threatened? I believe not. Twin studies show greater social closeness and affiliation between identical twins than between fraternal twins and virtually all other pairs of relatives, but social closeness does not imply loss of individuality. Parents have been frustrated by routine placement of their young identical twins in separate school classes because of educators' unsubstantiated concerns over diminished individuality and autonomy.[71] Most telling, some reunited identical twins worried over losing individuality before meeting their twin, but their concerns proved groundless. Some adolescent twins confront individuality and identity issues, as do adolescent nontwins, but most twins emerge unscathed from these episodes.

- Would novel family relationships generated by cloning prove harmful to the individuals involved? The answer to this question is unknown. The quality of relationships evolving between IGCs is uncertain because this particular human kinship has never existed. However, changed social values and advanced medical technologies have generated many new family arrangements that perhaps we can learn from. Researchers have compared parenting in ordinary birth families to parenting in families whose children were conceived by ART techniques.[72] *Greater* maternal warmth, emotional involvement, mother-child interaction and father-child interaction were found among parents who had undergone ART. Children in these families were only 2–8 years old so it may be that parent-child mismatches or other difficulties might emerge as children age. It will be fascinating to study characteristics of the families who continue to enjoy successful parent-child relations, as compared with those who do not, especially with regard to whether perceived similarities by parents and children make a difference.

- Would expectations of behavioral similarity in identical individuals (IGCs) prove psychologically damaging to children? Possibly, but simple answers to this question are unavailable. The greater average personality similarity of identical twins, relative to other individuals, suggests that the personalities of some pairs of IGCs would also be alike. However, identical twins are not exactly alike in personality because of differing environmental factors (e.g., popular identical twins are more extraverted than their cotwins[73]). Similarly, IGCs should show personality differences associated with different experiences, some due to their different generational rearing. An intriguing question is whether identical twins or IGCs would be more behaviorally similar. I suspect that for many traits identical twins would be more alike than IGCs primarily due to their common age and cohort. Identical twins raised apart are as similar in personality and in social attitudes as identical twins raised together. Therefore, identical twins' common rearing would not be the reason for their greater personality or attitudinal similarity, relative to clones. In contrast, identical twins reared apart are slightly less alike in intelligence than identical twins reared together. Therefore, identical twins would probably be more alike in intelligence than IGCs who would be reared separately and in different generations. I would not, however, be surprised if some identical twin pairs were *less alike* in some traits than some IGCs. For example, identical twins differing in prenatal trauma may differ in intelligence. These twins could conceivably be less alike in IQ than IGCs who would not have experienced multiples' stressful prenatal environments.

    The meaningful question is not whether IGCs' personalities would be alike or not, but *whether those who are alike might experience undue psychological distress because of it*. There is no evidence that identical twins who are more similar in personality than others are especially distressed—in fact, every year thousands of identical twins gather at national and international conventions to celebrate their twinship and their likenesses.

It would be prudent to engage identical twins' families in discussions of human cloning because they closely witness the benefits and liabilities of rearing identical twins. I would not be surprised if identical twins felt less threatened by possible adult human cloning than fraternal twins and nontwins because they were "doing cloning" all along. Furthermore, everyone can probably name similar parent-child pairs who capture crucial qualities of IGCs. A mother-daughter duo famous for preserving beauty and talent across generations is Ingrid Bergman and Isabella Rossellini.[74] These rare pairs might reveal the impact of watching a parent for even a partial glimpse of one's own developmental course. Another informative approach would include sibling sets in which older and younger siblings looked and behaved alike. The Baldwin brothers, Alec, William, Daniel and Steven, appear quite similar (especially

Alec and William) and all have chosen acting careers. This situation would replicate cloning children from the same donor at different times.

In the fall of 1997, I discovered another surprise source of possible insights into psychological consequences of human cloning. My Twinn Doll Company, based in Denver, Colorado, designs twenty-three-inch dolls to match photographs of boys and girls ages three to twelve.[75] Dolls' owners are in a "clonelike" situation, and their fondness for the figurines is worth investigating. Interestingly, the identical dolls are intended to *enhance* individuals' uniqueness (no one else can have the same toy), whereas some people have feared younger clones would diminish selfhood. Dolls are not people, but reactions to the toys offer possible models for probing feelings toward our identical others.

Twin research findings may dispel some psychological concerns raised over human cloning, but may not justify all aspects of the procedure. It would be inappropriate if done simply to satisfy an individual's vanity and without benefit to resulting children. However, neglecting cloning's promising fertility, health and food production benefits because of possible psychological or social concerns would not be the optimal solution.

A new season for making multiples is at hand, but seasons fade quickly. I expect 1980s and 1990s increases in twinning rates to subside in 2000 as improved techniques allow successful conceptions with fewer embryos. A possible antidote to supertwinning may be intracytoplasmic sperm injection (ICSI), in which a single oocyte from a natural cycle is injected with a single sperm incapable of penetrating an egg on its own. This procedure has enjoyed small-scale success. According to Dr. Bryan R. Hecht this alternative would represent the "pinnacle of efficiency in assisted reproductive technologies achieved to date."[76]

Another new and inexpensive technique, follicle aspiration, sperm injection and assisted rupture (FASIAR), may also reduce multiple birth risks.[77] FASIAR involves ovulation induction, followed by egg removal directly from the follicle. The egg and sperm are mixed inside a syringe, then injected into the uterus. This procedure proved successful for one thirty-six-year-old woman after two attempts, and seems a promising treatment.

Shapiro's discussion of Michael Jordan suggested that a unique blend of genetic and environmental influences separated athletic greatness from athletic skill. The basis of unusual athletic talent has occupied players and spectators for years, but only recently have there been answers from twin studies. Investigators have developed sophisticated measures and methods for assessing sports ability, transforming playing fields into research laboratories. What twin studies tell us about the making of athletes and about our own athletic skills are the focus of the next chapter.

Two-Base Hits and Triple Toe Loops: Physical Growth and Athletic Prowess

T wins Fever" swept through Minneapolis in mid-October 1987, infecting virtually everyone in its path. The Minnesota Twins were poised to capture the World Series title after sitting on the sidelines for twenty-two years. I do not follow baseball, but was mildly caught up in the excitement. On this particular morning, however, I was planning to travel to New York City for a party honoring my twin sister's recent marriage, and my thoughts were far from two-base hits and home runs when I stopped by my office at the University of Minnesota en route to the airport.

There was a knock on the door and I opened it to find a reporter and a photographer. The reporter introduced himself as Ira Berkow from the *New York Times*. Berkow is a prominent sports writer and author of several books, including *Hank Greenberg: The Story of My Life* (1991) and *To the Hoop* (1997). But since I did not read sports pages I insisted he show his identity card. He was miffed. Once I was satisfied that he was who he said he was, I invited him in. Berkow said he was looking for a psychological explanation of "Twins Fever." I started to laugh, wondering why he had chosen me to talk to. Apparently, he had asked to speak to someone about "the twins" and the department secretary had replied, "You want to see Nancy." The conversation soon became a comedy of errors. When Berkow encouraged me to discuss "the twins," I honestly asked, "reared apart or reared together?" The text of our conversation was printed several days later,[1] attracting nearly the same attention among my sister's party guests as the bride:

On the second floor of nearby Elliott Hall is the office of Nancy L. Segal, Ph.D. in psychology.
Did she follow the Twins?

"Which twins?" she asked.

"Is there more than one?"

"Of course."

"The Minnesota Twins."

"They're not the kind I study," she said. And that was true. She is the assistant director for the widely known Minnesota Center for Twin and Adoption Research.

"But I've been following them in the last few weeks," she said.

"How could you help it if you lived around here?"

Divided Loyalties

She is originally from Riverdale in the Bronx, and is, yes, divided in her loyalties, with the Twins on one hand and the Yankees and Mets on the other.

She said she liked Frank Viola, the Twins pitcher, because of his intensity. "He has this very penetrating stare," she said. "I'm sure the other guys are taught not to look at him."

Is Viola her favorite Twin?

"No," she said, "my sister, Anne, is."

Her sister Anne?

"Yes," said Dr. Segal. "I'm a twin."

In fact, Berkow was aware of at least one other type of twin beyond ball players. In September 1983 he wrote an inspiring piece, "Last Runner But Not Least," tracing the 11-hour, 54-second New York City marathon run of twenty-six-year-old identical twin Linda Down.[2] Linda was born with cerebral palsy (severe limb weakness and poor movement coordination), but navigated the 26.2-mile course by using her crutches like ski poles and pushing off with her legs. Higher proportions of twins than nontwins are affected with cerebral palsy,[3] although only 40% of affected identical twins have affected cotwins.[4]

I asked Berkow if identical twins had ever been elected to the Baseball Hall of Fame in Cooperstown, New York, but he was uncertain.[5] My question concealed a more important concern, namely the extent to which athletic abilities and interests are genetically influenced. Greater identical than fraternal twin similarity in muscle mass, running speed and athletic honors would support genetic contributions to sports performance. If individual differences in physical, intellectual and personality traits influence athletic skill, more realistic assessment of our sports potentials and shortcomings would be possible.

As a child I had wondered about athletic talent whenever I watched my fraternal twin sister, Anne, outrun our friends. Anne's skill at short sprints seemed to spring from nowhere, and no matter how hard I tried I could not compete at her level. Now, in adulthood, I overtake her in longer races, an achievement that surprises us both. Perhaps our different genetic backgrounds primed us for different physical feats that were designed to change with age and opportunity. These thoughts recall Sir Francis Galton's account of a newcomer's easy victory over seasoned runners, suggesting that natural talent, as well as circumstances and drive, influence athletic skill:

> Some years ago, the Highlanders held a grand gathering in Holland Park, where they challenged all England to compete with them in their games of strength. The challenge was accepted, and the well-trained men of the hills were beaten in the foot-race by a youth who was stated to be pure Cockney, the clerk of a London banker.[6]

Outstanding athletic performance by an individual is rare and breathtaking. Observing the same talent in identical twins, such as Phil and Steve Mahre, and Patricia and Sylviane Puntous, truly defies the odds. Their matched achievements became headlines:

> "Phil wins gold, Steve wins silver," echoed around the world, following the 1984 Olympic slalom skiing event in Sarajevo. Phil's combined time was 1 minute, 39.41 seconds, just .21 second faster than Steve's![7]

> Patricia and Sylviane lead the Hawaiian Ironman [triathlon] event, on October 6, 1984. [They] usually finish together and in front of just about everyone.[8]

Twin researchers have invested hours teasing apart athletic prowess to understand its separate physical and behavioral components, and how they fit together to produce a Carl Lewis (Olympic runner), a Nancy Kerrigan (Olympic figure skater) or a Shannon Miller (Olympic gymnast). Information uncovered so far has relevance for anyone cherishing Olympic dreams, running marathons for fun, or starting a weight loss program. Is it genetic likeness, hard work or just coincidence that identical twins turn in nearly duplicate performances?

My "Twins and Sports" file, assembled over the last fifteen years, reveals a corps of elite identical twin and triplet athletes. Greco-Roman wrestlers Dennis and Duane Koslowski won gold medals in the last six days of the 1988 Olympics. According to Duane, "Our legs give us a low center of gravity, giving us the power to go right after somebody, but making it difficult to push us around early."[9] Identical triplets Terri, Christine and Patty O'Reilly were stars of the 1980s Eastern regional junior tennis competitions.[10] Stunning parallel performances also characterize identical twin athletes competing at high school and college levels, such as Orono (Minnesota) High School's hockey players Ross and Rick Bonine, and Syracuse University's lacrosse stars Gary and Paul Gaits. Gary and Paul are famous for the Air Gait, a difficult shot resembling slamdunks in basketball. Their coach called them "super athletes who come along once in a lifetime."[11]

In contrast with the identical pairs, I found few outstanding fraternal twin athletes with similar talents or interests. High school tennis players Daniela and Alexandra Del Prete, ranked sixteenth and seventeenth in the Eastern Tennis Association sixteen-and-under division, are an exception.[12] I also discovered a fraternal quadruplet set, Jennie, Chrissie, Julie and Brian DeMichele of New Canaan, Connecticut, with matching sports interests, but differing sports activities.[13] The three females participate on their high school's soccer team, but they play different positions to avoid competing with one another. Their brother, Brian, plays ice hockey, a game the girls wanted to play until their mother insisted "ice hockey would be Brian's domain." The pattern of identical twins playing *with* each other, versus fraternal twins playing *against* each other, became familiar.

Identical twin resemblance in *rare* or *unusual* activities, such as Greco-Roman wrestling or the Air Gait, suggests contribution from genetic factors. Therefore, I suspected twins could tell a profound sports story, one going beyond the fascination of identical talent to the core of what explains physical performance. The real story is being unveiled by identical and fraternal twins whose physical traits, aptitudes and interests have been measured and monitored in exercise chambers and in research laboratories around the world. This information may bring us closer to the elusive algorithms separating victory from defeat, and fulfillment from frustration in Olympic games, in local competitions and in neighborhood contests.

My sports file also held a provocative 1995 letter from Dr. K. Anders Ericsson, of the Psychology Department at Florida State University. Dr. Ericsson, who studies the acquisition of expert performance, wrote, "In the traditional domains of Arts and Sciences the number of individuals (one or both members of identical and fraternal twin pairs) attaining the highest levels of achievement is very low and clearly below the frequency predicted by base rates. In sports I have found more examples of one or both twins reaching very high levels." His observation suggests that factors leading to excellence differ across domains, an issue sports-minded multiples might elucidate.

Twin studies of sports and exercise have proceeded at two levels: similarity in interests and achievement, and similarity in specific performance-related measures. Most reports prior to the mid-1970s compared identical and fraternal twins' resemblance in sports *interests*. Information was generally gathered by questionnaires, although compelling case material from early reared apart twin studies was available. Most later work examined activity-related physical characteristics (e.g., muscle fiber composition), fitness measures (e.g., maximal oxygen uptake) and hormonal changes (e.g., response to training and overfeeding). These studies brought twins from lawns to laboratories to collect information under highly controlled conditions.

Formal demonstration that genetic factors influence athletic interests was first provided by Hans von Grebbe, a 1950s German investigator. Using a small sample he found identical twin athletes engaged more frequently in the same sport and in the same branch of a sport than fraternal twins.[14] This pattern was repeated in a 1960 study of 97 identical and 227 fraternal Italian twins, conducted by Professor Luigi Gedda.[15]

Other dramatic suggestions of genetic influence upon athletic talents and choices also came from early reared apart identical twin studies. George and Millan each won boxing championships in his weight class before discovering that his twin existed. Esther and Elvira enjoyed dancing, as did Olive and Madge, who did not meet until after their interviews. Berta and Herta enjoyed standing before audiences, and while Berta danced and Herta sang both possessed the "stage presence" required by athletic and artistic performance.

It is worth revisiting the concept of emergenesis to understand why identical twins more often join the ranks of decorated athletes in the same sport than do fraternal twins and siblings. Recall that emergenesis describes unique traits associated with complex gene combinations, and odds are against the same gene assortment appearing in more than one family member. Parents and siblings of over 1,200 1968 Olympic athletes reported only average level physical and motor skills.[16] This is a somewhat surprising finding because while extraordinary talent might not repeat, I would expect most close relatives to be above average. Perhaps the more limited athletic opportunities in the 1960s prevented some people from knowing their true talents. Identical twins are the exception to the emergenic rule because they inherit the same genes and, consequently, the same gene combinations.

Only one twin can win any given contest in which both are competing, so comparing identical twins' performances may highlight major causes of minor differences. How do we explain Phil Mahre's .21-second advantage over Steve on the slopes, or Shigeru Soh's six-second edge over his twin brother, Takeshi, in Japan's 1983 marathon?[17] Did their performances reflect consistent differences in ability or training, or psychological factors on a particular day? Why did China's Li Xiaoshuang enter and win the men's 1996 Olympic gold medal in gymnastics while his identical twin brother, also an accomplished gymnast, cheered from the sidelines? Perhaps random events such as a slight change in snow conditions, a shoelace coming undone or a sudden case of nerves explain why identical twins' performances are just shy of identical.

Fraternal twins pose different questions. How did Mo Huilan, the Chinese gymnast who dazzled viewers at the 1996 Olympics, bypass her fraternal twin sister who showed greater early promise? Was she a more dedicated athlete, with greater drive and perseverance? Twin researchers can address these questions by "dissecting" sports performance and sports psychology into basic physical and behavioral elements. Their emerging insights may help us all enhance our athletic performance.

A modest but compelling laboratory analysis of twins' physical skills was an exception to the questionnaire format of early twin sports research. Reported in 1961 by Logan Wright, Professor of Psychology at Bethel College, the study compared the performances of a rare pair of reared apart ten-year-old identical twin boys with a pair of reared together nineteen-year-old identical twin women.[18] This design tested the extent to which shared environments affected athletic skill development. Wright concluded, "It is amazing how much identical twins tend to be alike in some abilities only to be so different in others. Even when their backgrounds are radically different (as in the case of twins 'F' and 'L'), they were still more alike than was originally hypothesized in some areas." Twins in both pairs were extremely similar in reaction time, agility and coordination, suggesting genetic influence on these measures. However, the reared apart "rural" twin outperformed his "urban" brother in strength and endurance, possibly due to greater physical activity.

Wright's twin study was too small to have significantly deepened our understanding of athletic performance.[19] However, he used a genetically sensitive design that anticipated analyses illuminating individual differences in sports-related measures.

• *Height.* Height significantly affects success in many activities. Even researchers who believe that practice and training contribute more to expert performance than genetically based physical traits view height as an exception. Short stature is favored in gymnastics for executing twists and turns, but tall stature is better in basketball for shooting balls into hoops. Six-foot, ten-inch Horace Grant and his identical twin brother, six-foot, nine-inch Harvey, play basketball for the Washington Wizards and for the Orlando Magic, respectively. They have been described as "among the country's most versatile and mobile big men."[20]

Studies show striking height resemblance in identical twins, relative to fraternal twins, suggesting that genetic factors explain 90% of individual differences.[21] Identical twin similarity in height is the same for males and females, and for twins reared together and apart. Early identical twin height differences may be explained by intrauterine hazards, such as unequal nutritional supply, but these effects usually lessen over time.

Many parents are awed by their identical twins' closely matched heights at virtually every developmental stage. Other parents are equally fascinated when identical twins alternate being slightly taller or slightly shorter at different ages. Swedish researchers found that, at age ten, height differences were .4 inches for identical males and .5 inches for identical females.[22]

Cotwins could differ by as little as zero, or as much as 2.3 inches. In contrast, height differences were 1.5 inches for fraternal males and 1.7 inches for fraternal females, with cotwin differences ranging from zero to 3.6 inches. The late Dr. Ronald S. Wilson at the University of Louisville gathered beautiful data showing more synchronized "spurts" and "lags" in height for identical twins than for fraternal twins.[23] ("Spurts" are periods of growth; "lags" are periods of stability.)

Genetic influence on height remains strong throughout adolescence and adulthood, although genetic effects decrease slightly in late adulthood. This happens because environmental influences unique to individuals, such as accidents or illnesses, may cause twins to differ. Reared apart identical Danish twins, Viggo and Oluf, differed by 1⅜ inches because Viggo suffered a severe hip lesion, leading to shortening of one leg, secondary scoliosis (sideways deviation of the backbone), and stooped posture.[24]

Proper health and diet are essential to normal growth. However, individual differences in height, within and between populations, persist despite dietary improvement, evidence of individuals' unique genetic effects. Eating beyond a certain point adds pounds, not inches.

• *Weight.* When the reunited identical Jim twins discovered sudden, simultaneous ten-pound weight gains at forty-five they wondered if their common genes might bear some responsibility. Had they never met, each might have blamed unknown dietary or lifestyle factors for their expanding waistlines.

Many people worry about gains and losses in weight. Blaming weight problems on biology rarely brings sympathy, but twin studies offer new answers to questions concerning weight gain and its control. Dr. David Allison of the Obesity Research Center at New York's St. Luke's/Roosevelt Hospital believes behaviors like eating and exercising lie between genetically based physiological factors and body weight.[25] This may help explain why some people lose weight easily by counting calories and lifting weights, while others following the same regimen lose weight more slowly. Genetically influenced personality traits may also distinguish conscientious from careless dieters.

Like height, weight can affect success in sports such as rowing and running because lighter athletes enjoy skill advantages. Low body fat composition helped make identical Olympian rowers Betsy and Mary McCagg well-suited to their sport.[26] Genetic influence on body weight also explains why heavier identical twins select and excel at certain sports, like the wrestling Koslowski twins who weigh 230 pounds (Dennis) and 245 pounds (Duane).[27]

Twin studies of weight replay twin studies of height in important ways. Some newborn identical cotwins show large birth weight differences, but they usually diminish over the first six months. Similarities in "spurts" and "lags" remain high after the first year, dropping somewhat between the ages of four and six. In contrast, fraternal same-sex twins' weight similarity declines over the first year as twins' unique genes start to express themselves. Not surprisingly, fraternal opposite-sex twins are least alike in birth weight, declining in similarity from birth to one year when males grow faster. However, opposite-sex twins become more similar in weight from ages one to four because females "catch up" to their brothers.[28]

Greater identical than fraternal twin similarity in weight also occurs in adolescence and adulthood. As with height, genetic influence upon weight appears stable during adulthood.[29] At eighteen, Swedish twins differed by 6.8 pounds (identical males); 5.4 pounds (identical females); 11.8 pounds (fraternal males); and 10.0 pounds (fraternal females). Cotwin differences ranged from 0.2 to 15.5 pounds for identicals, and from 0.8 to 64.5 pounds for fraternals. Twins' average weight differences increased at age thirty-eight, but identical twins remained more alike than fraternal twins; the largest difference was unusually large—over 100 pounds for one fraternal (female) pair.[30] Genetic influence on weight declines during late adulthood.

Most studies of twins reared together and apart show that genetic factors explain 50–80% of individual differences in weight.[31] There has been some evidence of greater genetic influence on weight in males than in females, especially in James Shields's 1962 reared apart twin study,[32] but the differences are often slight.[33] The life histories of female identical twins may fill gaps in this story.

Terri Bugbee and her identical twin sister, Debbie Apodaca, of Southern California are five-foot, one-inch blondes, first introduced in Chapter 1. Their weights have fluctuated idiosyncratically over the years, yielding differences between five and twenty pounds, but as much as ninety pounds during one twin's pregnancy. They blame their dissimilar weights on similar erratic eating habits during stress, and on their tendencies to gain weight easily. Researchers suspect that female twins' weight differences may also be linked with social pressures to diet and exercise, suggested by the greater frequency of eating disorders (e.g., anorexia nervosa and bulimia) in young girls and women than in young boys and men. Twin studies suggest that genetic factors, possibly personality traits such as impulsivity or introversion, may contribute to eating disorders.[34]

Environmental causes of males' weight differences have not been formally studied, but case histories offer insights. In 1979, I tested Edward and Gabriel Othon, eight-year-old identical twins. I was struck by the marked weight difference superimposed upon their identical faces and forms. Their mother Cira revealed that Gabriel, who had been bigger since birth, had a consistently larger appetite. During dinner I was impressed by the brothers' 3:1 servings ratio, and wondered if prenatal or postbirth nutritional or physiological factors may have affected hunger cues. Medical conditions, such as irritable bowel syndrome, explained weight differences in some reared apart male pairs in the Minnesota Study.

Identical twins who differ in weight offer a wealth of information on how excess pounds affect physical health. Identical male twins who gained more weight than their cotwins between ages twenty and forty-eight years had higher blood pressure and stored fat than their twin brothers, raising their cardiovascular risks.[35] In another study, identical female and male twins who outweighed their partners by 39.5 pounds, on average, showed disturbed glucose metabolism. These natural cotwin control designs bring welcome order to the search for disease susceptibility.[36]

• *Body Mass Index (BMI)*. Body mass index (weight in kilograms/height in meters^2) is a measure of obesity that adjusts for the fact that tall people weigh more than short people. Twin studies of BMI have shown genetic influence on BMI, ranging from 50–90%.[37] Genetic influence on BMI appears higher in adolescence than in adulthood, consistent with body weight patterns. Common features of home environments, such as meals and recreational sports, do not seem to affect BMI because reared apart identical twins are as similar as reared together identical twins.[38] This means that factors responsible for twin similarity reside in shared genes, and factors responsible for twin differences reside in nonshared environments. Some recent work has suggested greater BMI similarity in identical twins who spend more time together, but in this study it was unclear whether close contact led to similarity or if similarity led to close contact. Marital partners show slight BMI similarity *before* marriage, but not after, which suggests that living together does not make them alike.[39]

• *Other body fat measures*. There has been an influx of twins, siblings and other relatives into physiology laboratories, helping scientists find genetic and environmental influences on specific features of body size and composition. In addition to height and weight, measures have included skinfold thickness (body fat estimate made by measuring thickness of the skinfold at body areas, such as the back of the arm) and fat free weight. A tour of research centers reveals genetic influence on virtually all dimensions, but gene-environment contributions vary across traits and across studies.[40]

The nature and control of fatness are preoccupations of athletes, models, dancers and anyone concerned with health and appearance. A 1997 report showed increased obesity among children and adolescents, urging greater attention to diets and exercise.[41] This finding seems to conflict with twin research showing little effect of shared environments on body weight. Professor John Hewitt, at the University of Colorado, Boulder, explains that facilities reducing energy expenditure, such as televisions and computers, are present in nearly every home, *but* genetically influenced behavioral differences affect family members' use of these facilities.[42] In other words, the relative frequencies of television watching and sports participation are partly explained by genetic factors, so siblings may differ in their recreational choices despite sharing a home.

New twin studies are challenging old thoughts about who gains weight and why. According to identical twin wrestler Duane Koslowski, "We're big engines, and we need a lot of fuel. . . . In a day, we probably consume 1,500 to 2,000 calories more than most people."[43] It is reasonable to assume that the Koslowskis' intense workout schedules have kept these twin wrestlers muscular, not overweight, but perhaps their bodies use calories quite efficiently. Compelling twin research by Dr. Claude Bouchard, at Quebec's Laval University, has revealed genetically based differences in weight gain and in where weight goes. (Dr. Claude Bouchard is not related to Dr. Thomas Bouchard.)

• *Overfeeding and overexercising.* In 1990, Dr. Bouchard invited twelve identical male twin pairs, age 19–27 years, for a twelve-week feast, room included. He was looking at the body's response to overfeeding and lack of exercise.[44] The twins maintained diets that exceeded their normal intake by 1,000 calories each day, six days each week, for eighty-four days.

Body composition and fat deposition were measured frequently, yielding fascinating findings. The average weight gain was 17.8 pounds, but ranged from 9.5 pounds to 29.2 pounds. Most interesting was the fact that weight gain was more similar *within* twin pairs than *between* twin pairs—that is, individual twins were more similar to their twin brothers than to members of other pairs. Twin brothers also showed strong resemblance for body weight, percentage of fat and fat mass.

Bouchard's study may help vacationers, binge eaters, gourmets and gourmands understand why one person's three-course meal is another person's midnight snack. It is also not surprising that identical twins often enjoy similar foods and beverages that other people might find unusual:

• "Twin sin" is a specialty cocktail invented by reunited British Giggle Twins Barbara Herbert and Daphne Goodship. It includes one ounce of vodka, one ounce of blue curaçao, one ounce of crème de cacao, and one and one-half ounces of cream.
• Dining with reared apart identical twins Mark Newman and Jerry Levey at the Triplets Roumanian Steak House in New York, I learned that they shared a preference for *very* rare red meat.

Height, weight and diet affect athletic interest and performance, but cannot unlock the mysteries behind Tiki and Ronde Barber's stunning football careers. Nicknamed "Barbers of C'ville" at the University of Virginia in Charlottesville, the Barbers are the ninth twin pair to play in the National Football League (NFL)—Tiki is a New York Giants' running back and

Ronde is a Tampa Bay Buccaneers' cornerback.[45] Complex factors are also needed to explain the dramatic synchronized swimming of United States Olympians Karen and Sarah Josephson, the basketball artistry of University of Southern California's Pamela and Paula McGee, and the football prowess of North Central College's same-year teammates Ken and Greg Wilson, Don and Dave Ricks, Tim and Tom Franklin, and Frank and Wes Hobart.[46]

How can we understand the underpinnings of athletic ability? In his neurological story of sports performance, *Why Michael Couldn't Hit,* Dr. Harold L. Klawans asserted, "Nature determines the limits of what nurture can accomplish. That is an absolute. But at the same time nurture determines not only what nature can do but the way in which nature develops in order to do it."[47] In other words, genetic factors (nature) provide us with ability propensities, some of which must be activated before a certain age (nurture) in order to be developed fully. Because Michael Jordan spent his youthful years on basketball courts, not on baseball diamonds, he never developed the biological functions essential to great hitting. If Jordan had an identical twin devoted to joining bats and balls, his twin's baseball achievements might have been superior, but not equally legendary because his skills may have been better suited to basketball.

"If anyone beats me in the race, its okay if it's Jan." A 1987 television documentary, *Body Watch* (WGBH, Boston), featured Canadian identical twins Jan Girard and Dian Girard-Rives, superb athletes in running, swimming and cycling. Jan began triathletic events before Dian, but her sister achieved the same performance level after brief practice. This cotwin control "experiment" suggests that training benefits are partly under genetic control, explaining why some people take weeks to perform pirouettes, while others are adept within days.

Jan and Dian exemplify twin studies showing that training boosts endurance, but that the *amount* of improvement is genetically influenced. Dr. D. Prud'homme at Laval University recorded performance changes of male and female identical twin pairs before and after a two-week endurance-training program.[48] Participants' maximal aerobic power (MAP) changed substantially after training, but twin partners showed striking similarity in MAP gains. Genetic effects on endurance may come from specific genetic effects on bone length, lung functions, heart rate and other measures.[49]

Chapter 7 presented a reared apart twin study showing that genetic factors affected rate of learning, as well as pre- and postpractice performance. I believe this study has profound implications for athletic achievement. Assuming identical practice and training among athletes, then their ability differences should be more closely tied to genes than to experiences. Of course, practice methods vary across competitors and, as behavior geneticist Mike Miller proposed, choice of training may partly reflect genetically influenced traits (e.g., conscientiousness), possibly constraining achievement level. Runners learning the curves of future race courses may be better prepared than runners who do not.

The athletic talents of identical twin pairs also illustrate what we are learning from twin studies of performance and fitness. Nick and Pete Spanakos, the only identical twins winning boxing championships on the same night (February 21, 1955) in New York City, showed the same muscular contours on their five-foot, four-inch frames. "And they both fought the same [way]: busy, their hands always going. They were real crowd pleasers."[50] Identical twins David and Scott Hartle flaunted identical biceps at body-building camp, while preparing for the Teenage Mr. Western South Carolina and Mr. Olympia titles.[51] Forty-one-year-old identical twins Angela and Chris Hearn placed first and second in New York City's 1987 "Museum Mile" run.[52] Superior fitness may have favored their amazing finishes, as well as those of identical twin swimmers James and Jonathan DiDonato,[53] tennis players Tim and Tom Gullikson,[54] and hockey players Peter and Chris Ferraro.[55]

A 1997 study of ten-year-old Belgian twin pairs and their parents found both genetic and environmental influence on tests of physical performance (e.g., strength and running speed) and health measures (e.g., flexibility and oxygen uptake).[56] Genetic influence on performance measures ranged from 23% (running speed) to 72% (static strength); genetic influence on health measures ranged from 38% (flexibility) to 86% (skinfolds). Twins' shared experiences accounted for 32–46% of flexibility and running speed. Other twin research has disclosed information on muscle characteristics that the Spanakos and Hartle twins keep hidden from view. Surprisingly, these studies show that type and distribution of muscle fibers appear largely environmental in origin.[57] Further study of this finding will be of interest.

Evidence of genetic contributions to physical skills should not discourage parents and coaches from fostering fitness and sports participation in unathletic children. Short girls and boys may gain inches or strength in adolescence, acquiring sports advantages previously lacking. Furthermore, training and motivation improve skill and confidence in everyone, although gains vary across individuals. The trick may be creative matching of particular children to particular sports, sometimes specialized in nature. Everyone cannot be equally skilled, but everyone *can* be physically fit.

We also know that some athletes appear to be at greater injury risk than others, a circumstance twin research may help to explain. Genes affect pathological development of physical structures and processes, just as they affect the traits underlying outstanding athletic performance. Twin studies of sports-related injuries are unavailable, but some identical twins' fatalities after exercise reveal an interplay between abnormal physiology and behavior. Dr. Ernst Jokl has described twenty-year-old identical twin brothers suffering fatal heart attacks associated with physical activity. Their disorder's rarity in young adults, its similar timing and its coincidence with exercise implicated the twins' genetic design in their early deaths.

Scanning generations in our own families may also suggest common genetically influenced medical conditions that may be aggravated by exercise. Dr. Jokl's report included a three-generation family with six of ten sudden fatal collapses linked to exercise. A genetic defect causing irregular heartbeats was eventually identified.[58] Fortunately, most sports injuries are not fatal, such as the left wrist hamate bone fractures in baseball players José and Ozzie Canseco (happening two months apart),[59] back pains in basketball players Damon and Ramon Williams (appearing six months apart),[60] and stress fractures involving the same three vertebrae in hockey players Ron and Rich Sutter (occurring one week apart).[61] Incredibly, high school twins Pat and Mike Pearson pulled ligaments in their right ankles within one hour of each other, on the same step of the same agility exercise.[62] Another high school pair, Jason and Justin LaFerla, suffered similar leg fractures from basketball.[63] These examples suggest genetic influence on injuries in general, and on injury type in particular, despite the absence of genes specifically coding for these events. I believe athletic twins' common accidents and injuries suggest blended effects of inherited physical characteristics (e.g., cardiac anomalies or bone weaknesses), personality traits (e.g., aggressivity or risk-taking) and sports interests (tennis or basketball). Underlying the Sutters' fractures may be bone weaknesses aggravated by strain from the sport they both love.

Many people may recall the incredible silver medal win in pairs freeskating at the 1984 winter Olympics, in Sarajevo, Yugoslavia.[64] The award was won by Kitty and Peter Carruthers, a famous brother-sister ice skating team. The interesting twist was Kitty and Peter are not biologically related, having been adopted two years apart at age three months. Some might conclude that the $180,000 spent on intensive training guaranteed two ice skating champions, but the story is not that simple. Their mother, Maureen Carruthers, requested "active" children from the Home of Little Wanderers in Boston, and received exactly that. Peter was "always stronger than the other kids," while Kitty was "dancing before she could dance." They are a great example of natural ability uniting with opportunity to produce spectacular outcomes.

The McCaggs (female rowers), Koslowskis (male Greco-Roman wrestlers) and Carrutherses were more than natural athletes able to practice their sports. They were individuals with personalities and drives suited to particular activities and to intense competition. Twin studies show that individual differences in well-being, achievement, control, and stress reaction have a genetic basis, and combinations of these traits most likely affect athletic participation and success. Belief in one's ability to excel may also figure into the elusive athletic axiom. Identical twins show greater agreement on self-reported athletic competence, physical appearance and self-worth than fraternal twins, siblings and stepsiblings,[65] no doubt contributing to their similar sports successes and disappointments. Identical twins also show greater intellectual similarity than fraternal twins, probably affecting decision making and strategy in athletic contexts.

Not all identical twins are matched in athletic skill. An example is former Oakland A's baseball players José and Ozzie Canseco—José has been a "superstar," while Ozzie has mostly spent time in the minor leagues.[66] Not all identical twins prefer the same activity, such as high school students Kate and Nell Hirschmann-Levy—Kate practiced gymnastics since age seven and Nell chose soccer after trying track and swimming.[67] Some fraternal twins, such as tennis players Daniela and Alexandra Del Prete, are very much alike with adjacent rankings in their age division.[68] Exceptional cases are a good test of ideas about why we are the way that we are because they may highlight factors deciding success or failure, and participation or nonparticipation in different sports.

Another force driving athletic achievement springs from finely tuned interplay between teammates, or between performers and trainers. Is it trust, is it inspiration, is it love—or all three that fuel desire and confidence to reach new levels? I found amazing answers to these questions from twenty-eight-year-old Scot and Sean Hollonbeck, identical twins who embody athleticism and sportsmanship at their finest. They display a special side to *friendship extraordinaire* that enriches our lives beyond gymnasiums and race tracks.

Scot and Sean were born on November 5, 1969, at Fort Benning's Military Hospital near Atlanta, Georgia, but spent their childhood years in rural Rochelle, Illinois. The twins' older sister, Jamie, is thirty, and their younger brother, Lane, is twenty. They also had an infant brother who died when they were seven. Their parents, Susan Leith and Dr. Gary Hollonbeck, have divorced and each has since remarried.

Scot was born first with a six-pound weight that was double that of his twin. Sean's newborn health was poor, evidenced partly by his bluish skin tone which suggested oxygen insufficiency in his blood. The twins' size difference diminished, but did not disappear, as genetically based growth patterns overtook more unpredictable prenatal effects. Scot still leads in height, measuring five-feet, nine-and-one-half-inches (178 cm), while Sean measures five-feet, eight-and-one-quarter-inches (175 cm). However, Sean is twelve pounds (5.4 kg) heavier than Scot—a traumatic life event (to which I will return) reversed the twins' prenatal legacy, but not before their athletic abilities and interests blossomed.

Sean presented a detailed chronology of the twins' sports activities. Featured were "pee wee" baseball in first grade, swimming in third grade and basketball in fourth grade and beyond. Sean believes their abilities were

*Scot (left) and Sean Hollonbeck, shown at age twenty-eight, exemplify twin-
ship and athleticism at their finest.* PHOTO CREDIT: DEBORAH HANNA.

"equal" except for eighth grade basketball in which "for some reason Scot
was a better dribbler," dividing the brothers between "A" and "B" teams.
Sean disliked "B" status, but was never jealous of his twin. "If anything,
twinship makes you work that much harder to be faster and better," he said.

Where did the twins' shared athletic virtuosity come from? Their father
had excelled in football, basketball and track, becoming a sports legend in his
local high school. Their grandfather Loren ("Lefty") Hollonbeck held his
high school's title for fastest 800-meter run (2 minutes, 1.3 seconds), a record
unbroken for fifty-eight years until 1997.[69] Clearly their family provided both
the genes and the opportunities for developing athletic skills.

Shortly before their fifteenth birthday, on July 20, 1984, while Sean slept
in, Scot set out on his bicycle for early morning swim practice. Two hundred
meters from his home Scot was struck from behind by a wearied driver wan-
dering onto the opposite lane. Sean believes his powerlessness after his
brother's accident tightened his resolve to become a doctor, a desire kindled
when the death of his baby brother brought his family to the hospital many
times. He is now completing a medical residency in family practice.

Scot suffered permanent lower spinal cord injury, denying him use of his legs. He believes that on a "regular day" Sean would have biked with him, silencing the difficult "what if" questions that have arisen from his absence. Once out of rehabilitation, Scot's "hardest" challenge was watching his twin pursue football, track and wrestling, knowing that competition with Sean was no longer an option. Over the years I have learned that twin brothers and sisters of injured twins suffer different realities, a subject on which Scot shared incredible insight. He explained that able-bodied individuals cannot know the social stigmas and physical hardships paralysis imposes, leaving his twin with an "intimate wondering" of what daily tasks were like for him. He believes Sean understands him better than anyone, but people with similar disabilities would understand certain sides of him better than Sean.

Ironically, Scot's brilliant sports career was launched from his hospital bed in the intensive care unit two days after the accident. The 1984 Los Angeles Olympic Games broadcast the women's 800-meter wheelchair race, an event displaying "speed, skill, endurance, grace, and beauty," and convincing the fourteen-year-old his athletic days were not over. According to Sean, Scot continued high school swimming, stroking "strong and powerfully," and began playing wheelchair basketball. More remarkable, Scot raced in his wheelchair against his able-bodied classmates, outperforming them two and a half years later in all distances over 800 meters.

After high school, Sean entered Cornell College in Mount Vernon, Iowa, and Scot entered the University of Illinois in Champaign, Illinois, a trying separation. In addition to studying biomechanics, Scot's basketball talent earned him distinction as MVP (most valuable player). Sean transferred to the University of Illinois in his second year, and the twins were roommates once again. He accompanied Scot to approximately fifteen races each year, becoming an "unofficial wheelchair racing junkie," assisting his twin and other competitors with stretching exercises and equipment assembly. These races led to the 1992 Olympic and Paralympic Games in Barcelona.

Following a fifth place finish in the 1,500-meter Olympic race, Scot returned to Barcelona two weeks later for the Paralympic Games. (Paralympic Games occur two weeks after able-bodied Olympic Games and are held in the same venue. This event offers the highest level of competition for athletes with disabilities.[70]) Scot set world records in the 800-meter (1 minute, 40.63 seconds) and 1,500-meter races (3 minutes, 13.11 seconds), records standing unbroken for three years. Incredibly, Scot's performance in the 800-meter race was the *first time a wheelchair racer broke an able-bodied runner's 800-meter record*—Sebastian Coe from Great Britain finished this distance in the slightly greater time of 1 minute, 42.33 seconds in July, 1979, in Oslo, Norway.[71] Scot went on to earn silver medals in the 800-meter and 1,500-meter races in the 1996 Paralympic Games, and a silver medal in the 1,500-meter race in the 1996 Olympic Games, both in Atlanta. As of his performance in Barcelona, Scot now holds world titles for the second fastest 800-meter race

Scot Hollonbeck races toward the finish line at the 1996 Paralympic Games in Atlanta. PHOTO COPYRIGHT © CHRIS HAMILTON PHOTOGRAPHY, ATLANTA, GEORGIA.

and third fastest 1,500-meter race. He also set an IAAF (International Amateur Athletic Foundation) 5-kilometer (3.1 miles) world record in a road race (10 minutes, 28 seconds) in Carlsbad, California, at the 1997 Carlsbad 5000.[72] He placed first in the May 1998 Pittsburgh marathon (26.2 miles), finishing in 1 hour, 38 minutes, 23 seconds.

Scot's redirection of athletic skills, dedication to training, and optimistic outlook were crucial to the best development of his physical talents. He currently works for International Sport Productions in Atlanta, where he creates and promotes sporting events. Racing is in his future, especially events at the 2000 summer Olympic and Paralympic Games in Sydney, Australia. Sean is a medical resident at Fort Benning's Army Hospital, outside Atlanta. His athletic accomplishments include running the 1992 Chicago marathon in under four hours, and scoring 100% in the army's physical fitness tests in six separate years.

Scot and Sean actively contribute to changing the attitudes of people who associate disability with inability. Sean voiced the unappreciated truth that *greater* athleticism is often required of disabled athletes than able-bodied athletes to perform the feats they do. An example of this point occurred during their participation in Dr. William A. Bauman's twin study of spinal cord injury's (SCI) effects on metabolism at the Veterans Affairs Medical Center, in the Bronx, New York:[73] Sean set the record for able-bodies twins' exercise stress test performance, measured by arm and leg ergometers.[74] Scot shattered his brother's title, becoming the only SCI twin to outperform his nonSCI cotwin.[75]

Dr. Bauman's study is the only one in the world bringing a twin-based perspective to the medical consequences and clinical management of persons with SCI. I visited Dr. Bauman and his colleague, Dr. Ann Spungen,[76] in their laboratory in November 1997. Their study, launched in 1993, investigates how spinal cord injury affects cardiovascular risk and disease by comparing twins' blood sugar, energy expenditure, body composition, exercise endurance and cardiac stress. The nature of these changes and their consequences can be tracked more efficiently by contrasting identical twins, rather than by following nontwin individuals over many years (especially in the absence of information prior to injury), or by comparing SCI patients with unrelated controls. Sixteen twin pairs have been studied thus far, eleven male and five female, identified through SCI publications and referrals from colleagues. The twins range in age from 21 to 53 years, with an average age of thirty-eight years. Several new twin pairs have been identified and will be invited to the study when additional funding becomes available.[77]

Data analysis is under way, but important findings have already emerged. SCI twins weigh an average of 10.8 kg (23.8 pounds) less than nonSCI twins, reflected in BMIs lower on average by 3.5 kg/m². These differences reflect profound changes in SCI twins' body composition such as their decreased total body lean tissue and increased percentage of leg fat.[78] Scot and Sean's weight and BMI differences reflected these trends, but were below average due to Scot's unusually high activity level. The availability of identical twins also allows unique analyses of bone mineral density loss, a common cause of fractures in SCI patients due to their immobilization. It has been assumed that bone loss levels off after initial immobilization, but twin comparisons show that the degree of bone loss is associated with duration of injury, with progressive loss over time.

Drs. Bauman and Spungen assembled an incredible panorama of photographs, each showing a twin pair with the research team. It was a familiar display, reminding me of twin pairs decorating the desks and walls of twin laboratories everywhere. However, this exhibit suggested a mood different from the carefree poses I know so well. The twins' obvious warmth appears laced with regret, anger and frustration because life is not as it was meant to be. I shared my reactions with Scot who showed that emotions cannot always be read from photographs. "I feel none of these sentiments. . . . I am proud to be disabled, really—it is a natural part of the human experience."

The greatest tributes to twinship were quiet and personal. Virtually all of the able-bodied twins in the study privately approached Dr. Bauman, confiding in him that they would do anything to help their twin brothers and sisters. The successes of many of the injured twins may have been largely due to the love and encouragement of their twin brothers and sisters. Dr. Terry Winkler was one of the first disabled individuals in the United States to become a physician. He is famous for chaining his wheelchair to Governor Bill Clinton's desk in Little Rock, Arkansas, in 1990 to protest funding cuts for disabled persons. A female twin army officer, injured in an accident during maneuvers, went on to work in a Veterans Administration hospital and began tutoring. A female twin, Kari Krumweide, injured at age thirty-one when a falling tree damaged her body, drives a car, manages her home, and cares for her four sons. Injury may motivate disabled individuals and, as in sports, identical twins have only to look to their cotwins to see what they can achieve.[79] In some cases, the SCI twins' accomplishments exceeded those of their cotwins.

The behavioral features of paralysis have been examined by psychologist Cynthia L. Radnitz.[80] Eleven SCI and nonSCI cotwins did not differ in depression or alcohol misuse even though both have been associated with SCI patients' adjustments difficulties. Furthermore, SCI and nonSCI cotwins' scores did not differ across personality factors such as neuroticism and extraversion. These findings support theories that depression, alcohol misuse and personality characteristics (e.g., risk-taking tendencies) *predate* SCI, possible exposing some individuals to situations in which injury is likely.

Scot and Sean give depth and definition to identical twins' unique sports experiences:

- *Scot:* "Life as a twin is a life of competition. We were constantly compared to see who crawled first or who got better grades. But in sports, our competition meant staying abreast of one another. Having a twin made early morning runs and swims a lot easier, and we pushed each other rather than trying to beat each other. When I played basketball with Sean and he hit a three-pointer, I knew I could do it, too.

  "When I trained my teammates in Illinois I did it with the idea of making them better, not beating them, but pushing them to their limits just like I did with my twin. You can only do this with someone you completely trust. When I race against someone with whom I have no relationship, I try to beat him, but it was never that way with Sean. I once trained someone for two years who beat me at the Paralympic Games, which was okay, but not completely okay. I asked myself: Do I love that person that much? Did I get as much out of his win as he did? The answer was 'no.' If Sean had won it would have been completely okay and, in fact, I would not have thought of it in this way, I would not have asked myself these questions. With Sean it was all trust and friendship."

- *Sean:* "Having a twin is like having a training partner. You compete with your twin, but not against him, and not with the intention of beating him.

The goal is to be as good as you can be, and your twin provides inspiration to achieve that goal. Twinship is also a great setup because you practice more often than kids who do not have twins. I would go home and throw a ball with Scot, but others kids would go home and throw a ball alone. It's better than practicing with a brother or with a father because you're the same age, you experience the same thing, and you support each other.

"I never pursued sports in a selfish way. When Scot captured the gold medal in Barcelona I welled up inside with joy and tears."

Twins' comments and research findings have led me to recast concepts of athletic competition and glory. Many identical twins curb their selfish tendencies when competing with their cotwins, even as they seek personal triumph. Runner and identical twin Karen Peterson admits that when the gun sounds "it's everyone for themself. But I am also thinking of her (Jeanne) and how she is doing."[81] When identical twin Phil Mahre delivered a certain gold medal Olympic performance on the slopes in 1984, he told his twin brother, Steve, "Here's what you have to do to beat me." Fewer fraternal twins participate as pairs so less is known of their athletic dynamics.[82] However, high school tennis players Daniela and Alexandra Del Prete admit that their competition was once so fierce they left the court silent and angry. Today the twins have matured to the point that "Whatever happens on the court stays on the court."

The words of Karen Peterson and Phil Mahre recall the March 1989 *Twins* magazine cover story featuring Mike and Mark Hembd of Denver, who appear on the cover with Arnold Schwarzenegger. The occasion was the 1987 International Special Olympics, held in South Bend, Indiana.[83] (Special Olympics offers sports training and competition for children and adults who are mentally retarded.) In this issue, Sandy Hembd writes lovingly of her twin sons, born on December 16, 1968 with Down Syndrome. Mike and Mark learned basketball, swimming, skiing and weightlifting after joining Special Olympics at age eight, allowing them to compete with their high school swim team.[84] Sally is aware of four other twin pairs among Colorado's 4,000 Special Olympics participants, such as Stephanie and Holly Bakker who won gymnastics medals.[85] A fraternal twin pair with Down Syndrome, Hunter and Kyle Krei, from Denver, also participate in these games.[86] The chance that fraternal twins would be concordant for Down Syndrome is estimated to be 1/871,200,[87] but several cases have been reported.[88]

Twin research on sports fields and in exercise laboratories make us better positioned to understand how biology and psychology commingle to produce sensational performances in some people, and acceptable or uninspiring performances in others. A number of psychologists are taking new looks at the nature and origin of expert performance. Dr. K. Anders Ericsson claims that exceptional human performance in most fields requires ten years of deliberate practice, usually four or five hours each day. He argues that intense practice induces remarkable physiological adaptation in the tissues and organs of elite athletes, although the biological processes causing these adaptations also occur among the less elite. He also shows that experts structure their lives to make the most of rest and training, and that more accomplished individuals practice several years earlier than less accomplished individuals.[89] I find this evidence provocative, but not fully convincing. Everyone would agree that intense practice improves performance, but not all highly motivated individuals achieve similar results, and some high achievers perform admirably despite inconsistent practice. In fact, superior natural ability may motivate practice and training, rather than the other way around. However, I agree with Dr. Ericsson that genetically influenced activity level and temperament may affect individuals' ability to engage in and sustain deliberate practice.

I suspect training differences may better distinguish among elite athletes than among amateur athletes. In other words, there may be reduced variation in genetically based physical traits across accomplished athletes, allowing small differences in training to produce significant consequences in performance. Researchers studying skill acquisition might look to professional and nonprofessional identical and fraternal twin athletes for answers.

Earlier in this chapter, I mentioned Ericsson's suggestion that twins have made few outstanding artistic or scientific contributions, although they have had outstanding athletic achievements. The truthfulness of this claim has not been confirmed,[90] but I have heard discussion of his thoughts by other colleagues. Aside from twins' ideal training situations, partial answers to twins' athletic successes were suggested by Carolyn Waldo's 1988 Olympic synchronized swimming experience. Waldo, who teamed with Michelle Cameron to defeat Karen and Sarah Josephson, found the twins' physical identity intimidating because matched appearance is so crucial to her sport. Attempting to mimic twin advantages, Waldo and Cameron tried walking at the same pace and synchronizing their heartbeats through meditation and exercise, but Waldo "was more hyper."[91] Identical twin athletes also attract special attention, and being "on stage" may improve performance.

I once tried an experiment, covering one identical twin's face in a photograph. The remaining twin was still appealing, but the allure of the matched set was lost. I wonder if this phenomenon enhances identical twins' athletic performances in judges' minds.

It is possible that identical and fraternal twins' below-average intelligence test scores partly explain their seeming absence among noted artists and scientists. However, IQ does not perfectly predict unusual talent or achievement, and even scores exceeding 150 do not identify individuals with extreme giftedness or "genius."[92] Language difficulties experienced by some twins, especially identicals, may hinder their expression of ideas. More important, perhaps, while identical twins may intimidate athletes competing in events where appearance counts, they are unlikely to intimidate artists and scientists competing out of view in books and articles.

It would be interesting to know whether more fraternal twins than identical twins are socially or academically distinguished. Fraternal twins' accomplishments tend to attract attention only if they are extraordinary, not because of their twinship. There are, in fact, distinguished fraternals whose twinship is largely unknown. Actress Isabella Rossellini is a fraternal twin whose sister Ingrid has an advanced literature degree. The late world champion checkers player Marion Tinsley had a fraternal twin sister, Mary.[93] Identical twins' accomplishments may create interest *because of their twinship,* so perhaps we hold fraternals to higher standards.

Dr. Ericcson asserts that innovation in art and science fields is less frequent than mastery and maintenance of expert physical performance—but this would not explain twins' possible underrepresentation. He suggests, too, that being an identical twin may remove incentive for social recognition because twins' physical identity alone can accomplish that. This explanation *cannot* be correct because many identical twins have worked hard to become distinguished athletes. Attention to twin-singleton differences in achievement may sharpen thinking about routes to distinction in different fields.

Understanding the genetic and environmental underpinnings of physical ability does not demystify superb performance. Scientists may separate out measured components of athletic skill, but they have not yet furnished the formula that puts them together again. This mighty feat is accomplished only by performers whose personal prescriptions for superb performance may never be fully known. Triple toe loops remain miraculous in spectators' eyes.

Noah's Ark: Twins in the Nonhuman Animal Kingdom

In April 1987 I received a greeting card from my twin sister, Anne, showing orangutan twins *(Pongo pygmaeus)*. The card read: "Orangutan means 'man of the woods' in Malay. After a gestation period of more than nine months, the female usually gives birth to a single young which clings to her for at least two years as she moves around."[1] The appearance of these orangutan twins on the greeting card seemed a celebration of sorts, recognizing their rare birth.

A benefit of working in twin studies has been that my colleagues, students, relatives and friends were research partners in a real sense. The interest twins inspire in most people was heightened among individuals closest to me, guaranteeing a steady flow of scholarly reports, news clippings and sound bites on twin-related topics. Items ranged from the noteworthy ("twins provide clues on aging") to the mundane ("twin T-shirts made to order") to the extraordinary ("identical triplets reunited after nineteen years"). Their contributions also let me assemble an unexpected treasure: a nonhuman twinning library bearing fascinating findings on twin lambs, koalas, pandas and penguins.[2] I suspected that these sources might shed insights on aspects of human twinning. I began by examining some announcements of nonhuman multiple births:

- In October 1977 Dr. Jane Goodall announced the birth of male chimpanzee twins, Gyre and Gimble, to mother Melissa. Born at the Gombe Stream Reserve in Tanzania, they were the first recorded chimpanzee twins delivered in the wild.[3]

- In June 1985 a healthy panda pair, Pe-Pe and Ying-Ying, were born in Mexico City's Chapultepec Park. The larger firstborn twin was cared for by its mother, while the smaller secondborn twin was cared for by medical staff.[4]
- In August 1988 the Hellabrunn Zoo near Munich, Germany, announced the birth of snow leopard quintuplets to mother Eli. They were the first recorded quintuplets of their species, which inhabits the central Asian mountains.[5]
- In September 1988 Australian zookeeper David Pepper-Edwards revealed the birth of twin koala bears, Edward and Pooh, the second set born in captivity.[6]
- In December 1988 twin hippopotamuses were born at the Memphis City Zoo to mother Julia. Actress Cybill Shepherd, a native of Memphis, Tennessee, and mother of opposite-sex twins, would select the twins' names in a city-wide contest.[7]
- In July 1995 the Wildlife Conservation Society announced the birth of western lowland gorilla twins at New York's Bronx Zoo, only the second set born in the United States.[8]
- In February 1998 the Buffalo Zoo announced the December 1997 birth of polar bear twins, each weighing six pounds.[9] This seems striking, but twins are the most common birth in bears, and up to five young may be born at a time.[10]

Reports of nonhuman animal twinning also yielded surprises with human themes. A functionally infertile Friesian cow, artificially inseminated with Charolais semen and placed in the same area with a Simmental bull, delivered twins—a Charolais bull calf and a Simmental heifer calf. These superfecundated twins were conceived close in time by the same mother, but by different fathers, so they shared approximately 25% of their genes. Amazingly, the cow had been scheduled for slaughter when conception occurred, having been thought infertile![11]

Many nonhuman twin births are exceptional, but twinning occurs in a larger number of animals than people realize. Cattle often produce fraternal twins (about one in fifty births),[12] nine-banded armadillos almost always produce identical quadruplets,[13] and some wasps and flatworms normally produce thousands of identical descendants.[14] Thoroughbred horses have a higher incidence of twin conceptions (22%) compared with other breeds, such as standardbreds (14%) and quarter horses (10%).[15] Cats and dogs produce multiple offspring or litters, but their regular occurrence in these familiar animals may make them less special. Why frequency and twin type vary among animals is not fully known, but answers to these interesting questions are emerging. Polyembryony in nonhumans proved mysterious and enlightening.

Polyembryony is the splitting of one sexually produced embryo into many embryos. The offspring are genetically identical to each other, but are genetically different from both parents. Human analogues to polyembryony are

identical twins, triplets, quadruplets and quintuplets. Human identical twinning is, however, rare and sporadic, whereas polyembryony is frequent and
regular.[16] Polyembryony occurs repeatedly in only a few mammals, such as
nine-banded armadillos, but occurs often in several nonmammals, such as
bryozoans (marine animals) and parasitoid wasps (solitary insects).[17]

A lasting reproductive strategy should be advantageous, but polyembryony
poses a peculiar paradox for evolutionary theory: The original embryo is
formed by sexual reproduction which evolved to bring genetic variation to
populations through new gene combinations. Yet the process creates multiple
copies of an organism with untested survival value,[18] a result that evolutionary biologist Dr. George Williams likens to investing in identical lottery tick-
ets.[19] By the same token, parents of identical triplets have *one* chance to win
the healthy child raffle at a cost of three if they fail, while parents of two singletons have *two* chances at a cost of only two. The polyembryony paradox
may be resolved if the gains from producing many identical young exceed
losses from their lack of genetic variability.

Speculation surrounds the circumstances that might promote polyembryony.[20] According to Dr. Larry Slobodkin of the State University of New York
at Stony Brook, "Surprisingly, in more than a dozen cases, these animals
(wasps and flatworms) leave the number of offspring up to the kids."[21] His research team suggested that when females cannot judge their embryos' environmental circumstances then the *embryos* themselves may trigger twinning.
Human identical twinning is presumably random, yet unknown environmental conditions could cause its occurrence in some families. Perhaps parents of
identical multiples can "blame" their children for self-duplication—but
maybe their children were only "anticipating" their future surroundings. Theories of polyembryony await confirmation, but the efforts of Slobodkin and
his colleague Sean Craig have stirred the scientific community.

Evolutionary setbacks due to reduced genetic variability in populations
may partly explain identical twinning's infrequency in humans (1 in 250
births) and in some mammals. Identical twinning rates in cattle, sheep and
pigs may match those in humans, although this is uncertain because nonhuman identical twins may go unnoticed.[22] Extraordinary exceptions to the low
rate of mammalian identical twinning occur in the nine-banded armadillo and
the seven-banded mulita.

Armadillos are brilliantly described and beautifully depicted in *Vanishing
Animals,* an enchanting fusion of science and art.[23] In order to produce
quadruplets, the armadillo's fertilized egg divides several times after three
months' quiescence (delayed implantation). Amazingly, four identical babies
result nearly every time. This reproductive feat is rivaled only by the seven-
banded mulita, which produces seven to fifteen identical babies from one fertilized egg.[24] What enables armadillos to create their incredible litters? Unlike
many mammals who have a Y-shaped bicornuate uterus,[25] armadillos have a

single "kite-shaped" uterus with one implantation site. Armadillos may double ovulate, but double implantation has never been observed. Identical twinning may have evolved in armadillos to increase offspring number otherwise restricted by their uterine shape.[26]

Like their identical human counterparts who can differ in disease, hair whorl and handedness, armadillo quadruplets do not match exactly in all traits. One study showed that slow rejection of skin grafts occurred among coquadruplets in two sets, a surprising finding given their genetic identity.[27] The investigators suggested that the quadruplet set members might have different histocompatability antigens (foreign substances against which the body produces specific antibodies for protection). Skin grafting and organ transplantation enjoy high success rates among human identical twins who are uniquely perfect donor-recipient pairs.[28] If armadillos were easier to study we might be able to learn more about the mysteries lying behind transplantations performed between close relatives. We might also learn more about sibling relations from these striking quartets, a suggestion raised by zoologist Richard Dawkins over twenty years ago.[29]

W. J. Loughry of the Biology Department at Valdosta State University has reported some clever studies examining altruism in juvenile and adult armadillos.[30] The researchers first determined that young armadillos could tell their kin from nonkin, behavior that would allow altruism between animals sharing genes. They did so by showing that armadillos spent more time near pads containing their littermates' scents than pads containing strangers' scents. Then, contrary to what was expected, videotaped sessions (also a favorite of human twin researchers!) revealed that pairs of littermates did *not* interact more often or more harmoniously than pairs of strangers. The researchers suggested that littermates' genetic identity has little known consequence for their behavior, and that factors affecting altruism vary across animals and conditions.

Fraternal twinning seems a better evolutionary plan than identical twinning because genetic differences between siblings supply populations with precious variability. In fact, fraternal twinning is twice as frequent as identical twinning in humans (1/125 vs. 1/250 births) and in other large mammals. It would be misleading, however, to suggest that fraternal twinning offers obvious evolutionary advantages. This is because most primates (the order of mammals to which humans belong) have evolved to produce single offspring at advanced stages, thereby reducing litter size. Reduction in litter size is associated with uterine changes that support single fetuses. It also alters reproductive patterns, delaying sexual maturity by extending childhood and adolescence. This change allows longer time for brain development, but makes offspring more dependent upon parents. Consequently, multiple infants are less likely to survive the perils of uteri built for one, and twin survivors are more likely to suffer from disabilities or scarce resources. This may

explain why twins are rare among humans and among our closest primate an-
cestors.[31] A table summarizing frequencies of primate twinning is provided in
the notes for this chapter.

Twinning tendencies in various primates are variable. The near nonexis-
tence of twins among Old World primates catapults news of their births into
prominent science journals.[32] Twins were born on the night of March 18, 1946,
to a green guenon *(Cercopithecus sabaeus)* at the San Diego Zoological Gar-
dens. They were the first twins among forty births by eight *Cercopithecus* monkey species during the previous fifteen years. When the zookeeper discovered
the twins the next morning, they were no longer living, but their mother continued to carry and clean them. She finally abandoned the infants, who were
badly bruised and smaller than average, but otherwise appeared normal.[33]

Twins' continued presence poses other riddles. If their births are problematic throughout the animal world, why does fraternal twinning persist? This
leads to the question: Why is fraternal twinning genetically influenced in humans? It is possible that benefits of genes associated with fraternal twinning
offset its difficulties so genes associated with twinning are not eliminated.
For example, mothers of fraternal twins are taller than mothers of identical
twins and nontwins, which could be advantageous in some contexts.[34] Furthermore, mothers of fraternal twins seem to acquire resistance to breast cancer, so long as multiple births are not followed by single births.[35] Findings are
mixed on whether parents of twins live longer and bear more children than
parents of nontwins.[36]

Fraternal twinning is more frequent in older mothers, so I wonder if it is a
way of increasing genetic representation as menopause approaches. It turns
out that L. Scott Forbes of the University of Winnipeg in Canada has thought
about fraternal twinning with this idea in mind.[37] He sees fraternal twinning
as an "adaptive trade-off," namely that the benefits of successful pregnancies
in older women may offset the risks and costs of defective children. Forbes's
work, while controversial, challenges conventional wisdom that fraternal
twinning simply reflects an age-related increase in abnormal egg production.

Twins' novelty in the primate world may explain why we celebrate births
of twin gorillas, chimpanzees, orangutans and monkeys. I believe these nonhuman twins excite us by repeating the themes that make human twins special: We perceive their physical frailty, and hope they overcome survival
odds.[38] We recognize maternal dilemmas dividing attention in two, and smile
at creative solutions. We are fascinated by cotwins' developmental changes,
and indulge in sibling comparisons. It was not surprising that in July 1995 the
Bronx Zoo staged a nine-day festival welcoming male gorilla twins Ngoma
("to drum or dance") and Tambo ("to strut proudly") into their community.

Ngoma and Tambo were born at the Wildlife Conservation Society's Bronx
Zoo, in the Bronx, New York, on August 8, 1994. I learned of their birth from
a *New York Times* announcement, "They're rare, a pair and covered with

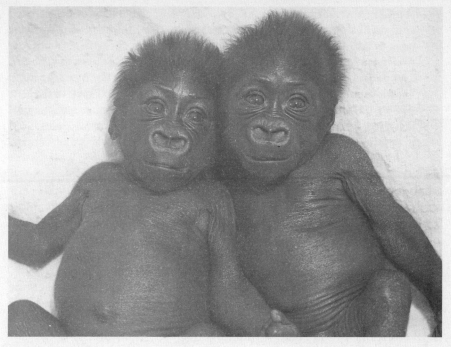

Four-month-old gorilla twins Ngoma (left) and Tambo were instant celebrities at New York's Bronx Zoo. They are the seventh recorded pair of gorilla twins born in captivity, and only the second pair in which both cotwins survived. PHOTO COPYRIGHT © WILDLIFE CONSERVATION SOCIETY.

hair."[39] Their matching wide-eyed stares are precious and powerful. Blood tests showed the twins were fraternal, but their physical likeness and rare delivery made their joint appearance alluring, as happens with humans. Most nonhuman (and human) primate births occur at night, so part of the surprise with the Bronx Zoo twins was their time of delivery—they arrived on a Sunday afternoon, witnessed by a keen visitor who reported the news to animal staff. The twins' mother, Pattycake, was seen carrying both twins while miraculously climbing through the door to the nighttime sleeping area. The first press releases (paraphrased below) were delayed until the twins' health received attention:

- *August 1994:* Ngoma and Tambo became the seventh and eighth infants born to twenty-two-year-old mother, Pattycake, and the third and fourth infants born to thirty-five-year-old father, Timmy. Pattycake was a "famous New Yorker," as the first gorilla arriving at the Bronx Zoo from New York's Central Park Zoo. Timmy was on breeding loan to the Bronx Zoo from the Cleveland MetroParks Zoo, in Cleveland, Ohio.
- *October 1994:* Soon after birth, Ngoma weighed four pounds, three ounces

and Tambo weighed three pounds, five ounces. (Lowland gorillas born in the wild usually weigh four and one-half to five pounds at birth. Gorilla twins born in 1967 in Frankfurt, Germany, had birth weights of three pounds, twelve ounces and four pounds.[40]) Their birth order could not be determined even though the delivery was captured on videotape. They were the sixth known set of western lowland gorilla twins, an endangered species (but see note 44). Few gorilla births occur in captivity. The only other gorilla twins delivered in captivity in the United States were four-pound, eight-ounce males;[41] two nontwin male gorillas born in captivity weighed four pounds, ten ounces and five pounds.[42]

Ngoma and Tambo were shielded from public view until July 1995 to assure their good health status. They spent their first twenty-four hours in the zoo health center before being transferred to a nursery to be cared for by a human surrogate mother. A part-time surrogate mother with identical twin daughters of her own was also delighted to assist in the gorillas' care. This step was essential for the twins' safety and survival, despite Pattycake's lifting of both babies after their birth. There was concern that Pattycake might drop one or both twins, and Timmy, who reached for one of them, could have put them at some risk.

The need for gorilla infants' good early treatment is underlined by the fact that only six twins from the other seven pairs are living today. Dr. Dan Wharton, Director of the Central Park Wildlife Center at New York's Central Park, provided me with a summary of these rare births.

Chronology of Gorilla Twin Births

Year of Birth	Location	Studbook Numbers[43]	Comments
1967	Frankfurt, Germany	294, 295	One twin survived newborn period and is alive today
1981	Barcelona, Spain	767, 768	One twin survived newborn period and is alive today
1981	Yerkes Primate Center Atlanta, Georgia	780, 1012	One twin stillborn, one twin lived one day
1983	Columbus, Ohio	835, 836	Both twins alive today

Continued on next page

Continued

Year of Birth	Location	Studbook Numbers[43]	Comments
1966[44]	Kansas City, Missouri	980, 981	Twin fetuses delivered at three months gestational age; gestation is usually 8.6 months
1987	Les Mathes, France	1031, 1032	Both twins stillborn
1994	Bronx, New York (Ngoma and Tambo)	numbers to be assigned	Both twins alive today
1999*	Oklahoma City, OK (Amiri & Ayana)	numbers to be assigned	Both twins alive today

*Information provided by Jack Grisham, General Curator of the Oklahoma City Zoo.

I visited the twins at the Bronx Zoo in December 1997. People closest to them, such as Dr. Colleen McCann, Assistant Curator of Primates, as well as the twins' full-time and part-time surrogate moms, described thrilling details of the infant twins.

Ngoma and Tambo were somewhat smaller than average newborn gorillas born in the wild, but their weights were within the normal range. They were small enough for their full-time human mother to place them both in a single incubator in her home. The twins were part of a quintet of infant gorillas reared together from birth. Their three companions included their half sister (one month younger and related through their father), and two unrelated females (four months younger and half sisters to each other). Ngoma and Tambo's greater social preferences for each other than for their mates developed increasingly over the first year.

The part-time surrogate mother was enamored of the pair, who reminded her of a litter of puppies, "like watching my own twins." Her most intriguing memories were of periodic shifts in the twins' dominance-submissiveness relations, "same as my twins." She was fascinated by Ngoma's left thumb-sucking and Tambo's right thumb-sucking, behavior sometimes shown by human twins. One twin has a crease on one nostril, while the other twin has two creases on his other nostril. Ngoma has four folds between his eyebrows, while Tambo has two. Both twins exhibited their father's teeth-grinding, a behavior he displayed in tense situations, even though they lacked early contact with him.

I wondered if there were certain features of the twins' parents, Pattycake and Timmy, that distinguished them from singletons' parents, but there appeared to be none. Pattycake had delivered six previous children, a risk factor in human fraternal twinning, but her birth history was typical of gorillas in captivity.

*   *   *

The twins have duplicate plaques outside their shared exhibit at the zoo, introducing the "rare pair" to onlookers: "Hard to tell apart from twin" and "Like most twins have a close bond;" and "Features: Square full face and large hands and feet" and "Disposition: Dependent upon his twin brother." The most impressive comments from Dr. McCann and the surrogate moms concerned the twins' striking physical similarity. For the first few months zoo staff assumed Ngoma and Tambo were identical twins because, unlike other infant gorillas, they were difficult to distinguish. Like parents of human twins, the caretakers used the twins' slight differences, such as Tambo's flatter shaped head and their number and location of nostril creases, to tell them apart. In contrast to human parents, Ngoma and Tambo's caretakers were still struggling to identify each twin three years later. Dr. Wharton was also struck by their unusually similar appearance. The part-time mother believed they were identical not only because of their matched appearance, but because of their matched dentition—gorillas show varied dental development, but Ngoma and Tambo were highly synchronized. Identical gorilla twins are presumably rare; according to Dr. Wharton twin-typing has been done only on the Columbus, Ohio, twins, who were fraternal.

When the twins' DNA profiles (patterns in certain DNA regions) were compared by Dr. George Amato, Bronx Zoo geneticist, they indicated fraternal twins. As Dr. Amato suggested, Ngoma and Tambo's slight physical differences may sharpen with maturity.

The public did not see Ngoma and Tambo during their first year of life, but progress reports were regularly released and closely followed:[45]

- *February 1995:* Tambo's weight increased to ten pounds, two ounces, and Ngoma's weight increased to ten pounds, seven ounces. They were "knuckle-walking" (supporting themselves on their knuckle joints), and were starting to sit and climb. They also discovered the "crib-gym" and each other.[46]
- *July 1995:* A city-wide twin-naming contest, sponsored by the *New York Daily News,* resulted in 30,000 submissions. The winning entry came from a five-year-old Brooklyn girl who found Swahili names, *Ngoma* and *Tambo,* in an African picture-word book.
- *May 1997:* Both twins weighed approximately fifteen and a half pounds. They were happy and playful, laughed a lot, and got along well with others.

The twins were reintroduced to adult and juvenile gorillas beginning at about one year of age. Living at the zoo they grew closely bonded, preferring time with each other to time with their three peers. During an observational study conducted on the five youngsters, Dr. McCann observed that social preferences followed kinship lines, with closest bonds between the twins, followed by the twins with their half sister, and the two half sisters with each other. The twins are well integrated into their social group, but remain each other's preferred playmate. Another male infant would have been an interesting addition.

The public's enthusiasm for the twins has not waned, as indicated by birthday notes, Christmas cards and even wedding invitations the pair regularly receive. It is likely they will be placed in a breeding situation when they begin maturing sexually at age eight. Most breeding groups have one male, but the twins may remain together because of their shared social history. Meanwhile, Ngoma and Tambo continue to thrive at the Bronx Zoo where they can be visited at the Ape House and new habitat, "The Congo Gorilla Forest." They weigh approximately forty-five pounds each, and are lively and fun to watch.

Chimpanzee twins Tom and Helene were another fascinating pair, encouraging new thoughts about what we do know, and what we can know, about behavior. In 1933 there were no confirmed records of twin births among the great apes (orangutans, chimpanzees and gorillas).[47] Therefore, the June 26 birth of opposite-sex fraternal chimpanzee twins Tom and Helene to parents Mona and Pan at Yale University's Anthropoid Experiment Station in Orange Park, Florida, was news.[48] The announcement indicated normally developing infants despite their 2–4 week premature birth at 210 ± 5 days gestation. Their birth weights were approximately 2–3 pounds each, just slightly below the typical 3.5-pound birth weight of newborn zoo chimps.[49] The twins' mother, Mona, was twenty years old, and weighed approximately 140 pounds which is heavy for females of her species *(Pan leucoprymnus)*. She had delivered three previous singleton infants. The twins' father, Pan, was age eleven and was described as "notably sexually vigorous." (I have heard several fraternal twin fathers claim physical credit for their multiples—"My wife had nothing to do with it!"—but sufficient sperm count is the only likely male requirement for conceiving multiples. Of course, unknown paternal genetic factors may be involved—for example, father's contributions to prenatal environments may stimulate ovulation despite conception, producing superfecundated twins.)

Wonderfully, experimental procedures were not employed so mother-twin observations were as naturalistic as possible within the confines of captivity. I have always enjoyed (human) parents and twins' private moments because of the potential for unplanned words and gestures which sometimes revise researchers' questions and explanations. For example, a father of identical twin boys insisted he never confused his sons, but when one boy engaged him in rough and tumble play he begged the "wrong" twin to stop. I realized that because fathers may see twins less often than mothers, they may be less sensitive to their distinguishing characteristics.

Highlights from chimpanzee mother Mona's first year with her twins, Helene and Tom, were available:[50]

- Mona's early nervousness affected her twins, causing both infants to cling to her. The source of her nervousness was not discovered, but seemed related to the northwest corner of the cage. It was also certain that caring for two infants at the same time was overwhelming to a mother who had already delivered three infants. Chimpanzee infants (born in the wild) are nursed for four or five years and are constantly carried by their mothers for three or four years, activities complicated by the birth of two.[51] (No wonder Mona was nervous!) A turning point occurred at month twelve when mother and twins were transferred to new quarters—afterward, the twins seemed less affected by their mother's mood and grew more independent of her. Remarkably, Helene then turned to Tom for protection, unusual behavior prior to weaning or separation.[52] Helene's substituting Tom for Mona may have been reinforced by Mona's tendency to "lessen" her maternal responsibilities toward the twins.

- Mona was a competent mother, evidenced by her twins' healthy development. Curiously, she showed less concern toward her twins than chimpanzee mothers usually show toward their nontwins. Mona's indifference might have reflected her previous maternal experience (motherhood was less novel), her unique behavioral traits (she tended toward reserve) or the unique effects of rearing twins (she found it overburdening). Interestingly, her time spent grooming self and twins was relatively brief, but all three animals were well groomed. Therefore, researchers suggested "economy of effort" might also explain Mona's behavior. (Human mothers of twins and near-in-age singletons will sympathize with Mona, recalling pressures to accomplish tasks with little time.)

- Helene's sucking difficulties brought extra maternal assistance, identifying her as Mona's favorite twin. This response on Mona's part was noteworthy since most mammals do not single out unhealthy offspring for special help—in fact, healthy offspring are more likely to reap benefits from parental investments. Investigators suggested Mona's solicitous behavior toward Helene may be unique to primates, or to anthropoid apes and humans. Examples of human mothers dedicated to caring for premature, frail or impaired infants are well known.[53]

- Most striking from the twins' birth through their first year of life was Mona's self-interested behaviors, namely discouraging infant clinging, grasping, sucking and begging. This uncharacteristic behavior possibly came from her conflict over personal freedoms and infant demands. At the risk of anthropomorphism, I sense in Mona the concerns and frustrations felt by many new mothers of twins, explaining the proliferation of support groups and hotlines for parents of multiples.

Helene and Tom were opposite-sex fraternal twins, and thus displayed developmental differences familiar to parents of two. For example, Helene's coloration was grayish, while Tom's was brownish; Helene was heavier than

Tom for the first half year, but they reversed positions when he adapted more readily to supplementary feedings; the twins showed matched dental development, with both developing eight deciduous incisors before six months of age.[54] Helene was also relatively timid, shy, slow to adjust to novelty and slow to benefit from success. (Helene took longer than Tom to drink from a cup, but once she acquired this skill her food intake still remained small.) In contrast, Tom was venturesome, aggressive, quick to adapt to novelty and quick to gain from mastery. At five months of age Helene was stronger than her brother, but clung to Mona's limbs, while Tom rode on her back. Helene was also less amenable than Tom to handling by observers.

Parents gazing at newborn twins delight in thinking about the shared pleasure the children will experience once they become social beings for each other. Social interest (e.g., vocalization) may occur sooner between human twins than between nontwins (three or four months vs. six months) because of their opportunities for close interaction with another newborn.[55] Helene and Tom appeared to befriend each other at month six, no longer treating each other as inanimate objects. (This is the age at which chimpanzee infants typically leave their mothers and approach other individuals.[56]) The circumstances proceeding this breakthrough are uncertain, but the emergence of twin-directed vs. mother-directed behavior signaled an important change. The first inkling of behavioral change occurred when Helene grabbed and bit Tom, who responded in kind. Thereafter, the frequency of joint play increased, including episodes of vocal and facial expressivity while manipulating each other's bodies. Tom initiated play periods in which Helene participated, even while she gave greater attention to Mona.

How Mona came to know her twins, and how they came to know one another remains a fascinating story. Some answers to questions of mother-infant identification and twin-twin recognition are coming from unusual sources, such as lambs.

Research has shown that ewes preferred their own familiar firstborn twin lambs who were reared with them, compared with the lambs' secondborn cotwins, who were raised apart in isolation since birth. Familiar lambs triggered greater licking readiness, more low bleats (baahs; signs of comfort often emitted by mothers reunited with their offspring), fewer high bleats (signs of distress), and less aggressive butting by their mothers. (Mothers are always excited to see their children!) It is remarkable that the ewes significantly favored their secondborn twin lamb taken from them at birth, compared with an isolated alien lamb or an alien lamb raised by its own mother. Investigators suggested that odors of the presumably fraternal twin lambs are similar, letting mothers recognize their lost twins.[57] In contrast, the alien lambs' odors probably differed from those of the familiar firstborn tw[...] lambs. The source of the firstborns' odors could have reflected ge[...]

based scents and/or acquired scents from delivery, sucking and being licked by their mother. Another possibility was that some separated twin lambs were opposite-sex, facilitating discrimination between twins.

Ingenious experiments using infant twin lambs and their mothers have teased apart some of these influences.[58] Following delivery, firstborn same-sex fraternal twins were immediately placed in a separate chamber in their mothers' presence. This allowed mothers to have access to these infants' odors, but prevented them from having physical contact. Secondborn twins were housed in isolation. Several hours later, ewes preferred their firstborn twins over their secondborn twins, as well as their secondborn twins over alien lambs. These findings supported the researchers' earlier conclusion that fraternal twin lambs share genetically influenced odors enabling their mothers to identify them. In these experiments, firstborns were preferred only because they remained with mothers while secondborns were isolated. There was nothing intrinsic to being a firstborn twin that would have affected ewes' preferences.

By now a wealth of studies show olfactory identification of kin by tadpoles, iguanas, mice and other animals. Olfactory recognition studies have also included humans, yielding some spectacular results. Mothers can use odors to correctly identify T-shirts worn by their two- to ten-day-old infants, and six-day-old infants can use odors to identify breast pads worn by their mothers.[59] Of course, people primarily rely upon vision and hearing to identify family members, but mother-infant sensitivities suggest that our sense of smell probably affected social attraction in early human history. In fact, body odor may play a larger role in our present social relations than we realize. Complex skin chemicals may underlie individuals' distinctive, recognizable odors.[60]

A fascinating series of studies shows that identical twins' scents generally confuse both human and canine noses, especially if twins are living together and eating the same foods.[61] There are also exceptions to the rule. Some mothers claim they sort identical twins' laundry by differences in smell, but this interesting assertion has not been tested. In one study, dogs were able to distinguish identical twins when tracking a twin's path after exposure to that twin's scent. In this case both twins' odor paths were present, possibly helping dogs identify the odors by contrast.

I became curious to know if the odors of garments worn by identical twins would be more difficult to distinguish than those of fraternal twins. However, I found no difference in judges' abilities to match shirts worn by adolescent fraternal and identical cotwins.[62] This result may reflect judges' lack of genetic and social relatedness to the twins. (For example, husbands and wives can identify spouses' T-shirts, so learning body odors of genetically unrelated cohabitants is possible.) This study may be improved by having twins themselves be the judges—my hypothesis is that identicals will be more accurate than fraternals in sniffing and selecting garments worn by their cotwins. Of course, the best kin study of odor recognition would use identical and fraternal twins reared apart because they would not have learned cotwins' odors through familiarity.

Most caretaking events, such as nursing and transporting infants, are less hidden than odor recognition. Infant care among marmosets and tamarins (small primates from Central and South America), in whom twinning is the rule, show fascinating parenting patterns.[63]

Marmoset and tamarin pregnancies last approximately 130–184 days. Many species have two births each year so mothers can become pregnant shortly after giving birth, even if nursing. Frequent multiple pregnancies, high infant birth weights, and carrying infants rather than leaving them in nests require dividing care responsibilities among parents and helpers. Fathers and helpers assist by carrying one or both twins, and by participating in feeding and protection. Larger groups enjoy greater reproductive success than smaller groups because greater assistance is available.

Cotton-top tamarins have tufts of white hair on their heads; I understand why they remind some animal researchers of punk-rockers. They have been studied more often than other members of their genus because they highlight certain pressures and dilemmas of multiple birth parenting. Maternal carrying-time in cotton-top tamarins is most influenced by number of children and, understandably, mothers without helpers carry twins less often than singletons. Additional caretakers also improve infant survival—in field studies, 40% of infants survive when cared for by parents plus one helper, while 100% of infants survive when cared for by parents plus three or more helpers. Interestingly, having helpers reduced carrying time by fathers, but not by mothers, possibly because maternal effort was lessened by one helper, while additional helpers assisted fathers. Carrying incurs costs in effort and energy to helpers (although infant benefits are presumed to be equally high), so I am not surprised that large groups rejected infants less often than small groups, and that singletons were rejected less often than twins. Twins' extra demands were underlined by mothers' earlier transfer of twins than singletons to other caretakers (day 3 vs. days 6–7 for cotton-top tamarins; days 9–11 vs. days 14–17 for lion tamarins).

Conflicts between parents and children following the births of younger siblings is a common theme in many households. Whether and by how much older children become upset are affected by age spacing, personality traits, parents' awareness, and other factors. Unfortunately, this issue has received scant attention in the human psychological literature. Therefore, I was delighted to discover that this problem has been examined in cotton-top tamarins.[64] A recent study observed twelve juveniles from five families, eight weeks before and twelve weeks after the birth of twins. Juveniles were 6.5 to 15 months old when twins were born. Twin births increased parent-child conflict, decreased child play, and increased nearness of siblings to parents and infants. The effects were sharpest on the twins' birthday, and faded during the next two weeks—by four to six weeks juveniles were carrying the twins. Interestingly, the elder siblings showed distress only when parents carried the twins, so conflict centered on parent-child competition over access to the newborn infants, rather than access to their parents or other resources. Siblings reacted the same way whether the newborns were twins or singletons.

I had always assumed that older siblings' jealousy over younger siblings was mostly due to reduced parental attention. It had not occurred to me that, in humans, older siblings' distance from new twins (and singletons), possibly enforced due to infants' fragile health, could contribute to siblings' adjustment difficulties when newborns come home. Of course, parallels between nonhumans and humans do not necessarily imply that similar behaviors share origins or functions. However, studies using different organisms complement one another by offering rich sources of questions and explanations.

My sister's greeting card showing healthy twin orangutans obscures the fact that not all twin births have happy outcomes. Only eight orangutan twin births have been recorded in captivity, one including a normal male with a behaviorally disabled female cotwin. The brother and sister, born on October 31, 1974 (Halloween), in Madison, Wisconsin's Vilas Park Zoo, were appropriately named Trick (male, firstborn) and Treat (female, secondborn).[65] Their birth weights of 1,250 grams and 1,000 grams were below the normal newborn orangutan birth weight of 1,300–1,500 grams. Unfortunately, their mother had difficulty nursing Treat so the twins were taken from her at two days of age for transfer to the University of Wisconsin Primate Laboratory for special care. Two months later they arrived at the Milwaukee Zoo, and were placed in adjoining areas with a glass divider. When they were five and a half years old, observers detected Treat's impaired fine motor skills and lack of coordination. She showed poor brachiation, the hand-over-hand arm-swinging movement children display in jungle gyms.[66] Trick appeared normal.

Standard learning tests revealed mental deficits in Treat and mental precocity in Trick. Treat could not develop relationships between tools and objects, and did not improve in problem solving. Trick completed tasks quickly and successfully, however, and improved his problem solving skills over time. Neurological tests also showed marked cotwin differences—Treat fell from a balance beam and failed to grasp food with thumb and forefinger, while Trick navigated the beam with ease and readily lifted small fruits and nuts.

Investigators concluded that Treat's mental and motor impairments were probably caused by oxygen deficiency at birth, especially since she showed no chromosomal anomalies. They also underlined the birth risks to secondborn twins, and the probability of disabled infants perishing quickly in the wild. Orangutan mothers might be unable to assist both infants, and probably choose to support the healthy infant who is likely to survive. Twins' greater birth hazards relative to singletons is a common explanation for the general rarity of multiple births in old world monkeys, apes and humans. Maternal abandonment has, however, not prevented the pademelon (a member of the kangaroo family) from bearing twins. An Australian newspaper pictured newborn twin Paddy being cared for by zoo staff after being thrown from her mother's pouch by her twin, Mel.[67]

Most nonhuman mammalian twins are fraternal, but methods for artificially creating identical twin cattle, rabbits, mice and sheep have recently proliferated.[68] Genetically identical animals offer potential insights into the causes and consequences of twinning, and the origins and treatments of disease. As discussed in Chapter 10, cloning interests escalated in 1997 following news that Dolly, a Scottish lamb, had been cloned in 1996 from a cell of an adult donor. This news caused early release of another groundbreaking story at the Oregon Regional Primate Research Center, in Beaverton—the development of cloning techniques for producing genetically identical monkeys.[69] Oregon researchers hoped to use cloned monkeys to develop cures for AIDS (Acquired Immune Deficiency Syndrome) and for retinitis pigmentosa (genetically influenced retinal degeneration). However, the fact that the *methods,* but not the *monkeys,* were available was misrepresented in the press. Nevertheless, the birth of the celebrated siblings Neti and Ditto meant that the birth of cloned monkey twins was imminent.

Dr. Don Wolf and his associates separated the eight cells from several embryos, removed genetic material from another monkey's eggs, fused the cells with these eggs, and implanted the embryos into a new mother. This process, called *nuclear transfer,* is a different procedure from the one used to create Dolly, the lamb. (Dolly was cloned from a single adult cell, whereas Neti and Ditto were created through embryo splitting.)

The term nuclear transfer explains how the monkeys were named—Neti stands for *nuclear embryo transfer infant* and Ditto means "the same." It was soon determined that Neti and her brother, Ditto, were not identical twins because their originating cells were from different embryos. The siblings were initially frightened following separation from their peers, introduction to one another, and exposure to the media. Therefore, a videotape was prepared for public viewing, and the monkeys themselves were returned to peaceful surroundings.

Beyond the pleasing stories of the gorilla twins, Ngoma and Tambo, and the koala twins, Edward and Pooh, nonhuman twinning holds answers to countless human twinning questions. Studies of natural-born and artificially created nonhuman animal twins have brought new perspectives to the evolutionary bases of twinning, parenting of twins, cotwin relations, and birth and delivery. Closest to the cutting edge are cloning experiments intended to un-

Embryo splitting led to the birth of Neti (left) and her brother, Ditto, rather than clones as researchers had hoped. This photo shows them at seven months. The siblings were named by Dr. Dan Wolf's daughter, Carla. PHOTO CREDIT: VINCE WARREN, OREGON PRIMATE RESEARCH CENTER.

cover disease characteristics and cures, and, possibly, new biological features of identical twinning.

I recall another greeting card in my nonhuman animal twin file. It shows two dinosaurs (*Allosaurus,* meat-eating dinosaurs living approximately 140 million years ago) who, according to the sender, are "twins waiting to be subjects in a research project." Dinosaur twins are unknown, but seeing these paired creatures evoked fond feelings, reminiscent of the interest twins of all species inspire.

The Other Half:
Noteworthy Twins

In the early 1980s Dr. Bernard J. Shapiro, Director of the Ontario Institute for Studies in Education, left his home in London, Ontario (Canada), to visit his twin brother, Dr. Harold T. Shapiro, President of the University of Michigan, in Ann Arbor. Students were protesting against the university's refusal to recognize a graduate student union, activities intended to draw President Harold Shapiro's attention. Arriving at the scene Bernard Shapiro was immediately mistaken for his twin brother, but "smiled benignly and kept walking." Protests meant for a university president were not entirely misdirected—in 1994, six years after Harold left Michigan to become eighteenth president of Princeton University, Bernard Shapiro was appointed fifteenth principal (president) and vice-chancellor of Canada's McGill University, in Montreal. The Shapiros may be the only twins in history to share distinction as heads of leading universities.

Twin studies of occupational interests and job satisfaction capture moments of career similarity and difference in twins' lives. These moments are "averages" of abilities, interests, events and choices over preceding years. I, therefore, believe that comparing identical and fraternal twins' *last* or *most prestigious* professions best reflects the interests and capabilities they share and do not share. Some twins taking different paths to common positions may be more alike at later than at earlier stages of their professional development. This is because varied work experiences help define work preferences, and because greater rank increases freedom of expression on the job.

Twin studies tell us that genetic influences affect job preference and satisfaction,[1] challenging predominantly environmental explanations of occupational choice. Twin research also shows genetic influence on changing jobs and occupations.[2] Formal studies cannot, however, convey the personal perceptions, daunting decisions and unplanned events underlying twins' career paths. Filtered through the eyes of twins and the people who know them, we find fascinating details surrounding identical and fraternal twins' acceptance, rejection, and creation of opportunities. Life histories of noteworthy twins may also illuminate our own job decisions, satisfactions and frustrations.

"A Pair of Presidents Keep It All in the Family" headlined a 1995 *New York Times Educational Life Supplement* article. I found the rare matched achievements of the Drs. Shapiro fascinating and compelling beyond words. Only a slim fraction of individuals meet strict standards set for the highest level of university advancement, so finding this accomplishment repeated in twins was extraordinary. Twin findings on intelligence and achievement led me to assume the Shapiros were identical twins, but the article began, "Fraternal twins, the Shapiro brothers grew up . . ." A second *New York Times* article announced, "Honorary degrees for fraternal twins with fraternal jobs."[3] I scrutinized the accompanying photographs for clues to their twin type, but this proved inconclusive—they looked very similar, but not exactly the same. I decided that either the articles' authors were wrong, or these similarly high-achieving twins were an exceptional fraternal pair. I did not solve the twin type dilemma until two years later, and when I did its outcome made me smile.

I met Harold Shapiro on September 24, 1997, in his office at Princeton University's Nassau Hall. His warm and gracious manner promised sincere and thoughtful dialogue on his twinship and his career. President Shapiro's office was the epitome of neatness and order, strikingly different from the typically cluttered halls of academe. I saw only one other such office, the one belonging to Bernard Shapiro, president of McGill. I met Bernard on October 28, 1997, in his McGill University office. He also welcomed me personally, showing the same friendliness and grace I enjoyed a month earlier. Opera music played in the background, an interest the twins shared, although Bernard's recent harpsichord mastery suggested greater musical involvement on his part than on his brother's. Both men took piano lessons as children, the only (small) source of jealousy either named. Bernard believed his twin had more natural musical talent, but "I was a better musician because I practiced." Bernard's tendency to study harder than his sports-minded twin was a familiar theme, designating him as "scholar" and his brother as "athlete" throughout childhood and adolescence.[4]

Bernard was ten pounds lighter than his brother, but the twins' appearance was more alike than the newspaper photographs suggested. Within moments of meeting him I was convinced the two were identical twins. I did not perform blood-typing, but my impression was confirmed by a standard physical resemblance questionnaire both twins filled out—Bernard indicated "frequent" confusion by casual friends (especially at airports and at

*In 1996, the Shapiro twins both received honorary degrees from Yeshiva University. From left to right: Bernard and Phyllis Shapiro, the twins'
mother, Mary Kantor, and Vivian and Harold Shapiro.* PHOTO COURTESY OF
MARY KANTOR.

meetings), while Harold indicated "occasional" confusion, answers tipping
their scores toward identical.

Why did I smile when I learned the Shapiros were identical? I was amused
that after sixty-two years of twinship, two such knowledgeable and distinguished individuals were "uncertain" of their twin type. It is a remarkable
truth that informed strangers know in minutes what close family and twins
overlook in a lifetime. The twins' mother, Mary (Tafler) Kantor, believed her
sons were fraternal twins. She told me, "They are similar, but not identical.
The family never confused them, only strangers did." The next day Bernard
shared a story with me that confirmed his mother's words: A University of
Michigan student once approached the "wrong" Shapiro requesting, and receiving, an extension on a class assignment. I also smiled because Mrs. Kantor's words divulged well-known relatives' sensitivity and strangers'
blindness to identical twins' slight differences. Her reasons for believing her
twins were fraternal were my reasons for believing they were identical.

There were significant distinctions between Harold and Bernard, but there
were profound commonalties. Their educational and professional careers oc-

casionally collided when, for example, they assumed joint management of
their father's restaurant business after his death (1956–61), and held department chairmanships during the same three-year period (1974–77).[5] There
were also near misses, such as Bernard's more scholarly bent, which earned
him higher grades and honors until college when his twin grew more academically inclined. Their most intriguing contrast was Harold's sports enthusiasm, evidenced by high school sports awards and championship of
collegiate athletics, and Bernard's lack of sports interest, typified by absence
from team sports and his refusal to kick off McGill's 1994 football season.
Bernard pursued individual sports, such as swimming and figure skating, but
Harold was a competitive swimmer and water polo player.

Like many identical twins the Shapiros presented unique versions of the
same score, their shared potentials differently shaped by unshared events. Interestingly, both twins delayed pursuing new opportunities until discussing
them with colleagues and with each other. As I reviewed their work histories,
I saw differences in details only, suggesting that their professional lives were
more similar than they or their families realized:

- In 1961, both twins entered top American graduate schools, but in different
  fields. Harold attended Princeton University in Economics, and Bernard attended Harvard University in Education. Both chose statistical specialization's within their disciplines (econometrics and psychometrics).[6] Both
  twins' attraction to topics requiring advanced mathematical skills prompted
  Harold's comment, "Something is going on here. I recognize long odds
  when I see them."
- Harold earned his Ph.D. degree in 1964, becoming assistant professor of
  Economics at the University of Michigan. Bernard received his Ed.D. degree in 1967, becoming assistant professor of Education at Boston University.
- The twins served as university provosts (high-ranking university administrative officers) in partially overlapping years, Harold at the University of
  Michigan and Bernard at the University of Western Ontario, in Canada.
- Harold initially declined the presidency of Princeton, and Bernard initially
  declined the presidency of McGill. Both universities pursued both twins,
  who eventually accepted second offers. Both twins are the first Jewish presidents of their universities.

Paradoxically, the Shapiros' *different routes* to university presidency were
similarly nonconventional. Neither twin sought the highest post in his academic institution, but opportunities came their way. Jack Lazare, a boyhood
friend, observed that while neither twin entertained presidential ambitions,
they probably asked the same important questions when offers came: Is this
job interesting? Could I make a contribution? Would I do it well?

*   *   *

When Harold joined the University of Michigan faculty as an assistant professor, his concerns were research and teaching, not university administration. Then a call came from the university's president, Dr. Robben W. Fleming, requesting that he serve as provost. Harold had no knowledge of what provosts did or where they worked, but after interviewing with President Fleming he found the job "intriguing" and decided to accept. He also had "no idea" why he was chosen. Two years later the president called him again to request that he head the Executive Committee of the University Medical Center. Harold accepted this offer, developing interests in health care finance, health care systems, and ethical values that underlie them. When the university presidency was proposed, his uncertainty turned to acceptance once he became convinced that the job promised an interesting life. His wife Vivian encouraged these career moves.

Harold rejected his first offer to become Princeton's president, but the second offer came when Michigan's campus was undergoing some change. This time Harold visited Princeton and according to Vivian, "was touched by something there—he would be closer to his academic interests, and to faculty and students." Harold echoed these thoughts, indicating that his challenges at Princeton would be contributing to the core curriculum and granting greater priority to undergraduate studies.[7]

After Bernard graduated from Harvard University he held faculty and administrative positions at Boston University for a ten-year period. In 1976, he returned to Canada as University of Western Ontario's dean of the Faculty of Education. Like his twin brother, Bernard's response to this offer was cautious at first, but he saw opportunities for personal growth. A succession of government (nonacademic) appointments followed.[8]

Bernard never intended to be a university president. He declined the first offer to become principal of McGill University, but he accepted a renewed invitation six months later. He thought he had "done it all," but the lure of "new challenges" was irresistible. His wife, Phyllis, remarked that he "had to accept it or the challenge of his career didn't make sense."

Challenge and change draw many people to new jobs. However, the Shapiros never mentioned status as a factor affecting their career choices, something many people would think important. I also noticed that neither twin expressed regret at sacrificing his personal research programs for administrative responsibilities, something many academics (including myself) find surprising. Their job changes and rises in status seem to have been byproducts of others' recognition of their talents, rather than something they thought seriously about. Both twins were inclined to embrace the research issues of their new positions, even as they continued their previous programs (albeit, on smaller scales). Thus, they never gave up personally meaningful projects, but adopted new ones wherever they went. Interestingly, neither twin mentioned that salary affected his job choice, so perhaps financial security allowed them the luxury of pursuing their interests. (Of course, their promotions came with higher salaries, setting a self-perpetuating process in motion—new offers, higher pay.) Nevertheless, the Shapiros could have taken many career paths, but they chose stimulating tasks that happened to bring them prominence and prestige.

Both twins viewed their accomplishments modestly, attributing their successes to hard work, but also to unquestioned acceptance of "authority" (i.e., their mother's expectations and goals), luck and circumstance. In a college paper examining factors responsible for "making me who I am," Harold wondered why he and his brother never questioned their mother's influence. Mrs. Kantor admitted that her sons' ready reception of her disciplined approach "made raising them so much easier." Less compliant children may not have flourished in the Shapiros' home circumstances.

The twins agreed that prevailing social conditions during their childhood and young adulthood had facilitated their accomplishments. Both said that having been born in 1935 to a prosperous middle-class family was a "stroke of luck." They attended fine schools, took music lessons, and traveled to Europe. They were too young for service in World War II or in the Korean War, and finished college in the middle 1950s when economic conditions were favorable. Harold also attributed his June 1996 selection as chair of the National Bioethics Advisory Commission (NBAC) to chance and circumstance. It is, however, likely that his health care expertise made him an attractive candidate for this position.

It seemed reasonable that identical brothers would also look to their identical genes for partial understanding of their successes, but neither twin did. This may be partly due to their rearing in an environment rich with resources. Of course, the Shapiros were also uncertain of their twin type, and like many identical twins downplayed similarities outsiders found striking. Bernard casually mentioned that both twins collected Eskimo sculpture and showed surprise at my interest. He also said that they arranged their homes the same way, but Harold said this was not true. Their disagreement on this point is curious and complex. Home furnishings and their placement variously reflect the tastes of both spouses, so the twins' homes probably had both common and unique characteristics. Perhaps Bernard and Harold had different home features in mind when addressing this question. It is also possible that Harold minimized their likeness in this area, especially since their offices showed the same exceptional order.

I pressed them for their views of behavioral-genetic theory, especially given Harold's recent service on the Cloning Commission (discussed in Chapter 10), and Bernard's knowledge of that work. Both brothers believed that genes affect behavior, hinting vaguely at genetic influence on their occupations and interests, but more specifically at genetic influence on their physical traits. Harold felt that their similar voices, confusing to their wives and mother, "could only be genetic—when Phyllis (Bernard's wife) answers the telephone I have to say 'it's Harold.' " Listening to Bernard in lecture, Harold was impressed by their similarities in hand motions and in construction of ideas. (I later learned that Bernard was unaware of their gestural likenesses.) Harold also believed that Bernard had the capacity, but not the drive, for athletic success which comes "mostly from motivation and work, given reasonable ability." Bernard listed coincidental, unexplained medical similarities between the twins, such as reduced red blood cell count and a skin disorder, as possibly genetic in origin. He also allowed that they shared a combination of "sufficient genes, but also shared an incredibly invigorating environment stressing high achievement." He suggested that the "same genes in different environments could produce different outcomes," restating concepts of *gene-environment interaction*.

Had the twins been raised in more modest surroundings, their genes might have predisposed them to seek challenging tasks, attaining comparable outcomes through different routes. Researchers believe that this process (active gene-environment correlation) partly explains achievement and work similarities in identical twins reared by separate but supportive families. A reared apart identical female twin from England grew up in a home filled with books, while her sister whose home lacked a literary environment was drawn to libraries. I suspect that adoptive siblings would have benefited from the Shapiro home's stimulating environment, but might have shown interests and goals differing from the twins'.[9]

The twins' mother, Mrs. Kantor, favored nurture over nature, but believed Bernard would have been scholarly regardless of his rearing. (She believed her sons "inherited" their father's brains, but emphasized hard work and obligation to succeed.) This was not the first time I heard someone unknowingly underline genetic influence despite their stated convictions to the contrary. Environmentally minded people often claim that certain traits "run in their family," but this observation supports genetic as well as environmental transmission.

I spent several hours with Mrs. Kantor in her Montreal home. I learned that Harold arrived at 10:21 A.M., nine minutes before Bernard who arrived at 10:30 A.M., and despite their prematurity both twins were healthy. A precious photograph of the twins at age four hangs in the hallway, showing perfectly matched little boys in sailor suits. The family was affluent due to the success of Ruby Foo's, a legendary Chinese restaurant on Montreal's Decarie Boulevard, owned and run by the twins' father, Max Shapiro, and their home was a gathering place for family and friends. Bernard wondered whether it was twinship or social life that put the twins at center stage, but when they were children probably both were responsible. I believe that he neglected a third factor, namely the twins' special abilities and engaging manners that drew attention beyond their family circles. Harold and Bernard were *invited* to enroll

Visitors to the Shapiros' childhood home will remember this portrait of four-year-old Harold (left) and Bernard, which hangs in the hallway. PHOTO COURTESY OF MARY KANTOR.

in LCC (Lower Canada College), a prestigious private boys' school in Montreal; thus, they bypassed the formal application process. This event distinguished the Shapiro twins early on, hinting that they would be conspicuous in crowds.

The Shapiro twins were continually noticed, but for different reasons. Their polarization according to scholarship (Bernard) and athleticism (Harold) emerged in early childhood. At age six Bernard was hospitalized for one month with measles and flu, but he still produced the highest grades in his class. He also maintained his first place academic ranking throughout high school. Mrs. Kantor learned that Bernard carved niches for himself at school, such as operating a wireless telegraph to avoid marching exercises. Dr. Robert J. Sternberg at Yale University believes intelligent people reshape their environments to make the most of their talents, something Bernard did very well.[10] Harold was never far behind Bernard scholastically, but did not work as hard as his twin. As a youngster Harold engaged in occasional fistfights with other boys, something his twin never did. Later, Harold distinguished himself in sports, becoming best swimmer and best all around high school athlete. Freshman year at McGill became a turning point for Harold when he met Vivian

Rapoport. Vivian's strong commitment to education was infectious, and soon transformed the erstwhile athlete into a more dedicated student.

These twins' life histories forced me to rethink concepts of twins' "likeness" and "unlikeness." Did early divergence in study habits and sports interests deservedly label Bernard as "scholar" and Harold as "athlete"? Harold also succeeded in school, so if he had been born a singleton he might have been a recognized "scholar." Bernard excelled in figure skating as a teenager, but singular sports attracted less attention than the traditional team sports Harold played. The Shapiros' differences may have been sharply and indelibly drawn in people's minds because they were the same age.

Polarization, identical twins' display of different behavioral roles relative to one another, is not uncommon. Caretakers identified the famous Dionne quintuplets as the "aggressor" (Annette), the "matriarch" (Yvonne), the "independent, happy-go-lucky" (Emilie), the "baby" (Marie) and the "unknown quantity" (Cécile) as early as two and one-half years of age.[11] These behaviors may be attempts at differentiating from the cotwin, but may be amplified by family and friends who are sensitive to twins' small differences.

Virtually all family and friends I interviewed, including Bernard and Harold, focused on the twins' behavioral differences. They may disagree with my view that while the Shapiros did show differences in attitude and in style, their abilities and temperaments were sufficiently alike for them to be solicited for the same prestigious positions that neither sought. At the same time, relatives and friends did not believe copresidencies were chance events. I suspect that Bernard and Harold's separation after college allowed each twin greater freedom of action, reducing differences arising from early cotwin comparisons.

The twins graduated from McGill in 1956 with highest honors in their respective faculties (majors). Shortly thereafter, they assumed management of their father's restaurant, Ruby Foo's. According to Harold, this five-year period was a lesson in interpersonal relations that would serve him well in later years.[12] Bernard enjoyed the colorful people frequenting the Bonsecours Market where he shopped.[13] Their friend, Jack Lazare, recalled a "crazy blend of American and Chinese food," and marvelous late night sessions of "world problem solving" over complimentary meals. After deciding graduate school promised the experiences and career choices they most desired, the Shapiros sold the restaurant. Harold entered a doctoral program in economics, and Bernard entered a master's program in education. Bernard's professors encouraged him to pursue a doctoral degree in education.[14] This is another example of opportunity in search of a receiver.

The twins married in 1957 within six weeks of one another. Harold's wife Vivian earned a doctoral degree in social work at Smith College in 1994, and maintains a private practice in Princeton. The couple have four daughters and eleven grandchildren. Bernard's wife Phyllis earned a doctoral degree in education at Boston University in 1967, and is a faculty member of McGill University's Department of Administration and Policy Studies. The couple have a son and a daughter, and five grandchildren.

The Shapiros' wives were described as "different" in personality, consistent with research findings on identical twins' spouses.[15] They were also described as bright and committed to academic professions when such paths were unusual for women. Both were also viewed as "influential" on their husbands' careers.

The Shapiros have been a focus of media interest since becoming university presidents, a phenomenon they understand, but something they (characteristically) do not seek. Less attention has been paid to their twin relationship as children and as heads of universities than to their similarities and differences in marital status and salary. When were the Shapiros first aware of being twins? Harold believes that twinship was first known to him in kindergarten, when his teacher remarked, "You are twins, but I do not know who is who." Bernard suspected that he knew he was a twin at age three or four when hearing adults' constant comparisons. "They did not pose the same questions to other brothers and sisters. I knew we were different because we were the same age and we looked alike."

As a young boy, firstborn Harold sometimes reminded his brother, "If we were royalty I would be king!" In *Born to Rebel,* Frank Sulloway describes birth order as a proxy for sibling differences in age, size, power and privilege. The relevance of his theory to twins is unknown, and clear birth order effects on twins' behaviors have not been found. Families with young twins know, however, that arrival on the "right" side of a minute can provoke teasing and taunting of secondborns by firstborns. Parents themselves may, however, unwittingly draw birth order distinctions. I wondered if Harold's kingly fancies foreshadowed predictable differences between the twins. Birth order issues surfaced at LCC where Bernard recalls that students were identified by last names, thus "Shapiro-1" and "Shapiro-2." "I resented it. It is silly, but those things come up all the time." It is conceivable that these secondborn sentiments, even if subtle, encouraged Bernard's studious bent and preference for nontraditional sports. Being a serious student upheld his family's values (typical of Sulloway's firstborn status), but Bernard's approach to schoolwork was unusual and his success brought parental approval. His maneuvers to avoid group sports were not rebellious, but were innovative and unconventional.

It is possible that twins' birth order remains a fragile, but forceful presence in their lives, as articulated by Lucius Bryant in Chapter 5. ("Just see the little hand resting upon brother's shoulder. . . . Get back there where you belong, Buster!") Harold recalled a Friday evening dinner with his mother and brother in which his mother turned to him as the older child to recite kiddush, the Jewish blessing over the wine. He sat at the head of the table. I wondered if their mother unknowingly made these distinctions in other situations.

Harold and Bernard's reflections on their twinship suggested quiet closeness, characterized by shared appreciation for books and music, issues facing higher education, and the importance of family. Occasionally, they seek each other's views on university matters, coauthoring a 1995 paper, "Universities in higher education: Some problems and challenges in a changing world."[16] "It was exciting working with Harold and easier working with him than with anyone else because we know each other so well." The 350 miles between the Shapiros prevent frequent visits, but family remains important. Harold admitted there are people he calls as often as Bernard, but "in some ways he is my best friend. I trust him completely."

Honorary degrees from some universities were simultaneously given to Bernard and Harold, prompting Bernard's mixture of pride and doubt: "I hope it is not twinness creating the judgments." Twins can enliven award ceremonies, but twinship per se cannot explain the Shapiros' separate illustrious careers. Harold and Bernard have lived and worked independently since college, effectively hiding their twinship until 1994 when Bernard joined McGill as president. Both have published over sixty scholarly papers and held numerous professional offices worthy of recognition. They earned some *separate* honorary degrees, both before and after 1994, distinctions apparently unaffected by their twinship and joint presidencies.

In Chapter 11, I suggested that identical twins may enjoy a competitive edge in sports where appearance counts, but this would not apply in arts and sciences where appearance does not count. Should twins reach the peaks of their professions, like the Shapiros, identical twinship could conceivably catch award committee's eyes. Future recognition of these twins and other noteworthy multiples will be fascinating to watch.

The career of one Shapiro could not have written a story with genetic scenes, especially because linking one individual's life events with his or her life circumstances is easy to do.[17] However, such explanations ignore contributions from genetically influenced abilities and behaviors mirrored in each twin brother. Individual twin pairs cannot assign relative worth to genetic and environmental influence in crafting careers, but they suggest that both make a difference. If challenging opportunities come our way, it may be that we attract them because of our talents and personalities, not just because our timing is right.

Matched achievements by identical twins are striking, but studying fraternal twins is also essential to understanding the origins of outstanding performance. My discovery of a prominent fraternal male professor-journalist pair came at the close of ABC's November 23, 1997, *This Week* program.[18] Ethics surrounding artificially conceived multiples were being debated, a topic prompted by the birth of Iowa's McCaughey septuplets in Des Moines five days earlier.[19] Cohost Cokie Roberts reminded viewers of reproductive medicine's new objective: Providing successful single pregnancies for childless couples, thus eliminating the risky (and costly) multiple conceptions used to improve delivery chances. She viewed this plan with some amusement, adding, "I am married to a twin, there are two of them." This was how I learned that Steven Roberts, one of my favorite television journalists, was a twin. Was he identical or fraternal?

If voices told the whole twin type story, Steve and Marc Roberts would rank among the most identical of twins that I know. Instead they are twins who present an unusual mix of similarities and differences that will challenge researchers and interest everyone. Their separate careers in writing, teaching, and public policy have become more alike over the years, but each twin retains distinct domains, styles and perspectives. I believe these individual differences tell the true story of the twins' professional paths, overshadowing their apparent job convergence since their early fifties.

Steve and Marc Roberts were born ten minutes apart on February 11, 1943, in Bayonne, New Jersey. Their father Will was twenty-six and their mother Dorothy twenty-four when the twins were born, Steve first and Marc second. They have a younger brother Glenn and a younger sister Laura. I spoke with Marc by telephone on December 13, 1997, and with Steve on January 8, 1998. I also watched a 1996 videotape of the twins delivering joint keynote speeches to the IHI (International Institute for Health Care Improvement) National Forum on health care policy.[20]

In the pre–polio vaccine days of 1949 when the twins were six, Marc was stricken with polio, "distinguishing us in profound ways from an early age." He lost muscle in his right leg, which was shortened by three-fourths of an inch. Consequently, Marc was sidelined from athletic events in which Steve excelled, especially basketball. Marc's illness deepened a slim, but conspicuous divide in the twins' personalities and interests. He tended toward "bookishness" as well as math and science pursuits; Steve tended toward athleticism as well as political and journalistic activities. "We were always thrown together, but at the same time we were different." As children, each twin complained to his mother that he "had no one to play with."

Marc and Steve completed a standard physical resemblance questionnaire which classified them as fraternal twins. This result should have been satisfactory, but their voices' indistinguishable quality haunted me. More important, the twins' illness-induced physical differences jeopardized their answers to questionnaire items concerning confusion by others. I had to see for myself.

The videotape of the Roberts twins' convention talks begins when the twins emerge from stage right. Marc appears first with Steve following, and they approach their podiums, positioned about twenty feet apart. This scene

Fraternal twins, Marc (left) and Steve Roberts, holding their infant twin nieces. PHOTO COURTESY OF LAURA ROBERTS.

is recorded from a distance, suggesting two nearly matching faces and figures, just as Marc said. Steve spoke first so I advanced the videotape to the close-up final portion of his speech where he relinquishes the floor to his brother. When Marc appeared I saw an altered "version" of Steve Roberts fill the screen. Marc was heavier and his hair was longer, but my first sense of their overall physical similarity overwhelmed their differences. I replayed this portion of the tape several times before deciding that they were similar looking fraternal twins.[21] Some of my colleagues who saw the tape disagreed.

Both Marc and Steve were intrigued when I raised the possibility that they could be identical because they had always believed they were fraternal twins. I offered to blood type them, an opportunity Marc accepted with interest and Steve declined without explanation. Then, joint photographs of Marc and Steve became available, clearly showing the facial contrasts I found with difficulty in the videotape.[22] The three of us agree that they present a provocative profile of similarities and differences in *fraternal* twin brothers.

In the videotape, IHI forum host Dan Wilson informed his audience that Marc was a professor and Steve was a writer, and that "both are educators and communicators with unique ideas and viewpoints." Wilson did not know that he had introduced the twin children as well as the adults. Marc was a university scholar when he was eight. Will Roberts watched his young son "delivering lectures" on the state of the world to anyone who would listen. Steve saw himself as a serious writer when he was nine, fulfilling this ambition as the editor of his sixth grade newspaper at twelve and as a reporter for a local journal at fourteen. Today, Professor of Political Economy Marc J. Roberts is a faculty member in Harvard University's School of Public Health, with a secondary appointment in the John F. Kennedy School of Government. Journalist Steven V. Roberts is a reporter for the *New York Daily News* and a frequent commentator on television news programs. In 1997 he accepted an endowed chair in political communications at George Washington University's School of Media and Public Affairs, "ironically coming back to a profession Marc was always in."

It seems remarkable that both twins practiced their different professions in grade school when college and careers were vague realities. However, strong talents erupt soon if opportunities allow, and the Roberts' home teemed with outlets for budding writers, politicians and teachers. Members of these professions filled many branches of their family tree, such as their great uncle, Marcus Rogowsky, a newspaper writer for whom Marc is named. (Steve would joke that this name was given to the "wrong" twin.)

The twins' father, Will Roberts, was a writer and publisher of children's books for the first ten years of his sons' lives. He combined their middle names to create his own byline, *Jeffrey Victor*. Actually, his sons' middle names have greater significance because they originated with an anticipated United States war victory (Jeffrey means "gift of peace," and Victor means "he who triumphs"). A major influence in both their lives, he passed away in the spring of 1997 at eighty. Steve feels his absence strongly: "It is painful still that he is not reading what I write. He was always my biggest fan." The twins' mother was a student at New York University when she met their father, leaving school several semesters before receiving her undergraduate degree.

They were "the twins" to their extended family and "the Roberts twins" to their friends in Bayonne. They shared bedrooms and classrooms, but Marc and Steve Roberts were an emotionally distant pair living separate lives from early childhood. Understanding their careers and their relationship begins by knowing that "the single biggest influence that divided us was Marc's illness." According to Marc, "It is fair to say that all through adolescence I could not do normal activities. I felt isolated, reading books and making model airplanes. Steve was very popular, great in basketball, a leader in many ways." For Steve, the "bicycle incident" became a metaphor for his parents' attempts to blur the twins' differences even as they treated them individually in many contexts. When they forbade Marc to ride a bicycle for safety reasons, they also decided that Steve should not ride a bike. Steve wondered if his parents' treatment in these situations was *similar* or *different,* and concluded that one could argue either way. I agree.

There were critical events and turning points in the twins' lives. High school teachers selected Marc, but not Steve, to represent the school at New Jersey's Boys State convention. Actually, both twins were entitled to attend, but because they were twins only one was chosen. Steve's resentment soared when Marc was elected Boys' State Governor, bringing publicity, lecture opportunities and college admission offers to his brother. The effects of this experience spiraled. Harvard was the only school to which both twins applied and when both were admitted, Marc was adamant about accepting and Steve was adamant about declining. According to Steve, "I always felt like the 'other brother'—if Marc were president, I was treasurer." Steve's father wisely assured him that, "Harvard is big enough for both of you." Arriving at Harvard in September 1960, Steve went to work for the *Crimson,* the school's daily newspaper, receiving a byline in his freshman year. When someone referred to Marc as "Steve's brother," then "I knew it would be okay."

Both twins remembered a Peter Bent Brigham Hospital twin study involving Harvard students, only Marc recalled it as rumor and Steve recalled it as fact. Marc heard that Harvard was interested in accepting twins in their graduating class so he wondered if that explained the twins' dual admission or "was I experiencing a paranoid fantasy?" Steve also questioned whether "twinness" affected the brothers' entry, but he was provided with plastic bottles to collect urine samples for the research. He never complied. Steve and Marc's answers to my questions were very consistent so their different renditions of this event were surprising.

I decided to investigate 1960s twin research at Harvard and turned to my colleague, Dr. Irving I. Gottesman of the University of Virginia. He reviewed old notes and suggested I contact Drs. Benjamin J. Murawski and Sanford Gifford. Both were unaware of twin recruitment among undergraduate applicants. Some participating twins may have joked about a research basis for their dual admission, hearsay that eventually reached Marc and Steve.

The Roberts twins' diverging intellectual interests and abilities steered them toward different pursuits at Harvard and beyond. Marc entered a multidisciplinary major spanning government, economics, history and sociology. Steve chose government and continued writing for the *Crimson,* becoming the Features Editor in his junior year. The twins graduated from Harvard in June 1964, Marc with highest honors (summa cum laude) and Steve with next highest honors (magna cum laude). According to Marc, there were two sources of "moderate jealousy" between the twins at this time, Marc's academic distinction and Steve's social success. The twins married three years apart, Marc at twenty and Steve at twenty-three. Marc has four children and

Steve has two children, most of whom have combined journalism and public policy with their studies or professions.

Where do the twins' differences come from? Both agreed that their careers are inextricable blends of talent and opportunity, but this is no longer news. It was fascinating that their separate interpretations accented different processes leading them to lecture halls and newsrooms. Marc's academic journey was largely self-driven, urged forward by deliberate choices he made to gain the experiences he sought. Steve's journalistic rise was also fueled by drive and determination, but he gave special credit to his father, his first mentor and his wife. It would be a mistake to think that Steve's career was "more environmental" than Marc's, although linking external events to personal outcomes offers simple, immediate behavioral explanations.[23] It would also be a mistake to attribute the twins' career differences to Marc's illness, because their individual abilities and preferences were evident early. The illness possibly sharpened Marc's penchant for solitary study, but did *not* create it. He admitted that he is more likely to be found "sitting in the bowels of the library" than Steve, acquiring more knowledge on narrow topics than anyone else, something Steve would not relish.

Marc's high school successes convinced him to stay in academics, but he toyed with the idea of a political career. His hope was to bring academic credibility to the political arena. His father was deeply involved in local political reform, and both his grandfathers were extremely attentive to political issues. Marc proved himself an able orator during student government days at Harvard, and today is proud of his public speaking skills, but regretful that they have been underexploited. When young Steve Roberts showed a spark of writing talent, Will Roberts reinforced it. Steve recognized his father's strong influence, but he also acknowledged that his own talents affected his success. After working for high school and college newspapers, Steve met James "Scotty" Reston at the *New York Times,* whom Steve would revere the rest of his life. Reston, the *Times*'s Washington Bureau chief from 1953 to 1964, gave Steve his first job in journalism after college. He was a great mentor and role model and "took such good care of me." Steve rose rapidly through the ranks of the *New York Times,* becoming a well-known Washington reporter.

The third major influence on Steve's career was his wife, Cokie Roberts, also a seasoned broadcast journalist. Cokie is the daughter of the late Hale Boggs, a Democratic congressman from Louisiana, and Corinne Morrison [Claiborne] Boggs who filled her husband's seat after his airplane disappeared in Alaska in 1972.[24] Steve's association with a celebrated political family and his marriage to a high-profile journalist drew him into a public world.[25]

The Roberts twins' careers converged in recent years as Marc became more of a writer and Steve became more of a teacher, culminating in their joint IHI Forum addresses in 1996. Steve examined expectations regarding legislation from the newly elected Republican majority Congress, and Marc explored the implications of new regulations for hospitals and physicians.

The brothers had a "blast." I suspect that Marc and Steve especially enjoyed their one-on-one dialogue after the talks. However, Marc's occasional use of technical jargon reminded us (and them) of the twins' different professional backgrounds. Steve joked that, "He [Marc] looks at me as if I know what he is talking about!"

The Roberts twins' careers do not show perfect convergence, only convergence to a point. They entered their teaching professions in different ways, Marc by choice at the start of his career and Steve by circumstance toward the latter part of his career. Both twins are skilled instructors—the twins' sister Laura gave rave reviews to Marc's guest lecture to her Boston University management class, and Steve's wife Cokie noted his popularity among Georgetown University students.[26] Steve wondered if Marc resented his entry into university life, blurring the boundaries between the separate worlds in which each had excelled. Understandably, Steve's appointment may have rekindled old conflicts.

I believe the Roberts twins' careers and the abilities they bring to their careers are deceptively similar. Both have been successful in positions demanding excellence in writing and speaking on public policy issues, but they are not a matched set. Marc claimed that he could never do what Steve does because "to be a reporter, to get information from people, is interpersonal. I have watched him do it, he remembers what people say, he is a master at it." I was, therefore, surprised when Steve described his brother as a "vibrant public speaker and a great teacher. People find it hard to believe that I am the quiet one."

Some people might argue that only individuals with certain intellectual and personality attributes become college professors, making the Roberts twins' careers impressively alike. I would argue that there are probably enough available professorships to suit most qualified twins and siblings—therefore, a pair of professors is less remarkable than a pair of presidents.

The Roberts' relationship as twins has grown closer over the years. However, childhood tensions reverberate even now. Their vision of their twinship hints at a special closeness they might share, blocked by an emotional distance they must share. I sense they fear discussing past tensions with each other, finding it easier to talk about their twinship with others. Their relationship as twins is in a "different place" now than it was four years ago, owing to time and to some significant talks about family matters. Their enjoyable venture at the IHI National Forum seems proof of how far they have come as twins since Bayonne. I also saw subtle "twinlike" behaviors on stage that perhaps only twins and some siblings can recognize. When time ran out, Marc, who had been speaking, thanked the audience on behalf of both twins as if to keep command of the situation, even if subtly. But perhaps this was just a momentary (and unavoidable) lapse in their delightful exchange. Marc walked over to Steve as they exited the stage and they embraced each other warmly.

When I ended their interviews I believed I knew more about the Roberts' twinship than they did, affirming their view that it is easier to tell someone who is not your twin.

"I didn't know she [Isabella] was a twin!" was a common response from people learning I had spoken with actress Isabella Rossellini's fraternal twin sister Ingrid.

I had known for many years that Ingrid and Isabella were the twin daughters of movie star Ingrid Bergman and film director Roberto Rossellini, but I knew little about their twinship. Isabella's 1997 autobiography, *Some of Me,* shows a photograph of her mother lovingly gazing at her infant pair, but this is the only allusion to Isabella's being a twin.[27] I have since learned that her sister, Ingrid Rossellini, received a doctoral degree in Renaissance Literature in 1993 from Columbia University in New York City. Ingrid's doctoral thesis was an analysis of metaphors and myths in *Rime Sparse,* by the fourteenth-century Italian poet Francesco Petrarch.[28] She also taught at Columbia for several years before becoming a full-time parent.

I was lucky to have met Ingrid Rossellini on Monday night, December 22, 1997, at the opening of Ingrid Bergman's film retrospective at New York's Museum of Modern Art. A highlight of this event was that both sisters would be introducing the program. A long line had formed outside the auditorium, but I found a seat behind the row reserved for special guests. I watched as Ingrid Rossellini entered. She was a different version of her mother than Isabella, taller and slimmer with a narrower face, so the twins were clearly fraternal. Her twin was unable to attend.

Ingrid told us wonderful details about *Stromboli* (1949), the first film collaboration of her parents. When the evening ended, Ingrid was surrounded by viewers eager for further news of her famous mother. After she fielded film-related questions, I brought up her twinship and she discussed it with pleasure. I wondered if Bergman's fans would think differently of her now, perhaps wondering how being a multiple-birth mother affected her life as a film star. I also wondered if they would think differently of her other daughter, Isabella, since discovering someone's twinship may cast them in a new light.

Ingrid and Isabella Rossellini were born in Italy on June 8, 1952. Ingrid Bergman grew extremely large during her pregnancy, leading her to anticipate the birth of an "elephant baby," but not twins. Only one heartbeat was detected, but her size probably led doctors to take an X ray just before delivery, revealing two infants. Ingrid keeps a copy of that X ray. Isabella was the firstborn twin by thirty minutes so she received the name her parents had chosen for a baby girl. Rossellini decided on the name *Isotta* for his second daughter; this was the make of his favorite car. Both parents preferred the name Ingrid, but Italian law did not allow children to take their parents' names. However, they always called her Ingrid as she was growing up.

*　　*　　*

Ingrid and Isabella are fraternal twins[29] with different personalities and, according to Ingrid, they were always that way. She described herself as shy and insecure, in contrast with Isabella who is outgoing and confident and who was the pair's spokesperson when they were small. Their parents tried to "make them the same" by dressing them alike and combing their hair the same way, but the twins turned out differently. Beyond the fact that Ingrid's hair is curly and Isabella's is straight, Ingrid believes that environments do not make you who you are. She recalled feeling unaffected by the glamour and publicity of her celebrity family, preferring to spend her time hidden in a library, reading books.

I asked Ingrid to consider why her career had diverged so greatly from her twin's and she was sure that this was a natural outcome of their different interests and styles. Despite their separate lives Ingrid and Isabella are good friends and share happy experiences especially with their children. Ingrid was extremely interested in being a twin because, as she explained, "We were born in the same place, but we are not the same."

I was unprepared for Ingrid's admission that she would have liked being an identical twin. There was little time for us to explore this issue because Ingrid was expected at a reception, but I suspect that many people envy identical twins' similarities and intimacies. Perhaps fraternal twins feel this more keenly than other people because they know that their births are special and they know that not everyone thinks so.

Many people asked Ingrid for her autograph, but between signings she told me that she was not used to doing this. Signing autographs is probably a familiar activity for her twin sister Isabella. I realized I had discovered another difference between these twins.

I met David H. Koch in his New York office in the early 1980s. David is a chemical engineer and executive vice-president of Koch Industries, the second largest closely held company in the United States.[30] The diversified company, founded in 1940 by his father, Fred Koch, operates oil refineries, manufactures chemicals and refining equipment and owns large cattle ranches. David expressed interest in the Minnesota Study of Twins Reared Apart so Bouchard asked me to arrange a meeting with him the next time I was in New York City visiting my family.

David told me that he had a fraternal twin brother, Billy, which explained his interest in twin studies. I wondered if Billy was as tall as David, who stood six feet, five inches tall and was an imposing presence. I also wondered if Billy was associated with the family company, or if he pursued different work. I knew little about the Koch family at that time.

I spoke on the telephone with David on January 24, 1998, and with Bill on February 11, 1998. I classified them as fraternal twins, based on their different hair colors (David's is brown and Bill's is strawberry blond). Both twins have blue eyes and Bill is six feet, four inches tall, just one inch shorter than his twin. They are occasionally confused by acquaintances, and as was true of the Roberts twins I could easily confuse them on the telephone.

Since my meeting with David in the early 1980s, the twins and their two brothers' business relations had been publicly probed in publications around the country. The brothers disagreed over the missions and goals of Koch Industries, projects to be supported by corporate funds, and the size of shareholders' dividends. Bill's attempt to gain control of the company's governing board failed, resulting in Bill and Fred selling all their shares in Koch Industries. These events culminated in a series of courtroom battles. I was interested in understanding the processes preceding the brothers' careers, and in exploring how their professional lives came apart in 1980. I also wished to consider the personal side of their differences.

David and Bill (William I.) Koch were born on May 3, 1940, in Wichita, Kansas, to Fred Koch and Mary Clementine Robinson Koch. Their father was forty and their mother was thirty-three when they were born, David first and Bill second by nineteen minutes. Their oldest brother Fred was seven, and their next older brother Charles was five when David and Bill joined the family.

The twins' behavioral differences emerged early. David was gregarious and athletic, Bill withdrawn and awkward; David was a good student from the start, Bill blossomed in high school and college; David's interests in people and activities were "mainstream," Bill's were "unusual." Fred Jr., the oldest brother, was a "supervisor" to the twins, "a disciplinarian, not a buddy." He broke away from his family's business tradition, pursuing English at Harvard and drama at Yale.[31] A childhood alliance developed between David and his older brother Charles, whom he emulated, growing naturally from their similarities in personality and interests. David and Charles's relationship persists to this day. Bill is now paired with Fred with whom he associates socially and shares art interests.

During their growing up years David and Bill competed in many ways, often engaging in unhealthy conflicts. These frictions were resolved when their parents sent the boys to different boarding schools. David attended Deerfield Academy in Deerfield, Massachusetts, and Bill attended Culver Military Academy in Culver, Indiana. During their years apart, David bragged to his friends about Bill's academic successes and Bill bragged to his friends about David's athletic successes. This turn of events may not be so surprising because the twins' differences caused clashes when they were living together, so living apart probably let them reevaluate their relationship and each other. They were on good terms when they were reunited as college students at the Massachusetts Institute of Technology (MIT) in Cambridge.

*   *   *

Fraternal twins Bill (left) and David Koch. The twins' diverging physical and behavioral characteristics that emerged in childhood were evident at age sixteen and beyond. PHOTO COURTESY OF THE KOCH FAMILY.

The twins' college years at MIT were their friendliest. Both David and Bill majored in chemical engineering, the same discipline their father had chosen when he attended that school. Both twins joined the same fraternity, Beta Theta Pi, and both lived at the fraternity house. Both twins also joined the college basketball team, David as captain and Bill as a team member. Bill's lesser skill sidelined him from playing much of the time, but he resolved not to take this out on his twin. Actually, Bill's basketball experience provided him with team management skills that would prove invaluable in later years.

Both twins give their father varying amounts of genetic and environmental credit for their mathematical and technical skills, and for their business interests. David believes that he and his twin inherited these special abilities from their father, and benefited from the "fascinating stories" Fred Sr. told them about his career. "It [chemical engineering] came naturally, I enjoyed it, it was perfect for me and perfect for Billy." By the time the twins completed college, Bill was more academically inclined than David, outperforming him at MIT and winning the prize for the most original chemical engineering thesis. Bill also decided to pursue a Ph.D. degree after both twins received their master's degrees in 1963.

Bill speculated that had he been raised by different parents he would have remained naturally inclined toward science and chemical engineering. He wondered, though, if a different home environment would have eased his fear of failure and increased his appetite for competition. Other parents may have encouraged Bill to be less fearful, but probably not fearless. Bill also revealed that the four brothers were left alone a great deal and did not learn to resolve their disputes, so different parenting behaviors may have been helpful in this regard.

David entered the business world after receiving his master's degree. He worked for a business consulting firm in Cambridge and for an engineering design firm in New York before joining Koch Industries in 1970. Bill joined Koch Industries as a consultant after completing his Ph.D. degree in 1971, later becoming corporate vice-president. Charles had been company president since 1966 and became chief executive when his father died in 1967. The nine years between 1971 and 1980, which began peacefully, turned turbulent for the three brothers at Koch Industries. Bill and Fred eventually sold their company shares in 1983, but accusations of business mismanagement and personal wrongdoing persisted between the brothers.

Bill left Koch Industries in 1980 to set up and head his own company, Oxbow Corporation, in 1983, now located in West Palm Beach. Its largest profit derives from the business of generating alternative energy sources.

The year 1980 marked the twins' last birthday celebration together. They gathered in a private room of New York City's 21 Club with close friends for what David called a "marvelous occasion." Their personal break came six months later and, according to David, the rift is "regrettable, a big loss" but sometimes you are forced to make such decisions. Bill remembers their fortieth birthday as a "nice one," and feels sad that so much in their lives is no longer shared. Still, Bill is adamant that David and Charles acted wrongly, although he feels less negatively toward his twin. "It strikes me as amazing that we are on opposite sides of a fence."

Bill and David have watched each other from a distance, disconnected from each other's accomplishments. Both twins are enormously talented, but in different ways. David went from being a competent, but undistinguished college student to top executive in a $30 billion business.[32] He has been active in politics, becoming the Libertarian Party's 1980 Vice-Presidential nominee.[33] He is also highly visible in New York City's social circles, as is his wife, Julia Flescher Koch, whom he married in May 1996 when she was thirty-three and he was fifty-six. This was the first marriage for both. With the birth of his son in June 1998, David joined his twin brother as a relatively older father (fifty-eight) of a young child—Bill married twice and has three children, his youngest son born when Bill was fifty-seven.

The greater surprise is that Bill went from being a below average athlete to becoming a world class professional sailor. His love of sailing began at the Culver Military Academy. After selling his Koch Industries shares he purchased a cruise boat and then a racing boat, the "biggest one" he could find. From 1984 to 1991 he established a research program at MIT to study principles of boat speed, attracting curiosity and criticism from seasoned sailors.

He raced in an existing boat, the *Matador,* and then developed the *Matador²* (as in second power) that traveled 2–3% faster than existing craft.[34]

In assembling a sailing team Bill recalled his MIT basketball coach's management theory, one that "took nerds with no skills and turned us into one of the best teams in the country." He achieved three second place wins in four Maxi World Sailing Championships (*Matador,* 1985–1988) and two first place wins (*Matador²,* 1990 and 1991), finally winning the 1992 America's Cup Race in San Diego—he was skipper on the winning boat, *America³* (to the third power). He went on to sponsor the first all female sailing team in the 1995 America's Cup race, which nearly beat elite sailor Dennis Conner.[35] Bill also chairs the Kansas Crime Commission and is considering running for the United States Senate, representing Kansas.

Some cordial moments have broken the twins' silence over the years. When Bill won the Challenger series against Conner, admitting him into the finals, he received a congratulatory telegram from his twin. David watched Bill's 1992 winning race against the Italians on television from a New York bar and, according to one of Bill's friends, bought celebratory drinks for everyone. Bill invited David to ride in the 1995 America's Cup race for free, a seat that sold for $150,000, but David declined.

The twins' legal battles resumed on April 6, 1998, in Topeka, in *Koch vs. Koch Industries*.[36] The trial lasted for nearly eleven weeks. Leslie Wayne, who covered the proceedings, observed that the opposing brother pairs avoided eye contact with one another. David also wept over his unhappy relationship with his twin. The jury held Koch Industries responsible for "misrepresentations and omissions," but determined they were insignificant and awarded no damages. Bill plans to appeal.

Two twins entered Koch Industries as young men, but only David remains there. He reflected that as children the twins received the same advantages and opportunities in their home, yet "we could not be more different in our behaviors, personalities and interests. If the environment has a major influence we should be similar, but we are more different than alike." Another pair with business disagreements are the opposite-sex Bernhard twins, Van Bernhard and Jean Bernhard Buttner. They recently settled a dispute over control of their family's company, Value Line, Inc.[37] The attentive sister and relaxed brother clashed continually over the years, speaking only through their attorneys.

I suspect that such family quarrels are less frequent than these pairs imply. It is possible that twins' involvement in these disputes attracts interest because most people expect twins to get along and are curious when they do not. In contrast with the Kochs and Bernhards are the five Blechman brothers, fraternal twins Steve and Ross, identical twins Neil and Brian, and their youngest brother, Dean.[38] The five brothers own and manage TwinLab, a $100 million dollar company that manufactures and sells vitamins and dietary supplements. Each brother performs a different but essential task, exemplifying the rare "fit" that all business partners desire, but few achieve.

In September 1994 my father gave me a newspaper article, "The Double Life of Dr. Swain," that electrified me as much as the Shapiro twins' double presidencies.[39] At age forty-five, Dr. Judith L. Swain became the only female chair of a major university's cardiology department (University of Pennsylvania), and the first female president of the American Society for Clinical Investigation. She has done groundbreaking animal research on *genomic imprinting,* the different expression of genes in offspring depending upon which parent they come from.[40] Even more inspiring, Dr. Swain has an identical twin sister, Dr. Julie A. Swain, the first female chief of cardiac surgery in an American medical center (Louisiana State University), and chair of the Food and Drug Administration's committee on circulatory system devices. She has also done significant research on brain function during cardiac surgery.[41]

Today Dr. Judith Swain is the Arthur L. Bloomfield Professor and chair of the Department of Medicine at Stanford University. Dr. Julie Swain is Professor of Surgery in the Division of Cardiothoracic Surgery at the University of Kentucky, in Lexington. Each woman's successes are extraordinary, but they gain meaning because they were made by identical twin sisters working in closely related, highly demanding fields. Beyond the fascination of these findings are the questions of how and why their careers came so closely together. I explored these issues on the telephone with Dr. Judith Swain on March 19, 1998, and with Dr. Julie Swain the following day.

Judith and Julie Swain were born on September 24, 1948, in Cypress, California, the only children of Joe and Christine Swain. Julie was born five minutes before her sister. The twins' father was a salesman and their mother was a librarian. Both twins recall being treated very much the same by their parents, like a "collective." They shared a close relationship with each other, maintaining a common pool of friends in their small town. Their confusion by others and their matching physical characteristics (e.g., height and hair color) classify them as identical twins.

The only obvious physical contrasts between the twins are their ten-pound weight difference and their opposite hand preference. Nevertheless, people confuse them. When Julie discussed her surgery research in a televised interview, Judith's colleagues wondered why "she" was speaking on a topic outside her specialty. More extraordinary was a dinner conversation during which Judith's spouse was convinced that Judith was Julie after she cut her hair like her sister's. A less obvious physical difference between the twins is Julie's spinal stenosis (constriction of the spine). She called this condition an "occupational hazard of being a surgeon." She explained that constant standing on her job aggravated a congenital defect that her twin sister should experience in about twenty years.

The Swains saw their mother as a role model, someone who set high standards for her own accomplishments. According to Julie, "If we were farmers we would be good farmers," suggesting that the family's work ethic was primarily responsible for the twins' determination and drive. It also seemed that twinship accentuated the Swains' naturally competitive spirit to be the best. Their school abilities were closely matched, but when one twin outperformed the other it provided an incentive to "be better." This outlook extended to sports, in which both twins excelled. Their father had played semiprofessional baseball so the twins played ball "before we could walk." Judith also told me that it helped to have a "twenty-four-hour practice partner," echoing Sean Hollonbeck in Chapter 11.

The twins felt more pride than jealousy in each other's successes, and achievement differences did not divide them. When Julie was a research presentation winner at the Southern California students' division of the American Chemical Society (an event in which her twin competed) the twins' relationship was unaffected. I wondered if Judith felt a twinge of envy when her sister won, but prevented it from intruding upon their lives. Perhaps controlling these feelings is part of the constellation of behaviors underlying identical twins' tranquility.

Julie and Judith received top grades at UCLA,[42] and were the only two students out of one thousand chemistry majors to receive special honors. After graduating, the twins parted for the first time, heading to different medical schools—Judith enrolled in the University of California in San Diego (UCSD) and Julie enrolled in Baylor University in Houston. The decision to separate was not made consciously, but reflected their attraction to the different schools to which they applied and were accepted. Separating was not traumatic because both twins were caught up in the excitement of their anticipated medical careers. They agree that their parents were not responsible for their medical interests, only for the high motivational levels that each twin brought to these interests. They credit their careers to the television shows *Dr. Kildare* and *Ben Casey,* in which the fictional doctors saved lives.

The twins' separate medical programs led to their only major career difference: their medical specialty. Judith followed the lead of UCSD's Dr. Eugene Braunwald to pursue cardiology, a branch of internal medicine concerned with the structures, functions and diseases of the heart. Her current research concerns finding ways to inhibit blood vessel formation to prevent cancer growth and stimulate blood vessel development to treat heart disease. Julie was inspired by Baylor's Dr. Michael DeBakey to practice cardiovascular and thoracic surgery, a part of medicine concerned with the circulation of blood and other body fluids. Her research concerns developing means to protect the brain during the subset of heart operations requiring stoppage of blood flow.

The twins' medical specialties are so distinct that they cannot collaborate or consult one another about their work. Both told me that their different medical areas are reflections of their medical school mentors and that they could easily imagine doing what their sister does. Julie also regrets that her area of cardiology includes fewer women than her twin's. Both twins work in their offices and laboratories from early morning until evening except when they are attending conferences or other work-related events. Some people might prefer a less frenetic lifestyle, but the twins thrive on this schedule. Clearly, they chose careers commensurate with their outstanding intellect, boundless ambition and unlimited energy. However, they set aside time on weekends for sports activities, especially golf and polo.

Judith married in 1980, and Julie married in 1984 and divorced two years later. In order to accommodate their devotion to their work both twins chose not to have children, opting to care for cats instead. The twins' schedules and the distance between them (California to Kentucky) leave them little time to visit with one another. They see each other only two or three times each year and speak on the telephone only every few weeks, but they exchange e-mail messages often. Their infrequent contact might suggest that the twins are not close, but Judith pointed out that she speaks to her twin more than to anyone else besides her spouse. The Swains' situation is unusual because at any given time one twin is probably attending a conference, and both twins spend long hours in their laboratories. Their decisions to seek their twin during their limited free moments show how much they care.

I was curious about the twins' views on the relative roles of genes and environments on career choice. Julie and Judith acknowledged that both influences are important, perhaps equally important, but they stressed their parents' values and encouragement in fashioning their own professional lives. Their parents gave them the freedom to excel at whatever they chose, but the highly motivated Swains would probably have shined in any supportive climate. Most compelling is that both twins filled slots reserved for a rare minority (first woman to head a major cardiac surgery department; first woman to head a major cardiology society). The fact that these twins are identical strongly suggests that their matched abilities and personalities, which are partly genetically influenced, contributed to their generally similar career paths and successes.

Julie's remark, "If we were farmers we would be good farmers" is worth a second look. I believe she meant that both twins would do the best possible job regardless of what that job was. I agree, except that the job would have to fit the drive and direction that is essential to both twins' satisfaction. It may be no accident that they are not farmers.

Most people do not know that a twin walked on the moon.[43] On April 16, 1972, identical twin Charlie (Charles) Duke, Jr., departed the Earth's atmosphere as a lunar module pilot (similar to a copilot on a commercial airliner) on Apollo 16, becoming the tenth individual to reach the moon's surface five days later. Only twelve people in the world can claim this distinction. It was "a thrilling, exciting experience," and its memory renewed the reverence Charlie felt twenty-six years ago. Retelling this story also revived his panic when he flipped over backward while jumping up and down on the moon in excitement.

Becoming an astronaut demands a unique blend of intelligence, endurance and drive as I discussed in Chapter 4. When I learned that Charlie's identical twin brother Bill (William) was a doctor I was curious to know what life events were responsible for their professional differences. I spoke with retired astronaut Charlie Duke by telephone on April 22, 1998, and with gastroenterologist Dr. Bill Duke the following day. Their voices matched in tone and volume, but Bill's stronger Southern accent made it easy to tell them apart.

The Duke twins were born on October 3, 1935, in Charlotte, North Carolina, but were raised in Lancaster, South Carolina, where Bill practices medicine. Their father, Charles M. Duke, Sr. (also Charlie), an insurance agent, was twenty-eight and their mother, Willie Waters Duke, the owner of a women's boutique, was twenty-five. Charlie, who is left-handed, was delivered six minutes before Bill, who is right-handed. They were called "the twins" by people who knew them and were dressed alike until the fourth grade. Their younger sister Betsy was born thirteen years later so the twins did not know her well while growing up.

I determined that the Dukes are identical twins based on their answers to a standard questionnaire. Both men are five feet, eleven and one-half inches tall and have the same brown eyes and thin, straight brown hair. One incident involving the twins' confusion is memorable. When Charlie was in transit to the moon the Duke family was allowed into mission control. The flight surgeon, knowing Bill was a doctor, invited him to review some medical materials. When Bill entered the laboratory, several staff members who did not know Charlie was a twin looked shocked, believing that he was thousands of miles away.

One physical difference between the twins had crucial consequences for their early development, twin relationship, and professional goals. Bill was born with a ventricular septal defect, a condition affecting communication between the heart's lower chambers. Bill's shortness of breath and reduced exercise tolerance precluded his participation in active team sports, such as football, although he enjoyed less strenuous individual games, such as golf. Bill's heart defect always kept him ten pounds lighter than Charlie, but the twins' physical identity overwhelmed this difference because many people confused them over the years. The absence of obvious physical differences caused by Bill's condition persuaded me that the physical resemblance questionnaire results were valid for this pair.

Bill's inability to join Charlie in athletic pursuits cast an early shadow on their twinship. Bill resented being restricted from sports events and sensed parental favoritism toward his more physically fit cotwin. The twins' evolving relationship included close moments (such as when they played golf, or went hunting or fishing), but it was marked by friction. This situation was resolved when Charlie left home to attend eleventh and twelfth grades at Admiral Farragut High School in St. Petersburg, Florida. His move was prompted by his tenth grade decision to become a military officer, not by a desire to avoid his difficult twinship, but the effect was the same. Bill believes that the twins' high school separation brought them together because it exposed each brother's positive qualities that physical closeness obscured. Bill did not fully resolve his conflicted family feelings until age thirty-three, with help from his newfound faith of Christianity. Charlie became a Christian several years later and the twins are now closer than ever.

Charlie's dream of becoming a military officer began in 1946 when he was eleven and his father returned from the navy. Charlie became fascinated with World War II military figures, and spent hours constructing paper airplanes and playing soldier. His resolve to become an officer grew stronger at age fifteen after he saw a Saturday afternoon film about life in the military. He entered the United States Naval Academy after graduating from high school, intent upon becoming a naval officer. Along the way he learned he could join the air force and "fell in love with flying" and with the goal of "serving my country." He accepted a mission in the United States Air Force and completed a master's degree in aeronautics and astronautics at the Massachusetts Institute of Technology (MIT). These events culminated in his selection for the 1972 Apollo 16 mission to the moon. According to Bill, the family was very proud, actually "exhilarated."

Dr. Bill Duke became a "future physician" when the fertilized egg split, triggering unusual developmental events that caused his heart defect. He believes that his constant presence in doctors' offices was behind his decision to enter the medical profession. Bill finished high school in Lancaster before enrolling in Davidson College's premedical program in Davidson, North Carolina. After graduating he attended medical school at the University of Pennsylvania, then completed an internal medicine residency at the University of Alabama in Birmingham. The influence of his mentor, Dr. Basil Hirschkowitz, lead to Bill's specialization in gastroenterology (study of the digestive system).

Bill married his wife, Georgianna, while he was in medical school and has three sons and one daughter. Charlie married his wife, Dottie, several years later and has two sons. Both twins have several grandchildren.

I was fascinated with Charlie and Bill as twins because their apparent differences in occupation and life events disguise their fundamental similarities in intelligence and personality. Both twins obtained top grades in their separate high schools, with Charlie becoming valedictorian and Bill graduating near the top of his class. They see themselves and each other as "inquisitive, studious and goal-oriented, dedicated to doing the best job possible." Charlie calls both twins "detail kind of guys" ("As a military pilot and astronaut you had to be attentive to detail."), but Bill believes this term applies more to himself ("My brother is not as detail-oriented as I am—I like things in 'cookbook' fashion.").

Bill believes that his twin displays their father's aggressive manner, while he expresses their mother's gentle style. It seems strange to think of identical twins resembling different family sides, because they have identical genes. Instead, the Duke twins' personalities are comprehensible in light of their health differences. Bill's condition precluded opportunities (e.g., military service or space travel) that might have attracted him had he been healthy. Like his twin, Bill worked hard toward a profession demanding high intellect, good judgment and great dedication, but his job choices were limited. His life experience may have dampened a naturally aggressive style, a conceivable conjecture given his twin's résumé—in fact, my opinion on this matter is possible only *because* Bill has a genetically identical twin who could reveal Bill's potentials in the absence of his defect.

I also asked both twins to consider the blend of genetic and environmental factors shaping their careers. Charlie said, "I really do not have a clue. I remember our parents and relatives being very supportive, but they let us make our own decisions." He could imagine doing what his brother does because being a doctor would be "interesting and rewarding." Bill senses that genetic propensities underlie behavioral differences among people. He was, however, always aware of the twins' personality contrasts and was curious about their source. He realizes that his condition "colored" his world, making it "hard to say" if he might otherwise have joined his twin in space.

Charlie is now retired, and lives with his wife in New Braunfels, Texas. He serves as a motivational speaker, an investor, and a member of various boards and committees. He and his wife also work with the Christian lay ministry. Bill practices medicine in Lancaster. He has less time for community activities than his twin, but he helps staff a church-based medical clinic and sponsors the building of a medical clinic for citizens of Togo. I view their lives as a natural cotwin control study, exposing the work of matched genes in different environments. Each twin mirrored a life that the other twin might have led, reminding us that different birth circumstances could have profoundly altered the progress of our own lives.

The Duke twins' experiences are also the closest we have come to conducting a fantastic test of the famous "twins paradox," first raised by Albert Einstein in 1905.[44] In this paradox one twin goes on a long space flight, traveling close to the speed of light and eventually returning to earth where the other twin has remained. According to Einstein's Special Theory of Relativity, time would have passed more slowly for the twin taking the space flight than for the twin staying on earth. Upon coming home the traveling twin would be younger than his earth-bound cotwin since aging is a function of time. The twins paradox is a real effect—Einstein's theory replaces absolute time with relative time that varies with an individual's location and speed of movement. Charlie Duke did not travel fast enough or long enough for any measurable change in his aging process to occur, relative to Bill's. Nevertheless, viewed against the backdrop of the twins paradox, Duke's mission recommends using identical twins to study the physical and psychological effects of space flight. Mark and Scott Kelly, accepted into NASA's astronaut training program, may shed light on these issues.

Noteworthy identical and fraternal twins can teach us more about human potentials and limits than noteworthy singletons because each was raised with a same-age partner. The identical Presidents Shapiro and Doctors Swain reached goals reserved for a select few, so their matched achievements are extraordinary. The chance that their unique blends of talent, personality and drive would repeat in fraternal cotwins is slim. The identical Dukes show that early health differences can chart separate goals for genetically matched individuals. We will never know if two twins might have made it to the moon had Bill's heart been intact, or if Lancaster would have gained a physician if the defect was shared. The fraternal Kochs, Robertses and Rossellinis present a range of professional similarities and differences, but none of these cotwins find themselves in the same place. These twins show us that jobs may be the same in name only, and that individual differences can emerge despite powerful family influences.

The search for long-term effects on behavior has taken some researchers outside the home to children's and adolescents' peer groups. Judith Harris has argued for closer looks at cultural norms making children similar to their friends (e.g., speech customs and television programs) and at group processes making children different from their friends (e.g., social comparisons and social rejection).[45] She believes that these influences have greater lasting impact on children than do their parents, and that "the universality of children's groups explains why development is not derailed by the wide variations in parental behavior found within and between societies." This view is consistent with evidence that family influences have limited effects on children's behaviors within the normal environmental range. The lives of the twins I discussed were clearly affected by what their friends were doing and what was happening in the world. Harold Shapiro's change in career goal was strongly influenced by his future wife, and Marc Roberts's and Bill Duke's physical restrictions affected their twin relationships and activities. Societal conditions were favorable for the careers of the Shapiro twins and their peers, but trying for Julie Swain and her female medical colleagues. Nevertheless, circumstances in some families cannot be overlooked—the Rossellini home was ideal for a budding actress, and the Koch brothers' careers were largely shaped by their father's business. The Koch brothers' persisting strife may also be partly explained by parental inattention to child-hood conflicts.

The life events of these six pairs are consistent with what twin studies on special skills and occupational choice tell us. Genetic factors shape our professional interests, as well as our abilities to find opportunities to express these interests. At the same time, environmental influences can alter genetic propensities for abilities and activities. Unfortunately, no one has studied the lives of prominent twins so it is uncertain if these pairs faithfully represent the larger twin population from which they were drawn. Julie Swain hinted that it would be interesting to learn if rearing by a prominent family would significantly raise one identical twin's occupational standing relative to his or her cotwin's—she correctly observed that most reared apart twins come from middle-class families. One could argue that had I interviewed other pairs—e.g., identical twins Peter and Anthony Shaffer (playwrights), identical twins Gunnar and Matthew Nelson (musicians and sons of singer Ricky Nelson), fraternal twins Donna Shalala[46] (United States Secretary of Health and Human Services) and her sister, or fraternal twin Seymour Hersch[47] (investigative reporter) and his brother—the conclusions may have differed, but I don't think so.

Double Indemnity: Twins in the Courtroom

It never occurred to me that psychological twin research might influence twins' legal outcomes. My first clue that twin studies were useful beyond parent-child issues and nature-nurture debates came in 1983, from law offices in San Francisco, California. An attorney representing an identical female twin grieving for the wrongful death of her twin sister contacted the Minnesota Center for Twin and Adoption Research for assistance. He wondered if twin research findings might clarify his client's behavior, possibly affecting legal arguments on her behalf. If research showed that identical twins share uniquely close relations, this might explain the unusual nature of her loss.

Ten months later I received a letter from a mental health professional specializing in legal issues. He was evaluating a twin whose sister had been killed in a sports accident. A parent witnessed the accident, the twin did not. The professional assigned to the case was interested in "exploring what it is like for this child to both grieve her sister and also assume many of her sister's traits."

I found these lawyers' requests challenging because they took twin research to a new domain, raising further questions about whom we grieve for and why. The Minnesota Twin Loss Study addressed these issues, but we had not considered its possible legal implications. Now it seemed clear to me that, in legal terms, research showing twins' unique social relations also implied twins' unique bereavement and loss. Of course, research *does not* imply that twins' lives are more valuable or worthwhile than nontwins' lives.

Legal interest in twin research was also exciting because it meant that these findings had previously unrecognized applications. Attention from attorneys also made me realize that events other than twins' wrongful deaths might be assisted by twin research, such as injury (one twin's disfigurement could alter twin relations) and custody (separate adoptions would deprive twins of their special relationship). I was to encounter several such cases over the years as awareness of twin research spread. I also believe that new fertility treatments producing multiples and the possibilities for human cloning anticipate novel legal skirmishes in which twin findings will star.

I started entering courtrooms as well as classrooms, instructing juries as well as students. I saw the sad sides of twinship, especially the high emotional costs of losing a treasured friend. I also encountered the dark sides of twinship, such as hostile behaviors by one, or both, twins directed at their cotwins, although such events are rare.

Moving from twin relations to twin legalities was a natural, but surprising byway. It demanded novel ways of thinking about twin research, especially showing relevance of group findings for individual cases. One attorney asked that I "describe the manner in which twins relate" and "particularize general concepts to . . . these particular twins."[1] If an identical twin was particularly grief-stricken about wrongful loss of his or her cotwin, was this reaction typical of identical twins? If a parent losing one infant twin was despondent despite bearing one healthy twin, was the response characteristic of other bereaved parents?

My role as expert witness was to assess the unique consequences of loss, accidents, injuries, separation and other events for twins and their parents and nontwin siblings. Most cases I examined involved twins' wrongful deaths, for which I developed a standard, but flexible plan. This includes administering a Twin Loss Survey; interviewing twins (usually by telephone); interviewing family members and other individuals about the surviving twin's grief reactions (and their own grief reactions); and reviewing depositions and medical records. Twin type is diagnosed by a modified physical resemblance questionnaire included in the Twin Loss Survey, supplemented by photographs. Nondeath cases include all of the above except the Twin Loss Survey, and blood group analysis usually determines twin type.[2]

Most cases were settled, but I always prepared with a view toward trial. Once trial dates were set I visited twins and families to improve my familiarity with their cases. My first court appearance involved the wrongful death of a twenty-six-year-old identical female twin, in the case *Fryover vs. Forbes*.[3] On the morning of September 25, 1986, identical twin Penny Fryover was driving to work. When she swerved to avoid hitting a dog her car struck a tree, killing her instantly. Penny was four months pregnant with her first child, and according to her twin sister Ginny "had so much going for her." Amazingly, Penny's husband Steven had driven past the car wreckage en route to work, but did not learn his wife was involved until later. He then called Ginny's home and asked for her husband, Norm, but he was working. Steven said nothing about the accident, only that "Penny wasn't sick anymore." He called Ginny again later that morning for Norm's work number, arousing her suspicions that "something was up." When Norm came home early she learned the difficult truth.

There were no eyewitnesses, but the accident was reconstructed by police experts assisted by a witness hearing the crash. The dog's owner, Steven Forbes, was charged with violating Michigan's law requiring owners to restrain pets taken off their property, and the deputy noted that his own wife had nearly hit the same dog at the same location nine days earlier. A lawsuit alleging Steven Forbes's negligence was filed on behalf of the deceased twin's spouse, mother, twin sister and half brother.

The night before trial I met Ginny and her mother at my hotel. I recognized Ginny immediately from a family photo taken at Penny's wedding. After dinner we talked for a long time. We reviewed Penny's death and its aftermath before reliving the episodes that make twins so fascinating. Ginny and her mother spoke with sparkle, ending the evening reluctantly. "They would not let me go," I later told Mark Verwys, their attorney. Telling twin tales kept Penny's memory alive for Ginny and her mother, a pleasure that would end once they stepped out of my door.

Loss of companionship, with reference to the special nature of identical twin relationships and the emotional consequences of twin loss, was central to my testimony. I described another unique feature of twin loss, namely that surviving twins remind family and friends of their deceased cotwins. *Fryover vs. Forbes* illustrated this point forcefully:

- *Steven Fryover (Penny's husband).* Steven's relationship with Ginny had been warm and friendly, but virtually ended after Penny's death. Steven insisted that he and Ginny testify in court on different days because the twins' similarities made Ginny a painful reminder of his former wife.
- *Ginny Corliss (Penny's twin).* Ginny never imagined the possibility of losing her twin until it happened, and then floods of twin-based media advertisements never let her forget. Her twinship was special—"above family"—because she and Penny were best friends, sharing thoughts even their husbands never knew. They met often despite living apart, and kept keys to each other's homes. After the accident, Ginny felt robbed of a relationship she loved, and often caught herself acting in ways more typical of her sister than herself.

  Ginny also felt deprived of the relationship she had anticipated with her twin's child. Ginny's biological relationship to the child would have been as her sister's because she and Penny were genetically identical. Loss of a potential niece or nephew troubled Ginny, persuading her to postpone her own pregnancy. Michigan law disallowed compensation for loss of a nonviable unborn child—the wrongful death claim concerning Penny's unborn child was heard by the state Court of Appeals, but to no avail.

- *Virginia Harvey (Penny's mother).* Many people assume that the death of a twin is less devastating to parents than the death of a singleton because surviving twins might lessen the loss. Research on newborn twins and nontwin infants has disproved this.[4] This issue has not been examined in adult twin loss cases, but there is no reason to expect any difference. Mrs. Harvey grieved for her twin daughter, recalling the special moments multiple birth parents experience when they are with their twins.

The resolution of *Fryover vs. Forbes* was inspiring and disappointing. The attorney representing defendant Steven Forbes offered $500,000 toward settlement for the Fryover family. According to Mr. Verwys, "Although I did not know it at the time, I have since learned that he did so primarily on the basis of his insurance company's reaction to the testimony of Marv [the economist analyzing future loss of support and services] and Nancy [Segal.] The insurance company representative who was present during trial on Thursday and Friday was apparently quite impressed and concerned with Nancy's testimony about the rupture of the twin relationship." Mr. Verwys rejected the $500,000 award, believing jurors would raise the amount. The jury favored Ginny and her family but, most meaningful to me, granted *highest compensation* to Ginny and Steven in *equal* amounts. Spouses usually receive greater compensation than siblings, so jurors were persuaded that twin loss is a devastating life event. Mrs. Harvey received a smaller award and the twins' half brother did not receive one. The case's disappointing outcome was reduction in awards to $300,000 for future loss of society and companionship. According to Verwys, "While the jury might have improperly speculated that Steve could remarry, there is nothing Virginia, Ginny or Vern [the twins' half brother] could do to affect their loss."

Still, I was gratified that twin research had made an important difference to Penny's family and to individuals present at trial. I was also pleased that *Fryover vs. Forbes* was summarized in the *Wall Street Journal,*[5] *Bureau of National Affairs Civil Trials Manual,*[6] and in *Medical Malpractice Law & Strategy*[7] because this approach was unknown to many attorneys. As a result of those publications and others, I was contacted by numerous lawyers, psychiatrists and social workers whose practices included bereaved twins. Some twins' identities have been disguised in the case summaries that follow.

T. vs. Northern State Power Company[8] concerned the July 1991 death of an identical twin in a tragic farming accident. Chad, the deceased, was twenty-four and attending a state university at the time of the incident. He and a coworker had been moving a grain auger that came in contact with a power line, fatally electrocuting him. His twin brother, Craig, was contacted by an emergency room staff member. "She said to come to the hospital quick, your brother's been in an accident. I asked how bad, and when all she could say was just come here, I knew." Chad and Craig were classmates, sports partners and best friends, and planned to share a summer lake home in the future.

A lawsuit was filed against the power company and grain bin manufacturer on behalf of Craig, his mother (also an identical twin) and his older brother—the twins' father had passed away in 1983. At issue were wrongful death, and loss of society and comfort. Like other multiples, Craig faced the unique twin loss legacy of *two* traumatic anniversaries—the date Chad died *and* the date they were born. The twins' mother had been thrilled to have twins and, being an identical twin herself, had rare understanding of her son's loss. The twins' older brother expressed greater rage at the accident than grief for the loss. This case went to trial, settling in favor of the family the day before I was to testify. The family's attorney indicated that the potential impact of my testimony, which had been disclosed to defense lawyers, was a significant factor in prompting the settlement.

C. vs. Salt Lake County concerned the death of a young twin boy and the unhappy consequences for his parents and siblings. Cameron and Corey were three-year-old identical twins, the fourth and fifth children of their parents, Mary and Jim. Mary told me her "towhead blonds" (individuals with soft whitish hair) were the "near perfect thing that ever happened to her." Her twin boys were close companions, creating fantasy worlds with Peter Pan and Lincoln logs. They were just acquiring social skills for including other children in their play.

On April 25, 1992, Mary, four of her children and two of their friends were visiting the historic Wheeler Farm in Salt Lake County.[9] Mary was photographing the boys when horses pulling a haywagon ride ran uncontrollably through the area. Corey's skull was crushed and, despite his mother's efforts to save him (Mary was a nurse), he died while she, his twin and his other siblings looked on. A lawsuit was filed against Wheeler Farm for inadequate management and maintenance of equipment by five families hurt in the accident. The twins' family additionally filed for "loss of care, comfort, society and protection" of their son, and for "mental and emotional distress,"[10] issues on which the lawyers instructed me to focus. I was also interested in learning more about how twin loss affected a young survivor. According to Mary, Cameron was "completely lost" without Corey—he did not eat all summer, did not know what to do in the bathtub, and showed reckless behavior. Cameron was also a constant reminder of his twin because they were so alike.

The case settled in favor of the family one week before I was to testify in court. Their attorney summarized the outcome: "In my opinion, your deposition testimony helped us in achieving a satisfactory settlement for the . . . family. As you are aware, we were primarily concerned with the impact of Corey's death on Jim and Mary. Although the loss was, and will continue to be traumatic for Cameron, we were only able to assert a claim on behalf of the parents for the loss of their twin son. Your testimony helped demonstrate to defense counsel the magnitude of that loss."

O. vs. Ford Motor Company also captured the unique emotional consequences following the loss of a young twin child. Kadie and Kymberly were a surprise identical twin birth for their parents, Rebecca and Karl.[11] At age three and a half years the twins were perfectly matched in their behavior, appearance, and enthusiasm for each other. Their only physical difference was the placement of birthmarks on their heads—one near the center and one near the side. This minor difference became major evidence in the heartbreaking loss of one twin.

On March 9, 1994, Karl and Rebecca were driving the twins and their older brother to school. Against her better judgment Rebecca seated the girls in the rear bench seat of the van when they insisted. They were wearing child restraints. Their van was hit by a car running a red light at 40–45 miles per hour, causing collision with a second car in the opposite lane. Kadie and Kymberly were thrown from the vehicle when the impact tore their seat loose. Soon after reaching the hospital, Kymberly died and Kadie was in a coma, leading to a lawsuit against Ford Motor Company for loss of society, pain and suffering. As the surviving twin improved Rebecca found it strange that Kadie behaved so much like her sister. It was only when Rebecca studied the child's birthmark that she knew a terrible mistake was made—*Kymberly* had survived and *Kadie* had perished. This happened two weeks after the accident and ten days after the funeral, so it was like losing a child all over again.

The case settled out of court in favor of the O. family. Attorneys concentrated on Kadie's wrongful death and Kymberly's physical trauma, not on the psychological consequences of Kymberly's twin loss. Information I provided on twin relationships and twin loss was included in settlement hearings. According to the attorney, this information did affect the outcome on behalf of the family, although the degree of influence was hard to assess. I have since learned from Marcia Kester-Doyle's moving article in *Twinsworld* that Kymberly recovered physically, but still cries for her twin.

O. vs. Drs. H. and K. concerned the medical circumstances and psychological aftermath following the sudden loss of an adult female twin. Fraternal twins Nina and Renee "did everything together" as children and as young adults. The twins were similar in appearance, both blond with blue eyes and nearly identical weights, but with a three-inch height difference. Their relationship was interrupted when Nina died in August 1983 at age nineteen, from alleged medical malpractice during a psychiatric hospitalization. The charge was that physicians neglected information warning against administration of certain medications due to family history—the twins' mother died following heart failure when they were nine, so some substances were potentially harmful to her children due to their shared genes. Nina had also demonstrated cardiac irregularity. I addressed the nature of twin relationships and twin loss during courtroom testimony.

The jury awarded compensation. The extent to which the twin relationship influenced the jurors' decision was not known, but their attorney believed it was significant.

Krasowskis vs. YMCA involved the disappearance and death of Andre, a twenty-one-year-old twin and seaman on leave from the Marine Corps. Andre was spending his summer as a camp counselor on a resort island off California at the time of his loss.

Andre was told to head out to sea to secure a tarp on a ski boat. However, the weather was stormy, he was alone, and he never returned. Sadly, his body was recovered several days later, tied to a dinghy. A lawsuit was filed against the YMCA for negligence. Losing her twin brother was devastating to Katrina, who worried that when her parents saw her they would also see Andre. Losing a twin son was also traumatic for Paul and his wife, Lidia. Paul told me that some people try to soften the hurt by saying "you have another child," but he answers, "I have a daughter, but not a son, and my daughter does not have a brother."

Nearly nine years after losing her twin, Katrina remembered Andre as her finest friend. Birthdays had been wonderful, but after Andre's death Katrina spent them alone. She did not share this day with her family again until age thirty, and what happened then reminded her of why she preferred to stay away. "Happy birthday to you, happy birthday to you, happy birthday dear . . ." Unhappy proof of Andre's loss was Katrina waiting for two names to be sung.

The Krasowskis' case has been pending for nearly a decade, and is still unsettled because of stubborn federal maritime legal issues unrelated to loss. Judgment was entered in favor of the Krasowskis family for $1,000,000 in deferral court. Insurance coverage issues are still pending. Neil Tardiff, one of the attorneys, believed information on twin loss substantially strengthened arguments in this regard.

Although I did not know it at the time, some twins' settlements affected legislation or influenced outcomes of other cases. Marc Kurzman's firm represented a family whose twin infant died from formaldehyde exposure. I was struck by his view that a twin's loss was so compelling that it urged policy makers to change regulations over particleboard gas levels. In another case, *Z. vs. McAbee,* a six-year-old identical twin boy was bitten on the face by his neighbor's dog. The scars he sustained made the twins easy to tell apart. Some features of their evolving twin relationship were also altered (e.g., the injured twin became reticent and the uninjured twin grew protective). The attorney, Donald P. Fedderly, believed that twinship had a substantial impact on the outcome of this case—$100,000 was awarded in arbitration, higher than the $25,000–30,000 compensation typically given to similarly situated individuals. Had the case gone to trial and produced a written opinion by the trial or appellate court, Fedderly believed such an opinion would have created new law regarding an unharmed twin's right to recover damages for injuries to his or her cotwin.

Years later, I also learned that *Fryover vs. Forbes*'s outcome (in which an identical twin was compensated for the wrongful loss of her sister) significantly affected the settlement of *O. vs. Cone Mill.* This case involved the disfigurement of a nineteen-month-old identical male twin.

Attorney John Steele's office in Minneapolis was a labyrinth of artwork and file folders, crammed into a two-story house near the Guthrie Theater. There I learned that on May 28, 1979, David and Johnny O.'s twinship changed forever. Left alone momentarily, the twins crawled onto the stove, with horrific consequences—David was badly burned on the face and chest. An ambulance was called twice, taking twenty minutes to travel ten blocks.

David and Johnny were ten years old when I worked on their case. Steele had delayed legal proceedings against Cone Mill in order to more accurately assess the physical and psychological damages. We used two complementary approaches to evaluating the effects of injury and disfigurement on the twins' behavior and relationship:

- The unaffected twin provided a "baseline" against which to compare the appearance and behaviors of the affected twin.
- The accident's current and future effects on the twin relationship were explored through interviews with the parents, twins, and others who knew the twins well.

Before the accident, David and Johnny were nearly identical in appearance, but after the accident their resemblance dropped dramatically. Clinical evaluation of the twins at age eight showed David's self-doubt, high parental dependence, and concern over bodily distortion. Johnny showed insecurity, sadness, and fear of injury.

I explored the twins' evolving relationship with their mother. Before the accident, David and Johnny had been "inseparable." As infants she would place them at opposite ends of their shared crib, but by morning she would find them with their heads together. When David was first hospitalized he placed Johnny's photograph near his bed and talked to the nurses about his twin. The first time that David was released from the hospital the twins held hands on the way to Burger King. Despite their initial closeness, the injury forced the twins in separate directions. David was prevented from playing football, and both boys regretted the lose of shared sports experiences. David was also taunted by children who called him "pizza face," remarks that brought Johnny to his rescue. The twins were no longer objects of excite-

David (left) and Johnny during David's treatment for severe facial burns. Johnny's protective attitude is typical of many twins whose cotwins suffer injury or illness. PHOTO COURTESY OF JOHN STEELE AND THE O. FAMILY.

ment, but objects of curiosity. For the rest of their lives, Johnny would remind David and his parents of what *could* and *should* have been.

Little behavioral research on twin children discordant for injury or disfigurement has been undertaken. One of the few available studies included six same-sex twin pairs discordant for hemifacial microsomia (abnormal development of the eyes, ears and jaw). The results replay many themes evident in David and Johnny's twinship.[12] Affected twins experienced more difficulties with friendship and self-esteem then their unaffected cotwins, partly due to teasing by peers. Affected twins also benefited from the emotional support offered by their cotwins. Unfortunately, the sample was small and the twins were not examined according to type.

Our knowledge of how one twin's injury, disfigurement or handicap affects their healthy cotwin is also limited, although some concerns have emerged in case reports.[13] Healthy or uninjured twins may develop insecurities following parental overindulgence, or they may show embarrassment when compared with their disabled or injured cotwins. Some twins see their cotwins as "caricatures" of themselves. Willingly or unwillingly, healthy twins often make "indirect sacrifices," such as forfeiting parental resources, or assuming responsibility for their cotwin's protection. Some healthy twins even exploit "good twin" roles to advantage, gaining parental favors in exchange for providing care.

Johnny suffered considerably following his twin's accident, albeit in ways that were not always obvious. He displayed cravings for physical affection, most likely due to reduced attention from his parents who focused on making his brother well. He was often cared for by his grandmother, who lived thirteen miles from his home, and he was denied access to his twin for the first month after the injury. His uncharacteristic "clinginess" persisted, changing to jealousy when David entered a camp for burned children and participated in other special programs. Johnny also experienced the loss of his unique relationship with David. Previously, Johnny was the idea "generator" while David was the "executor," but David's role was vacant after the accident.

O. vs. Cone Mill settled out of court, awarding $20,000,000 to David and $100,000 to his parents for medical care and emotional stress. The unique aspect of this case was recovery of $200,000 for Johnny for psychological damages, namely loss of twinship benefits associated with his twin's disfigurement. This was my first case involving physical injury to a twin rather than wrongful death, but it was not my last. A subsequent case involved an identical twin's mental and physical deterioration from a near drowning. Another case concerned an identical twin's cerebral palsy and seizure disorder from alleged medical malpractice during his mother's pregnancy. As the cases accumulated, it was increasingly clear that when twins are wrongly injured their twinship suffers too.

The pains of disrupted twinship are key issues in twin loss and twin injury cases. Therefore, I find it ironic that some families, health practitioners and judges do not object to placing twins in separate homes. My association with the Minnesota Study of Twins Reared Apart revealed that reunited twins resent their years alone, and that separate adoptions were often made simply for agencies' convenience. This is not right; every effort should be made to place twins together.

Twins' custody cases also showed that keeping pairs together is not always simple, and rare circumstances may favor their separation. Twins Carrie and Becky spent their first days of life in a neonatal unit for treatment of their breathing problems. Following discharge, they were placed in various foster homes when their biological parents could not care for them. At four months, Carrie and Becky entered their third foster homes, in which their respective fathers were brothers, living a few miles apart. A social worker asked one of the families to adopt one twin, not both, because of their health difficulties. The family objected to separating the twins so suggested that their nearby relatives adopt the other infant to keep them close together. This arrangement was challenged by a biological uncle and aunt who wished to adopt both. The focus of this case was *not* the advisability of rearing by biological or nonbiological kin, but the advisability of twins' separate or joint placement.

Separate adoptions were recommended by a clinical psychologist, based on the twins' successful adjustment to their new homes and assurance of the twins' frequent contact with one another. Contrary to this recommendation, at that time I favored placing Carrie and Becky together, to allow them to benefit from their relationship as twin sisters. I worried that unforeseen events, such as one family's leaving the area, might further divide the twins in the future. I also knew that they would be attending the same school so I wondered how classmates might view their unusual family situation. Still, each twin's contentment in their separate homes concerned me greatly because disrupting parent-child bonds can traumatize two-year-olds—thus, there was a trade-off between the twins' immediate versus long-term interests and well-being. The judge complied with the psychologist's recommendations, so Carrie and Becky were adopted separately.

Reflecting on this case years later, I believe the judge's decision was justified. The twins may have faced unforeseen behavioral problems if moved to yet a fourth residence in their short lives. In the years that followed, the twins' aunt voiced concerns over Carrie and Becky's adjustment to their separate rearing. In particular, she felt that they did not convey a clear sense of being twins. I also spoke with one of the adoptive mothers, who disagreed, insisting that Carrie and Becky's twinship was recognized by them and by those who knew them. She believed that they had adjusted well to their separate situations which had been familiar to them since they were two.

It will be interesting to learn the twins' views of their rearing as they grow older, and to consider the implications for other custody decisions involving twins. In the meantime, I received a case leading me to support twins' separation, a position I never anticipated.

An unusual custody battle over twin daughters challenged my thinking on placing some twins together or apart. Fraternal twin girls, Ellen and Karen, were the only children born to a professional midwestern couple, Frank and Greta Mann. The twins were eight years old when I become involved in struggles over their daughters' placement following their parents' divorce. Ellen, the firstborn twin, was a healthy child, while her twin sister Karen was severely brain damaged from birth. Karen's mental age equivalence was estimated to be six months—she was also blind and unable to communicate. The parents first separated when the twins were four, at which time joint legal custody was granted—Frank had physical custody of Ellen, and his wife Greta had physical custody of Karen. Both parents subsequently remarried, and Greta sought full custody of Ellen. At issue were the advisability of joint versus separate rearing of the twins, and Ellen's placement in the maternal or paternal household.

The case settled out of court with the recommendation that Ellen remain in her father's care. Frank requested, however, that I explore the twins' relationship with his daughter and other family members in the event of future family altercations. Based upon a Twin Relationship Interview[14] and Sibling

Statement Scale[15] given to Ellen, and interviews with her father and step-mother, I concurred with the court's judgment. I saw little evidence of meaningful past or present relationships between the twins, and little chance of any developing in the future. The voluntary time Ellen spent with Karen was minimal, and Ellen's visits to Karen's school left Ellen embarrassed because, despite the twins' extreme differences in physical development—the twins were five inches different in height, and sixty pounds different in weight—the staff emphasized the twins' similarities.[16] Furthermore, Karen's presence restricted family activities, impairing interactions between Ellen and her mother. I believed supportive relations between handicap-discordant twins should be encouraged, but not at the expense of healthy twins.[17]

Several years later Frank informed me of Karen's death at age ten when her heart and breathing stopped. Her twin sister and step-siblings were well prepared for the loss. Frank believed the loss was a mixed blessing because despite their grief, Karen no longer suffered and family activity was no longer affected.

Other legal cases raised a host of unique themes because twins were involved. A Russian émigré in the United States, Anatoly Rubchinsky, requested my help changing his twin nieces' immigration status, letting them leave Russia together for the United States. "Since they were born thirty-six years ago, these twin sisters have never been separated," he wrote. I prepared a letter on the twins' behalf for members of the Washington Processing Center and Congress, citing twin relationship and twin loss findings. The results were summarized in the uncle's marvelous note to his nieces, Laris and Frida: "You'll never know how much help she [Dr. Nancy Segal] gave me in my quest to get the two of you out of Russia *together*. My purpose in letting you know about her is to make you aware of how great kindnesses by unseen people can affect your lives."[18]

I opened Chapter 4 describing a father's distress over his identical twin sons' false accusation of cheating. The case progressed for only a short time until the university dismissed it suddenly for unknown reasons. Several months later I received a letter from him and, given the nature of his sons' case, I chuckled at his closing line: "By the way, they both called us tonight within a few minutes with practically the identical question." His communications over the years expressed his continued interest in twin research studies and findings. However, not everyone thinking about twin research in legal contexts showed the same appreciation.

Twin research had little effect on the settlement of *S. vs. Miller Brothers, et al.,* a case involving the death of an eighteen-year-old identical male twin in an automobile accident. Posttrial surveys showed that my testimony focused too strongly on general findings, rather than on specific details of the twins in question. I was, however, less surprised by the outcome in this case than I was by one judge's outright refusal to let me take the stand.

Attorney Timothy G. Riling was representing a family whose adult twin daughter, Betty, was killed in a car accident while her identical twin sister, Judy, was at the wheel. (The twin driving the car was not responsible for the accident.) Judy lay in a coma for six days, awakening to find her twin gone. Just prior to trial, I learned that I would not be allowed to testify because the presiding judge felt that uniting twin research and wrongful death was "too new." I realized that a vital task was to make the unfamiliar familiar by describing twin research's relevance to legal cases for broad professional audiences. Therefore, I published an article, "Implications of Twin Research for Legal Issues Involving Young Twins," in the journal *Law and Human Behavior*,[19] which I could supply to attorneys contacting me. I am convinced that most cases benefited from twin research findings. In one wrongful death case, just knowing a twin researcher was hired led the defense attorneys to settle the case quickly out of court.

Although legal experts' unfavorable reception of twin research never occurred again, there were occasional surprises. I declined involvement in several cases when the attorneys' understanding of twin research differed from mine. One lawyer reasoned that since twins are like everyone else, the experience of losing a twin or sibling must be the same. Another case involved the suicide of a forty-year-old identical male twin which led to severe disturbance in his twin brother. The surviving twin was later accused of sexual misconduct. I was asked to justify his behavior as an extreme reaction to his brother's suicide, but I refused because sexual misconduct is unacceptable in any context. I reminded the lawyer that none of the other fifty-five twins whose cotwins had committed suicide in my bereavement study showed such reactions.

Using twin research in court was new to my colleagues as well as to attorneys. Most were supportive and many were intrigued, but several raised questions. A few colleagues opposed giving twin relationships special weight, claiming that not every twin relationship is special. Some twins *are* closer than others. Over the years I have worked with more identical than fraternal twin loss cases, although fraternal twins are born more frequently.[20] Nevertheless, bereavement studies showed that twin loss brought greater grief to both identical and fraternal twins than the loss of other biological relatives. A more specific objection was that there are "no special relations between male-female pairs." Fraternal twins are generally not as close as identical twins; however, a slightly *higher* proportion of bereaved twins from fraternal male-female pairs (19%) than bereaved twins from fraternal same-sex pairs (15%) volunteered for the twin loss study. Later, I was amused to find an article by one of the critical colleagues entitled, "Separation Anxiety: The Twin Advantage."[21]

A few researchers challenged psychologists' ability to measure grief or loss reactions. Several well-crafted bereavement inventories and questionnaires are available, providing a valid sense of grief following loss.[22] In my own research, bereavement was measured in more than one way, and the results for identical and fraternal twins are consistent. Some questionnaires are superior to others, but sweeping criticism of bereavement research methods is unwarranted.

My legal file also includes several cases on which I worked briefly. Out-of-court settlements, withdrawals of complaints, or other factors could explain my limited contact with some attorneys and twins. I never learned the outcomes of these cases, but I never forgot their compelling details. One identical twin risked an unfair trial because his brother's previous conviction was known to the jurors who may have assumed that identical twins are always matched in crime. A foster family wished to adopt only one of the twins in their care, troubling case workers wishing to keep the twins together. Divorced parents each retained custody of one twin, and awaited final placement decisions.

In the future, twin research promises to become even more relevant to the law as the biomedical treatment of infertility advances. Multiple birth kinships created by new reproductive technologies are paving the way for new legal dilemmas. Novel legal tangles over infant twin survival, infant twin development, and twin family relations are certain. Possible human cloning would enlarge family law complexities by further revising parent-child and sibling relations.

An issue almost certain to end up in the courts concerns the selective reduction of multiple fetuses, such as quintuplets to twins. A possibility not addressed so far is legal action by surviving twins against parents for eliminating twin siblings, forfeiting their enjoyment of potentially significant relationships. Anecdotal evidence suggests that twin loss at birth or in early infancy poses psychological difficulties for some surviving twins, although the effects may differ from those linked to twin loss in adulthood.[23]

Organ transplantations are becoming more sophisticated and successful, raising unique legal issues for twins and their families. An unusual case of twins separated at birth begins a series of legal dramas and dilemmas based on relatives' varying biological compatibility.

An identical twin (Eric) and an unrelated nontwin (Pierre), born on the same 1941 evening, were accidentally "switched" as infants.[24] Watching a school parade six years later, the twins' father was astonished to see a child closely resembling one of his sons (Victor). Matched blood types and successful skin grafts confirmed the identical twinship of the separated pair. Eric and Pierre were both returned to their birth families.

The scarcity of compatible blood and organ donors is problematic,[25] but identical twins' identical genes make them fortunate exceptions to this concern. In 1990, Chris Singleton, then a University of Arizona NFL hopeful, donated bone marrow to his identical twin brother, Kevin, who had been stricken with leukemia.[26] In 1994, identical twin Martin Glasenapp underwent surgeries to correct a bowel condition caused by a tumor. His brother Donald donated three feet of his small intestine in an eight-hour procedure at the Veterans Affairs Medical Center, in Palo Alto, California. This may be the most successful bowel transplant on record,[27] but it may not surpass what another set of identical twin brothers accomplished.[28] A developmental error before birth left one twin without testicles, but a donated testicle from his cotwin enabled him to have children of his own.

Some fraternal twins and siblings are also good biological matches for one another. In 1996, the late Massachusetts senator Paul Tsongas received a bone marrow transplant from his twin sister, Thaleia, when he developed myelodysplasia (a complication from cancer involving bone marrow). The chance that fraternal twins and siblings show compatible donor-recipient relationships is, of course, variable.

Identical twins' perfect donor-recipient relationship raises unique legal themes.[29] When the outcomes of 130 cases involving identical twins' bone marrow transplantation proved favorable, investigators concluded, "Thus for twins with hematologic cancers the question is not *whether* to perform a transplant but *when* to do so."[30] Dr. Richard Morgan of the National Center for Human Genome Research is injecting specially treated blood from healthy identical twins into their AIDS-infected cotwins, hoping to find a cure.[31] However, if an identical twin was an unwilling donor, could a cotwin bring legal action claiming rights to lifesaving materials? Could he or she justify "joint ownership" of blood or organs because of their genetic identity?

Thus far the law forbids compelling twins to donate organs, but it allows states to order health insurers to pay for twin-twin transplants.[32] In August 1990 identical twin Thomas Bradley, a Long Island school teacher, won a court order requiring Empire Blue Cross and Blue Shield to cover the $150,000 cost of a bone marrow transplant from his identical twin brother, Robert. Tom had contracted AIDS, and his survival depended upon generating a new immune system with his twin's help. Blue Cross argued against payment on grounds that the treatment was too new, but Robert's ideal donor status affected the outcome in this case. Unfortunately, delayed legal proceedings postponed medical treatment, and Thomas died one year later at forty-seven.

The prospect of human cloning raises the issue of whether a clone can be forced to serve as an organ donor for his or her genetic double. This type of scenario reached the courts in 1990 when Nancy Curran refused genetic testing of her three-year-old twins, Jimmy and Allison, as potential bone marrow donors for their half brother, Jean-Pierre Bosze.[33] Curran feared subjecting her children to unnecessary medical procedures. Jean-Pierre, fatally stricken with leukemia, had been born to Tamas Bosze, who had fathered the twins in a previous relationship with their mother. The Illinois Supreme Court affirmed a lower court ruling that the twins' testing could not be coerced. It is likely that such decisions would also extend to cloned individuals.

Comparing relatives' willingness to donate blood or organs to one another tests evolutionary-based ideas about who helps whom, and why. Organ donation keeps relatives alive, allowing them to reproduce and indirectly transmit the donor's genetic material to their own offspring. Therefore, greater willingness to donate would be expected by identical twins than by fraternal twins, by mothers than by aunts, and by uncles than by cousins. In the case involving the testicle transplant, one twin's gift to his twin brother was not life-preserving, but it doubled his chances of having his genes represented in later generations. Of course, such decisions do not consciously include genetic relatedness, and are sometimes made quickly and emotionally.[34] Genetic relatedness may, however, underlie our affiliative feelings toward others, ultimately affecting these decisions.

Studies show that close relatives are usually willing donors,[35] yet some feel ambivalence. Mothers accept kidney donation as an "obligation" to their children, while some distant relatives, such as the spouses of potential donors, have opposed the decision.[36] These findings generally support evolutionary views of donation decisions, but fresh work is needed to test evolutionary-based hypotheses concerning willingness to donate organs. Twin, sibling and adoption studies will be revealing because they can explore donor attitudes while controlling for donor-recipient relatedness, age, gender, physical and behavioral similarity and other factors. Recipients' age may affect willingness to donate organs because recipients past their reproductive years would be unable to transmit donors' genes. If identical twins showed greater willingness to donate their organs to their cotwins, relative to fraternal twins and siblings, this would lend meaning to people's favoring close kin over distant kin in life-and-death situations.[37] Applying evolutionary psychology to medical decision making can help clarify why people act as they do. A new field, *evolutionary jurisprudence,* is helping us understand the nature of laws and legal decisions.

Evolutionary jurisprudence, described by law professor Jack Beckstrom, explores the common ground between evolutionary psychology and the law.[38] Evolutionary psychology can help us understand why fathers conceiving children out of wedlock may be less inclined to provide child support than divorced fathers conceiving children during marriage: Men uncertain of their biological relatedness to children would be less likely to nurture them than men who are certain. Legal systems might remedy these situations by offering paternity tests to putative fathers, whether they have overtly challenged their paternity or not.

Evolutionary-based analyses of other behaviors of interest, such as inheritance decisions, have been facilitated by existing data sets. The outcomes of current and future legal cases involving twins will, undoubtedly, further test evolutionary reasoning in legal contexts. We could compare court awards to twins, parents and nontwin siblings of deceased or injured identical and fraternal twins. The behaviors and feelings of twins unintentionally harmed by their cotwins might be contrasted with the behaviors and feelings of twins unintentionally harmed by nontwin relatives or unrelated individuals. I learned of an identical male twin who dozed at the wheel, causing a car accident and his cotwin's paralysis. The injured twin never considered a lawsuit, and the brothers continued to be close.[39] I wondered, however, if the injured twin would have taken legal action against a cousin, acquaintance or coworker. This issue could be investigated by presenting hypothetical situations to twins, siblings and other family members, and by examining real events. Twin cases often appear in the media, so tracking twins' behaviors for trends would be possible. An extreme test of identical twins' attachment showed they can forgive even when their cotwins threaten their lives.

Evolutionary psychology can help us make sense of some counterintuitive behaviors. In Chapters 5 and 6, I alluded to Jeen Han's failed murder attempt of her identical twin sister Sunny in 1996.[40] (Jeen allegedly planned to assume her twin's identity after the murder to escape her crime-filled past.) I was distressed by persistence of the "good twin–evil twin" theme in media reporting of this story, a convenient literary device with no basis in fact—Sunny had a history of credit card fraud. I had hoped for reasoned discussion of twins' behavior, fearing that families would think this atypical case was typical. A second surprise was Sunny's pardoning of her sister. Sunny told the press that she and Jeen, both former covaledictorians, were "best friends." An evolutionary psychological perspective might judge Sunny's forgiving behavior in light of their genetic identity, so that helping Jeen would ultimately be seen as working in Sunny's own genetic interest. Sunny might have been far less lenient had the attempt on her life been orchestrated by a distant relative or unrelated person.

New cases involving wrongful death and injury to twins have been referred to me by attorneys interested in exploring how a twin research perspective might illuminate the psychological aspects of their cases. Their observations that twins' reactions to unfortunate life events differ from those of nontwins are striking. The fact that their descriptions of twins' behaviors match evolutionary psychological predictions is also worth noting. Twins' legal cases promise to furnish revealing data bases advancing the field of evolutionary jurisprudence. They also raise larger societal issues, focusing attention on circumstances surrounding birth, adoption and other events in our daily lives.

15

Separate Minds in Shared Bodies: Conjoined Twins

The 1997 Broadway musical *Side Show* replayed the personal and professional triumphs and defeats of Daisy and Violet Hilton, *conjoined twins* and 1930s vaudeville stars.[1] Conjoining twinning is the appropriate medical term for the delayed division of the fertilized egg (splitting is thought to occur after day fourteen), resulting in identical twins who are physically connected.

Conjoined twins uniquely capture the conflict between our desires for intimacy and freedom. They are a rare form of identical twinning, one that brings heartbreak and challenge to affected twins and their families. Psychological and physical survival are tested daily as the twins practice cooperative locomotion, and parents weigh separation options.

Interest in conjoined twinning goes well beyond the curiosity raised by other deviations in human behavior and form. I believe our fascination with these pairs stems from witnessing their incredible tests of human coexistence at the extreme. For most of us, it is unimaginable how the well-known Bunker twins, Chang and Eng, joined at the chest, fathered twenty-one children between them.[2] It is equally inconceivable how Ruthie and Verena Cady, fused from sternum to waist, navigated a four-wheel walker at age two. Their mother Marlene tried to teach them to walk and sit, but soon learned that the girls developed better ways of doing things on their own.[3] The universal appeal of all twins, added to the premium we place upon individuality and independence, may also explain public preoccupation and satisfaction surrounding successful separations. Separation is not possible for all pairs, however. Families of such twins sometimes tell different, more compelling stories of patience, courage and companionship despite the extraordinary trials. The experiences of conjoined twins illuminate the lives of anyone raising children, confronting physical handicaps, or exploring social relationships.

Many people know conjoined twinning as *Siamese twinning,* a term made famous by Chang and Eng, born in 1811 in Siam (now Thailand).[4] Sadly, their appearance in P. T. Barnum's circus attractions lent freakish overtones to conjoined twins. Chang and Eng's death cast (a plaster mold of the twins' deceased bodies from the hips up) and liver are on display in the Mütter Museum at Philadelphia's College of Physicians. Professor Thomas Mütter hoped his anomaly collection would show viewers the limits of human variation, but it has been called a little museum of horrors by those misunderstanding his purpose.[5]

Conjoined twins are thought to originate from a single fertilized egg, so they will always be genetically identical and same-sex. Their one-egg origin is partly confirmed by frequent occurrence of *situs inversus,* or physical reversal of internal organs such as the heart or liver.[6] Recall that mirror-image reversal of traits such as handedness and hair whorl occur among 25% of normal identical twins. However, *situs inversus* does not occur more often in twins than in singletons, so its frequency in conjoined twins may be unique to some forms of conjoined twinning.[7] The finding that conjoined twins are typically connected in symmetrical (mirror-image) pose by corresponding body parts is also consistent with their one-egg derivation. Daisy and Violet Hilton were joined in the pelvic region, allowing them to stand back to back—they looked as if a slightly angled mirror had been placed next to one individual.

The reasons for twins' incomplete separation have puzzled physicians since the first recorded birth of conjoined male twins in tenth-century Byzantium.[8] The most widely accepted theory is the *fission hypothesis* involving delayed division of the fertilized egg. Other than delayed splitting, the same factors producing fully separated twins are believed to produce conjoined twins. A less convincing theory was the nineteenth-century *fusion hypothesis* involving partial joining of separately developed body parts.[9]

A possible exception to the same-sex rule was a conjoined male-female pair born in 1957, but pseudohermaphroditism (a condition in which external genitals resemble those of the opposite sex) was suspected in one twin. Conjoined twins in triplet and quadruplet sets have occurred,[10] perhaps not surprising in identical sets in which some zygotic divisions may occur later than others. One set included conjoined females who died shortly after birth, and a normal male cotriplet who thrived without complication.[11] Another triplet set also included conjoined identical female twins and a fraternal cotriplet, but all three infants died within eleven hours after delivery.[12] Of course, factors that might delay human zygotic splitting are uncertain. Toxic substances have induced conjoined twinning in hamsters, and increased water temperatures have caused conjoined twinning in zebra fish, but few leads are available in humans.[13]

In addition to current scientific theories of conjoined twinning, legendary views have attracted attention over the years. An intriguing story concerns the 1495 birth, near Worms, of female twins joined at the forehead. It was claimed that two women (one of whom was pregnant) were conversing when

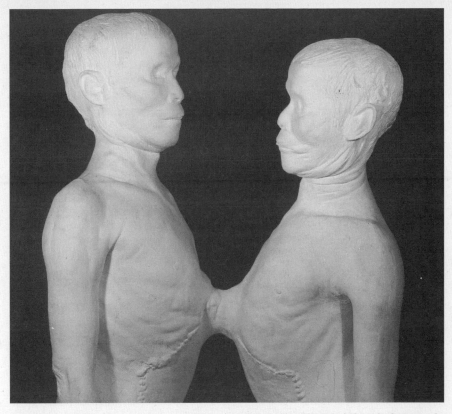

Plaster cast of conjoined twins Chang and Eng Bunker. They lived alternately in two farmhouses near Mount Airy, North Carolina, where they were respected by their neighbors for their "intelligence and industriousness." (Bryant, J. B. Asian Week. February 26, 1993.) PHOTO COURTESY OF THE MÜTTER MUSEUM, COLLEGE OF PHYSICIANS OF PHILADELPHIA.

their heads collided. The pregnant woman supposedly grew frightened, a reaction that transmitted the "mark of the concussion" to her unborn child, resulting in conjoined twins.[14]

The notoriety surrounding conjoined twins' deliveries masks their rarity. It is estimated that conjoined twins occur in 1/50,000 to 1/100,000 births, and in 1/200 identical twin births.[15] The scarcity of human conjoined twins may be due to spontaneous abortion of most affected pairs.[16] Among those delivered at term, 40–60% are stillborn (and mostly male), and 35% survive only one day.[17] The newborn survival rate varies between 5 and 25%, although not all pairs endure the first year and beyond.

Approximately 600 publications over nearly 500 years show that 70.7% of cases are female, 21.6% of cases are male, and 7.8% of cases are unidentified.[18] The steady rise in female representation from separated two-chorion twins to conjoined one-chorion twins is striking.[19] The reasons for the sex difference are uncertain, but possible explanations include greater male vulnerability to trauma, more frequently delayed splitting of female zygotes, or increased numbers of males born as Turner Syndrome females (XO instead of XY) after losing their Y chromosome. If delayed splitting is more common in female than in male zygotes, this would be an example of an atypical event (conjoined twinning) telling us about a typical event (complete twinning). The sex imbalance in conjoined twinning is also seen in chickens whose only cases are female.[20]

Physical variation among both ordinary identical and fraternal twin pairs is immense. However, the magnitude of conjoined twins' types and subtypes is even more staggering because they represent only a fraction of identical twin births. The broadest classification scheme includes two varieties of conjoined twins:[21]

- *Equal and symmetrical forms* (duplicatas completa *or* diplopagus). Twins show equal or nearly equal duplicate features so both twins are complete individuals. Chang and Eng Bunker displayed this type of twinning. These twins were joined at the chest by a band of tissue that allowed them to move freely, and to stand "half sideways."[22]
- *Unequal and symmetrical forms* (duplicatas incompleta *or* heteropagus). Twins show unequal duplication of features with different degrees of development. Sometimes twins' physical structures are equal, but each twin alone would lack the full complement of human features. For example, a pair may have two heads, two arms and two legs joined to a single body. This form of conjoined twinning also includes parasitic types in which parts of fetuses' anatomical structures are reproduced.[23]

More detailed conjoined twin classifications denote shared anatomical region, determined by location and degree of splitting. The terms are often followed by "-pagus," the Greek suffix meaning "fastened." The following groups, all equal in form, were defined by Drs. Alan F. Guttmacher and B. L. Nichols in 1967.[24]

- *A: Terata catadidymus.* Some twins share single features in the lower body and have duplicated features in the upper body (A.1 and A.2). Other twins are joined by a lower body portion (A.3 and A.4). There are four kinds of conjoined twins in this category.
  1. *Diprosopus.* Twins have one body with one head and two faces.
  2. *Dicephalus.* Twins have one body with two separate heads, usually with separate necks.
  3. *Ischiopagus.* Twins are joined by inferior margins of the coccyx (low-

est part of the backbone) and sacrum (part of the backbone above the coccyx).

4. *Pygopagus.* Twins are joined by a shared coccyx and sacrum, although the rest of the bodies are normally duplicated. These twins are positioned nearly back to back.

- **B: *Terata anadidyma.*** Some twins share upper body features, but have duplicated lower body features (B.1 and B.2). Some pairs may also be joined by part of the upper body (B.3). There are three kinds of conjoined twins in this category.

    1. *Dipygus.* Twins have a single head, thorax (chest) and abdomen with two pelvises, or two sets of reproductive organs, or four legs. One, two or all of these characteristics may occur.
    2. *Syncephalus.* Twins are joined by the face, which includes the right side of one face and the left side of the other face. Twins may otherwise be separate or joined at the chest.
    3. *Craniopagus.* Twins are joined at corresponding portions of the cranial vault (top of the head or skull), but are otherwise separate.

- **C: *Terata anacatadidyma.*** Twins are joined at the body's midportion, but are separate below and above. There are three kinds of conjoined twins in this category.

    1. *Thoracopagus.* Twins share part of the chest wall. Twins usually experience chest and upper abdominal abnormalities.
    2. *[Xiphopagus] Omphalopagus.* Twins are united from waist to lower breastbone.
    3. *Rachipagus.* Twins are joined by vertebral column (backbone or spinal column) anywhere above the sacrum.

The most common form of conjoined twinning is thoracopagus (C.1), occurring in about 40% of cases, and the least common form is craniopagus (B.3), occurring in about 2% of cases.[25] Xiphopagus (C.2) twins represent about 34% of conjoined twin pairs, pygopagus represent about 18%, and ischiopagus make up about 6%. The conjoined female twins of Worms displayed an extremely rare form of craniopagus conjoined twinning—their frontal juncture occurs in just 10% of these cases.[26]

Heteropagus (unequal and symmetrical) conjoined twins, which represent fewer than 10% of the cases, include one normal (or nearly normal) twin (autosite) and a partially developed, parasitic twin (parasite). Parasitic twins depend upon their cotwins for sustenance, and are usually attached to their front portion. Parasites could consist of arms or a head and arms attached to the stomach region of the other twin. Other parasitic twins may have developed within their cotwins' chest cavity, abdominal cavity or other region, and may be considered tumors.[27] *Fetus-in-fetu* refers to the presence of an abnormal fetus within another individual's body. An unusual example of this condition consisted of a tumor containing remnants of five fetuses, detected in a nineteen-day-old infant with hydrocephaly (excess fluid in the cranial cavity).[28]

Cephalodiprosopus is a very rare type of partial conjoined twinning in which a parasitic head is joined to the head of a normal cotwin. This condition was suggested in a male infant born with an occipital encephale (brain tissue mass inserted at the back of his head, approximately 1.5 times his head size).[29] The infant underwent successful surgical correction eight hours after an uneventful birth, and fared well during the next eight months. His physician, Dr. J. Lobo Antunes, from Columbia University's College of Physicians and Surgeons, uncovered only one similar case, described in a 1790 letter in the *Philosophical Transactions of the Royal Society of London.* Incredibly, a head attached to the head of an infant "seemed to sympathize with the child in most of its natural actions."

Donna Kopsell's healthy identical twin sons, David and Dean, participated in one of my early twin studies. Donna, who was unaware she was having twins, heard physicians counting her infants' ears after their delivery. She recalls mounting dread when the number of ears exceeded two, thinking she had given birth to conjoined twins or to one unusual infant. (Both of Donna's twins had the correct complement of ears, but the number went past two when her doctor counted the first ear of the second twin as "three.") Her experience is important because uneventful pregnancies can be deceptive preludes to the birth of conjoined twins. The surprise vaginal delivery of rare Janiceps twins to an Australian woman at thirty-two weeks' gestation illustrates this point well.[30]

The twenty-two-year-old mother of these twins was healthy, had one older child, and showed expected uterine size at seven weeks. She was treated for a urinary tract infection at eighteen weeks when enlarged uterine size suggested twins—however, an ultrasound performed at twenty-three weeks showed a single fetus. When labor began at thirty-two weeks vaginal delivery of the stillborn twins was possible due to their prematurity. Janiceps twins are a dipygus subtype, named after the Roman god Janus. In mythology, Janus "looked before and after," and is symbolized by two faces shown in profile. Janiceps twins are united face to face such that each face is divided down the middle with each half turned outward. The two final faces are formed by right and left halves of each twin.

Identifying pregnancy events that might signal conjoined twinning has concerned many medical investigators. A 300-year survey of thirty-six xiphopagus pairs (twins joined from navel to lower breastbone) showed an average gestational age of thirty-seven weeks; twins are nine times more likely to deliver before thirty-seven weeks than nontwins, most of whom deliver between thirty-seven and forty-one weeks.[31] Furthermore, conjoined twinning is unaffected by maternal age, ethnicity and number of previous

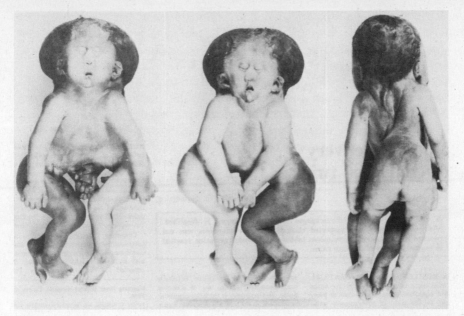

Janiceps conjoined twins. Photo Source: Greening, D. G., Vaginal delivery of conjoined twins. The Medical Journal of Australia 2, *356–359 (1981). Copyright* © The Medical Journal of Australia. *Reproduced with permission.*

children. Family history of conjoined twinning is also unrelated to producing conjoined twins, so genetic factors are not involved.[32] Compounding the mystery is that no known environmental agents or traumas have been reliably linked to this type of twinning. A 1945–65 New York State survey reviewed the reproductive histories of twenty-two mothers of conjoined twins. Results revealed seven stillbirths among fifteen mothers' thirty-two previous deliveries (22%), a figure exceeding the expected 2% rate.[33] The high percentage of stillbirths suggests that abnormal prenatal events may be affecting these women's pregnancies.

The search for causes of conjoined twinning has also led researchers to examine birth patterns in different geographical areas. A provocative South African report revealed that fifteen of the thirty-one conjoined pairs (48%), born between 1974 and 1982 were clustered between 1974 and 1976 in a remote region of Zimbabwe.[34] Seasonal variation and living styles were unrelated to conjoined twinning so unidentified environmental agents were presumed responsible. Time effects were also reported by the New York State survey which found six pairs born in 1959, and thirteen pairs born between 1957 and 1960.[35] The possibility of geographical, seasonal or temporal factors being associated with conjoined twinning is compelling, but incomplete reporting or chance events may explain the patterns and inconsistencies seen across studies.

The few symptoms associated with conjoined twins during pregnancy are hard to interpret because they may also occur with normal twins. Polyhydramnios[36] (increased amniotic fluid levels) occurred in 50–70% of conjoined twinning cases, and in 75% of thoracopagus twins (twins sharing a chest wall) described in the 1960s medical journals. Interestingly, the 300-year review of thirty-six xiphopagus pairs (twins joined from waist to lower breastbone), born between 1689 and 1978, reported only an 11% incidence of polyhydramnios, similar to normal twinning. (Polyhydramnios affects 2% of normal singleton pregnancies.) According to Dr. Michael Crenin, polyhydramnios is becoming a less significant sign of conjoined twinning because current cases are identified by ultrasound during the first or second trimesters.

Most conjoined twins born today are detected during routine prenatal examination that includes sonography. However, before sonograms were available only 50–70% of conjoined twinning cases were identified before birth.[37] Ultrasound, also used to confirm suspected multiple births, first diagnosed conjoined twins in 1976 at thirty-seven weeks' gestation.[38] More recently, conjoined twins have been diagnosed as early as nine weeks (dicephalus: twins with separate heads and one body) and eleven weeks (thoraco-omphalopagus: twins joined from chest to lower breastbone),[39] although detection in the third trimester is the most reliable.[40]

Some physicians urge careful study of all twin pregnancies for possible conjoining, especially if amnions are shared.[41] Diagnosing twins' number of amnions (one or two) can be done by ultrasound; vaginal ultrasound can enhance images of slender amnions in first trimester, one-amnion identical twins. All conjoined twins have single amnions, but only 5–10% of twins with single amnions are conjoined. The criteria for detecting conjoined twins by modern ultrasound techniques have been summarized by Dr. William L. Koontz.[42] They include: lack of a separate membrane between twins; inability to separate fetal bodies; detection of more than three vessels in a single umbilical cord; detection of fetal anomalies; and identification of specific X-rayed features (e.g., fetal heads at the same level and body plane).

Commenting on the first conjoined twins in a triplet pregnancy diagnosed by ultrasound, Dr. Koontz noted that two bodies with one identifiable head was the most conclusive sonographic evidence of conjoined twinning.[43] (This set included conjoined female twins who died shortly after birth, and a normal male cotriplet who survived.) Most ultrasonic criteria listed above do not apply to craniopagus twins (twins joined at the head). The few telltale sonographic signs include fetal heads positioned at the same level and nonseparable continuous skin contour.[44] In fact, the defining feature in the first craniopagus twin pair diagnosed by both ultrasound and computed tomography (use of layered X rays to clarify structural details at particular body depths) was stable fetal head positioning.[45] This was also the first occurrence of anencephaly (absence of skull bones and cerebral hemispheres) with encephalocele (brain tissue mass) in one female craniopagus twin. Anencephaly may be increased among identical twins and conjoined twins, relative to fraternal twins and singletons, so common causes may link these events.

Like the Australian mother of Janiceps twins, this mother's pregnancy experience was unremarkable. Ultrasound at ten weeks, conducted to assess fetal age, showed a normal single fetus. The history of twins in her family led her to seek a thirty-week ultrasound for multiple pregnancy, although all previously born twins were normal. The second examination indicated craniopagus twins, and computed tomography clarified the heads' bony mass. The mother chose cesarean delivery immediately following diagnosis of conjoined twins, delivering stillborn females.

It would be misleading to suggest that sonography always tells the truth.[46] Some conjoined twins appear in sonograms as single fetuses, with or without malformations. For example, dicephalus twins (twins with a single body and two heads) might go undetected if one twin's head is positioned higher than the other's. I am, however, unaware of any mistakes ever having been made in the opposite direction, i.e., a diagnosis of conjoined twins proving false upon delivery of a normal singleton or normal twins. Fortunately, improved ultrasound is better able to detect conjoined twins early in pregnancy, allowing more thoughtful postnatal treatment of the infants. However, optimal management of conjoined twins is not simple.

Public debates on the physical and psychological treatment of conjoined twins have engaged physicians, families and reporters in triadic tangles over pregnancy termination, surgical separation, and postoperative management. Bioethicists, theologians and historians have defined and debated ethical and moral issues, such as: Is it right or wrong to sacrifice one twin to save another, invest scarce resources in uncertain operations, and live life as a conjoined twin or not at all? However, these individuals do not provide all the answers. It is unfortunate that the voices of the twins themselves have been largely silent in the professional literature, where they might affect practices and policies. According to Dr. Alice D. Dreger of Michigan State University, many people believe conjoined twins experience "living hell," but she finds this view to be narrowly conceived.[47] The Schappell twins, Lori and Reba, tell a different story from the dismal world that is often envisioned.

Thirty-six-year-old Lori and Reba (Dori) Schappell of Reading, Pennsylvania, force hard looks at life quality and life satisfaction under conjoined twins' extraordinary circumstances.[48] These twins are the only living adult conjoined pair in the United States joined at the head. They have individual brains, but their shared blood supply and brain tissue makes separating them impossible. Reba is much shorter in height, requiring her to sit in a special stool, steered by her sister. Reba is also paralyzed from the waist down and was born with some internal organs outside her body.

The words of the Schappell twins and other conjoined pairs have echoed in the popular press, confirming difficult challenges, but revealing astonishing achievements. I spoke with Lori and Reba by telephone on June 18, 1998. Their achievements are extraordinary irrespective of their physical situation, and some of their stories will sound familiar, as well as amusing, to twins everywhere.

They were born in Reading Hospital, in Reading, Pennsylvania, on September 18, 1961. Their mother, who had delivered three previous children, found this pregnancy uneventful. Lori and Reba cannot pinpoint their first awareness of their unusual twinship, but they always knew they were "different." Their presence brought unkind comments and stares, but they were taught to ignore them.

Lori was responsible for arranging the telephone interview with me. She is the "open, extraverted twin" who fields questions about conjoined twinning. Reba is the "shy, private twin" who will only discuss her budding musical career, but who will assert herself when the situation demands it. According to Lori, "She [Reba] always encouraged me to pursue my career [as a ward clerk or nurse receptionist], and now I want to focus on hers." Today Lori accepts occasional part-time positions, freeing her to concentrate on her sister's singing engagements. Reba received a 1997 L.A. Music Award for best new country artist, and is now producing a CD, *Momma Taught Me*.

The twins' behavioral differences are extensive—Lori likes to watch television, Reba does not; Lori loves to shop, Reba does not; Lori craves sweets, Reba does not. Perhaps their physical proximity fuels their psychological separation, over and beyond what ordinary twins experience; their behavioral differences recalled those revealed in many conjoined twins' biographies.[49] The Schappells' physician, Dr. John M. Templeton, Jr., a former pediatric surgeon at Children's Hospital, also found the twins' differences striking. He mentioned Lori's earlier computer interests and Reba's former medical ambitions. Reba, once an aspiring physician, designed support equipment for physically disabled individuals.

When I asked the twins to list some similarities, Lori replied, "We have the same last name and we love each other." They call their relationship a "compromise," a plan any couple must learn, "only we learned it from the beginning." What is the most important message the twins would like the world to hear? It is that they are *handicapable,* a term coined by Reba. Handicapable means that they are successful, but slower, at doing what other people do. We may wrongly think of these twins as impossibly doomed, rather than as people simply trying to live their lives.

My conversation with Lori and Reba ended humorously. They recalled Reba's attempt to pay for a gift, an alcoholic beverage they wished to bring to a friend. The cashier requested proof of age, but when he saw Lori's face he decided that she looked old enough—and allowed her to pay instead! I suspect that identical twins differing in dress or demeanor have similar stories to tell.

Some conjoined twins' life satisfaction matches David Lykken's research showing that our happiness levels are partly influenced by genetic factors, and that life events affect happiness in transitory ways.[50] I do not believe anyone would downplay the difficulties these twins face, nor deny the value of surgical separation when it is likely to succeed. In fact, legal and ethical experts generally support "reasonable medical attempts" to separate conjoined twins, as well as surgical intervention on behalf of one twin (i.e., operations that sacrifice one twin for the other when survival chances are otherwise minimal for both.)[51] At the same time, the satisfactory psychological adjustment of some inseparable pairs encourages a search for the factors promoting their well-being, and respect for their extraordinary circumstances.

Greater attention to the medical support and public reaction new families of conjoined twins can expect may help prepare them and their children for the uncertainties lying ahead. Conjoined Twins International, based in Prescott, Arizona, dispenses advice and support to twenty-seven of fifty families with conjoined twins living in the United States.[52] The organization was established by Will L. Degeraty after his daughter delivered conjoined female twins in 1987. Her first physician seemed unsympathetic, causing her to seek support elsewhere.

The life histories of some conjoined twins describe the shock and sorrow of mothers and fathers first learning of their children's condition. Marlene Cady recalled the long silence in the delivery room as she waited for news of the twins she expected.[52] Patty Hensel, mother of eight-year-old Abigail and Brittany who share their bloodstream and organs below the waist, expected a single baby—a sonogram did not reveal conjoined twins, because one head was probably hidden by the other.[54] Under sedation she heard the word "Siamese" and, failing to understand, asked if she had delivered cats. Her husband also reports a painful first account of the girls' condition from doctors. The delivering physicians in both cases were as surprised as the parents, so their poor communications were perhaps understandable, if not excusable. Still, these stories call for improvement in informing and assisting families.

As families begin to adapt to their situations new emotional hardships may be introduced by others, sometimes before the babies come home. Marlene Cady describes onlookers' curious comments and stares when she exited the hospital with her daughters. Abigail and Brittany, and Lori and Reba draw attention in public places, but both families and twins have resolved to live as normally as possible. Abigail and Brittany swim, hike and bicycle. Lori and Reba pursue careers, and Lori, who can bear children, hopes to do so, despite discouragement from others.

The outlooks of these twins and their families are lessons in the strength and flexibility of human will and determination. However, those we hear from may not speak for all. The unhappiness and despair endured by twelve-year-old conjoined male twins are unsettling. (The twins were joined from waist to lower breastbone.)[55] The twins' mother was "violently rejecting" of them, and their father took them on tour ("What else can you do with them?"). The effects of conjoined twins on other siblings is also of concern. Maria Cady, the older sister of Ruthie and Verena, was sometimes upset by the attention her sisters attracted, making her feel less special. Maria's situation parallels those of other siblings yielding spotlights to younger twin siblings. Parents should provide extra care to the brothers and sisters of conjoined twins, especially if these siblings are ridiculed by others.

Parents and physicians also struggle over whether or not to separate conjoined twins. Separation was first attempted in the tenth century on the first recorded conjoined pair in history, identical males joined from waist to abdomen.[56] The twins resided in Constantinople where they were admired as a curiosity, but they were later exiled when it was believed they were a bad omen. They later returned to Constantinople, where one twin's death prompted surgical separation, with the survivor dying three days later. The first *successful* separation of conjoined twins occurred in 1689 when German physician G. König severed twins' connection at the waist.[57]

Some people may be surprised to learn that some adult conjoined twins resist separation. Born in 1100, Elisa and Mary Chulkhurst, the "Biddenden Maids" of Kent, may be the first conjoined British pair. The Chulkhurst Charity, established after their death at thirty-four years, distributes Easter biscuits embossed with the twins' likeness. Following one sister's death, the other refused separation with the words, "As we came together, we will also go together."[58] Chang and Eng Bunker once asked their family physician to separate them, but when he refused to sever their common band exactly in half the matter was dropped. Chang died first, on January 17, 1874, at age sixty-three, after suffering from a stroke and severe lung illness. Eng, whose health had been favorable until that time, died two hours later.[59]

Several questions concerning separation should be asked in all cases.[60] They are: What are the nature and degree of connection between the twins? Are the twins both healthy? How experienced is the surgical team?

Nearly two hundred surgical separations of conjoined twins have been attempted, with approximately 90% occurring after 1950.[61] Survival of one or both twins has occurred in close to 150 cases.[62] A 1988 review of thirteen cases in which ten operations were performed showed 50% survival in newborns and 90% survival in infants older than four months. Six deaths occurred during a ten-year postoperative period, mainly due to heart failure.[63] A 1998 update added eight new cases and six new operations to that review. The new analysis showed 50% survival in four pairs under four months of age, 90% survival in eight pairs 6–14 months of age, and 100% survival in four pairs over two years of age. No late postoperative deaths have occurred thus far.[64]

In the past, operations have generally been delayed until twins reached six to twelve months of age to improve their trauma tolerance, and to avoid newborn care complexities. The extra time required was also critical for allowing expansion of twins' skin (by skin expanders, 6–8 weeks before surgery), operation dress rehearsals, and further evaluation of twins' condition. Currently, however, we are seeing trends toward earlier surgeries.

The recent availability of life-support systems and sophisticated diagnostic techniques such as computed tomography for revealing relationships among shared organs, are allowing earlier separations. The advantages of early surgeries are reduced chances of infection, scoliosis (backbone deviation), and emergency complications.[65] A disadvantage remains young twins' reduced physiological maturity, lessening their chances of withstanding difficult medical procedures. Immediate separation is typically advised when one twin is stillborn, one twin's health status threatens the cotwin's survival, or abnormalities threaten the progress of one or both twins.[66] Separation of conjoined twins prior to their awareness of their condition is believed to promote their psychological well-being. Following surgery, twins are often kept in close physical and visual proximity, sometimes assisted by mirrors.[67] These recommendations are reasonable, although evaluating the behavioral consequences of time and proximity is difficult.

Successful surgeries are on the rise, allowing twins like Carmen and Rosa Taveras to lead independent lives. Carmen and Rosa, from the Dominican Republic, were joined at the pelvis, but did not share vital internal organs.[68] Chang and Eng, the conjoined twins from Siam, could have easily been separated with modern technologies.[69] Recent separated pairs include Doris and Betsy Gonzalez (formerly joined at the head)[70] and an anonymous Texas pair (joined at the chest and abdomen).[71] Some pairs such as Yvonne and Yvette MacArthur could not, however, be safely separated.

Yvonne and Yvette, born in 1949 in Los Angeles, had separate hearts and brains, but were fused at the head. Their mother had been advised to institutionalize them, but refused and instead helped them to walk and to accept their situation. The twins received home tutoring, but eventually completed college degrees in nursing. They died from heart failure in January 1993 at age forty-three. Yvonne, who had an enlarged heart, apparently died first, but no other details are available.[72]

Dilemmas surrounding separation decisions came to the fore in a famous 1993 case. Amy and Angela Lakeberg were born on June 29, 1993, at Loyola University's Chicago Medical Center. Their conjoined status was determined during their seventeenth prenatal week—the twins shared a liver and a malformed heart, but had separate brains, lungs, kidneys and gastrointestinal tracts. Following their birth, the twins showed little chance of survival, but an operation unlikely to save one or both twins was eventually performed at Children's Hospital, in Philadelphia. The surgery was undertaken knowing that Amy, the weaker twin, would be sacrificed to save Angela, the stronger twin; however, Angela died shortly before her first birthday. Loyola University physicians who delivered the twins recommended against surgery because of the twins' poor survival chances and potentially poor life quality. Children's Hospital of Philadelphia physicians felt an ethical responsibility to attempt separation despite the long odds.[73]

A host of ethical quandaries formed the core of this case: Was it appropriate to try separating the twins, knowing one twin would not survive and the other twin would probably not survive? Did availability of technical procedures for separating conjoined twins mean that they must be used?[74]

Media attention escalated when the twins' father received compensation for bringing a videocamera into the neonatal unit. The film was broadcast nationally and Mr. Lakeberg used the money to purchase drugs, although this was not immediately known. Dr. David C. Thomasma, Director of Medical Humanities at Loyola University, suggested that public interest might have desensitized the parents to their twins' poor condition. The Children's Hospital's role as care provider was also publicly scrutinized, possibly affecting its provision of costly treatment for a risky procedure. As a result of this case, Thomasma urged hospital ethicists to work more closely with reporters covering future cases. The Lakeberg twins were, unfortunately, cast into the spotlight because of their father's unconscionable behavior.

Aside from the controversy raised by the Lakebergs, the twins' welfare was a priority for everyone involved. The lesson that separation decisions deserve confidential, private parent-surgeon collaboration may be the most important outcome from their story. Dr. John Raffensperger has described other conjoined twin cases in which the media, family and physicians played roles differing from those in the Lakeberg case. The parents of an ischiopagus conjoined pair (twins joined by the backbone) working with their physicians decided against life-prolonging treatment. This news led the local state attorney to file murder charges against the parents, giving the state responsibility for the twins' care. The hospital's lawyers then had the District Attorney's office agree that the operating surgeon would not be prosecuted for homicide, and the surgeon reached a similar agreement with the hospital ethics committee.[75] Neither twin survived the operation. In another case involving an ischiopagus pair, early legal complications followed the decision to donate shared organs to the stronger twin. However, surgeons refused media contact and forbade cameras in the operating room. The surviving boy had various surgeries during childhood, but seems well-adjusted and has played high school hockey. He was told about decisions surrounding his separation from his twin.[76]

*   *   *

"What is it like being a twin?" This question, often asked by curious singletons, brings amusement and impatience to ordinary twins. "What is it like not being a twin?" they counter. This question is unanswerable because twins do not know otherwise. The same is true for twins living inextricably attached to one another. However, while most identical twins get along well, many conjoined twins are masters at negotiation, cooperation and compromise. At the same time, their separate brains allow psychological separateness and selfhood, feelings crucial to all humans. I was intrigued, but not surprised, that families highlighted conjoined twins' personality differences. I suspect physical connection intensifies identical twins' needs to distinguish between themselves, as well as their parents' needs to distinguish between them.

Elisa and Lisa Hansen were the first twins fastened at the brain to be successfully separated.[77] Before separation, the sisters' individual but corresponding actions made them like one. Their crawling was highly coordinated, with one twin advancing and the other twin retreating. Following separation at nineteen months, their mother still saw "a real closeness between them"—the girls had their own beds, but preferred falling asleep while hugging each other. The twins were, however, differently described by their mother as passive vs. aggressive, and thoughtful vs. physical. Their behavioral differences could be tied to prenatal factors, as well as to behavioral contrasts that developed between them as they interacted. These observations dispel notions that identical twins' psychological closeness means psychological fusion.

Eight-year-old Abigail and Brittany Hensel are another case of coordination par excellence.[78] They are a rare dicephalus pair, with a single body and two separate heads and necks, sharing organs below the waist. Each twin controls one of the two arms and two legs they have between them. The twins' collaborations impress their teachers, parents and playmates, especially since each controls one side of the body. They learned to walk at age fifteen months without instruction; one twin holds paper while the other twin uses a scissors; and each twin controls a different shoelace while negotiating double knots. Their physical skills baffle physicians, but it is possible that their separate spinal cords have connections that facilitate joint activity.

Abigail and Brittany's physical and emotional connections do not thwart psychological independence. They work separately on class assignments and occasionally argue like all twins and siblings. One twin prefers pink, while the other prefers blue, and one twin enjoys animals, while the other likes art. Their differences extend to academics, leadership, and eating habits. Of course, Abigail and Brittany are still young children, protected by conscientious parents. Their father worries about their inability to forge separate social relations as teenage years approach.

Chang and Eng Bunker worked to maintain harmony with one another, sometimes by playing chess with strangers to curb their mutual tensions. When their wives quarreled, they alternated three-day visits in the separate households, an arrangement they maintained for years. However, scholars disagree over how frequently the brothers fought—contention arose due to Chang's heavy drinking, which once led to a fistfight.[79] The twins' interviews and others' recollections reveal that both were "self poised, agreeable and perceptive," but differed in irritability and intellectual vigor.

How similar are conjoined twins, and what do they tell us about human physical and behavioral development? Some assume that conjoined twins should be the most physically similar identical twin group, but research evidence has challenged this view. In 1928, twin researcher H. S. Reichle was a victim of such reasoning—when he observed significant differences in conjoined cotwins' palm and sole patterns, he lost confidence in this method of diagnosing twin type. Horatio H. Newman, Biology Professor of the University of Chicago in the early 1900s, presented striking examples of conjoined twins' physical differences, especially in height and head size. He found that right-handed twins (in both separate and conjoined pairs) had larger heads and faces.[80] I have seen little discussion of these issues in the current literature, which is more focused on surgical and ethical management of conjoined twins' separations. Available case reports can be informative when viewed against the backdrop of ordinary twin studies, but they leave a blurred development picture.

Dr. Helen Koch was one of the few investigators to administer physical and psychological tests allowing conjoined twin–ordinary twin comparisons.[81] Her study concerned fourteen-year-old conjoined twins Daisy and Violet Hilton, joined in the pelvic region. Koch compared the twins' scores and score differences on physical and behavioral measures with those of ordinary twins (identical and fraternal twins combined), high school students and college students. The results revealed an uneven pattern of similarities and differences. Daisy and Violet's head measurement differences were *less* than those shown by 75% of the twin pairs. In contrast, their height difference exceeded the twin pairs' average height difference.[82] Daisy's intellectual and scholastic ability scores were consistently higher than Violet's. The twins' differences on some mental ability tests were large, relative to the comparison twins, but were small on others. The twins' temperament profiles were "strikingly similar," but they did not show the same amount of match across the twelve parts of the inventory. Few conclusions about how conjoined twinning affects behavioral and physical development can be drawn from this study. Improved efforts along these lines may be possible given the increasing survival rate of conjoined twins.

Dr. J. David Smith, now Dean of Education at Longwood College, in Farmville, Virginia, has consolidated scattered psychological reports on conjoined twins.[83] His summary suggests that conjoined twins' personality differences are more pervasive than their similarities. Smith cautions that methodological differences make each case hard to judge. He reasons that because conjoined twins have identical genes and the most similar environments possible, their behavioral differences largely reflect their differences in free will (i.e., individuals' purposeful construction of their environments).

The literature suggests that conjoined twins' environments are probably *less* alike than Smith supposes. Vaudeville twins Daisy and Violet Hilton sometimes engaged in different activities, such as when one twin read while the other slept.[84] The larger member of the twelve-year-old conjoined male pair suffered petit mal seizures (brief unconscious spells), while his brother did not. Lori and Reba Schappell vary dramatically in size and in physical abilities, facing vastly different constraints upon their development.

Behavioral-genetic researchers have provided evidence that siblings' unique genetic propensities guide them toward different experiences and events. Such opportunity-seeking seems akin to Smith's concept of free will in which individuals construct personally desirable settings. Of course, conjoined twins do not differ for genetic reasons, only for environmental ones. It is likely that their early size or health differences underlie their behavioral differences, and the kinds of environments they prefer. Conjoined twins may *seem* to have the most identical environments possible, but this appears unlikely. For example, Lori and Reba both attended Lori's college classes and Reba's musical recitals, but they participated very differently in these two settings.

I believe a crucial element missing from Smith's discussion is that control groups of *ordinary twins* and *separated conjoined twins* are required for judging the degree of difference between unseparated conjoined twins. It would be intriguing to know if, and for what traits, unseparated conjoined twins were less alike than twins in the other two groups. Some marked behavioral differences between unseparated conjoined twins might be expected since their unusual biological origins probably leave lasting developmental effects. At the same time, these twins' desires for individuation might be intensified by their physical connection. Psychological adjustment and well-being should also be compared among the three twin groups, an effort that might disclose fewer differences than we might expect. Until research sorts out these issues, our knowledge of conjoined twins' lives will continue to come from those who are willing to tell us.

"What the Audience Won't Watch" headlined news of *Side Show*'s early closing in January 1998 after a three-month run. Were audiences "unwilling to see a musical about a subject they considered distasteful"? Did "mass squeamishness over[ride] all the old barometers of good reviews"?[85] I believe both suggestions partly explain *Side Show*'s demise, reflecting common views of conjoined twins as abnormal and distressing. Interestingly, conjoined twins' lives have fascinated people for years, but medical news and magazine articles allow a comfortable distance between readers and twins that live theater may diminish. Furthermore, although public exhibitions no longer occur, the theme of conjoined twins as "freaks" lingers. A 1995 advertisement for Van Halen's compact disc *Balance* showed young female twins attached at the hips, one expressionless, the other in pain.[86]

Most twins seem capable of confronting unique situations associated with their physical and behavioral similarity. I believe this situation also applies to conjoined twins. Left to their own devices, many conjoined twins can (and have) found separate identities and different dreams. Some conjoined twins were uninterested in separation or refused separation following their cotwin's illness or death. Mary and Margaret Gibb, born in 1912 and joined at the buttocks, survived together until age fifty-four although their separation became medically possible. They preferred to stay attached even after Margaret developed cancer, dying minutes apart in 1967.

I was especially moved by nurses' reactions to conjoined male twins Lin and Win Hut, from Burma: "Once we overcame our initial reaction to their deformity we were struck by their normalcy." However, following the twins' separation (in which Win was assigned as female) the twins appeared "badly deformed," even "handicapped."[87] These nurses had discovered the twins' humanity.

Double Entendre:
Twinship's Many Meanings

F*riendship Extraordinaire* is the title of my sixth chapter. However, the words and the phrase—friendship extraordinaire; extraordinary friend-ship—have touched every theme and thread of twins in science, in society and in our daily lives, even becoming the book's working title for a time. Twin studies' findings have broad relevance. They have challenged our views of intelligence and personality, and reshaped our thoughts on family and law. They have altered our explanations of athletic skill, and inspired timeless artistic and literary works. Twin studies have also launched bitter debates over human behavioral origins, and twins have strained some parents' patience and resources.

Twin research brings fresh images and new realities to our understanding of human development. Identical twins' matched running speeds, fraternal twins' varied biological origins and conjoined twins' incredible accomplishments are inspiring and provocative, daring us to make sense of what seems insensible. But like a double entendre, twin research may produce equivocal results, allowing different interpretations and truths. Twin research findings have also segued into the media as metaphors for curious nontwin episodes. Above all, twin findings have raised our awareness of human behavioral consistences and oddities, and what they might mean. We begin by looking at twin studies' role in nature-nurture debates.

It is no longer appropriate to ask *if* genes affect mathematical skills, sociability or longevity. Twin studies support genetic influence upon nearly all measured behaviors (although love styles and mate choice are notable exceptions). In response to behaviorist and Nazi movements, genetic views of human behavior were denounced and then discarded through much of the twentieth century.[1] John Watson's 1930's behaviorism viewed human traits as environmentally determined and as infinitely malleable. Contemporary psychologists reject pure environmental determinism, but many lean toward experience as behavior's primary cause. Nazism's horrific medical experiments in the 1930s and early 1940s drew on its misguided notion that Jews, gypsies, homosexuals and the handicapped were biologically inferior. Nazi doctor Josef Mengele's deplorable concentration camp twin studies sullied other researchers' legitimate efforts to understand why we are the way that we are. I will say more about this dark side of twin research, based on my interviews with some surviving twin victims.

Meanwhile twin, family and adoption studies continued, supporting roles for both genes *and* environments in human behavioral development. The data proved compelling, admitting behavioral genetic research into psychology's mainstream in the 1980s.

Twin study findings lie at the heart of the nature-nurture debate, a controversy dividing some colleagues and friends. Genetic views of human behavior have been deplorable, even frightening, to people taking this view to mean that their efforts to change old habits or influence their children would be wasted. The idea of genetic effects can also be welcome—even comforting— to people learning that their child's depression or timidity may be linked to genes, as well as to parenting. Genetic influence *does not* mean that behaviors are fixed, but the ease, immediacy and magnitude of behavioral change vary from trait to trait, and from person to person. Unfortunately, such messages are often missed amidst the debate's emotional tenor. Furthermore, some media reports are sensationalized or oversimplified, exchanging insight and reason for confusion and concern. One of my first television appearances taught me this hard lesson.

In 1986, I discussed reared apart twin studies on a nationally televised morning program. Twenty seconds of airtime remained when I heard the complex question: "How much of behavior is genetic and how much is environmental?" Condensing the substance of my fifteen-week graduate seminar into a meaningful sound bite was impossible. I, therefore, said that answers to that question depended upon the particular behavior in question. This prompted the host's response, "Whatever that means!" thus ending the show on an uncertain note. Had there been time, I would have explained that more stable, reliably measured behavioral characteristics, such as general intelligence, show higher degrees of genetic influence (50–70%) than less stable, less reliably measured behaviors, such as personality traits (50%), occupational interests (40%) and social attitudes (34%).[2] Greater genetic than environmental influence on behavior does not imply that behavior resists change.

I have been asked by some audiences if identical twins have extrasensory perception (ESP). Some people believe that ESP explains why twins often say or do things simultaneously, even without the cotwin present. There is *no evidence* that twins' similarities are caused by mental communication between them. One early study showed that brain wave patterns produced in one member of two identical male pairs (out of fifteen) were induced in their cotwins, but this report was later retracted because of methodological problems.[3] I do not question the occurrence of twins' "ESP-like" behaviors. I do wonder why some people endorse ESP in the face of more compelling data from twin studies.

My television experience was great cocktail party conversation, but it identified roadblocks to accurately explaining twin research findings. I believe more focused television programs and news articles would clear confusion. I am intrigued by the new "Gene Shop" in England's Manchester Airport, designed to promote understanding of inherited disorders such as hemophilia (genetic disorder in which blood clots slowly) and Marfan's syndrome (genetic disorder of connective tissue characterized by excessive height and long fingers.)[4] Such exhibitions raise appreciation for the intricacies of nature-nurture debates which require mastering certain concepts and ideas. These points are easy to grasp, but they are mostly buried in textbooks and professional journals:

- Individual differences characterize virtually every measured trait.
- Paradoxically, some highly genetically influenced traits have heritability equal to zero. Everyone has two eyes, two legs and one nose because our genes specify this anatomy as part of the human plan. If we compared similarity between normal identical and fraternal twins for these traits, they would show no variability. Remember, heritability refers to genetic *variability* among people.
- Individual differences in behavior are due to differences in genes *and* to differences in environments. As people's environments become more similar, genetic factors play more important roles in explaining individual differences.
- Both genes and environments affect behavioral variability, but the extent to which each contributes varies across traits. Twin studies have shown that genetic factors shape individual differences in intelligence to a greater degree than individual differences in personality. Genetic factors shape individual differences in personality to a greater degree than individual differences in job satisfaction.
- One-to-one correspondence between genes and complex behaviors, such as intelligence or mental disorder, usually does not occur. Therefore, genetic predisposition for certain behaviors does not guarantee that those behaviors will be expressed. An exception is Huntington's chorea, a central nervous system disorder that always affects people carrying the gene if they live until about age forty, when the gene is expressed.
- Specific environmental events must trigger complex behaviors. You may have inherited a genetic potential for smoking from your late father, but if

your environment has been tobacco-free you will not smoke. Also remember that if identical twins are schizophrenic, their cotwins have less than a 50% chance of developing the disease, and whether cotwins become sick or stay healthy depends upon their environments and experiences. The relationship between genes and behavior is *probabilistic,* not *deterministic.*

- The degree to which genetic factors influence trait variability, or *heritability,* can be estimated using groups or populations. High heritability means individual differences among group members are largely due to genetic factors, while low heritability means individual differences are largely due to environmental factors. If a group's heritability for extraversion is 50% this means half of the *group's* variability in that trait is associated with differences in their genetic factors. It does *not* mean that half of *your* extraversion level is explained by your genes. Genetic and environmental effects are inseparable in single individuals.

- Heritability is not a fixed value. It may vary across populations, tests and time. Identical twins reared apart yield higher IQ heritability that identical and fraternal twins reared together, although the reasons for this are unknown. IQ heritability increases with age, perhaps because early genetic effects strengthen and parenting effects weaken.[5]

- Genetic influence on a trait does not mean that it resists change. The best example of this concept is phenylketonuria (PKU), an inborn (genetic) metabolic error. Left untreated, affected children do not convert the substance phenylalanine into tyrosine, leading to mental retardation. Newborns are routinely screened for this disorder and administering phenylalanine-free diets early in life offsets this mental defect. Some foods contain information about product safety for affected individuals. Recent research suggests, however, that even children receiving the proper treatment for PKU may show some residual effects.

- Environmentally based behaviors are *not* always easily altered. Imagine that the rules of the road suddenly changed, requiring you to stop at green lights and advance at red lights. It is likely that many traffic accidents would result because previous response patterns, based on learning, were deeply ingrained. At the same time, some motorists might respond faster to this change than others due to genetically based differences in their concentration or flexibility. Similarly, most people driving in some foreign countries find it difficult to drive on the opposite side of the road, but some adapt more readily than others.

- Human individual differences "can simply be accepted as differences and not as deficits."[6] The wise words of behavioral geneticist Sandra Scarr, echoed by evolutionary biologist Theodosius Dobzhansky, should be repeated often in nature-nurture discussions. Genetically based differences among people *do not* warrant value judgments, they are simply differences. Who can say that verbal facility or physical agility is "better" than mathematical giftedness or musical talent? I believe values can be assigned only in specific circumstances. If I were lost in a cave I would want my rescuer to have excellent spatial orientation, not perfect pitch.

- Human differences, whatever their source, should be celebrated, not denigrated. Variation in genetically based traits insures species' survival since some members will successfully adapt to changing conditions. Many of us take people's diverse talents and temperaments for granted, but their differences keep us interested, as well as alive.

Twins have advanced progress in solving gene-environment formulas for the range of human behaviors. It is extraordinary that simply arranging twins into various combinations and permutations (e.g., concordant vs. discordant identical pairs; fraternal same-sex vs. fraternal opposite-sex pairs) has provided clues to weight gain, mood quality and leadership skill. Twin methods are, however, powerful beyond detecting genetic and environmental influences on behavior. They also help us track developmental processes when we compare identical and fraternal twins' similarity over time. And twin studies have been recently used by evolutionary psychologists to explore affiliation, reproduction, parenting, and personality. I teamed up with Linda Mealey to show that there is greater genetic influence on males' than on females' reproductive behaviors, consistent with their different reproductive strategies.[7]

Neither evolutionary psychology nor twin research has been embraced by all members of the academic community. Controversy surrounding evolutionary arguments centers largely around the *naturalistic fallacy,* the notion that natural or adaptive behaviors are necessarily good in a moral or social sense. People misperceiving evolutionary interpretations in this way worry that they generate complacency toward aggressive or antisocial acts.[8] Evolutionary researchers *do not* dismiss or condone such behaviors, but try to understand their presence in light of our evolved history, that is, if and how they may have contributed to human survival and reproduction in the past. They also assert that the significance of past behaviors may be very different in modern times, and believe that understanding factors promoting these behaviors may help to control them. If medical and psychological professionals know that mothers favor healthier preterm twins, they can encourage parents to give extra care to less advantaged cotwins. The misconception that behavior is fixed also explains the cool reception given to evolutionary psychology, as well as to behavioral genetics. Research in both these disciplines shows the opposite to be true.

Socially unacceptable behaviors may be present for other reasons, such as a gene having more than one effect, a concept called *pleiotropy.* In other words, a gene providing some benefits may exact a price in the form of reduced fitness. The gene for sickle cell anemia is lethal when inherited from both parents, but protects against malaria if inherited from only one.[9] It is also possible that some unfavorable or morally reprehensible behaviors represent malfunction or maladaptation. Some skeptics also believe that evolutionary psychology is inconsistent with more traditional social or psychological explanations. However, evolutionary psychology can infuse behavior with fresh meaning, supplementing not denying other perspectives. Martin Smith, now at Canada's University of Victoria, explained that children may learn aggressive tendencies from their environment, but males may be more evolutionarily disposed toward observational learning of aggression.[10]

Twin studies' success rests on fulfilling the *equal environments assumption,* a goal questioned by some critics. Twin designs also have some imperfections, causing some people to reject the findings and implications outright. Some objections to twin research may come from the method, not from the message. I suspect, however, that some people's resistance to genetic effects prompts their exaggeration of twin studies' limitations, and their neglect of the "big picture." By "big picture" I mean consistency of findings among twin and nontwin studies, and across behaviors.[11] Examining twin studies' disputed features can help decide if they are minor blemishes or major defects.

Three frequent challenges to twin research have been labeled *social biases, primary biases* and *recruitment biases:*

- *Social biases.* When researchers compare identical and fraternal twins' mental or medical similarities they assume that environmental influences (e.g., parental discipline or teacher expectations) affecting traits are the same for identical and fraternal twins.[12] This is called the *equal environments assumption (EEA).*[13] If this assumption is not fulfilled, twin studies could yield false estimates of genetic and environmental influence on behavior because of an undetected environmental effect. If teachers expected more similar achievement by identical twins than by fraternal twins, this could increase identical twins' similarity relative to fraternal twins, overestimating genetic effects. This is precisely what critics of twin studies argue. They conclude that *similar treatment* not *similar genes* causes identical twins' behavioral resemblance.[14] Conversely, they reason that because fraternal twins look different people treat them differently; thus, fraternal twins show less similarity due to environmental effects, not genetic ones. Critics, therefore, believe that identical and fraternal twins' unequal treatment violates the EEA and invalidates findings.

    Many twin researchers have subjected the EEA to close scrutiny. It is not surprising to learn that identical twins *are* dressed alike more often than fraternal twins—but, *dressing alike or dressing differently has little effect upon identical twins' personality similarity.* Researchers have found that twins' similarity on most measured intellectual abilities, interests and medical traits is unrelated to their similarity in rearing, appearance or interpersonal closeness.[15] (Some twin data on bulimia and delinquency suggest EEA violation, but these behaviors are exceptions.[16]) What is surprising is critics' neglect of the EEA's substantial empirical support that refutes their claims.

As recently as 1997, Jay Hook, Research Director of Harvard University's Continuing Education Division, worried that the "face to feedback to self-fulfilling prophecy," may weaken twin studies' heritability estimates. He proposed, but did not conduct, a "face-judging" study to test his notions.[17] David Rowe, twin researcher at the University of Arizona, reminds us that faces and brains are not one, so similar treatment will not affect biological functions underlying personality. Rowe asked, "If we gathered ten Elvis lookalikes together, would they be alike in personality at all?"[18] Even if identical twins are treated more similarly than fraternal twins, this may reflect other peoples' responses to their matched behaviors, not conscious efforts to "make" them alike.

- *Primary biases.* In 1950 and 1978 psychologist and statistician Bronson Price claimed that "in all probability the net effect of most twin studies has been underestimation of the significance of heredity in the medical and behavioral sciences."[19] This declaration may be a chilling revelation to opponents of twin research. Primary biases include three categories of prenatal and birth events that produce differences between identical twins, namely birth factors (fetal position and order of delivery), lateral inversions (physical reversals) and mutual circulation (transfusion of blood from one identical twin fetus to the other). It is counterintuitive, but true, that sharing a womb *reduces,* rather than enhances, identical twin resemblance.

Primary biases have been understood for nearly fifty years, but have been neglected by some investigators. As recently as 1997 Dr. Bernard Devlin of the University of Pittsburgh erred when he claimed that twins' shared prenatal environments increased their IQ similarity more than was previously suspected, and that other researchers overestimated genetic influence on intelligence.[20] Prenatal environments may affect twins' IQs, but they *do not* increase their IQ similarity.[21] His twin-sibling IQ comparison neglected differences in identical and fraternal twins' prenatal circumstances, as discussed in Chapters 2 and 4.

The precise effects of primary biases upon behavior are unknown and may vary from trait to trait. Since Price's work, we know that identical (and fraternal) twin fetuses are not at equal risk for contracting HIV from infected mothers. This is an extraordinary special effect. However, despite prenatal factors making identical twins different, *identical twins are more alike in most traits than fraternal twins or siblings.*

- *Recruitment biases.* While walking to school, fraternal twin brothers— wearing matched jackets—were surprised when onlookers exclaimed, "See the twins!" The boys wondered who they were talking about, and started searching for this interesting pair.

This story shows that some fraternal twins do not readily think of themselves as twins. Their thoughts partly explain the finding that two-thirds of twin pairs volunteering for research are identical, and two-thirds are female.[22] Believing birth rates of identical and same-sex fraternal twins are the same, researchers have worried that fraternal twins seeking research opportunities may be more similar in appearance and in behavior than fraternal twins who do not. Dr. David Lykken found that twin pairs concordant for returning mailed questionnaires were *not* more psychologically or demographically similar than pairs in which one or both twins declined. Recruitment problems may persist, however, when twins are asked to participate in person,[23] perhaps because twins who are highly committed to research may be more alike than twins generally.

Twin sample sizes have been troubling because two hundred pairs are needed to confidently show genetic influence on traits. Early twin studies did not show genetic influence on female alcoholism, but more recent studies with larger samples have found the same 70% heritability for alcoholism in females and males.[24]

Today, adult twin recruitment problems may be lessening due to our understanding of twinning rates, i.e., decreases in fraternal twinning and slight increases in identical twinning over the last few decades.[25] Current excesses of identical twins in research may, therefore, approach the proportions of twin types in populations. Of course, recording and interpreting shifting twinning rates is complicated by advances in fertility treatments which improve chances for multiple births, mostly fraternal. The next wave of adult twin studies might include increasing proportions of fraternal twins. Fortunately, population-based twin registries have been established in the United States, Australia, Europe, Sri Lanka, Japan and elsewhere, letting researchers find twin samples whose characteristics match larger twin and nontwin populations. There are also state-wide twin rosters such as the Minnesota Twin Registry and the Wisconsin Twin Panel, and national and international registries of HIV-exposed infant twins, elderly twins, twins with chronic fatigue syndrome and World War II veteran twins.[26]

Studies have shown that the effects of primary biases on twin research are largely exaggerated. Nevertheless, some misconceptions about twin research linger:

- Twin studies have been criticized for inappropriately applying findings to nontwins. Individual twins are hidden in crowds, but their biological beginnings and social circumstances distinguish them from singletons. Zygotic splitting and shared circulation partly explain some identical twins' opposite hand preferences and neurological problems. Language development may be delayed in some identical and fraternal twins because of reduced verbal interaction with parents. However, most behavioral and physical traits do not show significant twin-singleton differences in frequency or in severity, so twin studies are suitable for studying the origins of most traits.

Twin and other studies showing genetic influence on IQ have been chastised for neglecting environmental effects on intelligence in impoverished children. The majority of twin samples (and research samples generally) represent middle-class families, so findings are *not* generalizable to individuals at population extremes. Most twin investigators have been careful to include this caveat in their reports.

- Twin methods (and other behavioral genetic designs) have been disparaged for not revealing the developmental processes linking genes and behaviors. Twin, sibling and other family methods are *first steps* toward solving developmental mysteries. Once gene-environment contributions to behavioral differences are identified, elucidating genetic and environmental factors and the ways they are expressed over time will become possible.[27] Twin studies have shown that genetic differences explain 50% of personality differences among people. The biggest surprise has been that identical twins raised apart and together are *equally similar,* revealing that common genes, not common rearing, underlie relatives' resemblance.[28] Separated parents and children may also resemble one another for genetic reasons.

- Twin studies have been reproached for failing to find specific major genes tied to complex behaviors such as reading disability or extraversion. Their identification would allow researchers to learn how different environments affect expression of these genes, possibly by comparing behaviors of identical twins reared apart. Twin analyses recently linked reading disability to chromosome 6.[29] Future twin studies may lead us to particular genes underlying particular behaviors, improving knowledge of why we vary, and how to help people at risk. Finding major genes would also stimulate the search for proteins produced by these genes, and how these proteins influence our daily behaviors.[30]

In the past, finding major genes required large, multigeneration families to track genetic paths from grandparents to parents, parents to children, and children to grandchildren. Knowing identical twins resembled one another more than fraternal twins demonstrated genetic influence, but did not reveal which genes influence behavior, or how genes travel through family lines. Recently, advanced statistical tools and molecular genetic methods have discovered ways in which twin studies can find genes explaining differences in complex behaviors. Specifically, using twins and their families lets researchers test whether certain genes or gene combinations "fit" family resemblance patterns.

I believe quarrels over twin studies' power and productivity vary in merit, but the majority have been resolved. Most importantly, separate complaints lose significance from the perspective of the big picture. Twin studies consistently show greater identical than fraternal twin similarity for most behaviors, although the degree of difference may vary. In Drs. Thomas J. Bouchard, Jr., and Matt McGue's mega twin summary, reared together identical twins' IQ correlations ranged from .58 to .94, and fraternal twin's IQ correlations ranged from .20 to .85.[31] Reasons for the spread in the correlations were unresolved, but type of test (group administered or individually administered) and sex of fraternal twins (same or opposite) were ruled out. More complete stories about twins' IQ resemblance are told by identical and fraternal twins' *average* correlations of .86 and .60. Adding to this picture is a survey of twin studies published between 1967 and 1985, showing increasing identical twin IQ similarity with age.[32] Again, pooled findings from accumulated studies are better approximations to truth than findings from single studies.

There is currently greater professional and public acceptance of twin research and what it reveals about human development than in times past. Ninety-fine percent of over 1,000 psychologists, sociologists and educators interviewed in 1987 endorsed genetic contributions to intelligence.[33] Like Dr. Jerome Kagan of Harvard University, a former environmentalist who was "dragged by the [genetic] data," I believe many environmentally oriented psychologists and psychiatrists are finding twin research difficult to ignore.[34] I also find that twins, parents of twins, and parents of two or more children "instinctively" embrace genetic contributions to behavior, perhaps because they "live" the evidence firsthand. At the same time, there is a perception that "daily discoveries" of genes underlying different behaviors revitalizes Nazi themes of genetically based desirability of some traits and some people. In the last few years we have learned of genes for Alzheimer's disease, novelty-seeking and sex reversal.[35] There is also fear that genetic progress leaves little room for experience and for free will.

I always tell the story of Mengele's twins in psychology classes and seminars. Dr. Josef Mengele conducted brutal experiments on twins in the Auschwitz-Birkenau concentration camp in Poland, between spring 1943 and January 1945.[36] These experiments included X rays, blood transfusions and typhus injections to one twin, with both twins later killed to compare their organs. Mengele's goals have been debated by historians who concluded they were meant to confirm Aryan superiority. Some people suggested that Mengele tried to unravel the biological bases of twinning to increase Aryan numbers, but I disagree because he did not study twins' parents who would hold the key to twinning processes. Most importantly, experts agree that there is no scientific merit to information gathered by applying horrendous procedures to helpless victims.[37]

I learned of Mengele's twin children in March 1984 from a radio program on their planned fortieth anniversary liberation reunion. The twins' reunion would include tours of Auschwitz-Birkenau in January 1985, followed by a three-day hearing on Mengele's war crimes, held at Yad Va Shem (Hand and

Name), Jerusalem's Holocaust memorial and research center. Minutes after hearing the broadcast I *knew* I was going—this opportunity had a powerful hold on me because as Jewish twins, in another time and place, Anne and I might have suffered at Mengele's hands. In addition, I was studying twins reared apart and some separated Holocaust twins hoped for reunion with their twin siblings.

Approximately 110 of the 157 twin children released from the camps were located. They represent a fraction of the 1,500 twin pairs (3,000 twins) who had been held there. The stories I heard were horrifying and heartbreaking. Blood transfusions sickened recipients, and X rays caused their sterilization. Twins' body parts were measured as they stood for long hours, humiliated and dehumanized. Some twins returning to Auschwitz in 1985 brought their own children to honor grandparents' graves. Twins also came to confront a part of their lives that had remained silent, but not forgotten, for forty years. Meeting other twins was their best therapy because each understood the unique physical and emotional trials of the past. They also appreciated twinships' extraordinary importance—keeping one's cotwin alive in Auschwitz was crucial to one's own survival because twins whose cotwins died were slaughtered for medical purposes.

The potential for abuse of research subjects and methods plagues every domain of human knowledge. Recalling past tragic episodes may be the best way to prevent them from recurring. Many of my students plan careers working with human subjects, which is why I believe they must know about Mengele's twin children.

On July 19, 1991, the telephone rang in the University of Minnesota twin research office. I was stunned to discover actor Marlon Brando on the other end. Brando was familiar with behavioral similarities between twins reared apart, and wanted to know how to reconcile genetic effects with free will. I explained that our genetic predispositions for risk-taking or for divorce do not mean we necessarily engage in these behaviors. Our decisions to bungee jump or to leave partners are under our control, our genes do not force us to make them. Individuals exercising or dieting to overcome heart conditions or obesity are also attempting to control their genetic tendencies through conscious choice. Of course, some people are more committed to avoiding risk or to exercising than others, partly due to their genetically based personality traits.

The finding that shared environments contribute little to most behavioral similarities among relatives has raised concerns over parents' and educators' influence on children's lives.[38] However, small shared environmental effects on behavior do not mean that environments do not matter. We now know that our unique, idiosyncratic experiences exert significant impact upon our behavioral development. Winning the lottery or losing an election may alter the course of our lives and how we think about ourselves. Furthermore, supportive circumstances insure that children will nourish their interests and skills. Parents contribute to their children's development by encouraging aggressive youngsters to calm down, and by prompting shy youngsters to speak up. It is unlikely that shy and aggressive children will switch places, but each may enjoy a more successful life with parental help. I told all this to Marlon Brando, who seemed satisfied.

We delight in seeing young twins in their parents' arms. We envy children their built-in playmates, easing families' worries over their loneliness or boredom. There are other amazing unseen advantages to having twins, known only to their families. Jonathan Black, Managing Editor of *Playboy* magazine, charmed *New York Times* readers with tales of traveling with his two-month-old twins.[39] Arriving at Kelmscott Manor in England (home of designer William Morris) he was disappointed to learn that the rooms were closed. However, the gift shop attendant pronounced his twins "marvelous" and granted entry. My father, Al Segal, has a similar story. Anne and I were ten months old when our family left Boston for Philadelphia. Unfortunately, the landlord refused to release us from our apartment contract without penalty. When my father mentioned the difficulties of moving with young twins the landlord smiled, revealed he was a twin, and terminated the contract.

No doubt most families with twins have similar stories to tell. Young twins please people, sometimes opening opportunities that might otherwise be unavailable. Perhaps the sight of a small couple amplifies the infants' helplessness, igniting our inclinations to offer assistance. Or perhaps we hope to penetrate the special connectedness twin partners convey. I do not understand all of the phenomena twins' stories pose, but some seem to stir our desire for the intimacy we believe twins enjoy. Once we know why twins intrigue us we may know more about ourselves.

Watching twins smile and squirm, some people become oblivious to the care, expenses, and sibling jealousies accompanying their births. Most multiple-birth parents relish the special pleasures their children bring, but some face endless struggles.

Raizy Kornitzer's tearful radio appeal to New York Mayor Rudolph Giuliani brought diapers, formula and sitters for her two-month-old triplets and two-year-old twins.[40] Her husband's income as a nursery school teacher could not meet the family's financial demands, and Raizy told listeners, "Sometimes I do feel like I'm going to jump off a bridge." Not all multiple birth families have found relief. A mother of five children abandoned infant twins in the hospital when she became "overwhelmed" by her circumstances. The fourteen-year-old Kienast quintuplets' father, William, committed suicide, attributed to his personal bankruptcy and impending eviction.[41] A three-and-a-half-year-old New York girl was suspected in her newborn twin brothers' deaths, but jealousy was dismissed because of her previous affection toward the boys.[42]

Over the last fifteen years, we have learned that child abuse rates are higher for twins than for singletons. (This does *not* mean that all parents with twins are potentially abusive, it means that twins more than singletons may trigger abuse by parents with predisposed personalities and circumstances.) Investigators have linked this finding to the increased stress caused by caring for two infants simultaneously, particularly if families' resources are limited. Surprise twin deliveries can be further debilitating since families have not planned for two children.[43] A Japanese national survey revealed that 10% of 231 abuse cases were multiple birth children, but only rarely were both twins abused.[44] Instead, one twin's maltreatment was mostly associated with serious medical problems, or with undesirable physical or personality traits. In contrast, the few cases involving abuse of both twins were explained by parental or family problems. A British study did not find twin-singleton differences in nonaccidental injury.[45]

Twins' differential abuse recalls some societal practices in which twin births necessitate infanticide due to maternal overburdening. In these cases, secondborn twins, weaker twins, or female twins in opposite-sex pairs (but not both twins) are usually sacrificed. Evolutionary psychologists have suggested that this behavior may enhance parents' reproductive fitness (transmission of their genes) by letting them nurture healthier infants under better rearing conditions.[46] (Evolutionary interpretations may explain, but do *not* condone such practices. Furthermore, such decisions have not been made casually in any known society.) The fact that some twin and nontwin children in families face greater abuse risk than others requires researchers to find the factors placing them at risk. I believe twins may help this effort.

Relations between parent-child bonding and child abuse could be explored in families whose twins differ in health and maturity. Extended hospitalization of premature or unhealthy cotwins may disrupt parent-child attachment, possibly setting the stage for abuse or neglect. Some studies find that parents prefer the twin arriving home first (usually the healthier twin),[47] possibly because their cotwin arriving home second disrupts established routines. Recall that Janet Mann found that mothers vocalized more to healthy twin infants than to their less healthy cotwins. Her findings *do not* suggest abuse, but they suggest that twins' distinctions can become important in potentially abusive families.[48] It is also possible that parents' reduced stimulation of less healthy twins is beneficial to these infants who might otherwise become overwhelmed.

Stepparenting has also been linked to increased child abuse. Evolutionary psychologists explain this as reflecting resentment at investing in genetically unrelated children. Differential abuse among biological children may be associated with differences in bonding, possibly associated with parents' perceived resemblance to their children.[49] Abused same-sex fraternal twins can test the hypothesis that abuse is more frequently directed to children perceived to be different from parents. Such twins would provide better tests than abused same-sex siblings since family stressors are matched for twins.

Parents of twins know the benefits and liabilities of twinship. Many mothers and fathers welcome "instant families," and enjoy the attention that twins attract. However, onlookers' comments may undermine parents' efforts to treat twins fairly. My friend Ellen (also a mother of twins) and one of her friends (Pat) passed a stroller bearing identical male infant twins. Pat insisted to the twins' father that the boy on the left was "the one with personality." The father seemed uncomfortable, replying that the other twin was also "a good guy." As a parent of twins, Ellen was sensitive to such remarks, but Pat said he was "only a baby" and she would not have commented had he been older. However, these words can hurt parents and divide twins trying to maintain a healthy cotwin balance.

The good news is that mothers up to age fifty-five are less likely to contract breast cancer if they have had twins.[50] The bad news is that mothers of twins show increased depression, relative to mothers of nontwins, when children are five years old.[51] Depression is also higher in mothers of singletons if children are close in age, but lower than in mothers of twins. Maternal depression is unrelated to social class, partner presence, mothers' age or number of children in the home, suggesting that twins pose extra demands on caretakers. These findings do not imply that all mothers bearing twins risk depression—it is more likely that raising twins activates some women's depressive tendencies.

Little research exists on twins' siblings, so case reports may leave false impressions of inevitable jealousy and distress, because it is only the unhappy siblings who seek professional attention. Parents tell me that older siblings suffer more than younger ones since older children forfeit their parents' focused attention. Of course, some younger siblings may feel excluded from the twins' special relationship, and wish that they too had a partner. When the McCaughey septuplets were born in November 1997 there was public concern for their two-year-old sister Mikayla, dethroned by the extraordinary set of seven. In a television interview, I suggested that Mikayla might benefit from this experience. After all, she was the only older sister in America with younger septuplet siblings, so playmates' curiosity might make her a popular friend. She would surely learn parenting skills, but remembering that she was a little girl would be important for her parents.

Sibling jealousies can, but need not, tarnish twins' first days at home. We may never know what propels young singleton siblings to harm twins, but their sense of neglect is a possibility. Making nontwins in twins' families feel special is a crucial task for their parents.

*   *   *

Raizy Kornitzer's cry for help with her twins and triplets shows that the needs of multiple-birth parents are not always met. Their needs are financial and emotional, and the two are closely related. I applaud national, state and local twin and triplet clubs for their generous efforts on behalf of disadvantaged families, and I salute Pat Malmstrom, Director of Twin Services in Berkeley, California, for disseminating information to the public and to legislators. Twin Services and some parents' groups also maintain hotlines for dispensing support to overwhelmed families. Similar organizations exist in major cities around the world, but their resources are limited. I believe families with twins will face more difficult hardships, given recent shifts toward increasing multiple birth rates and rising medical costs.

I was disheartened by news that the Dilley sextuplets of Indianapolis would no longer attend nursery school due to their family's financial struggles.[52] I was also distressed that the first black sextuplet parents, Linden and Jacqueline Thompson of Washington, D.C., were ignored by the media and by companies offering products to higher multiple birth families.[53] Ironically, the McCaugheys' birth brought belated attention to the Thompsons when their children were eight months old, so now they enjoy groceries, toys and future college scholarships. It is possible that the early death of one Thompson child caused their withdrawal from the media, or that "only" five babies made their birth less special in the public's eyes—after all, the Dilley sextuplets were thriving by then. It remains an unpleasant but real possibility that the McCaugheys would have struggled silently had only six infants survived.

I believe the time is right for creative solutions to multiple-birth families' problems. I have seen some wonderful programs over the years, but there are too few.

- In 1982 Lake Erie College in Painesville, Ohio, offered "two-for-one" scholarships to twins.[54] An anonymous donor offered to pay for one twin if cotwins paid their own way. Four such scholarships are offered each year, renewable for three years.
- In 1992 the Polish insurer Warta offered a "twins protection policy."[55] Families paid the equivalent of $35.00 for returns of $4,200.00 if pregnancies brought twins.
- In 1996 the Eagle Star Insurance Company in the United Kingdom offered a policy to provide monetary benefits to parents expecting multiples.[56]
- In 1997 One Step Ahead, a company manufacturing toys and care products, established their Twins and Triplets Club.[57] Members save 20% when ordering a second item and 30% when ordering a third item, with incremented discounts for quadruplets and more. A new product line, Tykes Alike, is available for families with multiples.

Two-for-one medical bills and museum passes would help to offset costs for families needing assistance. I also look forward to routine DNA analysis of newborn same-sex twins for determining their twin type. Twin type and chorionicity can be assessed in the first trimester of pregnancy, allowing physicians to anticipate physical risks that are common among one-chorion identical pairs.[58] Knowing twin type is also vital to parents and educators because it affects their management of twins' behaviors. Until twin-typing is standard practice, I encourage insurance companies to finance this procedure for multiple birth families. Increased attention to twins' well-being might be society's repayment for their use of twin images and twinlike phrases in the media and in advertising.

"What gives you guys the right to look alike?" My friend Alan Forsyth and his identical twin brother, John, were riding the New York subway when their "right" to physical resemblance was jokingly questioned by another passenger. Of course, twins' matched appearance is not a *right,* it is a developmental outcome of their identical genes. Nevertheless, this special effect was interpreted differently by their fellow rider, prompting his unusual response.

The passenger's question typifies the intrigue and interest trailing identical twins wherever they go. Fraternal twins, both same-sex and opposite-sex, inspire different concerns, such as "How can you be twins?" or "Do you feel like twins?" No doubt twins are amused, but weary of the excitement surrounding their circumstances. Many twins instinctively know that genes affect behaviors, and some show impatience toward cloning controversies since they were "doing cloning" all along. Most twins treasure their mutual trust and companionship, but some people forget that twins also pursue individual hopes and dreams. Perhaps human and scientific interest in twins is the price twins pay for their *friendship extraordinaire.*

Afterword: Part of Me

I began this book saying I could not recall my first awareness of being a twin. Except for reared apart twins learning this news as adults, no one has pinpointed that moment of realization. Marc Roberts, professor of political economy and twin of Steve Roberts, journalist and commentator, came close—his early memories included hitting someone with arms and legs flailing while lying side by side. Most people cannot recollect events before age three so perhaps knowledge of one's twinship dawns gradually at about that time. Like most twins I cannot recall a time when being a twin was not a constant psychological presence. I did not wear twinship on my sleeve, probably because Anne and I differed in appearance, in ability and in outlook. Instead, twinship was a background factor for me, something like my neighborhood or nationality—gaining gravity when celebrated or threatened, but mostly subtle even while significant. Our shared birthdays brought twinness into the foreground, and our individual jealousies sometimes kept it there. But most often our differences in behavior and in communicating with each other were just part of the picture. However, this picture was ever present, always changing as Anne and I grew up, and the process was interesting and exhilarating. All twins produce such pictures, providing raw materials that keep researchers active and absorbed.

Anne was a key contributor to *Entwined Lives* in that our early experiences as twins became my later preoccupations and projects. These sixteen chapters have come swiftly, following years of research and writing. But, perhaps not surprisingly, the preface was written reluctantly because of its intimate bent. Anne and I had not discussed our twinship for years even though we were closer than ever, and writing about our relationship brought thoughts about being a twin into a new foreground. This time around our twinship was neither celebrated, nor threatened—instead, it became a personal (and public) prelude to twins' scientific significance—so it was important I get it right. Anne's enthusiasm for the preface pleased me beyond words, freeing me to produce the volume I had envisioned over the years.

I was surrounded by events that made writing *Entwined Lives* lively and exciting:

- In February 1997 the 1996 birth of Dolly, a lamb cloned from an adult cell, was revealed. This changed human cloning from a virtual uncertainty to a real possibility.
- In November 1997 the McCaughey septuplets were born, raising higher order multiple births to new limits.

Anne (left) and I during one of our rare moments together, June 19, 1998.
PHOTO CREDIT: MICHAEL KEEL.

- In November 1997 identical twins and football stars Tiki (New York Giants running back) and Ronde Barber (Tampa Bay Buccaneers cornerback) expected to play on opposing sides at Giants Stadium, an occasion they viewed with fascination and restraint.
- In February 1998 twins Rhea Spohner and Ruth Emblow (who claim to be fraternal) celebrated their 100th birthday, a milestone reached by only one in one hundred thousand twin pairs.
- In March 1998 the three surviving Dionne quintuples, Yvonne, Cécile and Annette, accepted a $2.8 million settlement as compensation for their exploitation as a tourist attraction in the 1930s and 1940s.
- In April 1998 researchers announced that Dolly, the cloned lamb, was pregnant. A successful birth would mean that cloning produces healthy, fertile animals that will advance the manufacture of drugs and other medical products.
- In July 1998 University of Hawaii researchers announced the multigenerational cloning of fifty mice (i.e., clones of clones).

- In July 1998 the Jane Goodall Institute announced the birth of female chimpanzee twins, Golden and Glitta, to mother Gremlin, at the Gombe Stream National Park in Tanzania.
- In September 1998 twenty-eight-year-old twin Ronaldo da Costa, from Brazil, set a world record at the Berlin marathon, winning the 26.2 mile race in 2 hours, 6 minutes and 5 seconds. He believes he and his brother Romildo are fraternal twins.

Each event was separately stirring, but gained consequence in light of twins' messages for human behavior. Dolly demonstrated new reproductive possibilities, but made us ponder identity and individuality, issues twins have long illuminated. Ronde and Tiki Barber thrilled fans with their closely matched athleticism that twin studies have explained partly by genes. Their scheduled confrontation on Thanksgiving Sunday, 1997, also made us wonder if these identical twins would tackle each other in competition, a theme twin research has explored. The Barbers did not discuss this prospect jointly, but their separate speculations showed that twinship was on their minds. (Ultimately, the twins never played that game because of Ronde's injuries.) I saw these events as part of larger developmental questions, helping us understand our different behaviors *and* why we think about them as we do.

Twin research's timeliness and momentum were also evident in several cutting edge projects I discovered, some not far from New York University, where I enjoyed part of my sabbatical while writing this book. Dr. Darrick Antell, a plastic surgeon in private practice, was exploring factors causing aging of the skin by studying identical twins with different degrees of damage. Dr. William Bauman, physician at the Bronx Veterans Affairs Medical Center, was measuring effects of spinal cord trauma on physical functions by using identical twins discordant for injury. Interestingly, neither investigator came from a twin study background, but their unique nature-nurture questions charted their unplanned arrivals.

Talking with twins in these projects revealed rich sources of untapped data. Identical twins Ynette Sapp and Olvette Mahan were completing final visits to Dr. Antell's office when I met them in November 1997. These fifty-one-year-old twins had sought his assistance primarily to look younger, but also to look more alike— "before" photographs revealed subtle facial differences. I wondered if evolutionary psychologists might join plastic surgeons to elucidate our conflicting desires for resemblance and distinction. Dr. Bauman offered me the chance to talk with Kari Krumweide and her twin sister, Kathi Nordgaard, included among the pairs in his project whose situations (Kari's paralysis) unveiled their deep affiliation and loyalty. Evolutionary anthropologists Napoleon Chagnon and Paul Bugos once suggested that traumatic events were the best settings for disclosing our true feelings toward family members. We may be predisposed toward supporting close genetic relatives, so family members' assistance may vary by degree of relatedness. I believe the stories of Dr. Bauman's exceptional twins comprise common themes recognizable in our unlucky moments.

I have always studied humans, so the affinity I felt for nonhuman twins was surprising at first. Some of the experiences I had while writing that chapter were among the most memorable. Ngoma and Tambo, the Bronx Zoo's gorilla twins, were endearing and entertaining. In fact, my enthusiasm surprised me—the two matched forms triggered the same fascination I felt with human twins. Watching them at play, I was eager to see how much they approached, protected, and confronted one another, and what they might tell us about human twinning. I was also amazed to discover the varied patterns and purposes twinning assumed throughout the animal kingdom.

Entwined Lives was also an opportunity to rediscover the books and essays that have left indelible marks on twin research methods and findings. Sir Francis Galton's 1875 work, "The History of Twins as a Criterion of the Relative Powers of Nature and Nurture," is rich with concepts that have been confirmed by modern investigators. It was Galton who was first to ask whether dogs distinguished identical twins' scents, studies others would conduct later.

Two books I return to often are Newman, Freeman, & Holzinger's *Twins: A Study of Heredity and Environment* (1937) and Daniel G. Freedman's *Human Infancy: An Evolutionary Perspective* (1974). Favorite papers include von Bracken's "Mutual Intimacy in Twins" (1934) and J. Paul Scott's "Social Genetics" (1977).

Twins offered an incredible blend of data and detail on identical and fraternal twins raised together, and identical twins raised apart. *Human Infancy* was a fresh look at what newborns reveal about the contexts and functions of human behavior. In both books statistical analyses, human interest stories, twins' photographs and investigators' speculations entice as well as inform readers. This level of description is, unfortunately, lost in most modern publications. I prefer things the former way, when narration and images made research findings more accessible and versatile. I sense that other researchers also miss the appealing but informative explication omitted from current scientific accounts.

"Mutual Intimacy in Twins" was a marvelous study, revealing varieties of cooperation and competition in identical and fraternal twins working alongside, and apart from, their cotwins. I believe it remains a fine, but overlooked, conceptual and methodological investigation of young twins' social relatedness. And "Social Genetics" was an elegant essay on social behaviors resulting from interactions between canines with similar and dissimilar genetic backgrounds. Early on I was intrigued by both these studies' implications for twin research on social relations, and was elated when Dan Freedman encouraged me to pursue these themes in my doctoral thesis.

*   *   *

Revisiting former friends was another benefit of my activities over the past year. Sometimes this meant reviewing old notes, tapes and files, making "meetings" one-sided, but remarkable nevertheless. I rekindled the fondness I have felt for twins passing through my life over the years, especially the 105 pairs of twin children I worked with whose efforts helped award my Ph.D. degree. Leafing through their folders revived memories of my train rides to Chicago suburbs (once to redo one fingerprint for one twin!), my anticipation of each pair's responses to puzzles and tests, and my amazement at how much twins reveal just by acting naturally.

I have kept track of some of these twins over the years. I congratulated one mother on her daughter's artistic talents and advised another mother of her daughters' relationship difficulties. I also shared one family's pain following the loss of one twin daughter. As for the rest, I wondered if their participation in twin research had made a difference in their lives. I suspected it did for at least one twin who approached me later as a colleague in twin studies. I also took comfort in the fact that these blood-tested twins will have always known their twin type.

Other twins have been unforgettable in different ways. Reliving life histories with Minnesota's reared apart twins during their week-long assessments made them my friends forever. I was thrilled to reconnect with some pairs at Professor Bouchard's Briggens House reunions outside London. I have received holiday cards and telephone calls from some twins, and I have delighted in their shared experiences following reunion. A rare moment was fielding a question from a familiar separated twin while I was a guest on a live radio talk show on twinship.

The up-close relationships I shared with many twin pairs over the years taught me that caring for participants does not jeopardize the scientific objectivity required for truthful findings. I also learned this from my advisors (now colleagues), Dan Freedman and Tom Bouchard, who were so concerned with getting research right. Of course, twins' tests and interviews should be administered and scored by separate examiners to curb bias from knowing twin type or cotwins' performance. At the same time, research is a partnership between twins and researchers in which best efforts yield best results. I believe my best efforts came easily because I sincerely loved the twins. They, in turn, were always trusting and generous with their time and attention.

I have also learned that researchers can talk comfortably about being twins themselves, although this knowledge was late in coming. When I left graduate school, colleagues cautioned me against discussing my twinship in papers, lectures and interviews. They reasoned that personal perspectives might diminish my scientific credibility because I could be perceived as other than objective or dispassionate. When I was a new investigator with a slim résumé that may have been true. With scientific papers and experience behind me, I realize that my own twinship has been a rare source of insights and ideas. It has also strengthened my commitment to producing research meaningful to twins, to families and to people asking developmental questions.

I have been fortunate that my career has been so professionally engaging and personally gratifying. Dan Freedman's best advice to me and to his other students has been "follow your bliss." I have done exactly that, knowing twin studies will always be part of me.

Glossary

Altruism (evolutionary view): Behavior resulting in assistance to individual(s) at the benefactor's expense; selfless behavior within species.

Alzheimer's Disease: A progressive form of mental decline occurring in middle age or later, characterized by intellectual deficit and loss of short-term memory.

Amnion: The inner membrane surrounding the embryo, developing on about the seventh day after conception. Amniotic fluid cushions the developing embryo.

Assisted Reproductive Techniques: Procedures that help infertile couples conceive.

Assortative Mating: The tendency for individuals to choose partners with similar behavioral and physical traits.

Behavioral Genetics: The discipline devoted to studying the relative contributions of genes and environments underlying individual differences in behavior.

Body Mass Index (BMI): A body fatness measure that adjusts for the fact that tall people weigh more than short people.

Chimerism: The presence of two different cell lines in an individual. This can occur in fraternal twins due to prenatal blood exchange or the fusion of two embryos.

Chorion: The outer membrane surrounding the embryo, forming on the fourth or fifth day after conception. It nourishes the embryo until the placenta develops.

Chromosome: Structures in cells that contain our genetic material, DNA. Humans have 23 pairs of chromosomes for a total of 46.

Conjoined Twins: Identical twins who fail to separate completely during the first two weeks after conception.

Continuous Trait: A trait influenced by many genes, such as intelligence and height; also called a polygenic trait. Members of a population vary on these measures.

Correlation: A statistical measure of relationship between two things.

Cotwin Control Study: The administration of different treatments to identical cotwins to study the effects on development while controlling for genetic background.

DNA (deoxyribonucleic acid): The double helical molecule carrying each individual's genetic information.

DNA Profile: Each individual's unique DNA banding pattern. DNA profiles are used to establish twin type, as well as paternity by comparing DNA characteristics of cotwins, or fathers and children. Identical twins have the same banding patterns.

Down Syndrome: This condition, also called trisomy 21, affects individuals who have inherited an extra twenty-first chromosome. Characteristic features include mental retardation and short stature. Mothers older than thirty-five are at increased risk for delivering Down Syndrome infants.

Embryo: In humans, the name used for the developing organism from the second through the eighth week of gestation. During this time the body's main structures and organs are formed.

Emergenesis: The effect of complex gene combinations, leading to unique behavioral and physical traits. Resemblance in *emergenic traits* is expected to be high for identical twins and low for fraternal twins.

Equal Environments Assumption: The premise that environmental influences affecting trait development are the same for identical and fraternal twins.

Evolutionary Psychology: A discipline concerned with the origins and functions of human behavior, with a view toward discovering which traits helped human survival in the past.

Fetal Transfusion Syndrome: Shared prenatal blood circulation between one-chorion identical twins. Depending upon its severity, this condition can lead to unequal growth, or even death of one or both fetuses.

Fingerprint Ridge Count: The number of lines or "ridges" across all ten fingers. This trait is highly genetically influenced, but may be modified by prenatal effects.

Follicle: A small sac in the ovary where egg cells are produced.

Fraternal Twins: Twins resulting from the fertilization of two eggs by two spermatozoa. These twins share half their genes, on average, by descent; also called *dizygotic twins.*

Freemartin Effect: In some nonhuman twins, the masculinization of female members of opposite-sex pairs from prenatal exposure to male hormones.

Gene: A hereditary unit that occupies a specific place on a chromosome.

Gene-Environment Correlation: The tendency for individuals with certain genetic predispositions to have, to seek, or to receive particular experiences.

Gene-Environment Interaction: The differing effects of environments on individuals with different genetic backgrounds.

Genomic Imprinting: The different expression of the same stretch of genetic material in a child depending upon whether it was inherited from the mother or father.

Heritability: An estimate of the proportion of trait variation in a population associated with genetic differences among the members.

Higher Order Multiples: Individuals born as part of a set of triplets, quadruplets or more; also called *supertwins.*

Identical Twin Half-Sibling Family: A family formed by the marriages and children of identical twins. Children are "genetic half-siblings," as well as first cousins.

Identical Twins: Twins resulting from the splitting of a single fertilized egg during the first two weeks after conception. These twins share all their genes; also called *monozygotic twins.*

Implantation: Attachment of the embryo to the intrauterine lining six to eight days after ovulation.

In Vitro Fertilization (IVF): Removal of eggs from a woman's ovaries, followed by laboratory fertilization of these eggs by sperm and transfer of resulting embryos to the uterus.

Inclusive Fitness: The reproductive benefits (genetic gains) acquired by an individual from helping genetic relatives; help given to relatives favors their chances for reproducing, thereby increasing the individual's genetic representation in future generations.

Mirror-Imaging: Reversals in physical features observed in some identical twin pairs, such as hand preference, hair whorls and fingerprint patterns. (The term *mirror-image twins* is a misnomer because physical reversal does not affect every physical trait, only some physical traits.)

Mitochondrial DNA: DNA found in energy-producing cellular structures. Mitochondria are transmitted from mother to child through the egg so identical and fraternal twins and siblings have the same mitochondria.

Multifetal Pregnancy Reduction: Elimination of one or more embryos in higher order multiple pregnancies to improve the survival chances of others.

Mutation: A heritable change in genetic material.

Nature–Nurture Debate: A long-standing, often bitter controversy over the relative extent to which behaviors are influenced by genetic and environmental events.

Nonshared Environments: Unique experiences that family members have apart from one another that make them differ in behavior.

Oocyte: The maternal cell that divides to form the egg or ovum containing one-half of the mother's chromosomes.

Ovulation: Release of an oocyte from a mature ovarian follicle.

Parity: The number of pregnancies a woman has completed.

Parkinson's Disease: A degenerative disorder associated with aging.

Paternity Uncertainty: Males' questionable relatedness to their children owing to the fact that they do not give birth. Paternity uncertainty has been associated with males' reduced investment in some children, relative to females.

Phenylketonuria: A recessive metabolic disorder leading to mental retardation if a phenylalanine-free diet is not provided early in life.

Placenta: Organ in the uterus which provides nutrition, eliminates wastes, and exchanges respiratory gases for the fetus.

Pleiotropy: The influence of a single gene on the expression of multiple traits.

Polar Body Twinning: Twins that may result from the fertilization of an egg cell and polar body, a small cell produced during maturation of the egg. Polar bodies are usually not fertilized.

Prenatal Insult: Events that may adversely affect fetal development, such as intrauterine crowding, insufficient nutrition and maternal infections.

Reproductive Fitness: An individual's capacity to produce offspring who will survive to adulthood and also reproduce.

Rule of Two-Thirds: The observation that volunteer twin samples are characteristically two-thirds female and two-thirds identical.

Shared Environments: Experiences that family members have in common that make them similar in behavior.

Single Gene Trait: A trait influenced by the expression of one gene, e.g., phenylketonuria (PKU).

Situs Inversus: Reversal of internal organs.

Superfecundation: The fertilization of two eggs by two spermatozoa at different times within the same menstrual cycle. This may produce twins conceived at different times, sometimes by different fathers.

Superfetation: The release of two eggs several weeks apart, and their fertilization by two spermatozoa. This is thought to produce twins differing markedly in maturity.

Tay-Sachs Disease: A single-gene disorder causing blindness, mental retardation and death in infants.

Tourette Disorder (Gilles de la Tourette Syndrome): A condition characterized by vocal and motor tics, and sometimes involuntary obscene language.

Turner Syndrome (XO): A condition in females lacking a second X chromosome, leading to short stature, infertility and spatial ability deficit (e.g., poor sense of direction).

XX: The normal complement of sex chromosomes in females. A female receives one X chromosome from her mother and one from her father.

XY: The normal complement of sex chromosomes in males. A male receives his X chromosome from his mother and his Y chromosome from his father.

Zygote: A fertilized egg that will develop into an embryo, a fetus and eventually a mature organism.

Notes

INTRODUCTION

[1]Daly, M., & Wilson, M. (1983). *Sex, evolution, and behavior.* Boston: Willard Grant Press.

[2]Bouchard, T. J., et al. (1990). Sources of human psychological differences: The Minnesota Study of Twins Reared Apart. *Science, 250,* 223–228.

[3]Bouchard, T. J., Jr. (1997). The genetics of personality. In K. Blum, & E. P. Noble (Eds.) *Handbook of psychiatric genetics* (pp. 273–296). Boca Raton, FL: CRC Press.

[4]The Indian mathematician Ramanajan (1887–1920) is legendary because his exceptional talent flourished despite the absence of a formal education.

[5]Plomin, R., DeFries, J. C., McClearn, G. E., & Rutter, M. (1997). *Behavioral genetics.* 3rd ed. New York: W.H. Freeman & Co.; American Psychological Society. Cross cutting issues in basic psychological research: Behavioral genetics. *American Psychological Society Observer,* February 1998, pp. 37–38.

[6]Darwin, C. (1859). *On the origin of species by means of natural selection, or, preservation of favoured races in the struggle for life.* London: Murray.

[7]Hamilton, W. D. (1964). The genetical evolution of human behaviour. *Journal of Theoretical Biology,* 7, 1–16; 17–52.

[8]Smith, M. (1987). Evolution and developmental psychology: Toward a sociobiology of human development. In C. Crawford, M. Smith, & D. Krebs (Eds.) *Sociobiology and psychology: Ideas, issues, and applications* (pp. 225–252.) Hillsdale, NJ: Erlbaum.

[9]Rowe, D. C., Woulbroun, E. J., & Gulley, B. L. (1994). Peers and friends as nonshared environmental influences. In E. M. Hetherington, D. Reiss, & R. Plomin (Eds.) *Separate social worlds of siblings: The impact of nonshared environment on development.* (pp. 159–173). Hillsdale, NJ: Erlbaum.

[10]Bryan, E. M. (1983). *The nature and nurture of twins.* London: Baillière Tindall.

[11]Martin, N. et al. (1997). A twin-pronged attack on complex traits. *Nature Genetics, 17,* 387–392; Torrey, E. F., Bowler, A. E., Taylor, E. H., & Gottesman, I. I. (1994). *Schizophrenia and manic-depressive disorder: The biological roots of mental illness as revealed by the landmark study of identical twins.* New York: Basic Books; Tysk, C., et al. (1986). Ulcerative colitis and Crohn's disease in an unselected population of monozygotic and dizygotic twins. A study of heritability and the influence of smoking. *Gut, 29,* 990–996; Newman, B., et al. (1987). Concordance of type 2 (non-insulin-dependent) diabetes mellitus in male twins. *Dibetologia, 30,* 763–768.

[12]Marshall, E. (1993). NIH told to reconsider crime meeting. *Science, 262,* 23–24.

[13]Segal, N. L. (1985). Holocaust twins: Their special bond. *Psychology Today, 19,* 52–58.

CHAPTER 1

[1]Galton, F. (1875). The history of twins as a criterion of the relative powers of nature and nurture. *Journal of the Anthropological Institute, 5,* 391–406.

[2]Martin, N., et al. (1997). A twin-pronged attack on complex traits. *Nature Genetics, 17,* 387–392.

[3]Bryan, E. M. (1983). *The nature and nurture of twins.* London: Baillière Tindall.

[4]Blatz, W. E. (1937). *Collected studies of the Dionne quintuplets.* Toronto: University of Toronto Press.

[5]See Stockard, C. R. (1921). Cited in Campbell, D. (1988). Aetiology of twinning. In I. MacGillivray, D. M. Campbell, & B. Thompson (Eds.) *Twinning and twins* (pp. 27–36). London: John Wiley & Sons, Ltd; Bulmer, M. G. (1970). *The biology of twinning in man.* Oxford: Clarendon.

[6]Hall, J. G. (1992). Symposium, Jackson Laboratory, Bar Harbor, ME; Hall, J. G. (1996). Twins and twinning. *American Journal of Medical Genetics, 61,* 202–204.

[7]See Bryan (1983).

[8]Bomsel-Helmreich O., & Mufti, W. A. (1995). The mechanism of monozygosity and double ovulation. In L. G. Keith, et al. (Eds.) *Multiple pregnancy: Epidemiology, gestation and perinatal outcome* (pp. 25–40). New York: Parthenon.

[9]Carter-Saltzman, L. (1979). Mirror-twinning: Reflection of a genetically mediated embryological event? *Behavior Genetics, 9,* 442–443. A recent study found an excess of identical twins born to mothers who were identical twins, and suggested independent genetic influences on identical and fraternal twinning; see Lichtenstein, P., et al. (1996).

[10]Hall, J. G. (1996). Twins and twinning. *American Journal of Medical Genetics, 61,* 202–204.

[11]Burn, J., & Corney, G. (1988). Zygosity determination and the types of twinning. In I. MacGillivray, et al. (Eds.) (pp. 7–25).

[12]See Bryan (1983). The peak fraternal twinning age for Nigerian women is 30–34 years.

[13]Corney, G., et al. (1979). Maternal height and twinning. *American Journal of Human Genetics, 43,* 55–59.

[14]Campbell, D. (1988). Aetiology of twinning. In I. MacGillivray, et al. (Eds.) (pp. 27 36).

[15]Nylander, P. P. S. (1971). Biosocial aspects of multiple births. *Journal of Biosocial Science Supplement, 3,* 29–38; Allen, G. (1981). The twinning and fertility paradox. In L. Gedda, et al. (Eds.) *Twin research 3A: Twin biology and multiple pregnancy* (pp. 1–13). New York: Alan R. Liss, Inc.; also see MacGillivray, I., et al. (1988). Factors affecting twinning. In I. MacGillivray, et al. (Eds.) (pp. 67–97).

[16]Derom, R., et al. (1995). The epidemiology of multiple births in Europe. In L. G. Keith, et al. (Eds.) (pp. 145–162); MacGillivray, et al. (1988). Factors affecting twinning. In I. MacGillivray, et al. (Eds.) (pp. 67–97).

[17]Bryan, E. M. (1983); Lewis, C. M., et al. (1996). Genetic contribution to DZ twinning. *American Journal of Medical Genetics, 61,* 237–246; Lichenstein, P., et al. (1996). Twin births to mothers who are twins: A registry based study. *British Medical Journal, 312,* 879–881; Lambalk, C. B., et al. (1996). Increased levels and pulsatility of follicle-stimulating hormone in mothers of hereditary dizygotic twins. *Journal of Clinical Endocrinology and Metabolism, 83,* 481–486. A search for specific genes associated with fraternal twinning is in progress by Dr. Nicholas G. Martin, Queensland Institute of Medical Research, Australia.

[18]Nylander, P. P. S. (1979). The twinning incidence in Nigeria. *Acta Geneticae Medicae et Gemellologiae, 28,* 261–263; Ugwonali, O. F. C., et al. (1998). White yams (*Discora Rotundata*) and socioeconomic status as risk factors for twin births in southwest Nigeria. *Ninth International Congress on Twin Studies.* Helsinki, Finland; also see Bryan (1983); Lummaa, V., et al. (1998). Natural selection on human twinning. *Nature, 394,* 533–534.

[19]Allen, G., & Schachter, J. (1970). Do conception delays explain some changes in twinning rates? *Acta Geneticae Medicae et Gemellologiae, 19,* 30–34; James, W. H. (1986). Dizygotic twinning, cycle day of insemination, and erotic potential of orthodox Jews. *American Journal of Human Genetics, 39,* 542–544.

[20]James, W. H. (1992). Coital frequency and twinning. *Journal of Biosocial Science, 24,*

135–136. An earlier study did not find a relationship between twinning and frequency of sexual intercourse; Bonnelyke, B., et al. (1990). *Journal of Biosocial Science, 22,* 191–196.

[21]James, W. H. (1980). Seasonality in twin and triplet births. *Annals of Human Biology, 7,* 163–175; also see MacGillivray, I., et al. (1988). Factors affecting twinning. In I. MacGillivray, et al. (Eds.) (pp. 67–97).

[22]Mosteller, M., et al. (1981). Twinning rates in Virginia: Secular trends and the effects of maternal age and parity. In L. Gedda, et al. (Eds.) *Twin research 3A: Twin biology and multiple pregnancy* (pp. 57–69). New York: Alan R. Liss, Inc.

[23]James, W. H. (1972). Secular changes in dizygotic twinning rates. *Journal of Biosocial Science, 4,* 427–434.

[24]Boklage, C. E. (1981). On the distribution of nonrighthandedness among twins and their familes. *Acta Geneticae Medicae et Gemellologiae, 30,* 167–187.

[25]Nylander, P. P. S., & Corney, G. (1977). Placentation and zygosity of twins in Northern Nigeria. *Annals of Human Genetics, 40,* 323–329; Bomsel-Helmreich O., & Mufti, W. A. (1995). The mechanism of monozygosity and double ovulation. In L. G. Keith, et al. (Eds.) (pp. 25–40).

[26]Centers for Disease Control (June 1998), Associated Press on-line; Births (Statistical Summary). *Monthly Vital Statistics Report, 46:1 Supplement.*

[27]I calculated these figures based on a 1996 world population of 5,789,662,862 (adjusting for a 1.5% yearly increase), using the 1/80 frequency of twin births and 1/40 frequency of individual twins. Johnson, O. (1997). (Ed.) *Information please almanac.* 50th ed. New York: Houghton-Mifflin.

[28]Ball, H. L., & Hill, C. M. (1996). Reevaluating "twin infanticide." *Current Anthropology, 37,* 856–863; Hill, C. M. & Ball, H. L. (1996). Abnormal births and other "ill omens." *Human Nature, 7,* 381–401.

[29]Landy, H. J., & Nies, B. M. (1995). The vanishing twin. In L. G. Keith, et al. (Eds.) (pp. 59–71).

[30]Groothuis, J. (1985). Twins and twin families: A practical guide to outpatient management. *Clinics in Perinatology, 12,* 459–474.

[31]Plomin, R., DeFries, J. C., McClearn, G. E., & Rutter, M. (1997). *Behavioral genetics.* 3rd ed. New York: W.H. Freeman & Co.

[32]Scarr, S. (1966). Environmental bias in twin studies. In M. Manosevitz, G. Linzey, & D. D. Thiessen (Eds.) *Behavioral-genetics: Method and research* (pp. 597–605). New York: Appleton-Century-Crofts; Goodman, R., & Stevenson, J. (1989). Parental criticism and warmth toward unrecognized monozygotic twins. *Behavioral and Brain Sciences, 14,* 394–395.

[33]Segal, N. L. (1984). Zygosity diagnosis: Laboratory and investigator's judgment. *Acta Geneticae Medicae et Gemellologiae, 33,* 515–520.

[34]Race, R. R., & Sanger, R. (1975). *Blood groups in man.* Oxford: Blackwell.

[35]Lykken, D. T. (1978). The diagnosis of zygosity in twins. *Behavior Genetics, 8,* 437–463.

[36]Nichols, R. C., and Bilbro, W. C., Jr. (1966). The diagnosis of twin zygosity. *Acta Genetica et Statistica Medica, 16:* 265–275.

[37]Bracha, H. F., et al. (1992). Second-semester markers of fetal size in schizophrenia: A study of monozygotic twins. *American Journal of Psychiatry, 149,* 1355–1361.

[38]Cellmark Diagnostics. "DNA fingerprinting for twintyping." Germantown, MD.

[39]Richards, B., et al. (1993). Multiplex PCR amplication from the CFTR gene using DNA prepared from buccal brushes/swabs. *Human Molecular Genetics, 2,* 159–163.

[40]See Segal, N. L. & Topoloski, T. (1995). A twin research perspective on reading and spelling disabilities. *Reading and Writing Quarterly, 11,* 209–227.

[41]Mittler, P. (1971). *The study of twins.* Baltimore, MD: Penguin Books.

[42]Gessell, A. L., & Thompson, H. (1941). Twins T and C from infancy to adolescence: A

biogenetic study of individual differences by the method of co-twin control. *Genetic Psychology Monographs, 24.*

[43]Carr, A. B., et al. (1981). Vitamin C and the common cold: A second MZ cotwin control study. *Acta Geneticae Medicae et Gemellologiae, 30,* 249–255.

[44]Ball, J. D., et al. (1987). Neuropsychological effects of cold water near-drowning in an identical twin. *International Journal of Clinical Neuropsychology, 9,* 71–73.

[45]Dumont-Driscoll, M., & Rose, R. J. (1983). Testing the twin model: Is perceived similarity due to genetic identity? *Behavior Genetics, 13,* 531–532.

[46]Watson, J. D. (1990). The Human Genome Project: Past, present, and future. *Science, 248,* 44–49.

[47]Wilson, R. S. (1983). The Louisville Twin Study: Developmental synchronies in behavior. *Child Development, 54,* 298–316.

[48]See Segal, N. L. (1990). The importance of twin studies for individual differences research. *Journal of Counseling and Development, 68,* 612–622, and references therein.

[49]Young, B. K., et al. (1985). Differences in twins: The importance of birth order. *American Journal of Obstetrics and Gynecology, 151,* 915–921; Makano, R., & Takemura, H. (1988). Birth order in delivery of twins. *Gynecologic and Obstetric Investigation, 25,* 217–222.

[50]Goedert, J. J., et al. (1991). High risk of HIV-1 infection for first-born twins. *Lancet, 338,* 1471–1475; Duliège, A.-M., et al. (1995). Birth order, delivery route, and concordance in the transmission of human immunodeficiency virus type 1 from mothers to twins. *Journal of Pediatrics, 126,* 625–632. Twins delivered by cesarean section are at lower risk for HIV infection than twins delivered vaginally (15% vs. 35% for firstborn twins, and 8% vs. 16% for secondborn twins. Note that cesarean delivered firstborn twins and vaginally delivered secondborn twins are at equal risk.

[51]Thomas, P. A., et al. (1990). Pediatric acquired immunodeficiency syndrome: An unusually high incidence of twinning. *Pediatrics, 86,* 774–777.

[52]Goedert, J. J., et al. (1991).

[53]James, W. H. (1992). Coital frequency and twinning. *Journal of Biosocial Science, 24,* 135–136.

[54]Segal, N. L. (1992). Twinning and AIDS: Alternative explanations. *Human Biology, 64,* 623–624.

[55]Lallemant-Le Coeur, S., & Mallemant, M. (1992). Twinning among HIV-infected mothers. *Lancet, 339,* 66–67.

[56]Coren, S., & Halpern, D. (1991). Left-handedness: A marker for decreased survival fitness. *Psychological Bulletin, 109,* 90–106.

CHAPTER 2

[1]Hall, J. G. (1996). Twins and twinning. *American Journal of Medical Genetics, 61,* 202–204.

[2]Keith, L., & Machin, G. (1997). Zygosity testing: Current status and evolving issues. *Journal of Reproductive Medicine, 42,* 699–707.

[3]Boklage, C. E. (1980). The sinistral blastocyst: An embryologic perspective on the development of brain-function asymmetries. In J. Herron (Ed.) *Neuropsychology of left-handedness* (pp. 115–137). New York: Academic Press.

[4]Dr. Walter E. Nance, personal communication (July 1998), based on a presentation by Dr. Robert G. Edwards at the *Fifth International Congress on Twin Studies,* September 15–19, 1986, Amsterdam, the Netherlands; also see Burn, J., & Corney, G. (1988). Zygosity determination and the types of twinning. In I. MacGillivray, D. M. Campbell, & B. Thompson (Eds.) *Twinning and twins* (pp. 7–25). Chichester: John Wiley & Sons; Nance, W. E. (1990). Do twin lyons have larger spots? *American Journal of Human Genetics, 46,* 646–648.

[5]Bryan, E. M. (1983). *The nature and nurture of twins.* London: Baillière Tindall; Springer, S., & Deutsh, G. (1985). *Left brain, right brain.* New York: W.H. Freeman & Co.

[6]Machin, G. A. (1996). Some causes of genotypic and phenotypic discordance in monozygotic twin pairs. *American Journal of Medical Genetics, 61,* 216–228.

[7]Staley, R. N., et al. (1998). Brief communication: Type II tooth cusp occurrence asymmetry in a human monozygotic twin pair. *American Journal of Physical Anthropology, 105,* 93–95; Cidis, M. B., et al. (1997). Mirror-image optic nerve dysplasia with associated anisometropia in identical twins. *Journal of the American Optometry Association, 68,* 325–329; Morison, D., et al. (1994). Mirror-image tumors in mirror-image twins. *Chest, 106,* 608–610, and a reply by Segal, N. L. (1995). *Chest, 107,* 1181.

[8]Schinzel, A. G. L., et al. (1979). Monozygotic twinning and structural defects. *Journal of Pediatrics, 95,* 921–930.

[9]Nance, W. E. (1981). Malformations unique to the twinning process. In L. Gedda, et al. (Eds.) *Twin research 3A: Twin biology and multiple pregnancy* (pp. 123–133). New York: Alan R. Liss, Inc.

[10]Gangestad, S. W., & Thornhill, R. (1996). The evolutionary psychology of extrapair sex: The role of fluctuating asymmetry. *Evolution and Human Behavior, 18,* 69–88.

[11]Mealey, L., et al. (in press). Symmetry and perceived facial attractiveness. A monozygotic co-twin comparison. *Journal of Personality and Social Psychology.*

[12]Coren, S., & Halpern, D. (1991). Left-handedness: A marker for decreased survival fitness. *Psychological Bulletin, 109,* 90–106.

[13]Ross, P. E. I can read your face. *Forbes,* December 19, 1994, p. 304–305.

[14]Burke, P., & Hughes, C. (1987). The effect of congenital cardiac disease on facial growth in a monozygotic twin pair, studied by stereophotogrammetry. *European Journal of Orthodontics, 9,* 97–103.

[15]Steinmetz, H., et al. (1995). Brain (A)symmetry in monozygotic twins. *Cerebral Cortex, 5,* 296–300.

[16]Kee, D. W., et al. (1998). Multi-task analysis of cerebral specialization in monozygotic twins discordant for handedness. *Neuropsychology, 12,* 468–478.

[17]Edelman, G. (1987). *Neural Darwinism: The theory of neuronal group selection.* New York: Basic Books.

[18]Sokol, D. K., et al. (1995). Intrapair differences in personality and cognitive ability among young monozygotic twins distinguished by chorion type. *Behavior Genetics 25,* 457–466.

[19]Derom, C., et al. (1996). Handedness in twins according to zygosity and chorion type: A preliminary report. *Behavior Genetics, 26,* 407–408; Carlier, M., et al. (1996). Manual performance and laterality in twins of known chorion type. *Behavior Genetics, 26,* 409–417.

[20]Satz, P., et al. (1985). The pathological left-handedness syndrome. *Brain and Cognition, 4,* 27–46.

[21]Derom, R., & Thiery, M. (1974). Intrauterine hypoxia—a phenomenon proper to the second twin. *Acta Geneticae Medicae et Gemellologiae, 28,* 54.

[22]Christian, J. C., et al. (1979). Association of handedness and birth order in monozygotic twins. *Acta Geneticae Medicae et Gemellologiae, 28,* 67–68; Orlebeke, J. F., et al. (1996). Left-handedness in twins: genes or environment. *Cortex, 32,* 479–490.

[23]Segal, N. L. (1989). Origins and implications of handedness and relative birth weight for IQ in monozygotic twin pairs. *Neuropsychologia, 27,* 549–561.

[24]See Springer, S. P., & Deutsch, G. (1985). *Left brain, right brain.* New York: W. H. Freeman & Co.; Springer, S. P., & Searleman, A. (1980). Left-handedness in twins: Implications for the mechanisms underlying cerebral asymmetry of function (pp. 139–158). In J. Herron (Ed.) *Neuropsychology of left-handedness.* New York: Academic Press.

[25]Derom, C., et al. (1996). Handedness in twins according to zygosity and chorion type: A preliminary report. *Behavior Genetics, 26,* 407–408 (twins vs singletons: 17% vs. 8%); Davis, A., & Annett, M. (1994). Handedness as a function of twinning, age and sex. *Cortex, 30,* 105–111 (no difference); Perelle, I. B., & Ehrman, L. (1994). An international study of human handedness. *Behavior Genetics, 24,* 217–227 (no difference).

[26]Lauterbach, C. E. (1925). Studies in twin resemblance. *Genetics, 10,* 525–568.

[27]Bryan, E. M. (1983).

[28]Machin, G. A., et al. (1996). Correlations of placental anatomy and clinical outcomes in 69 monochorionic twin pregnancies. *American Journal of Medical Genetics, 61,* 229–236.

[29]Torrey, E. F., Bowler, A. E., Taylor, E. H., & Gottesman, I. I. (1994). *Schizophrenia and manic-depressive disorder: The biological roots of mental illness as revealed by the landmark study of identical twins.* New York: Basic Books.

[30]Cameron, A. H. (1968). The Birmingham Twin Study. *Proceedings of the Royal Society of Medicine, 61,* 229–234.

[31]Wilson, R. S. (1986). Twins: Genetic influence on growth. In R. M. Malina, & C. Bouchard (Eds.) *Sports and human genetics* (pp. 1–21) Champaign, IL: Human Kinetics.

[32]Babson, S. G., et al. (1964). Growth and development of twins of dissimilar size at birth. *Pediatrics, 33,* 327–333.

[33]Plomin, R., DeFries, J. C., McClearn, G. E. (1990). *Behavioral genetics: A primer.* 2nd ed. New York: W. H. Freeman & Co.; Plomin, R., DeFries, J. C., McClearn, G. E., & Rutter, M. (1997). *Behavioral genetics.* 3rd ed. New York: W. H. Freeman & Co.

[34]Uchida, I. A., et al. (1983). 45,X/46XX mosaicism in discordant monozygotic twins. *Pediatrics, 71,* 413–417.

[35]Nance, W. E., & Uchida, I. (1964). Turner's syndrome, twinning, and an unusual variant of glucose-6–phosphate dehydrogenase. *American Journal of Human Genetics, 16,* 380–392. Also see Nielsen, J., & Dahl, G. (1976). Twins in the sibships and parental sibships of women with Turner's syndrome. *Clinical Genetics, 10,* 93–96; Goodship, J., et al. (1996). X-inactivation patterns in monozygotic and dizygotic twins. *American Journal of Medical Genetics, 61,* 205–208.

[36]Bryan, E. M. (1983), Little, J., & Bryan, E. (1986). Congenital anomalies in twins. *Seminars in Perinatology, 10,* 50–64.

[37]Dallapiccola, B., et al. (1985). Discordant sex in one of three triplets. *Journal of Medical Genetics, 22,* 6–11.

[38]Blakeslee, S. "Power Plants of the Cell Become Suspect in Baffling Disease." *New York Times,* November 6, 1990; Brown, M.D., et al. (1996). Mitochondrial DNA sequence analysis of four Alzheimer's and Parkinson's disease patients. *American Journal of Medical Genetics, 61,* 283–289.

[39]Bergem, A. L. M., et al. (1997). The role of heredity in late-onset Alzheimer disease and vascular dementia. *Archives of General Psychiatry, 54,* 264–270; Gatz, M., et al. (1997). Heritability for Alzheimer's Disease: The study of dementia in Swedish twins. *Journal of Gerontology, 52a,* M117–M125.

[40]Korenke, G. C., et al. (1996). Cerebral adrenoleukodystrophy (ALD) in one of monozygotic twins with an identical ALD genotype. *Annals of Neurology, 40,* 254–257.

[41]Diamond, M., & Sigmundson, H. K. (1997). Sex reassignment at birth: Long-term review and clinical implications. *Archives of Pediatric and Adolescent Medicine, 151,* 298–304; Gorman, C. (1997). "A Boy Without a Penis." *Time Magazine,* March 24, 1997.

[42]Gartler, S. M., & Riggs, A. D. (1983). Mammalian X-chromosome inactivation. In H. L. Roman, A. Campbell, & L. M. Sandler. (Eds.) *Annual Review of Genetics, 17,* 155–190; Tuckerman, E., et al. (1985). Frequency and replication status of the fragile X, fra (X)

(q27–28), in a pair of monozygotic twins of markedly differing intelligence. *Journal of Medical Genetics, 22,* 85–91.

[43]Herzing, L. B. K., et al. (1997). *Xist* has properties of the X-chromosome, inactivation centre. *Nature, 386,* 272–275.

[44]Tuckerman, E., et al. (1985).

[45]Burn, J., et al. (1986). Duchenne muscular dystrophy in one of monozygotic twin girls. *Journal of Medical Genetics, 23,* 494–500; Pedersen, P. J., et al. (1980). Monozygotic twins with dissimilar phenotypes and chromosome complements. *Acta Obstetrica Gynecologia Scandinavica, 59,* 459–462; Jørgensen, A. L., et al (1992). Different patterns of X inactivation in MZ twins discordant for red-green color-vision deficiency. *American Journal of Human Genetics, 51,* 291–298.

[46]Walls, G. L. (1959). Peculiar color blindness in peculiar people. *Archives of Opthalmalogy, 62,* 41–60.

[47]Richards, C. S., et al. (1990). Skewed X inactivation in a female MZ twin results in Duchenne muscular dystrophy. *American Journal of Human Genetics, 46,* 672–681.

[48]Trejo, V., et al. (1994). X chromosome inactivation patterns with fetal-placental anatomy in monozygotic twin pairs: Implications for immune relatedness and concordance for autoimmunity. *Molecular Medicine, 1,* 62–70; Derom, C. (1998). X chromosome inactivation patterns in monozygotic twin girls (abstract). *Twin Research, 1,* 101.

[49]Monteiro, J., et al. (1998). Commitment of X inactivation precedes the twinning event in monochorionic twins. *American Journal of Human Genetics, 63,* 339–346.

[50]Nance, W. E. (1990); Richards, C. S., et al. (1990).

[51]Monteiro, J., et al. (1998).

[52]Skuse, D. H., et al. (1997). Evidence from Turner's syndrome of an imprinted X-linked locus affecting cognitive function. *Nature, 387,* 705–708.

[53]Piontelli, A. (1992) *From fetus to child: An observational and psychoanalytic study.* London: Tavistock.

[54]Arabin, A., et al. (1996). The onset of inter-human contacts: Longitudinal ultrasound observations in early twin pregnancies. *Ultrasound Obstetrics and Gynecology, 8,* 166–173; Arabin, B., et al. (1998). Intrauterine behavior of multiples. In A. Kurjack (Ed.) *Textbook of perinatal medicine,* vol. 2 (pp. 1506–1531). New York: Parthenon Press.

[55]Frothingham, R. (1997). A medical mystery. *New England Journal of Medicine, 337,* 1666; Kassirer, J. P. (1998). Medical mystery—the answer revealed. *New England Journal of Medicine, 338,* 266–267.

[56]Wilson, R. S. (1979). Twin growth: Initial deficit, recovery, and trends in concordance from birth to nine years. *Annals of Human Biology, 6,* 205–220.

CHAPTER 3

[1]Archer, H. (1810). Facts illustrating a disease pecular to the female children of Negro slaves. *Medical Repository, 1,* 319–323.

[2]Bulmer, M. G. (1970). *The biology of twinning in man.* Oxford: Clarendon Press.

[3]Shearer, L. "Mixed Twins." *Parade Magazine,* October 23, 1983, p. 8.

[4]Hester, J. "Twin Born, 84 Days After First." *New York Times,* February 9, 1996.

[5]Nance, W. E. (1981). Malformations unique to the twinning process. In L. Gedda, et al. (Eds.) *Twin research 3A: Twin biology and multiple pregnancy* (pp. 123–133). New York: Alan R. Liss, Inc.

[6]Nance, W. E. (1981); Terasaki, P. I., et al. (1978). Twins with two different fathers identified by HLA. *New England Journal of Medicine, 299,* 590–592.

[7]Okamura, K., et al. (1992). A probable case of superfecundation. *Fetal Diagnosis and Therapy, 7,* 717–720.

[8]Phelan, M. C., et al. (1982). Discordant expression of fetal hydantoin syndrome in heteropaternal dizygotic twins. *New England Journal of Medicine, 307,* 99–101.

[9]Baker, L. K. "The Twins With Two Fathers." *Ladies Home Journal,* February, 1996, pp. 112–115, 174–176.

[10]Daly, M., & Wilson, M. (1987). Evolutionary psychology and family violence. In C. Crawford, M. Smith, & D. Krebs (Eds.) *Sociobiology and psychology: Ideas, issues and applications* (pp. 293–309). Hillsdale, NJ: Erlbaum.

[11]Christenfeld, N. J. S., & Hill, E. A. (1995). Whose baby are you? *Nature, 378,* 669.

[12]Bellis, M. A., & Baker, M. A. (1990). Do females promote sperm competition? Data for humans. *Animal Behavior, 40,* 996–997.

[13]Rhine, S. A., et al. (1974). Familial twinning: A possible example of superfetation in man. *First International Congress on Twin Studies, October 28–November 2, 1974,* Rome, Italy.

[14]Krenn, V., et al. (1995). Superfetation occurring in connection with gamete intrafallopian transfer: a case report. *Virchows Archives, 426,* 647–649.

[15]Reuters. "Twins, Conceived a Month Apart." November 11, 1997; Dr. Richard de Chazal (Personal communication, November 13, 1998).

[16]Boklage, C. E. (1995). The frequency and survival probability of natural twin conceptions. L. G. Keith, E. Papiernik, D. M. Keith, & B. Luke (Eds.) *Multiple pregnancy: Epidemiology, gestation and perinatal outcome* (pp. 41–50). New York: Parthenon.

[17]Fisher, R. A. (1919). The genesis of twins. *Genetics, 4,* 489–499; Fisher, R. A. (1925). The resemblance of twins, a statistical examination of Lauterbach's measurements. *Genetics, 10,* 569–579.

[18]Fisk, N. M. (1996). Molecular genetic etiology of twin reversed arterial perfusion sequence. *American Journal of Obstetrics and Gynecology, 174,* 891–894.

[19]Bulmer, M. G. (1970).

[20]Bieber, F. R., et al. (1981). Genetic studies of an acardiac monster: Evidence of polar body twinning in man. *Science, 213,* 775–777.

[21]Fisher, K. M., & Polesky, H. F. (1979). Polar body conceptions and fertility drug twins. *American Society of Human Genetics,* October 3–6, 1979, Minneapolis, MN.

[22]Boklage, C. E. (1981). On the distribution of nonrighthandedness among twins and their families. *Acta Geneticae Medicae et Gemellologiae, 30,* 167–187.

[23]Gregory, K. E., et al. (1995). Effects of twinning on dystocia, calf survival, calf growth, carcass traits, and cow productivity. *Journal of Animal Science, 74,* 1223–1233; also see Gandelman, R. (1992). *Psychobiology of behavioral development.* New York: Oxford University Press.

[24]See Race, R. R., & Sanger, R. (1975). *Blood groups in man.* 6th ed. Oxford: Blackwell.

[25]van Dijk, B. A., et al. (1996). Blood group chimerism in human multiple births is not rare. *American Journal of Medical Genetics, 61,* 264–268.

[26]See Bryan, E. M. (1983). *The nature and nurture of twins.* London: Baillière Tindall.

[27]Bird, G. W. G., et al. (1980). Another example of haemopoietic chimaerism in dizygotic twins. *British Journal of Haematology, 46,* 439–445.

[28]Dunsford, I., et al. (1953). A human blood-group chimera. *British Medical Journal, 2,* 81.

[29]Gilgenkrantz, S., et al. (1981). Cytogenetic and antigenic studies in a pair of twins: A normal boy and a trisomic 21 girl with chimera. In L. Gedda, et al. (Eds.) *Twin research 3A: Twin biology and multiple pregnancy* (pp. 141–153). New York: Alan R. Liss, Inc.

[30]Barth, J. "Some Reasons Why I Tell the Stories the Way I Tell Them Rather Than Some Other Sort of Stories Some Other Way." *New York Times Book Review,* May 9, 1982, pp. 29–33.

[31]Miller, E. M. (1994). Prenatal sex hormone transfer: A reason to study opposite-sex twins. *Personality and Individual Differences, 17,* 511–529.

[32]Kinsley, C., et al. (1986). Prior intrauterine position influences body weight in male and female mice. *Hormones and Behavior, 20,* 201–211; Gandelman, R. (1992).

[33]Clark, M. M., & Galef, B. J., Jr. (1994). A male gerbil's intrauterine position affects female response to his scent marks. *Physiology and Behavior, 55,* 1137–1139.

[34]Loehlin, J. C., & Martin, M. G. (1998). A comparison of adult female twins from opposite-sex and same-sex pairs on variables related to reproduction. *Behavior Genetics, 28,* 21–27.

[35]Christensen, K., et al. (1998). Fecundability of female twins. *Epidemiology, 9,* 189–192; Rose, R. J., et al. (1994). Femininity and fertility in sisters of twin brothers: Neither prenatal androgenization nor cross-sex socialization. *International Society for the Study of Behavioral Development,* June 28–July 2, 1994, Amsterdam, the Netherlands.

[36]Resnick, S. M., et al. (1993). Sensation seeking in opposite-sex twins: An effect of prenatal hormones? *Behavior Genetics, 23,* 323–329.

[37]McFadden, D. (1993). A masculinzing effect on the auditory systems of human females having male co-twins. *Proceedings of the National Academy of Sciences, USA, 90,* 11900–11904. SOAEs have no known function themselves.

[38]Cole-Harding, S., et al. (1988). Spatial ability in members of opposite-sex twin pairs. *Behavior Genetics, 18,* 710.

[39]Miller, E. M. (1995). Reported myopia in opposite-sex twins: A hormonal hypothesis. *Optometry and Vision Science, 72,* 34–36.

[40]Boklage, C. (1985). Interactions between opposite-sex dizygotic fetuses and the assumptions of Weinberg difference method epidemiology. *American Journal of Human Genetics, 37,* 591–605.

[41]Geschwind, N., & Behan, P. (1982). Left-handedness: Association with immune disease, migraine, and developmental learning disorder. *Proceedings of the National Academy of Sciences, 79,* 5097–5100.

[42]Davis, A., & Annett, M. (1994). Handedness as a function to twinning, age and sex. *Cortex, 30,* 105–111.

[43]Orlebeke, J. F., et al. (1995). Sinistrality in twins: Evidence for nongenetic transmission of lefthandedness. *Behavior Genetics, 25,* 281–282; Orlebeke, J. F., et al. (1996). Left-handedness in twins: genes or environment. *Cortex, 32,* 479–490.

[44]Koch, H. (1966). *Twins and twin relations.* Chicago: University of Chicago Press.

[45]Elizabeth, P. H., & Green, R. (1984). Childhood sex-role behaviors: Similarities and differences in twins. *Acta Geneticae Medicae et Gemellologiae, 33,* 173–179.

[46]Henderson, B. A., & Berenbaum, S. A. (1997). Sex-typed play in opposite-sex twins. *Developmental Psychobiology, 31,* 115–123.

[47]Collaer, M., & Hines, M. (1995). Human behavioral sex differences: A role for gonadal hormones during early development? *Psychological Bulletin, 118,* 55–107; Bryden, M., et al. (1994). Evaluating the empirical support for the Geschwind-Behan-Galaburda model of cerebral lateralization. *Cognition and Behavior, 26,* 103–167.

CHAPTER 4

[1]Wilson, R. S. (1983). The Louisville Twin Study: Developmental synchronies in behavior. *Child Development, 54,* 298–316; also see McCartney, K., et al. (1990). Growing up and growing apart: A developmental meta-analysis of twin studies. *Psychological Bulletin, 107,* 226–237.

[2]McClearn, G. E., et al. (1997). Substantial genetic influence on cognitive abilities in twins 80 or more years old. *Science, 276,* 1560–1563.

[3]Cherny, S. S., & Cardon, L. (1994). General cognitive ability. In J. C. DeFries, R. Plomin, & D. W. Fulker (Eds.) *Nature and nurture during middle childhood* (pp. 46–56). Oxford: Blackwell; Cardon, L. (1994). Specific cognitive abilities. In J. C. DeFries, et al. (Eds.) (pp. 57–76).

[4]Boomsma, D. I., & van Baal, G. C. (1998). Genetic influences on childhood IQ in 5- and 7-year-old Dutch twins. *Developmental Neuropsychology, 14,* 115–126.

[5]Spurious correlations occur when two things are related statistically, but not meaningfully.

[6]Bouchard, T. J., Jr., & McGue, M. (1981). Familial studies of intelligence. *Science, 212,* 1055–1059; McGue, M., & Bouchard, T. J., Jr. (1998). Genetic and environmental influences of human behavioral differences. *Annual Review of Neuroscience, 21,* 1–24.

[7]Wilson, R. S. (1983).

[8]Fulker, D. W., et al. (1993). Continuity and change in cognitive development. In R. Plomin & G. E. McClearn (Eds.) *Nature, nurture, and psychology* (pp. 77–79). Washington, D.C.: American Psychological Association Press.

[9]Petrill, S. A., et al. (1998). Exploring the genetic and environmental etiology of high general cognitive ability in fourteen- to thirty-six-month-old twins. *Child Development, 69,* 68–74.

[10]Bock, R. D. (1978). Familial resemblance in patterns of growth in stature. In W. E. Nance, G. Allen, & P. Parisi (Eds.) *Twin research, Part A: Psychology and methodology* (pp. 211–216). New York: Alan R. Liss, Inc.

[11]Cherny, S. S., & Cardon, L. (1994).

[12]McClearn, G. E., et al. (1997). Substantial genetic influence on cognitive abilities in twins 80 or more years old. *Science, 276,* 1560–1563.

[13]*New York Times,* May 3, 1996.

[14]Binet, A., & Simon, T. (1916). *The development of intelligence in children.* Baltimore: Williams & Wilkins. Reprinted in W. Kessen & G. Mandler (Eds.) (1965). *The Child.* New York: John Wiley & Sons, Inc.

[15]Segal, N. L. (1985). Monozygotic and dizygotic twins: A comparative analysis of mental ability profiles. *Child Development, 56,* 1051–1058; Bouchard, T. J., Jr., & McGue, M. (1981).

[16]Bouchard, T. J., Jr., et al. (1990). Sources of human psychological differences: The Minnesota Study of Twins Reared Apart. *Science, 250,* 223–228.

[17]Loehlin, J. C. (1989). Partitioning environmental and genetic contributions to behavioral development. *American Psychologist, 44,* 1285–1292. Loehlin, J. C., et al. (1997). Heredity, environment, and IQ in the Texas Adoption Project. In R. Sternberg & C. Grigorenko (Eds.) *Intelligence: Heredity and environment* (pp. 105–125). New York: Cambridge University Press.

[18]See Bouchard, T. J., Jr. (1997). IQ similarity in twins reared apart: Findings and responses to critics. In R. Sternberg & C. Grigorenko (Eds.) (pp. 126–160).

[19]Segal, N. L. (1997). Same-age unrelated siblings: A unique test of within-family environmental influences on IQ similiarity. *Journal of Educational Psychology, 89,* 381–390.

[20]Bouchard, T. J., Jr. (1998). Genetic and environmental influences on adult intelligence and special mental abilities. *Human Biology, 70,* 253–275.

[21]Plomin, R. (1990). *Nature and nurture.* Pacific Grove, CA: Brooks/Cole Pub. Co.

[22]Newman, H. H., Freeman, F. N., & Holzinger, K. J. (1937). *Twins: A study of heredity and environment.* Chicago: University of Chicago Press.

[23]Hirsh, S. "For Some, Ceremony is Tiny Part of the Story." *New York Times,* May 26, 1997.

[24]Devlin, B., et al. (1997). The heritablity of IQ. *Nature, 388,* 468–471.

[25]See Dennis, M., & Barnes, M. A. (1994). Neurological function in same-sex twins discordant for perinatal brain damage. *Developmental and Behavioral Pediatrics, 15,* 124–130. Their statement that "same-sex twins share a similar (if not identical) prenatal history" is incorrect.

[26]Taffel, S. M. (1995). Demographic trends in twin births: USA. In L. G. Keith, E. Papiernik, D. M. Keith, & B. Luke (Eds.) *Multiple pregnancy: Epidemiology, gestation and perinatal outcome* (pp. 133–143). New York: Parthenon; Keet, M. P., et al. (1986). Follow-up study of physical growth of monozygous twins with discordant within-pair birth weights. *Pediatrics, 77,* 336–344.

[27]Scarr, S. (1969). Effects of birth weight on later intelligence. *Social Biology, 16,* 249–256.

[28]Wilson, R. S. (1979). Twin growth: Initial deficit, recovery, and trends in concordance from birth to nine years. *Human Biology, 6,* 205–220.

[29]Amiel-Tison, C., & Gluck, L. (1995). Fetal brain and pulmonary adaptation in multiple pregnancy. In L. G. Keith, et al. (Eds.) (pp. 585–597).

[30]Bartley, A. J., et al. (1997). Genetic variability of human brain size and cortical gyral patterns. *Brain, 120,* 257–269.

[31]Nash, J. M. "Fertile Minds." *Time Magazine,* February 3, 1997.

[32]Mann, J. (1992). Nurturance or negligence: Maternal psychology and behavioral preference among preterm twins. In J. H. Barkow, L. Cosmides, & J. Tooby (Eds.) *The adapted mind: Evolutionary psychology and the evolution of culture* (pp. 367– 390). New York: Oxford University Press.

[33]Holden, C. (1997). "Overstimulated by brain research?" *Science, 278,* 1569, 1571.

[34]Rowe, D. C. (April 17, 1997). Electronic communication; Harrington, G. (April 17, 1997). Electronic communication.

[35]Furlow, B. F., et al. (1997). Fluctuating asymmetry and psychometric intelligence. *Proceedings of the Royal Society of London, B264,* 823–829; Blinkhorn, S. (1997). Symmetry as destiny—taking a balanced view of IQ. *Nature, 387,* 849–850.

[36]Loehlin, J., & Nichols, R. (1976). *Heredity, environment and personality: A study of 850 sets of twins.* Austin: University of Texas Press.

[37]See Willerman, L. (1979) *The psychology of individual and group differences.* San Francisco: W. H. Freeman & Co.

[38]Sisk, R. "Fair Law, Thanks to Twins." *New York Daily News,* June 5, 1997.

[39]See Bouchard, T. J., Jr., & Segal, N. L. (1985). IQ and environment (pp. 391–464). In B.B. Wolman (Ed.) *Handbook of Intelligence.* NY: John Wiley & Sons.

[40]IQ variability is the same for twins and nontwins. IQ variability may, however, be restricted in some twin samples because of exclusion of disadvantaged pairs.

[41]Plomin, R., & DeFries, J. C. (1980). Genetics and intelligence: Recent data. *Intelligence, 4,* 15–24.

[42]Jensen, A. (1997). The puzzle of nongenetic variance. In R. J. Sternberg, & E. L. Grigorenko (Eds.) (pp. 42–88). Cambridge; also see Bailey, J. M., & Horn, J. M. (1986). A source of variance in IQ unique to the lower-scoring monozygotic (MZ) twin. *Behavior Genetics, 16,* 509–516.

[43]Record, R. G., et al. (1970). An investigation of the differences in measured intelligence between twins and single births. *Annals of Human Genetics, 34,* 11–20.

[44]Myrianthpoulos, N. C., et al. (1972). Intellectual development of a prospectively studied population of twins and comparison with singletons. In J. de Grouchy, F. J. B. Ebling, & I. W. Henderson (Eds.) *Human genetics: Proceedings from the Fourth International Congress of Human Genetics* (pp. 243–257).

[45]Bouchard, T. J., Jr., et al. (1990).

[46]Jensen, A. R. (1998). *The g factor: The science of mental ability.* Westport, CT: Praeger.

[47]Segal, N. L. (1997).

[48]Bakker, P. (1987). Autonomous languages in twins. *Acta Geneticae Medicae et Gemellologiae, 36,* 233–238; Lytton, H., et al. (1977). The impact of twinship on parent-child interaction. *Journal of Personality and Social Psychology, 35,* 97–107.

[49]See Dodd, B., & McEvoy, S. (1994). *Journal of Child Language, 21,* 273–289.

[50]"Ginny and Gracie Go to School." *Time Magazine,* December 10, 1979.

[51]"The Strange Speech of Former Fremont Ladies." *Fremont Journal,* December 17, 1903.

[52]Malmstrom, P. M., & Silva, M. N. (1986). Twin talk: manifestations of twin status in the speech of toddlers. *Journal of Child Language, 13,* 293–304.

[53]Lytton, H. (1980). *Parent-child interaction: The socialization process observed in twin and singleton families.* New York: Plenum; Bornstein, M. H., & Ruddy, M. G. (1984).

Infant attention and maternal stimulation: Prediction of cognitive and linguistic development in singletons and twins. In H. Bouma & D. Douwhuis (Eds.) *Attention and performance x: Control of Language processes* (pp. 433–445). London: Erlbaum; Tomasello, M., et al. (1986). Linguistic envirnoment of 1– to 2–year-old twins. *Developmental Psychology, 22,* 169–176.

[54] Bornstein, M. H., & Ruddy, M. G. (1984).

[55] McDiarmid, J. M., & Silva, P. A. (1979). Three-year-old twins and singletons: A comparison of some perinatal, environmental, experiential, and developmental characteristics. *Australian Paediatric Journal, 15,* 243–247; Douglas, J. E., & Sutton, A. (1978). The development of speech and mental processes in a pair of twins: A case study. *Journal of Child Psychology and Psychiatry, 19,* 49–56.

[56] Barton, M. E., & Strosberg, R. (1997). Conversational patterns of two-year-old twins in mother-twin-twin triads. *Journal of Child Language, 24,* 257–269.

[57] Lytton, H., et al. (1977); Bishop, D. V. M. (1997). Pre- and perinatal hazards and family background in children with specific language impairments: A study of twins. *Brain and Language, 56,* 1–26.

[58] Wallace, M. (1986). *The silent twins.* New York: Prentice Hall.

[59] This condition was originally called *elective mutism,* but the name was changed to *selective mutism* in 1994 to reflect the fact that individuals' failure to speak may be situation-dependent; Dummit, E. S., III, et al. (1997). Systematic assessment of 50 children with selective mutism. *Journal of the Academy of Child and Adolescent Psychiatry, 36,* 653–660.

[60] Miller, C. M., & Newman, S. (1997). Understanding selective mutism. *Selective Mutism Foundation, Inc.;* West, H. I. "The Silence of the Lambs." *New York Daily News,* September 9, 1991, p. 23. Information can be obtained by sending a self-addressed envelope with two stamps to Sue Newman, P.O. Box 450632, Sunrise, FL 33345–0632.

[61] Dummit, E. S., III, et al. (1996). Fluoxetine treatment of children with selective mutism: An open trial. *Journal of the Academy of Child and Adolescent Psychiatry, 35,* 615–621.

[62] Wilson, R. S. (1975). Twins: Patterns of cognitive development as measured on the WPPSI. *Developmental Psychology, 11,* 126–134; Segal, N. L. (1985).

[63] Bouchard, T. J., Jr. (1998).

[64] Plomin, R., et al. (1997).

[65] Rowe, D. C. (1994). *The limits of family influence.* New York: Guilford Press.

[66] Ho, H.-Z., et al. (1988). Covariation between intelligence and speed of cognitive processing: Genetic and environmental influences. *Behavior Genetics, 18,* 247–261; Petrill, S. A., et al. (1995). The genetic and environmental variance underlying elementary cognitive tasks. *Behavior Genetics, 25,* 199–209.

[67] Rowe, D. C. (1994).

[68] Vander Zanden, J. W. (1980). *Educational psychology in theory and practice.* New York: Random House. (See Public Law 94–142).

[69] See Segal, N. L. & Topoloski, T. (1995). A twin research perspective on reading and spelling disabilities. *Reading and Writing Quarterly, 11,* 209–227; Alarcón, M., et al. (1997). A twin study of mathematics ability. *Journal of Learning Disabilities, 30,* 617–623.

[70] Farber, S. L. (1981). *Identical twins reared apart: A reanalysis.* New York: Basic Books.

[71] Bishop, D.V.M. (1997); Dale, P.S., et al. (1998). Genetic influence on language delay in two-year-old children. *Nature Neuroscience, 1,* 324–328.

[72] Johnson, C. (Personal communication, April 25, 1998).

[73] Horowitz, W. A., et al. (1965). Identical twin—"idiot savants"—calendar calculators. *American Journal of Psychiatry, 121,* 1075–1079.

[74] Sacks, O. (1985). *The man who mistook his wife for a hat.* New York: Summit Books.

[75] Lykken, D. T., et al. (1992). Emergenesis: Genetic traits that may not run in families. *American Psychologist, 47,* 1565–1577.

[76]Plomin, R., et al. (1997).

[77]See Sternberg, R. J. (1997). Educating intelligence: Infusing the triarchic theory into school instruction. In R. Sternberg & C. Grigorenko (Eds.) (pp. 343–362); Gardner, H. (1993). *Multiple intelligence: The theory in practice.* New York: Basic Books; Goleman, D. (1998). *Working with emotional intelligence.* New York: Bantam Books.

[78]Cardon, L., et al. (1994). Quantitative trait locus for reading disability on chromosome 6. *Science, 266,* 276–279.

[79]Plomin, R., & Petrill, S. A. (1997). Genetics and intelligence: What's new? *Intelligence, 24,* 53–77; Gottesman, I. I. (1997). Twins: En route to QTLs for cognition. *Science, 276,* 1522–1523; Chorney, M. J., et al. (1998). A quantitative trait locus associated with cognitive ability in children. *Psychological Science, 9,* 159–166. The effect of the gene on intelligence is estimated to explain about 2% of the variation between people.

[80]Pinker, S. (1997). *How the mind works.* New York: W.W. Norton & Co.

[81]Loehlin, J., & Nichols, R. (1976).

[82]Segal, N. L., & MacDonald, K. B. (1998). Behavioral genetics and evolutionary psychology: Unified perspective on personality research. *Human Biology, 70,* 157–182.

[83]Associated Press. "No, You're Not Seeing Double." *New York Times,* March 20, 1991.

[84]Segal, N. L., & Russell, J. M. (1992). Twins in the classroom: School policy issues and recommendations. *Journal of Educational and Psychological Consultation, 3,* 69–84.

[85]Schwarz, J. C. (1972). Effects of peer familiarity on the behavior of preschoolers in a novel situation. *Journal of Personality and Social Psychology, 24,* 276–284.

[86]Sanger, Lillie-Beth. "Twins' Separation Debated." *The Daily Oklahoman,* May 10, 1993.

[87]Bouchard, T. J., Jr., et al. (1990).

CHAPTER 5

[1]*Léa e Maura* (circa 1940) was painted by Brazilian artist Alberto de Veiga Guignard.

[2]Galton, F. (1875). The history of twins as a criterion of the relative powers of nature and nurture. *Journal of the Anthropological Institute, 5,* 391–406.

[3]Saudino, K. J., & Plomin, R. (1996). Personality and behavioral genetics: Where have we been and where are we going? *Journal of Research in Personality, 30,* 335–347.

[4]Plomin, R., & Daniels, D. (1987). Why are children in the same family so different from one another? *Behavioral and Brain Sciences, 10,* 1–16.

[5]Jockin, V., et al. (1996). Personality and divorce: A genetic analysis. *Journal of Personality and Social Psychology, 71,* 288–299.

[6]Rushton, J. P., et al. (1986). Altruism and aggression: The heritability of individual differences. *Journal of Personality and Social Psychology, 50,* 1192–1198; Segal, N. L. (1997). Twin research perspective on human development. In N. L. Segal, G. E. Weisfeld, & C. C. Weisfeld (Eds.) (1997). *Uniting psychology and biology: Integrative perspectives on human development* (pp. 145–173). Washington, D.C.: American Psychological Association Press.

[7]Robinson, J. L., et al. (1992). The heritability of inhibited and uninhibited behavior: A twin study. *Developmental Psychology, 28,* 1030–1037.

[8]Tesser, A. (1993). On the importance of heritability in psychological research: The case of attitudes. *Psychological Review, 100,* 129–142.

[9]Waller, N. G., et al. (1990). Genetic and environmental influences on religious interests, attitudes, and values: A study of twins reared apart and together. *Psychological Science, 1,* 138–142.

[10]Waller, N. G., & Shaver, P. R. (1994). The importance of nongenetic influences on romantic love styles: A twin-family study. *Psychological Science, 5,* 268–274.

[11]Losoya, S. H., et al. (1997). Origins of familial similarity in parenting. A study of twins and adoptive siblings. *Developmental Psychology, 33,* 1012–1023.

[12]Plomin, R., et al. (1990). Individual differences in television viewing in early childhood. *Psychological Science, 1,* 371–377; Loehlin, J., & Nichols, R. (1976). *Heredity, environment and personality: A study of 850 sets of twins.* Austin TX: University of Texas Press.

[13]Kendler, K. S., et al. (1993). A twin study of recent life events and difficulties. *Archives of General Psychiatry, 50,* 789–796; Saudino, K. J., et al. (1997). Can personality explain genetic influences on life events? *Journal of Personality and Social Psychology, 72,* 196–206.

[14]Phillips, K., & Matheny, A. P., Jr. (1995). Quantitative analysis of injury liability in infants and toddlers. *American Journal of Medical Genetics, 60,* 64–71.

[15]Dunne, M. P., et al. (1997). Genetic and environmental contributions to variance in age at first sexual intercourse. *Psychological Science, 8,* 211–216.

[16]Bouchard, T. J., Jr. (1996). Genetics and evolution: Implications for personality theories. In J. Newman (Ed.) *Measures of the five factor model and psychological type* (pp. 19–39). Gainsvile, FL: Center for the Application of Psychological Type; Segal, N. L., & MacDonald, K. B. (1998). Behavior genetics and evolutionary psychology: Unified perspective on personality research. *Human Biology, 70,* 157–182.

[17]Benjamin, J., et al. (1996). Population and familial association between the D4 dopamine receptor gene and measures of novelty seeking. *Nature Genetics, 12,* 81–84.

[18]Mittler, P. (1971). *The study of twins.* Harmondsworth, England: Penguin Books.

[19]Rowe, D. C. (1994). *The limits of family influence.* New York: Guilford Press.

[20]Rowe, D. C. (1994).

[21]Buss, D. M. (1995). Evolutionary psychology: A new paradigm for psychological science. *Psychological Inquiry, 6,* 1–30.

[22]Barkow, J. H. (1997). Happiness in evolutionary perspective. In N. L. Segal, et al. (Eds.) (1997) (pp. 397–418).

[23]Nesse, R., & Williams, G. C. (1995). *Why we get sick: The new science of Darwinian medicine.* New York: Times Books.

[24]Bergeman, C. S., et al. (1988). Genotype-environment interaction in personality development: Identical twins reared apart. *Psychology and Aging, 3,* 399–406.

[25]Reiss, D., et al. (1995). Genetic questions for environmental studies: Differential parenting and psychopathology in adolescence. *Archives of General Psychiatry, 52,* 925–936; Pike, C., et al. (1996). Using MZ differences in the search for nonshared environmental effects. *Journal of Child Psychology and Psychiatry, 37,* 695–704; also see Vernon, P. A., et al. (1997). Environmental predictors of personality differences: A twin and sibling study. *Journal of Personality and Social Psychology, 72,* 177–183.

[26]Riese, M. (1990). Neonatal temperament in monozygotic and dizygotic twin pairs. *Child Development, 61,* 1230–1237.

[27]Dr. Kimberly Saudino suggests that greater reliability (repeatability) of recent methods for measuring temperament may have contributed to the observed increase in genetic influence over time.

[28]Lykken, D. T., & Tellegen, A. (1996). Happiness is a stochastic phenomenon. *Psychological Science, 7,* 186–189; also see Lykken, D. T. (1999). *Happiness.* NY: Golden Books.

[29]Lewis, M. (1987). Interview on "What Makes Us Tick? The Biology of Personality." WNET, Newark, NJ, January 28, 1989.

[30]Kagan, J., et al. (1993). The idea of temperament: Where do we go from here? In R. Plomin & G. E. McClearn (Eds.) *Nature, nurture and psychology* (pp. 197–210). Washington, D.C.: American Psychological Association Press.

[31]Lewis, M., & Ramsay, D. S. (1995). Developmental change in infants' responses to stress. *Child Development, 66,* 657–670.

[32]Robinson, J. L., et al. (1992). The heritability of inhibited and uninhabited behavior: A twin study. *Developmental Psychology, 28,* 1020–1037.

[33]Loehlin, J., & Nichols, R. (1976).

[34]Tellegen, A., et al. (1988). Personality similarity in twins reared apart and together. *Journal of Personality and Social Psychology, 54,* 1031–1039.

[35]Lykken, D. T., et al. (1993). Heritability of leisure interests. *Journal of Applied Psychology, 78,* 649–661.

[36]See McGue, M., & Bouchard, T. J., Jr. (1998). Genetic and environmental influences on human behavioral difference. *Annual Review of Neuroscience, 21,* 1–24.

[37]Lykken, D. T. (1995). *The antisocial personalities.* Mahwah, NJ: Erlbaum.

[38]Salzinger, S., et al. (1993). The effects of physical abuse on children's social relationships. *Child Development, 64,* 169–187; Alessandri, S. M., & Lewis, M. (1995). Differences in pride and shame in maltreated and nonmaltreated preschoolers. *Child Development, 67,* 1857–1869.

[39]Shields, J. (1962). Monozygotic twins: Brought up apart and brought up together. London: Oxford University Press.

[40]See Willerman, L. (1979). *The psychology of individual and group differences.* San Francisco: W. H. Freeman & Co.

[41]Kaprio, J., et al. (1990). Change in cohabitation and intrapair similarity of monozygotic (MZ) twins for alcohol use, extraversion, and neuroticism. *Behavior Genetics, 20,* 265–276.

[42]E. Mavis Hetherington, D. Reiss & R. Plomin (Eds.) (1994). *The separate social worlds of siblings.* Hillsdale, NJ: Erlbaum.

[43]See Segal, N. L. (1982). Cooperation, competition, and altruism within twin sets: A reappraisal. *Dissertation Abstracts International, 43–06B,* 2034, and references therein.

[44]McConigle, M. M., et al. (1993). Hostility and nonshared family environment: A study of monozygotic twins. *Journal of Research in Personality, 27,* 23–34.

[45]Sulloway, F. J. (1996). *Born to rebel.* New York: Pantheon Press.

[46]LaLumière, M. L., et al. (1995). Why children from the same family are so different from one another. *Human Nature, 7,* 281–290.

[47]Very, P. S., & Van Hine, N. P. (1969). Effects of birth order upon personality development of twins. *Journal of Genetic Psychology, 114,* 93–95.

[48]Taketoshi, T. (1971). Some Japanese studies on twin research. *Zeitschrift für Experimentelle und Angewandte Psychologie, 18,* 670–677. (Abstract).

[49]Segal, N. L., & MacDonald, K. B. (1998).

[50]Plomin, R., et al. (1976). Resemblance in appearance and the equal environments assumption in twin studies of personality traits. *Behavior Genetics, 6,* 43–52.

[51]Heath, A. C., et al. (1992). Evidence for genetic influences on personality from self-reports and informant ratings. *Journal of Personality and Social Psychology, 63,* 85–96; Angleitner, A., et al. (1995). Cited in Plomin, R., DeFries, J. C., McClearn, G. E., & Rutter, M. (1997). *Behavioral genetics.* 3rd ed. New York: W. H. Freeman & Co.

[52]Freedman, D. G., & Keller, B. (1964). Inheritance of behavior in infants. *Science, 140,* 196–198.

[53]Jockin, V., et al. (1996).

[54]Trumbetta, S. L., & Gottesman, I. I. (1997). Pair-bonding deconstructed by twin studies of marital status: What is normative? In N. L. Segal, et al. (Eds.) (1997) (pp. 485–491).

[55]Waller, N. G., et al. (1990).

[56]Saudino, K. J., et al. (1997).

[57]Phillips, K., & Matheny, A. P., Jr. (1995).

[58]Hur, Y. H., & Bouchard, T. J., Jr. (1997). The genetic correlation between impulsivity and sensation seeking traits. *Behavior Genetics, 27,* 455–463. Genetic influence was found for disinhibition, boredom susceptibility, and experience seeking, but not for thrill and adventure seeking.

[59]Dunne, M. P., et al. (1997).

[60]Kallman, F. J. (1952). Twin and sibship study of overt male homosexuality. *American Journal of Human Genetics, 4,* 136–146.

[61]Shields, J. (1962).

[62]Juel-Nielsen, N. (1966). Individual and environment: A psychiatric-psychological investigation of monozygotic twins reared apart. *Psychiatrica et Neurologica Scandinavica, Monograph Supplement 183.* Kaj did not believe his twin had homosexual leanings.

[63]Segal, N. L., et al. (1990). A summary of psychiatric and psychological findings from the Minnesota Study of Twins Reared Apart. Proceedings from the *World Psychiatric Association Regional Symposium: Etiology of Mental Disorder,* August 23–26, 1990, Oslo, Norway, 183–200.

[64]Bailey, J. M., & Pillard, R. C. (1991). A genetic study of male sexual orientation. *Archives of General Psychiatry, 48,* 1089–1096; Bailey, J. M., et al. (1993). Heritable factors influence sexual orientation in women. *Archives of General Psychiatry, 50,* 217–223.

[65]Bailey, J. M., & Pillard, R. C. (1991).

[66]Bailey, J. M., et al. (1993).

[67]Bailey, J. M., et al. (submitted). Sex differences in the distribution and determinants of sexual orientation in a national twin sample.

[68]Hershberger, S. L. (1997). A case study of the cognitive profiles of a set of male monozygotic triplets discordant for sexual orientation. *Behavior Genetics Association,* July 10–13, 1997, Toronto, Canada.

[69]Bailey, J. M., & Pillard, R. C. (1991); Bailey, J. M., et al. (1993).

[70]LeVay, S. (1991). A difference in hypothalamic structure between heterosexual and homosexual men. *Science, 253,* 1034–1037.

[71]Hamer, D., et al. (1993). A linkage between DNA markers on the X chromosome and male sexual orientation. *Science, 261,* 321–327; Hu, S., et al. (1995). Linkage between sexual orientation and chromosome Xq28 in males but not in females. *Nature Genetics, 11,* 248–256; also see Sanders, A. R., et al. (1998). Genetic linkage study of male homosexuality. *American Psychiatric Association,* May 30–June 4, 1998, Toronto, Canada.

[72]See Byne, W., & Parsons, B. (1993). Human sexual orientation: The biologic theories reappraised. *Archives of General Psychiatry, 50,* 228–239, and Blanchard, R., et al. (1995). Birth order and sibling sex ratio in homosexual male adolescents and probably prehomosexual feminine boys. *Developmental Psychology, 31,* 22–30.

[73]Bem, D. J. (1996). Exotic becomes erotic: A developmental theory of sexual orientation. *Psychological Review,* 103, 320–335.

[74]Blanchard, R., et al. (1995).

[75]Waller, N. G., & Shaver, P. R. (1994).

[76]*Nightline,* ABC. October 2, 1989.

[77]Rowe, D. C. (1994).

[78]Rosenthal, D. (Ed.) (1963). *The Genain quadruplets.* New York: Basic Books; DeLisi, L. E., et al. (1984). The Genain quadruplets 25 years later: A diagnostic and biochemical followup. *Psychiatry Research, 13,* 59–76.

[79]Dr. David Rosenthal was affected with Alzheimer's Disease and passed away in 1996.

[80]Gottesman, I. I. (1991). *Schizophrenia genesis.* New York: W. H. Freeman & Co.

[81]Bertelsen, A., et al. (1977). A Danish twin study of manic-depressive disorders. *British Journal of Psychiatry, 130,* 330–351; Kendler, K. S., et al. (1993). A pilot Swedish twin study of affective illness, including hospital- and population-ascertained subsamples. *Archives of General Psychiatry, 50,* 699–706. Findings were based on strict diagnostic criteria.

[82]Relatives of patients with unipolar depression are not at increased risk for bipolar depression; relatives of patients with bipolar depression are at increased risk for unipolar depression.

[83]Fromm-Reichman, F. (1948). Notes on the development of treatment of schizophrenics by psychoanalytic therapy. *Psychiatry, 11,* 263–273.

[84]Gottesman, I. I., and Bertelsen, A. (1989). Confirming unexpressed genotypes for schizophrenia. *Archives of General Psychiatry, 46,* 867–872. The mental health of the twins' spouses did not affect the findings; Gottesman, I. I. (Personal communication, 1995).

[85]Torrey, E. F., Bowler, A. E., Taylor, E. H., & Gottesman, I. I. (1994). *Schizophrenia and manic-depressive disorder: The biological roots of mental illness as revealed by the landmark study of identical twins.* New York: Basic Books.

[86]Myra showed the least pathology during hospitalization, and Hester showed the most. Nora and Iris alternated between second and third positions, but Iris ranked third more often.

[87]Holzman, P. S., et al. (1988). A single dominant gene can account for eye tracking dysfunction and schizophrenia in offspring of discordant twins. *Archives of General Psychiatry, 45,* 641–647.

[88]See Gottesman, I. I. (1991). *Schizophrenia genesis.* New York: W. H. Freeman & Co.; Torrey, E. F., et al. (1994); also see commentary by Holzman, P. S., et al. (1997). Smooth pursuit eye tracking in twins. *Archives of General Psychiatry, 54,* 429–431.

[89]A 1996 Danish study showed a 28% higher rate of first hospital admissions for schizophrenia among twins than singletons. However, findings were based on a small twin sample and applied to females only; see Kläning, O., et al. (1996). Increased occurrence of schizophrenia and other psychiatric illnesses among twins. *British Journal of Psychiatry, 168,* 688–692.

[90]Holm, N. V. (Personal communication, June 17, 1998).

[91]Reveley, A., et al. (1981). Mortality and psychosis in twins. In L. Gedda, et al. (Eds.) *Twin research 3B: Intelligence, personality, and development* (pp. 175–178). New York: Alan R. Liss, Inc.

[92]Segal, N. L., et al. (1990). Tourette disorder in reared apart triplets: Genetic and environmental influences. *American Journal of Psychiatry, 147,* 196–199.

[93]*Diagnostic and statistical manual of mental disorders* (1994). 4th ed. Washington, D.C.: American Psychiatric Press.

[94]Price, R. A., et al. (1985). A twin study of Tourette Syndrome. *Archives of General Psychiatry, 42,* 815–820.

[95]Le Couteur, A., et al. (1996). A broader phenotype of autism: The clinical spectrum in twins. *Journal of Child Psychology and Psychiatry, 37,* 785–801.

[96]Singer, H. S., et al. (1998). Brain antibodies provide new clues to origins of Tourette's. *Neurology, 50,* 1618–1624.

[97]Roy, A. (1986). Suicide in twins. *American Journal of Psychiatry, 143,* 557.

[98]United States Bureau of the Census (1991). *Statistical abstract of the United States: 1991.* Washington, D.C.: U.S. Government Printing Office.

[99]Roy, A., et al. (1991). Suicide in twins. *Archives of General Psychiatry, 48,* 29–32.

[100]Roy, A., et al. (1995). Attempted suicide among living co-twins of twin suicide victims. *American Journal of Psychiatry, 152,* 1075–1076.

[101]Statham, D. S., et al. (1998). Suicidal behavior: An epidemiological and genetic study. *Psychological Medicine, 28,* 839–855.

[102]Segal, N. L., & Roy, A. (1995). Suicide attempts in twins whose co-twins' deaths were non-suicides. *Personality and Individual Differences, 19,* 937–940.

[103]Kety, S. (1986). Genetic factors in suicide. In A. Roy (Ed.) *Suicide* (pp. 41–45). Baltimore, MD: Williams & Wilkins.

[104]Roy, A., et al. (1997). Genetic studies of suicidal behavior. *Psychiatric Clinics of North America, 20,* 595–611.

[105]"Mike Bell of Chiefs Is Arrested." *New York Times,* November 21, 1985; "Bell Brothers in Jail." *New York Times,* August 12, 1986.

[106]Schreiner, B. "Twin Brothers Caught Swapping Roles at Nebraska Penitentiary." *Minneapolis Star & Tribune,* October 5, 1984.

[107]Diaz, K. "Identical Identities Cause Court Confusion." *Minneapolis Star & Tribune,* December 1, 1984.

[108]Bray, D. "Brother's Keeper." *Los Angeles Times,* January 7, 1994.

[109]Noah, P. "Trial Ordered for Twin Accused of Murder Plot." *Los Angeles Times,* April 9, 1997; Hernandez, G. "Identical Stories." *Los Angeles Times Magazine,* July 12, 1998, pp. 20–21, 40–44.

[110]Gottesman, I. I., et al. (1997). A developmental *and* a genetic perspective on aggression. In N. L. Segal, et al. (Eds.) (1997). (pp. 107–130).

[111]Cloninger, C. R., & Gottesman, I. I. (1987). Genetic and environmental factors in antisocial behavior disorders. In S. A. Mednick, T. E. Moffit, & S. A. Stack (Eds.) *The causes of crime: New biological approaches* (pp. 92–109). Cambridge: Cambridge University Press.

[112]Rowe, D. C. (1983). Biometrical genetic models of self-reported delinquent behavior. *Behavior Genetics, 13,* 473–489. Gottesman et al. (1997) point out that Rowe gathered self-report data on delinquent acts, whereas other studies identified delinquent twins.

[113]See Segal, N. L. (1995). Pathways to sociopathy: Twin analyses offer direction. *Behavioral and Brain Sciences, 18,* 574–575.

[114]Mapes, D., & Bonapace, R. "I Became a Wife and Mother . . . She Became a Killer." *Woman's World,* 41, 19.

[115]Brunner, H. G., et al. (1993). Abnormal behavior associated with a point mutation in the structural gene for monoamine oxidase A. *Science, 262,* 578–580.

[116]Hamer, D. (1997). The search for personality genes. *Current Directions in Psychological Science, 4,* 111–114.

[117]van den Ord, E. J. C. G., et al. (1996). A genetic study of maternal and paternal ratings of problem behaviors in 3-year-old twins. *Journal of Abnormal Psychology, 105,* 349–357; Edelbrock, C. et al. (1995). A twin study of competence and problem behavior in childhood and early adolescence. *Journal of Child Psychology and Psychiatry, 36,* 775–785.

[118]*Diagnostic and statistical manual of mental disorders.* 4th ed. (1994).

[119]Slutske, W., et al. (1997). Modeling genetic and environmental influences in the etiology of conduct disorder: A study of 2,682 adult twin pairs. *Journal of Abnormal Psychology, 106,* 266–279.

[120]Lyons, M., et al. (1995). Differential heritability of adult and juvenile antisocial traits. *Archives of General Psychiatry, 52,* 906–915.

[121]Carvajal, D. "Records as Long as 7–Year-Old Arm." *New York Times,* March 9, 1996.

[122]Rowe, D. C., & Rodgers, J. L. (1989). Behavioral genetics, adolescent deviance, and "d": Contributions and issues. In G. R. Adams, R. Montenayor, & A. Gullotta (Eds.) *Biology of adolescent behavior and development* (pp. 38–67). Newbury Park, CA: Sage.

[123]Jarvik, L. F., & Deckard, B. S. (1977). The Odyssean personality: A survival advantage for carriers of genes predisposing to schizophrenia? *Neuropsychobiology, 3,* 179–191.

[124]Holden, C. (1997). A gene is linked to autism. *Science, 276,* 905.

[125]Freedman, D. G. (1979). *Human sociobiology: A holistic approach.* New York: Free Press; Baron-Cohen, S., et al. (1997). Is there a link between engineering and autism? *Autism, 1,* 101–109.

[126]Feierman, J. R. (1994). A testable hypothesis about schizophrenia generated by evolutionary theory. *Ethology and Sociobiology, 15,* 263–282.

[127]Marks, I. M., & Neese, R. (1994). Fear and fitness: An evolutionary analysis of anxiety disorders. *Ethology and Sociobiology, 15,* 247–261.

[128]Mealey, L. (1995). The sociobiology of sociopathy: An integrated evolutionary model. *Behavioral and Brain Sciences, 18,* 523–541; also see commentaries.

[129]Sherman, D. K. et al. (1997). Twin concordance for attention deficit hyperactivity dis-

order: A comparison of teachers' and mothers' reports. *American Journal of Psychiatry, 154,* 532–535.

[130]Berrettini, W. (1998). Genetic aspects of anorexia nervosa and bulimia nervosa. *Directions in Psychiatry, 17,* 53–57. This paper indicated a 50% concordance rate for identical twins, but this was an unweighted average. I recalculated the value to consider the number of twin pairs in the separate studies reviewed.

[131]Kendler, K. S., et al. (1991). The genetic epidemiology of bulimia nervosa. *American Journal of Psychiatry, 148,* 1627–1637.

[132]Berkovic, S. F., et al. (1998). Epilepsies in twins: Genetics of the major epilepsy syndromes. *Annals of Neurology, 43,* 435–445.

[133]Heath, A. C., et al. (1997). Genetic and environmental contributions to alcohol dependence risk in a national sample: Consistency of findings in women and men. *Psychological Medicine, 27,* 1381–1396.

[134]Swan, G. E., et al. (1997). Heavy consumption of cigarettes, alcohol and coffee in male twins. *Journal of Studies on Alcohol, 58,* 182–190.

[135]Kendler, K. S., et al. (1993). Panic disorder in women: A population-based twin study. *Psychological Medicine, 23,* 397–406.

[136]Gatz, M., et al. (1997). Heritability for Alzheimer's disease: The study of Swedish twins. *Journal of Gerontology, 52A,* M117–M125.

[137]Treolar, A. S., et al. (1998). Longitudinal genetic analysis of menstrual flow, pain, and limitation in a sample of Australian twins. *Behavior Genetics, 28,* 107–116. The medical name for Premenstrual Syndrome is Premenstrual Dysphoric Disorder; see *Diagnostic and statistical manual of mental disorders.* (1994); also see Dalton, K., et al. (1987). Incidence of the premenstrual syndrome in twins. *British Medical Journal, 295,* 1027–1028; Condon, J. T. (1993). The premenstrual syndrome: A twin study. *British Journal of Psychiatry, 162,* 481–486.

[138]Smalley, S. L., et al. (1988). Autism and genetics: A decade of research. Archives of General Psychiatry, 45, 953–961.

[139]Gillberg, C. (1983). Identical triplets with infantile autism and the fragile-X syndrome. *British Journal of Psychiatry, 143,* 256–260; Wing, L. (1981). Asperger's syndrome: A clinical account. *Psychological Medicine, 11,* 115–129.

[140]Holden, C. (1997). A gene is linked to autism. *Science, 276,* 905.

CHAPTER 6

[1]Darwin, C. (1859). *On the origin of species by means of natural selection, or preservation of favoured races in the struggle for life.* London: Murray.

[2]Trivers, R. L. (1985). *Social evolution.* Menlo Park, CA: Benjamin/Cummings Publishing Co.

[3]Hamilton, W. D. (1964). The genetical evolution of human behaviour. *Journal of Theoretical Biology, 7,* 1–16; 17–52.

[4]Dawkins, R. (1989). *The selfish gene.* 2nd ed. Oxford: Oxford University Press.

[5]Barkow, J. H. (1989) *Darwin, sex and status: Biological approaches to mind and culture.* Toronto: University of Toronto Press.

[6]Rushton, J. P., et al. (1986). Altruism and aggression: The heritability of individual differences. *Journal of Personality and Social Psychology, 50,* 1192–1198; Zahn-Waxler, C., et al. (1992). The development of empathy in twins. *Developmental Psychology, 28,* 1038–1047; Pérusse, D., et al. (1994). Human parental behavior: Evidence for genetic influence and potential implication for gene-culture transmission. *Behavior Genetics, 24,* 327–335; Losoya, S. H., et al. (1997). The origins of family similarity in parenting: A study of twins and adoptive siblings. *Developmental Psychology, 33,* 1012–1023.

[7]Fraternal twins or siblings can theoretically share 0–100% of their genetic makeup, but a more realistic range is 25–75%; see Pakstis, A., et al. (1972). Genetic contributions to morphological and behavioral similarities among sibs and dizygotic twins: Linkages and allelic differences. *Social Biology, 19,* 185–192.

[8]Pinker, S. (1997). *How the minds works.* New York: W. W. Norton & Co.

[9]Dawkins, R. (1989).

[10]Barash, D. P. (1979). *The whisperings within.* New York: Harper and Row.

[11]Cimons, M. "Families Make Adoption Their First Option." *Los Angeles Times,* February 14, 1998.

[12]Segal, N. L., Weisfeld, G. E., & Weisfeld, C. C. (1997). Pursuing the big picture. In N. L. Segal, G. E. Weisfeld, & C. C. Weisfeld (Eds.) (1997). *Uniting psychology and biology: Integrative perspectives on human development* (pp. 3–18). Washington, D.C.: American Psychological Association Press.

[13]Burlingham, D. (1945). The fantasy of having a twin. *Psychoanalytic Study of the Child, 1.* 205–210.

[14]Paluszny, M., et al. (1977). Twin relationships and depression. *American Journal of Psychiatry, 134,* 988–990; Mowrer, E. (1954). Some factors in the affectional adjustment of twins. *American Sociological Review, 19,* 468–471.

[15]Loehlin, J., & Nichols, R. (1976). *Heredity, environment and personality: A study of 850 sets of twins.* University of Texas Press, Austin.

[16]Freedman, D. G. (1979). *Human sociobiology: A holistic approach.* New York: Free Press.

[17]McClintock, M. K. (1971). Menstrual synchrony and suppression. *Nature, 260,* 244–245. Some subsequent studies by other investigators have not confirmed this finding.

[18]van den Akker, et al. (1987). Genetic and environmental variation in menstrual cycle: Histories of two British samples. *Acta Geneticae Medicae et Gemellologiae, 36,* 541–548; Sneider, H., et al. (1998). Genes control the cessation of a woman's reproductive life: A twin study of hysterectomy and age at menopause. *Journal of Clinical Endocrinology and Metabolism, 83,* 1875–1880.

[19]Segal, N. L. (1988). Cooperation, competition and altruism in human twinships. A sociobiological approach. In K. B. MacDonald (Ed.) *Sociobiological perspectives on human development* (pp. 168–206). New York: Springer-Verlag.

[20]Loehlin, J., & Nichols, R. (1976); Hettema, J. M., et al. (1995). Physical similarity and the equal-environment assumption in twin studies of psychiatric disorders. *Behavior Genetics, 25,* 327–335.

[21]Loehlin, J., & Nichols, R. (1976).

[22]Freedman, D. G. (1979); Freedman, D. G. (1997). Is nonduality possible in the social and behavioral sciences? Small essays on holism and related issues. In N. L. Segal, et al. (Eds.) (pp 47–80).

[23]Lee, A. "The Emperor of Dreams." *The New Yorker Magazine,* July 28, 1997, pp. 42–53.

[24]Bonhall, B. "Her Work Has Her Seeing Double." *Los Angeles Times,* May 4, 1997.

[25]von Bracken, H. (1934). Mutual intimacy in twins. *Character and Personality, 2,* 293–309.

[26]Scott, J. P. (1977). Social genetics. *Behavior Genetics, 7,* 327–346.

[27]Segal, N. L. (1988); Segal, N. I. (1997).

[28]Segal, N. L. (1984). Cooperation, competition and altruism within twin sets: A reappraisal. *Ethology and Sociobiology, 5,* 163–177; Segal, N. L. (1988).

[29]Segal, N. L., & Hershberger, S. L. (in press). Cooperation and competition in adolescent twins: Findings from a Prisoner's Dilemma game. *Evolution and Human Behavior.*

[30]See Axelrod, R., & Hamilton, W. D. (1981). The evolution of cooperation. *Science, 211,* 1390–1396.

[31]Daniel G. Freedman used this phrase in discussions of human individual differences.

[32]Argyle, M. (1991). *Cooperation: The basis of sociability.* London: Routledge.

[33]The quote is from Alan and Alvan Chow, identical concert pianists. Abbe, K. M., & Gill, F. M. (1980). *Twins on twins.* New York: Clarkson N. Potter, Inc.

[34]Goldstein, P. "They All Have A Secret." *Los Angeles Times Calendar,* March 15, 1998.

[35]Segal, N. L. (1988); Segal, N. L. (1997).

[36]Rowe, D. C., et al. (1994). Peers and friends as nonshared environmental influences. In E. M., Hetherington D., Reiss. & R. Plomin (Eds.) *Separate social worlds of siblings* (pp. 159–173). Hillsdale, NJ: Erlbaum.

[37]Freedman, D. G. (1979).

[38]Lykken, D. T., et al. (1992). Emergenesis: Genetic traits that may not run in families. *American Psychologist, 47,* 1565–1577.

[39]Examples of emergenic traits are positive emotionality (having an upbeat outlook on life), and self-rated artistic talent (how you view your own ability in the creative arts compared with others).

[40]Scarr-Salapatek, S. (1975). Commentary I. In K. W. Schaie, V. E. Anderson, G. E. Mc-Clearn, & J. Money (Eds.) *Developmental human behavior genetics* (pp. 77–83). Lexington, MA: Lexington.

[41]Segal, N. L. (1993). Twin, sibling and adoption methods: Tests of evolutionary hypotheses. *American Psychologist, 48,* 943–956. Twin-family designs have been used to study intelligence, mental disorder and physical development; see Rose, R. J., et al. (1979). Genetic variance in nonverbal intelligence. *Science, 205,* 1153–1155; Gottesman, I. I., and Bertelsen, A. (1989). Confirming unexpressed genotypes for schizophrenia. *Archives of General Psychiatry, 46,* 867–872; Magnus, P. (1984). Causes of variation in birth weight: A study of offspring of twins. *Clinical Genetics, 25,* 15–24.

[42]Leek, M., & Smith, P. K. (1989). Phenotypic matching, human altruism, and mate preference. *Behavioral and Brain Sciences, 12,* 534–535; Leek, M., & Smith, P. K. (1991). Cooperation and conflict in three-generation families. In P. K. Smith (Ed.) *The psychology of grandparenthood: An international perspective* (pp. 177–194). London: Routledge.

[43]Daly, M., & Wilson, M. (1987). Evolutionary psychology and family violence. In C. Crawford, M. Smith, & D. Krebs (Eds.) *Sociobiology and psychology: Ideas, issues and applications* (pp. 293–309). Hillsdale, NJ: Erlbaum.

[44]Sorosky, A. D., et al. (1978.) *The adoption triangle.* Garden City, NY: Doubleday; Merker, P. The realities of adopting twins. *Twins Magazine, 2,* November/December, 1985, pp. 32–33, 52–55.

[45]Chen, E. "Twins Reared Apart: A Living Laboratory." *New York Times Magazine,* December 9, 1979, pp. 112–124.

[46]Serock, E. "Brother Firefighters Meet Their Match." *Firehouse.* April, 1986, pp. 80–81.

[47]Gonyo, B. (1987). "Genetic Sexual Attraction." *American Adoption Congress "Decree," 4,* 1, 5.

[48]The chromosomes of each individual carry, on average, two sites with lethal recessive genes; see Wilson, E. O. (1998). *Consilience: The unity of knowledge.* New York: Knopf.

[49]Shepher, J. (1983). *Incest: A biosocial view.* New York: Academic Press.

[50]Wolf, A. P. (1995). *Sexual attraction and childhood association: A Chinese brief for Edward Westermarck.* Stanford, CA: Stanford University Press.

[51]Thornhill, N. W., & Thornhill, R. (1987). Evolutionary theory and rules of mating and marriage pertaining to relatives. In C. Crawford, M. Smith, & D. Krebs (Eds.) *Sociobiology and psychology: Ideas, issues and applications* (pp. 373–400). Hillsdale, NJ: Erlbaum.

[52]Wilson, E. O. (1998).

[53]Amery, D. "Couple Wed 20 Years Discover They're Twins." *Sun,* December 17, 1985.

[54]McMillan, T. "Newlyweds Learn They Are Brother and Sister." *Weekly World News,* February 4, 1986.

[55]Beasley, M. "After 30 Years of Marriage, Couple Discover They're Brother and Sister." *Sun,* May 1, 1990.

CHAPTER 7

[1]Information in this chapter was available in public sources, or was provided to me by the reared apart twins and included with their permission. Some names have been disguised to preserve confidentiality.

[2]Lackey, M. "Identical Twins, Separated as Babies in 1939, Reunited." *Lima News.* February 19, 1979; Clark, M. "Double Take." *Newsweek.* March 12, 1979.

[3]Newman, H. H., Freeman, F. N., & Holzinger, K. J. (1937). *Twins: A study of heredity and environment.* Chicago: University of Chicago Press; Shields, J. (1962). *Monozygotic twins: Brought up apart and brought up together.* London: Oxford University Press: Juel-Nielsen, N. (1966). *Individual and environment: Monozygotic twins reared apart.* New York: International Universities Press.

[4]Mischel, M. (1981). *Introduction to personality.* 3rd ed. New York: Holt, Rinehart & Winston.

[5]A Tale of Twin Brothers" (Letters to the Editor). *New York Times Magazine,* January 20, 1980; p. 78; Bazell, R. "Sins and Society." *New Republic,* December 21, 1987, pp. 17–18.

[6]*Nightline,* ABC. October 2, 1989.

[7]Begley, S., & Kasindorf, M. "Twins: Nazi and Jew." *Newsweek,* December 3, 1979.

[8]*Oskar and Jack.* Lichtfilm, Wolfgang Bergmann, 1995.

[9]Bouchard, T. J., Jr., et al. (1986). Development in twins reared apart: A test of the chronogenetic hypothesis. In A. Demirjian (Ed.) *Human growth: A multidisciplinary review* (pp. 299–310). London: Taylor & Francis, Ltd.

[10]Langinvainio, H., et al. (1984). Finnish twins reared apart I: Validation of zygosity, environmental dissimilarity, and weight and height. *Fourth International Congress on Twin Studies,* June 28–July 1, 1983, London, England; Pedersen, N. L., et al. (1985). Separated fraternal twins: Resemblance for cognitive abilities. *Behavior Genetics, 15,* 407–419; Pedersen, N. L., et al. (1991). The Swedish Adoption Twin Study of Aging: An update. *Acta Geneticae Medicae et Gemellologiae, 40,* 7–20; Hayakawa, K. & Shimizu, T. (1987). Blood pressure discordance and lifestyle: Japanese identical twins reared apart and together. *Acta Geneticae Medicae et Gemellologiae, 36,* 485–491.

[11]Bouchard, T. J., Jr., et al. (1990a). Sources of human psychological differences: The Minnesota Study of Twins Reared Apart. *Science, 250,* 223–228; Bouchard, T. J., Jr. (1997). IQ similarity in twins reared apart. Findings and responses to critics (pp. 126–160). In R. J. Sternberg, & E. L. Grigorenko (Eds.) *Intelligence, heredity and environment.* New York: Cambridge University Press.

[12]Tellegen, A., et al. (1988). Personality similarity in twins reared apart and together. *Journal of Personality and Social Psychology, 54,* 1031–1039; Bouchard, T. J., Jr., et al. (1996). Genes, drives, environment, and experience. In C. P. Benbow, & D. Lubinski (Eds.) *Intellectual talent: Psychometrics and social issues* (pp. 5–43). Baltimore: Johns Hopkins University Press.

[13]Loehlin, J. C., et al. (1994). Differential inheritance of mental abilities in the Texas Adoption Project. *Intelligence, 19,* 325–336.

[14]Leary, L. "Portland Man Part of Longest-Separated Twins." *Senior Spectrum,* April 1992.

[15]Committee Finds Rambam Babies Were Switched." *Jerusalem Post,* August 15, 1978.

[16]*Prime Time Live,* ABC. April 7, 1994.

[17]Associated Press. "Surrogate Mom Has Twins; Girl Taken, Boy Rejected." *Minneapolis Star & Tribune,* April 23, 1988.

[18]Bonner, R. "Tales of Stolen Babies and Lost Identities." *New York Times,* April 13, 1996.

[19]Bryan, E. M. (1983). *The nature and nurture of twins.* London: Ballière-Tindall.

[20]Steadman, L. (Personal communication, June 5, 1997).

[21]Lohr, S. "Creating Jobs." *New York Times Magazine,* January 12, 1997, pp. 14–19.

[22]Jerome, R., et al. "The Blood Knot." *People Magazine,* December 12, 1994, pp. 73–74.

[23]Noonan, K. M. (1987). Evolution: A primer for psychologists. In C. Crawford, M. Smith, & D. Krebs (Eds.) *Sociobiology and psychology: Ideas, issues and applications* (pp. 31–60). Hillsdale, NJ: Erlbaum. Group living also has disadvantages, such as increased competition for resources.

[24]Botham, N. "Chance in a Million. Identical Twins, 64, Meet for 1st Time—By Accident." *National Enquirer.* April 9, 1985; *Body Watch,* WGBH. Boston, MA, January 31, 1987.

[25]"Separated at Birth, 19-year-old Triplets Reunited." *The Record,* September 24, 1980.

[26]Saul, S. "In the Name of Research." *Newsday, 58.* October 12, 1997, pp. A5, A48.

[27]Abrams, S. (1986). Disposition and the environment. In P. B. Neubauer & A. J. Solnit (Eds.) *Psychoanalytic study of the child, 41* (pp. 41–60). New Haven: Yale University Press; Neubauer, P. B., & Neubauer, A. (1990). *Nature's thumbprint.* Reading, MA: Addison-Wesley.

[28]Lykken, D. T., et al. (1990). Recruitment bias in twin research: The rule of two-thirds reconsidered. *Behavior Genetics, 17,* 343–362.

[29]"After 25 Years, Sisters Are Reunited." *Picture Week,* November 25, 1985.

[30]Addams, C. (1981). "Separated at Birth, the Mallifert Twins Meet Accidentally." In *Creature Comforts.* NY: Simon & Schuster; © 1981, The New Yorker Magazine, Inc.

[31]Plomin, R., DeFries, J. C., McClearn, G. E., & Rutter, M. (1997). *Behavioral genetics.* 3rd ed. New York: W. H. Freeman & Co.

[32]Lykken, D. T., & Tellegen, A. (1993). Is human mating adventitious or the result of lawful choice? A twin study of mate selection. *Journal of Personality and Social Psychology, 65,* 56–68.

[33]Bouchard, T. J., Jr., et al. (1990b). Genetic and environmental influences on special mental abilities in a sample of twins reared apart. *Acta Medicae Geneticae et Gemellologiae, 39,* 193–206.

[34]Bouchard, T. J., Jr. (1984). Twins reared together and apart: What they tell us about human diversity. In S. W. Fox (Ed.) *Individuality and determinism* (pp. 147–184). New York: Plenum; Waller, N. G., et al. (1990). Genetic and environmental influences on religious interests, attitudes, and values. A study of twins reared apart and together. *Psychological Science, 1,* 138–142; Betsworth, D. G., et al. (1994). Genetic and environmental influences on vocational interests assessed using adoptive and biological families and twins reared apart and together. *Journal of Vocational Behavior, 44,* 263–278; Hur, Y. H., & Bouchard, T. J., Jr. (1995). Genetic influences on perceptions of childhood family environment: A reared apart twin study. *Child Development, 66,* 330–345.

[35]Segal, N. L., et al. (1991). Psychiatric investigations and findings from the Minnesota Study of Twins Reared Apart. In M. Tsuang, K. Kendler, & M. Lyons (Eds.) *Genetic issues in psychosocial epidemiology, Vol. 8.* (pp. 247–266). New Brunswick: Rutgers University Press.

[36]Hanson, B., et al. (1989). Genetic factors in the electrocardiogram and heart rate of twins reared apart and together. *American Journal of Cardiology, 63,* 606–609.

[37]Stassen, H. H., et al. (1988). Genetic determination of the human EEG. *Human Genetics, 80,* 165–176; Lykken, D. T., et al. (1988). Habituation of the skin conductance response to strong stimuli: A twin study. *Psychophysiology, 25,* 4–15; Lykken, D. T., et al. (1992). Emergenesis: Genetic traits that may not run in families. *American Psychologist, 47,* 1565–1577; Bouchard, T. J., Jr. (1996). Behaviour genetic studies of intelligence, yesterday and today: The long journey from plausibility to proof. *Journal of Biosocial Science, 28,* 527–555.

[38]Grove, W. M., et al. (1990). Heritability of substance abuse and antisocial behavior: A study of monozygotic twins reared apart. *Biological Psychiatry, 27,* 1293–1304.

[39]Heath, A. C. (1995). Genetic influence on alcoholism risk. *Alcohol Health and Research World, 19,* 166–171.

[40]DiLalla, D., et al. (1996). Heritability of MMPI personality indicators of psychopathology in twins reared apart. *Journal of Abnormal Psychology, 105,* 491–499.

[41]Bouchard, T. J., Jr., et al. (1990a).

[42]Segal, N. L., & Russell, J. (1991). IQ similarity in monozygotic and dizygotic twin children: Effects of the same versus separate examiners: A research note. *Journal of Child Psychology and Psychiatry, 32,* 703–708.

[43]McGue, M., & Bouchard, T. J., Jr. (1998). Genetic and environmental influences on human behavioral differences. *Annual Review of Neuroscience, 21,* 1–24.

[44]Plomin, R., et al. (1997).

[45]Bouchard, T. J., Jr. (1998). Genetic and environmental influences on adult intelligence and special mental abilitities. *Human Biology, 70,* 253–275.

[46]Hearnshaw, L. S. (1979). *Cyril Burt, psychologist.* London: Hodder & Stoughton.

[47]Joynson, R. B. (1989). *The Burt affair.* London: Routledge; Fletcher, R. (1991). *Science, ideology and the media: The Cyril Burt scandal.* New Brunswick, NJ: Transaction Books.

[48]See N. K. MacKintosh (Ed.) (1995). *Cyril Burt: Fraud or framed.* Oxford, England: Oxford University Press; Samelson, F. (1996) *Contemporary Psychology, 41,* 1177–1179; Horowitz, I., et al. (1997). *Contemporary Psychology, 42,* 655–656.

[49]Bouchard, T. J., Jr., et al. (1990a).

[50]Denis, M., & Barnes, M. A. (1994). Neuropsychological function in same-sex twins discordant for perinatal brain damage. *Developmental and Behavioral Pediatrics, 15,* 124–130; Hoffman, L. W. (1991). The influence of the family environment on personality: Accounting for sibling differences. *Psychological Bulletin, 110,* 187–203.

[51]Farber, S. L. (1981). *Identical twins reared apart: A reanalysis.* New York: Basic Books.

[52]Taylor, H. F. (1980). *The IQ game: A methodological inquiry into the heredity environment controversy.* New Brunswick, NJ: Rutgers University Press.

[53]Bouchard, T. J., Jr. (1983). Do environmental similarities explain the similarity in intelligence of identical twins reared apart? *Intelligence, 7,* 175–184; also see Bouchard, T. J., Jr. (1997).

[54]Eckert, E. D., et al. (1986). Homosexuality in twins reared apart. *British Journal of Psychiatry, 148,* 421–425; Segal, N. L., et al. (1991).

[55]Hanson, B. R., et al. (1984). Rhythmometry reveals heritability of circadian characteristics of heart rate of human twins reared apart. *Italian Journal of Cardiology, 29,* 267– 282.

[56]Hanson, B., et al. (1991). Atopic disease and immunoglobulin E in twins reared apart and together. *American Journal of Human Genetics, 48,* 873–879.

[57]Hopp, R. J., et al. (1984). Genetic analysis of allergic disease in twins. *Journal of Allergy and Clinical Immunology, 73,* 265–270.

[58]Eckert, E. D., et al. (1981). MZ twins reared apart: Preliminary findings of psychiatric disturbances and traits. In L. Gedda, et al. (Eds.) *Twin research 3B: Intelligence, personality, and development (pp. 179–188).* New York: Alan R. Liss, Inc.

[59]Farber, S. L. (1981).

[60]Boraas, J. C., et al. (1988). A genetic contribution to dental caries, occlusion, and morphology as demonstrated by twins reared apart. *Journal of Dental Research, 67,* 1150–1155; Conry, J. P., et al. (1993). Dental caries and treatment characteristics in human twins reared apart. *Archives of Oral Biology, 38,* 937–943.

[61]Michalowicz, B. S., et al. (1991). Periodontal findings in adult twins. *Journal of Periodontology, 62,* 293–299; Michalowicz, B. S., et al. (1991). A twin study of genetic variation in proportional radiographic alveolar bone height. *Journal of Dental Research, 70,* 1431–1435.

[62]Farber, S. L. (1981).

[63]Knobloch, W. H., et al. (1985). *Ophthalmic Paediatrics and Genetics, 5,* 89–96.

[64]Meyers, S. M., & Zachary, A. A. (1988). Monozygotic twins with age-related macular degeneration. *Archives of Opthalmology, 106,* 651–653; *American Journal of Opthalmology, 125,* 353–359.

[65]Koch, H. (1966). *Twins and twin relations.* Chicago: University of Chicago Press; also see Miller, E. M. (1995). Reported myopia in opposite-sex twins: A hormonal hypothesis. *Optometry and Vision Science, 72,* 34–36.

[66]Good, W. V., et al. (1996). Cortical visual impairment by twin pregnancy. *American Journal of Ophthalmology, 122,* 709–716.

[67]Nance, W. E., et al. (1982). Distribution of common eye diseases in the families of Norwegian twins. *Birth Defects,* 18, 669–678; Lin, L. L. -K., & Chen, C. J. (1987). Twin study of myopia. *Acta Geneticae Medicae et Gemellologiae, 36,* 535–540; Teikari, J., et al. (1990). Study of gene-environment effects of development of hyperopia: A study of 191 adult twin pairs from the Finnish twin cohort study. Acta Geneticae Medicae et-Gemellologiae, 39, 133–136.

[68]Fox, P. W., et al. (1996). Genetic and environmental contributions to the acquisition of a motor skill. *Nature, 384,* 356–358.

[69]Moster, M. (1991), cited in Bouchard, T. J., Jr. (1997). Genetic influence on mental abilities, personality, vocational interests and work attitudes. In C. L. Cooper & I. T. Robertson (Eds.) *International Review of Industrial and Organizational Psychology, 12* (pp. 373–395). New York: John Wiley & Sons.

[70]McGue, M., & Bouchard, T. J., Jr. (1984). Information processing abilities in twins reared apart. *Intelligence, 8,* 239–250; McGue, M., & Bouchard, T. J., Jr. (1989). Genetic and environmental determinant of information processing and special mental abilities: A twin analysis. In R. J. Sternberg (Ed.) *Advances in the Psychology of Human Intelligence, 5,* 7–45.

[71]Wilson, E. O. (1975). *Sociobiology: The new synthesis,* Cambridge, MA: Harvard University Press.

[72]See Trivers, R. L. (1985). *Social evolution.* Menlo Park, CA: Benjamin/Cummings Publishing Co.; Trivers, R. L. (1997). Section II conclusion. In N. L. Segal, G. E. Weisfeld, & C. C. Weisfeld (Eds.) (1997). *Uniting psychology and biology: Integrative perspectives on human development* (pp. 175–183). Washington, D.C.: American Psychological Association Press.

[73]Freedman, D. G. (1979). *Human sociobiology.* New York: Free Press.

[74]Segal, N. L. (1988). Cooperation, competition and altruism in human twinships: A sociobiological approach. In K. B. MacDonald (Ed.) *Sociobiological perspectives on human development* (pp. 168–206). New York: Springer-Verlag.

[75]Blood-typing results were not available until after the twins left Minnesota.

[76]Hur, Y. -H., et al. (1998). Genetic and environmental influence on morningness-eveningness. *Personality and Individual Differences, 25, 917–925.*

[77]Arvey, R. D., et al. (1989). Job satisfaction: Environmental and genetic components. *Journal of Applied Psychology, 74,* 187–192; Waller, N. G., et al. (1990). Genetic and environmental influences on religious interests, attitudes, and values: A study of twins reared apart and together. *Psychological Science, 1,* 138–142; Keller, L. M., et al. (1992). Work values: Genetic and environmental influences. *Journal of Applied Psychology, 77,* 79–88; Betsworth, D. G., et al. (1994); Arvey, R. D., & Bouchard, T. J., Jr. (1994). Genetics, twins, and organizational behavior. In B. A. Staw & L. L. Cummings (Eds.) *Research in organizational behavior, Vol. 16* (pp. 21–33). Greenwich, CT: JAI Press.

[78]See Bryan, E. M. (1983); "Plautus" *Britannica Online,* June 25, 1998.

[79]Bouchard, T. J., Jr. (1987). Diversity, development and determinism: A report on identical twins reared apart. In M. Amelang (Ed.) *Proceedings of the German Psychological Association, 1986* (pp. 417–436). Heidelberg, Germany.

[80]Popenoe, P. (1922). Twins reared apart. *Journal of Heredity, 5,* 142–144.

[81]Muller, M. J. (1925). Mental traits and heredity. *Journal of Heredity, 16,* 443–448.

CHAPTER 8

[1]It turned out that "B" had been adopted at five years of age, thus eliminating her and two of the pairs (B-C and B-A) from the study.

[2]Bernstein, L. " 'Are the Babies Twins?' 'Well, No. Not Really.' " *New York Times,* December, 1991.

[3]Ceci, S. J. (1991). How much does schooling influence general intelligence and its cognitive components? A reassessment of the evidence. *Developmental Psychology, 27,* 703–722.

[4]Kolata, G. "Clinics Selling Embryos Made for 'Adoption.' " *New York Times,* November 23, 1997.

[5]Simini, B. (1997). Italian surrogate "twins." *Lancet, 350,* 1307.

[6]Miller, M. B. (1998). News, views and comments. *Twin Research, 1,* 78–79.

[7]Achenbach, T. M. (1991). *Manual for the Child Behavior Check List/4–18 and 1991 Profile.* Burlington, VT: T. M. Achenbach.

[8]Gough, H. G. (1952). *The Adjective Check List.* Palo Alto: Consulting Psychologists Press.

[9]Daniels, D., & Plomin, R. (1984). *Sibling Inventory of Differential Experience (SIDE).* Boulder: Institute for Behavioral Genetics.

[10]McGuire, et al. (1992). *Sibling Inventory of Differential Experiences: Childhood Version (SIDE-C).* (unpublished).

[11]Segal, N. L. (1997). Same-age unrelated siblings: A unique test of within-family environmental influences on IQ similarity. *Journal of Educational Psychology, 89,* 381–390.

[12]Plomin, R., & DeFries, J. C. (1980). Genetics and intelligence: Recent data. *Intelligence, 4,* 15–24.

[13]Boomsma, D. I., & van Ball, G. C. M. (1998). Genetic influences on childhood IQ in 5- and 7-year-old Dutch twins. *Developmental Neuropsychology, 14,* 115–126.

[14]See Jensen, A. R. (1998) *The g factor: The science of mental ability.* Westport, CT: Praeger. Adoptive siblings' .25 IQ correlation is based on several studies.

[15]See Horn, J. M., et al. (1982). Aspects of inheritance of intellectual abilities. *Behavior Genetics, 12,* 479–516 (support); Loehlin, J. C., et al. (1997). Heredity, environment, and IQ in the Texas Adoption Project. In R. Sternberg & C. Grigorenko (Eds.) *Intelligence: Heredity and environment* (pp. 105–125) New York: Cambridge University Press (mixed support); Bouchard, T. J., Jr., & McGue, M. (1981). Familial studies of intelligence. *Science, 212,* 1055–1059 (no support).

[16]Giordani, P. J. (1997). *An analysis of problem behaviors in unrelated siblings reared together from infancy of the same age (UST-SA).* M.A. Thesis: CSU, Fullerton.

[17]Edelbrock, C., et al. (1995). A twin study of competence and problem behavior in childhood and early adolescence. *Journal of Child Psychology and Psychiatry, 36,* 775–785.

[18]Sullivan, P. F., et al. (1995). Adoption as a risk factor for mental disorders. *Acta Psychiatrics Scandinavica, 92,* 119–124.

[19]Sorosky, A. D., et al (1978). *The adoption triangle.* Garden City, NY: Doubleday.

[20]Sharma, A. R., et al. (1998). The psychological adjustment of United States adopted adolescents and their nonadopted siblings. *Child Development, 69,* 791–802.

[21]Bernstein, L. (1997); Johnson, P. I. (1997). "Artificial Twinning: An Instant Family at What Price?" *Adoptive Families,* May/June, 1997, pp. 20–23.

CHAPTER 9

[1]Engel, G. L. (1975). The death of a twin: Mourning and anniversary reactions. Fragments of 10 years of self-analysis. *International Journal of Psychoanalysis, 56,* 23–40.

[2]Mowrer, E. (1954). Some factors in the affectional adjustment of twins. *American Sociological Review, 19,* 468– 471.

[3]See Littlefield, C. H., & Rushton, J. P. (1986). When a child dies: The sociobiology of bereavement. *Journal of Personality and Social Psychology,* 51, 797–802.

[4]Sanders, C. M., Mauger, P. A., & Strong, P. N., Jr. (1985). *A manual for the Grief Experience Inventory.* Charlotte, NC: The Center for the Study of Separation and Loss.

[5]Littlefield, C. H. (1984). When a child dies: A sociobiological perspective. *Dissertation Abstracts International, 45–08B,* 2734.

[6]Archer, J. (1999). *The nature of grief: The evolution and psychology of reactions to loss.* London: Routledge.

[7]Buss, D. M. (1994). *The evolution of desire: Strategies of human mating.* New York: HarperCollins Publishers, Inc.

[8]Nesse, R. M. (1991). What are emotions for? *Psycholoquy, 2;* Nesse, R. M. (1994). An evolutionary perspective on substance abuse. *Ethology and Sociobiology, 15,* 339–348; Nesse, R. M., and Williams, G. C. (1994). *Why we get sick: The new science of Darwinian medicine.* New York: Times Books.

[9]Barkow, J. H. (1997). Happiness in evolutionary perspective. In N. L. Segal, G. E. Weisfeld, & C. C. Weisfeld (Eds.) *Uniting psychology and biology: Integrative perspectives on human development* (pp. 397–418). Washington, D.C.: American Psychological Association Press.

[10]Barash, D. P. (1979). *The whisperings within.* New York: Harper and Row.

[11]Whitmer, P. O. (1996). *The inner Elvis: A psychological biography of Elvis Aaron Presley.* New York: Hyperion.

[12]Lindeman, B. (1969). *The twins who found each other.* New York: William Morrow & Co., Inc.

[13]Rebecca Spiegel, University of Chicago graduate student, has been collecting information on identical twins discordant for physical defects.

[14]Segal, N. L., et al. (1995). Comparative grief experiences of bereaved twins and other bereaved relatives. *Personality and Individual Differences, 18,* 511–524.

[15]Fraternal twins share exactly 50% of their genes with their children, and an average of 50% of their genes with their twin.

[16]Segal, N. L., & Ream, S. L. (1998). Decrease in grief intensity for deceased twin and non-twin relatives: An evolutionary perspective. *Personality and Individual Differences, 25,* 317–325.

[17]Surprisingly, decrease in grief was less for uncles than for twins, but the effect size (meaningfulness of the difference) was slight.

[18]Woodward, J. (1988). The bereaved twin. *Acta Geneticae Medicae et Gemellologiae, 37,* 173–180; also see Woodward J. (1997). *The lone twin.* London: Free Association Books.

[19]Farmer, P. (1996). *Two or the book of twins and doubles: An autobiographical anthology.* London: Virago Books.

[20]Jones, E. M. (1987). *My twin and I.* New York: Carlton Press.

[21]Taffel, S. M. (1995). Demographic trends in twin births: USA. In L. G. Keith, E. Papiernik, D. M. Keith, & B. Luke (Eds.) *Multiple pregnancy: Epidemiology, gestation and perinatal outcome* (pp. 133–143). New York: Parthenon. The sex ratio is based on 1987 data.

[22]See Segal, N. L. (1998). Gender differences in bereavement response and longevity: Findings from the California State University Twin Loss Study. In Ellis, L., & Ebertz, L. (Eds.) *Males, females, and behavior: Toward biological understanding.* (pp. 195–212). Westport, CT: Praeger.

[23]Tiger, L., & Fox, R. (1971). *The imperial animal.* New York: Delta.

[24]Lusk, J., et al. (1988). Resource appraisal among self, friend and leader: Implications for an evolutionary perspective on individual differences. *Personality and Individual Differences, 24,* 685–700.

[25]Salmon, C. A., & Daly, M. (1996). On the importance of kin relations to Canadian women and men. *Ethology and Sociobiology, 17,* 289–297.

[26]McGue, M., et al. (1993). Longevity is moderately heritable in a sample of Danish twins born 1870–1880. *Journal of Gerontology, 48,* B237–244.

[27]Sanders, C. (1993). Risk factors in bereavement outcome. In M. S. Stroebe, W. Stroebe, & R. O. Hansson, (Eds.) *Handbook of bereavement: Theory, research, and intervention* (pp. 255–267). Cambridge: Cambridge University Press.

[28]Wilson, A. L., et al. (1982). The death of a newborn twin: An analysis of parental bereavement. *Pediatrics, 70,* 587–591.

[29]Zeitlin, M. "Hope After Death." *USA Today,* July 30, 1986.

[30]Van Gelder, L. "Learning About a Dead Twin, and Affirming Life." *New York Times,* May 14, 1998. The production was by the Netherlands's Speeltheater.

[31]"Twins Die Together While Dining." *New York Daily News,* May 28, 1996.

[32]Some previously diagnosed SIDS deaths (in nontwins) have proven to be abuse cases. It is possible that some infant twins' concurrent deaths were due to nonbiological causes. See Southall, D. P., et al. (1997). Covert video recordings of life-threatening child abuse: Lessons for protection. *Pediatrics, 100,* 735–760.

[33]Henderson, W. G., et al. (1990). The Vietnam Era Twin Registry: A resource for medical research. *Public Health Reports, 105,* 368–373.

[34]Kaprio, J., et al. (1981). Cancer in adult same-sexed twins: A historical cohort study. In L. Gedda, et al. (Eds.) *Twin research 3C: Epidemiological and clinical studies* (pp. 217–223). New York: Alan R. Liss, Inc., Lichtenstein, P., et al. (1998). The Nordic Cancer in Twins Project: The importance of genes and environments. *Ninth International Congress on Twin Studies,* June 3–5, 1998, Helsinki, Finland; also see Dunn, J., & Plomin, R. (1990). *Separate lives: Why siblings are so different.* New York: Basic Books.

[35]Finch, C. E., & Tanzi, R. E. (1997). Genetics of aging. *Science, 278,* 407–411.

[36]Wyshak, G. (1978). Fertility and longevity in twins, sibs, and parents of twins. *Social Biology, 25,* 315–330. Twin type (identical or fraternal) was not indicated in this study.

[37]Christensen, K., et al. (1995). Mortality among twins after age 6: fetal origins hypothesis versus twin method. *British Medical Journal, 310,* 432–436.

[38]Simmons, S. F., et al. (1997). Selection bias in samples of older twins? *Journal of Aging and Health, 9,* 553–567.

[39]Sorensen, T. I., et al. (1988). Genetic and environmental influences on premature death in adult adoptees. *New England Journal of Medicine, 318,* 727–732; also see commentary by Williams, R. R. (1988). Nature, nurture, and family predisposition. *New England Journal of Medicine, 318,* 769–771.

[40]Perls, T. T., et al. (1998). Siblings of centarians live longer. *Lancet, 351,* 1560.

CHAPTER 10

[1]"Woman Gives Birth for Daughter." *New York Times,* October 13, 1991.

[2]Centers for Disease Control and Prevention. (1997 Report); also see Stolberg, S. G. "U.S. Published First Guide to Treatment of Infertility." *New York Times,* December 19, 1997.

[3]Pregnancy attempts include in vitro fertilization and embryo transfer.

[4]Assisted/Advanced Reproductive Technology (ART) refers to "laboratory handling of human oocytes and/or embryos." American Fertility Society (1990), cited in Hecht, B. R.

(1995). The impact of assisted reproductive technology on the incidence of multiple gestation. In L. G. Keith, E. Papiernik, D. M. Keith, & B. Luke (Eds.) *Multiple pregnancy: Epidemiology, gestation and perinatal outcome* (pp. 175–190). New York: Parthenon.

[5]This estimate is based on 1994 data from Ventura, S. J., et al. (1996). Advance report of final natality statistics, 1994. *Monthly Vital Statistics Report, 44,* and the SART/ASRM (1998). Assisted reproductive technology in the United States and Canada: 1995 results generated from the American Society for Reproductive Medicine/Society for Assisted Reproductive Technology. *Fertility and Sterility, 69,* 389–398.

[6]An embryo is the developing organism from the second through the eighth gestational week, but this definition is not strictly followed in the assisted reproductive technology literature.

[7]United States Department of Health and Human Services, Centers for Disease Control and Prevention, and National Center for Chronic Disease Prevention and Health Promotion (1997). *1995 Assisted Reproductive Technology Success Rates.* Vol. 3.

[8]Hecht, B. R. (1995). The impact of assisted reproductive technology on the incidence of multiple gestation. In L. G. Keith, et al. (Eds.) (pp. 175–190); Society for Assisted Reproductive Technology. (1991). In vitro fertilization-embryo transfer (IVF-ET) in the United States: 1989 results from the IVF-ET Registry. *Fertility and Sterility, 55,* 14–23.

[9]Hecht, B. R. (1995). SOURCE is not a widely used term.

[10]Hecht, B. R. (1995).

[11]Stolberg (December 19, 1997); Mead, R. "Annals of Reproduction: Eggs for Sale." *New Yorker Magazine,* August 9, 1999, pp. 56–65.

[12]Kolata, G. "Clinics Selling Embryos Made for 'Adoption.' " *New York Times,* November 23, 1997.

[13]Kolata, G. "Successful Births Reported with Frozen Human Eggs." *New York Times,* October 17, 1997.

[14]Belkin, L. "Pregnant with Complications." *New York Times Magazine,* October 26, 1997, pp. 34–39, 48–49, 67–68.

[15]Kolata, G. (October 17, 1997).

[16]Centers for Disease Control and Prevention. 1997 Report.

[17]Dodson, M. "Fertility Patient OKs $460,000 UC Settlement." *Los Angeles Times,* February 20, 1998.

[18]Centers for Disease Control and Prevention. 1997 Report.

[19]Kolata, G. (November 23, 1997).

[20]SART/ASRM (1998).

[21]Hecht, Bryan R. M.D. (Personal communication, fall. 1997).

[22]D'Emilio, F. "No Regrets About Having Her Baby at 62." *Los Angeles Times,* July 27, 1997.

[23]*Dateline NBC.* December 9, 1997.

[24]"Woman, 50, Gives Birth to Triplets." *New Zealand Multiple Births Foundation Newsletter,* February 1993.

[25]George, T. "Family Woes After Birth of Quints." *Daily News,* July 21, 1997.

[26]"Actor Tony Randall is becoming a father at age 77." *New York Times,* November 12, 1997.

[27]Fenwick, L. B. (1998). *Private choices, public consequences.* New York: Dutton.

[28]Taylor, H. "The Baby Gamble: Day 3." *Albany Times Union,* March 11, 1997.

[29]Belluck, P. "Heartache Frequently Visits Parents With Multiple Births." *New York Times,* January 3, 1998.

[30]Scott-Jupp, R., & Field, D. (1991). Multiple pregnancies resulting from assisted conception: burden on neonatal units. *British Medical Journal, 302,* 1079.

[31]Reuters. "Crib Death Increased in Twins." May 8, 1997. Recent work suggests that a lag in maturation of neurotransmitters (chemical substances that assist in sending information between nerves) may be involved; see Panigrahy, A. (1997). Decreased kainate re-

ceptor binding in the arcuate nucleus of the sudden infant death syndrome. *Journal of Neuropathy and Experimental Neurology, 56,* 1253–1261.

[32]Beal, S. (1989). Sudden infant death syndrome in twins. *Pediatrics, 84,* 1038–1044.

[33]Southall, D. P. (1997). Covert video recordings of life-threatening child abuse: Lessons for child protection. *Pediatrics, 100,* 735–760.

[34]"Septuplet Cost Estimate: $1 Million for 18 years." *New York Times.* December 24, 1997.

[35]Lemonick, M. D. "It's a Miracle." *Time Magazine,* December 1, 1997; Times Wire Reports. "Oldest Septuplet Has Eye Surgery." *Los Angeles Times,* January 18, 1998.

[36]Associated Press. "Two Saudi Septuplets in Critical Condition." January 17, 1998.

[37]Associated Press. "Mother-to-be in Mexico Expecting Eight or Nine Babies." February 14, 1998; Reuters News Service. "Mexican Mother Expects Seven Babies Instead of Nine." February 17, 1998; Reuters News Service. "Sextuplets Born to Mexican Mother." February 28, 1998.

[38]Hecht, B. R. (1995); also see Derom, C., et al. (1987). Increased monozygotic twinning rate after ovulation induction. *Lancet, 2,* 1236–1238; and Edwards, R. G., et al. (1986). Identical twins and in vitro fertilization. *Journal of In Vitro Fertilization and Embryo Transfer, 3,* 114–117.

[39]Wenstrom, K. D., et al. (1993). Increased risk of monochorionic twinning associated with assisted reproduction. *Fertility and Sterility, 60,* 510–514.

[40]Hecht, B. R., & Magoon, M. W. (1998). Can the epidemic of iatrogenic multiples be conquered? *Clinical Obstetrics and Gynecology, 41,* 126–137.

[41]Strain, L., et al. (1998). A true hermaphrodite chimera resulting from embryo amalgamation after in vitro fertilization. *New England Journal of Medicine, 338,* 166–170.

[42]Sperm counts have dropped 1.5% each year for American males, and 3% each year for European males. *Time Magazine.* December 8, 1997.

[43]Lloyd, O. L., et al. (1988). Twinning in human populations and in cattle exposed to air pollution from incinerators. *Journal of Industrial Medicine, 45,* 556–560.

[44]MacGillivray, I., Samphier, M., & Little, J. (1988). Factors affecting twinning. In I. MacGillivray, D. M. Campbell, & B. Thompson (Eds.) *Twinning and twins* (pp. 67–97). Chichester, England: John Wiley & Sons.

[45]Luke, B. (1994). The changing pattern of multiple births in the United States: Maternal and infant characteristics, 1973 and 1990. *Obstetrics and Gynecology, 84,* 101–106; Jewell, S. E. (1995). Increasing trends in plural births in the United States. *Obstetrics and Gynecology, 85,* 229–232.

[46]Taylor, H. "The Baby Gamble: Day 1." *Albany Times Union,* March 9, 1997.

[47]James, W. H. (1995). Are 'natural' twinning rates continuing to decline? *Human Reproduction, 10,* 3042–3044.

[48]Evans, M. I., et al. (1995). Multifetal pregnancy reduction and selective second-trimester termination. In L. G. Keith, et al. (Eds.) pp. 359–366); Evans, et al. (1990). Selective termination: Clinical experience and residual tasks. *American Journal of Obstetrics and Gynecology, 162,* 1568–1575; Taylor, H. "Fetal Reduction: Birth of a Controversy" (Baby Gamble). *Albany Times Union,* March 10, 1997. Also see Sebire, N. J., et al. (1997). Effects of embryo reduction from trichorionic triplets to twins. *British Journal of Obstetrics and Gynaecology, 104,* 1201–1203.

[49]Alikani, M., & Wiemer, K. (1997). Embryo number for transfer should not be strictly regulated. *Fertility and Sterility, 68,* 782–783; De Jonge, C. J., & Wolf, D. P. (1997). Embryo number for transfer should be regulated. *Fertility and Sterility, 68,* 784–786.

[50]Simons, M. "Uproar Over Twins, and a Dutch Couple's Anguish." *New York Times,* June 28, 1995.

[51]Dr. Vincent S. E. Falger of the University of Utrecht provided this translation.

[52]A black couple in Brazil took legal action against an in vitro fertilization clinic because the mother delivered a white child. Reuters News Service. November 30, 1994.

[53]Segal, N. L. (1997). Behavioral aspects of intergenerational cloning: What twins tell us. *Jurimetrics, 38,* 57–67; Segal, N. L. "Double Trouble." *New York Times Book Review* (letter), January 18, 1998.

[54]Blanchard, R., et al. (1995). Birth order and sibling sex ratio in homosexual male adolescents and probably prehomosexual feminine boys. *Developmental Psychology, 31,* 22–30.

[55]*ABC News.* February 16, 1998; *Today Show,* NBC. February 17, 1998; Golden, F. "The Ice Babies." *Time Magazine,* March 2, 1998, p. 65.

[56]National Bioethics Advisory Commission (1997). "Cloning Human Beings." Rockville, MD.

[57]Silver, L. (Personal communication, January 16, 1998).

[58]Brown, M.D., et al. (1996). Mitochondrial DNA sequence analysis of four Alzheimer's and Parkinson's disease patients. *American Journal of Medical Genetics, 61,* 283–289; Shoffner, J. M., et al. (1990) Myoclonic epilepsy and ragged-red fiber disease (MERRF) is associated with a mitochondrial DNA tRNA (Lys) mutation. *Cell, 61,* 931–937.

[59]Wilmut, I., et al. (1997). Viable offspring derived from fetal and adult mammalian cells. *Nature, 385,* 810–813.

[60]Kolata, G. (1998). *Clone: The road to Dolly and the path ahead.* New York: William Morrow & Company, Inc.

[61]Researchers raised concerns that attempts to repeat the Dolly experiment had failed. They questioned whether, in fact, Dolly truly resulted from adult human cloning: see Sgaramella, V., & Zinder, N. D. (1998). Dolly confirmation. *Science, 279,* 635, 637. The success of adult human cloning has, however, been demonstrated in recent work; see Kolata, G. "Cloning Pioneer is Focused and Creative in his Research." *New York Times,* July 24, 1998.

[62]Specter, M., & Kolata, G. "After Decades and Many Missteps, Cloning Success." *New York Times,* March 3, 1997.

[63]Twin calves have lower survival rates than nontwin calves, posing problems for twinning technologies aimed at increasing beef supply; see Gregory, K. E., et al. (1996). Effects of twinning on dystocia, calf survival, calf growth, carcass traits, and cow productivity. *Journal of Animal Science, 74,* 1223–1233. Cloning would circumvent these difficulties.

[64]"Cloned Sheep May Help Human Hemophiliacs." *New York Times,* December 19, 1997.

[65]Johannes, L. "Cows Are Cloned From Altered Genes In Move With Practical Applications." *Wall Street Journal,* January 21, 1998.

[66]Associated Press. "Dutch Banning Genetic Technique That Cloned Calves." February 28, 1998.

[67]Robertson, J. A. (1997). A ban on cloning and cloning research is unjustified. Testimony presented at the National Bioethics Advisory Commission. Washington, D.C.

[68]Most newspaper reports describe the Shapiros as fraternal. Based on standard physical resemblance questionnaires I administered to these twins, they proved identical; see Chapter 13.

[69]Kestenbaum, D. (1998). Cloning plan spawns ethics debate. *Science, 279,* 315; "A Cloning Plan Lead to Vows to Outlaw It." *New York Times,* January 12, 1998.

[70]Chen, E. "Clinton Urges Quick Ban on Human Cloning." *Los Angeles Times,* January, 1998; "A Slapdash Proposal on Cloning." *New York Times,* February 10, 1998; Chen, E. "Human Cloning Ban Runs Into Wall of Science." *Los Angeles Times,* February 11, 1998.

[71]Segal, N. L. & Russell, J. M. (1992). Twins in the classroom: School policy issues and recommendations. *Journal of Educational and Psychological Consultation, 3,* 69–84.

[72]Golombok, S., et al. (1995). Families created by the new reproductive technologies:

Quality of parenting and social and emotional development of the children. *Child Development, 66,* 285–298; Golombok, S. (in press). New Family forms: Children raised in solo mother families, lesbian mother families and in families created by assisted reproduction. In L. Balter & C. Tamis-LeMonde (Eds.) *Child psychology: Handbook of contemporary issues.* New York: Garland; van Balan, F. (1996). Child-rearing following in vitro fertilization. *Journal of Child Psychology and Psychiatry, 37,* 687–693.

[73]Baker, L. A. & Daniels, D. (1990). Nonshared environmental influences and personality differences in adult twins. *Journal of Personality and Social Psychology, 58,* 103–110.

[74]"Double Take" (NBC *Extra*) showed two unusually similar mother-daughter pairs. The women enjoyed close social relationships with their partners.

[75]My Twinn Workshop. Fall 1997/Spring 1998 catalogue. David Liggit, Public Relations Department of My Twinn, provided information on the identical dolls.

[76]Hecht, Bryan R., M.D. (Personal communication, Fall, 1997).

[77]Paulson, R. J. & Thornton, M. H. (1997). Follicle aspiration, sperm injection, and assisted rupture (FASIAR): a simple new assisted reproductive technique. *Fertility and Sterility, 68,* 1148–1151.

CHAPTER 11

[1]Berkow, I. "In Minneapolis, Hankies and Hysteria." *New York Times,* October 16, 1987.

[2]Berkow, I. "Last Runner but Not Least." *New York Times,* September 22, 1983.

[3]Williams, M. C., & O'Brien, W. F. (1998). Low weight/length ratio to assess risk of cerebral palsy and perinatal mortality in twins. *American Journal of Perinatology, 15,* 225–228.

[4]Torrey, E. F., Bowler, Taylor, E. H., & Gottesman, I. I. (1994). *Schizophrenia and manic-depressive disorder: The biological roots of mental illness as revealed by the landmark study of identical twins.* New York: Basic Books.

[5]Three brother pairs have been inducted into the Baseball Hall of Fame: R. Paul (1952) & Lloyd Waner (1957); George (1937) & William (Harvey) Wright (1953); Andrew "Rube" (1981) & Willie ("Bill") Foster (1996).

[6]Galton, F. (1891). *Hereditary genius: An inquiry into its laws and consequences.* 2nd ed. New York: D. Appleton & Co.

[7]Thornton, R. "Mahre Brothers Sweep Olympic Slalom." *Minneapolis State Tribune,* February 20, 1984.

[8]Hobbs, M. "You Have to Put in Lots of Miles to Keep up with Julie Olson." *Minneapolis Star Tribune,* October 14, 1984.

[9]Levy, P. "Double Threat for the Olympics." *Minneapolis Star Tribune Sunday Magazine,* April 26, 1987, pp. 7–28.

[10]Christine O'Reilly was killed in an automobile accident at age 25, in Irvine, California, in 1993. Finn, R. "Secret Sharer: O'Reilly is Dead, but Her Gift Lives On." *New York Times,* October 15, 1993.

[11]Wallace, W. N. "Twin Killing in College Game." *New York Times,* April 12, 1990.

[12]Sullivan, T. "Del Prete Twins Serve up Cup for Mann." *New York Daily News,* June 2, 1997.

[13]Berkow, I. "Making Room for Four." *New York Times,* November 15, 1997.

[14]von Grebe, H. (1955). Sport bei zwillingen. *Acta Geneticae Medicae et Gemellologiae, 4,* 275–295.

[15]Gedda, L. (1960). Sports and genetics: A study on twins. *Acta Geneticae Medicae et Gemellologiae, 9,* 387–406.

[16]Bouchard, C., & Malina, R. M. (1984). Genetics and Olympic athletes: A discussion of methods and issues. *Medicine and Sport Science, 18,* 28–38.

[17]"Marathon to Seko; Salazar Places Fifth." *New York Times,* December 1983.

[18]Wright, L. (1961). A study of special abilities in identical twins. *Journal of Genetic Psychology, 99,* 245–251.

[19]Wright, L. (1961).

[20]Jacobs, B. "Twins go separate ways on and off basketball court." *New York Times,* February 2, 1987.

[21]Plomin, R. (1990). *Nature and nurture.* Pacific Grove, CA: Brooks/Cole.

[22]Data are from Dr. Siv Fischbein and Anders Skarlind of the Stockholm Institute of Education.

[23]Wilson, R. S. (1979). Analysis of longitudinal twin data. *Acta Geneticae Medicae et Gemellologiae, 28,* 93–105.

[24]Juel-Nielsen, N. (1980). *Individual and environment: Monozygotic twins reared apart.* New York: International Universities Press.

[25]Comuzzie, A. G., & Allison, D. B. (1988). The search for human obesity genes. *Science, 280,* 1374–1377.

[26]Kearny, J. T. (1996). Training the Olympic athlete. *Scientific American, 274,* 52–63.

[27]Weiner, J. "Koslowskis wrestle to make ends meet." *Minneapolis Star Tribune,* September 11, 1998.

[28]Wilson, R. S. (1979)

[29]Carmichael, C. M., & McGue, M. (1995). A cross-sectional examination of height, weight, and body mass index in adult twins. *Journal of Gerontology, 50A,* B237–B244.

[30]Weight data were unavailable for opposite-sex pairs at age eighteen. At thirty-eight, cotwin differences were zero to forty-eight pounds for identicals, and zero to over one hundred pounds for fraternals, and zero to twenty-nine pounds for opposite sex twins. Weight data were self-reported at age thirty-eight.

[31]Allison, D. B., et al. (1996). The heritability of body mass index among an international sample of monozygotic twins reared apart. *International Journal of Obesity and Related Metabolic Disorders, 20,* 501–506; Maes, H. H. M. (1997). Genetic and environmental factors in body weight and human adiposity. *Behavior Genetics, 27,* 325–351.

[32]Shields, J. (1962). *Monozygotic twins: Brought up apart and brought up together.* London: Oxford University Press.

[33]See Carmichael, C. M., & McGue, M. (1995).

[34]Crisp, A. H., et al (1985). Nature and nurture in anorexia nervosa: A study of 34 pairs of twins, one pair of triplets, and an adoptive family. *International Journal of Eating Disorders, 4,* 5–27.

[35]Newman, B., et al. (1990). Nongenetic influences of obesity on other cardiovascular disease risk factors: An analysis of identical twins. *American Journal of Public Health, 80,* 675–678.

[36]Ronnemaa, T., et al, (1997). Glucose metabolism in identical twins discordant for obesity. The critical role of visceral fat. *Journal of Clinical Endocrinology and Metabolism, 82, 383–387.*

[37]See Maes, H. H. M. (1997).

[38]Price, R. A., & Gottesman, I. I. (1991). Body fat in identical twins reared apart. *Behavior Genetics, 21,* 1–7; Macdonald, A., & Stunkard, A. (1990) Body-mass indexes of British separated twins. *New England Journal of Medicine, 322,* 1530; also see Allison, D. B., et al. (1996).

[39]Allison, D. B., et al. (1996). Assortative mating for relative weight: Genetic implications. *Behavior Genetics, 26,* 103–111.

[40]Maes, H. H. M., et al. (1996). Inheritance of physical fitness in 10–year-old twins and their parents. *Medicine and Science in Sports and Exercise, 28,* 1479–1491.

[41]Ogden, C. L., et al. (1997). Prevalance of overweight among preschool children in the United States, 1971 through 1994. *Pediatrics, 99,* E1.

[42]Hewitt, J. K. (1997). The genetics of obesity: What have genetic studies told us about the environment. *Behavior Genetics, 27,* 353–358; also see Boomsma, D. I., et al. (1989).

Resemblance of parents and twins in sports participation and heart rate. *Behavior Genetics, 19,* 123–141.

[43]Levy, P. (1987).

[44]Bouchard, C., et al. (1990). The response to long-term overfeeding in identical twins. *New England Journal of Medicine, 322,* 1477–1482.

[45]NFL twin pairs include: Mark and Mike Bell, Keith and Kerry Cash, Gene and Tom Golsen, Devon and Ricardo McDonald, Raleigh and Reggie McKenzie, Rich and Ron Saul, Hal and Herb Shoener, and Paul and Phil Tabor. Freeman, M. "Giants' Tiki Barber Now Must Make It on His Own." *New York Times,* April 27, 1997. NFL Communications staff believe all pairs are identical (Personal communication, November 14, 1997).

[46]"Seeing Double." *Campus Highlights,* October 1985.

[47]Klawans, H. L. (1996). *Why Michael couldn't hit.* New York: W. H. Freeman & Co.

[48]Prud'homme, D., et al. (1984). Sensitivity of maximal aerobic power to training is genotype-dependent. *Medicine and Science in Sports and Exercise, 16,* 489–493.

[49]Bouchard, C., & Lortie, G. (1984). Heredity and endurance performance. *Sports Medicine, 1,* 38–64.

[50]Kennedy, J. "Quick-fisted Twins From Brooklyn Recall Their Days of Hard Knocks." *New York Times,* September 15, 1996.

[51]Alexander, R. "Body-building Camp: A Week to Better Biceps." *New York Times,* August 1, 1996.

[52]Thomas, R. M. *New York Times,* September 27, 1987.

[53]"Twins in the Swim." *New York Times,* August 1, 1981.

[54]Tim Gullikson passed away from inoperable brain cancer in 1996 at age 44. Finn, R. "Tim Gullikson, 44, Tennis Coach and Player." *New York Times,* May 4, 1996.

[55]Peter, but not Chris, was selected to play on the 1994 United States Olympic hockey team. Tokatch, J. "A Long Road to Success." *Mothers of Twins Club Notebook,* Fall, 1994.

[56]See Maes, H. M. M., et al. (1996).

[57]Bouchard, C., et al. (1986). Genetic effects in human skeletal muscle fiber type distribution and enzyme activities. *Canadian Journal of Physiology and Pharmacology, 64,* 1245–1251.

[58]Jokl, E. (1978). Twin research in cardiology with a comment on the role of genetic design in physiology and pathology. In W. E. Nance, et al. *Twin research, Part C: Clinical studies* (pp. 49–55). New York: Alan R. Liss, Inc.

[59]"Pain in the Wrist." May 9, 1989 (Media Report).

[60]"VMI's Twin Terrors Stick Together." *Asheville Citizen.* February 27, 1990.

[61]Moran, T. (1989). Hockey's Sutter twins: When one is hurt, the other knows it." *Canadian Medical Association Journal, 140,* 1216.

[62]*Indiana Daily Student,* January 1978.

[63]Brennan, S. "An Identical Choice." *New York Daily News,* November 13, 1997.

[64]Anderson, D. "Skaters Spun Parents' Dreams Into Silver." *Minneapolis Star & Tribune,* February 13, 1984.

[65]McGuire, S., et al. (1994). Genetic and environmental influences on perceptions of self-worth and competence in adolescence: A study of twins, full siblings, and step-siblings. *Child Development, 65,* 785–799.

[66]Scarton, D. "Identical Twins Often Have Similar Athletic Ability." *The Pittsburgh Press.* July 22, 1990. José Canseco is now a free agent, playing for the Tampa Bay Devil Rays. Ozzie Canseco played most recently for the Duluth-Superior Dukes.

[67]Lipsyte, R. "Twins, but With Little Resemblance." *New York Times,* January 11, 1998.

[68]See Sullivan (1997).

[69]Mrs. Wilma Hollonbeck, Scot and Sean's grandmother, kindly provided this information.

[70]Information about the Paralympic Games is available on the internet: (www.usoc.org/sports/).

[71]Coe, S., & Miller, D. (1981). *Running free.* New York: St. Martin's Press.

[72]Babbit, B. "Slingshot." *Competitor Magazine,* May 1997, pp. 32–35.

[73]Dr. William A. Bauman is Professor of Medicine and Rehabilitation Medicine, Mt. Sinai School of Medicine, New York, NY, and Director of the Spinal Cord Damage Research Center at the Veterans Affairs Medical Center, Bronx, New York.

[74]An arm ergometer is a bicycle designed for arm work, during which oxygen, carbon dioxide and total volume of air exhaled were measured. A leg ergometer is a bicycle pedaled by the legs and used for testing nonSCI twins only.

[75]Scot's extensive training and larger body size enabled him to outperform his twin brother. Personal communication, investigators (November 7, 1997).

[76]Dr. Ann M. Spungen is an Assistant Professor of Medicine and Rehabilitation Medicine, Mt. Sinai School of Medicine, New York, NY, and a physiologist (whose area specialties are exercise physiology and statistics) at the Spinal Cord Damage Research Center at the Veterans Affairs Medical Center, Bronx, New York.

[77]The SCI twin study has been supported by the Spinal Cord Research Foundation and the Eastern Paralyzed Veterans Association. The Bronx Veterans Affairs Medical Center provided food and lodging for participants, without which the project would not have been possible.

[78]Spinal Cord Damage Research Center. Annual Report, July 1, 1996–June 30, 1997.

[79]Simonton, D. K. Creative expertise: A life-span developmental perspective. In K. A. Ericsson (Ed.) (1996). *The road to excellence: The acquisition of expert performance in the arts and sciences, sports, and games* (pp. 227–253). Mahwah, NJ: Erlbaum.

[80]Radnitz, C. L., et al. Depression and alcohol use in persons with SCI: A study of monozygotic twins. (abstract) *American Association of Spinal Cord Injury Psychologists and Social Workers,* September, 1997, Las Vegas, Nevada; Hollick, C., et al. (in progress). The effects of spinal cord injury on personality: A study of monozygotic twins. SCI and nonSCI twins' scores on the five major scales of the revised NEO (Neuroticism-Extraversion-Openness) Personality Inventory were within the average range. In this modest sample average scores for depression (Beck Depression Inventory) and alcohol use (Alcohol Use Disorders Investigative Test) were not elevated, but a few twins' individual scores may have been somewhat high.

[81]Kilgannon, C. "Can a Doublemint Ad Be That Far Behind?" *New York Times,* February 5, 1996.

[82]Kujala, U. M., et al. (1998). Relationship of leisure-time physical activity and mortality: The Finnish twin cohort. *Journal of the American Medical Association, 279,* 440–444.

[83]Special Olympics was developed in the 1960s by Eunice Shriver, sister of former President Kennedy, whose sister and child were mentally retarded. (www.special olympics.org).

[84]Hembd, S. Cheering the family spirit of Special Olympics. *Twins Magazine, 5,* 62–63; Ladlub, L. Let the games begin. *Tuesday's Child, 1,* Summer 1997, 3335.

[85]Twins adopted through the CAP (Children Awaiting Parents, Inc.) Book triumph with support of can-do family. *CAP Book, 11,* Fall 1997, 1–2.

[86]*Today Show,* NBC. November 29, 1997.

[87]Meyers, C., et al. (1995). Congenital anomalies and pregnancy loss. In L. G. Keith, E. Papiernik, D. M. Keith, & B. Luke (Eds.) *Multiple pregnancy: Epidemiology, gestation and perinatal outcome* (pp. 73–92). New York: Parthenon.

[88]Spender, Q., et al. (1995). Impaired oral-motor function in children with Down's syndrome: A study of three twin pairs. *European Journal of Disorders of Communication, 30,* 77–87.

[89]Some peopole might count training as environmental, but a genetic component is suggested.

[90]Dr. Ericsson acknowledged that additional study of twins' scholarship is needed. (Personal communication, October, 1997).

[91]Bondy, F. "Double Image Swims for Gold." *New York Times,* August 4, 1992.

[92]Feldman, D. H. (1984). A follow-up of subjects scoring above 180 IQ in Terman's "Genetic Studies of Genius." *Exceptional Children, 50,* 518–523.

[93]Thomas, R. M. Jr. "Marion Tinsley, 68, Unmatched as Checkers Champion, Is Dead." *New York Times,* April 8, 1995.

CHAPTER 12

[1]Paper House Productions: Woodstock, NY, 1986.

[2]I endorse the essential continuity of humans and other animals, so the terms human animals and nonhuman animals are used throughout the chapter; see Dess, N. K., & Chapman, C. D. (1998). "Humans and animals"? On saying what we mean. *Psychological Science, 9,* 56–57.

[3]*Leakey Foundation News.* "Double Trouble." Fall. 1978; Goodall, J. (1986). *The chimpanzees of Gombe: Patterns of behavior.* Cambridge, MA: Belnap Press. Gyre, always the weaker twin, died at ten months of age.

[4]Associated Press. "Twin Pandas Born in Mexico City." *Minneapolis Star and Tribune,* June 27, 1985.

[5]"Leopard Quints." *Minneapolis Star and Tribune,* August 13, 1988.

[6]Associated Press. "A Couple of Koalas." *Minneapolis Star and Tribune,* September 15, 1988.

[7]"Cybill to Name Hippos." *Minneapolis Star and Tribune,* January 16, 1989.

[8]*Wildlife Conservation Society.* "Come Celebrate Gorillas Gorillas." *New York Times,* July 14, 1995.

[9]*NBC News.* February 1, 1998.

[10]"Mammals: Major mammal orders; Bears." *Britannica Online,* May 1998.

[11]Rudram, N. (1997). Mixed breed twins. *The Veterinary Record, 140,* 408.

[12]Twinning rates in cattle vary with the breed. See Scheinfeld, A. (1973). *Twins and supertwins.* Baltimore, MD: Pelican Books, and Lloyd, O. L., et al. (1988). Twinning in human populations and in cattle exposed to air pollution from incinerators. *Journal of Industrial Medicine, 45,* 556–560.

[13]Armadillo means "little tank." Warhol, A., & Benirschke, K. (1986). *Vanishing animals.* New York: Springer-Verlag. An alternative meaning is "little armored one." Smith, L. L., & Doughty, R. W. (1984). *The amazing armadillo: Geography of a folk critter.* Austin: University of Texas Press.

[14]Craig, S. F., et al. (1995). The 'paradox' of polyembryony: A review of the cases and a hypothesis for its evolution. *Evolutionary Ecology, 11,* 127–143.

[15]Jones, W. E. (1988). The trauma of twinning. *Horsemen's Journal, 39,* 16, 68.

[16]Craig, S. F., et al. (1995).

[17]Bryozoans are sessile (permanantly attached), marine or fresh water animals; parasitoid wasps are solitary insects living off hosts.

[18]Craig, S. F., et al. (1995).

[19]Williams, G. C. (1975). *Sex and evolution.* Princeton, N.J.: Princeton University Press.

[20]Craig, S. F., et al. (1995).

[21]Cohen, P. "Animals Cloning Around." *Newsday,* June 17, 1997.

[22]Bulmer, M. G. (1970). *The biology of twinning in man.* Oxford: Clarendon. Identical twins occur in about 1% of twin births in some domestic sheep. Lévy, F., et al. (1996). Physiological, sensory, and experiential factors of parental care in sheep. In J. Z. Rosenblatt, & C. T. Snowdon (Eds.) *Advances in the study of behavior* (pp. 385–422). New York: Academic Press.

[23]Warhol, A. & Benirschke, K. (1986).

[24]Benirschke, K. (1981). Lessons from multiple pregnancies in mammals. In L. Gedda, et al. (Eds.) *Twin research 3A: Twin biology and multiple pregnancy* (pp. 135–139). New York: Alan R. Liss, Inc.

[25]A bicornuate uterus has two hornlike projections that meet in a common space. In human females, this describes an abnormal uterus divided into two halves at the upper end. Human females have a unicornuate uterus adapted for single birth pregnancies, characteristic of primates.

[26]Craig et al. (1995); Loughry, W. J., et al. (1998). Polyembryony in armadillos. *American Scientist, 86,* 274–279.

[27]Anderson, J. M., & Benirschke, K. (1962). Tissue transplanation in the nine-banded armadillo, *Dasypus novemcinctus. Annals of the New York Academy of Sciences, 99,* 399–414.

[28]Fefer, A., et al. (1986). Identical-twin (syngeneic) marrow transplantation for hematologic cancers. *Journal of the National Cancer Institute, 76,* 1269–1273. Unequal distribution of histocompatibility factors in later splitting identical twins might explain their occasional transplant rejection; see Warhol, K. & Benirschke, K. (1986).

[29]Dawkins, R. (1989). *The selfish gene.* 2nd ed. New York: Oxford University Press.

[30]Loughry, W. J., et al. (1998).

[31]Bulmer, M. G. (1970).

[32]Stott, K. (1946). Twins in green guenon. *Journal of Mammalogy, 27,* 394.

[33]Sources of twins' abuse were not mentioned in the article.

[34]Bulmer, M. G. (1970).

[35]Jacobson, H. I., et al. (1989). Multiple births and maternal risk of breast cancer. *American Journal of Epidemiology, 129,* 865–873. A later study also found that twin births protected mothers against breast cancer, but did not find that the effect vanished following subsequent singleton births; see Murphy, M. F. G., et al. (1997). Breast cancer risk in mother of twins. *British Journal of Cancer, 75,* 1066–1068.

[36]Wyshak, G. (1978). Fertility and longevity in twins, sibs, and parents of twins. *Social Biology, 25,* 315–330; Haukioja, E., et al. (1989). Why are twins so rare in homo sapiens? *American Naturalist, 133,* 572–577; also see Lummaa, V., et al. (1998). Natural selection on human twinning. *Nature, 394,* 533–534.

[37]Forbes, L. S. (1997). The evolutionary biology of spontaneous abortion in humans. *Trends in Ecology and Evolution, 12,* 446–450.

[38]Humans are close descendants of chimpanzees, with approximately 99% of genetic material in common. However, minor genetic differences can have major behavioral and physical consequences. Of course, similarities in humans and chimps do not necessarily imply common structures or functions; see Pinker, S., & Bloom, P. (1992). Natural language and natural selection. In J. H. Barkow, L. Cosmides, & J. Tooby (Eds.) *The adapted mind: Evolutionary psychology and the evolution of culture* (pp. 451–493). New York: Oxford University Press.

[39]*New York Times.* July 14, 1995.

[40]Napier, J. R. & Napier, J. H. (1967). *A handbook of living primates.* New York: Academic Press.

[41]*Minneapolis Star and Tribune.* October 27, 1997.

[42]Napier, J. R., & Napier, J. H. (1967).

[43]The studbook records zoo animals' births, deaths, parents, locations and transfers. It also provides genetic and demographic information used in the management of animals.

[44]This twin birth occurred in 1996, but was not recorded at that time because of the stillbirths. Recording policies were later changed, so the higher studbook numbers reflect time of entry.

[45]I am grateful to the Bronx Zoo/Wildlife Conservation Society staff for making these reports available. I also wish to acknowledge Dr. Colleen McCann, Assistant Curator of Primates at the Bronx Zoo; Allison Hart, Senior Keeper of the Ape House; and the surrogate mothers for additional information on Ngoma and Tambo.

[46]First-year skill development is similar in sequence for gorillas and humans, but gorillas

develop faster and with greater strength. "Gorilla Twins Growing by Leaps and Bounds at Bronx Zoo/Wildlife Conservation Park." Wildlife Conservation Society Press Release, February 6, 1995.

[47]Some chimpanzee twins may have been born in the wild and not survived. Chimpanzee twinning rates may exceed human twinning rates, although most births are single. Twelve out of three hundred births at the Yerkes Regional Primate Center (4%) were multiples (eleven twin sets and one triplet set); most infants were stillborn or died soon after birth; see Goodall, J. (1986).

[48]Yerkes, R. M. (1934). Multiple births in anthropoid apes. *Science, 79,* 430–431.

[49]Kuroda, S. (1989). Developmental retardation and behavioral characteristics of pygmy chimpanzees. In P. G. Heltne & L. A. Marquardt, (Eds.) *Understanding chimpanzees.* (pp. 184–193). Cambridge, MA: Harvard University Press.

[50]Tomlin, M. I., & Yerkes, R. M. (1934). Chimpanzee twins: Behavioral relations and development. *Journal of Genetic Psychology, 46,* 239–263.

[51]Teleki, G. (1989). Population status of wild chimpanzees (*Pan Troglodytes*) and threats to survival. In P. G. Heltne & L. A. Marquardt (Eds.) (pp. 312–353).

[52]Chimpanzees in the wild do not achieve full independence until age eight; Teleki (1989).

[53]Mann, J. (1992). Nurturance or negligence: Maternal psychology and behavioral preference among preterm twins. In J. H. Barkow, et al. (Eds.) (pp. 367–390).

[54]Dental development proceeds more quickly in chimpanzees than in humans, but the developmental sequence is similar.

[55]Brazelton, T. B. "It's Twins." *Redbook Magazine,* February 1980, pp. 80, 83–84; Vandell D. L., & Mueller, E. C. (1995). Peer play and friendships during the first two years. In H. C. Foot, A. J. Chapman, & J. R. Smith (Eds.) *Friendship and social relations* (pp. 181–208). New Brunswick, NJ: Transaction Publishers.

[56]Kuroda, S. (1989). Developmental retardation and behavioral characteristics of pygmy chimpanzees. In P. G. Heltne, & L. A. Marquardt (Eds.) (pp. 184–193).

[57]Porter, R. H., et al. (1991). Individual olfactory signatures as major determinants of early maternal discrimination in sheep. *Developmental Psychobiology, 24,* 151–158.

[58]Romeyer, A., et al. (1993). Recognition of dizygotic and monozygotic twin lambs by ewes. *Behavior, 127,* 119–139.

[59]Porter, R. H., et al. (1983). Maternal recognition of neonates through olfactory cues. *Physiology and Behavior, 30,* 151–154; Macfarlane, A. (1975). Olfaction in the development of social preferences in the human neonate. *Parent-infant interaction, 33,* 103–113. (Ciba Foundation Symposium), New York: Elsevier; also see Porter, R. H. (1991). Human reproduction and the mother-infant relationship: The role of odors. In T. V. Getchell (Ed.) *Smell and taste in health and disease* (pp. 429–442). New York: Raven Press.

[60]Nicolaides, N. (1974). Skin lipids: Their biochemical uniqueness. *Science, 186,* 19–26.

[61]Segal, N. L., & Topolski, T. D. (1995). The genetics of olfactory perception. In R. L. Doty (Ed.) *Handbook of clinical olfaction and gustation* (pp. 323–343). New York: Marcel Dekker, Inc. See references therein.

[62]Segal, N. L., Grimes, M. V., and Topolski, T. D. (1995). Twin study of genetic relatedness and odor similarity. *Aromachology Review, 4,* 2, 10–12.

[63]Snowdon, C. T. (1996). Infant care in a cooperative breeding species. In J. Z. Rosenblatt & C. T. Snowdon (Eds.) *Advances in the study of behavior* (pp. 643–689). New York: Academic Press.

[64]Achenbach, G. G., & Snowdon, C. T. (in press). Response to sibling birth in juvenile cotton-top tamarins (*Saguinus oedipus*). *Behaviour.* A comparable study using human mothers and children would be of interest.

[65]Savage, A., & Snowdon, C. T. (1982). Mental retardation and neurological deficits in a twin orangutan. *American Journal of Primatology, 3,* 239–251.

[66]Rosen, S. I. (1974). *Introduction to the primates: Living and fossil.* Englewood Cliffs, N.J.: Prentice-Hall, Inc.

[67]"Paddy Gets the Boot." *South-West News,* May 6, 1998.

[68]Nagashima, H., et al. (1984). Production of monozygotic mouse twins from microsurgically bisected morulae. *Journal of Reproduction and Fertility, 70,* 357–362; Yang, X., & Foote, R. H. (1987). Production of identical twin rabbits by micromanipulation of embryos. *Biology of Reproduction, 37,* 1007–1014.

[69]Center reveals nuclear embryo transfer success; "Cloned" monkeys meet the world. *Oregon Regional Primate Research Center: A Newsletter for Employees, 22,* March 10, 1997.

Primate Twinning

Prosimians		New and Old World Monkeys		Apes and Humans	
Family	**Common name**	**Family**	**Common name**	**Family**	**Common name**
Tupiidae	tree shrews–1	*Callitrichidae*	marmosets–1	*Hylobatidae*	common gibbons–5
			tamarins–1		siamang–5
Lemuridae	true lemurs–4	*Cebidae*	capuchin monkey–4	*Pongidae*	orangutan–4
			squirrel monkey–4		chimpanzee–4
	mouse lemurs–1				gorilla–4
	dwarf lemurs–1		titi–5		
			owl monkey–5	*Hominidae*	humans–4
Indriidae	indris–5				
	sifaka–5		uakari–5		
	ampongi–5		saki–5		
			bearded saki–5		
Daubentoniidae	aye-aye–5				
			howler monkey–4		
Lorsidae	slender loris–2				
	slow loris–4		spider monkey–5		
	angwantibo–5		wooley spider monkey–5		
	potto–5				
	galago–3	*Cercopithecidae*	guenon–4		
			baboon–5		
Tarsidae	tarsier–5		patas–5		
			macaque–5		
			langur–5		

Key: 1 = Twins or other multiples occur "commonly." 2 = Twins occur "occasionally." 3 = Twins are "common" in some subspecies. 4 = Single births are the rule, but twins have been recorded, or are "rare." 5 = No twin births recorded or data unavailable. (*Note*: The terms "commonly," "occasionally" and "rarely" are from the texts and do not reflect specific frequencies. Sources did not always distinguish between twin births in captivity or in the wild.) Prosimians and Anthropoidea are suborders of the order Primates. It is believed New World and Old World Monkeys had a common ancestor millions of years ago, but then evolved separately. Their common inheritance and adaptation to similar environments make them appear superficially similar. Their history is called *parallel evolution.* Entries grouped together denote members of common subfamilies and/or families; lists are not exhaustive. Data are from Napier, J. R., & Napier, J. H. (1967). *A handbook of living primates.* New York: Academic Press; Bulmer, M. G. (1970). *The biology of twinning in man.* Oxford: Clarendon; Rosen, S. I. (1974). *Introduction to the primates: Living and fossil.* Englewood Cliffs, NJ: Prentice-Hall; and literature cited in chapter 12. The table is adapted from Rosen, S. I. © 1974, p. 25, by permission of Prentice Hall, Upper Saddle River, New Jersey.

CHAPTER 13

[1]Genetic factors explain about 50% of individual differences in intellectual, social and enterprising features of vocational interest. (Plomin, R., DeFries, J. C., McClearn, G. E., & Rutter, M. (1997). *Behavioral genetics.* 3rd ed. New York: W. H. Freeman & Co). Reared apart twin studies reveal more modest, but significant, genetic influence on intrinsic features of job satisfaction (e.g., challenge and achievement), but not on extrinsic features of job satisfaction (e.g., work conditions and supervision); see Arvey, R. D., et al. (1989). Job satisfaction: Environmental and genetic components. *Journal of Applied Psychology, 74,* 187–192; Arvey, R. E., et al. (1994). Genetic influences on job satisfaction and work values. *Personality and Individual Differences, 17,* 21–33.

[2]McCall, B. P., et al. (1997). Genetic influences on job and occupational switching. *Journal of Vocational Behavior, 50,* 60–77.

[3]"Honorary Degrees for Fraternal Twins with Fraternal Jobs." *New York Times,* May 21, 1996.

[4]Swoboda, V. "Tall, Dark and Principal." *McGill News,* Spring 1994, pp. 10–13.

[5]Harold chaired the Economics Department of the University of Michigan, and Bernard chaired the Humanistic and Behavioral Studies Department at Boston University.

[6]Econometrics is the application of statistical methods to the study of economic data and problems. Psychometrics is the psychological theory or technique of mental ability measurement.

[7]Carmody, D. "New Head of Princeton." *New York Times,* April 29, 1987.

[8]See Swoboda, V. (1994).

[9]Adopted children's IQ scores generally fall below those of birth children in their families; see Segal, N. L. (1997). Same-age unrelated siblings: A unique test of within-family environmental influences on IQ similarity. *Journal of Educational Psychology, 89,* 381–390.

[10]Sternberg, R. J. (1997). Educating intelligence: Infusing the Triarchic Theory into school instruction. In R. J. Sternberg, & E Grigorenko, (Eds.) *Intelligence, heredity, and environment* (pp. 343–362). New York: Cambridge University Press.

[11]Blatz, W. E. (1938). *The five sisters.* New York: William Morrow & Co.

[12]McLarin, K. J. (1995). "A Pair of Presidents Keep it All in the Family." *New York Times Educational Life Supplement,* April 2, 1995, pp. 20–21, 38.

[13]Swoboda, V. (1994).

[14]McLarin, K. J. (1995).

[15]Lykken, D. T., & Tellegen, Al. (1993). Is human mating adventitious or the result of lawful choice? A twin study of mate selection. *Journal of Personality and Social Psychology, 65,* 56–68.

[16]Shapiro, B. J., & Shapiro, H. T. (1995). Universities in higher education: Some problems and challenges in a changing world. In T. Courchene (Ed.) *Policy frameworks for a knowledge economy* (pp. 81–108). Kingston, Ontario: Queen's University Press.

[17]Plomin, R. (1990). *Nature and nurture: An introduction to behavioral genetics.* Pacific Grove, CA: Brooks/Cole Publishing Company.

[18]Guests were Dr. Arthur Haney, President of the American Society for Reproductive Medicine, and Dr. Arthur Caplan, Director of the Center for Bioethics, University of Pennsylvania.

[19]Lemonick, M. D. "It's a Miracle." *Time Magazine,* December 1, 1997.

[20]The IHI is a nonprofit organization based in Boston, Massachusetts. It sponsors conferences and educational programs in quality management and improvement in health care. The forum in which the twins participated took place in New Orleans, December 5, 1996.

[21]Intriguing experiments show that distinguishing identical twins can be induced by train-

ing; see Stevenage, S. V. (1998). Which twin are you? A demonstration of induced categorical perception of identical twin faces. *British Journal of Psychology, 89,* 39–57.

[22]The twins' sister Laura and their mother Dorothy made these photographs available. Five twin researchers examined them and three (including me) judged Marc and Steve to be fraternal.

[23]Plomin, R. (1990).

[24]"Roberts, Cokie." (1994). In J. Graham (Ed.) *Current biography yearbook* (pp. 486–489). New York: H. W. Wilson Co. Corinne (Lindy) Boggs became the American Ambassador to the Vatican at eighty-one.

[25]In her 1998 book *We Are Our Mothers' Daughters,* ABC's *This Week* host Cokie Roberts writes, "It's uncomfortable for me to be with Steven and have someone recognize me and not him, though he's a pretty familiar face to news junkies."

[26]Interview on *Charlie Rose,* KCET. May 18, 1998.

[27]Rossellini, I. (1997). *Some of me.* New York: Random House.

[28]Rossellini, I. I. (1993). Nel "Trapassar del Segno" della poesia Petrarchesca: Per una lettura delle "Rime Sparse." *Dissertation Abstracts International, 54–07A,* 2603.

[29]The twins' differences in hair texture (curly vs. straight) identified them as fraternal.

[30]Tomsho, R. "Koch Family Is Roiled by Sibling Squabbling Over Its Oil Empire." *Wall Street Journal,* August 8, 1989; Wayne, L. "Brothers at Odds." *Business World,* December 7, 1986, pp. 82–83, 100, 102.

[31]Wayne, L. (December 7, 1986).

[32]Bumiller, E. "Woman Ascending a Marble Staircase." *New York Times Magazine,* January 11, 1998, pp. 18–21.

[33]Wayne, L. (December 7, 1986).

[34]Larsen, P. C. *To the third power.* Gardiner, ME: Tilbury House Publishers.

[35]Huntington, A. S. (1996). *Making waves.* Arlington, TX: Summit Publishing Group. The *Mighty Mary* did beat Conner's boat in the first trial leading to the Cup.

[36]Wayne, L. "Brother Versus Brother." *New York Times,* April 28, 1998; Wayne, L. "Zero is the Verdict in $2 Billion Koch Family Feud." *New York Times,* June 20, 1998.

[37]Henriques, D. B. "Twin v. Twin, Company at Stake." *New York Times,* July 3, 1996; Henriques, D. B. "Long and Bitter Sibling Rivalry at Value Line Ends in a Deal." *New York Times,* November 28, 1996.

[38]Ono, Y. "TwinLab Finds Itself A Lucrative Niche in Health-Food Pills." *Wall Street Journal,* August 8, 1995.

[39]Kolata, G. "The Double Life of Dr. Swain; Work and More Work." *New York Times,* September 27, 1994.

[40]See Swain, J. L., et al. (1987). Parental legacy determines expression and methylation of an autosomal fusion gene carried by a transgenic mouse. *Cell, 50,* 719–727.

[41]Swain, J. A., et al. (1993). Low flow cardiopulmonary bypass and cerebral protection: A summary of investigations. *Annals of Thoracic Surgery, 56,* 1490–1492.

[42]Kolata, G. (September 27, 1994).

[43]Dr. Julie Swain acquainted me with the Duke twins.

[44]Hawking, S. W. (1988). *A brief history of time.* New York: Bantam Books; Davis, P. (1995). *About time: Einstein's unfinished revolution.* New York: Touchstone.

[45]Harris, J. R. (1995). Where is the child's environment? A group socialization theory of development. *Psychological Review, 102,* 458–489; Harris, J. R. (1998). *The nurture assumption: Why children turn out the way they do.* NY: Free Press.

[46]"Shalala, Donna." (1991) In C. Moritz (Ed.) *Current biography yearbook* (pp. 514–518). New York: H. W. Wilson Co.

[47]"Hersh, Seymour (Myron)." (1984) In C. Moritz (Ed.) Current biography yearbook (pp. 159–161). New York: H. W. Wilson Co.

CHAPTER 14

[1]Wexler, T. W. (Personal communication, April 23, 1987).

[2]Blood-typing may not have been performed in occasional cases in which my involvement was limited. In these cases I made every effort to learn twin type through the physical resemblance questionnaire, inspection of twins' photographs, or other methods.

[3]Fryover vs. Forbes, Michigan Circuit Court, Kent City (No. 86–53236NI), March 2, 1998.

[4]Wilson, A. L., et al. (1982). The death of a newborn twin: An analysis of parental bereavement. *Pediatrics, 70,* 587–591.

[5]Stevens, A. "Wrongful-death Suits and Custody Cases Spotlight Special Relationship of Twins. *Wall Street Journal.* January 18, 1993.

[6]"Auto Accident." *Bureau of National Affairs Civil Trial Manual, 4,* 163–165, May 4, 1988.

[7]Cohen, N. "Twins' 'Special Bond' Stressed in Litigation." *Medical Malpractice Law & Strategy, 10,* 3, February 1993.

[8]Cohen, N. (1993).

[9]McCann, S. "5 Families File Suit After Tragedy at Wheeler Farm." *Salt Lake Tribune,* September 22, 1992.

[10]Nebeker, S. B., & Rose, R. L. (1992). Complaint and Jury Demand. September 21, 1992.

[11]Downey, W. J., III., Esq. *Settlement Brochure,* March 16, 1995; Kester-Doyle, M. (1996). An unusual story of mistaken identity. *Twinsworld, 2,* December 1996, 19–25.

[12]Maris, C. L., et al. (1998). Manuscript in progress.

[13]Bryan, E. M. (1984). *Twins in the family: A parent's guide.* London: Constable; Bernabei, P., & Levi, G. (1976). Psychopathologic problems in twins during childhood. *Acta Geneticae Medicae et Gemellologiae, 25,* 381–383.

[14]Segal, N. L. & Russell, J. (1991). IQ similarity in monozygotic and dizygotic twin children: Effects of the same versus separate examiners: A research note. *Journal of Child Psychology and Psychiatry, 32,* 703–708.

[15]Wilson, J., et al. (1989). Siblings of children with severe handicap. *Mental Retardation, 27,* 167–173.

[16]The twins' obvious behavioral and physical differences made impressions of similarity ludicrous, but probably hurtful to E.

[17]Bryan, E. M. (1984).

[18]Twins' uncle. (Personal communication, 1992).

[19]Segal, N. L. (1993). Implications of twin research for legal issues involving young twins. *Law and Human Behavior* (Special Issue: Law, psychology and children), *17,* 43–58.

[20]It is possible that only unusually close fraternal twins file for loss of companionship in the event of wrongful death.

[21]Matheny, A. P. (1993). Separation anxiety: The twin advantage. *Twins Magazine, 9,* 40–41.

[22]See, for example, Faschingbauer, T. R., et al. (1987). The Texas Revised Inventory of Grief. In S. Zisook (Ed.) *Biopsychosocial aspects of bereavement* (pp. 109–124). Washington, D.C.: American Psychological Association Press, Inc.

[23]Woodward, J. (1988). The bereaved twin. *Acta Geneticae Medicae et Gemellologiae, 37,* 173–180.

[24]McIndoe, A., & Franceschetti, A. (1949). Reciprocal skin homografts. *British Journal of Plastic Surgery, 2,* 283–289; Scheinfeld, A. (1973). *Twins and supertwins.* New York: Pelican Books.

[25]Borgida, E., et al. (1992). Understanding living kidney donation: A behavioral decision making perspective. In S. Spacepan, & S. Oskamp (Eds.) *Helping and being helped: Naturalistic studies* (pp. 183–212). Beverly Hills, CA: Sage Publications.

[26]Anderson, A. "The Bone-Marrow Transplant Twins." *New York Times,* April 22, 1990. Chris Singleton was a linebacker for the New England Patriots (1990–1993) and the Miami Dolphins (1993–1996). He is now a free agent.

[27]Department of Veterans Affairs, New York Regional Office of Public Affairs. "Twins DNA Match in Unusual Bowel Transplant Reduces Risk of Organ Rejection." 1994.

[28]Silber, S. J. (1978). Transplantation of a human testis for anorchia. *Fertility and Sterility, 30,* 181–187; Silber, S. J., & Rodriguez-Rigau, L. J. (1980). Pregnancy after testicular transplant: Importance of treating the couple. *Fertility and Sterility, 33,* 454–455.

[29]Organ rejection between identical twins is possible due to infection.

[30]Fefer, A., et al. (1986). Identical-twin (syngenic) marrow transplantation for hemotologic cancers. *Journal of the National Cancer Institute, 76,* 1269–1273.

[31]Morgan, R. A., et al. (1997). An AIDS gene therapy trial in HIV-1 discordant identical twins. *Blood, 90,* 405a; "Twin H.I.V. Study." *New York Times,* March 7, 1995. Temporary increases in healthy cells have been observed in affected twins.

[32]Lambert, B. "Court Orders Blue Cross to Pay for Transplant in AIDS Case." *New York Times,* August 1, 1990; Prial, F. J. "Thomas J. Bradley, 47, a Teacher Fought Blue Cross for Transplant." *New York Times,* October 23, 1991.

[33]Wilkerson, I. "In Marrow Donor Lawsuit, Altruism Collides With Right to Protect Child." *New York Times,* July 30, 1990; Lambert, W., & Hayes, A. S. "Bone Marrow test." *Wall Street Journal,* October 1, 1990.

[34]Fellner, C. H., & Marshall, J. R. (1981). Kidney donors revisited. In J. P. Rushton & R. M. Sorrentino (Eds.) *Altrusim and helping behavior: Social, personality and developmental perspectives* (pp. 351–356). Hillsdale, NJ: Erlbaum; see Borgida, et al. (1992).

[35]Fellner, C. H., & Marshall, J. R. (1981).

[36]Simmons, R. G., et al. (1971). Family tension in the search for a kidney donor. *Journal of the American Medical Association, 215,* 909–912.

[37]Burnstein, E., et al (1994). Some neo-Darwinian rules for altruism: Weighing cues for inclusive fitness as a function of the biological importance of the decision. *Journal of Personality and Social Psychology, 67,* 773–789.

[38]Beckstrom, J. H. (1989). *Evolutionary jurisprudence.* Urbana: University of Illinois Press; Jones, O. D. (1997). Evolutionary analysis in law: An introduction and application to child abuse. *North Carolina Law Review, 75,* 1117–1242. The Gruter Institute for Law and Behaviorial Research publishes literature on selected topics in law and biology, and hosts conferences that introduce legal thinkers to law-relevant aspects of evolutionary biology and psychology.

[39]Spungen, A. M. (Personal communication, 1997).

[40]Stryker, J. "Twin Pique: Yin, Yang and You." *New York Times,* September 7, 1997. Jeen Haan was sentenced to twenty-six years in prison on May 8, 1998.

CHAPTER 15

[1]Brantley, B. "7 Days Ago, Broadway's New Hit Musical Arrived." *New York Times,* October 23, 1997.

[2]Wallace, I., & Wallace, A. (1978). *The two.* New York: Bantam Books.

[3]Cady, M. "The Pure Joy of Being Alive." *People Magazine,* July 3, 1989, pp. 64–71.

[4]Creinin, M. (1995). Conjoined twins. In L. G. Keith, E. Papiernik, D. M. Keith, & B. Luke (Eds.) *Multiple pregnancy: Epidemiology, gestation and perinatal outcome* (pp. 93–112). New York: Parthenon.

[5]Rubin, J. C. Little museum of horrors. *Time Magazine,* November 7, 1994, p. 20.

[6]Newman, H. H. (1923). *The physiology of twinning.* Chicago: University of Chicago Press; Smith, D. W., et al. (1976). Monozygotic twinning and the duhamel anomalad (imperforate anus to sirenomelia): A nonrandom association between two aberrations in

morphogenesis. In D. Bergsma & R. N. Schimke (Eds.) *Cytogenetics, environment and malformation syndromes* (pp. 53–56). New York: Alan R. Liss, Inc.

[7]Cuniff, C., et al. (1988). Laterality defects in conjoined twins: Implications for normal asymmetry in human embryogenesis. *American Journal of Medical Genetics, 31,* 669–677; Fitzgerald, E. J., & Cochlin, D. L. (1985). Conjoined twins: Antenatal diagnosis and a review of the literature. *British Journal of Radiology, 58,* 1053–1056.

[8]Pentogalos, G. E., & Lascaratos, J. G. (1984). A surgical operation performed on Siamese twins during the tenth century in Byzantium. *Bulletin on the History of Medicine, 58,* 99–102.

[9]Body symmetry of many conjoined twins renders the fusion hypothesis unlikely; Newman (1923).

[10]Little, J., & Bryan, E. M. (1988). Congenital anomalies. In I. MacGillivray, D. M. Campbell, & B. Thompson (Eds.) *Twinning and twins* (pp. 207–240). Chichester, England: John Wiley & Sons; also see Rudolph, A. J. (1967). Obstetric management of conjoined twins. *Birth Defects, 3,* 28–37.

[11]Koontz, W. L., et al. (1985). Antenatal sonographic diagnosis of conjoined twins in a triplet pregnancy. *American Journal of Obstetrics and Gynecology, 153,* 230–231.

[12]Seo, J. W., et al. (1985). Cardiovascular system in conjoined twins: An analysis of 14 Korean cases. *Teratology, 32,* 151–161.

[13]Viljoen, D. L., et al. (1983). The epidemiology of conjoined twinning in Southern Africa. *Clinical Genetics, 24,* 15–21. See references therein.

[14]Calagan, J. L. (1983). The conjoined twins born near Worms, 1495. *Journal of the History of Medicine and Allied Sciences, 38,* 450–451.

[15]Bryan, E. M. (1983). *The nature and nurture of twins.* London: Ballière Tindall; O'Neill, J. A., Jr., et al. (1988). Surgical experience with thirteen conjoined twins. *Annals of Surgery, 208,* 299–312.

[16]Creinin, M. (1995).

[17]Freeman, N. V., et al. (1997). *Pediatric Surgery International, 12,* 256–260; O'Neill, J. A., Jr. (1998). Conjoined twins. In J. A. O'Neill, M. Rowe, J. L. Grosfeld, E. W. Fonkalsrud, & A. G. Coran (Eds.) *Pediatric Surgery, Vol. 2.* 5th ed. (pp. 1925–1938). Philadlephia, PA: Mosby Yearbooks, Inc.

[18]Hoyle, R. M. (1990). Surgical separation of conjoined twins. *Surgery, Gynecology and Obstetrics, 170,* 549–562. The twins' sex was probably not recorded for some early cases. Complex connection of the pelvic region can lead to ambiguous genitalia, but this is rare; see Cunniff, C., et al. (1989).

[19]Machin, G. A. (1996). Some causes of genotypic and phenotypic discordance in monozygotic twin pairs. *American Journal of Medical Genetics, 61,* 216–228.

[20]Creinin, M. (1995).

[21]Creinin, M. (1995).

[22]Guttmacher, A. F. (1967). Biographical notes on some famous conjoined twins. *Birth Defects, 3,* 10–17.

[23]See, for example, Stephens, T. D., et al. (1982). Parasitic conjoined twins, two cases, and their relation to limb morphogenesis. *Teratology, 26,* 115–121.

[24]Harper, R., et al. (1980). Xiphopagus conjoined twins: A 300–year review of the obstetric, morphopathologic, neonatal, and surgical parameters. *American Journal of Obstetrics and Gynecology, 137,* 617–629; see Guttmacher & Nichols (1967); Creinin (1995).

[25]Hubinot, C. et al. (1984). Dicephalus: Unusual case of conjoined twins and its prepartum diagnosis. *American Journal of Obstetrics and Gynecology, 149,* 693–694; Greening, D. (1981). Vaginal delivery of conjoined twins. *The Medical Journal of Australia,* 357–360; O'Neill, et al. (1988); also see Hoyle, R. M. (1990).

[26] Calagan, J. L. (1983).

[27]Creinin, M. (1995).

[28]See Meyers, C., et al. (1995). Congenital anomalies and pregnancy loss. In L. G. Keith, et al. (Eds.) (pp. 73–92).

[29]Antunes, J. L., et al. (1983). Occipital encephale—a case of conjoined twinning? *Neurosurgery, 13,* 703–707.

[30]Greening, D. (1981).

[31]Harper, R., et al. (1980); Papiernik, E. (1995). Reducing the risk of preterm delivery. In L. G. Keith, et al. (Eds.) (pp. 437–452).

[32]Creinin, M. (1995). There has been only one report of two sets of conjoined twins born in the same family.

[33]Milham, S., Jr. (1966). Symmetrical conjoined twins: An analysis of the birth records of twenty-two sets. *Journal of Pediatrics, 69,* 643–647.

[34]Viljoen, D. L., et al. (1983).

[35]Milham, S., Jr. (1966).

[36]Creinin, M. (1995); Harper, R., et al. (1980).

[37]Creinin, M. (1995).

[38]See Chatterjee, M. S., et al. (1983). Prenatal diagnosis of conjoined twins. *Prenatal Diagnosis, 3,* 357–361.

[39]Creinin, M. (1995).

[40]O'Neill, J. (1998).

[41]Apuzzio, J. J., et al. (1984). Prenatal diagnosis of conjoined twins. *American Journal of Obstetrics and Gynecology, 148,* 343–344; Sabbagha, R. E. (1995). Pregnancy dating and evaluation by ultrasonography. In L. G. Keith, et al. (Eds.) *Multiple pregnancy: Epidemiology, gestation and perinatal outcome* (pp. 215–238). New York: Parthenon.

[42]Koontz, W. L., et al. (1983). Ultrasonography in the antepartum diagnosis of conjoined twins: A report of two cases. *Journal of Reproductive Medicine, 28,* 627–630; Koontz, W. L., et al. (1985). Radiographic features are from Gray (1950), cited in Koontz, et al. (1983).

[43]Koontz, W. L., et al. (1985).

[44]Creinin, M. (1995).

[45]Abrams, S. L., et al. (1985). Anencephaly with encephalocele in Craniopagus twins: Prenatal diagnosis by ultrasonography and computed tomography. *Journal of Ultrasound Medicine, 4,* 485–488.

[46]Creinin, M. (1995).

[47]Dreger, A. D. (1997). The limits of individuality: Ritual and sacrifice in the lives and medical treatment of conjoined twins. *Studies in History and Philosophy of Science, 29,* 1–29.

[48]Charlanza, B. "Lori, Dori Make Their Way." *Reading Eagle,* September 18, 1988; Angier, N. "Joined for Life, and Living Life to the Full." *New York Times,* December 23, 1997.

[49]Smith, J. D. (1988). *Psychological profiles of conjoined twins: Heredity, environment, and identity.* Westport, CT: Praeger.

[50]Lykken, D. T., & Tellegen, A. (1996). Happiness is a stochastic phenomenon. *Psychological Science, 7,* 186–189.

[51]Annas, G. J. (1987). Siamese twins: Killing one to save the other. *Hastings Center Report, 17,* 27–29.

[52]Gorman, T. "Familes of Twins Joined at Birth Help Each Other." *Los Angeles Times,* February 24, 1998.

[53]Cady, M. (1989).

[54]Wallis, C. "The Most Intimate Bond." *Time Magazine.* March 25, 1996; Miller, K. "Together Forever." *Life Magazine.* April 1996, p. 44–56.

[55]Cleveland, S. E., et al. (1964). Psychological appraisal of conjoined twins. *Journal of Projective Techniques, 18,* 265–271.

[56]Pentogalos, G. E., & Lascaratos, J. G. et al. (1984).

[57]König, G. (1689), cited in O'Neill, J. (1998).

[58]Guttmacher, A. F. (1967). Biographical notes on some famous conjoined twins. *Birth Defects, 3,* 10–17; Bryan, E. M. (1983); Thomasma, D. C., et al. (1996). The ethics of caring for conjoined twins: The Lakeberg twins. *Hastings Center Report, 26,* 4–12.

[59]Wallace, I., & Wallace, A. (1978); Chichester, P. "A Hyphenated Life." *Blue Ridge Country,* November/December, 1995, pp. 16–21, 54.

[60]Creinin, M. (1995).

[61]Thomasma, D. C., et al. (1996); Raffensperger, J. (1997).

[62]O'Neill (1998).

[63]O'Neill (1998); also see Cywes, S., et al. (1997). Conjoined twins—the Cape Town experience. *Pediatric Surgery International, 12,* 234–248.

[64]O'Neill, J. A., Jr. (1998). Dr. O'Neill provided me with details on the surgical outcomes of his new cases.

[65]Raffensperger, J. (1997).

[66]Creinin, M. (1995); Cywes, S., et al. (1997); also see Slovut, G. (1988). "One Twin Survives Desperate Surgery." *Minneapolis Star and Tribune,* March 17, 1988.

[67]Pepper, C. K. (1967). Ethical and moral considerations in the separation of conjoined twins. *Birth Defects, 3,* 128–134; Cywes, S., et al. (1997).

[68]Tanne, J. H. "Free at Last." *New York Magazine,* November 15, 1993.

[69]Guttmacher (1967). P. T. Barnum had no intention of separating the twins and destroying his famous circus act.

[70]"Doctors Separate Twins Joined at the Head." *New York Times,* September 15, 1996.

[71]"Conjoined Twins, Successfully Separated, Head Home." *Houston Chronicle* (Nando.net), April 18, 1997.

[72]"Yvette McCarther, Yvonne McCarther." (Obituary). *New York Times,* January 6, 1993; Stumbo, B. "The Amazing Grace of Two Lives." *New York Times,* January 17, 1993.

[73]Chance of survival was estimated at 1%; see Raffensperger, J. (1997).

[74]Thomasma, D. C., et al. (1996).

[75]Annas, G. J. (1987). This case was the first attempted criminal prosecution of a physician for withholding newborn treatment.

[76]Raffensperger, J. (1997).

[77]Associated Press. "They'll Risk Life Apart—or Death." *Chicago Star & Tribune,* April 30, 1979; Kotulak, R. "Once Joined at Head, Twins Still Display a Special Bond." *Chicago Star & Tribune,* November 9, 1980.

[78]Wallis, C. (1996); Miller, K. (1996).

[79]Guttmacher, A. F. (1967).

[80]Newman, H. H. (1931). Differences between conjoined twins in relation to a general theory of twinning. *Journal of Heredity, 22,* 201–215; Reichle, H. S. (1928), cited in Newman (1921); Newman, H. H., Freeman, F. N., & Holzinger, K. J. (1937). *Twins: A study of heredity and environment.* Chicago: University of Chicago Press.

[81]Koch, H. L. (1927). Some measurements of a pair of Siamese twins. *Journal of Comparative Psychology, 7,* 313–333.

[82]Professor Newman found the Hiltons to be the least physically similar conjoined pair in his series, based on attractiveness, height and weight. Other investigators found them very similar in height, weight, hair, eyes, expression, shoe size, and dentition; see Seeman, E., & Saudek, R. (1932). The self-expression of identical twins in handwriting and drawing. *Character and Personality, 1,* 91–128. Note: Newman recorded the twins' height difference as 1.5 inches, while Seeman & Saudek recorded it as 1.0 inch.

[83]Smith, J. D. (1988); also see a review of this book by DiLalla, D. (1986). Conjoined twins: Metaphor or data. *Contemporary Psychology, 35,* 332–333.

[84]Seeman, E., & Saudek, R. (1932). The self-expression of identical twins in handwriting and drawing. *Character and Personality, 1,* 91–128.

[85]Lyman, R. "What the Audience Won't Watch." *New York Times,* January 4, 1998.

[86]*Los Angeles Times,* January 22, 1995.

[87]Cited in Dreger, A. D. (1997).

CHAPTER 16

[1]Plomin, R., DeFries, J. C., McClearn, G. E., & Rutter, M. (1997). *Behavioral genetics.* 3rd ed. New York: W. H. Freeman & Co.: Segal, N. L. (1992). Twin research at Auschwitz-Birkenau: Implications for the use of Nazi data today. In A. Caplan (Ed.) *When medicine went mad* (pp. 281–299). Totowa, N.J.: Humana Press.

[2]Bouchard, T. J., Jr., et al. (1990). Souces of human psychological differences: The Minnesota Study of Twins Reared Apart. *Science, 250,* 223–228.

[3]Duane, T. D., & Behrendt, T. (1965). Extrasensory electroencephalographic induction between identical twins. *Science, 150,* 367; Duane, T. D., & Behrendt, T. (1966). Letter to the Editor. *Science, 151,* 28, 30.

[4]"Airport 'Gene Shop' Teaches Genetics." Reuters, New York. January 21, 1998.

[5]Plomin, R. et al. (1997).

[6]Scarr-Salapatek, S. (1971). Unknowns in the IQ equation. *Science, 174,* 1223–1228; Dobzhansky, T. (1973). *Genetic diversity and human equality.* New York: Basic Books.

[7]Mealey, L., & Segal, N. L. (1993). Heritable and environmental variables affect reproduction-related behaviors, but not ultimate reproductive success. *Personality and Individual Differences, 41,* 783–794.

[8]Smith, M. (1987). Evolution and developmental psychology: Toward a sociobiology of human development. In C. Crawford, M. Smith, & D. Krebs (Eds.) *Sociobiology and psychology: Ideas, issues and applications* (pp. 225–252). Hillsdale, NJ: Erlbaum.

[9]Plomin, R., et al. (1997).

[10]Smith, M. S. (1987).

[11]Also see Segal, N. L., et al. (1997). Pursuing the big picture. In N. L. Segal, G. E. Weisifeld, & C. C. Weisfeld (Eds.) *Uniting psychology and biology: Integrative perspectives on human development* (pp. 3–18). Washington, D.C.: American Psychological Association Press.

[12]Plomin, R., et al. (1997).

[13]Behavioral geneticists' use of the abbreviation EEA should not be confused with its use by evolutionary psychologists, who refer to the *environment of evolutionary adaptiveness.*

[14]Farber, S. L. (1981). *Identical twins reared apart: A reanalysis.* New York: Basic Books; Hoffman, L. W. (1991). The influence of the family environment on personality: Accounting for sibling differences. *Psychological Bulletin, 110,* 187–203.

[15]Loehlin, J. C., & Nichols, R. (1976). *Heredity, environment and personality: A study of 850 sets of twins.* Austin, TX: University of Texas Press; Hettema, J. M., et al. (1995). Physical similarity and the equal-environment assumption in twin studies of psychiatric disorders. *Behavior Genetics, 25,* 327–335; LaBuda, M. C., et al. (1997). Twin closeness and cotwin risk for substance use disorders: Assessing the impact of the equal environment assumption. *Psychiatry Research, 70,* 155–164.

[16]Rowe, D. C., & Gulley, B. (1992). Siblings effects on substance use and delinquency. *Criminology, 30,* 217–233; also see Hettema, et al. (1995).

[17]Hook, J. (1997). On twins, faces, and expectations: A reinterpretation of heritability. *Society for Research in Child Development,* Washington, D.C., April 3, 1997.

[18]Rowe, D. C. (1994). *The limits of family influence: Genes, experience, and behavior.* New York: Guilford Press.

[19]Price, B. (1950). *American Journal of Human Genetics, 2,* 293–352; Price, B. (1978). *Acta Geneticae Medicae et Gemellologiae, 27,* 97–113.

[20]Devlin, B., et al. (1997). The heritability of IQ. *Nature, 388,* 468–471.

[21]Bouchard, T. J., Jr. (1997, unpublished manuscript). Meta-analysis and model-fitting comment on Devlin, B., et al. (1997).

[22]Lykken, D. T., et al. (1987). Recruitment bias in twin research: The rule of two-thirds reconsidered. *Behavior Genetics, 17,* 343–362.

[23]Lykken, D. T., et al. (1990). The Minnesota Twin Family Registry: Some initial findings. *Acta Geneticae Medicae et Gemellologiae, 39,* 35–70.

[24]Martin, N., et al. (1997). A twin-pronged attack on complex traits. *Nature Genetics, 17,* 387–392.

[25]Hur, Y. M., et al. (1995). Unequal rate of monozygotic and like-sex dizygotic twin births: Evidence from the Minnesota Twin Family Study. *Behavior Genetics, 25,* 337–340.

[26]*Eighth International Congress on Twin Studies* (Abstracts), May 28–June 1, 1995, Richmond, Virginia; Boomsma, D. I. (1998). Twin registers in Europe: An overview. *Twin Research, 1,* 34–51; National Twin Register, Sri Lanka (Summary Brochure), March 1997; Ando, J., & Ono, Y. (1998). Keio Twin Project: A preliminary report. (Abstract). *Twin Research, 1,* 81; Goldsmith, H., & Lemery, K. S. (1998). The Wisconsin Twin Panel: Temperament in context. *Behavior Genetics Association,* Stockholm, Sweden.

[27]Plomin, R. (1988). A stake in the heart: A review of *The Ontogeny of Information. Developmental Psychobiology, 21,* 93–95.

[28]Tellegen, A., et al. (1988). Personality similarity in twins reared apart and together. *Journal of Personality and Social Psychology, 54,* 1031–1039.

[29]Cardon, L. R., et al. (1994). Quantitative trait locus for reading disability on chromosome 6. *Science, 266,* 276–279.

[30]Plomin, R., et al. (1997).

[31]Bouchard, T. J., Jr. and McGue, M. (1981). Familial studies of intelligence. *Science, 212,* 1055–1059.

[32]McCartney, K., et al. (1990). Growing up and growing apart: A developmental meta-analysis of twin studies. *Psychological Bulletin, 107,* 226–237.

[33]Snyderman, M., & Rothman, S. (1987). Survey of expert opinion on intelligence and attitude testing. *American Psychologist, 42,* 137–144.

[34]Ellis, M. V., & Robbins, E. S. (1990). In celebration of nature: A dialogue with Jerome Kagan. *Journal of Counseling and Development, 68,* 623–627.

[35]Marshall, E. (1998). Alzheimer's Research; The Alzheimer's Disease puzzle. *Science, 280,* 1002; Benjamin, J., et al. (1996). Population and familial association between the D4 dopamine receptor gene and measures of novelty-seeking. *Nature Genetics, 12,* 81–84; Swain, A., et al. (1998). *Daxl* antagonizes *Sry* action in mammalian sex determination. *Nature, 391,* 761–767.

[36]Segal, N. L. (1985). Holocaust twins: Their special bond. *Psychology Today, 19,* 52–58.

[37]Segal, N. L. (1992).

[38]Baumrind, D. (1993). The average expectable environment is not good enough: A response to Scarr. *Child Development, 64,* 1299–1317; Jackson, J. F. (1993). Human behavioral genetics, Scarr's theory, and her views on interventions: A critical review and commentary on their implications for African American children. *Child Development, 64,* 1318–1332.

[39]Black, J. "Having Second Thoughts in the Air." *New York Times,* January 4, 1998.

[40]Roane, K. R. "Mother's Plea Moves Mayor to Act." *New York Times,* November 8, 1997.

[41]" 'Kienast Quintuplets' Father Found Dead, Apparently a Suicide." *Minneapolis Star & Tribune,* March 4, 1984.

[42]Purdum, T. S. "Sister Suspected in Twins' Death." *New York Times,* April 17, 1986.

[43]Groothuis, J. (1985). Twins and twin families: A practical guide to outpatient management. *Clinics in Perinatology, 12,* 459–474.

[44]Tanimura, M., Matsui, I., & Kobayshi, N. (1990). Child abuse in one of a pair of twins in Japan. *Lancet 336,* 1298–1299; also see Becker, J. C., et al. (1998). Shaken baby syndrome: Report on four pairs of twins. *Child Abuse and Neglect, 22,* 931–937.

[45]Bryan, E. M. (1984). *Twins in the family: A parent's guide.* London: Constable.

[46]Scrimshaw, S. C. M. (1984). Infanticide in human populations: Societal and individual concerns. In G. Hausfater & S. B. Hrdy (Eds.) *Infanticide: Comparative and evolutionary perspectives* (pp. 439–462). New York: Aldine; Daly, M. & Wilson, M. (1984). A sociobiological analysis of human infanticide. In G. Hausfater & S. B. Hrdy (Eds.) *Infanticide: Comparative and evolutionary perspectives* (pp. 487–502). New York: Aldine; also see Ball, H. L., & Hill, C. M. (1996). Reevaluating "twin infanticide." *Current Anthropology, 37,* 856–863; Eibl-Eibesfeldt, I. (1989). *Human ethology.* New York: Aldine de Gruyter.

[47]Hay, D. A., & O'Brien, P. J. (1986). Early influence on the school social adjustment of twins. *Fifth International Congress on Twin Studies,* September 15–19, 1986, Amsterdam, the Netherlands.

[48]Favored twins in Mann's study were equally likely to be first or second twins home; however, her sample included only seven twin pairs.

[49]Daly, M., & Wilson, M. (1987). Evolutionary psychology and family violence. In C. Crawford, et al. (Eds.) (pp. 293–309).

[50]Jacobson, H. I., et al. (1989). Multiple births and maternal risk of breast cancer. *American Journal of Epidemiology, 129,* 865–873; Murphy, M. F. G., et al. (1997). Breast cancer risk in mothers of twins. *British Journal of Cancer, 75,* 1066–1068.

[51]Thorpe, K., et al. (1991). Comparison of prevalence of depression in mothers of twins and mothers of singletons. *British Medical Journal, 302,* 875–878.

[52]*Prime Time Live,* ABC, October 29, 1997.

[53]Seelye, K. Q. "First Black Sextuplets Belatedly Win Public Notice." *New York Times,* January 8, 1998.

[54]"College Bargain." *New York Times,* June 6, 1982; Lake Erie College Financial Aid Office (Personal communication, February 6, 1998).

[55]"Double Indemnity." *Wall Street Journal,* November 5, 1992.

[56]Coppard, J. A. (Personal communication, June 5, 1996).

[57]*One Step Ahead* (catalogue). Summer 1998.

[58]Keith, L., & Machin, G. (1997). Zygosity testing: Current status and evolving issues. *Journal of Reproductive Medicine, 42,* 669–707.

Index